This thoroughly updated new edition provides a comprehensive introduction to contemporary social policy and addresses its historical, theoretical and contextual foundations. Divided into four sections, it opens with a survey of the socio-economic, political and governmental contexts within which social policy operates, before moving on to look at the historical development of the subject. The third section examines contemporary aspects of providing welfare, whilst the final part covers European and wider international developments. The text explores the major topics and areas in contemporary social policy, including:

- work and welfare
- education
- adult health and social care
- children and families
- crime and criminal justice
- health
- housing
- race
- disability

Issues are addressed throughout in a lively and accessible style and examples are richly illustrated to encourage the student to engage with theory and content and to help highlight the relevance of social policy in our understanding of modern society. It is packed with features including 'Spotlight', 'Discussion and review' and 'Controversy and debate' boxes, as well as further readings and recommended websites. A comprehensive glossary also provides explanations of key terms and abbreviations.

Social Policy is an essential textbook for undergraduate students taking courses in social policy and related courses such as criminology, health studies, politics, sociology, nursing, youth work and social work.

Hugh Bochel is Professor of Public Policy at the University of Lincoln, UK.

Guy Daly is Professor and Dean of the Faculty of Health and Life Sciences at Coventry University, UK.

SOCIAL POLICY

Third Edition

Edited by
Hugh Bochel and Guy Daly

Routledge
Taylor & Francis Group

LONDON AND NEW YORK

First and second edition published 2005, 2009
by Pearson Education Limited

This edition published 2014
by Routledge
2 Park Square, Milton Park, Abingdon, Oxon, OX14 4RN

and by Routledge
711 3rd Avenue, New York, NY 10017

Routledge is an imprint of the Taylor & Francis Group, an informa business

British Library Cataloguing in Publication Data
A catalogue record for this book is available from the British Library

Library of Congress Cataloging in Publication Data
 Social policy / edited by Hugh Bochel, Guy Daly. – Third Edition.
  pages cm
 1. Great Britain–Social policy. I. Bochel, Hugh M., editor of compilation.
 II. Daly, Guy, editor of compilation.
 HV248.S264 2014
 320.60941–dc23

2013032289

ISBN: 978-0-415-73382-3 (hbk)
ISBN: 978-1-447-92957-4 (pbk)
ISBN: 978-1-315-81913-6 (ebk)

Typeset in Garamond
by Swales & Willis Ltd, Exeter, Devon, UK

MIX
Paper from responsible sources
FSC
www.fsc.org FSC® C013056

Printed and bound in Great Britain by
TJ International Ltd, Padstow, Cornwall

Contents

FIGURES AND TABLES

Figures

Tables

Contributors

Catherine Bochel is Principal Lecturer in Policy Studies at the University of Lincoln.

Hugh Bochel is Professor of Public Policy at the University of Lincoln.

Michael Cahill is Reader in Social Policy at the University of Brighton.

Harry Cowen is an Honorary Research Fellow at the University of Gloucestershire, and was formerly Principal Lecturer in Social Policy and Sociology.

Guy Daly is Professor and Dean of Faculty, Health and Life Sciences, Coventry University.

Paul Daniel is a Senior Lecturer at the University of Roehampton.

Nick Ellison is Professor and Head of the Department of Social Policy and Social Work at the University of York.

Norman Ginsburg is Professor of Social Policy at London Metropolitan University.

Jon Glasby is Professor of Health and Social Care and Director of the Health Services Management Centre, University of Birmingham.

Edwin Griggs has taught social policy full-time and, more recently, part-time at a number of higher education institutions, latterly at Birmingham University.

Kevin Gulliver is Research and Development Director at the Human City Institute. HCi is an independent research agency that researches the nature and extent of exclusion, disadvantage, and inequality and seeks to promote practical and realistic solutions.

Bernard Harris is Professor of Social Policy at the University of Strathclyde.

Stephen McKay is Distinguished Professor of Social Research at the University of Lincoln.

Robert M. Page is Reader in Democratic Socialism and Social Policy at the University of Birmingham. He has a long-standing interest in the political history of the post-1945 British welfare state.

Martin Powell is Professor of Health and Social Policy at the Health Services Management Centre and School of Social Policy, University of Birmingham.

Alan Roulstone is Professor of Disability Studies at Leeds University and holds honorary professorial positions at Swansea University and the European School of Public Health (Paris-Rennes).

Karen Rowlingson is Professor of Social Policy at the University of Birmingham.

Peter Squires is Professor of Criminology and Public Policy at the University of Brighton.

Karen West is a Senior Lecturer in the Sociology and Social Policy Group at Aston University.

Sharon Wright is Senior Lecturer in Public Policy at the University of Glasgow. She specialises in the critical study of welfare reform and conditionality, the implementation of employment services, devolution and poverty in the context of inequality and wealth.

PREFACE

Social policy is an academic field that everyone encounters in one way or another, even if we do not immediately recognise it. Conversations at home, at work or with friends are frequently related, directly or indirectly, to areas considered by the discipline. This includes when we consider:

- whether education is being 'dumbed down';
- why different parts of the United Kingdom have different tuition fees for higher education and what their impact is on the participation of people from poorer backgrounds;
- whether the state should provide free child care;
- whether pensions should be provided by the state or should depend upon individuals making provision for themselves;
- whether social security benefits are too generous;
- what roles the individual, society, and the state should play in tackling social harms arising from environmental change;
- whether welfare services should be provided to people depending upon their means ('selective' or 'means-tested' provision) or 'free', irrespective of their income and wealth ('universal' provision).

This book therefore provides an introduction to the subject of social policy for students studying specifically for a degree in social policy and for those encountering the subject within their broader studies, such as part of a nursing, social work, criminology or youth work qualification. We hope that those studying social policy for the first time will find it a gentle and useful introduction to the subject.

After the introductory chapter, the book is in four parts. The first contains four chapters that provide the broad context necessary to understand current debates in social policy. The three chapters in Part 2 consider the development of the subject, particularly over the nineteenth and twentieth centuries. Part 3 examines contemporary aspects of providing welfare, including areas where both government policies and provision, and the academic subject, are developing. The final part is concerned with European and wider international developments, and the Conclusion seeks to draw together some of the ideas presented throughout the book.

While we would hope that some readers will work through the book from beginning to end, it has also been designed so that it can be used for particular topics, by focusing on key chapters or sections. To help to understand and explore the subject matter there are a variety of features, such as the 'Controversy and debate', 'Spotlight', and 'Discussion and review' features that both highlight and remind the reader of important arguments and examples. The Glossary at the end of the book provides explanations of some of the key terms and abbreviations that are part and parcel of the language of social policy. Finally, each chapter also has guidance on further reading and web sites where additional information can be found.

Overall, we hope that the book is interesting and enjoyable, since, in our view, while clearly important, social policy should be 'serious fun'.

Hugh Bochel and Guy Daly

CHAPTER 1

Introducing Social Policy

Hugh Bochel and Guy Daly

Learning objectives

- To introduce the subject of social policy
- To consider how and why the subject has changed and developed over the past three decades

Chapter overview

Social policy is one of the social sciences, together with, for example, politics and sociology. It is sometimes studied on its own, sometimes jointly with another subject, and also is frequently delivered as part of another subject. It is often taken as part of professional training, such as in nursing or social work. This chapter seeks to provide a consideration of the subject of social policy, how it relates to other cognate subjects, and what it means to be studying it. The chapter, therefore:

- explores the nature of the subject, including the way in which it has developed as an academic discipline over time;
- outlines the structure of the remainder of the book.

What is social policy?

The almost inevitable starting point for a book such as this is the question, 'What is social policy?' While such a question is equally likely for a book on one of the other social sciences, there is perhaps a greater importance for social policy, in part because the subject itself has developed and changed direction considerably since the 1980s, in part because the actions of governments and others impact upon what might be considered 'social policy' (see, for example, Chapters 20 and 21), and in part because these considerations continue to have significant resonance within the subject as it and its subject matter evolve further.

As an academic subject social policy is clearly related to other social science disciplines, including economics, politics, and sociology, but it also has a resonance with many professional courses, such as those focusing on social work, housing or nursing. Given the connections, it is not surprising that the study of social policy often draws upon concepts and insights that come from all of these areas, but at the same time it brings its own distinctive approach to the understanding and analysis of the world. In the same way, a subject such as criminology, which has largely emerged in UK higher education since the 1990s, also draws upon a range of subjects, including social policy, but is itself developing and debating its boundaries (see, for example, Chapter 14).

Although it may draw upon a range of cognate areas, social policy as an academic discipline can be seen as differing from others in a number of ways. For example, it is different from sociology in its focus upon the formulation, implementation, and delivery of policies that affect the circumstances of individuals, groups, and society; it differs from politics in its focus upon welfare and wellbeing; and it is different from economics, because it is less concerned with the production of goods and services, and because of its emphasis upon social or welfare policies and their outcomes. This is not to say that there are not sometimes closely related interests, and social policy academics and courses may be located in departments with a variety of labels in different higher education institutions, while social policy departments may in turn contain individuals who draw heavily upon or who originate from other subjects. There are also many institutions where social policy is in a department jointly with one or more other subjects, such as criminology, politics, social work or sociology. These all reflect the complexity and breadth of the subject.

Notwithstanding the discussion above, the nature of the subject has changed considerably over time. For much of the twentieth century, 'social administration', as it was then called, was strongly associated with the Fabian tradition, itself linked to social democratic thought, including the Labour Party (see Chapter 8). Many social administration academics were therefore seeking not merely to study social policy, but also to influence it in a direction that fitted generally with Fabian beliefs, often using their research and analysis to support their political arguments. These could roughly be characterised as a belief in the role of the state as a central pillar of welfare provision (the 'welfare state'), generally located in a mixed economy, and a commitment to research and analysis that was concerned with the identification of needs and the impact of state welfare in attempting to meet those needs. This classic welfare state was often conceived of in relation to policies of income maintenance and social security, health care, the personal social services, education and training, employment, and housing; and social policy was widely seen as what the welfare state did. However, in the second half of the twentieth century, a more critical approach emerged within the subject, and by the 1970s and 1980s it was possible to identify a number of theoretical challenges to the association of Fabianism and the study of social administration and social policies linked to the welfare state. These included:

- The New Right and other 'anti-collectivists' – one of the most significant attacks on state provision of welfare (see Chapters 7 and 8) came from the right, and in particular from think tanks such as the Adam Smith Institute, the Centre for Policy Studies, and the Institute for Economic Affairs. These critiques took a number of forms, but could generally be seen as arguing that: the welfare state was a burden on the economy and that it demanded too high levels of public expenditure and an excessive tax burden upon entrepreneurs and citizens; that it damaged individual choice, in contrast to the market, which is seen from this perspective as promoting it; and that it weakens the family and encourages dependency. The strategies that the New Right put forward as alternatives typically involved cuts in income tax, a shift away from state provision to individuals providing for themselves and their families through the private market, direct charging for services such as education and health, and the replacement of most of the benefits and services provided by the state with alternatives from the private and voluntary sectors.

- On the left there also emerged a number of criticisms – some began to accept that the role of the state remained problematic in the provision of welfare, and while in some instances state intervention had been valuable in changing social conditions, in others it had not always been so beneficial. Some argued that one answer was the injection of more resources to help tackle problems more successfully, while others favoured alternative approaches, such as the decentralisation of power and the encouragement of self-help for particular groups. One view, associated with a Marxist approach, suggested that in reality state welfare reflected the needs of capitalism for an educated, healthy workforce, and that this explained the failure of the welfare state to solve social problems.

- The centre – critiques of the welfare state also emerged from centrist positions, often focusing upon the view that the large bureaucratic organisations that were often responsible for delivering welfare were inefficient and inflexible and were remote from the needs of consumers, and that they tended to be run in the interests of professionals and administrators rather than users or citizens. From this perspective, proposed solutions generally involved a shift towards a pluralistic, decentralised, and more participative pattern of provision, including a much greater role for the voluntary sector.

- Other critical perspectives – for example, feminists pointed out that there were a number of assumptions behind the provision of many services, including education, health care, and the personal social services, such as that it was 'natural' for women to provide care for children, disabled people and older people, and that they would often provide this care free at home while men went out to work to earn the household income. The state, therefore, could be seen as exploiting and encouraging the 'caring role' of women. Even when women did work (often in the 'caring services'), there was a tendency for them to do so in the less-well paid jobs, while men dominated the higher-status, better-paid positions. In a similar manner, it could also be pointed out that many welfare services failed to recognise particular needs of minority ethnic groups, disabled people, and others.

In addition, there were other developments that encouraged reflection within the subject. These included other New Right critiques, in particular of bureaucracies, which have been important in the delivery of state welfare. New Right thinkers have argued that bureaucrats are primarily concerned with promoting their own interests, and that they do this at the expense of the public interest. Furthermore, they suggest that political control of state bureaucracies is often ineffective. From the perspective of the New Right, these combine to increase the pressure for higher levels of public expenditure, which itself is seen as problematic and a drain on the economy. Given the large bureaucracies often associated with state welfare provision, these arguments, if accepted, raise significant questions over the mechanisms used for delivering welfare.

It is also worth noting here that while the academic subject of social policy, and indeed many social policies, has been concerned with improving the welfare of citizens, or leading to greater social justice, there is nothing necessary or inevitable about this. Social policies and other measures, such as taxation (see Chapter 9), can equally be designed to ignore or even to increase inequalities.

From the 1970s, there also came to be a much greater awareness of the relevance of comparison to the study and understanding of social policy. In part, this resulted from the United Kingdom's membership of the European Union, which inevitably focused greater attention upon Europe and other European states. However, increasingly this interest spread to other areas of the world, and in particular sought to learn from the experiences and policies of other states. For some, for example, the Scandinavian states provided models for state welfare founded in a social democratic approach. For others, the more market-oriented approach of the United States appeared to present a more appropriate path for the UK. Whatever the approach, it became apparent that there was a great diversity of forms of welfare provision, with very different mixes of provision by the public, private, voluntary, and informal sectors. The comparative approach to social policy has developed greatly in recent years and is now a major strand within the subject (see Chapters 22 and 23), while concerns over international trends such as globalisation have been seen as having implications for the shape of social policies, and thus for the academic subject (see Chapter 24). In addition, there are many examples of policy transfer, with governments drawing upon ideas and policies from other countries, such as elements of Labour's New Deal, which drew on the experience of the United States, and the Coalition government's 'free schools', which drew on the establishment of similar schools in Sweden and the United States.

The impact of all of these developments has inevitably affected the academic subject of social policy. Over a period of time it came to reflect and respond to these debates, arguably becoming broader and, in some respects at least, more critical. It is therefore not surprising that during the 1980s there was considerable debate about the nature of the discipline. However, the subject has not lost entirely its traditional links, with a number of university departments and awards continuing to use the term 'social administration', while the government bodies that fund and oversee much of higher education, such as the Higher Education Funding Council for England and the Quality Assurance Agency for Higher Education (QAA), often refer to 'social policy and administration'. Indeed, the QAA's subject benchmark statement (see Spotlight, below), which seeks to outline the nature and characteristics of the subject and the attributes and capabilities that an honours graduate in social policy should possess, is for social policy and administration. As illustrated elsewhere in this book, the boundaries and relevance of social policy and its insights continue to evolve.

SPOTLIGHT

Social policy and administration subject benchmark: the nature and extent of the subject

Social policy and administration is about the study of the distribution and organisation of welfare and wellbeing within societies. Its focus is on the ways in which different societies understand and meet the needs of their populations. The discipline is characterised by the following principles:

- the rigorous linking of theoretical analysis with empirical enquiry
- the identification and understanding of different value positions
- a willingness to engage with a range of intellectual traditions and social science disciplines
- the belief that students should acquire the skills and qualities which enable them to become active and informed citizens.

Social policy is an interdisciplinary and applied discipline which is concerned with analysing the distribution and delivery of resources in response to social need. The subject draws on ideas and methods from sociology, political science and economics, while also using insights from a range of disciplines including social anthropology, human geography, social psychology and social work. As a discipline in its own right, social policy studies the ways in which societies provide for the social needs of their members through structures and systems of distribution, redistribution, regulation, provision and empowerment. It seeks to foster in its students a capacity to assess critically evidence from a range of social science disciplines and to appreciate how social policies are continuously reconstructed and changed. Students will understand the contribution to these processes from those who come from different value positions and different social, cultural and economic backgrounds. They will also appreciate the fact that some social groups are more able to protect, alter or advance their value positions more effectively than others.

(QAA, 2007, p. 2)

Interestingly, consideration of the benchmark statement demonstrates both the academic and the applied nature of the subject, since the statement attempts to set out academic characteristics, but does so in response to a policy imperative in the form of pressure from governments to measure and maintain standards in higher education (see Chapter 11).

However, attempts to define the subject also need to recognise that social policy exists outside the academic world, and that much of what governments and other bodies do is social policy. Policies can be designed to help people, although even those that are intended to do so may not always achieve their aims, for a variety of reasons. Others may be 'technocratic' in nature – designed to improve a mechanism, perhaps to achieve something more efficiently or economically, or even to improve the nature of policy-making itself. And social policies can be used to control people, as we have seen in recent years with demands to control or deter asylum seekers and migrants, or with regard to anti-social behaviour. One of the things that students and analysts of social policy need to do, therefore, is to examine policies critically – to look at their intentions and impacts and consider the extent to which they achieve their goals, and the reasons why this might or might not be the case. As the QAA benchmark statement suggests, we must therefore sometimes try to set aside our personal views and opinions, and recognise that it can be useful to try to see things from the perspectives of others. For example, we can seek to understand why some people feel strongly about individual choice and others favour collective provision, or why politicians, managers and health professionals in the National Health Service may clash over the best way to meet particular goals. We can try to put ourselves in the place of politicians who sometimes have to make difficult decisions about the level of resources that should be spent on welfare (and other areas of activity) and how the money for this should be raised, or the people who then have to deliver services, or those who are recipients. Each of these may provide us with very different perspectives on social policies. However, we also have to recognise that we all have our own values and attitudes, our own visions of what a good society should be like, and that the study of social policy is likely to involve us in both seeking to be objective and in maintaining our beliefs, and that at times there is likely to be a tension between the two.

The structure of this book

While the discussion above has outlined the complexity of the study of social policy, this book is written on the assumption that most students of social policy have little or no knowledge of the academic subject, even if all have inevitably come into contact with social policies. Given that social policy exists in a social, political, and economic environment, the chapters in Part I set out the background, including social and economic changes and the political context within which social policies are made and delivered, including the new framework that has emerged from devolution.

Part II focuses on the development of social policy, beginning with changes in the provision of welfare and changing attitudes to the role of the state, and then considering key influences upon social policy in the form of the ideas that have underpinned Conservative and Labour governments and their approaches.

Part III consists of a series of chapters that can be broadly characterised as focusing primarily upon the delivery and impacts of social policy. While inevitably reflecting the legacy of previous governments and policies, these examine in particular social policy under Labour from 1997 to 2010 and developments under the Conservative–Liberal Democrat Coalition government from 2010 to the present. In many respects, therefore, these chapters are concerned not only with changes and priorities in social policy, but also with social policies as they affect individuals.

Reflecting the preceding discussion about the broader international scope of interests in social policy, Part IV examines European and international developments, including the European Union and its impact upon social policy development, comparisons between the UK and other states, and debates about globalisation and its implications for social policy.

Each chapter is designed to provide information and also to encourage you to think for yourself about its subject matter. Each also gives directions to additional sources of information, both written and via the Internet, to allow students to follow up areas in which they have a particular interest.

Summary

This chapter has outlined the development of the subject of social policy and provided a brief history of the welfare state in the UK. It has shown that:

- The academic study of social policy has moved away from a focus upon the welfare state towards a much broader consideration of provision by the public, private, voluntary, and informal sectors.
- Theoretical debates have been and continue to be important, not only in improving our ability to understand and explain social policy, but also in influencing the decisions of policy-makers, as was reflected in the move away from the post-war consensus over the social democratic state towards a view that has been more influenced by New Right thinking.
- Our understanding of social policy has been affected further by the growth of an international dimension, which itself has been affected by the greater awareness of the range of modes of welfare provision (and different systems of payment for welfare) in different states, and by the UK's involvement in the European Union.

Discussion and review

- What is social policy?
- In what ways do social policies affect your everyday life?
- How useful is the concept of the 'welfare state'?

Reference

Quality Assurance Agency for Higher Education (2007) *Social Policy and Administration*, QAA, Gloucester.

Further reading

Alcock, P., Erskine, A. and May, M. (eds.) (2002) *The Blackwell Dictionary of Social Policy*, Blackwell, Oxford. This is a useful source of definitions of a range of ideas relevant to social policy.

Alcock, P., May, M. and Wright, S. (eds.) (2012) *The Student's Companion to Social Policy*, Blackwell, Oxford. This book contains a number of concise but comprehensive discussions, including over many key aspects of social policy.

Fraser, D. (2009) *The Evolution of the British Welfare State*, Palgrave Macmillan, Basingstoke. This title provides a comprehensive history of welfare policy in Britain.

Useful websites

http://www.gov.uk – intended to be the first port of call for access to government, this site provides links to government departments and other organisations responsible for social policy and services throughout the UK.

http://www.oecd.org – the Organisation for Economic Cooperation and Development site contains considerable amounts of information relevant for comparisons across countries.

http://www.qaa.ac.uk/Publications/InformationAndGuidance/Pages/Subject-benchmark-statement-Social-policy-and-administration.aspx – this is the QAA benchmark statement for 'Social Policy and Administration'.

http://www.social-policy.org.uk/ – this is the website for the Social Policy Association (SPA), which is the professional association for teachers, researchers, students, and practitioners of social policy.

PART 1
CONTEXT

- THE SOCIO-ECONOMIC CONTEXT OF
  SOCIAL POLICY

- THE POLITICS AND GOVERNANCE OF
  SOCIAL POLICY

- DEVOLUTION AND SOCIAL POLICY

- RESEARCH, EVIDENCE, AND POLICY

CHAPTER 2

The Socio-economic Context of Social Policy

Nick Ellison

Learning objectives

- To illustrate the interaction between social and economic phenomena and policies
- To explore changing social patterns and the issues that they raise for social policy and policy-makers
- To provide some wider context for the UK situation
- To consider the extent to which social and economic change and welfare dependency are leading to new policy responses

Chapter overview

Changing patterns of employment, the changing shape of families and family life, the impact of key demographic changes on national communities, each of these phenomena carries profound implications for how social policy is perceived and understood. Why should this be so? How is it that welfare policies are so closely connected to issues of employment and family life?

There is a constant 'dialogue' between social and economic phenomena that make up the context of social policy-making and the organisation of social policy itself. So, briefly taking changes in employment patterns as an example, the majority of welfare systems in the mid to late twentieth century were constructed around particular assumptions about the nature of work and the respective roles of men and women in the labour market. Unfortunately (for policy-makers at least), these assumptions quickly became outdated. What constituted 'work' and who did it changed rapidly and radically – and it is no exaggeration to say that the majority of welfare states have been playing catch-up ever since the 1960s when these changes first became evident.

This chapter demonstrates how rapidly things can change in the modern world and how relatively *slowly* welfare arrangements seem to respond to these changes. The result, of course, is that welfare states, despite having their roots in the radical, progressive politics of the first half of the twentieth century can appear rather 'conservative' and unresponsive to social and economic change. The chapter explores the following key issues:

- changing patterns of work in the UK and elsewhere;
- the impact of employment changes on key social divisions;
- changing family structures;
- demographic change.

Changing employment patterns

Work is absolutely central to social policy. Why? Because ensuring the availability of paid employment is the most obvious way of reducing the risk of poverty for individuals and their families. While this statement needs to be qualified in a number of ways – it may not be possible for literally everyone to work even if jobs are available, because some people suffer from physical impairments that prevent them from working and women carry out a vast amount of *unpaid* domestic and caring work in the home – it is the case, nevertheless, that paid employment underpins social policy-making in all the developed welfare states.

This stress on employment is as old as 'social policy' itself – and of course it continues to play a central role in current debates about 'welfare reform' in the UK and elsewhere. In England, the Elizabethan Poor Law of 1601 saw the appointment of overseers in each parish who were charged with the task of finding work for the able-bodied unemployed, while the 'New Poor Law' of 1834 actively forced the able-bodied into the employment market by making conditions in the new workhouses so bad that only those on the verge of complete destitution would contemplate entering them (see Chapter 6). Poor Law arrangements of one kind or other existed in most parts of Europe into the twentieth century, only being gradually overtaken by organised welfare systems that aimed to produce full employment as part of a wider strategy of economic management. Certainly by the end of the Second World War in 1945, governments in Northern and Western Europe, in addition to those in Australia, New Zealand, Canada, and the USA, had come to recognise that they had a major role to play in maintaining employment. How they did this varied among the different countries, but between roughly the late 1940s and the late 1970s 'full employment' was a major policy goal in these states. Following broadly Keynesian economic policies throughout this period, governments actively managed the 'demand side' of their economies in efforts to achieve it.

The real issue, however, is what sort of 'employment' governments were attempting to sustain. In the early part of the post-war period, almost without exception, the (unstated) goal was full *male* employment, and it is no great exaggeration to suggest that the welfare systems that developed in Europe and elsewhere took for granted the fact that men worked while married women remained at home. Consequently, income provision for unemployment, sickness, and old age largely depended on the size and continuity of the male wage. In the majority of welfare states, the employed 'breadwinner' would pay insurance contributions from his wages either directly to the state or into special insurance funds to provide pensions and other benefits for both himself and his wife. Outside these arrangements, which were quite generous in countries like Germany and France, although less so in Britain, there were only means-tested forms of 'social assistance' to support those who were not able to work or who had gaps in their employment record.

Whether or not this understanding of 'full employment' is defensible in terms of the clear gender bias that characterises it is not the issue here – important though this matter is. In terms of the socio-economic context of social policy, the significant point is that, from the 1960s onwards, *structural changes* in the majority of the developed economies meant that full male employment became increasingly hard to sustain. These changes favoured new forms of work, were less dependent on the male industrial worker, and if anything, were more disposed towards the employment of women.

The key shift concerned the dramatic decline of 'Fordist' manufacturing industry – characterised by the virtually all-male, unionised workforce engaged in production line assembly – and the rise of 'post-Fordist' or 'post-industrial' forms of employment, usually based in the service industries (Amin, 1994). Although the causes of this change are complex and cannot be addressed in detail here, it is important to appreciate that a number of factors contributed to it. It is highly likely that rising global economic competition meant that many manufactured goods could be produced more cheaply in the developing economies; but it is also the case that 'post-industrial' changes *within* many advanced economies were also significant factors. The emergence of new labour-saving technologies reduced reliance on human labour for example, while changes in patterns of consumption as incomes rose and consumers became more discerning, meant that demand for mass-produced standardised goods gave way to a range of new 'wants' for evermore sophisticated 'niche' products and services. To meet these changing consumption patterns, producers had to become more 'flexible' – able to shift product lines and re-focus workforce skills according to market demands. Underpinning these changes has been the dramatic rise of the 'knowledge economy', which has entailed a need to move workforces away from the traditional skills associated with heavy industry and mass production towards a very different range of abilities concerned with 'informationalisation', knowledge exploitation, creativity, and above all, the capacity continually to 're-skill' in response to constantly shifting consumption patterns.

The following tables provide an insight into the nature and timing of this move from male-based industrial production to service sector employment – a process that became visible around the early 1960s, developed throughout that decade, and gathered speed across the 1980s and early 1990s. The trends continue to this day, although, with much of the transformation complete, the pace of change has inevitably lessened in recent years. Table 2.1 provides data, gathered by the Organisation for Economic Cooperation and Development (OECD), which demonstrate how employment in industry fell as a percentage of civilian employment in a number of key economies between 1960 and 2011.

With the exception of Japan (which is something of an anomaly in the table on manufacturing employment because, during the 1960s and 1970s in particular, the country benefited from having a large and cheap workforce, an advantage lost during the late 1980s and 1990s as other Asian and South East Asian countries – South Korea, Taiwan, Malaysia, and now of course China – overtook Japan in their ability to produce cheap manufactured goods), all countries experienced a loss of industrial employment in the early part of the period, but it is worth acknowledging how serious the decline was

Table 2.1 Civilian employment in industry as a percentage of civilian employment

	1960	1974	1986	1994	2000	2006	2011
USA	35.5	32.5	27.7	24.0	23.0	19.9	17.3
Japan	28.5	37.0	34.5	34.0	31.2	28.0	26.0
Germany	47.0	46.7	40.8	37.7	33.7	29.8	28.4
France	37.6	39.4	31.4	24.5 (e)	22.5 (e)	20.8 (e)	—
Italy	33.9	39.3	33.1	34.3	32.4	30.5	28.5
UK	47.7	42.0	34.1	27.6	25.2	22.1	19.1
Canada	33.1	30.5	28.2	22.3	23.1	23.6	19.8
Australia	38.9	34.9	26.5	23.4	21.7	21.4	20.7
Denmark	36.9	32.3	31.4	24.5 (e)	26.4	23.6	18.6
Sweden	40.3	37.0	29.8	25.1	24.6	22.0	19.9

Source: Adapted from OECD (2012).

in the United States, the United Kingdom, Canada, and Australia. However, the rise in service sector employment over the same period is very clear, as Table 2.2 illustrates.

Employment in industry, then, has plainly declined in the major economies. In addition, service sector work, which includes a wide variety of employment from the highly paid banking and legal sectors to low-paid jobs in catering, cleaning, and leisure services, increased markedly in all cases between 1960 and the early 1990s, and has continued to do so through to 2011, albeit at a slower pace.

Table 2.3 shows how the percentage of women in the workforce has risen as the nature of employment has changed. In fairly simple terms, as male employment in the manufacturing sector declined, employment in the service sector increased and this shift allowed more women to enter the workforce. Although the change was by no means an unalloyed good for women, because

Table 2.2 Employment in services as a percentage of civilian employment

	1960	1974	1986	1994	2000	2006	2011
USA	56.2	63.4	69.3	73.1	75.2	78.5	81.1
Japan	41.3	50.1	57.1	60.2	63.7	67.7	70.2
Germany	39.1	46.3	54.8	59.1	63.7	67.9	69.0
France	39.9	49.9	61.3	68.4	74.2	76.4	—
Italy	33.5	43.2	56.0	59.7	62.2	65.2	67.8
UK	47.6	55.1	66.7	72.4	73.3	76.6	79.7
Canada	54.1	63.1	69.9	73.3	73.6	75.3	78.1
Australia	50.1	58.0	66.9	71.3	73.4	75.2	76.4
Denmark	44.8	58.0	65.9	68.1	70.2	73.4	79.2
Sweden	44.0	56.3	65.7	71.6	73.0	76.0	78.1

Source: Adapted from OECD (1996, Table 2.12), OECD (2012).

Table 2.3 Civilian employment of women as a percentage of civilian employment

	1960	1974	1986	1994	2000	2006	2011
USA	33.3	38.9	44.4	46.0	46.0	46.5	46.9
Japan	40.7	37.7	39.8	40.5	40.8	41.6	42.2
Germany	37.8	38.1	39.5	42.1	44.1	45.5	46.3
France	34.8	37.2	42.3	45.3	45.9	47.2	48.2
Italy	30.9	29.2	33.8	35.0	37.2	39.8	40.8
UK	33.4	38.4	42.5	45.6	46.1	46.3	46.5
Canada	26.8	35.7	42.8	45.3	46.0	47.0	47.5
Australia	—	34.4	39.3	42.6	44.1	45.1	45.5
Denmark	31.8	41.5	45.3	46.0	45.9	47.2	48.2
Sweden	—	41.6	47.6	48.7	46.5	47.6	47.4

Source: Adapted from OECD (2012).

Table 2.4 Rate of unemployment as a percentage of the civilian labour force

	1960	1974	1986	1994	2000	2006	2011
USA	5.5	5.6	7.0	6.1	4.0	5.8	7.6
Japan	1.4	1.4	2.8	2.9	4.7	4.1	4.5
Germany	1.0	2.2	6.6	8.5	7.8	10.3	5.9
France	1.3	2.6	9.6	10.6	9.3	8.6	9.1
Italy	5.7	5.4	11.2	11.2	10.4	6.9	8.4
UK	1.4	2.6	10.8	9.6	5.4	5.4	7.9
Canada	7.0	5.3	9.7	10.4	6.8	6.3	7.4
Australia	1.4	2.7	8.1	9.7	6.3	4.8	5.1
Denmark	2.0	3.6	5.5	8.1	4.4	4.1	7.8
Sweden	1.7	2.0	2.9	9.8	5.6	7.1	8.9

Source: Adapted from OECD (2012).

many service sector jobs are non-unionised, part-time or casual, with the low wages that these working conditions imply, it nevertheless had the effect of radically altering prevailing assumptions about the nature of work.

A further table (Table 2.4) is necessary because it is important to see how the changes discussed here affected overall rates of employment. In essence, from a low base in the early 1960s, unemployment rose in the majority of the advanced economies from the late 1970s through the 1980s and 1990s as industry shed workers. Although the service sector helped to stem the resulting unemployment, the fact that work in this sector tends to be less secure and non-unionised has meant that service jobs have never fully offset the combined effects of the decline in industrial employment and (with more women coming into the labour market) the rising numbers of people seeking work. The period from the late 1990s to the recession created by the banking crisis in 2008 saw unemployment fall as a percentage of the civilian labour force – but not to the low levels that were considered 'normal' in the immediate post-war years.

Changing social divisions

The discussion above suggests that the changing nature of work, including the rising incidence of unemployment, has had a clear impact on the employment structures of the developed economies, but what changes have taken place and who has been most affected? These are complex questions and only fairly brief answers can be provided here. It is important to appreciate, however, how traditional socio-economic class divisions have changed over the past 30 years or so, while the impact of post-industrial employment patterns on gender divisions, alluded to above, need to be explored in more detail.

Where 'social class' is concerned, there are many ways of defining the term (see Giddens, 2006), but for present purposes 'occupation' and particularly the division between manual and non-manual employment is the most useful. The decline in industrial employment implies a decline in manual work and the system of class-based industrial relations associated with it. In short, as 'working-class' manual occupations based in manufacturing declined, the strength of organised labour was simultaneously reduced. This process was hastened and exacerbated in the UK in the 1980s by Conservative governments' attacks on trade unions, the 1984–85 miners' strike being the most dramatic example of the assault on organised labour at a time when the days of the traditional unionised, male working class were already numbered. The speed of the decline of trade union membership in the UK is marked. In 1979, membership stood at 13.3 million, with 55 per cent of employees belonging to a union. By 2011 these figures were 6.4 million and 26 per cent respectively (Brownlie, 2012). An indicative aspect of this process is that, as union strength has waned, those areas of employment that have remained relatively highly unionised have been the professions and public sector occupations (lawyers, doctors, teachers, civil servants), as opposed to what remains of the manufacturing sector. In addition, women are now more likely than men to be members of a trade union, with females in professional occupations being one-and-a-half times more likely to be union members than their male counterparts (Self and Zealey, 2007).

Similar patterns of trade union decline can be detected in many, although not all, developed economies. The USA, for instance, has seen a marked reduction in union membership from 36 per cent of the labour force in the 1950s to 16 per cent in the 1990s, and according the US Bureau of Labor Statistics, 11.3 per cent in 2012. Particularly steep declines can be detected in manufacturing and construction. Elsewhere, union membership fell in Sweden and Germany – but actually increased in Denmark and the Netherlands. According to the Federation of European Employers (2012), membership rates are generally falling across Europe, with a dramatic – if unsurprising – collapse in trade union membership in the latest countries to join the European Union from Eastern Europe. While this decline cannot be attributed *solely* to changing employment patterns – after all, political changes in Eastern Europe have clearly influenced matters in the post-Communist states – this dimension is crucial.

What, then, does the post-industrial socio-economic landscape look like in terms of social structure? With the old unionised class politics in abeyance, if by no means entirely absent, the picture is highly fragmented. The growth of flexible and casual work has meant that individuals across a range of areas and income groups have been affected by unemployment and insecurity. With the threat of unemployment ever-present for *all* sectors of the labour market, it has been easier for employers to demand more from their employees, with the result that the amount of hours spent at work has risen while the amount of work actually carried out during those hours has also gone up. This intensification of work has been accompanied by greater income inequalities. Although it is important to note that absolute living standards in the UK and other developed economies have risen for most people over the past 30 years, the absence of strong labour movements to maintain income levels for the low paid has meant that income distribution has been increasingly 'stretched'. According to Carrera and Beaumont (2010, p. 3), 'GDP per head in the UK more than doubled in real terms' between 1970 and 2009 – although it is important to remember that, as a result of the economic downturn following the banking crisis, gross domestic product (GDP) per head had dropped by 5.5 per cent to just below its 2004 level. However, according to information derived from the Institute for Fiscal Studies, the Gini Coefficient – the measure of overall income inequality in the UK – has risen to its highest level since 1979, from 26 to 41 points (The Poverty Site, 2010).

In place of the single most significant twentieth-century division between manual and non-manual occupations have come more fine-grained divisions among different income groups. While those in certain professions – law, financial services, medicine, and the higher echelons of business – have seen their incomes rise markedly, even in the period of economic recession associated with the banking crisis of 2008, others in the lower reaches of the service sector, where employment patterns tend to be more casual, have fared less well. Employment among young people has fallen in the UK, with 16- to 17-year-olds experiencing a 24.9 per cent fall in employment rates between 1992 and 2011 (Spence, 2011). Of course, many women work in these latter occupations, as do individuals from minority ethnic communities, with the result that income divisions tend to be gendered and racialised. As Self and Zealey (2007, p. 65) make clear,

> . . . in 2004/5 in Great Britain, all ethnic minority groups had greater than average likelihood of being in the bottom quintile group, with the Pakistani/ Bangladeshi group being particularly at risk. In addition, groups with greater than average risks of being in the bottom quintile group in the UK were single parent families and families where one or more adults and one or more of the children were disabled.

The only way in which this picture of more subtle income divisions needs to be qualified concerns not so much a divide between social classes, as one between those who work (or have access to work) and those who do not. As Rowlingson (2003, p. 15) stated, 'another fairly new phenomenon in the 1980s and 1990s was the *workless household* [original emphasis]. Work has polarised across households, as there has been a rise in the number of dual-earner households and the number of no-earner households'. Rowlingson goes on to note that 'there has been a substantial increase in worklessness among couples over the last 30 years' with about 'two-thirds . . . of the change [being] caused by variations in access to employment for different types of household'. Essentially, in better-off households women joined their partners in employment, whereas 'in worse-off households, men were joining their partners in the home'.

If lone parents, who are another group that suffers from high unemployment rates, are added to those in workless households, it is possible to portray the resulting divide between the 'work rich' and 'work poor' as a variation on more traditional *class* divides. The phraseology used by some commentators, such as Charles Murray in the USA, is considered by others – especially in the UK – to be pejorative (Deacon, 2002; Lister, 2004). Murray (1994) refers to certain key segments of the workless poor (he particularly singles out African-Americans) as an 'underclass', arguing that individuals in this 'class' are distinguished by high rates of single parenthood, high divorce rates, high crime rates, poor educational achievement, and dependency on welfare benefits. One way of encouraging different behaviours, according to Murray, would be to remove welfare support so that individuals had little choice but to find work – in other words, the important issue is to alter the behaviour of *irresponsible individuals*. Others, including the US sociologist William Julius Wilson (1987), for example, while accepting that an 'underclass' might exist, nevertheless do not ascribe its existence to individual behaviour but to key 'structural' factors of the kind discussed in this chapter – most obviously the decline of manufacturing employment and the associated rise of unemployment and casual, low-paid jobs. Wilson also acknowledges that, in the USA, additional difficulties have been arisen owing to the close association between 'race' and poverty, although he argues that these, too, owe more to structural failings of the economy than to the behaviours of African-American individuals and communities.

Yet others (see Bagguley and Mann, 1992; Deacon, 2002; Lister, 2004; Alcock, 2006) argue that the use of the term 'underclass' is dangerous and should be avoided. For one thing, there is little empirical evidence to suggest that the 'underclass' is a coherent class at all, but rather a series of different groups (lone parents, the unemployed) who may experience particular kinds of misfortune at different stages of the life cycle. Again, it is not clear that the apparent behaviours associated with the 'underclass', such as lone parenthood and high divorce rates, differ much from those found in other sections of society. More importantly, perhaps, the tendency to use flimsy evidence to label vulnerable people as irresponsible and 'undeserving' itself separates and excludes them from the social mainstream – and this stigmatizing process can hardly be expected to result in greater social inclusion or better understanding of the challenges facing the most deprived sections of society.

Debates of this kind, stimulated as they are by the ever-changing socio-economic environment, are highly significant, and relate directly to social policy. In view of the sweeping changes that have occurred in the world of work over the past 30 years, how should governments respond? Is it really the case that the welfare states of the post-war era created a dependent 'underclass'? How should governments balance employers' demands for a 'flexible' workforce with the problems, particularly for women, disabled people, and minority ethnic communities, generated by unemployment and low pay? Is there a way for welfare provision both to support the 'new economy' *and* protect the interests of the most vulnerable?

CONTROVERSY AND DEBATE

Charles Murray's 'underclass' thesis rests on the assertion that a distinct and separate class exists outside 'normal' society. This 'class' is characterised by certain types of behaviour, which Murray deems unacceptable. High rates of single parenthood, divorce, fatherless families, illegitimacy, crime, and welfare dependency mean that this 'class' is both economically and culturally segregated. (For further details, see Murray, 1996a, 1996b.) Others, such as Buckingham (1999), also argue that there is evidence of the existence of an 'underclass' in the UK. Buckingham's analysis of the National Child Development Study indicated that there is good reason to distinguish between a 'working class' and an 'underclass' in the UK – and evidence to suggest that there are distinct patterns of family formation, commitment to work, and political allegiance between the two classes.

Many academics, especially in the UK, have challenged these views. They argue that there is no real evidence to support the conclusions advanced by Murray and Buckingham, pointing to the fact that rising rates of divorce, single parenthood, and illegitimacy are by no means confined to an 'underclass', but characterise changes throughout society. They also argue that to stigmatise groups and individuals in this way is inherently counter-productive. (For further details, see Bagguley and Mann, 1992; Lister, 1996, 2004; Deacon, 2002; Levitas, 2005; Prideaux, 2005; Alcock, 2006.)

Examine the evidence that Murray uses to argue for the existence of an 'underclass' and then assess the evidence discussed by Buckingham. Consider how accurate both accounts are by considering the arguments against the existence of an 'underclass' by the critics mentioned above.

The changing nature of the welfare state

The changes discussed above have, over time, resulted in wide-ranging alterations to the role and purpose of social policies in the developed economies. What follows concentrates mainly on the UK because it constitutes one of the more marked examples of how welfare arrangements developed in the late 1940s have changed to accommodate the challenges posed by changing economic conditions and employment patterns. However, it is important to understand that the majority of welfare states in the developed economies have been confronted with the same difficulties and have responded in similar, although not identical, ways.

At the most general level of analysis, social policies in the UK and other welfare states have shifted from an orientation around 'social protection' to one that is more concerned with 'competition'. Commentators such as Jessop (1994, 2002) and Cerny (1990, 2000) have discussed the ways in which states, faced with the mounting costs of welfare support in the face or rising unemployment and falling economic growth, turned to forms of 'welfare' that would support the changing economic environment rather than compensate the victims of it. Jessop (1994) suggested that there has been a shift from what is frequently referred to as the 'Keynesian Welfare State' to the 'Schumpeterian Workfare State', while Cerny (1990) refers simply to the emergence of the 'competition state'. In both cases, the point being made is that the role of the state in the newly competitive capitalist world economy is one of securing and maintaining the *conditions* for economic growth. In particular, the extension of the free market and retreat from direct state intervention in economic management has characterised state economic strategies in the developed economies, and the conduct of social policy has been a key aspect of – indeed, almost a metaphor for – this change. As Evans and Cerny (2003, p. 26) state:

> The creation of the competition state involves a policy agenda which seeks to provide the conditions that will help the state to adapt state action to cope more effectively with what [are perceived] as global 'realities'. Particular types of policy change have thus risen to the top of the policy agenda . . . [including] a shift . . . in the focal point of party and governmental politics away from the general maximisation of welfare within a nation (full employment, redistributive transfer payments and social service provision) to the promotion of enterprise, innovation and profitability in both private and public sectors.

In other words, where competition is becoming increasingly global, domestic economies 'post-industrial', and the nature of the workforce changing as a result, social policy is used to work with the grain of the new economy rather than to act as a countervailing force. It is in this way that those claiming unemployment benefit have been turned into 'job-seekers' and labour market policies have been re-orientated to 'activate' the unemployed. In the UK, the Job-Seekers Allowance (1996) was the first attempt by policy-makers to 'encourage' those claiming unemployment benefit actively to seek work. Under the New Labour governments between 1997 and 2010, this formula was increasingly refined in the shape of various 'New Deals' (for the young unemployed, the long-term unemployed, lone parents, and disabled people), which have required claimants to attend regular work-based interviews and take active responsibility for finding paid employment – with penalties being imposed on those who refused to attend interviews or accept job offers. This approach has been considerably strengthened, but by no means radically altered, by the Conservative-Liberal Democrat Coalition government that came to office in May 2010. Similar systems have developed in many other countries, including the USA and Australia (from which the UK learned a great deal), and also Germany and France. In each case, too, these policy changes have been accompanied by a political rhetoric that emphasises the dangers of welfare dependency and lack of individual responsibility, while stressing the benefits of work, the free market, low taxation, and workforce flexibility.

On one reading, then, welfare has become more 'conditional' (Dwyer and Ellison, 2009). Certain goods and services are not supplied as of *right* but according to acceptable behaviour, and there is a greater awareness of how welfare support can create dependency, as 'right-of-centre' think tanks such as Policy Exchange make clear (see Doctor and Oakley, 2011). Do these changes mean that Murray's 'underclass' thesis has been vindicated? The short answer is 'not entirely'. Although New Labour governments in the UK clearly endorsed elements of the 'underclass' analysis, and this approach has been further elevated by the 'strivers' and 'shirkers' rhetoric of the UK Coalition government (Osborne, 2013), it is too simplistic to argue that welfare reform over the past decade has been driven entirely by it. Ruth Levitas (2005), for instance, is correct to point out that although evidence of a 'moral underclass discourse' can be found in New Labour governments' social policies – the stress on 'conditionality' stands as evidence of this tendency – it is equally clear that other 'discourses' have been present in discussions of welfare reform.

For example, the emphasis on *social inclusion* was a key feature of welfare debates during the New Labour years, as governments reacted to the need to maintain social stability and cohesion in the face of increasing global economic pressures. And it could be argued that the theme of inclusion has been maintained, albeit in a rather different idiom, by David Cameron's apparent favouring of the 'Big Society' (Ellison, 2011) – although at the time of writing, it appears that this dimension of the Coalition government's social policy in the UK has atrophied in the face of the perceived need to cut welfare spending. Nevertheless, in the current environment of economic austerity, it is clear that, in their efforts to cut welfare spending, governments quickly point to the drawbacks of 'welfare dependency' in a manner that would not have been contemplated a generation or two ago. UK governments, for instance, have followed their counterparts in the USA and Australia, in encouraging a number of social groups hitherto not embraced by welfare-to-work policies – disabled people and lone parents being the key examples – to take offers of work or face penalties for not doing so.

Further challenges: social policy, family structures, and demographic change

Whether in fact the stress on paid employment is really a panacea for 'solving' economic and social challenges that owe their existence, as suggested, to the changing employment structures of post-industrial economies is, to say the least, unclear. Although the central objectives of welfare reform in many countries have undoubtedly been to improve access to work – and the take-up of work – it is evident that other changes in economy and society also have an impact on how social policy is understood and perceived – and here it is not so obvious that paid work offers a solution to the difficulties that welfare states are currently facing. The discussion that follows explores two key changes. First, the changing structure of the family has forced policy-makers to confront traditional assumptions about the role of women and the nature of 'care'. Second, certain demographic changes have led to the emergence of greater ethnic and cultural diversity, while other demographic shifts are beginning to impact upon the ability of post-war welfare systems to provide security in old age.

The changing family

With the partial exceptions of the Scandinavian systems, post-war welfare states essentially allocated women to the private sphere of the home. The necessary corollary of the full-time, permanently employed male 'breadwinner' is the unpaid female domestic worker who takes care of the children and other family members. In return, she receives certain types of support in the form of access to health care and an old age pension *not* in her own right but as a function of contributions taken in the form of social insurance from her husband's income. Superficially, it could be argued that this system worked. Certainly for the first 20 years or so after the end of the Second World War, the breadwinner model was not explicitly challenged, and welfare states in the UK, USA, Australia, and the greater part of Western Europe established social insurance arrangements that essentially confined married women to the home. However, from around the mid 1960s onwards, changes began to occur that were to result in mounting criticism of both the model and the assumptions about the family and the role of women in society that underpinned it.

These assumptions about the structure of the family in the post-war world were largely based on quite recent perceptions of its role – family structures in previous eras being radically different (Steel and Kidd, 2000; see also Chapter 14). So, for example, the ideal type of family unit was perceived to be the small 'nuclear family' consisting of two adults and roughly two children. The relationship between the husband/father and wife/mother was typically portrayed as based on sexual attraction and romantic attachment, with responsibility for the family's economic wellbeing allocated to the male worker and for its emotional or 'affective' wellbeing to the wife and mother. A number of potentially problematic issues with this depiction of the family were taken for granted. These included:

- all families in all cultures either are, or should be, based on the nuclear unit;
- women are essentially domestic creatures, content in their caring and nurturing roles;
- all families are based on primary (hetero)sexual attachments;
- (hetero)sexual attachments should be monogamous;
- the nuclear family is the most stable social unit yet to have evolved and, by virtue of its flexibility and capacity for mobility, is better suited than other family types to the demands of industrial society.

There is no need to go into too much detail here to see how misplaced assumptions of this kind have turned out to be. Leaving aside the fact that the nuclear family is mainly a Western phenomenon – different family structures operate in different cultures and parts of the world – it has become clear over the past 30 years that the perception of gender roles that lies at the heart of the nuclear family is open to challenge. From the mid 1960s, with their increasing ability to control contraception as a result of the pill, and with the labour market beginning to offer greater opportunities than had existed hitherto, women began to speak out against the oppressive nature of 'a domestic life bound up with child care, domestic drudgery and a husband who only occasionally put in an appearance and with who, little emotional communication was possible' (Giddens, 2006, p. 211). This 'speaking out' took a number of forms. Certainly the emergence of feminism as a major social movement, starting in the USA and spreading to the UK and the Western world, served to crystallise and advance women's demands for greater equality both within the home and outside it. Betty Friedan's *The Feminine Mystique* (1963) and Germaine Greer's *The Female Eunuch* (1969) formed the intellectual basis for a range of increasingly radical demands for equality of opportunity and equal pay to an end to male patriarchy in the private and public spheres (Barrett and McIntosh, 1991). Radical feminists, in particular (Firestone, 1970), not only challenged assumptions about the domestic orientation of women but also their predisposition to monogamous heterosexual attachments, while socialist feminists argued that the patriarchal nuclear family was essentially a creature of industrial capitalism, using female domestic labour to 'reproduce' the male workforce and so perpetuate the capitalist mode of production.

Looking specifically to the changing context for social policy, it is clear that the nuclear family, understood as a stable, monogamous, heterosexual unit comprising two married adults and their offspring, began a rapid decline from the 1970s onwards. The erosion of this institution is relatively easy to trace in the form of the rising incidence of divorce, single parenthood, and cohabitation. In the UK, 'first marriage' rates (where both partners are marrying for the first time) have fallen from a peak of 426,000 in 1940 to 150,000 in 2009. Overall marriage rates have fallen from a high of 480,000 in 1940 to 230,000 in 2009. Divorce rates rose dramatically from a low of 24,000 in 1958, climbing to 50,000 by 1968, rising steadily to a peak of 165,000 in 1993. Thereafter, however, the rate has fallen consistently, standing at 155,000 in 2000 and 113,900 in 2009 (Beaumont, 2011a). Of course, divorce rates are by no means the only indicator of the 'state of marriage' and the changing state of the family. According to the UK's Office for National Statistics, following the Civil Partnership Act of 2004, there are now 66,000 same-sex couples in civil partnerships (ONS, 2012), suggesting a desire on the part of these couples for formal recognition of their relationship. It is also the case that there has been a rise in the number of individuals forming new relationships and either choosing to re-marry or cohabit. Remarriages for one or both partners increased by a third (to 120,000) between 1971 and 1972, and peaked at 141,000 in 1988. Since that time the figures have fallen somewhat – to approximately 80,000 in 2009. Perhaps the most dramatic figures are those that chart the rise of cohabitation. The numbers of non-married men and women under the age of 60 who are cohabiting has risen from 1.5 million in 1996 to 2.9 million in 2012 (ONS, 2012). Significantly, too, the percentage of dependent children in cohabiting couples rose from 8 per cent in 1996 to 14 per cent in 2012. Finally, there has also been a marked rise in the numbers of people who form single-parent families. The proportion of children living in lone-parent families increased from 7 per cent in 1972 to 24 per cent in 2012 (ONS, 2012).

Changes of the kind discussed here can also be observed elsewhere in the developed economies, although not always to such a marked extent. Thus, divorce rates have risen throughout the European Union, although the pattern is uneven. Northern countries typically have higher rates of divorce than those in Catholic Southern Europe, and marked rises can also be seen in certain former communist states, such as Poland and Slovakia. Numbers of divorces have also risen in the USA, although there has been a consistent, if slight, decline since the mid 1990s. Again, lone-parent families have increased in Europe with the UK, Ireland, Denmark, and Finland leading the way, while 'in the EU-27 some 38.3% of children were born outside marriage in 2010' – the corresponding figure for 1990 being 17.4 per cent (Eurostat, 2012, p. 24).

To this already complex picture should be added the important dimension of ethnic and cultural diversity. Certainly in Britain, but also in many other countries, populations have become increasingly diverse as those migrant groups that arrived in the early years of the post-war period become settled second- and third-generation communities. New waves of migration have added to these communities over the years, while new migrant populations are emerging as a result of the expansion of the European Union into the former communist countries of Eastern Europe. Clearly, attitudes to marriage and the family differ among different groups. Indian, Pakistani, and Bangladeshi communities display higher rates of marriage than either White or mixed communities, and significantly lower rates of cohabiting and single parenthood. Conversely, Black African and Black Caribbean populations have lower rates of marriage and cohabiting and higher rates of lone parenthood – but these trends need to be understood in the cultural context of the extended family structures and kinship networks that characterise Black Caribbean groups in particular. On a different note, in the more sexually tolerant climate of the later 1990s and early twenty-first century, gay and lesbian couples have begun to adopt children in greater

STOP AND THINK

The changing nature of the family
Arguments that there has been a 'revolution' in the nature of the family and family life are not exaggerated – but why should social policies accommodate these changes?

Perhaps, as the right-leaning Centre for Social Justice has suggested, social policies should protect 'core values' – including marriage and the traditional family. On this reading, social policies should aim to rebuild fragile relationships, encourage marriage and responsible fatherhood, and discourage divorce and the formation of 'non-traditional' families.

See Centre for Social Justice (2006), *Breakdown Britain*, and Centre for Social Justice (2007a, 2007b), *Breakthrough Britain*.

numbers, while individuals who may have had children in heterosexual relationships are rather more likely to redefine their sexuality and move with their
offspring into same-sex relationships.

Taking all these changes into account, it appears that the 'traditional'
nuclear family is far from being the typical family form in many, if not all, of
the developed economies. In fact, sociologists have been arguing for some
time that this model – if it ever really was dominant – has now given way to
very different types of family structure characterised not only by 'natural'
parents and their offspring, but also by step-parents, half-brothers and half-
sisters, and the grandparents and other family members associated with past
marriages and cohabitations (Williams, 2004). The most important feature of
contemporary family life, perhaps, is its innate 'flexibility'. When discussing
changes of the kind considered here – and especially when categorising social
groups in particular ways – it is easy to suppose that these groups are somehow
'fixed' and unchanging. Of course, nothing could be further from the truth.
Rising divorce rates have to be set in the context of re-marriage, cohabitation,
and changes in the shape of the families involved (Smart and Neale, 1999).
While it continues to be true that, at any one time, the majority of families
continue to be two-parent, heterosexual couples and their children, these
'families' are increasingly likely to be 'reconstituted' with step-children,
ex-husbands/wives/partners participating – one way or another – in 'family
life'. Where lone parents are concerned, rising overall numbers say little about
the key feature of lone parenthood – that it is a potentially fluid state.
Depending on the reasons why women become lone parents – covering a
range of possibilities from widowhood, through divorce or separation to active
choice – this type of family is the most likely to be reconstituted through (re)
marriage or cohabitation.

Where social policy is concerned, the changes to the family examined here
present serious challenges (discussed in greater detail in Chapter 13). Without
doubt, the breadwinner model of welfare is not appropriate to family structures that have become so far removed from the traditional 'nuclear family'. In
its place, and over time, governments have begun (more or less reluctantly) to
recognise that a more individualised system of welfare support is required if
women are to have the recognition that they deserve as both paid workers and
unpaid carers, and children are also to be properly supported. However,
progress has been piecemeal at best, with social policy provision tending to lag
behind the social and economic changes that have been the key subject of this
chapter. As Rowlingson (2003) suggests, the following features are necessary
for an approach to social policy that would treat the *individual*, and no longer
the family, as the prime unit of welfare:

- gender equality and justice in the welfare state and within the family;
- work–life balance;
- labour supply;
- anti-poverty alleviation;

the value that should be attributed to care and caring by government on behalf of society as a whole.

With the exception of Sweden, which treats both men and women as individual citizens able to receive benefits, goods, and services in their own right, the majority of welfare systems are some way from being able to make such a claim. Precisely how the welfare system operates in the UK will be discussed in later chapters, but suffice it to say here that much greater and more generous attention would need to be paid to the following matters if British social policy was to be moved permanently beyond the post-war breadwinner model:

- rights to maternity and paternity leave, with fathers in particular having the right to substantial periods of time for child care duties;
- the availability and affordability of care for children under five years of age;
- more generous remuneration for those who undertake caring roles in the home;
- rules governing the payment of tax credits and other income-enhancing measures (which remain subject to *couple-based* assessment).

Demographic change

The final area of crucial significance for an understanding of the socio-economic context of social policy concerns 'demography'. Demographic changes are particularly important 'because they alter the size and composition of the population who contribute to and use the services provided by welfare states' (Liddiard, 2007, p. 132). In short, in the context of (inevitably) scarce resources, the precise amount of spending on different services is partly dictated by the numbers of potential users involved. So, for example, numbers of school children will influence the amount and nature of expenditure on education, while a rise or fall in the numbers of retired people will impact upon health and pensions policies. Certain aspects of population change in the UK and other developed economies over the past 50 years or so have been dramatic – and two examples will be examined here. First, migration in and out of a country can result in the emergence (and in some cases the decline) of communities with different cultural assumptions and lifestyles, and movements of this kind are likely to influence social and political debates about the nature of welfare as well as the kinds of support that society may be expected to provide. Second, perhaps the most compelling issue in terms of its urgency is population ageing – and this will be discussed in some detail below.

UK migrations patterns altered considerably over the course of the twentieth century. For much of the century, more people left Britain than entered the country but this pattern had reversed by the 1990s. As Beaumont (2011b, p. 8) notes, between 1993–94 and 2009–10 'there has been a bigger inflow to the UK than outflow', the most dramatic incidence being the 260,000 people who entered the UK from the EU Accession countries in 2006. However, since that year, the apparent increase in net migration (the difference between those entering and leaving the country) can be explained by a fall in emigration rather than increases in the numbers of people coming into the UK. Of course not all inward-migration comes from the European Union. The need to attract those from overseas with particular skills that the UK labour market lacks, together with the greater awareness among those in developing countries of the relative wealth of Northern and Western economies, and consequences of (civil) war and political oppression in key parts of the world, have all contributed to increased inward-migration. In social policy terms, increasing numbers of migrants can increase demand for social goods and services, which, in turn, can lead to short-term difficulties for service providers in those areas where new migrant populations settle (although it is equally the case that immigration can bring important skills and other benefits to destination countries). Conversely, those groups which over a period of time move from first-generation 'immigrant' status to become settled second- and third-generation *citizens*, present rather different issues. In the UK, for example, although individuals from different minority ethnic groups comprise about 8 per cent of the total population, the great majority have been born in the UK and enjoy full UK citizenship. Here, as initial phases of immigration give way to increasingly settled, permanent communities, the population as a whole comes to be characterised by greater ethnic and cultural diversity.

Demographic changes of this kind raise a number of issues for social policy, not least because the needs of different minority ethnic groups have to be understood and accommodated differently (see also Chapter 17). Although individuals from all established minority ethnic communities generally fare less well than their counterparts in the majority White population in terms of access to employment and welfare goods and services, differences of treatment *among* these communities, as well as *between* them and the White population, are marked. For example, although all minority ethnic groups suffer from higher levels of unemployment than the White population, Bangladeshi communities experience the highest incidence of worklessness (closely followed by the Pakistani and Black Caribbean populations). Again, looking at educational attainment rates, large differences can be found among ethnic groups. At GCSE level, African-Caribbean, Pakistani, and Bangladeshi

STOP AND THINK

A way forward for immigration?
As at early 2013, the UK used a points-based system to facilitate judgements about immigration decisions. Points are awarded to individuals according to their status defined in the following categories:

- **Tier 1**: 'High value migrants' – investors, entrepreneurs and exceptionally talented people can apply to enter the UK without the need of a job offer.

- **Tier 2**: Contains four categories of skilled worker: general, Minister of Religion, sportsperson, intra-company transfer.

- **Tier 4**: Overseas students with confirmed acceptance from an approved institution to study in the UK.

- **Tier 5**: Youth mobility and various categories of temporary workers: people coming to the UK to satisfy primarily non-economic objectives.

- **'Other'**: Domestic workers, contract seamen, representatives of overseas business.

How necessary is a system of this type in the UK today?

children do less well than White students – but Indian and Chinese students do better than any of these groups. Where the highest qualifications are concerned, 34 per cent of Chinese men and 32 per cent of Indian men had a degree in 2005 compared with 9 per cent of Black Caribbean and 13 per cent of Bangladeshi men; figures for women are similar (Self and Zealey, 2007). While it is certainly true that greater attention has been paid recently to how welfare institutions treat people from minority ethnic communities – much greater attention being paid to the incidence of 'institutional racism', for example – the challenge is to ensure that social policies provide different communities with the resources and opportunities required to eradicate poverty and allow individuals to realise their full potential. Many of these issues are discussed in greater depth in Chapter 17.

A different, and in some ways more challenging, demographic problem now confronting most developed economies is population ageing. This phenomenon has two main causes. First, it is certainly the case that people in the developed economies of the West and North now live longer than their parents or grandparents did. Second, however, fertility rates have been declining for some time; indeed, fertility fell for much of the twentieth century – with the marked exception of the post-war 'baby boom'. The combination of these two factors is expected to lead to a near-doubling of the 'old age dependency ratio' (OADR) in many countries, which in simple terms means that there will be fewer and fewer people of working age to support increasing numbers of people in retirement and old age. Of course, now that the first cohorts of the baby boom generation are beginning to hit retirement, the potential difficulties are easy to see. As Pierson (2001, p. 91) writes:

> The key argument in relation to ageing societies is that at some point in the next fifty years in all developed societies and many developing countries the costs of supporting a growing elderly population out of the current production of a much smaller active workforce will place on the latter a burden which is either unsustainable or . . . politically unacceptable.

Any examination of population ageing can quickly become highly technical and impenetrable – and it is important to point out that some commentators are more sceptical about its possible impact than others (Bonoli, 2000). Nevertheless, it is important to consider two particularly significant issues that impinge directly on social policy. First, in many countries – Australia and the USA as well as Northern and Western Europe – rising OADRs mean that the arrangements for old age pension provision put in place in the aftermath of the Second World War are likely to be inadequate. In short, the money produced by working populations through taxation and other surpluses from increased production will not be sufficient to pay the pensions and associated costs of health and social care for those either in, or nearing, retirement. Second, however, to change arrangements that have been established for the best part of 50 years is exceedingly difficult. Any dramatic alteration in pensions policies can have a significant impact on those who, having contributed through taxation or social insurance contributions to preceding generations' pensions, see their own assumptions about their income in old age undermined. To do nothing, on the other hand, would impose equally unacceptable costs on younger generations who would be faced with much higher taxes and insurance contributions. National governments, in other words, are caught between a rock and a hard place! Failure to act could lead to the disenchantment of economically active populations and the collapse of the unspoken inter-generational agreement about paying for old age, while to alter existing systems could provoke the wrath of those nearing retirement.

In the event – and unsurprisingly – governments appear to be opting for a mixture of policies that will certainly reduce state pension commitments over time as greater reliance is placed upon occupational and private provision. So, in the UK, for example, governments have discouraged over-reliance on the contributory state pension for the past 25 years, shifting away from an earnings-related system in the 1980s to a minimal (and declining) basic state pension that can be enhanced by means-tested supplements for those without alternative sources of income in old age. Meanwhile, UK governments have also attempted to persuade those in work to make provision for occupational pensions where employers offer them, or take out private pensions plans. Elsewhere, governments have been more generous, although the principle that a pensions system should be arranged among a number of 'tiers' – state, occupational, and private – rather than relying too heavily on any one of these is becoming universal. Australia, for example, alongside the basic 'Age Pension', has established a system of mandatory superannuation, with employers and employees contributing to approved private funds, which now covers the vast majority of Australians. After a lengthy consultation process that lasted throughout the latter part of the 1990s, Sweden radically reformed its pension system to cater for the difficulties posed by population ageing – although the full effects of the new system will not be felt for some years. Again, various tiers are involved, including a reorganised 'Guaranteed Pension' that sits alongside a contributory scheme that has both state- and privately-funded elements. Other policies being adopted – particularly in France, Italy, and Germany – involve downward pressure on early retirement, an increase in the official retirement age (or encouragement to work past the official age of retirement), and the general encouragement of 'active ageing' (Ellison, 2006).

Generally speaking, the phenomenon of population ageing offers a particularly good example of how social policy constantly needs to be adjusted to take account of wider social and economic changes. In the case of pensions, it is important to understand that the pace of change is in fact quite slow – after all, the retirement of the baby boom generation will take over 10 years to complete and the impact of changing OADRs will continue for at least another 30 years. However, this apparently gradual process has to be understood in the context of how long certain forms of social policy take to establish and properly embed. Once embedded, whole generations develop expectations about life in retirement based on the policies they have grown up with. It is not surprising, then, that decisions to alter social policies, although they may be deemed necessary by an analysis of the changing socio-economic environment, are intensely complex, involving significant political as well as economic calculations about the impact of new arrangements as well as an assessment of likely policy 'winners' and 'losers'.

Conclusion

This chapter has examined some important dimensions of the changing socio-economic context of social policy. Looking back over the past 30–50 years, it is clear just how much societies in the economically developed world have altered. Indeed, it is not an exaggeration to argue that assumptions about the nature of working life, the relationships between genders and generations, what is understood by the 'family' and family life – and even the character of entire national populations – have changed out of all recognition.

So, what does attention to the socio-economic environment say about the nature of social policy? For one thing, it points to an area of politics and policy-making that is, of necessity, dynamic. Social policies are never 'settled' for long and, of course, in a world increasingly characterised by a range of global pressures (see Chapter 24), it is important that welfare systems remain able to respond flexibly to the needs of vulnerable populations even as policy-makers struggle with inevitably scarce resources. Second, in contrast to the welfare pioneers of 60 years ago, who believed that welfare states were inherently progressive, providing welcome relief from the rigours of market solutions for vulnerable sections of the populations, it is possible to see now that this perception is not always accurate. Indeed, welfare systems can be highly conservative forces depending on their institutional make-up. It is clear from the discussion of the changing nature of employment, or changing family structures, that social policies make assumptions about work and gender roles that turn out to be based on particular understandings of social needs and values that themselves are historically specific. Far from always being at the forefront of societal change, welfare arrangements can act as brakes upon it – although whether this fact is necessarily problematic is a matter for debate. Finally, it is important to be clear that welfare states are inherently *political* projects. If the socio-economic environment contributes significantly to establishing the overall framework within which discussion can take place, *how* this environment is 'interpreted', *who* does the 'interpreting', and the *priorities* subsequently established are decided through political argument and struggle. For this reason, debates about the role and purpose of social policy should not be confined to the realm of representative politics but should extend into broader forms of 'social politics', because decisions about welfare affect such a vast range of populations, communities, interests, and movements.

Summary

This chapter has shown how a range of socio-economic factors creates an overarching framework for political arguments about the role and nature of social policy. The discussion has also established how rapid social and economic changes can make welfare systems and the assumptions that informed their development appear outdated. The key issues explored here include:

- The changing nature of employment in many economically developed countries, the decline of full male employment in manufacturing industry in particular. This decline has been offset by a rise in service sector employment – the change also being accompanied by the increasing numbers of women in some form (full-time, part-time or casual) of work. Rising female and falling male employment has challenged the basis of the 'breadwinner model' of welfare – forcing national governments to develop social policies that are less dependent on the male earner.

- These changes were associated with others – specifically the emergence of a central division between 'work rich' and 'work poor' households. A key argument is whether the shift in employment patterns has led to the development of an 'underclass', as those most vulnerable to unemployment in the 'new economy' become increasingly dependent on welfare.

- While it is difficult to argue that a distinct 'underclass' has emerged, particularly in the UK and European societies, it is nevertheless clear that changing employment patterns have altered the nature of social policy and the shape of welfare states. Specifically, welfare systems have become less 'protective' and more 'competitive' – and in so doing it may be that neoliberal and conservative critiques of the dangers of welfare dependency have at least partly influenced policy-makers.

- Changing employment patterns are partly, but by no means wholly, responsible for changing family structures. Greater access to employment has encouraged women to leave the home in ever-increasing numbers, but a higher degree of economic independence has been accompanied by greater sexual freedom as a result of the universal availability of contraception in many countries. Both of these factors contributed to nothing less than a revolution in women's perception of their roles and a 'cultural revolution' that saw the traditional model of the 'nuclear family' rapidly undermined in favour of a range of family types arising from the increasing incidence of divorce and re-marriage, single parenthood, civil and same-sex partnerships.

- Demographic changes associated with the emergence of second- and third-generation minority ethnic communities stemming from initial periods of inward migration have contributed to greater ethnic and cultural diversity in many of the developed economies. The presence of settled ethnic communities raises issues about the nature of social policy and whether policies are sufficiently sensitive to minority ethnic needs.

- A further dimension of demographic change concerns population ageing. That the numbers of those either in or nearing retirement are rising is not in doubt – the real issue is how governments are responding to rising OADRs. Whether or not population ageing poses a 'real' threat to existing arrangements in the developed welfare states is not entirely the point. The issue is that governments *think* that ageing populations will create difficulties in time to come, and are consequently taking measures to reduce their commitments to those nearing retirement while encouraging individuals to provide for themselves in old age by contributing to different 'tiers' of provision. In many countries, these developments have led to significant changes in traditional post-war pensions policies.

Discussion and review

- What have been the key changes in employment patterns over the past 50 years and how have these affected welfare state organisation in developed welfare systems?
- In what ways have women's roles changed over the past 50 years and what factors in your view have been responsible for the changes?
- To what extent have changing employment patterns contributed to the emergence of an 'underclass'?
- Consider how family structures have changed since the 1960s. What implications do the changing structure of the family have for social policy?
- Why might demographic changes such as the increasing size of minority ethnic communities or population ageing have an impact on perceptions of welfare and social policy-making?

References

Alcock, P. (2006) *Understanding Poverty*, Palgrave, Basingstoke.

Amin, A. (ed.) (1994) *Post-Fordism*, Blackwell, Oxford.

Bagguley, P. and Mann, K. (1992) 'Idle thieving bastards? Scholarly representations of the "underclass" ', *Work, Employment and Society*, Vol. 6, No. 1, pp. 113–26.

Barrett, M. and McIntosh, M. (1991) *The Anti-social Family*, Verso, London.

Beaumont, J. (2011a) 'Households and families', in J. Beaumont (ed.) *Social Trends 41*, Office for National Statistics, London.

Beaumont, J. (2011b) 'Population', in J. Beaumont (ed.) *Social Trends 41*, Office for National Statistics, London.

Bonoli, G. (2000) *The Politics of Pension Reform*, Cambridge University Press, Cambridge.

Brownlie, N. (2012) *Trade Union Membership 2011*, Department for Business, Innovation and Skills, London.

Buckingham, A. (1999) 'Is there an underclass in Britain?', *British Journal of Sociology*, Vol. 50, No. 1, pp. 49–75.

Carrera, S. and Beaumont, J. (2010) 'Income and wealth', in J. Beaumont (ed.) *Social Trends 41*, Office for National Statistics, London.

Centre for Social Justice (2006) *Breakdown Britain: Interim Report on the State of the Nation*, Centre for Social Justice, London.

Centre for Social Justice (2007a) *Breakthrough Britain: Ending the Costs of Social Breakdown: Overview*, Centre for Social Justice, London.

Centre for Social Justice (2007b) *Breakthrough Britain: Ending the Costs of Social Breakdown: Vol. 1. Family Breakdown*, Centre for Social Justice, London.

Cerny, P. (1990) *The Changing Architecture of Politics*, Sage, London.

Cerny, P. (2000) 'Restructuring the political arena: globalization and the paradoxes of the competition state', in R. Germain (ed.) *Globalization and its Critics*, Macmillan, Basingstoke.

Deacon, A. (2002) *Perspectives on Welfare*, Open University Press, Buckingham.

Doctor, G. and Oakley, M. (2011) *Something for Nothing: Reinstating Conditionality for Jobseekers*, Policy Exchange, London.

Dwyer, P. and Ellison, N. (2009) 'Work and welfare: the Rights and responsibilities of unemployment in the UK', in M. Giugni and P. Statham (eds.) *The Politics of Unemployment in Europe: Policy Issues and Collective Action*, Ashgate, Aldershot.

Ellison, N. (2006) *The Transformation of Welfare States?*, Routledge, London.

Ellison, N. (2011) 'The Conservative Party and the "Big Society" ', in C. Holden, M. Kilkey and G. Ramia (eds.) *Social Policy Review 23*, Policy Press, Bristol.

Eurostat (2012) *Marriage and Divorce Statistics*, available at http://epp.eurostat.ec.europa.eu/statistics_explained/index.php/Marriage_and_divorce_statistics [accessed 3 April 2013].

Evans, M. and Cerny, P. (2003) 'Globalization and social policy', in N. Ellison and C. Pierson (eds.) *Developments in British Social Policy 2*, Palgrave, Basingstoke.

Federation of European Employers (2012) *Trades Unions in Europe*, available at http://www.fedee.com/tradeunions.html [accessed 5 April 2013].

Firestone, S. (1970) *The Dialectic of Sex*, Bantam, New York.

Friedan, B. (1963) *The Feminine Mystique*, Penguin, Harmondsworth.

Giddens, A. (2006) *Sociology*, Polity, Cambridge.

Greer, G. (1969) *The Female Eunuch*, Flamingo, London.

Jessop, B. (1994) 'The Schumpeterian workfare state', in R. Burrows and I. Loader (eds.) *Towards a Post-Fordist Welfare State?*, Routledge, London.

Jessop, B. (2002) *The Future of the Capitalist State*, Polity, Cambridge.

Levitas, R. (2005) *The Inclusive Society? Social Exclusion and New Labour*, Palgrave, Basingstoke.

Liddiard, M. (2007) 'Welfare, media and culture', in J. Baldock, N. Manning and S. Vickerstaff (eds.) *Social Policy*, Oxford University Press, Oxford.

Lister, R. (ed.) (1996) *Charles Murray and the Underclass: The Developing Debate*, IEA Health and Welfare Unit, London.

Lister, R. (2004) *Poverty*, Polity, Cambridge.

Murray, C. (1994) *Losing Ground* (10th anniversary edition), Basic Books, New York.

Murray, C. (1996a) 'The emerging British underclass', in R. Lister (ed.) *Charles Murray and the Underclass: The Developing Debate*, IEA Health and Welfare Unit, London.

Murray, C. (1996b) 'Underclass: the crisis deepens', in R. Lister (ed.) *Charles Murray and the Underclass: The Developing Debate*, IEA Health and Welfare Unit, London.

OECD (1996) *Historical Statistics, 1960–1994*, OECD, Paris.

OECD (2012) *Employment and Labour Statistics*, available at http://0-www. oecd-ilibrary.org.wam.leeds.ac.uk/employment/data/oecd-employment-and-labour-market-statistics_lfs-data-en [accessed 5 April 2013].

Office for National Statistics (ONS) (2012) *Statistical Bulletin: Families and Households, 2012*, available at http://www.ons.gov.uk/ons/rel/family-demography/families-and-households/2012/stb-families-households.html [accessed 3 April 2013].

Osborne, G. (2013) Speech on Changes to the Tax and Benefit System, 2 April, available at http://www.hm-treasury.gov.uk/press_35_13.htm [accessed 7 April 2013].

Pierson, C. (2001) *Hard Choices: Social Democracy in the 21st Century*, Polity, Cambridge.

Prideaux, S. (2005) *Not So New Labour? A Sociological Critique of New Labour's Policy and Practice*, Policy Press, Bristol.

Rowlingson, K. (2003) '"From cradle to grave": social security over the life cycle', in J. Millar (ed.) *Understanding Social Security: Issues for Policy and Practice*, Policy Press, Bristol.

Self, A. and Zealey, L. (eds.) (2007) *Social Trends 37*, Office for National Statistics, London.

Smart, C. and Neale, B. (1999) *Family Fragments?*, Polity, Cambridge.

Spence, A. (2011) 'Labour market', in J. Beaumont (ed.) *Social Trends 41*, Office for National Statistics, London.

Steel, L. and Kidd, W. (2000) *The Family*, Palgrave, Basingstoke.

The Poverty Site (2010) *Income Inequalities*, available at http://www.poverty.org.uk/09/index.shtml [accessed 31 March 2013].

Williams, F. (2004) *Rethinking Families*, Calouste Gulbenkian Foundation, London.

Wilson, W.J. (1987) *The Truly Disadvantaged*, University of Chicago Press, Chicago, IL.

Further reading

Crompton, R., Gallie, D. and Purcell, K. (1996) *Changing Forms of Employment: Organisations, Skills and Gender*, Routledge, London. This work looks at the trends that underlie pressures around changes to employment and employment-related institutions.

Deacon, A. and Williams, F. (eds.) (2004) Themed section on 'Care, values and the future of welfare', *Social Policy and Society*, Vol. 3, No. 4. This section of the journal draws on a 5-year research programme to consider changes in parenting and partnering and their policy implications.

Levitas, R. (2005) *The Inclusive Society? Social Exclusion and New Labour*, Palgrave, Basingstoke. This book examines differing conceptions of social inclusion under the New Labour governments and the ways in which they responded to social exclusion.

Murray, C. (1996) 'The emerging British underclass', in R. Lister (ed.) *Charles Murray and the Underclass Debate*, IEA Health and Welfare Unit, London. Murray's work was influential in sparking debate about the 'underclass'.

Pierson, C. (2001) *Hard Choices: Social Democracy in the 21st Century*, Polity, Cambridge. Within a consideration of social democracy, this book examines the challenges posed by demographic change and globalisation.

Williams, F. (2004) *Rethinking Families*, Calouste Gulbenkian Foundation, London. This book outlines the major trends around families, the effects of these, and their implications for social policy.

Useful websites

http://www.guardian.co.uk/ – this general reference to *The Guardian*'s website (Guardian Unlimited) is included mainly because the easy search facilities provide swift access to news and commentary about key social policy issues. *Guardian Society*, published each Wednesday, also carries important news and information about social policy matters.

http://0-www.oecd-ilibrary.org.wam.leeds.ac.uk/employment/data/oecd-employment-and-labour-market-statistics_lfs-data-en – the OECD is an excellent source of comparative statistical material. This website provides employment data about all OECD countries in historical and contemporary perspective.

http://ons.gov.uk/ons/rel/social-trends-rd/social-trends/social-trends-41/index.html – the current issue of *Social Trends* can be downloaded free. It carries a wealth of detail about core areas of UK society and social policy.

http://www.statistics.gov.uk/ – a more challenging website that provides access to the full range of UK Government statistical information.

CHAPTER 3

The Politics and Governance of Social Policy

Catherine Bochel and Guy Daly

Learning objectives

- To describe the structures within which social policies are made
- To explore changes to the government of social policy from 1979
- To consider a range of influences on the making and implementation of social policies
- To introduce a number of models that can help us understand the nature of the governance of social policy

Chapter overview

Both social policy and politics are closely tied to decisions about the make-up of society and the distribution of resources (including income and wealth) within it. Each is therefore concerned with the appropriateness of social arrangements and the means by which these are determined. Within the political system there are a variety of forces that impact upon social policy – changes of government inevitably bring different policy priorities and approaches, pressure groups lobby governments to achieve their aims, the media also seek to influence government and to highlight issues, and as implied above, individuals and groups can also participate in different ways. In addition, there have been significant changes in recent years in the mechanisms of social policy formulation and implementation, with devolution to Scotland, Northern Ireland, and Wales being a clear instance of this, and these also have implications for social policy.

This chapter examines:

- the role of political parties, pressure groups, and the media with regard to social policy;
- developments in approaches to the government of social policy under Conservative, Labour, and Coalition administrations;
- the use of models of governance that can assist us in our understanding of the formulation and implementation of social policies.

SPOTLIGHT

Does politics matter?

Whether we realise it or not, politics impacts on the lives of all of us. The media report daily on issues that include: taxation, immigration, ID cards, funding of services, health, schools, climate change, the economy, the EU, elections, conflict in countries around the world, human rights, refugees, trade unions, and so on. These, directly or indirectly, affect us all, and this is why politics matters.

In the 2010 general election, only 65 per cent of people in the UK who were entitled to vote did so. However, participation in politics is not limited to voting, and many more people chose to participate by belonging to pressure groups and by taking part in protests and campaigns, whether an ad hoc group fighting the closure of a local school or hospital, an organised campaign to fight a new airport runway or train line, or pig farmers demonstrating against food companies importing cheap foreign bacon. Other action might include campaigns against roads, rubbish tips, housing developments, supermarkets, and animal experiments.

In these ways, people are choosing to get involved and participate. They are electing representatives from different political parties who will make decisions on their behalf, about issues that will affect their lives, and/or they are directly participating in pressure groups and campaigns to try to influence the decisions that will be taken on their behalf by government.

How politics affects...
your night out

It decides where and when you can buy an alcoholic drink • **says at what age you can buy an alcoholic drink** • sets the amount of tax that you have to pay every time you buy one • **decides where and when you can listen to music and whether it can be played live** • controls how loud that music can be and whether or not you're allowed to dance to it • **decides whether your local town can have its own casino** • decides what is acceptable behaviour when you're under the influence and what is liable to get you arrested • **affects the number of police officers patrolling town centres at night** • says what substances are illegal and what will happen to you if you're caught with them • **says how much you can legally drink and still drive home** • decides what time trains and buses stop running and whether or not there will be a night service • **controls the licensing of taxis** • controls the licensing of doormen and bouncers • **sets hygiene standards for restaurants, pubs and takeaways.**

www.dopolitics.org.uk

The
Electoral
Commission

There is considerable evidence that many people, especially younger people, are less engaged with 'politics', or at least with 'mainstream politics', than was previously the case. Yet, as the Electoral Commission poster highlights, politics, broadly defined, affects all of our lives.

It is almost impossible to consider social policy divorced from 'politics', as social policy is concerned with, among other things, the distribution of goods, services, and life chances, all of which are affected by 'political' decisions.

Attempts to define 'politics' can develop into complicated debates in the same way as can occur with definitions of social policy. However, for now we can adopt a simple view. Politics can be seen as the arena within which conflicts and differences are expressed and, to a greater or lesser extent, resolved. If politics is sometimes defined as 'who gets what, when, and how', this illustrates well the inevitable link between politics and social policy. Similarly, given the centrality of social policy concerns in contemporary society, with issues such as education, employment, immigration, housing, health, welfare benefits, and pensions frequently at the core of political debate, this is clearly a two-way relationship.

There are, of course, many aspects of politics that could be considered in relation to social policy. For present purposes, we concentrate on political parties, pressure groups, and the media, as these can be seen as having a direct impact upon social policies. Later in this chapter, some of the institutions and mechanisms of government will also be examined, together with a number of models that can help us analyse and understand how they operate.

Political parties

Perhaps surprisingly, there is a relative paucity of literature on political parties and social policy, and in looking at this area students of social policy are therefore often reliant upon more general literature drawn from political science. However, although a little dated now, Bochel and Defty's (2007) *Welfare Policy Under New Labour* provides an example of links between political parties and social policy, particularly at the parliamentary level, while Jones and MacGregor (1998), although older, provides an example of a linkage from the social policy perspective, focusing in particular upon the 1997 general election. A few other books, such as those edited by Powell (1999, 2002, 2008) on New Labour, and Bochel (2010) on the Conservatives, focus on particular parties and their social policies. This section draws out some of the key characteristics of parties as they might be seen to relate to social policy.

The functions of parties

The functions of political parties can be categorised in a number of ways, many of which can be seen to have some relationship with social policy, although for some the connection is more apparent and perhaps more important. If we examine three of these, the nature of the links with social policy can be illustrated:

- *Representation*: political parties seek to organise within the electorate and to provide meaningful choices that enable voters to elect governments. In reality, most voters cast their vote for a party rather than for an individual candidate. These votes may be cast for a number of reasons, such as judgements on party policies (including those that relate to social policy), the parties' likely effectiveness to govern, and, perhaps increasingly, their leaders.
- *Participation*: parties also provide a significant form of participation, varying from voting at general elections to membership and working for a party through attending meetings, campaigning, and even standing for election.
- *Elaboration of policies*: parties develop programmes and policies to present to the electorate as part of their attempts to achieve office. These range from fairly general statements of intent to more detailed policy proposals. Any examination of political debates or party manifestos over the post-war period demonstrates that social policies have been a fundamental part of this function.

Ideology and political parties

The close relationship between politics and social policy is further illustrated by the importance of ideas to parties and the impact that these have had upon their policies. Chapters 7 and 8 examine this in some detail in relation to the Conservative and Labour parties. However, if we briefly examine the post-war period, while it is quite apparent that ideology has impacted upon social policy, it may not always do so as extensively, or in quite the ways, that might be supposed.

The Labour government elected in 1945 is often depicted as creating the welfare state in the UK, or at least with doing so on the foundations laid by previous governments, and in particular the Liberal government of 1906–14. Whichever of these views is accepted, there can be little doubt that Clement Attlee's Labour government, itself influenced by the Beveridge Report of 1942, did fundamentally shape the welfare state as it developed in the post-war years. However, while it was the Labour Party that became associated with the creation of the welfare state, the very idea appeared to have widespread support so that even when Labour was defeated at the general election of 1951, there followed a period that has often been described as one of 'consensus'. This implied a general acceptance of broadly social democratic ideals that included a commitment to the welfare state and to a continued expansion of state welfare provision as the economy grew, as well as to the role of government in maintaining low levels of unemployment through Keynesian economic policies.

While the extent and basis of this 'consensus' might be questioned, for the next 30 years there was a general maintenance and expansion of the role of the state in the provision of welfare. However, by the mid 1970s a number of challenges had emerged to the welfare state, including practical problems, such as reduced economic growth and oil price rises, and political and ideological questions about the extent to which the welfare state had been successful and whether it was the most appropriate way of meeting needs. From the mid 1970s the Conservative Party began to move more to the political right, influenced by 'New Right' ideas (see Chapter 7), and when it returned to power in 1979 under the leadership of Margaret Thatcher it had a commitment to the free market and the private sector and to reducing state intervention in society. The period from 1979 to 1997 thus saw attempts to roll back and reshape the frontiers of the state, including welfare provision, using a variety of instruments such as privatisation (for example, sales of council homes), increased use of means-testing (in social security), restructuring (including the NHS and local government), greater use of performance measurement (school and hospital 'league tables'), and the introduction of internal markets (such as in health and social care).

Following the election of Tony Blair as leader of the Labour Party in 1994, many commentators have suggested that the party shifted to the political right, and that the creation of 'New Labour' (see Chapter 8) included acceptance of some of the ideas that had emerged from New Right critiques of the state, and of the welfare state, and the continuation of policy trends that had originated under the Conservatives, such as means-testing and a commitment to an increased role for the private and voluntary sectors in the provision of welfare services and the encouragement of an active welfare state in which citizens accepted that in return for certain rights to welfare, they had obligations to society. However, it is also possible to argue that under the Blair and Brown premierships there were some changes that contrasted with the position under the Conservatives, such as significant increases in public expenditure and attempts to redistribute from the rich to the poor (see Chapters 2 and 9).

Following their election defeat in 2001, the Conservative Party in turn began to adapt its policies, seeking to develop itself as a more inclusivist party, with successive leaders at least paying lip-service to the recognition that the United Kingdom had changed and that some of the party's perceived political excesses during the 1980s and 1990s were no longer appropriate. After another election defeat in 2005, David Cameron's leadership appeared to reinforce this, with a shift towards a recognition that there is a significant role for the state in social welfare, breaking with the dominant stream of Conservative thinking in this area from the late 1970s. Following the general election of 2010, Cameron's Conservative Party formed a Coalition government with the Liberal Democrats. The Coalition's dominant discourse has been that of 'austerity'. Through this, despite pre-election appearances, they have pursued a programme of significant cuts in welfare and other areas of public expenditure, arguably with the exception of the National Health Service (NHS), which the Coalition has said it will protect. As a result, since 2010 we have seen a significant 'rolling back' of the welfare state and the privatisation of provision – both to individuals and families and also to private and independent sector providers.

CONTROVERSY AND DEBATE

It is often difficult to be clear exactly what new policy directions different governments might take. The amount of taxation that different groups in society pays raises issues around equality, fairness, and social responsibility, and affects the level of resources available for public expenditure, including upon welfare services such as health and education.

Although tax evasion is illegal, tax avoidance is not. In recent years, governments have sought to reduce levels of tax avoidance by individuals and companies, although at the same time they have sometimes used it and the tax system to encourage what they see as positive behaviour, such as paying money into pension schemes.

Visit the websites of the three major parties (www.conservatives.com; www.libdems.org.uk; www.labour.org.uk) and consider how each might address the issue of tax avoidance, why they might take different approaches to this, and what effects this might have on policy.

Party leaders

From the 1960s onwards, it has frequently been argued that Britain has been moving towards a 'prime ministerial' – or even 'presidential' – style of government, with the Prime Minister occupying an increasingly central and powerful position. This has arisen at least in part from the increasing emphasis on the party leaders in the media, and thus in the eyes of the public, not only at election time, but continuously as part of the political debate, a shift that has been intensified by the increased role of television as a means of communication. The apparent dominance of prime ministers such as Harold Wilson in the 1960s and 1970s, Margaret Thatcher in the 1980s, and Tony Blair in the late twentieth and early twenty-first century, has helped reinforce this impression.

It is clear that prime ministers can bring significant influence to bear upon welfare policies. It was Margaret Thatcher's commitment to New Right ideas, and her use of right-of-centre think tanks, such as the Adam Smith Institute and the Institute for Economic Affairs, that encouraged the adoption of policies such as the 'right to buy' council houses, the creation of internal markets in health and social care, and the use of league tables of performance in education. The example of Margaret Thatcher pushing the poll tax through Parliament against the wishes of her ministerial colleagues and many in her party illustrates the power than prime ministers can exert, but her removal from power in 1990 also serves to demonstrate that even dominant prime ministers rely upon the support of their Members of Parliament, and if they lose that they risk being removed from office by their own parties.

One of the characteristics of the Blair governments, much commented upon, was the strengthening of control through the growth of the Prime Minister's Office. However, despite this apparent strengthening, and Blair's attempts to define and develop a 'third way' (see Chapter 8), in many respects the government was not dominated by the Prime Minister alone, but also by the Chancellor of the Exchequer, Gordon Brown. While the Prime Minister did make occasional forays into the social policy arena, the government also saw the Treasury, under Brown, developing an almost unprecedented role in social policy, ranging from initiatives such as tax credits, largely designed to help the 'working poor', to public service agreements requiring other government departments to establish targets for delivery of services.

Clearly, with a Conservative-Liberal Democrat Coalition government, Prime Minister David Cameron is not alone in exercising power and control. First, he has had to work closely with his Deputy Prime Minister, the leader of the Liberal Democrats, Nick Clegg. In addition, there is the power and influence of the Chancellor, the Conservative George Osborne, as well as the Chief Secretary to the Treasury, the Liberal Democrat Danny Alexander. Indeed, these four politicians have been described as the 'Quad' of decision-makers at the heart of the Coalition.

Pressure groups

A central feature of liberal democracies such as the United Kingdom is that it is often argued that power is widely distributed among different groups (sometimes called pluralism) and that at any one time there are a variety of interests competing to influence decision-making. Outside the party political arena there exists a huge number of pressure or interest groups. These can usually be differentiated from political parties by the fact that they generally seek to influence government, rather than to govern themselves. They can range in size from small, ad hoc groups, such as those which sometimes form to campaign against the closures of local schools or hospitals, or to fight for or against particular local forms of provision, to the large, well-known groups that feature regularly in the media (see Spotlight below). Pressure groups are an alternative and important form of participation, with the memberships of pressure groups far exceeding those of the political parties.

SPOTLIGHT

Examples of pressure groups

Cause groups

- Child Poverty Action Group (CPAG) – a cause group which campaigns for the abolition of poverty among children and young people in the UK and for the improvement of the lives of low-income families. Its membership consists of individuals and organisations. It is funded predominantly from membership subscriptions, sales of CPAG publications, and grants and donations (see www.cpag.org.uk).

- Amnesty International UK – a cause group, launched in 1961, with around 265,000 financial supporters in the UK. It works to improve human rights worldwide. It is funded predominantly through membership subscriptions, appeals and donations, events and community fundraising, and from legacies (see www.amnesty.org.uk).

- Voice For Choice – a cause group that is an example of a national coalition of organisations, including the British Pregnancy Advisory Service, Abortion Rights, and Education for Choice. It works alongside the All Party Parliamentary Pro-Choice and Sexual Health Group (see www.vfc.org.uk).

Sectional groups

- British Medical Association (BMA) – a sectional organisation founded in 1832, the BMA is a professional association of doctors, representing their interests and providing services for its 128,000 members. It is funded through membership subscriptions (see www.bma.org.uk).

- National Union of Teachers (NUT) – a sectional organisation that represents teachers, the NUT has a membership of 290,000. It is represented on national education bodies and makes representations to government on all matters affecting teachers and schools, particularly education policy at national and local level. It is funded through membership subscriptions (see www.teachers.org.uk).

While pressure groups can be characterised in a number of ways, it is perhaps useful to consider them as 'cause' and 'sectional' groups, as illustrated above:

- *Cause groups* – those organisations that seek to promote causes based upon particular values or beliefs, such as Child Poverty Action Group, Age Concern, Fathers 4 Justice, and Shelter. It is this category that would normally include the ad hoc groups mentioned above.

- *Sectional groups* – those bodies that represent the interests of particular groups in society, such as trade unions, or professional organisations, such as the British Medical Association or the British Association of Social Workers.

Groups are also often described as 'insider' or 'outsider', a terminology that refers to the nature of their relationship with government. Insider groups are those that are seen by government as legitimate, are regularly consulted, and which are most likely to have their voices heard. An example might be Child Poverty Action Group. Outsider groups do not have, or in some cases do not wish to have, a close relationship with officials and policy-makers. The gay rights group OutRage is one such example.

In relation to social policy, it is apparent that there are a host of pressure groups that campaign on a wide variety of issues at both central and sub-central government levels. Following the 1997 general election, the emphasis on 'partnership' under Labour appeared to offer a better prospect for consultation and partnership with regard to policy-making and implementation for some groups, although the extent to which this occurred in practice was sometimes questionable. Indeed, it is difficult to assess the impact of pressure groups on social policy as their influence may vary with a variety of factors, including the proximity of their ideas to governments' policy proposals, the resources available to the group, the acceptability of their views to the media and the public, and the external economic and political environment. The cause group Action on Smoking and Health (ASH) might be seen as successful in working towards eliminating the harms caused by tobacco. It has campaigned to ban tobacco advertising, which is now illegal in the UK, and workplace smoking bans have been implemented in Scotland (March 2006), Wales and Northern Ireland (April 2007), and England (July 2007). But, despite the undoubted success of ASH in working towards this, other factors and pressure groups, including, for example, the British Medical Association, will also have played a role in this achievement, serving to underline the difficulty in assessing the precise impact of particular factors and groups. Easton's (1965) black box model (a simplified model is shown in Figure 3.1) illustrates how ideas from the wider environment can become inputs (such as demands from parties, the media, and pressure groups), which in turn are changed by demands from within the political system, and may become policy outputs and outcomes.

Despite the complexity and range of factors that influence policy-making, the continued existence and activities of pressure groups in the social policy field clearly requires some consideration of their role.

The media

The media has become a key part of British society. Together, newspapers, magazines, radio, television, and the Internet provide us with a myriad of sources of information. However, it is important to recognise that the role of the media is not confined to the provision of information – it also has the potential to influence the way in which we interpret issues and debates, and perhaps even set the agenda for decision-makers and influence decisions themselves.

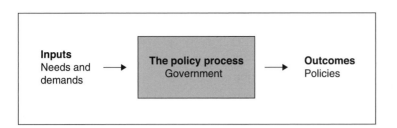

Figure 3.1 The black box approach to policy-making
Source: Ham and Hill (1993)

Despite the potential importance of the media to social policy, there has been limited research into this relationship. There remain a number of important questions, including: What is the role of the media in setting the agenda? What influence does the media have upon those who make policies? And what might this tell us about the exercise of power in contemporary society?

A good example of media coverage of social issues is Cohen's (2002) study of Mods and Rockers in the 1960s, which highlighted the role of the media in creating and amplifying what he termed 'folk devils' and 'moral panics'. Cohen (2002, p. 1) argued:

> Societies appear to be subject, every now and then, to periods of moral panic. A condition, episode, person or group of persons emerges to become defined as a threat to societal values and interests; its nature is presented in a stylised and stereotypical fashion by the mass media; the moral barricades are manned by editors, bishops, politicians and other right-thinking people; socially accredited experts pronounce their diagnoses and solutions . . . Sometimes the panic passes over and is forgotten, except in folklore and collective memory; at other times it has more serious and long-lasting repercussions and might produce such changes as those in legal and social policy or even in the way the society conceives itself.

From roughly the same period, another well-known example of the role of the media is that of the television drama, *Cathy Come Home*, which has frequently been credited with leading to the creation of the charity Shelter, and having a substantial impact on the issue of homelessness and the introduction of legislation in the 1970s. Other examples of media coverage and involvement range from portraying increased immigration to the UK as a threat to society (including in respect of crime and jobs), the effects of designer drugs such as ecstasy, campaigns to name and shame paedophiles, and, more recently, the depiction of the recipients of welfare benefits as 'benefit scroungers'. Given the variety of media and the complexity of their roles and influences, the remainder of this section seeks to provide some framework through which we can seek to analyse and understand their relationship with social policy.

The media and public opinion

There is perhaps a general assumption by both the media and by many commentators that the media is important in bringing issues to public attention, and that it is to some extent influential in changing attitudes and perceptions, and even of affecting policy. However, the extent to which this might be the case is not easy to gauge. For example, there are major differences, not just between, say, TV and the press, but also within the press, for example between coverage in the tabloids and the broadsheets, or between left and right leaning papers, and increasingly within TV broadcasters with the development of satellite and digital broadcasting. The same story can be portrayed in a variety of different ways, and differ not only in respect of the level of detail and accuracy of coverage, but also in terms of political perspectives, with some papers, such as *The Guardian* and the *Daily Mirror* being seen as tending to favour the Labour Party, while others such as the *Daily Mail* and *The Times* tend to be seen as favouring the Conservative Party. The public also make distinctions, with evidence to suggest that they are generally more likely to believe TV news reporting than newspaper coverage.

The media are often accused of trivialising or distorting issues, either to make headlines or as a form of entertainment. Sometimes this may be positive, as a way of bringing an issue to public attention, but often it can create or reinforce misconceptions or stereotypes, or may personalise or individualise what could be seen as *social* issues or problems. However, this may not entirely be the media's fault – for example, many agencies view the media as being in a position of power, able to influence public opinion and policy-making. They may thus seek to attract media interest, and this in turn may mean accepting media agendas and a subsequent modification of their messages and concerns. Journalists may therefore use crude and stereotypical images of, say, homeless or disabled people as a way of making good copy, attracting attention or making a point; but importantly, some agencies may collude with these images to attract coverage (or, in the case of some charities, coverage and potentially funds).

There are a number of perspectives in seeking to assess the overall impact of the media upon public opinion:

- *Direct effects* – the view that the media has a direct impact on public attitudes is now largely discredited; the public does not form a passive audience that unquestioningly absorbs and accepts whatever it is fed to them by the media.
- *Reinforcement* – it is now widely accepted that the public selects and interprets media messages in accordance with their existing viewpoints; in other words, that we actively interpret the information that the media provides. In addition, it is mainly those media messages that reinforce what we

already believe that we select. Thus individual members of the public can interpret the same media coverage very differently.

- *Agenda-setting* – in general, this view accepts that the public has its own agenda, but that the media can influence its priorities, especially on matters about which the public knows relatively little.

- *Framing* – progressing from the agenda-setting standpoint, this view suggests that the media is able to affect political life (including social policy) and the way that people see and understand it. This may occur in different ways: (a) interpretation – the same event might be presented in different ways to give it a completely different meaning, and the effect may be both unintentional and unconscious; (b) bad news – the mass media concentrates on bad news, conflict, and violence because these sell newspapers and attract TV audiences, but negative news can create cynicism, disillusion, distrust of politicians and professionals, and apathy; (c) the 'fast forward syndrome' – news and reaction to it now spreads so rapidly that policies can be launched in the morning news, criticised at lunchtime and buried by the evening, and at the same time there is so much 'news' that the public cannot cope with or understand such a flow of events; (d) personalisation and trivialisation – the mass media concentrate not on problems, issues or policies but on personalities and appearances, so that politicians and others may sometimes be less concerned with policy options than with looking and sounding right.

Whichever interpretation we accept, for social policy one of the important abilities of the media is its potential to reach millions of people who may not otherwise be involved or interested in an issue.

The media and policy-making

So to what extent do the media impact upon policy-makers? Does coverage of issues such as immigration, homelessness or hospital waiting lists influence either their agendas or decisions? Again, these questions are difficult to answer because it is hard to measure the extent of influence, since it is dependent on many factors. These factors include the type of issue (e.g. child abuse or cruelty to animals may gain the sympathy and support of the public to a greater extent than homelessness or poverty), the intensity of coverage, and the extent to which the public and policy-makers trust the source. However, it could be said that the media is most likely to have an impact at the stage where there is an emerging issue. It is at this point that pressure groups will strive to get the media on their side and to use them to push the issue further up the agenda of both

STOP AND THINK

Different parts of the mass media portray topics in different ways. Look at the ways in which different newspapers have recently portrayed groups such as women, young people, migrant workers, benefits recipients or asylum seekers.

What messages do these portrayals send to their readers and to policy-makers?

the public and the politicians. Despite this, it is difficult to identify many concrete examples of the media having an impact on social policy, and it is arguable that the media has most impact when the ideas that it is pushing are compatible with the general socio-economic and political environment. The media may have only a limited impact upon policy-making, but can perhaps play a role in setting the parameters for policy debates and in framing policy discussions.

Ownership and regulation

Freedom of the press is often presented as one of the central tenets of liberal democracy, yet, at the same time, one of the major concerns of many academics and others has been the ownership and control of the media and the impact of this. Initially, concerns often focused around the power of press barons to directly influence politics, for example through persuading people to vote for particular parties or candidates or the perceived need of political leaders to have the support of particular media owners and organisations, such as Rupert Murdoch and News International, but others have argued that the major influence of newspapers has been their 'cumulative support for conservative values' (Curran and Seaton, 1991, p. 61) and the status quo. In addition, it is clear that newspapers, for example, are able to select particular issues for discussion and to marginalise or ignore others. This latter point is perhaps of significance to social policy, as it is sometimes said that it is radical or progressive voices that receive least space in the press.

For the written media, control and regulation have rested largely with the media themselves. Recent years have seen ongoing debates about the extent to which parts of their coverage are acceptable, for example in relation to privacy, of both public figures and private individuals, and there have been calls for greater regulation. The Leveson Inquiry, the subsequent report (Leveson, 2012), and the debates about the implementation of its recommendations, served to highlight the concerns of many on different sides of the arguments about the role of the print media.

As with the press, the broadcasting media, and television in particular, have also seen a concentration of ownership, with News International's dominance of satellite broadcasting within the United Kingdom being seen as problematic by many (especially when combined with its strong press presence). One difference here is the existence of the state-funded BBC, with its responsibility to provide public service broadcasting, although it has been argued that this has been – and will continue to be – undermined by the pressure to maintain audiences and the increased choice available to viewers. In addition, at least for party politics, the terrestrial broadcasters have a statutory duty to provide 'balanced coverage', although this does not necessarily apply to the satellite broadcasters, which it would clearly be difficult for a national government to control in any case.

Debates over the role and control of the media are further complicated by the widespread availability of the Internet. The Internet provides opportunities for the collection and dissemination of ideas and information, but raises additional questions over the regulation of content. In addition, the Internet is used to campaign in both old and new manners, for example by anti-globalisation protesters (see Chapter 24). In other respects, there is clearly potential for a whole range of individuals and groups to have much wider access to a great variety of information, and potentially for more inputs into policy-making. However, there are also fears that existing inequalities might be reinforced by unequal access (see Chapter 21).

The governance of social policy

While the preceding section has demonstrated the importance of politics to social policy (by and large, *politics matters*), this section seeks to illustrate that the mechanisms by which policies are made and implemented can also be significant. If we reflect on the period since 1979, it is possible to identify not only major shifts in policy under Conservative, Labour, and Coalition govern-ments, but also changes in the way in which social policy is 'governed'. Butcher (1995, p. 155) described the traditional mode of operation of government in the social policy arena before 1979 as '. . . the public administration model of welfare delivery . . . in which the five core social services . . . were delivered by a combination of national and local governmental organizations'. However, increasingly, discussion has moved from talking about 'government' to using the term 'governance', in recognition of the increasingly fragmentary nature of policy-making and implementation. Richards and Smith (2003, p. 15) provide a useful definition:

'Governance' is a descriptive label that is used to highlight the changing nature of the policy process in recent decades. In particular, it sensitizes us to the ever-increasing variety of terrains and actors involved in the making of policy. Thus, governance demands that we consider all the actors and loca-tions beyond the 'core executive' involved in the policy making process.

The remainder of the chapter seeks to discuss the governance of social policy since 1979, including a consideration of the extent to which there has been continuity or change and the implications of these developments for social policy in the future.

The Conservatives, 1979–97

From 1979 to 1997, styles of governance can be seen to have moved through two main phases. Until 1988, the emphasis was largely on 'managerialism', reflected in the focus of initiatives which drew upon what the government perceived to be 'private sector values' and based upon the belief that business performance tools from the private sector could be transferred to the public sector to make it more efficient and effective at both central government and local government levels. From around 1988, there was a shift towards a style of governance based on 'the new institutional economics' (Hood, 1991) with concepts such as markets and consumer choice being central to this (Rhodes, 1996). At the same time, there were attempts by the government to encourage a greater range of service providers across public, private, and voluntary sectors, making the organisation, implementation, and delivery of services more complex and dependent on a much wider network of organisations. Many of these changes were encapsulated in the term 'the new public management', a concept that encompasses features such as devolution of responsibility towards lower-level agencies, budgetary limits, incentives to collaborate with the private sector, competition between providers, concentration on core services and privatisation of non-essential functions, use of performance measurement, and greater consumer choice. These reforms resulted in significant change to both the structures and styles of governance, including the introduction of internal markets in the NHS and education, privatisation, a greater use of performance measures and standards, the increased use of arms length government including quangos and Next Steps agencies, the centralisation of power, reform and residualisation of local government, and the introduction of a variety of mechanisms designed to give consumers a greater say in the operation and delivery of services.

There are a variety of issues that arise from this approach. One of the most important is that the actual process of governing becomes more complex because of the number and variety of organisations involved, which raises concerns such as: the extent to which these organisations are accountable to the state and the public; the relationship between the state and these organisations; and the inter-dependence and fragmentation created by the complexity of organisations and the structures of governance.

New Labour, 1997–2010

The changes to the mechanisms of policy-making and implementation that took place under the Conservatives may have been substantial, but in the early years of the Labour government the pace accelerated further, with constitutional reforms, new emphases, such as on partnership and 'joined-up government', and continued use of measures such as performance 'league tables' that had been introduced under the Conservatives. While some commentators characterised Labour's social policies as displaying a high degree of continuity with those of the Conservatives, despite the fact that some of the Conservatives' reforms were retained and even enhanced, the same could not be said about the government's approach to the policy process.

The Labour government's commitment to improving the quality of policy-making might be perceived of as drawing upon a 'rational' approach (Simon,

1957). Such an approach assumes that any policy will be tackled by progressing logically through a series of steps, eventually selecting the most appropriate outcome at the end of the process. The notion of 'joined-up' government – that each department is aware of what is going on within other departments and can take account of the work each is undertaking – served to reinforce this approach. The use of public and pressure group consultations and the incorporation into legislation (Department of the Environment, Transport and the Regions, 1998) of a duty for local authorities to consult with local communities can be seen as further dimensions of an inclusive approach. However, the extent to which this apparent commitment to different modes of decision-making, evidence-based policy, and participation was realised in practice remains a matter for debate.

More specifically, there were a number of other changes in policy-making under Labour. One was the greater role for the Treasury, which, in particular under Gordon Brown as Chancellor of the Exchequer, played a significant part in directing social policy through the Comprehensive Spending Reviews and public service agreements, as well as the use of the tax system to deliver 'income support' such as via the working tax credit.

Partnership was seen by Labour as one of the key mechanisms for the implementation and delivery of policy, and there were a variety of attempts to encourage partnerships across the public, private, and voluntary sectors in health, education, housing, crime prevention, and so on. These were viewed by the government as appropriate for tackling particular social problems and in improving the quality of public services. The Private Finance Initiative (PFI) was one of the more controversial initiatives, with the private sector building schools, which were then leased to local authorities, and hospitals, which were leased to the NHS, before reverting to the public sector after a set period. Critics have claimed that such initiatives have proved more costly than if they had been undertaken wholly by the public sector.

The government also saw the development of ICT as opening up opportunities, and it sought to maximise provision of government services electronically. While this does appear to have a number of potential benefits for citizens, there remain concerns about a number of issues, including equality of access.

Constitutional and structural change

Immediately after coming to office in 1997, Labour introduced or outlined a number of changes that had significant implications for the governance of social policy. These included devolution, incorporation of the European Convention of Human Rights into UK law, and acceptance of the Agreement on Social Policy (originally signed at Maastricht in 1992 by the then other 11 members of the European Union). Shortly after becoming Prime Minister, Gordon Brown signed the European Union Reform Treaty (the Lisbon Treaty), designed to replace the failed European Union Constitution, which had been rejected by French and Dutch voters in 2005.

DEVOLUTION

It is important to note that the different constituent parts of the United Kingdom have always possessed some social, economic, legal, and political features that have distinguished them from each other. These were to some extent recognised by the existence of the Northern Ireland Office, the Scottish Office, and the Welsh Office as part of the governmental machinery, seeking to take account of at least some of these differences. However, it was only under Labour that these differences were reflected in terms of elected legislative bodies.

Following referendums in the autumn of 1997, the Scottish Parliament and the National Assembly for Wales came into being on 1 July 1999. In Northern Ireland, as part of the ongoing peace process, an Assembly came into existence on 2 December 1999, although it had a rather on–off existence for a period, reflecting the vagaries of the peace process. Devolution therefore played a major part in Labour's attempts to modernise government. This is discussed in greater detail in Chapter 4.

As a consequence of devolution, we now have an even greater variety of approaches to social policy across the United Kingdom, including differences on NHS commissioning, funding of higher education, prescription charges, testing of school pupils, and the use of tables of school performance. Following the 2007 elections to the devolved administrations in Scotland and Wales, political control of the Scottish Government passed from Labour to the Scottish National Party, who retained power at the 2011 elections, while Plaid Cymru shared power with Labour in Wales until Labour formed a minority government from 2011. It seems likely that in future the diversity of policies and methods of policy implementation and delivery will continue, particularly as political control in the different administrations will be likely to change over time.

THE HUMAN RIGHTS ACT 1998

Although the United Kingdom ratified the European Convention of Human Rights (ECHR) in 1951, successive governments refused to incorporate it into UK law. Citizens who felt that their human rights had been infringed were therefore not able to use the domestic courts, although they were able to appeal to the European Court of Human Rights in Strasbourg, an expensive and time-consuming process. The Court found against the UK Government on many occasions, on issues varying from censorship of prisoners' mail to different ages of consent for heterosexuals and homosexuals, and, although the UK was not bound to comply with the decisions of the Court, it consistently did so and UK law was changed to reflect the judgments. However, the Human Rights Act 1998 finally incorporated the ECHR into UK law, thus making it possible for individuals who believe that their human rights have been infringed to pursue this in the domestic courts, speeding up the time scale and reducing the costs. While much of the early media coverage of the impact of the Act involved the rights (or otherwise) to privacy of often high-profile individuals, the effects of the Act were rapidly seen in a number of areas of social policy, including mental health, where patients detained under the Mental Health Act do not now have to demonstrate that they should no longer be detained, but it is now incumbent upon those detaining them to demonstrate that they have a case. Similarly, many public authorities were forced to change some of the ways in which they operate and interact with the public because of the requirements of the Act and the ECHR.

LOCAL GOVERNMENT

Many of Labour's changes also affected local government, particularly in England. Local government in the United Kingdom has always been subservient to central government. It has no independent right to exist and all of its functions and activities can be changed by Parliament. Despite this relative weakness, and even following 18 years of Conservative government that saw large-scale restructuring of local government in England, Scotland, and Wales, a reduction in its ability to raise its own income, and a reduced responsibility for the direct provision of services, local government retained a significant role in social policy under Labour. At its most basic, it was still possible under Labour to identify a number of services that clearly related to social policy for which local authorities had a responsibility, including education, the personal social services, housing and planning.

To a considerable extent, these responsibilities were retained, although Labour followed the approach of the previous Conservative governments in continuing to stress the role of local authorities as enablers of services rather than as providers. Labour's enthusiasm for 'modernisation' was also apparent, with local authorities encouraged to adopt new structures for decision-making, so that by the late 1990s many councils had moved away from the traditional model of services overseen by a committee of councillors towards a leader and cabinet model, with most councillors having primarily a responsibility for scrutinising decisions made by the cabinet. Labour did also reintroduce London-wide government, with an elected mayor and the Greater London Assembly, although the emphasis was primarily on strategic economic and to some extent transport policy, with the London boroughs retaining responsibility for local government's social policy commitments.

As with other areas of social policy, there was an emphasis on 'partnerships' and collaboration across public, private, and voluntary sectors as a way of tackling problems and meeting needs. And there was continued use of mechanisms of external audit and inspection as a major driver, from the government's perspective, of improving standards and quality. Although there may have been a rather less critical view of local government than before 1997, nevertheless the government's attitude showed an unwillingness to trust local government to deliver improvements on its own.

WOMEN IN POLITICS

Under Labour there were was also a significant increase in the numbers of women elected to the House of Commons and to the devolved administrations. In Westminster, the proportion of MPs who were women rose significantly from 9 per cent in 1992 to 18 per cent in 1997, remaining around that level for the 2001 and 2005 parliaments. It is important to note that much of this increase was down to the Labour Party adopting more women as candidates, so that in 2007, 27 per cent of Labour MPs were female, compared with 14 per cent of Liberal Democrats and 9 per cent of Conservatives. The advent of devolution has also resulted in significant female representation in the Scottish Parliament (33 per cent in 2007) and the National Assembly for Wales (47 per cent in 2007), again in large part due to larger numbers of Labour women candidates. This led some to anticipate different approaches to decision-making, with perhaps a more consensual and less adversarial approach, and different policy emphases, such as a greater stress on family-friendly policies, although the extent to which these were realised is perhaps questionable.

New Labour: an overview

Overall, many of the issues that can be identified with the Conservatives' approach to the governance of social policy were also applicable to Labour. The complexity of networks continued to pose questions about the mechanisms that governments seek to use to implement policy, as did the contradiction between centralising and devolving tendencies that were particularly apparent under New Labour. And, despite the apparent commitment to improving the quality of policy-making, questions remained over the extent to which this was being achieved in practice.

Governance under the Coalition, 2010–

Following the 2010 general election, the emergence of a Coalition government almost inevitably necessitated some changes to policy-making, not least because the two governing parties, and their leaders, were forced to rely upon each other, rather than being free to make entirely their own decisions. This was evidenced right from the start of Coalition with the publication of *The Coalition: Our Programme for Government* (Cabinet Office, 2010), which set out the new government's programme.

Some of the themes identified from the Labour governments remain apparent; although at the same time can be viewed quite differently under the Coalition. Where devolution is concerned, the Conservative-Liberal Democrat government at Westminster has pursued very different approaches from those taken by the Scottish, Welsh, and Northern Irish governments (see Chapter 4), with much greater enthusiasm for the involvement of the private sector in the provision of public services and the delivery of social policies. Following the 2011 elections to the devolved administrations, the Scottish National Party retained power in Scotland, while in Wales Labour formed a minority government. Yet, the fact that Westminster retains control over economic policy, and over key areas such as social security and pensions, means that the devolved areas are inevitably affected by the Coalition's policies, so that the major cuts in public expenditure, while they may to some extent have been delayed and can be delivered somewhat differently in the devolved areas, will nevertheless have a major impact, as will initiatives associated with welfare reform, such as the 'bedroom tax' and the Work Programme (see Chapters 10 and 11). However, at the same time the Coalition government accepted the report of the Calman Commission (2009) for a further transfer of financial powers to the Scottish Parliament and legislated for that in the Scotland Act 2012.

One obvious area of compromise between the two parties was the Human Rights Act. At the 2010 general election, the Conservatives promised to replace the Human Rights Act with a Bill of Rights for the United Kingdom. However, with the Liberal Democrats being supportive of the Act, it has remained in place.

Austerity

While under the Labour government's the Treasury's role in social policy was perhaps greater than it had ever been, particularly under Gordon Brown as Chancellor, it has remained significant under the Coalition, although for very different reasons. From 2010, the driving force for many of the Coalition's social policies was 'austerity', with the perceived answer to the financial crisis and the deficit being seen as major cuts in the level of public expenditure. However, given the importance of social provision in public spending, the inevitable consequence of this was cuts in spending on social policies. Indeed, the Coalition's commitment to maintaining spending on the NHS and education in real terms itself meant that other areas would be hit disproportionally.

Localism and the Big Society

The Coalition government's policies can generally be portrayed as further weakening the role of local government in social policy. This is perhaps particularly the case with regard to school age education, where the encouragement of schools to become academies takes them away from local government control, and the creation of free schools further limits the powers of local authorities to plan education provision in their areas. More generally, the apparent enthusiasm for localism and the 'Big Society' in England, particularly in the early years of the Coalition government, were widely seen as encouraging the provision of services by local groups rather than by local authorities, and, taken together with unprecedented cuts in local government expenditure, were likely to result in the increasing residualisation of the role of local government, including in the delivery of social policies. While the idea of the Big Society and other mooted initiatives, such as the development of mutual organisations to provide public services (sometimes termed the 'John Lewis model') did not really take root, and the extent to which 'localism' was likely to become a reality was also questioned, the impact of the Coalition's other policies meant that by the third year of the government local authorities were facing a future of yet more limited powers and funding.

The Coalition: an overview

Although at the time of writing we have only witnessed some three years of Coalition government, we have seen certain continuities with and discontinuities from previous governments. The Coalition has pursued cuts in welfare and the privatisation of provision, often within the guise of the need to cope with the challenges of 'austerity'. It has also promoted, through its 'localism' and 'Big Society' agendas, a diminished role for local government together with an associated aspiration that communities and localities with take on the responsibility for running services and representing communities – an aspiration that has yet to demonstrate any significant impact.

Models of governance

The preceding section presented an account of the various approaches to making and implementing social policy. This section now presents various governance models. Models can be useful in helping us to analyse and understand our world. They are unlikely to reflect precisely how governments act and what they do, but they enable us to compare those things with 'ideal-types' and to draw conclusions from that.

Newman (2001) suggested that there have historically been four types of governance arrangements: hierarchies, markets, networks, and partnerships:

- traditional public administration – the hierarchical model;
- markets – the rational goal model;
- networks – the open systems model;
- partnerships – the self-governance model.

Newman also suggested that these four models can be distinguished with reference to two 'dimensions of difference':

- power – centralised or decentralised;
- disposition to change – stability or innovation.

She maps the four models of governance against these two axes (see Figure 3.2).

The discussion below outlines these different governance models. However, it is important to note that it would be overly simplistic to depict or overlay

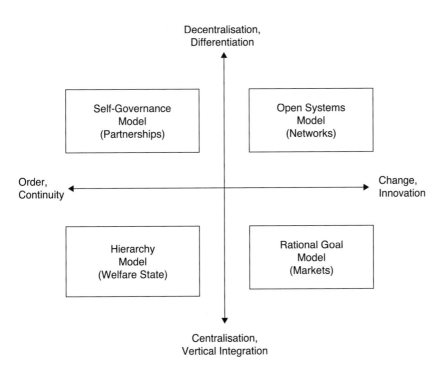

Figure 3.2 Newman's models of governance

particular epochs, ideologies or governments with particular governance models. As Richards and Smith (2003, p. 9) have observed, '[in] reality there is no distinct temporal breach between each [model of governance]. The reality is there is a great deal of fuzziness and overlap'.

Traditional governance structures – hierarchies

The last four decades have seen a shift away from the traditional, centralised, hierarchical structures of government. During and in the immediate aftermath of the Second World War, the state's role had been extended to the control of the production of many goods, such as health services, housing, child care, and food production, while government had also taken on the responsibility for managing demand, for example for food and fuel. In many respects, 'the Warfare State had become the Welfare State'. There was a general belief, informed by Keynesian economic theory, that the state could control both demand and supply rather than leave it to the market to balance supply to individual demand.

At the core of hierarchical government was the sovereignty of government at Westminster. On this perspective, governments are elected and held accountable through periodic elections with the majority party taking power. Government takes place through a strong cabinet (the Executive), supported by the doctrines of collective responsibility and ministerial responsibility. In theory ministers, as elected politicians with democratic legitimacy, make policy, which is then implemented by non-political civil servants. In the case of much social policy, this saw the development of large bureaucratic (and hierarchical) organisations for the delivery of services, such as the NHS and social security at central government level, and for education and social care within local government.

However, by the mid 1970s this model was subject to a range of criticisms, including its perceived failure to allow citizens to shape and influence the nature of public services. The New Right-influenced governments of Margaret Thatcher and John Major, the New Labour governments, and the Conservative-Liberal Democratic Coalition government have all argued that public services should cease to be monolithic, inefficient, unresponsive, and dominated by providers rather than by users.

DISCUSS AND DO

Problems with hierarchical governance

What criticisms could you make and what examples can you give of the traditional, hierarchical welfare state. Think of a particular service, for example housing, the NHS, education, and relate the service to criticisms of the traditional welfare state in terms of the service being:

- monolithic – 'one size fits all'

- inefficient – slow, costly, bureaucratic

- unresponsive – no choice, long queues

- supplier dominant – serving the interests of providers, e.g. welfare professionals.

Governance through markets

The New Right-influenced Conservative governments of 1979–97 (see also Chapter 7) sought to redefine the nature of welfare provision and public services more generally. For them the solution was to be found in the promotion of market-type mechanisms, including privatisation, the new managerialism, and empowerment of users.

The 1980s and 1990s therefore saw the privatisation of many industries and services. In addition, local authorities, the NHS, and other public services were required to 'contract out' many of their services. And, where it was not seen as appropriate for the private sector to take over, there was the creation of 'quasi-markets' (Le Grand and Bartlett, 1993). Other services were either taken out of the direct control of central government by being set up as agencies or made independent of local authorities, often being recast as local quangos.

The New Right sought to privatise welfare in terms of repositioning parts of it back in the private realm, by making individuals, families, and communities responsible for meeting their own welfare needs.

Another aspect of the New Right's approach was the attempt to exert greater control on social welfare and other public service providers through stronger management. The new mangerialism typically featured 'attention to outputs and performance rather than inputs and personal authority to line managers' (Clarke *et al.*, 2000, p. 6) and an emphasis on reducing budgets, 'getting more for less', and freeing up managers to manage and deliver outputs and outcomes (to 'get results') almost irrespective of how this was to be achieved.

Alongside these changes the New Right sought to return power and responsibility to the individual, including through changes in social policy, with the avowed intention of empowering individuals – for example, as parents, school governors, tenants, patients, and clients. The argument was that an emphasis on consumer choice (as opposed to supplier control) and a mixed economy of welfare provision would consequently lead to increased responsiveness from welfare providers (Hill, 1994).

However, the marketisation of welfare and other public services let to greater fragmentation of control mechanisms. The state, and government more specifically, could not control or command the provision of social welfare in the way that it had in the past. As a result, governments had to develop new forms of control, including greater managerial control and audit and regulation by new bodies.

STOP AND THINK

The New Right-influenced Conservative governments from 1979 to 1997 took three approaches to the reform of social policy: privatisation, managerialism, and user empowerment. How might each of these approaches be seen to be able to improve the provision and governance of welfare services? Choose a particular service area and consider the impact of each of the following approaches:

- Privatisation – in order to make provision more efficient and responsive

- Managerialisation – which challenges the power of suppliers – professionals and technocrats

- User involvement – whereby users get what they want, when they want it, and are able to influence the nature of provision more generally.

Governance through networks

Alongside the changes introduced by governments in the United Kingdom were other developments, including globalisation, the growth of international and supranational organisations, and changes in public expectations and demands. Richards and Smith (2003, p. 276) were thus able to argue that in this new world:

[P]ower is . . . dispersed: the once unified state is fragmented and networks have replaced hierarchy. The policy process has become much more complex: rather than being a linear process with decisions being made in the centre, it

> has become one where a range of actors are involved . . . [P]olicy decisions now involve public and private sector actors, agencies, privatised industries, regulators, officials, and ministers. The process of policy-making and policy delivery has become more complex.

The authority, autonomy, and power of the nation-state's government was being 'hollowed out' or dispersed: outwards, via privatisation and quasi markets; downwards, via the creation of quangos and government agencies; upwards, to the supranational level, for example, the EU. It could be argued that the 'hollowed out state' had led to a 'differentiated polity', the main features of which were (Richards and Smith, 2003, p. 276):

- an emphasis on governance, rather than government
- power dependence, and thus exchange relationships
- policy networks
- a segmented executive
- intergovernmental relationships
- a hollowed out state.

Government could no longer 'govern from the centre', controlling both demand and supply, and instead had to relinquish command over service delivery, steering through policy networks, and acting as an enabler within networks:

> These networks are made up of organisations which need to exchange resources (for example, money, information, expertise) to achieve their objectives . . . As British government creates agencies, bypasses local government, uses special purpose bodies to deliver services, and encourages public–private partnerships, so networks become increasingly prominent among British governing structures.
>
> (Rhodes, 1997, p. 658)

Governance through partnerships

When Labour returned to power in 1997, 'it promised forms of governance that would offer a "third way" between traditional forms of public and social administration *and* the reliance on markets as mechanisms to reform the delivery of public services' (Driver, 2005, p. 265), and this was to be governance through partnerships. As Newman (2001, p. 105) said:

> . . . a more distinctive feature of Labour's approach was a more explicit focus on partnership as a way of governing. This focus was evident in the strengthening of the partnership rhetoric and in the [Labour] government's approach to the delivery of public policy.

Of course, partnership and partnerships can be viewed in very different ways. And indeed Labour proposed different forms of partnership, including: horizontal, for example across government departments; vertical, for example between central and local government; and with stakeholders, including users, citizens, private and not-for-profit organisations, and communities.

It can be argued that partnership working does have the potential to improve the governance and delivery of social policy, such as through bringing together expertise and contribution from different partners, by helping ensure integrated and coordinated approaches and breaking down 'silos', by enabling a wider involvement of stakeholders, and by potentially increasing the financial resources by drawing in different organisations (Newman, 2001). However, even early in the government's existence, an Audit Commission (1998) report, *A Fruitful Partnership*, argued that making partnerships work well is challenging, and identified a number of difficulties that included:

- getting partners to agree on priorities for action;
- keeping partners actively involved;
- preventing the partnership from becoming a talking shop;
- making decisions that all partners endorse;
- deciding who will provide the resources to achieve the objectives;
- linking the work of the partnership with the mainstream activities and budgets of the partners;
- monitoring the partnership's effectiveness;
- working out whether what is achieved justifies the costs involved;
- avoiding partnership overload, particularly where organisations are involved in large numbers of partnerships.

These, and other issues, are reflected in the significant literature on partnership and collaboration that developed during this period. There are also other questions about Labour's approach to partnership, perhaps particularly around the controlling and centralising role played by the government.

Indeed, there are some significant questions about partnerships in general, such as whether it is possible ever to be egalitarian or democratic, the distribution of resources (financial, legal, skills, etc.) means that some partners will inevitably be more equal than others, what to do if some partners decide not to get involved or withdraw their involvement, and how to enable poorer or less well resourced groups or individuals to engage in meaningful and rewarding ways. As with markets and networks, it seems that in many respects the rhetoric of an approach to governance is likely to be different from its work in practice.

Lessons from these models

If we apply these models to the Coalition government, it is apparent that in some respects we have seen a return to the market-type approach, as with the Conservative governments of the 1980s and 1990s. For example, the reforms to the NHS that took place from April 2013 allowed greater involvement of the private and third sectors. At the same time, user involvement and choice have continued to be promoted in health and social care and in education, while the privatisation of responsibility to individuals and families has been a significant feature of government policy. Yet, at the same time, the Coalition has sought to continue to exercise control from the centre, whether in relation to control of the curriculum and assessments in education, the funding of and service provision by local government, or the distribution of rights and responsibilities in terms of welfare and work.

While we have undoubtedly seen major changes in the ways in which governments and the state command (steer) and control (row), it is worth noting that it is still government and the state that are controlling, notwithstanding the pressures upwards (supranationally), downwards (to regions, localities, communities, and individuals), and outwards (to other state and non-state actors). And while social policy may increasingly be delivered via market, network, and partnership arrangements, the relationship between government and other organisations remains asymmetrical, with government, typically, remaining the most powerful. In that sense, therefore, it is arguably still the hierarchical state that determines whether market, network or partnership governance approaches are pursued.

Conclusion

While social policy as an academic subject may not always pay considerable direct attention to 'politics', or to the mechanisms by which policies are made and implemented, social policy and politics are inseparable. Politics inevitably affects social policy, but so too is it intimately concerned with social policy. Many key contemporary issues are social policy issues, and even those that may not on the face of it appear to be, such as climate change or the development of technology, may have significant social policy implications (see, for example, Chapter 18). This means that in order to fully comprehend what is going on in social policy, we need to have a broad understanding of the world of politics and government, the influence of the media and pressure groups, and generally the ways in which power and influence work, including via networks, partnerships or markets.

Summary

This chapter has outlined a variety of features of politics and government in the United Kingdom and related these to the making and implementation of social policy. It has suggested that:

- There are a variety of ways in which social policy can be affected by politics, not only directly through political parties and the process of governing, but also by influences such as pressure groups and the media.
- Under the Conservative governments of 1979–97, there was an emphasis upon what were seen as the virtues of the private sector, and in particular markets and marketisation, with the 'consumer' at the centre, and this was reflected in social policy through initiatives such as privatisation, compulsory competitive tendering, attempts to create 'internal markets', greater managerialism, and use of quangos and 'Next Steps' agencies for the delivery of some services.
- The New Labour government elected in 1997 demonstrated a significant degree of radicalism in its approach to the policy process, most notably through the introduction of devolution to Northern Ireland, Scotland, and Wales, the passage of the Human Rights Act, and an emphasis on 'better' policy-making and implementation, making terms such as 'joined-up government', 'evidence-based policy', 'partnership' and 'modernisation' part of the social policy lexicon.
- The use of models can assist us in analysing and understanding the ways in which the governance of social policy has developed over recent decades.

Discussion and review

- How do political parties and pressure groups differ in their attempts to influence social policy?
- What is the role of sub-central government (the devolved administrations and local authorities) in the making and implementation of social policy?
- What were the principal differences between the Conservative governments of 1979–97 and the Labour governments that followed in their approaches to the government of social policy?
- What can the four models of governance presented in this chapter tell us about the approach of the Coalition government to the making and implementation of social policy?

References

Audit Commission (1998) *A Fruitful Partnership: Effective Partnership Working*, Audit Commission, London.

Beveridge, W. (1942) *Social Insurance and Allied Services* (The Beveridge Report), Cmd. 6404, The Stationery Office, London.

Bochel, H. (ed.) (2010) *The Conservative Party and Social Policy*, Policy Press, Bristol.

Bochel, H. and Defty, A. (2007) *Welfare Policy under New Labour*, Policy Press, Bristol.

Butcher, T. (1995) *Delivering Welfare: The Governance of Social Services in the 1990s*, Open University Press, Buckingham.

Cabinet Office (2010) *The Coalition: Our Programme for Government*, Cabinet Office, London.

Calman Commission (2009) *Serving Scotland Better: Scotland and the United Kingdom in the 21st Century*, Commission on Scottish Devolution, Edinburgh.

Clarke, J., Gewirtz, S. and McLaughlin, E. (2000) 'Reinventing the welfare state', in J. Clarke, S. Gewirtz and E. McLaughlin (eds.) *New Managerialism, New Welfare*, Sage, London.

Cohen, S. (2002) *Folk Devils and Moral Panics*, Routledge, London.

Curran, J. and Seaton, J. (1991) *Power Without Responsibility: The Press and Broadcasting in Britain*, Routledge, London.

Department of the Environment, Transport and the Regions (1998) *Modern Local Government: In Touch with the People*, The Stationery Office, London.

Driver, S. (2005) 'Welfare after Thatcher: New Labour and social democratic politics', in M. Powell, L. Bauld and K. Clarke (eds.) *Social Policy Review 23*, Policy Press, Bristol.

Easton, D. (1965) *A Systems Analysis of Political Life*, Wiley, New York.

Ham, C. and Hill, M. (1993) *The Policy Process in the Modern Capitalist State*, Harvester Wheatsheaf, Hemel Hempstead.

Hill, D. (1994) *Citizens and Cities: Urban Policy in the 1990s*, Harvester Wheatsheaf, Hemel Hempstead.

Hood, C. (1991) 'A public management for all seasons?', *Public Administration*, Vol. 69, No. 1, pp. 3–19.

Jones, H. and MacGregor, S. (1998) *Social Issues and Party Politics*, Routledge, London.

Le Grand, J. and Bartlett, W. (eds.) (1993) *Quasi Markets and Social Policy*, Macmillan, Basingstoke.

Leveson, B. (2012) *An Inquiry into the Culture, Practices and Ethics of the Press* (The Leveson Report), The Stationery Office, London.

Newman, J. (2001) *Modernising Governance*, Sage, London.

Powell, M. (ed.) (1999) *New Labour, New Welfare State?*, Policy Press, Bristol.

Powell, M. (ed.) (2002) *Evaluating New Labour's Welfare Reforms*, Policy Press, Bristol.

Powell, M. (ed.) (2008) *Modernising the Welfare State*, Policy Press, Bristol.

Rhodes, R. (1996) 'The new governance: governing without government', *Political Studies*, Vol. 44, No. 4, pp. 652–67.

Rhodes, R. (1997) *Understanding Governance: Policy Networks, Governance, Reflexivity and Accountability*, Open University Press, Buckingham.

Richards, D. and Smith, M.J. (2003) *Governance and Public Policy in the UK*, Oxford University Press, Oxford.

Simon, H. (1957) *Administrative Behaviour*, Macmillan, New York.

Further reading

Alaszewski, A. and Brown, P. (2012) *Making Health Policy*, Polity, Cambridge. Usefully applies ideas around the policy process to UK health (and social care).

Bochel, H. and Duncan, S. (eds.) (2007) *Making Policy in Theory and Practice*, Policy Press, Bristol. Presents a range of academic and practitioner perspectives on policy analysis.

Hill, M. (2009) *The Public Policy Process*, Pearson, Harlow. Provides a discussion and evaluation of the policy process and the exercise of power in contemporary society.

Hudson, J. and Lowe, S. (2009) *Understanding the Policy Process*, Policy Press, Bristol. Provides a valuable coverage of the policy process, and is particularly useful in relation to social policy.

Moran, M. (2011) *Politics and Governance in the UK*, Palgrave, Basingstoke. One of a number of comprehensive textbooks on British politics, this book provides a thorough introduction to the subject.

Newman, J. (2001) *Understanding Governance*, Sage, London. Provides a comprehensive exploration of the shifting agendas of governance under New Labour.

Useful websites

The main political parties throughout the UK each have their own websites, including:

http://www.conservatives.com, www.labour.org.uk, www.libdems.org.uk, www.snp.org.

http://www.gov.uk – this site provides access to a vast amount of information about government and services, with links to most central and local government sites, including those in the devolved administrations of Northern Ireland, Scotland, and Wales.

http://www.electoralcommission.org.uk – the body responsible for oversight of elections also provides access to its publications and research, including on elections and party financing.

CHAPTER 4

Devolution and Social Policy

Sharon Wright

Learning objectives

- To consider why and how devolution matters in all countries of the UK
- To appreciate what devolution can tell us about how social policies are influenced and formed
- To understand how some policies have diverged following devolution and why there are constraints to divergence
- To understand why some important policy areas remain under central UK control
- To view social policies as products of particular political, institutional, and socio-economic contexts

Chapter overview

This chapter will outline why devolution matters to everyone in the UK. First, it will define devolution and describe the different arrangements for governing England, Scotland, Wales, and Northern Ireland that have developed following public votes in favour of transferring power away from

London in 1997. Crucial questions will be asked about how welfare needs can be met in the different parts of the UK and whether the UK can still be said to have a 'national' or UK-wide welfare state. The chapter will then look at what has changed since devolution (including both policies and political processes) and why this matters to all countries of the UK, including England.

CONTROVERSY AND DEBATE

University students in England have to pay their own tuition fees, which can amount to £9,000 a year, whereas Scottish residents studying in Scotland do not.

- Is this fair?
- What sorts of potential students are advantaged or disadvantaged by these policies?
- Are the English and Scottish approaches sustainable?

Alex Salmond (2011), Scotland's First Minister, said that the tradition of free higher education in Scotland should be 'not just for Christmas but for all time'. He called falling university admissions in England, following the introduction of up-front student-paid fees, a 'catastrophe south of the border' (http://news.stv.tv/politics/206962-scotlands-free-higher-education-is-not-just-for-christmas/).

- Who should pay for university education?
- Which issues do governments need to consider when making decisions about who pays for higher education?

Why does devolution matter?

There is a temptation to think of devolution as a minority concern for the 5.3 million citizens of Scotland, 3.1 million citizens of Wales, and 1.8 million citizens of Northern Ireland, rather than a central feature of twenty-first-century social life for the majority of the 53 million of the UK population based in England. However, devolution (meaning here the transfer of powers from the central UK Government in London to the newly elected government in Scotland and administrations in Wales and Northern Ireland in the late 1990s) provides a rare opportunity to observe a live policy drama unfold. Devolution offers us a unique viewpoint to try to understand what new policy developments mean in the devolved countries of the UK (the 'United Kingdom' means England, Scotland, Wales, and Northern Ireland together, whereas 'Britain' refers to England, Scotland, and Wales, without Northern Ireland). Devolution also offers new perspectives on the possibilities that are available for change in England. This is why some analysts have referred to devolution as a 'policy laboratory' (ESRC, 2004) in which to observe how different actions can be taken in relation to similar social problems. Not only this, but the development of different political systems and welfare arrangements allows us to fundamentally question our taken-for-granted assumptions about what a welfare state is, how welfare systems operate, why policies are formed as they are, and whether or not they have to remain the same in future. Devolution also disrupts the idea of 'nationality' in relation to welfare states. In short, devolution allows us to compare different countries *within* the UK in the sort of way that was only previously possible by looking overseas (e.g. to Europe, the USA or Australia). In this way, devolution can turn the obvious into the interesting by 'familiarising the distant' and 'distancing the familiar' (Gouldner, 1971). Devolution, therefore, offers great potential to observe and learn about what is and what might be.

What is devolution and how has it developed?

Until the late 1990s, the UK differed from many comparable rich nations in having an especially strong central unitary state, with few opportunities for anyone other than elected politicians from the ruling party or senior civil servants to influence social policies. This meant that social policies could be changed relatively quickly and dramatically (as happened in the 1980s, when sudden large-scale cutbacks were made by the Conservative governments) without meaningful consultation or negotiation with representatives such as trade unions or employers (as would be usual in several European and Scandinavian countries). Furthermore, regional and local authorities were limited in the extent to which they could intervene in the welfare of people living within their boundaries.

In 1997, however, the UK Government (led then by New Labour Prime Minister Tony Blair) proposed to change this state of affairs by offering voters in Scotland, Wales, and Northern Ireland the opportunity to choose to have greater control over many issues relating to welfare. In all three cases, there was support for the transfer of some powers away from London, although the stories of policy change are unique in each country and devolution has been asymmetrical. Ultimately, the UK Parliament has retained significant powers over all parts of the UK, including direct control of financial and economic matters and several social policy areas that are of fundamental importance to citizens' wellbeing, such as social security (except for Northern Ireland, where distinct policy-making is possible), employment law (except in Northern

Ireland), and immigration and asylum. Strangely, devolution in the UK has not undermined the very powerful central state to the extent that might have been expected. Instead, the Westminster government continues to exert strong control in many ways (including, under the Conservative-Liberal Coalition, from 2010 to the present, deep cuts to welfare provision far beyond those made under the Conservative governments in the 1980s). However, devolution *has* led to very significant changes for everyone living in the UK, which we will now consider in greater depth.

Table 4.1 provides an overview of the key social policy powers (for full details of devolved powers, see Cabinet Office *et al.*, 2013) of the devolved administrations in Scotland, Wales, and Northern Ireland. It is important to compare the last two columns of the table, England and the UK, since it is a common mistake to assume that English policies apply to other areas (e.g. Wales) or to the whole of the UK. The table shows that most of the key social policy issues are now controlled by multiple legislatures. It has been argued that concern over social issues created the main thrust of support for the intro-duction of devolution and now, looking back over more than a decade of devolution in practice, that social policies have been the main business of the devolved governments (Chaney and Drakeford, 2004; Birrell, 2009; Scott and Mooney, 2009). Arguably, this means that there is substantial scope for the development of different policies, influenced directly by more varied pro-cesses and political values/priorities than ever before in the history of the post-war welfare state. In the devolved administrations, policies are directed by distinct mixes of political influence, which are guided by different values and priorities than those of the Westminster government (see below). In fact, some analysts have questioned whether we now can consider there to be a 'British' welfare state at all (Stewart, 2004). Whether or not we judge there to

Table 4.1 Quick guide to devolved powers over key social policy issues

Policy area	Scotland: Scottish Government	Wales: Welsh Assembly Government	Northern Ireland: Northern Ireland Assembly	England: UK Parliament	United Kingdom: UK Parliament
Health	✓	✓	✓	✓	
Education	✓	✓	✓	✓	
Housing	✓	✓	✓	✓	
Social security			✓		✓
Employment			✓		✓
Training	✓	✓	✓	✓	
Justice and policing	✓		✓	For England and Wales	
Equal opportunities			✓		✓

be an enduring core of a shared welfare state in the UK, we certainly have to acknowledge what Williams and Mooney (2008) call a 'decentring of social policy', since it no longer makes sense to talk of UK-wide social policy in any of the traditional key areas of welfare provision. However, Table 4.1 only shows whether or not devolved powers exist in relation to key areas of social policy, rather than the type or extent of these powers, or whether these powers have led to any observable policy changes or outcomes in practice (which will be considered below).

Processes

It is also important to view devolution as an ongoing process, rather than being a one-off event that determines the scope or nature of all future developments. The original devolution settlements that were agreed in law have already changed over time, and the character of policy-making has also been influenced by shifting electoral support for a range of political parties, many of which were relatively unfamiliar on the UK political scene. In all three countries, increased powers have been transferred after the initial establishment of devolution. Devolution did not just bring change to the substance of policies, but also brought new policy-making processes into being, creating a long-lasting legacy of *how* social policies are made. In Scotland, Wales, and Northern Ireland, the mechanisms of democracy were designed to increase cooperation, voter engagement, and community involvement. Broader committee structures within the legislatures were aimed at encouraging policy-making with greater transparency, openness, and responsiveness. Crucially, the 'first-past-the-post' system used to elect members of the UK Parliament was rejected in favour of proportional representation (or at least more proportional systems; for further detail, see Cabinet Office *et al.*, 2013). This made it more difficult for a single party to dominate and hence encouraged power-sharing and cooperative approaches. However, this well-intentioned development has met challenges, since powerful party political allegiances have proved hard to shake off. Although new alliances have had to be built between different parties to make governance possible, oppositional debates can be swung by the smallest of minority parties, whose casting vote can thus be more decisive than public support warrants. Politically, in the early stages of devolution, the Labour Party formed a key part of governments at UK level and in Scotland and Wales. However, after 2007, the Labour Party lost its hold in the devolved countries and since the election of the Conservative-Liberal Democrat Coalition government at Westminster in 2010, there has been a wide gap between the values and ideologies of the UK and devolved governments, especially that in Scotland.

Scotland

Scotland is the largest of the three countries (by population and landmass, including a combination of large urban areas and sparsely populated remote highlands and islands) and the most powerful of the new legislatures (see Mooney and Scott, 2005; Keating, 2010). The Scottish Parliament was established in 1999 (with 129 elected members) together with a civil service arm, the Scottish Executive (renamed by the Scottish National Party as the Scottish Government in 2007). Scotland presents a very interesting case because even *before* devolution it had separate legal and educational systems, meaning that fresh policies built on existing arrangements in 1999, rather than being completely new (Mooney and Wright, 2009). At the time of writing, the First Minister of the Scottish Government is Alex Salmond, leader of the Scottish National Party majority government. The Scottish Government has control over a range of policy issues, including: health; education; housing; social work; criminal justice and policing; environmental affairs, culture and sport; training; local government; and economic development (Cabinet Office/ Scotland Office, 2013). There is at present fierce debate about whether Scotland should separate from the rest of the UK after the October 2014 vote on full independence (Scott and Wright, 2012). This question of independence is vital to the future of the UK as a state.

Wales

The National Assembly for Wales (with 60 elected members) was legislated for in 1998, but initially its powers were limited. Greater powers were transferred in 2007 after a review of devolution in Wales (the Richard Commission) and a separate Welsh Government (with executive functions) was established. In 2011, further new powers were transferred enabling the Welsh Assembly to make laws in all of its devolved areas. Currently, a minority Labour government holds power in the Welsh Assembly, led by First Minister of Wales, Carwyn Jones. The Welsh Government now has power over a broad range of matters, including: rural development; culture; economic development; education and training; the environment; health; housing; local government; public administration; social welfare; and sport (Cabinet Office/Wales Office, 2013). Demands for increased powers continue.

Northern Ireland

Devolution took a more complex and contested course in Northern Ireland, where it was connected with a broader peace process, following a long period of political and civil unrest, in which Northern Ireland's relationships with Britain and Ireland were a focal point for decades of intense struggle that involved paramilitary and counter-terrorist violence. In May 1998, the Good Friday Agreement, also known as the Belfast Agreement, was voted in. Devolution was a key part of this agreement. However, support for the first version of a devolved administration was far from universal. For example, the then leader of the Democratic Unionist Party, the Reverend Ian Paisley, objected vocally to the idea 'that armed gunmen, thugs and murderers, with their hands dripping with the blood of their fellow countrymen . . . be given office in government' (Hansard, 1999, col. 269). With political and sectarian tensions running high, the first governments collapsed or were suspended, before a workable devolution settlement was found. At the time of writing, the First Minister, Peter Robinson of the Democratic Unionist Party, and Deputy First Minister, Martin McGuinness of Sinn Féin, hold equal power and must agree before changes can be made. The Northern Ireland Executive (with 108 elected members) differs from governments in Scotland and Wales, in being led by the four largest political parties who all share power: the Democratic Unionist Party (DUP), Sinn Féin, the Ulster Unionist Party (UUP), and the Social Democratic Labour Party (SDLP). This power sharing is 'best described as an involuntary coalition' (Birrell, 2009, p. 2) and involves an adversarial dynamic that is qualitatively different from the other countries of the UK. Although Northern Ireland is the smallest of the devolved regions (in terms of population and landmass), devolved social policy powers are the broadest of the three devolved administrations, including: health and social services; education; employment and skills; social security (which was separately administered *pre*-devolution, and presents a very interesting case study; see Wiggan, 2012 and below); pensions and child support; housing; economic development; local government; the environment; transport; culture and sport; equal opportunities; local government; and, since 2010, policing and criminal justice (Cabinet Office/Northern Ireland Office, 2013).

Funding devolution

Funding is of crucial importance to the scope and type of changes that might be possible under devolution – after all, politicians can promise much, but what they can deliver depends on what can be afforded. Currently, all three of the devolved legislatures rely on the UK Government for their main funding (a block grant), which is agreed by HM Treasury as part of the Comprehensive Spending Review (see McLean *et al.*, 2008). HM Treasury allocates money according to its funding policy (HM Treasury, 2007), which is based on a formula accounting for the size of population and proportion of comparable spending in England. Some degree of local funding is also possible, such as through non-domestic rates, local authority or public body borrowing, and European Structural Funds. The Scottish Parliament is unique in having the power to vary income tax (which could be used to increase or decrease income tax by three pence for those living in Scotland). However, to date, these powers have not been used (see Scottish Government, 2009a). The Northern Ireland Executive has extra borrowing powers that the Scottish Parliament and Welsh Assembly do not have. However, in 2016 the Scottish Government will gain new powers to borrow money and to levy a variable rate of income tax (Cabinet Office *et al.*, 2013). The devolved administrations decide how to allocate the funds they receive (for further detail on the financing of social policies in devolved countries, see Birrell, 2009).

What does devolution mean for England?

Although England has been referred to as a 'black hole' (Trench, 2008, p. 7) for its lack of devolution action, this is not the whole story. Devolution has also impacted on people in England in a number of important ways, which may not be immediately apparent. There is a sense in which England has missed out on the potential advantages of decentralised policy-making. Certainly, there have been loud calls from some quarters for more localised decision-making powers in parts of England (e.g. the rejected proposal for an Assembly for the North East). However, in the decade that has passed since devolution to Scotland, Wales, and Northern Ireland, much less has materialised in England. The main example of localised decision-making has been in London, where a new 25-member London Assembly and Mayor of London role was established in 2000. Following devolution, there have, however, been serious questions about the role of the Westminster Parliament. For example, does the apparatus of government that was designed to govern the whole of the UK now mainly service England? And is it fair for Members of Parliament from the devolved countries to vote on matters of policy that will only be implemented in England? Although of a somewhat different nature from devolution in Northern Ireland, Scotland, and Wales, the Coalition government passed the Localism Act 2011 in order to:

> achieve a substantial and lasting shift in power away from central government and towards local people. They include: new freedoms and flexibilities for local government; new rights and powers for communities and individuals; reform to make the planning system more democratic and more effective, and reform to ensure that decisions about housing are taken locally.
>
> (Greg Clark MP, UK Minister for Decentralisation; Communities and Local Government, 2011, p. 1)

While this has been criticised by some, including for a lack of clear vision of what localism would look like in practice, and for allowing different government departments to interpret localism as it suits them (Communities and Local Government Committee, 2011), it nevertheless shares some of the rhetoric of devolution (see Greer, 2010).

Local solutions to local problems?

Thus, the principle of devolution has come to be supported by most political parties. The main idea is that decentralising power offers the opportunity to develop better solutions to engage with local factors – that is, local solutions to local problems. However, this raises an important question about the extent to which social problems are spatially fixed or territorial in nature.

STOP AND THINK

How local are social problems?

To what extent are social problems (which prompt social policy interventions) created at local or national levels?

- Think of a social problem that interests you (e.g. poverty, crime, domestic violence, teenage pregnancy).

- Name as many potential causes of this social problem as you can think of.

- Can any of these causes be located at the following levels:

    individual
    family
    structures (e.g. welfare system, economic conditions/events, labour market)
    local area
    region
    nation
    global?

- Can all causes be isolated at one level (e.g. personal, group, community or geographical level) or are they interconnected with processes at other levels?

- How successful do you think action at devolved country level would be in tackling the social problem you chose?

Are social issues determined by local factors, or can some or all of the causes of local problems be located outside of regional, or even national, boundaries? Although debates about nationhood and nationality cannot be reduced to locality, it is worth considering the underlying assumption that most causes of social problems can be geographically placed in some way. For example, local authorities or devolved governments may seek to tackle poverty in their area, but will be limited in their success because it is impossible to eradicate poverty in capitalist societies without ensuring adequate income to meet basic needs. Since ultimately the UK Government controls minimum levels of wages, benefits, and tax credits (even in the case of Northern Ireland, Westminster holds the purse strings), there is little that the devolved administrations can do to change this fundamental factor that influences the prevalence and experience of poverty. This demonstrates that the causes of social problems are a mix of individual and structural factors and may be mainly located in broader systems (such as the design of the UK-wide welfare system, or the global economic system), structures (e.g. expectations about freedom to accumulate personal wealth) or events (e.g. the 2008 economic recession), rather than localities. So can devolved administrations make any difference? The extent to which devolved decision-making bodies can take action on social issues is related to their formal powers, the political context, type and degree of funding, and relationships with the central UK Government.

What difference has devolution made?

Devolution has clearly altered political processes and generated a wealth of policy documents with bold aspirations, but to what extent has it actually impacted on the welfare needs and wellbeing of people in Scotland, Wales, and Northern Ireland? This is difficult to assess, particularly given the interconnections between policies at UK and devolved levels, combined with causes and potential solutions located outside of the UK entirely. However, the dawn of devolution was surrounded by optimism, with ambitions for *fairer* and *better* social outcomes in Scotland (Scottish Executive, 1999a, 1999b, 2003), Wales (Welsh Assembly Government, 2000, 2003, 2007), and Northern Ireland (Northern Ireland Executive,

2001, 2008). Thus, there were high expectations that devolution would deliver not only policy departures but divergence of a particular kind – towards progressive universalism (Birrell, 2009). Some politicians and commentators felt this might offer opportunities for the devolved countries of the UK to become more socially democratic – potentially more like their Scandinavian neighbours than like England, perhaps (for a critical discussion of these ideas, see Mooney and Poole, 2004). On the other hand, there was a counter-argument that devolution would create a 'race to the bottom' in social provision.

Let us now consider how these expectations have played out in practice.

Distinct divergence

Devolution has certainly created policy divergence (Ledge and Schmuecker, 2011), but as Mooney and Scott (2012, p. 8) demonstrate, 'in its first decade, devolution has not produced radically different forms of government across the UK, nor has policy making across the devolved countries and England been as significantly divergent as was anticipated'. Overall, Scotland has been the most active of the three countries in passing social policy legislation (Birrell, 2009). In all three of the devolved countries, most spending has gone into health and education (Birrell, 2010), which, together with personal social services, reflects the core of devolved powers and activities (see Table 4.1). Distinct policies can be found in each of the devolved countries. Some of the most popular and well-known examples (for more comprehensive accounts of divergence, see Drakeford, 2005, 2006; Williams, 2011; Knox, 2010; Mooney and Scott, 2012) include universal services or benefits in kind like free personal care for older people in Scotland, free prescriptions in Wales, and free bus and rail travel for the over 60s (as well as free prescriptions) in Northern Ireland. In several areas, the devolved governments have introduced policies that did not previously exist within the UK. Wales led the UK in establishing a dedicated independent Children's Commissioner in 2002. This unique approach was triggered by child abuse scandals and as a response to the UN Convention on the Rights of the Child. Later, similar roles were established for children's commissioners in Northern Ireland (2003), then Scotland and England (2005) (see Birrell, 2009). This highlights policy transfer between the countries of the UK. Similarly, a Wales-specific strategy resulted in the world's first independent Older People's Commissioner. Scotland was at the international forefront of progressive rights for homeless people by legislating in 2003 to establish entitlement to permanent re-housing. This included a target for all unintentionally homeless people to have the right to settled accommodation by 2012 (Anderson, 2007). Northern Ireland integrated health and social care and developed an existing outstanding approach to equal opportunities (employment and sex equality) and anti-discrimination legislation (covering grounds of religious, political, gender, race, and disability); these were brought together after devolution in the 2000 Northern Ireland Equality Commission.

STOP AND THINK

Problems and policies – similar or different?

How similar or distinctive are social problems/issues and social policies in England, Scotland, Wales, and Northern Ireland?

- Think of one example of a social problem or issue that is experienced *differently* in England than the other parts of the UK.

- Think of one example of a social problem or issue that is experienced *similarly* in all parts of the UK.

- Give three examples of *policies* that are different in different parts of the UK.

- Give three examples of *contexts* that are different in the devolved areas (e.g. political, socio-economic, physical environment).

- Why have different policies developed?

This encouraged comprehensive and detailed practices of monitoring for equality in employment, affirmative action, and complaints procedures. In these examples, we can see that devolution facilitated social action that may not otherwise have occurred.

In terms of policy outcomes, McCormick and Harrop (2010) demonstrate the impact that devolution has had for those on a low income, who are often the target of social policies. Overall, Scotland is the country that has made most progress in achieving successful social policy outcomes – scoring best on three indicators and worst on only one. Northern Ireland fared best on two of the indicators and worst on five. Wales did not score best on any of the indicators and was worst on two. However, caution must be used to avoid overstating results because: the long-term impacts of policies (for example, in health and education) will take much longer timescales to show; results are influenced by existing historical inequalities; and the extent to which better outcomes can be attributed only to *devolved* policies is limited. Between 1998 and 2008, Scotland showed the greatest improvement on poverty and social exclusion indicators (McCormick and Harrop, 2010), with Wales and Northern Ireland showing no net improvement, and the least progress made in certain regions of England (the Midlands, the South East, and East Anglia).

New connections with supranational social policy frameworks

Devolution has also created potential for different types of connections to be made with supranational organisations (e.g. the European Union) and international social policy frameworks and agreements, such as the UN Convention on the Rights of the Child (see above). The ability of Scotland, Wales, and Northern Ireland to pass their own laws means that they do not have to follow the style of supranational engagement that is traditional for the UK Government. For example, some aspects of the Human Rights Act 1998, which incorporated the European Convention on Human Rights into UK law, have been engaged with (e.g. in the constitutional framework) in Scotland, Wales, and Northern Ireland in ways that have not been accepted by the UK Government (SHRC, 2013). In this way, Scotland, Wales, and Northern Ireland are arguably ahead of England and UK law in addressing international conventions on the economic and social treatment of citizens and European conventions on civil and political rights.

Pressures against policy innovation

Despite the debate and controversy surrounding the establishment of the devolved governments, there was also a palpable sense of hope that the mix of politics, greater powers, and more participatory processes might offer a fresh start to design different policies – *better policies* – offering people living in Scotland, Wales, and Northern Ireland more of what they wanted and needed for better wellbeing. However, translating these aspirations into observable policy outcomes (e.g. lower poverty or better health) has not been a straightforward process. In fact, policy innovation has been much more limited in the decade of devolution than was originally anticipated by many. Two major tensions have influenced the formation of policies in all devolved areas. First, oppositional politics has operated to limit the extent to which cooperation for innovation has been possible. In Northern Ireland, deep political and sectarian divides have led to unworkable alliances. In Scotland and Wales, proportional representation made it difficult for clear party majorities (particularly before 2007) to justify strong policy mandates – meaning that compromises had to be made in every respect of policy change. This seems to have created a pressure against extensively implementing risky new ideas (which may be unacceptable to the values/ ideologies of opposing parties). Second, strong talk of action has been limited by the availability of funding. This can be understood partly in relation to the limits imposed by the conventions for transferring block grants from Westminster (i.e. using the Barnett Formula). However, this is not the whole story, since devolved governments have been very reluctant to use their powers to increase funding through additional borrowing or increases in taxation (which are an option available to the Scottish Government) and have even restricted income to local authorities by freezing Council Tax for consecutive years.

Contested convergence

Paradoxically, devolution highlights both the potential for change and the pressure to conform. It is clear that the 'reserved' areas of policy convergence involve enduring tensions, in which the central UK Government and the governments of Scotland, Wales, and Northern Ireland are caught in ongoing struggles. It is important to recognise both the existence of high-profile social policy divergence and the evidence of varied outcomes in England, Scotland, Wales, and Northern Ireland (see above). However, we still need to interpret these changes in relation to the broader UK, Westminster-controlled contexts in several important respects. For example, what does devolution really mean? Does it represent tinkering at the edges of the welfare state, or has it funda-mentally altered the character and dynamics of welfare systems throughout the UK? We cannot answer this question without acknowledging the other side of the picture – the UK and English developments that have not been transformed by devolution. Since policies and politics are continually in a state of flux, we cannot consider the social policies that were 'reserved' to Westminster control in 1999 as having stayed the same. But we can consider the character of shared social provision and the values and priorities that have shaped its parallel development over the devolution years. Here, welfare reform and immigration policies present illuminating case studies (see also Chapters 10, 11, and 18).

Welfare reform and devolution case study

Several important social policy areas remain reserved to the Westminster government. However, this does not indicate that there is necessarily any agreement between Westminster and the devolved countries in their views on the issues in question. One crucial shared, but contested, area is welfare reform, including social security, mechanisms to top-up inadequate wages (i.e. previously tax credits, being incorporated within the universal credit system in 2013; see Department for Work and Pensions, 2010), and minimum wages (see Chapters 10 and 11). UK policies dictate arrangements and payment levels for these areas in England, Scotland, and Wales. The Scottish Government and Welsh Assembly have powers to design complementary policies and services, particularly area-based anti-poverty initiatives, training and childcare, that can influence transitions into and out of work, but are heavily constrained by the British Department for Work and Pensions and Jobcentre Plus organisational structures. Interestingly, Northern Ireland has a long, *pre*-devolution, history of having its own control over employment policy, employment services (i.e. jobs and benefit offices), and social security (Scottish Government, 2011a, 2011b). UK-controlled welfare reform has prioritised cost-cutting and 'work first' conditionality (Lindsay *et al.*, 2007; Wright, 2012) for a sustained period under both Labour (1997–2010) and Coalition (2010–present) administrations. However, despite this long-established (and recently expanded) form of devolution, Northern Irish policies in this field have not diverged radically from those in the rest of the UK. This is mainly because Westminster mediates the funding of policies and has very strong policy and administrative frameworks that create ongoing constraints, which always involved 'implicit acceptance of parity in social security' meaning that 'radical potential' only resulted in 'gentle divergence' (Wiggan, 2012, pp. 66–8). Furthermore, the Welsh Assembly and Scottish Government (see Dryburgh and Lancashire, 2011) have highlighted the detrimental impact of recent welfare reforms on their populations and have opposed key new developments, such as the 'bedroom tax' (Scottish Government, 2013). Shared policies like the 'bedroom tax' may also have different impacts in different countries of the UK; for example, in Northern Ireland families tend to be larger and the Housing Executive has few small properties for people to 'downsize' to. As the political priorities of devolved countries increasingly depart from the values of Westminster power holders, welfare reform is likely to be a main battleground in coming years.

Immigration and devolution case study

Immigration policy is a matter reserved to the UK Government in Westminster, and which the devolved legislatures have no control over. However, it has been the site of considerable conflict between the Scottish Parliament and Westminster because UK immigration policy is developed with reference mainly to the traditional English experience of net in-migration (immigration), rather than the Scottish traditional experience of net out-migration (emigration). Scotland, therefore, has greater need for migrant workers, particularly in rural areas, than England (de Lima and Wright, 2009). This has led to campaigns to attract migrant workers and international students, which is at odds with the limitations sought by Westminster. Although the situation in Scotland has changed in recent years, with significant increases in the number of people coming into the country (exceeding the numbers leaving) and the proportion of births increasing, debate has continued (Scottish Government, 2009b). The UK Government has capped the numbers of migrants in ways that limit opportunities for professionals and international students, which the Scottish Government believes will harm the Scottish economy (Scottish Government, 2010).

SPOTLIGHT

Social policy and nationalism

The initial drive for devolution and the development of divergent social policy trajectories (perhaps even leading to independence in the Scottish case after 2014) has been connected with struggle in the forms of deep, combative debate and even violent clashes (in the case of Northern Ireland). But how are concerns of identity and 'nation' (also see Chapter 18) connected to the welfare systems and devolution projects of the countries of the UK?

Compare the following approaches from the Scottish and Welsh leaders (see also Mooney and Williams, 2006):

'With the partial independence the Scottish Parliament has in health, education, justice, business support and social services, we have achieved much – and with the full measure of independence we get by voting Yes, we will achieve much more for Scotland . . . Scotland's date with destiny . . . September 18 2014 is the day when every one of us will be asked to take the future of our country into our hands' (First Minister of Scotland Alex Salmond, 2013).

'As First Minister, my job is to deliver my Programme of Government for the people of Wales. Everything I say about constitutional reform needs to be set in this context. We are striving to use the powers we have to create jobs, support the economy and sustain public services in an economic and fiscal context which is extremely challenging. This means using our legislative and executive powers to full effect. It also means standing up for Wales when the decisions of the UK Government are in our view ill-judged or plain wrong, as in the area of welfare reform' (First Minister of Wales Carwyn Jones, 2013).

With the view that:

'nationalist movements are likely to focus on social programmes as a specific target for decentralisation . . . First, social programmes are more likely than other types of programme to touch people in their everyday life. As a consequence, governments running these programmes can establish direct and tangible links with a population. Social policy is, in other words, a potent nation-building tool. Second, discussion around specific social policy alternatives can easily be conducted as a debate over core values, principles and identities. In this respect, the language of social policy is similar to discourse of nationalism insofar as one group can argue to have more of a certain quality (for example, egalitarian or entrepreneurial) than the other' (Béland and Lecours, 2007, p. 415).

Conclusions

This chapter has introduced devolution and considered the extent to which transferring power to the Scottish Parliament, Welsh Assembly, and Northern Ireland Executive has brought about meaningful changes in political processes, policy design, and social outcomes. Devolution has been shown to matter to both those living in the devolved countries *and* those living in and beyond England. Studying devolution, particularly being aware of which parts of the welfare system are determined in Westminster and which are governed by the devolved administrations, has been shown as a valuable way of comparing how social policies operate and what the options for innovation might be in similar but distinct socio-political contexts. Pressures against policy innovation have been considered, before focusing on the role of nationalism in devolved welfare debates. The future, of course, is uncertain, with question marks over how the Westminster Parliament deals with policies that relate solely to England, and over the extent of the further devolution of powers to Northern Ireland, Scotland, and Wales, as well as the referendum on independence for Scotland in 2014.

Summary

This chapter has outlined the powers, remits, and funding of each of the devolved administrations in terms of their relationships with the central UK state. It has:

- Considered the implications of these for England, and highlighted new forms of decentralisation through English localism.

- Questioned the issue of territorially based social intervention in relation to the extent to which social problems and their solutions can be seen as caused or being solvable at local level.

- Assessed the social policy achievements of the devolved administrations, including highlighting examples of divergent approaches (e.g. different institutional arrangements in each country for health; free personal care for older people in Scotland; the independent Children's Commissioner in Wales; and equal opportunities policies in Northern Ireland) and of contested convergence (e.g. welfare reform and immigration).

- Highlighted the different positioning of the UK central state and the devolved legislatures in relation to supra-national social policy agendas and conventions.

Discussion and review

- To what extent are social policies determined at UK level?

- Why have some policy areas remained UK-wide, while others have diverged dramatically in England, Scotland, Wales, and Northern Ireland?

- What does devolution tell us about the potential for social policies to develop in new ways?

References

Anderson, I. (2007) 'Sustainable solutions to homelessness: the Scottish case', *European Journal of Homelessness*, Vol. 1, No. 1, pp. 163–83.

Béland, D. and Lecours, A. (2007) 'Federalism, nationalism, and social policy decentralisation in Canada and Belgium', *Regional and Federal Studies*, Vol. 17, No. 4, pp. 405–19.

Birrell, D. (2009) *The Impact of Devolution on Social Policy*, The Policy Press, Bristol.

Birrell, D. (2010) 'Devolution and approaches to social policy', in G. Lodge and K. Schmuecker (eds.) *Devolution in Practice 2010*, IPPR, London.

Cabinet Office/Northern Ireland Office (2013) *Devolution Settlement: Northern Ireland*, available at https://www.gov.uk/devolution-settlement-northern-ireland [accessed 21 March 2013].

Cabinet Office/Scotland Office (2013) *Devolution Settlement: Scotland*, https://www.gov.uk/devolution-settlement-scotland [accessed 21 March 2013].

Cabinet Office/Wales Office (2013) *Devolution Settlement: Wales*, available at https://www.gov.uk/devolution-settlement-wales [accessed 21 March 2013].

Cabinet Office/Northern Ireland Office/Scotland Office/Wales Office (2013) *Devolution of Powers to Scotland, Wales and Northern Ireland*, available at https://www.gov.uk/devolution-of-powers-to-scotland-wales-and-northern-ireland [accessed 21 March 2013].

Chaney, P. and Drakeford, M. (2004) 'The primacy of ideology: social policy and the first term of the National Assembly for Wales', in N. Ellison, L. Bauld and M. Powell (eds.) *Social Policy Review 16*, The Policy Press, Bristol.

Communities and Local Government (2011) *A Plain English Guide to the Localism Act*, Department for Communities and Local Government, London.

Communities and Local Government Committee (2011) *Localism*, The Stationery Office, London.

de Lima, P. and Wright, S. (2009) 'Welcoming migrants? Migrant labour in rural Scotland', *Social Policy and Society*, Vol. 8, No. 3, pp. 391–404.

Department for Work and Pensions (2010) *Universal Credit: Welfare that Works*, The Stationery Office, London.

Drakeford, M. (2005) 'Wales and a third term of New Labour: devolution and the development of difference', *Critical Social Policy*, Vol. 25, No. 4, pp. 497–506.

Drakeford, M. (2006) 'Health policy in Wales: making a difference in conditions of difficulty', *Critical Social Policy*, Vol. 26, No. 3, pp. 543–61.

Dryburgh, K. and Lancashire, M. (2011) *The Impact of the Welfare Reform Bill on Scotland's People and Services*, Citizen's Advice Scotland, Edinburgh.

Economic and Social Research Council (ESRC) (2004) *Devolution: What Difference has it Made?*, University of Birmingham, Birmingham.

Gouldner, A.W. (1971) *The Coming Crisis of Western Sociology*, Heinemann, London.

Greer, S.L. (2010) 'How does decentralisation affect the welfare state? Territorial politics and the welfare state in the UK and US', *Journal of Social Policy*, Vol. 39, No. 2, pp. 181–201.

HM Treasury (2007) *Funding the Scottish Parliament, National Assembly for Wales and Northern Ireland Assembly: Statement of Funding Policy*, The Stationery Office, London.

Jones, C. (2013) 'Delivering for Wales within a United Kingdom', Speech 26 March, available at http://wales.gov.uk/newsroom/firstminister/2013/130326psa/?lang=en [accessed 27 March 2013].

Keating, M. (2010) *The Government of Scotland: Public Policy Making after Devolution* (2nd edn.), Edinburgh University Press, Edinburgh.

Knox, C. (2010) *Devolution and the Governance of Northern Ireland*, Manchester University Press, Manchester.

Ledge, G. and Schmuecker, K. (2011) *Devolution in Practice 2010*, IPPR, London.

Lindsay, C., McQuaid, R.W. and Dutton, M. (2007) 'New approaches to employability in the UK: combining "human capital development" and "Work First" strategies', *Journal of Social Policy*, Vol. 36, No. 4, pp. 539–60.

McCormick, J. and Harrop, A. (2010) *Devolution's Impact on Low-income People and Places*, Joseph Rowntree Foundation, York.

McLean, I., Lodge, G. and Schmuecker, K. (2008) *Fair Shares: Barnett and the Politics of Public Expenditure*, Institute for Public Policy Research, Newcastle.

Mooney, G. and Poole, L. (2004) '"A land of milk and honey"? Social policy in Scotland after devolution', *Critical Social Policy*, Vol. 24, No. 4, pp. 458–83.

Mooney, G. and Scott, G. (eds.) (2005) *Exploring Social Policy in the 'New' Scotland*, The Policy Press, Bristol.

Mooney, G. and Scott, G. (eds.) (2012) *Social Justice and Social Policy in Contemporary Scotland*, The Policy Press, Bristol.

Mooney, G. and Williams, C. (2006) 'Forging new "ways of life"? Social policy and national building in devolved Scotland and Wales', *Critical Social Policy*, Vol. 26, No. 3, pp. 608–29.

Mooney, G. and Wright, S. (2009) 'Introduction. Social policy in the devolved Scotland: towards a Scottish welfare state?', *Social Policy and Society*, Vol. 8, No. 3, pp. 361–5.

Northern Ireland Executive (2001) *Programme for Government: Making a Difference*, Office of the First Minister and Deputy First Minister, Belfast.

Northern Ireland Executive (2008) *Building a Better Future: Draft Programme for Government 2008–2011*, Office of the First Minister and Deputy First Minister, Belfast.

Salmond, A. (2011) *Alex Salmond interview: 'England's a great country'*, video available at http://www.guardian.co.uk/politics/video/2011/oct/09/alex-salmond-interview-video.

Salmond, A. (2013) 'Independence Speech', 23 March, available at http://news.stv.tv/politics/218734-alex-salmond-outlines-independence-vision-at-snp-conference/ [accessed 27 March 2013].

Scott, G. and Mooney, G.C. (2009) 'Poverty and social justice in the devolved Scotland: neo-liberalism meets social democracy?', *Social Policy and Society*, Vol. 3, No. 4, pp. 379–89.

Scott, G. and Wright, S. (2012) 'Devolution, social democratic visions and policy reality in Scotland', *Critical Social Policy*, Vol. 32, No. 3, pp. 440–53.

Scottish Executive (1999a) *Making it Work Together: A Programme for Government*, Scottish Executive, Edinburgh, available at http://www.scotland.gov.uk/Publications/1999/09/3423/File-1 [accessed 25 March 2013].

Scottish Executive (1999b) *Social Justice: A Scotland Where Everyone Matters*, Scottish Executive, Edinburgh, available at http://scotland.gov.uk/Publications/1999/11/4174/File-1 [accessed 25 March 2013].

Scottish Executive (2003) *A Partnership for a Better Scotland: Partnership Agreement*, Scottish Executive, Edinburgh, available at http://www.scotland.gov.uk/Publications/2003/05/17150/21952 [accessed 25 March 2013].

Scottish Government (2009a) *Fiscal Autonomy in Scotland: The Case for Change and Options for Reform*, Scottish Government, Edinburgh, available at http://www.scotland.gov.uk/Resource/Doc/261814/0078318.pdf.

Scottish Government (2009b) *Trends in Migration*, available at http://www. gro-scotland.gov.uk/files2/stats/high-level-summary/j11198/j1119806. htm [accessed 28 March 2013].

Scottish Government (2010) *Immigration Cap*, available at http://www. scotland.gov.uk/News/Releases/2010/11/23162746 [accessed 28 March 2013].

Scottish Government (2011a) *Welfare Reform Scrutiny Group*, Paper WRSG 1-04 (rev), Analytical Note on Welfare Reform, Lifelong Learning Analytical Services Unit, Edinburgh, available at http://www.scotland.gov. uk/Topics/People/welfarereform/Initialanalysis#top.

Scottish Government (2011b), *Welfare Reform*, news release, available at http://www.scotland.gov.uk/News/Releases/2011/12/21150319 [accessed 26 January 2012].

Scottish Government (2013) *UK Welfare Reform in Scotland*, available at http://www.scotland.gov.uk/Topics/People/welfarereform [accessed 29 March 2013].

Scottish Human Rights Commission (SHRC) (2013) *The Future of Human Rights in Scotland*, SHRC, Glasgow.

Stewart, J. (2004) *Taking Stock*, The Policy Press, Bristol.

Trench, A. (ed.) (2008) *The State of the Nations 2008*, Imprint Academic, Exeter.

Welsh Assembly Government (2000) *A Better Wales*, Welsh Assembly Government, Cardiff.

Welsh Assembly Government (2003) *Wales: A Better Country: The Strategic Agenda of the Welsh Assembly Government*, Welsh Assembly Government, Cardiff.

Welsh Assembly Government (2007) *One Wales: A Progressive Agenda for the Government of Wales*, Welsh Assembly Government, Cardiff.

Wiggan, J. (2012) 'A kingdom united? Devolution and welfare reform in Northern Ireland and Great Britain', *Policy and Politics*, Vol. 40, No. 1, pp. 57–72.

Williams, C. (2011) *Social Policy for Social Welfare Practice in a Devolved Wales*, Venture Press, Birmingham.

Williams, C. and Mooney, G. (2008) 'Decentring social policy? Devolution and the discipline of social policy, a commentary', *Journal of Social Policy*, Vol. 37, No. 3, pp. 489–507.

Wright, S. (2012) 'Welfare to work, agency and personal responsibility', *Journal of Social Policy*, Vol. 41, No. 2, pp. 309–28.

Further reading

The best comprehensive starting point for understanding the evolving social policy implications of devolution in all four countries of the UK is Birrell, D. (2009) *The Impact of Devolution on Social Policy*, Policy Press, Bristol. For Scotland, try Mooney, G. and Scott, G. (eds.) (2012) *Social Justice and Social Policy in Contemporary Scotland*, Policy Press, Bristol. This offers in-depth analyses of the main social policy areas from a social justice perspective. For Northern Ireland, see Knox, C. (2010) *Devolution and the Governance of Northern Ireland*, Manchester University Press, Manchester. This has a broader approach, but includes key issues of social policy. For Wales, start with Williams, C. (2011) *Social Policy for Social Welfare Practice in a Devolved Wales* (2nd edn.), Venture Press, Birmingham. Broader guides dealing with all issues of devolution are useful for context, identifying key issues, and providing detail on processes and outcomes; see Lodge, G. and Schmuecker, K. (2011) *Devolution in Practice 2010*, IPPR, London; and Béland, D. and Lecours, A. (2008) *Nationalism and Social Policy: The Politics of Territorial Solidarity*, Oxford University Press, Oxford.

Useful websites

http://news.bbc.co.uk/1/hi/uk_politics/election_2010/first_time_voter/
8589835.stm – the BBC Beginner's Guide to devolution.
http://www.gov.uk/devolution-of-powers-to-scotland-wales-and-northern-
ireland – the UK Government pages on devolution.
http://home.scotland.gov.uk/home – the Scottish Government.
http://www.northernireland.gov.uk/ – the Northern Ireland Executive.
http://wales.gov.uk/ – the Welsh Government.
http://www.devolution.ac.uk/ – this site provides access to the findings of a
major research programme into devolution and constitutional change from
2000 to 2006.
http://www.guardian.co.uk/politics/scottish-independence-essential-guide –
The Guardian (2012) 'Scottish independence: the essential guide'.

CHAPTER 5

Research, Evidence, and Policy

Hugh Bochel and Guy Daly

Learning objectives

- To highlight the sometimes problematic links between research, evidence, and policy-making
- To consider efforts to develop evidence-based policy-making
- To outline critiques of the idea of evidence-based policy
- To discuss the importance of policy evaluation

Chapter overview

Each of the chapters in this book has drawn on a variety of evidence to support the arguments that they make. Many have also reflected the types and varieties of evidence that are used by policy-makers in making decisions about the extent and shape of social policies and provision. Inevitably, they have reflected that the use of evidence and research is selective, and that ideologies and values play a major role in determining policies. However, research, evaluation, and other forms of evidence remain fundamental in helping us understand the nature and extent of social problems and in assessing the extent to which policies do or do not achieve their goals. This chapter therefore:

- outlines some of the links between policy and evidence;
- considers different approaches to policy-making by governments over the past 50 years;
- highlights some of the challenges to the pursuit of 'evidence-based' policy-making;
- considers some of the critiques of the idea of 'evidence-based' policy.

CONTROVERSY AND DEBATE

Alistair Darling MP, Secretary of State for Trade and Industry, in evidence to a select committee enquiry, gave an example of a politician's take on evidence-based policy:

'There is a huge body of evidence that speed cameras save lives and save serious injuries; whatever way you want to do it, that has been established. You remember, there is an issue which has still to come before this House, it was brought by secondary legislation, in relation to whether or not you ought to get three points regardless of whether you were doing 36 miles an hour or 86 miles an hour. I announced, I think in the autumn of 2004, that I thought we should have a graduated system; however, there were many people who said "All the evidence is that these cameras save lives, therefore there's no excuse for having something graduated." I took the view that general fairness and the general public perception of how these cameras operated demanded that we ought to have a graduated approach. That is something the House is going to have to decide on shortly. It is a case where I strongly defend my right, as the Secretary of State, a Member of an elected Government, to form a judgement as to what I think is the right thing to do, and the Commons and the Lords will decide. Let me give you another example, in a completely different area. There is stem-cell research. I could cite, and I would cite, a lot of evidence to suggest that we need to pursue this line of research because it could bring immense gains. It is perfectly open to, and I respect the right of, any Members of the House who might say, because of deeply-held convictions, "No, this is wrong; you ought not to be doing it," to say so. We are entitled, as ministers, as MPs, to reach a judgement, but what you will want to do in each case, I hope, is look at the evidence. If I put it this way, if the entire thing was automatic, I suppose you could argue you did not need any governments at all; now there are some people who might think it is a jolly good idea, but I do not think that actually life works like that.'

Science and Technology Committee (2006) *Scientific Advice, Risk and Evidence Based Policy Making*, House of Commons, London, Minutes of Evidence, 5 July 2006, Q1315.

Policy and evidence

Both the Labour governments of 1997–2010 and the Coalition government that succeeded them made significant claims, certainly before taking power and in the early years of government, about basing policy on evidence. Indeed, the idea of 'evidence-based' policy has sometimes been seen as contrasting with 'opinion-based' policy, which critics have depicted as more typical of British policy-making, accusing it of being based upon selective use of evidence, or the untested views of powerful individuals and groups.

However, as discussed later in the chapter, while there was a significant degree of change under Labour, it is important to note that there had been developments under previous governments that paid attention to research and evidence, particularly during the 1960s and 1970s, when rationalistic approaches were receiving attention from governments. For example, the establishment of the Social Science Research Council (the forerunner of the Economic and Social Research Council) arose from the Heywood Committee's (1965) recommendation for greater government support for the social sciences; the Rothschild Report (1971) examined the relationship between research and policy and led to new structures for the commissioning and funding of research across central government, and it also emphasised the importance of 'science', in its widest sense, to the policy process; and the Central Policy Review Staff, established in the Cabinet Office in 1971, sought to develop a strategy for the coordination of social policy, although the attempt only lasted for a handful of years. However, from the mid 1970s, and particularly with the election of the Thatcher governments from 1979, there was a new ideological impetus, combined with a degree of scepticism about the potential of a 'social engineering' role for governments and research. At the same time, a significant growth in the numbers and scope of 'think tanks' that sought to offer a variety of 'solutions' to problems meant that the Thatcher governments had a number of new and sympathetic sources of policy advice.

The return to power of the Labour government in 1997 brought a new emphasis to the relationship between evidence and policy. However, while this may sound like a sensible aim, and clearly arguments for policy based on dogma, guesswork or hunches, rather than on evidence, would be problematic, the links between policy and evidence are far from clear. Indeed, a simple consideration of the way in which the term 'policy' is used highlights definitional challenges. For example, Hogwood and Gunn (1984) noted that policy could be used in many different ways, including as:

- a label for a field of policy, such as economic policy, health policy, or transport policy;
- an expression of a desired state of affairs, with the Coalition government, for example, stating that 'We are reforming the welfare system to help more people to move into and progress in work, while supporting the

most vulnerable' (https://www.gov.uk/government/policies/simplifying-the-welfare-system-and-making-sure-work-pays);

- specific proposals, with the Liberal Democrats' 2010 manifesto promising to 'scrap unfair university tuition fees for all students taking their first degree' (p. 39), while the Conservatives' 2010 manifesto undertook to 'raise taxes on those drinks linked to anti-social drinking' (p. 55);

- formal authorisation, as with the passage of an Act of Parliament which permits a particular activity to take place.

Similarly, as discussed later in the chapter, 'evidence' can be construed as very different things, with some academics, for example, seeing something of a hierarchy, with 'scientific' approaches such as randomized control trials and systematic review towards the top, and smaller one-off studies and expert opinion lower down. However, not all agree with such a view, and in the social sciences in particular, some would argue that qualitative approaches can help us understand things like individuals' motivations and beliefs in a way that quantitative methods alone might not (see Becker *et al.*, 2012). For politicians and policy-makers, 'evidence' might also take an even wider variety of forms, including information that comes from constituents, from lobbyists and pressure groups, and the media.

'Evidence-based' policy is sometimes seen as contrasting with 'opinion-based' policy, which has sometimes been viewed as more typical of British policy-making, with critics accusing the latter of being based upon selective use of evidence, or the untested views of powerful individuals and groups.

Given these definitional challenges, the relationship between evidence and policy is not as straightforward as might sometimes be imagined. In addition, Davies *et al.* (2000) suggest four key ways in which evidence can have an influence:

> **STOP AND THINK**
>
> It has sometimes been claimed that anti-social behaviour orders (ASBOs) were introduced as a result of Labour MPs experiencing complaints from constituents that neither the police nor councils were able to tackle anti-social behaviour. Is that an example of evidence-informed policy-making?

- *instrumental* evidence, where research leads to a policy decision, while perhaps being the most straightforward, is perhaps the least common;

- *conceptual* evidence, where research leads to changes in knowledge, understanding or attitude, tends to be gradual in its impact;

- *mobilisation*, where evidence stimulates policy action, is when something grabs the attention of policy-makers, for example through media attention; and

- *wider influence*, is where evidence leads to larger-scale shifts in thinking.

These conceptualisations help to highlight that the links between policy and evidence may be indirect, are often slow to have an impact, and often lead to gradual changes in approach rather than to direct policy innovation or change.

Post-war policy-making

During the 1960s and early 1970s, there was some concern over the processes of policy-making in the United Kingdom, and there were a number of attempts to improve policy-making, including, for example, to make it more rational in nature (broadly speaking, identifying policy preferences and choosing the best means of achieving the chosen aims), expanding the use of planning units in government departments, and seeking to improve collaboration between government departments (with the Joint Approach to Social Policy being one example of that). In addition, in 1968 the Fulton Committee suggested that the Civil Service was a product of a nineteenth-century philosophy (reflecting a cult of the amateur and the generalist) and that this was inadequate for the demands of the twentieth century. Following the report, a series of reforms were introduced, including the creation of a civil service department and a civil service college to provide training for civil servants. The Central Policy Review Staff was established within the Cabinet Office in 1971, with the intention that it should define government strategy and produce a framework for policy formulation, and in 1975 a Policy Unit was created to provide advice specifically to the Prime Minister.

Under the Conservative governments from 1979 to 1997, there were not only major changes in policy, as made clear in many chapters in this book, including a shifting of responsibility towards individuals and families and away from the state, which, together with privatisation, led to a consequent reduction in the role of the state, but there were also changes to the processes of policy formulation and implementation (see Chapters 3 and 7). One of the most obvious was the greater reliance upon the private sector and the market, but this itself required the creation of new regulatory mechanisms, such as the Office of Gas and Electricity Markets (OFGEM), OFTEL (the Office of Telecommunications), later to become part of OFCOMM, the regulator of the communications industries, and the Office of Water Services (OFWAT). The Conservatives also sought to make greater use of the private and not-for-profit sectors in the delivery of services, such as care of older people and social housing.

Another significant development was the increased emphasis on providers being accountable to consumers, rather than simply through the traditional primary route of elected representatives. Mechanisms that sought to use or replicate market-type activities were introduced, such as parental choice of schools, and these implied or required new sources of information for consumers, which became typified in league tables and other quality ratings. This, accompanied by a wider focus on the use of audit and inspection to maintain and improve quality, meant that more and new information was made available to consumers to help them to make 'informed' choices, such as school 'league tables' and star ratings for local authority services.

New Labour: modern policy-making?

When Labour returned to power in 1997, they took on and developed many of the Conservatives' ideas, including around choice. However, they also placed what was arguably an unprecedented emphasis on the processes of policy-making and implementation and introduced considerable structural and constitutional change, including devolution (see also Chapters 3 and 4). This happened for a variety of reasons, including a view that better policy-making would result in better policies and better implementation, and was arguably underpinned to a considerable extent by the view associated with writers such as Lasswell (1958) and Simon (1945, 1957), that better policy-making can be achieved through improvements in instrumental rationality, and a more 'technocratic' approach to the policy process.

As a result, particularly in the early years of the Labour government, there were a number of publications from within government that highlighted the importance of the processes of policy-making (see, for example, Bochel and Duncan, 2007). One of the first of these was the *Modernising Government* White Paper (Cabinet Office, 1999), which highlighted the importance of improving the policy process in order to produce better policies and better public services. A series of subsequent publications continued to build upon the idea of developing better policy-making.

Many of the ideas associated with these developments became familiar phrases during the first two terms of the Labour government, including ideas such as 'evidence-based' policy, 'what works', and 'joined-up' government. These phrases in themselves clearly imply a greater commitment to the use of research and other forms of evidence in policy-making and implementation. Yet, even at the height of the desire for better policy-making, there was an awareness that it was not unproblematic, with the Cabinet Office's Performance and Innovation Unit (2000), for example, noting that if policy is to be based on evidence, then that evidence has to be of good quality, and that would require analysts and policy-makers to work differently from in the past, and, while making the case for evidence-based policy, also recognising the range of pressures and constraints on policy-making, including political pressures.

While many of the ideas developed under Labour were potentially of significance for the making and implementation of social policy, a number were of particular relevance for this chapter. The Cabinet Office Strategic Policy Making Team produced a paper, *Professional Policy Making for the Twenty First Century* (1999), which set out nine key principles for policy-making: forward looking; outward looking; innovative, flexible, and creative; evidence-based; inclusive; joined-up; reviews; evaluates; learns lessons. Although there was not always clarity about what these involved, and there was considerable overlap between these features, they nevertheless help us understand what was construed as 'better' policy-making.

In some respects, as noted earlier, Labour's approach drew on some of the developments already introduced by the previous Conservative governments. For example, in relation to policy-making looking outward, the idea of 'policy

STOP AND THINK

The media often pay attention to the performance of the United Kingdom's nations in international 'league tables' of educational performance. What might be the advantages and problems arising from the use of such data?

transfer', drawing upon the experience of other jurisdictions and making cross-national comparisons, was used by the Conservatives prior to the introduction of the Child Support Agency in 1993, but became considerably more widespread under Labour, including in relation to major initiatives such as the New Deal and Sure Start.

Like the Conservatives, Labour also sought to make changes to the Civil Service, although while the former had sought to introduce stronger management and more market-oriented approaches, Labour introduced the 'Professional Skills for Government' programme to improve the core skills of senior civil servants, including around policy-making, with 'analysis and use of evidence' being listed as among the core skills that all civil servants should possess.

Labour also developed the use of performance measurement, audit, and inspection, which had been encouraged under the preceding Conservative governments, with a much greater use of targets for public services and an increased role for audit and inspection mechanisms to ensure that services were providing efficient and effective services and good value for money, including in defining some organisations as 'failing'. Critics, however, questioned the validity and utility of such approaches, noting, for example, that while targets can help establish priorities and enable measurement against them, excessive, inappropriate or conflicting targets can create problems, including driving organisations towards meeting targets rather than working towards other ends (for example, Appleby and Coote, 2002; Clarke, 2004), including focusing on the measurable, as opposed to the softer, more human aspects of service delivery (for example, Harrison and Smith, 2004), and placing too great a burden of inspection and performance measurement on organisations.

While customer 'choice' continued to be seen as an important means of empowering users and of driving improvements in the quality of services under Labour, at the same time there was also an awareness that the exercise of choice is affected by and can replicate economic, social, and political inequalities, with some recognition that a simple shift towards market-type mechanisms may be problematic. Indeed, in relation to inclusive policy-making, while Labour's approach in some areas, such as the encouragement of active citizenship, was broadly in line with that of the Conservatives, in others, such as the extent of consultation, the widespread use of impact assessments, and the emphasis on partnerships for the delivery of policy, it was arguably considerably different from that of their predecessors.

Labour also made extensive use of policy reviews to examine policy and practice, although, as Powell and Maynard (2007) have noted, the term 'review' was used in such a variety of ways and for such different purposes that it is hard to assess its value. The number of policy evaluations also grew greatly under Labour, both of process and to some extent of outcomes, with one significant element of this being the much greater use of 'policy pilots'. Although there was some development of these under the Conservatives, under Labour these were more widely used across a range of policies, including aspects of the New Deal and Sure Start and some changes to social security benefits.

Yet, despite all of these initiatives, even half-way through the Labour government, a Select Committee on Science and Technology (2006) report suggested that the use of evidence in government departments was variable, and pointed out that some of its witnesses had identified areas where evidence might not support existing government policy. After 13 years of Labour governments it was arguable that, while the direction of travel might have been altered somewhat, with greater awareness of the potential value of better informed policy-making (and indeed better policy-making and implementation as a whole), policy-makers and politicians frequently continued to select evidence that accorded with their views and priorities, while ignoring, or at least paying less attention to, that which might have contradicted them.

Evidence and the Conservative-Liberal Democrat Coalition government

Following the formation of the Coalition government in 2010, a number of ministers claimed to support the idea of evidence-based policy. Indeed, the Higher Education Minister, David Willetts (2012), argued that 'Evidence should be the bread and butter of policymakers'. Yet critics have argued that the government's use of evidence has not reflected this, with policies such as the creation of more academies and the development of 'free schools' being highlighted for being highly partial and selective in the use of evidence, including international experience (for example, Exley and Ball, 2011). At the same time, some argued that evidence on those who were being hit hardest by the economic downturn and by public expenditure cuts was not taken into account by the government, including around levels of child poverty and changes to the tax and benefits systems (Bamfield, 2012).

Perhaps the one area where there was a further significant development from the Labour years was in the idea of 'behavioural economics', often associated with the idea that it is possible to 'nudge' people towards better behaviour [described in the Coalition's *Programme for Government* (Cabinet Office, 2010) as helping people to make better choices for themselves], with the creation of a Behavioural Insights Team in the Cabinet Office and projects including encouraging people to pay their income tax on time and working to encourage unemployed people to find jobs more quickly.

Critiques of approaches to evidence-based policy

As is apparent from the discussion above, there are many challenges to the idea of evidence-based and research-informed policy. Indeed, there are also a number of significant critiques of the idea. One of the most important of these is that arguments for the idea of evidence-based policy have drawn upon medical and scientific ideas of what constitutes evidence, have been highly positivist and quantitative in nature, have made assumptions about the links between measurement and policy success or failure (for example, for some proponents of the idea, 'what works' is largely what can be measured), and have ignored questions around social construction and social control. Parsons (2002, p. 57) has noted that in the social world things are more complex, and that

'What works' is about: what works, for whom, when and how?; or what kind of evidence works for what kind of problem/policy in what context, and for whom.

He also argues that a real move towards evidence-based policy would also have to address the very difficult question of 'who gets what, when and how' (Lasswell, 1958).

Parsons' argument also helps highlight the important question of the role of values in policy-making. For example, individuals with strong ethical or ideological beliefs might wish to place them above particular evidence about whether a policy works. So, for example, those who favour greater income equality might feel that there is a case for supporting progressive income tax even if it were demonstrated that such an approach might reduce economic growth, or those who believe strongly that inequality is inevitable and desirable might oppose redistributive measures even if they could be shown to reduce poverty.

It is also potentially the case that values will affect not just the interpretation of evidence, but also the mechanisms by which policies are made and implemented, with a preference for market-type approaches likely to favour particular types of evidence and forms of policy-making, while a preference for collaborative approaches might lead to methods of policy-making that seek to be more consensual. This might arguably have been reflected in the 1979–97 Conservative government, and the Coalition government's significant use of market and market-type mechanisms and the emphasis on consumers and individual choice, as opposed to some elements of Labour's approach, such as the greater use of partnership, or to more collectivist ideas or those which might involve greater devolution of decision-making to democratically elected local authorities.

And there are risks that highly technocratic policy-making mechanisms might, like the Conservatives' use of markets, give a particular type of legitimation to government decisions and the distribution of resources, effectively depoliticising decisions about policies and about resource allocation, when, by their nature, these decisions are inevitably highly political.

Obstacles to evidence-based policy-making

While the idea of evidence informing policy may on the face of it appear appealing and straightforward, the relationship is actually very complex. As Duncan (2005, p. 11), who was Chief Government Social Researcher for a time under the Labour government, has noted:

> Other factors aside, social science evidence doesn't tend to provide the black and white answers that could potentially be useful to policy – we can't always say unequivocally 'what works'.

She also highlights that there is not a simple uni-directional link between knowledge and policy, and equally importantly reminds us that research is only one of the influences upon policy:

> Research which informs policy rarely if ever points to a single and unequivocal course of action – it all depends upon what policies are trying to achieve, how much money is available, which solution is workable and publicly acceptable, and how a chosen policy solution will impact upon other policy areas. Research and analysis will only ever be one of the influences upon policy (ibid.).

As this suggests, policy-makers and politicians have to take account of a wide range of factors and influences, other than simply research. These are likely to include the costs of particular actions or inactions, public opinion, fit with political ideology and values, the experience of practitioners, and pressures associated with other problems and policies. Mulgan (2005), who was Director of the Prime Minister's Strategy Unit, also highlights the broader framework of knowledge used by policy-makers, of which social research and evidence is only one element, with a typology that includes:

- statistical knowledge, for example of population size and migration;
- policy knowledge, such as what works in reducing reoffending;
- scientific knowledge, for example on climate change;
- professional knowledge, which may be informed by rigorous testing, such as on the impact of vaccination;
- public opinion, including both quantitative and qualitative data;
- practitioner views and insights, for example police experience in tackling organised crime;
- economic knowledge, such as on which sectors are likely to grow and contract;

▨ classic intelligence, such as on the capabilities and intentions of hostile states or terrorist networks.

Yet, even if it is accepted that policy should be based on evidence, quite apart from questions of the quality of evidence and uncertainties over cause and effect in the social sciences, there remain a number of significant obstacles.

In liberal democracies such as the United Kingdom, policy decisions are normally made in a political environment, with ministers in charge of departments and dictating the overall priorities and policies to be followed, although they may be directly involved in only a very small proportion of day-to-day decisions. Government, at central, devolved, and local levels is subject to political control and direction. Policy is therefore inevitably going to be affected by ideological positions, political beliefs, values, and other considerations, including electoral and public opinion.

There is clearly likely to be tension between ideology and values on the one hand, and evidence from social research on the other. For example, attitudes to crime and to punishment will inevitably be affected by social and ethical judgements, whatever evidence might tell us about the success or failure of different approaches. Many politicians recognise this, but assert that it is for ministers appointed from Parliament to decide on policy, as has long been seen as a key part of representative democracy.

Indeed, some have suggested that the emphasis on evidence-based policy was itself politically driven, as it can be argued was the emphasis on markets and choice under the Conservatives from 1979 to 1997, elevating particular approaches, with the former drawing on a belief in models of 'rational' decision-making and the latter on models of individual rational choice, both of which have been widely critiqued, and with both approaches to some extent depoliticising decision-making, with one based upon evidence and expertise, and the other on individuals acting as consumers. Indeed, some have argued that rather than using the phrase 'evidence-based', the term 'evidence-informed' policy-making is more appropriate as it reflects the wider range of influences on the policy process.

Another important element in policy-making has been judgement informed by experience and expertise, including that of civil servants. Traditionally, senior civil servants had long experience in the system, and worked in a collegiate and collaborative way in making judgements about decisions. In recent years, increasing numbers of experts from outside the Civil Service have been drawn into the system, and senior civil servants change jobs and departments more regularly, working against such a system. Nevertheless, some ministers have continued to complain that the civil service's way of working works against them. Indeed, one response by politicians to this has been an increase in the number of political advisors appointed to support ministers, with both Labour and Coalition governments making significant use of this approach.

Perhaps one of the most significant obstacles to evidence-based decision-making is the need to make decisions based upon finite and often scarce resources. While many of those who produce evidence, such as academics and think tanks, are in many respects isolated from the direct impact of having to make such decisions, politicians and some other policy-makers are almost inevitably faced with this, so that, for example, while there might be good evidence to suggest that a particular approach might be effective in tackling a problem, only half of the finance necessary to implement it in full might be available. What decision should be made then – partial implementation, slower implementation, or a completely different approach? Indeed, it is not only finance that is a scarce resource; skills and staffing, for example, may be equally problematic. Time too can be a further pressure, for example because of the electoral cycle, which may mean that politicians will be judged over a far shorter term than might be required for a policy to work properly, while if legislation is required for a particular course of action, ministers have to seek to be able to find time in what is often a very crowded parliamentary timetable.

As noted elsewhere, the competing set of actors seeking to influence policy can also be problematic for evidence-based or evidence-informed policy. These include lobbyists, pressure groups, consultants, and think tanks. All of these groups may make use of evidence, but are likely to select it according to their aims and potentially in a less systematic manner than supporters of evidence-based policy might wish.

In its report on evidence-based policy, the Select Committee on Science and Technology (2006) noted that some of its witnesses queried whether evidence-based policy-making was actually possible, given political and other constraints: critics highlighted the lack of evidence to support policy direction, while even strong proponents recognised that there was progress still to be made. The Committee's report acknowledged that many policies would be driven by factors other than evidence, and agreed that such an approach was necessary. However, it suggested that there should be greater openness about the use of evidence, or otherwise, in policy-making:

> We have detected little evidence of an appetite for open departure from the mantra of evidence based policy making. It would be more honest and accurate to acknowledge the fact that while evidence plays a key role in informing policy, decisions are ultimately based on a number of factors – including political expediency. Where policy decisions are based on other such factors and do not flow from the evidence or scientific advice, this should be made clear.
>
> (Select Committee on Science and Technology, 2006, p. 47)

Evidence-based or evidence-informed policy?

The emphasis on evidence-based policy under Labour clearly had important implications for the use of social research in government, for example in encouraging policy transfer, experimentation and policy pilots, such as those associated with the introduction of the educational maintenance allowance for 16- to 18-year-olds (Middleton *et al.*, 2005), some aspects of which survived under the Coalition government, while attempts to use behavioural economics also became more prominent. However, it is arguable that 'evidence-informed policy' is, and perhaps always was, a more accurate depiction of policy-making than 'evidence-based policy'. Evidence-based policy appears to offer more than it can, or perhaps should, deliver. There are inevitably obstacles, some of which are an inherent part of the policy-making process, which will inhibit the use of evidence. Some of these stem from the democratic system, including the values and ideologies of politicians, for which they are held to account at elections as well as their policy successes or failures; some may arise from the perhaps justifiable scepticism of policy-makers about the extent to which evidence and expert knowledge are always appropriate guides to correct actions; others may arise from the need to make quick decisions and to be seen to be acting quickly in some circumstances, including where evidence to support a particular response may be partial or lacking.

Evaluation

Although there has been some discussion of evaluation above, and although the evaluation of policy is also seen as an important part of evidence, it is arguably important enough and used widely enough to deserve some consideration on its own. Those views that see a policy cycle (for example, from agenda-setting through policy formulation, policy implementation, monitoring and evaluation back to agenda-setting) have tended to see evaluation (and to some extent evidence) as central to the policy-making process. For example, HM Treasury utilises the ROAMEF model (Rationale, Objectives, Appraisal, Monitoring, Evaluation and Feedback) in the *Green Book* (a set of guidance for central government for the appraisal and evaluation of policies and projects), which has, at least implicitly, the use of evidence as part of 'appraisal', while evaluation is clearly identified as a key part of the cycle. This close fit with a 'rational' view of policy-making helps explain why, under the Labour governments, evaluation was seen as an important element of policy-making.

Evaluation can be characterised as falling into three broad types:

- *Prospective evaluation* – this takes place before the introduction of a policy and seeks to assess what has worked in the past or in other areas.
- *Formative evaluation* – takes place while a policy is being implemented and provides feedback that might help improve its implementation.
- *Summative evaluation* – is intended to assess the impact and outcome of a policy and takes place following implementation.

However, many government policies do not have evaluation built into them. As a result, some policies may never be formally evaluated, while for many policies evaluations are often undertaken by a variety of more or less independent organisations. Some evaluations may be undertaken within the organisation or organisations responsible for the policy; others may be done externally, including by academics and consultants; and yet others may be done by interest groups or think tanks. It is important to be aware of the strengths and weaknesses of these different approaches.

For example, internal evaluations may have advantages such as a knowledge of the organisation and the policy, and access to key individuals, but there may also be a lack of independence. Evaluations undertaken by academics or external consultants may be more independent, but may not have the immediate level of knowledge and access available to internal evaluators, and may themselves face some pressures directing them towards particular assessments; while interest groups and think tanks are likely to have their own agendas.

> **STOP AND THINK**
>
> Why might many policies receive no formal evaluation?

There are a number of elements of evaluation that can help differentiate it from research more generally:

- Although some is prospective, as noted above, evaluation tends to be reactive, coming after a policy has been implemented, rather than proactive, in the sense of coming before decisions about the shape of a policy.
- It tends to focus on a particular policy or programme, rather than on a broader policy area.
- It tends to focus on questions such as why and to what extent a policy or programme has had an impact on a problem or issue.
- It helps provide judgements of the extent of success or failure of particular policies or programmes.
- It tends to draw on a more limited range of research techniques, and is sometimes criticised for an emphasis on quantitative approaches that seek to mirror those of the sciences.

Evaluation research, therefore, is frequently subject to the same critiques as are made of evidence-based policy-making and rational approaches as a whole. These include the methodological challenges of measurement and establishing cause and effect in the social world, and the more 'political' challenges of influencing policy-making. In addition, there are often likely to be moral and ethical problems in such work. It is likely to be hard to justify, for example, as part of a randomised control trial or experiment, randomly allocating to or withholding services from individuals who may be among the poorest and most vulnerable sectors of society. Other problems, familiar from the broader discussion of evidence and policy, can also be identified – the timescale of elected politicians, who are required to face the electorate on a regular basis, may not fit easily with the longer time periods required to undertake substantial evaluations of the effectiveness, or otherwise, of a policy, evaluation can be costly, it can be hard to identify the aims of a policy, and so on. As a result, while there is often widespread support for the idea of policy evaluation, it is not as commonplace or as thoroughgoing as might be expected.

Conclusions

As is apparent, there has been a considerable history of attempts to try to link evidence from research and evaluations to policy. Yet, despite the apparent desirability of this, it remains highly problematic. In part this arises from the difficulties of defining particular 'policy' and what constitutes 'evidence', in part from the difficulty of providing clear answers to 'what works' in social policy, and in part from the variety of influences upon policy-makers and politicians. At the same time, governments continue to suggest that they believe in using evidence to inform policy. There therefore continue to be significant questions over whether and to what extent policy should be 'evidence-based', 'evidence-informed' or 'evidence-inspired'?

Summary

This chapter has traced the development of ideas of evidence and policy over the past five decades. It has argued that the level of attention paid to the process of policy-making from 1997 to 2010 was unprecedented, but, despite this, reflecting on that period, the evidence base for policy remained partial. It is therefore possible to suggest that:

- The idea of using evidence to support policy-making is arguably widely accepted, but it is important to recognise that there are a wide range of other influences that impact upon the decision-making process to a greater or lesser extent and at different times.
- While studies have shown that there are many examples of good practice within government departments and across tiers of government, there are also many examples where there is little clear linkage between evidence and policy.
- The very idea of 'evidence' is itself open to interpretation, ranging across a variety of approaches, methods, and techniques, from very small-scale to very large projects, and consequently very different judgements about quality, effectiveness, and so on.
- There are a range of obstacles to the greater use of evidence in policy-making, including the capability of government departments, the availability of evidence, the impact of values and ideologies among policy-makers and the public, and the many other pressures and competing influences on policy-making in liberal democracies.

▧ The extent to which policy-making is, or perhaps even should be, evidence-driven, or even evidence-based, is highly contestable, so that it might be more appropriate to characterise the desired situation as 'evidence-informed'.

Discussion and review

▧ When should a policy-maker's values outweigh 'evidence'?

▧ Are some forms of evidence better than others? Why?

▧ To what extent should social policies be 'evidence-based'?

References

Appleby, J. and Coote, A. (2002) *Five Year Health Check: A Review of Health Policy, 1997–2002*, King's Fund, London.

Bamfield, L. (2012) 'Child poverty and social mobility: taking the measure of the Coalition's "New Approach"', *Political Quarterly*, Vol. 83, No. 4, pp. 830–7.

Becker, S., Bryman, A. and Ferguson, H. (2012) *Understanding Research for Social Policy and Social Work*, Policy Press, Bristol.

Bochel, H. and Duncan, S. (2007) *Making Policy in Theory and Practice*, Policy Press, Bristol.

Cabinet Office (1999) *Modernising Government*, The Stationery Office, London.

Cabinet Office (2010) *The Coalition: Our Programme for Government*, Cabinet Office, London.

Cabinet Office Strategic Policy Making Team (1999) *Professional Policy Making for the Twenty First Century*, Cabinet Office, London.

Clarke, J. (2004) *Changing Welfare, Changing States*, Sage, London.

Conservative Party (2010) *Invitation to Join the Government of Britain: The Conservative Manifesto 2010*, Conservative Party, London.

Davies, H., Nutley, S. and Smith, P. (2000) 'Introducing evidence based policy and practice in public services', in H. Davies, S. Nutley and P. Smith (eds.) *What Works? Evidence-based Policy and Practice in Public Services*, Policy Press, Bristol.

Duncan, S. (2005) 'Towards evidence inspired policy', *Social Sciences*, No. 61, pp. 10–11.

Exley, S. and Ball, S.J. (2011) 'Something old, something new: understanding Conservative education policy', in H. Bochel (ed.) *The Conservative Party and Social Policy*, Policy Press, Bristol.

Harrison, S. and Smith, C. (2004) 'Trust and moral motivation: redundant resources in health and social care', *Policy and Politics*, Vol. 32, No. 3, pp. 371–86.

Heywood Committee (1965) *Report of the Committee on Social Studies*, HMSO, London.

Hogwood, B. and Gunn, L. (1984) *Policy Analysis for the Real World*, Oxford University Press, Oxford.

Lasswell, H. (1958) *Who Gets What, When and How*, Meridian Books, Cleveland, OH.

Liberal Democrat Party (2010) *Liberal Democrat Manifesto 2010*, Liberal Democrats, London.

Middleton, S., Perren, K., Maguire, S., Rennison, J., Battistin, E. *et al.* (2005) *Evaluation of Education Maintenance Allowance Pilots: Young People Aged 16 to 19 Years. Final Report of the Quantitative Evaluation*, Department for Education and Skills, Nottingham.

Mulgan, G. (2005) 'Government, knowledge and the business of policy making: the potential and limits of evidence-based policy', *Evidence and Policy*, Vol. 1, No. 2, pp. 215–26.

Parsons, W. (2002) 'From muddling through to muddling up – evidence based policy making and the modernisation of British government', *Public Policy and Administration*, Vol. 17, No. 3, pp. 43–60.

Performance and Innovation Unit (2000) *Adding it Up*, London, Performance and Innovation Unit.

Powell, M. and Maynard, W. (2007) 'Policy review', in H. Bochel and S. Duncan (eds.) *Making Policy in Theory and Practice*, Policy Press, Bristol.

Rothschild, Lord (1971) *The Organisation and Management of Government Research and Development* (The Rothschild Report), HMSO, London.

Select Committee on Science and Technology (2006) *Scientific Advice, Risk and Evidence Based Policy Making*, The Stationery Office, London.

Simon, H. (1945) *Administrative Behaviour*, Free Press, New York.

Simon, H. (1957) *Administrative Behaviour* (2nd edn.), Free Press, New York.

Willetts, D. (2012) 'Research evidence is the antidote to sloppy thinking of sofa government', available at http://www.guardian.co.uk/higher-education-network/blog/2012/oct/22/evidence-based-policy-david-willetts [accessed 19 April 2013].

Further reading

Becker, S., Bryman, A. and Ferguson, H. (eds.) (2012) *Understanding Research for Social Policy and Social Work*, Policy Press, Bristol. This book provides a comprehensive overview of the importance of research, as well as explaining how it should be conducted.

Evidence and Policy – a journal that focuses on the relationship between research, policy, and practice (see http://www.policypress.co.uk/journals_eap.asp).

Glasby, J. (ed.) (2011) *Evidence, Policy and Practice: Critical Perspectives in Health and Social Care*, Policy Press, Bristol. Drawing primarily on examples from the fields of health and social care, this short volume provides a useful critique of the idea of 'evidence-based' policy.

Nutley, S., Walter, I. and Davies, H. (2007) *Using Evidence: How Research can Inform Public Services*, Policy Press, Bristol. Explores how research can be and is used in public services, particularly in parts of the field of social policy.

Palfrey, C., Thomas, P. and Phillips, C. (2012) *Evaluation for the Real World: The Impact of Evidence in Policy Making*, Policy Press, Bristol. This book examines the impact of evaluation on public policy, including recognising the variety of pressures on policy-makers.

PART 2
THE DEVELOPMENT OF
SOCIAL POLICY

CHAPTER 6

The Development of Social Policy, 1800–1945

Bernard Harris

Learning objectives

- To provide an overview of the historical development of social policy in the United Kingdom
- To consider the impact of key ideas on social policy
- To describe the creation of the classic welfare state
- To explore the foundations of contemporary social policy

Chapter overview

The period between 1800 and 1945 saw many changes in welfare policy. At the start of this period, most people relied on their families and local communities for support in times of need, and central government played very little role in the provision of welfare services. However, by 1945 the state played a much greater role in the provision of a wide range of services, covering all the main areas of social policy. This chapter provides an introduction to the development of public welfare policy during this period by examining the following issues:

- the initial growth of state welfare intervention before circa 1870;
- changing attitudes to welfare provision between 1870 and 1900;
- the Liberal welfare reforms of 1906–14;
- the development of social policy between 1914 and 1939;
- the impact of the Second World War on the development of the 'welfare state'.

Introduction

During the last 20 years, the historiography of British welfare provision has been transformed by a growing emphasis on the provision of welfare outside the state. Geoffrey Finlayson (1994, p. 6) argued that Britain had always 'possessed what is now called a "mixed economy of welfare"' and that 'within that mixed economy, the state was only one element – and, arguably, for much of the nineteenth century, and even the twentieth century, it was not the most important element'. Other historians have echoed this view. Jane Lewis (1995, p. 3) claimed that Britain has 'always . . . had a mixed economy of welfare, in which the state, the voluntary sector, the family and the market have played different parts at different points in time', and Joanna Innes (1996, p. 140) concluded that 'a mixed economy of welfare' persisted throughout Western Europe from the sixteenth century onwards (see also Harris and Bridgen, 2007).

However, it is also important to recognise the extent to which the state's role within this mixed economy has developed and expanded since the end of the eighteenth century. At the beginning of this period, the majority of people relied on their families and their local communities for welfare support, and central government played a very limited role in the provision of welfare services (Brewer, 1989, p. 40). However, over the course of the next 150 years, the extent of state intervention increased dramatically. It included the introduction of measures to regulate conditions of work and establish minimum standards for the construction of new housing, as well as the provision of public services, such as public health and education, and the introduction of new forms of income support, such as unemployment insurance and health insurance. These developments meant that, despite their deficiencies, Britain still possessed a more comprehensive set of social services than almost any other democratic country on the eve of the Second World War (Stevenson and Cook, 1994, p. 83).

This chapter presents an overview of the growth of state welfare provision between circa 1800 and 1945 (see Appendix 1 for changes in prime ministers and political control and Appendix 2 for significant events over the period). The next section summarises the main developments in social policy during

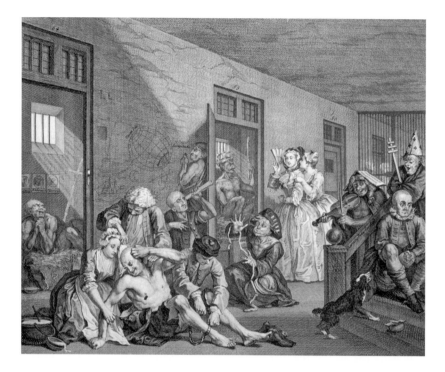

'Scene in Bedlam', from the series *A Rake's Progress* by William Hogarth
Source: © Historical Picture Archives/CORBIS

the first seven decades of the nineteenth century, including changes in the methods of poor relief and the development of attempts to regulate living and working conditions, the history of public educational provision, and the introduction of public health reforms. The various changes that occurred in the provision of poor relief between 1870 and 1906 are then explored, together with new developments in the history of public health and housing and the acceptance of state responsibility for the provision of elementary education under the Forster Education Act of 1870. This is followed by an examination of the history of the 'Liberal welfare reforms' of 1906–11, including the intro-duction of school meals and school medical inspection, old age pensions, the Housing and Town Planning Act, a radical set of tax reforms, and the creation of statutory health and unemployment insurance schemes. The chapter then explores the development of welfare provision in inter-war Britain, including the expansion of both the extent and the coverage of the unemployment insurance scheme, the introduction of a contributory pension scheme for those between the ages of 65 and 70, the changing nature of poor relief (or public assistance, as it became known), the reform of hospital services, the introduction of subsidised forms of council housing, and the partial reorgani-sation of the education system. The final section of the chapter discusses social policy during the Second World War, and the impact of those changes on the development of welfare provision after 1945.

One of the ways in which we can 'measure' the growth of public welfare provision is by looking at the statistics of public expenditure. During the nineteenth century, most additional expenditure on social services was incurred by local authorities (Szreter, 2002a, p. 29), but in the twentieth century a much larger share of the burden was borne by central government (see Table 6.1). In 1790, central government expenditure on social services probably amounted to no more than 1 per cent of the country's total national income, but this proportion more than doubled between 1790 and 1900, and by 1938 it had reached 10.7 per cent, before increasing still further after the Second World War. This expenditure reflected a degree of public intervention in welfare provision that would have been almost unthinkable at the end of the eighteenth century.

The years between 1800 and 1945 were also characterised by some important changes in methods of taxation. At the start of the eighteenth century, the government obtained most of its income from indirect taxes in the form of customs and excise duties, supplemented by smaller amounts of income from direct taxes on land and other forms of assessable wealth and stamp duties, but in 1799 William Pitt the Younger introduced the first income tax. This was originally intended as a means of raising emergency revenue for the Napoleonic War and it was abandoned during the Peace of Amiens in 1802–3 and again following the end of the war in 1816, before being reintroduced by Robert

Table 6.1 Government expenditure on social, economic, and environmental services in the United Kingdom, 1790–2000

	As a percentage of total expenditure		As a percentage of GDP	
	Social services	Economic and environmental services	Social services	Economic and environmental services
1790	8.7	8.7	1.0	1.0
1840	9.4	9.4	1.0	1.0
1890	20.9	14.8	1.9	1.3
1900	18.0	17.3	2.5	2.4
1910	32.8	19.2	4.0	2.3
1920	25.9	14.4	6.9	3.8
1930	42.3	14.9	10.3	3.6
1938	37.6	12.7	10.7	3.6
1950	41.9	15.7	14.1	5.3
1960	46.1	15.1	16.9	5.5
1970	47.1	25.5	20.0	10.8
1980	54.3	16.2	25.4	7.6
1990	55.0	12.5	21.9	5.0
2000	60.3	9.8	22.9	3.7

Source: Harris (2004, pp. 12–13)

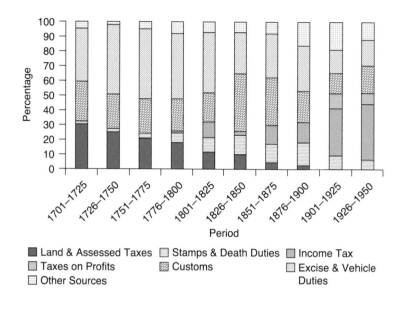

Figure 6.1 Sources of government finance, 1701/25–1926/50

Source: Harris (2004, p. 10)

Peel in 1842. Peel believed that income tax could provide an alternative to more traditional forms of taxation, but the Liberal government of 1906–11 decided to expand the scope of the income tax system as part of its plans for funding increases in welfare spending. This was one of the main reasons why the percentage of total revenue derived from income tax rose from 13.5 per cent in the final quarter of the nineteenth century to 37.5 per cent in the second quarter of the twentieth century (see Figure 6.1).

Victorian origins of the welfare state

Although it is conventional to assume that the 'welfare state' only came into being in Britain after 1945, some historians have argued that a form of welfare state existed much earlier. Paul Slack (1999) claimed that England already possessed a 'local welfare state' by the end of the eighteenth century, and David Roberts (1960) suggested that the foundations of a national welfare state were laid between 1833 and 1854, but other historians have rejected this view. Ursula Henriques (1979, p. 268) argued that it was difficult to apply the label 'Victorian origins of the welfare state' to the mid nineteenth century, when 'the welfare state represents, at least in theory, the total reversal of nineteenth-century attitudes', and Pat Thane (1982, p. vii; 1996, p. xii) claimed that it was only around 1870 'that important demands began to arise for the state . . . to take a permanent, as distinct from a temporary and residual, responsibility for the social and economic conditions experienced by its citizens'. However, despite these reservations, the period between 1800 and 1870 witnessed a number of developments that had profound implications for the role of the state in the provision of welfare services. These developments were particularly apparent in relation to the administration of the Poor Law, and to the identification of the state's responsibility for the promotion of education and the protection of public health.

One of the main challenges posed by this chapter is the need to recognise the existence of different welfare traditions, and different systems of education and health administration, in different parts of the United Kingdom. This is particularly true of the history of poor relief. In both Ireland and Scotland, the provision of poor relief was largely dependent on voluntary arrangements before the 1830s (Luddy, 1998; Mitchison, 2000). However, in England and Wales, the Poor Law Acts of 1597 and 1601 had conferred a legal obligation on the churchwardens of every parish to 'set the poor on work', make arrangements for the apprenticeship of pauper children, and maintain those who were unable to work. The creation of this system led the French writer, Alexis de Tocqueville, to observe in 1835 that England was 'the only country in Europe which has systematised and applied the theories of public charity on a large scale'. He also claimed that this was one of the main reasons why, in his view, the level of indigence was much greater than elsewhere (Harris 2004, pp. 40–1).

During the eighteenth century, the estimated cost of this system rose from just under 2 shillings (10 pence) per head in 1696 to nearly 9 shillings (45 pence) in 1802–3 (Kidd, 1999). This increase fuelled a growing debate about the provision of poor relief, which culminated in the passage of the Poor Law Amendment Act in 1834. This Act aimed to curtail the welfare entitlements of able-bodied men by requiring them to enter a workhouse, or submit to some other form of deterrent test, in order to qualify for relief, and it led to a sharp reduction in the number of able-bodied men who featured on the relief rolls (Williams, 1981; Harris, 2004). However, it also witnessed some important changes in the administrative structure of the Poor Law, including the reorganisation of individual parishes into Poor Law Unions, the establishment of the central Poor Law Commission, and the appointment of Assistant Commissioners who were then able to exercise a significant influence over the development of local relief policies (Harling, 1992). Even though these measures were originally designed to prevent the growth of welfare expenditure, they also reflected the view that there ought to be a nationally agreed framework for the possession of welfare rights that could be applied across the entire country.

The 1830s and 1840s also saw the extension of the Poor Law to Ireland and changes in the Scottish system

STOP AND THINK

The Poor Law Amendment Act has been described as 'one of the great watersheds in English social policy' (Jones, 1990, p. 13). One of its main aims was to establish a framework for the introduction of policies that would lead to a dramatic reduction in Poor Law expenditure. However, when the Poor Law Commissioners tried to introduce the new Act in the north of England, they encountered opposition from members of both the working and middle classes (Rose, 1966; Edsall, 1971). Why might middle-class ratepayers have been opposed to the changes the Commissioners wished to introduce?

of poor relief. The Poor Relief (Ireland) Act of 1838 allowed the Poor Law Commissioners for England and Wales to establish Poor Law Unions in Ireland and make new arrangements for the construction of workhouses. The original Act prohibited the granting of outdoor relief, but this restriction was removed, following the outbreak of the Irish Potato Famine, when the Irish Poor Relief Extension Act was passed in 1847. A new Poor Law Act had been passed regarding Scotland two years earlier. That Act created a central Board of Supervision to oversee the provision of poor relief (section 2), and required every burghal parish or group of parishes to appoint a Parochial Board of Managers of the Poor to administer the Poor Law in their area (section 17). In 1929, the Labour MP, Tom Johnston, claimed that the 1845 Act granted the Scottish working class a legal right to state welfare, but this right was explicitly denied to 'able-bodied persons out of employment' (section 68) and, as Ian Levitt (1988) has argued, the number of people receiving relief in 1890 was lower than at any time since the 1830s.

The first half of the nineteenth century also witnessed a number of other developments. In 1802, Parliament passed the Health and Morals of Apprentices Act, which sought to limit the working hours of apprentices and prevent them from working through the night, and this was followed by a series of other measures, including the Factory Acts of 1819, 1825, and 1833 (Harris, 2004). The government established a Board of Commissioners for National Education in Ireland in 1831 (Considine and Dukelow, 2009), and the first state grant for public education in England and Wales was introduced in 1833. Even though the size of the grant was very small (only £20,000), both the extent and the scope of education grants increased significantly in the ensuing years. In 1839, Parliament established a Privy Council Committee on Education to supervise the expenditure of public funds, and after 1843 schools were permitted to request public support for the purchase of new equipment as well as the construction of new buildings (Harris, 2004).

Important as these developments were, it is arguable that the most important example of the growth of state intervention in this period lay in the sphere of public health. During the course of the eighteenth century, Britain had witnessed a sharp reduction in the incidence of what demographers call 'crisis mortality' (i.e. years in which mortality rates are exceptionally high) and there was a gradual improvement in the underlying rate of mortality between circa 1780 and 1820, but these developments were placed in jeopardy by the rapid growth of large towns and cities (Flinn, 1965; Fogel, 1994). It has been estimated that at the beginning of the nineteenth century just over one-third of the total population of England and Wales lived in towns or cities containing more than 2500 inhabitants, and there was only city – London – whose population exceeded 100,000. However, over the course of the next 50 years, the number of 'large' towns and cities increased to ten, and the proportion of the total population that was classified as 'urban' increased to 54 per cent (Harris, 2004). These changes were seen to represent a major threat to the overall standard of public health because the death rates experienced by people living in large and rapidly growing towns were significantly higher than those experienced elsewhere (Szreter and Mooney, 1998).

The threat which the growth of large towns posed to the health of the population was one of the major causes that lay behind the development of the campaign for public health reform between 1800 and 1850, culminating in the passage of the first Public Health Act in 1848. This Act led to the creation of the first central government health department – the General Board of Health – and granted it the power to conduct its own investigations into the sanitary condition of areas where more than 10 per cent of ratepayers requested such an enquiry, or where the local death rate had exceeded 23 deaths per thousand living over a seven-year period. However, the Act only applied to England and Wales and, although it was undoubtedly a major watershed in the history of social policy, its practical significance can easily be exaggerated. In the five years after the Act came into operation, the initiation of enquiries by the General Board of Health led to the establishment of local Boards of Health in 14 areas where the local death rate had exceeded 23 deaths per thousand and 168 areas where an enquiry had been requested by local ratepayers, but the combined population of these areas accounted for less than one-eighth of the total population of England and Wales at the time of the 1851 census (Harris, 2004).

Welfare provision 1870–1906

As the previous section has demonstrated, the period between 1800 and 1870 witnessed a number of important changes in the role played by the state in the establishment of minimum standards and the development of welfare services, but there were still major gaps in the development of public welfare provision, and this is why Pat Thane argued that it was only after 1870 that the state came under concerted pressure 'to take a permanent . . . responsibility for the social and economic conditions . . . [of] its citizens' (Thane, 1982, p. vii; 1996, p. xii). Although some commentators were calling for the introduction of tighter controls on the distribution of poor relief, others were advocating an enhanced role for the state in the improvement of housing standards and the provision of health and education services, and these demands exerted a major impact on the development of social policy between 1870 and 1906.

As we have already seen, the introduction of the Poor Law Amendment Act in 1834 led to a sharp reduction in the number of able-bodied men in receipt of outdoor relief, and a significant decline in the overall level of Poor Law expenditure in England and Wales, but the number of paupers began to rise once more during the 1860s, and this led to renewed calls for a return to the 'principles of 1834' and a further crackdown on relief payments (Harris, 2004, pp. 53–4). However, although the number of claimants fell by more than 300,000 (from 917,890 to 571,892) between 1871 and 1877, the late-1860s and 1870s also witnessed a number of other developments that may have been less eye-catching in themselves, but also betokened the emergence of a rather different attitude to the question of poor relief. Perhaps the most important of these was the gradual separation, in London at any rate, of the poor relief functions of the Poor Law from its medical functions, with the creation of the Metropolitan Asylums Board. This measure created a separate administrative authority for the organisation of hospital services, and marked the first stage in a process that gradually enabled an increasing number of people to receive medical assistance from the public authorities without suffering any loss of personal or civic status (Harris, 2004).

In addition to the gradual extension of medical rights under the Poor Law (reinforced by the decision to admit non-paupers to infectious disease hospitals after 1871 and the promulgation of the Medical Relief (Disqualifications Removal) Act of 1885), the last three decades of the nineteenth century also witnessed a series of other developments which bore directly on the question of poverty itself. In 1870, when Parliament introduced the Forster Education Act, it gave school boards the power to remit fees for children whose parents were unable to afford the cost of sending them to board schools, and after 1891 the vast majority of children in England and Wales became exempt from the payment of elementary school fees altogether. At the same time, new measures were initiated to deal with the problems of unemployment and to investigate the incidence of poverty in old age. In 1886, Joseph Chamberlain issued the first of a series of circulars authorising the establishment of public works schemes during periods of cyclical unemployment, and in 1894 the Royal Commission on the Aged Poor was charged with investigating the problem of poverty in old age. Once again, it would be easy to exaggerate the practical importance of these initiatives, particularly in the short term, but they were nevertheless indicative of a growing awareness of the limitations of existing approaches to social policy (Harris, 2004).

The 1870s and 1880s also witnessed a number of other significant developments in the area of health policy. As we have seen, the provision of therapeutic services by public authorities continued to be closely linked to the Poor Law, but many local authorities began to build their own infectious disease hospitals (which came under municipal rather than Poor Law control), and it became much easier to receive medical assistance without suffering the stigma or disabilities associated with pauperism (Harris, 2004). However, the most radical changes occurred in relation to the preventive or environmental medical services. The Sanitary Act of 1866 extended some of the provisions of the 1848 Public Health Act to Ireland and expanded the legal definition of 'nuisances' prejudicial to health, but its main innovation was the decision to compel local authorities to inspect their districts and exercise their basic powers (Harris, 2004; Considine and Dukelow, 2009). The growing importance of public health was also underlined by the passage of the Public Health (Scotland) Act of 1867 and the Public Health Act of 1875, and by the introduction of a series of Acts addressing such issues as the sale of food and drugs, the prevention of lead poisoning, and the purification of the water supply. The period also witnessed a substantial increase in the value of the loans contracted by local authorities for public works, including the construction of new sewers (Harris, 2004).

Although Szreter's (2002b, p. 4) suggestion that the period between 1870 and 1914 witnessed 'colossal and ever-increasing investments' in the improvement of local housing stock may be a little misleading, the period was nevertheless notable for a series of legislative innovations. In 1868 and 1875, Parliament introduced the first slum clearance Acts, but these had only a limited impact because of the failure to build substantial numbers of new properties to replace those that had been demolished. However, the Housing of the Working Classes Act of 1890 gave local authorities the power to construct additional housing for more affluent workers in suburban areas in the hope that this would 'free up' housing at the bottom of the market for the more poorly paid. In Ireland, a new body – the Congested Districts Board – was set up in 1891 to deal with problems of congestion and overcrowding in western districts. As in many other cases, the practical impact of much of this legislation was limited (only around 5 per cent of all the houses constructed between 1890 and 1914 were built by local authorities), but the legislation pointed the way for the much more significant expansion of local authority housing after 1919 (Harris, 2004; Considine and Dukelow, 2009).

Perhaps the most important policy innovation between 1870 and 1900 was the introduction of the Forster Education Act of 1870. This Act gave local ratepayers the power to establish school boards in areas where the existing level of elementary education was deemed inadequate and allowed them to raise money for the support of these schools from local rates, and similar changes were introduced to Scotland in 1872. Forster's Act did not make elementary education compulsory or free, but it paved the way for both, and by 1900 more than half of all the children between the ages of 5 and 12 years who were attending publicly supported schools in England and Wales were attending board schools, and many school boards were also providing voluntary classes for children above this age (Harris, 2004). It is not surprising, therefore, that observers such as A.V. Dicey (1962) should have regarded the passage of Forster's Act as the true beginning of what subsequently came to be seen as late-Victorian and Edwardian collectivism.

STOP AND THINK

The Education Act of 1870 has often been regarded as one of the major landmarks in the history of state welfare intervention. It enabled school boards to establish their own public elementary schools and gave them the power to make education compulsory for children between the ages of 5 and 10 years in their areas. However, many parents resented the introduction of compulsory education and this led to several prosecutions for non-attendance (see, for example, Hurt 1979; Humphries, 1981; Davin, 1996). Why might some parents have been reluctant to take advantage of the opportunities the Act provided?

Liberal welfare and the 'social service state'

By the early twentieth century there was a growing recognition of the problems faced by the Poor Law, coupled with an increasing awareness of the extent of working-class poverty and its implications for the country's ability to maintain social stability and protect its economic and military interests. However, despite these pressures, the main changes in welfare provision were not implemented within the structure of the Poor Law itself but alongside it, and this had profound implications for its longer-term future.

It is customary for historians to begin their accounts of the 'Liberal welfare reforms' with the Education (Provision of Meals) Act of 1906. This was a relatively brief measure (containing only three clauses) designed primarily to encourage greater cooperation between local authorities and voluntary agencies, and its main aim was not so much to provide free school meals, as to facilitate the provision of meals to paying children that could be provided at cost price. However, the third clause of the Act recognised that there was also a minority of children who were 'unable by reason of lack of food to profit from the education provided for them', and whose parents were unable to pay, and for this reason the Act also allowed the local education authority to raise a small amount of money (not more than the yield of a halfpenny rate) to feed these children without charge. Similar changes were introduced to Scotland (under the Education (Scotland) Act) in 1908 and to Ireland (under the Education (Provision of Meals) (Ireland) Act) in 1914. These Acts did not lead to any huge increase in the number of children who received free meals at school, but they did represent a marked break with Poor Law orthodoxy, since meals were being provided to the children without any penalty to the parents, and this undoubtedly enraged many conservative commentators (Harris, 2004). As Dicey observed in 1914:

> No-one can deny that a starving boy will hardly profit from the attempt to teach him the rules of arithmetic. But it does not necessarily follow that a local authority must therefore provide every hungry child at school with a meal . . . [or] that a father who first lets his child starve, and then fails to pay the price legally due from him for a meal . . . should, under the Act of 1906, retain the right of voting for a Member of Parliament. Why a man who first neglects his duty as a father and then defrauds the state should retain his full political rights is a question easier to ask than to answer.
>
> (Dicey, 1962, p. l)

Although the Liberals also introduced a number of other measures affecting children (including the establishment of a national system of school medical inspection, the introduction of free places in secondary schools, and the Children Act of 1908), these measures were probably rather less important than the introduction of old age pensions in 1908. The new Act provided a non-contributory pension of 5 shillings a week to pensioners who were over the age of 70 and whose annual income was less than £21, with a sliding scale of payments for individuals whose annual income was between £21 and £31.10s. When the scheme was first introduced it was limited to individuals who met a small number of 'character' tests and who had not recently been in

'The Dawn of Hope' – poster produced by the Liberal Party to promote the 1911 National Insurance Act

Source: The National Archives, www.nationalarchives.gov.uk, PRO: PIN 900/42. Reprinted with permission

receipt of poor relief, but these measures were rescinded over the next few years (Harris, 2004). Although Pat Thane (1982, p. 83; 1996, p. 77) argued that the Act only provided a comparatively small pension to 'the very poor, the very respectable and the very old', it was nevertheless a further breach in the wall of traditional Poor Law thinking, and it prompted the Prime Minister, Herbert Asquith, to insist that it was not a final destination, but a 'new departure' on an 'unmeasured road of future social progress' (Parliamentary Debates, 1908, cols. 828–9, see also Pugh, 2002).

Following the passage of the Old Age Pensions Bill, the government was able to turn its attention to a range of issues connected with the labour market. In 1909, Parliament approved legislation covering the establishment of labour exchanges, a Development Fund for the promotion of public works programmes during periods of cyclical unemployment, and trade boards, with the power to set minimum wages in a range of 'sweated industries'. The government also introduced a major new housing measure, the Housing and Town Planning Act. This Act reinforced many of the provisions introduced by earlier Acts, such as the Housing of the Working Classes Acts of 1890, 1900, and 1903, but it broke new ground by giving official encouragement to the principle of town planning, and also sought to strengthen the local administration of public health services by preventing newly appointed Medical Officers of Health from engaging in private practice and granting them greater security of tenure (Harris, 2004).

Although each of these measures was undoubtedly important, none was more so than the Finance Bill which the Chancellor, David Lloyd George, presented to Parliament in the same year. During the nineteenth century, the government had derived the bulk of its revenue from indirect taxation, but the growth of new obligations forced politicians of all parties to consider new ways of generating the revenue on which public expenditure depended. In 1903, Joseph Chamberlain had persuaded the Conservative Party to abandon its historic support for free trade in favour of tariff reform, but the Liberals believed that new revenue could best be raised by introducing a more graduated form of income tax and increasing death duties. The new proposals, which were finally approved in 1910, led to a significant increase in the proportion of all revenue that was derived from income tax, and in the proportion of income tax revenue derived from higher earners (Harris, 2004).

The long-drawn-out passage of what became known as the 'People's Budget' enabled the government to proceed with its plans for the creation of a new system of national insurance. During the nineteenth century, a growing proportion of working-class men (together with a much smaller number of working-class women) had sought to protect themselves against the financial hazards of sickness and old age (and, to a much lesser extent, unemployment) by taking out voluntary insurance through friendly societies or trade union benefit schemes and these schemes formed the basis – to some extent, at least – of the national scheme that the government introduced in 1911 (Harris, 2004). Part I of the National Insurance Act established a national health insurance scheme that was to be financed by contributions from workers, employers, and the state, and which offered a range of health-related benefits, including free accommodation in a tuberculosis sanatorium, general practitioner treatment, a maternity allowance for insured women and the wives of insured men, and, most importantly, cash benefits of 10 shillings a week for men and 7s.6d a week for women for the first 26 weeks of any incapacitating illness. Part II of the Act introduced a much more limited scheme, covering approximately 2.25 million workers, to deal with the problem of unemployment. This scheme was also financed by contributions from workers, employers, and the state, and offered a flat-rate benefit of 7 shillings a week for up to 15 weeks in any 52-week period (Harris, 2004).

Although national insurance has long been regarded as the flagship of the Liberal welfare reforms, it has not been without its critics. The flat-rate nature of the employees' contributions meant that the cost of insurance bore most heavily on those with the lowest incomes (Harris, 1972), and Paul Johnson (1996) has complained that the introduction of national insurance substituted an 'individualistic' system of social protection for the more 'solidaristic' nature of the Poor Law. However, while neither of these criticisms should be treated lightly, it is also important to remember that the Poor Law was only able to preserve its 'solidaristic' features by imposing a highly deterrent framework on the administration of poor relief and by stigmatising the recipients of poor relief. In view of this, it is perhaps less surprising that so many people should have been willing to accept the principle of national insurance as a welcome and worthwhile alternative to traditional Poor Law policies (Roberts, 2000).

CONTROVERSY AND DEBATE

Working-class attitudes and the Liberal welfare reforms

In a famous article, Henry Pelling (1968, pp. 1–2) once argued that 'the extension of the power of the state at the beginning of . . . [the twentieth] century . . . was by no means welcomed by members of the working class' and may even have been undertaken 'over the critical hostility of many of them, perhaps of most of them'. He claimed that this hostility was rooted in 'working class attitudes of suspicion or dislike towards existing institutions' – such as the Poor Law and the public vaccination service – 'which were the expression of national social policy'.

One of the major limitations of this debate is that it is often very difficult to find direct evidence of working-class views. Pelling's account was largely dependent on evidence obtained from official enquiries, such as the Royal Commission on the Poor Laws and the Interdepartmental Committee on Partial Exemption from School Attendance, observations by middle-class observers, such as the district nurse, Margaret Loane, and from his analysis of the main topics discussed during general elections between 1886 and 1914. However, other authors have been able to move beyond this, using evidence from oral historians, working-class autobiographies, and surveys carried out among the members of trade unions and friendly societies, and their investigations have yielded a rather more nuanced view. Pat Thane (1984, pp. 879, 882–92) concluded that 'many poorer people . . . were grateful for any amelioration of their hard lives', and that it was the leaders of trade unions who tended to be most sceptical of the motives of those advocating reform. However, even those who were hostile to state intervention were forced to recognise that some form of state welfare provision was necessary to improve the conditions of the very poor, and during the 1890s and 1900s trade unionists and friendly society members played an increasingly important role in campaigns for the introduction of such measures as school meals and school medical inspection, old age pensions, the abolition of the Poor Law, the establishment of trade boards, and measures to reduce unemployment (Harris, 2004, p. 154).

Although it is clear that working-class pressure was *one* of the reasons for the introduction of the Liberal welfare reforms, it was not the only one, and Thane (1984, p. 896) also pointed out that the reforms themselves 'were far from being complete victories for Labour; they were granted very much on Liberal terms'. It is also important to recognise the extent to which they were designed to fend off calls for more fundamental change, as Winston Churchill explained in relation to the introduction of unemployment insurance in 1909:

'The idea is to increase the stability of our institutions by giving the mass of industrial workers a direct interest in maintaining them . . . This scheme . . . will help to remove the dangerous element of uncertainty from the existence of the industrial worker. It will give him an assurance that his home, got together through long years and with affectionate sacrifice, will not be broken up, sent bit by bit to the pawnshop, just because . . . he falls out of work. It will make him a better citizen, a more efficient worker, [and] a happier man' (quoted in Harris, 1972, pp. 365–6).

▪ How did working-class people view the prospect of increased state intervention in welfare provision?

▪ What role did working-class pressure play in the introduction of the Liberal welfare reforms?

▪ What other factors also contributed to the introduction of these measures?

Welfare between the wars

Although the Liberal welfare reforms represented a major shift in the history of British social policy, their impact was almost immediately overshadowed by the outbreak of the First World War. The war severely disrupted many welfare services and forced the government to take a number of emergency measures, but it also generated a new sense of entitlement on the part of many working-class people and fuelled a wide-ranging debate on the future of welfare provision.

One of the most important changes (if not the most important change) in the infrastructure of welfare provision after 1918 was the expansion of the unemployment insurance scheme. As we have already seen, the original unemployment insurance scheme was set up under Part II of the National Insurance Act of 1911, and was designed to provide a short-term flat-rate benefit for a limited number of workers employed in a selected range of industries, but during the course of 1920 and 1921 this scheme was transformed by a series of changes which meant that by the end of 1921 it covered approximately 75 per cent of the employed workforce, and provided benefits that were intended not only to cover both short- and long-term periods of unemployment, but also to cater for the needs of both unemployed workers *and* their dependants. During the remainder of the 1920s and 1930s, the government introduced a number of other changes, many of which were designed to restrict access to the unemployment insurance fund and reduce overall levels of expenditure, but in spite of this the basic principle that had been established by the reforms of 1920 and 1921 remained intact, and by the end of the inter-war period the overwhelming majority of unemployed workers were receiving benefits under the statutory unemployment insurance scheme (Harris, 2004).

Although the expansion of unemployment insurance represented the most dramatic change in the state's response to the problem of poverty, the period also witnessed important developments in other areas of anti-poverty policy. The number of workers covered by national health insurance increased from 15.9 million in 1918 to 21.6 million in 1938, and there were also some significant (although by no means universal) improvements in the provision of municipal welfare benefits, such as school meals and the distribution of nutritional supplements at maternity and child welfare centres. One of the most important innovations was the development of a contributory pension scheme for those between the age of 65 and 70. This scheme was grafted on to the existing health insurance scheme and provided a basic pension of 10 shillings a week for insured workers, the wives of insured men (where the man was over the age of 65 and his wife was aged between 65 and 70), and the widows of insured men, with additional allowances for widows' children and orphans (Harris, 2004).

These changes in the overall framework of welfare support had profound implications for the oldest form of statutory welfare provision, the Poor Law. As we have already seen, the main ethos of the New Poor Law after 1834 had been one of deterrence, but this attitude came under growing attack during the 1890s and early 1900s, and became increasingly difficult to sustain in many parts of the country after the end of the First World War. The role of the Poor Law (or public assistance, as it became known after 1930) was also affected by the development of alternative welfare systems. During the nineteenth century, the Poor Law had formed the bedrock of statutory welfare support, but during the inter-war period it acted more as a back-up, providing supplementary benefits to individuals who received the majority of their support from one of the contributory schemes, but still required additional support to 'make ends meet'. In this respect, then, it is at least arguable that there was rather more continuity between the public assistance scheme of the late 1930s and the national assistance scheme of the 1940s and 1950s than post-war welfare rhetoric might suggest (Harris, 2004).

The inter-war years also witnessed important developments in the provision of hospital services. Although the number of publicly controlled hospital beds remained largely unchanged, an increasing proportion of these hospitals began to develop acute medical services, with the result that the number of patients treated in public hospitals increased substantially. There were also important changes in the administrative structure of public hospital provision. During the nineteenth and early twentieth centuries, the majority of public sector hospitals had been under the control of Poor Law authorities, but in 1929 these were transferred to the local county, county borough or burgh councils, and these authorities were also given the power to transfer responsibility for hospital administration from their public assistance committees to their public health committees. There has been some debate over the extent and pace of the process of transfer, or 'appropriation', but by the end of the 1930s more than half the public sector hospital beds in England and Wales were under public health control (Levitt, 1988; Harris, 2004).

These changes in the development and administration of the public sector hospital service were matched by equally significant changes in the voluntary hospital sector. The voluntary hospitals originated during the eighteenth and nineteenth centuries as privately controlled institutions supported by voluntary contributions, but during the inter-war years they began to see themselves not so much as charitable institutions for the deserving poor, but rather as general medical institutions for the population at large. This change in the character of the voluntary hospitals encouraged new demands for better coordination between the public and voluntary hospital sectors and also for the management of voluntary hospitals to become more accountable to the populations they served, and these twin demands for coordination and accountability played an important part in the debates over the plans for a national health service during the Second World War (Harris, 2004).

In legislative terms, some of the most dramatic changes in welfare policy affected the area of housing. Although local authorities had enjoyed at least the theoretical power to construct their own houses since the mid nineteenth century, only around 0.25 per cent of all householders lived in municipally owned accommodation on the eve of the First World War. However, in 1919 Parliament passed two Acts, the Housing and Town Planning, etc. Act, and the Housing (Additional Powers) Act, which provided central government subsidies to local authorities and private builders to enable them to build new homes for working-class use, and in 1930 the second Labour government introduced the Greenwood Housing Act, which earmarked separate subsidies for the construction of replacement housing for individuals who were to be evicted from their existing properties under slum clearance schemes. More than 1.1 million homes were built by local authorities between 1 January 1919 and 31 March 1939, and more than 2.8 million homes were built by private builders, of which approximately 430,000 were constructed with the aid of government subsidies (Harris, 2004).

Historians of social policy have often seen the inter-war period as a wasted period in terms of educational development, and this has led some commentators to conclude that it is not worthy of consideration (see Gilbert, 1970). The reduction in the birth rate should have enabled inter-war governments to achieve significant improvements in educational provision, but there was only a small increase in the number of pupils attending selective secondary schools, and the school-leaving age remained fixed at 14 despite a series of attempts to raise it. However, the period did see some important changes in the organisation of the elementary school system. During the first half of the 1920s, the majority of children remained in the same 'all-age' schools throughout their educational careers, but in January 1925 the Board of Education argued that all children should pass from 'junior' to 'senior' education at the age of 11, and the Board's Consultative Committee (the Hadow Committee) called for a similar break to be made between 'primary' and 'secondary' education when it published its report on *The Education of the Adolescent* (1926) in the following year. This report contributed to the process which became known as 'Hadow reorganisation', and by the end of the 1930s more than 60 per cent of the pupils attending elementary schools in England and Wales were being educated in schools that had undergone some form of reorganisation along these lines (Harris, 2004).

The inter-war period also witnessed some important changes in children's experience of education and the development of educational facilities. Although very few new schools were constructed during the immediate post-war period, education authorities were able to embark on a substantial new building programme from the mid 1920s onwards, and by the middle of the following decade a substantial proportion of children were being educated in schools that had either been newly constructed or significantly refurbished since the end of the First World War. These developments were central to such reorganisation as did occur, and they played an important role in helping to reduce class sizes and facilitate the introduction of more modern methods of teaching. In 1925, more than 14 per cent of elementary school children attended classes containing more than 50 pupils, but by 1938 this proportion had fallen to less than 1.5 per cent, and the number of 'blacklisted' schools that were still awaiting replacement had fallen by more than 70 per cent (from 2827 to 844) (Harris, 2004).

The Second World War and after

By 1939 it was clear that the structure of the British welfare services had expanded considerably, but there were still large numbers of people who lived in squalid and overcrowded accommodation, who were unable to obtain adequate medical care, or who continued to depend on means-tested public assistance benefits. The outbreak of war heightened public awareness of the implications of many of these issues and led to the publication of a series of reports with proposals for change.

Of all the reports issued during the war, none is more famous that the Beveridge Report of 1942 (Parliamentary Papers, 1942). William Beveridge was one of the architects of the Labour Exchanges Act of 1909, and had been summoned out of retirement to advise the wartime Minister of Labour, Ernest Bevin, in 1940. In June 1941, however, he was invited by Arthur Greenwood, Minister-without-Portfolio, to chair an enquiry into the development of a consolidated scheme of social insurance. According to his biographer, José Harris (1977), Beveridge was initially quite reluctant to take on this role, but he soon realised that it offered him a unique opportunity to develop proposals for a much more fundamental reform of welfare provision.

The primary aim of the Beveridge Committee was to frame proposals for the development of a more consolidated scheme of social insurance. Beveridge advocated a single scheme providing insurance against sickness, unemployment, and old age, and said that it should provide benefits to the entire population, not just manual workers. He also argued that these benefits should be sufficient to meet the recipients' subsistence needs, and this became the focus of particular controversy during the remainder of the war years (Harris, 2004).

Beveridge also included two other sets of recommendations – one implicit and one explicit – which had major implications for the government's welfare role. He argued that the new scheme of social insurance would only work if it was supported by action in three other areas: the provision of family allowances for all families with children, whether they were in work or not; the development of a comprehensive health and rehabilitation service to enable every individual to maintain themselves in good health and obtain adequate medical care when they needed it; and the prevention of mass unemployment. He also said that 'Want' was only one of the 'five giants' on the road to social reconstruction, and that the government's attack on Want had to be accompanied by a parallel assault on the giants of Ignorance, Disease, Idleness, and Squalor (Harris, 2004).

The attack on Idleness was one of the most important 'Assumptions' on which the Beveridge Report was based. During the 1920s and 1930s, unemployment had been a major cause of hardship and the cost of supporting unemployed people and their families had been a significant drain on the government's finances, but the Treasury argued that there was very little which governments could do to reduce unemployment, other than by seeking to restore normal trading conditions. However, in June 1944 the government published a White Paper on Employment Policy (Parliamentary Papers, 1944a), which represented a major departure from the 'Treasury view'. It marked the first official acceptance of the idea that governments had a legitimate role to play in maintaining a high and stable level of employment under normal peacetime conditions.

After Idleness and Want came Ignorance. As we have already seen, the inter-war period witnessed a number of important changes in the organisation of public education but the process of 'Hadow reorganisation' remained incomplete and the school leaving age had still not been raised since 1918. However, in 1943 the government published a White Paper on Educational Reconstruction (Parliamentary Papers, 1943), and this formed the basis of the Education Act, which the President of the Board of Education, 'Rab' Butler, introduced in the following year. Although the new Act ignored the position of the country's private fee-paying schools and sidestepped the controversial question of the structure of secondary education beyond the age of 11, it did introduce a number of important changes. It removed one of the major barriers to the coordination of primary and secondary education by placing responsibility for both forms of education in the hands of a single education authority in each area; it insisted that all children should move from primary school to some form of secondary school at the age of 11; and it raised the status of education at the level of central government by converting the Board of Education into a full-fledged Ministry. It also abolished the payment of fees in all state secondary schools and raised the school leaving age from 14 to 15, and gave the Minister of Education the power to raise the school leaving age to 16 as soon as circumstances permitted (Harris, 2004). In Scotland, similar changes were introduced under the Education (Scotland) Act of 1945. However, although this Act also drew a clear distinction between primary and secondary education, it did not stipulate the age at which children should move from one to the other (see Education (Scotland) Act, 1945, section 1).

Although some historians have suggested that the politics of educational reform were comparatively straightforward, the reform of health provision was much less so. This was partly the result of the attitude of the medical profession itself. During the 1930s, there was a growing consensus that the existing system of national health insurance needed to be extended to provide better access to medical care for those sections of the population – principally women and children – who were not already covered by it, but it was also assumed that there would continue to be significant scope for the continuation of private medical practice. However, when Beveridge published his report in 1942, he argued that the new social insurance scheme should cover the entire population, in which case the whole population would become entitled to free medical care. This proposal attracted fierce opposition within the medical profession, because it was believed that it would lead to the erosion of private practice and pose a significant threat to medical independence.

This was not the only way in which the Beveridge Report affected the debate over health care. During the inter-war period, the voluntary hospitals had begun to derive an increasing proportion of their income from patients' payments and contributory insurance schemes, but Beveridge's proposals threatened to undermine these sources of income by suggesting that everyone would be covered by the government's social insurance scheme. The British Medical Association also believed that people would be much less inclined to support the voluntary hospitals as charitable institutions in the atmosphere created by what it called 'the government's "free-for-all" propaganda' (Harris, 2004, pp. 294–6).

In view of these difficulties, it is perhaps not surprising that the development of concrete plans for the reform of the country's health services should have proceeded more slowly than the development of plans for educational reform, but it is still important to recognise the importance of the changes that did occur. In February 1944, the Ministry of Health and the Department of Health for Scotland published a joint White Paper in which they set out their initial proposals for the development of a comprehensive system of health care. Although many of the details of these proposals were subsequently changed, the White Paper nevertheless established the basic principles on which the National Health Service would develop after 1948. Its opening paragraph read as follows:

> The Government have announced that they intend to establish a comprehensive health service for everybody in this country. They want to ensure that in future every man and woman and child can rely on getting all the advice and treatment and care which they may need in matters of personal health; that what they get shall be the best medical and other facilities available; that their getting these shall not depend on whether they can pay for them, or on any other factor irrelevant to the real need – the real need being to bring the country's full resources to bear upon reducing ill-health and promoting good health in all its citizens.
>
> (Parliamentary Papers, 1944b, p. 1)

The last of Beveridge's five giants was Squalor. Although significant progress had been made before 1939, many people continued to live in insanitary and overcrowded conditions on the eve of the Second World War, and these problems were exacerbated by the outbreak of hostilities. The war diverted resources from the construction of new housing and it has been estimated that approximately 475,000 homes (out of a total of approximately 11.5 million) were either destroyed or rendered uninhabitable by enemy action. In 1944, the Prime Minister, Winston Churchill, announced plans for the immediate construction of 500,000 prefabricated houses and promised to build 200,000–300,000 permanent homes during the first two years of peace, but the Labour Party promised to build between four and five million new homes, the majority of which would be supplied by local authorities. This marked a reversion to an earlier view of the role of council houses, in which local authorities would build homes for general needs, and not just for the poorest sections of the population (Harris, 2004).

CONTROVERSY AND DEBATE

Consensus and social policy during the Second World War

In 1950, one of the pioneering figures of academic social policy in Britain, Richard Titmuss, published a magisterial survey of the history of social policy during the Second World War. In it, he not only provided a vivid account of the social challenges posed by the war, but also attempted to draw a connection between the events of war and the development of the post-war welfare state. He was particularly impressed by the importance of three critical events in the first year of war: the evacuation of mothers and children in September 1939; the evacuation of British soldiers from Dunkirk; and the Blitz. He claimed that the popular reaction to these three events generated what he called 'the war-warmed impulse of people for a more generous society' (1950, pp. 507–8).

In addition to exploring the specific effect of the Second World War on the development of social policy, Titmuss also attempted to develop a more general theory, based on the ideas of the sociologist, Stanislaw Andrzejewski (1954), about the relationship between war and social policy more generally. In a lecture originally delivered in 1955, he wrote that:

> 'The aims and content of social policy, both in peace and in war, are thus determined – at least to a substantial extent – by how far the cooperation of the masses is essential to the successful prosecution of war. If this cooperation is thought to be essential, then inequalities must be reduced, and the pyramid of social stratification must be flattened' (Titmuss, 1987, p. 111).

While few historians would deny that the war saw some changes in social policy, many have questioned the extent to which all classes and all sections of the population shared Titmuss's concept of a 'war-warmed impulse to a more generous society' (see, for example, Harris, 1981; Macnicol, 1986; Jefferys, 1987). At the same time, it is also clear that the war did have some effect in helping to alert official minds to the extent of existing social problems. As authors of a London County Council survey explained in 1943:

> 'The experience of evacuation has – in advance of the Beveridge Report – brought home to social workers, and indeed to the nation at large, how real and formidable are the giants of Want, Ignorance and Squalor, and how sadly they are hindering, in town and country alike, the well-being of the rising generation' (quoted in Welshman, 1997, p. 53; see also Harris, 2004).

In 1990, Rodney Lowe attempted to reconcile these conflicting accounts by examining the extent of consensus at three different levels: among politicians, within the Civil Service, and among the public at large. He concluded that 'at all levels of society and in each area of welfare policy, consensus – defined as an historically-unusual degree of agreement – was not a mirage in the 1940s' (Lowe, 1990, p. 180). However, he also argued that this was an increasingly passive consensus, and that the failure to develop a more active consensus after 1945 lay at the heart of Britain's problems in the post-war era (pp. 181–2).

- How did the outbreak of war affect the debate over social policy?
- Did it promote the existence of a wartime 'consensus'?
- How radical were the policies that were promoted during the war?
- What impact did these policies have on the development of social policy after 1945?
- What were the limitations of the 'wartime consensus' and how were these reflected in the development of peacetime policies?

Conclusion

At the end of the Second World War, Britain emerged victorious but shattered from six years of hostilities. However, despite these difficulties it also possessed a series of plans for the reform of social policy and the development of what came to be known as the 'welfare state' (Lowe, 2005). These plans provided the initial starting point for many of the policies that are discussed in the following chapters of this book.

Summary

This chapter has examined the history of social welfare provision in Britain from the beginning of the nineteenth century to the end of the Second World War. Although the chapter has recognised the importance of the 'mixed economy of welfare' and the contributions made by the different elements within this mixed economy, including the informal and voluntary sectors, the family, and the market, the main focus has been on the role of the state. This has been reflected in a number of ways, including:

- The acknowledgement of a basic level of responsibility for welfare provision in England and Wales under the Poor Laws of 1597 and 1601.
- The regulation of living and working conditions through such measures as the Factory Acts of 1819, 1825, and 1833, and the introduction of building bye-laws under successive Public Health Acts.
- The provision of public services, such as the development of public education and the expansion of public health service provision.
- The introduction of new forms of income support and other changes in welfare policy as part of the Liberal welfare reforms of 1906–14.
- The introduction of publicly subsidised local authority housing and the gradual expansion of other forms of public welfare provision between 1914 and 1939.
- The emergence of plans for the establishment of a more comprehensive 'welfare state' between 1939 and 1945.

Discussion and review

- In what sense, if any, is it appropriate to talk about the 'Victorian origins of the welfare state' in Britain between circa 1800 and 1870?
- Did the period between 1870 and 1906 witness any important changes in attitudes to the relief of poverty or other aspects of social policy?
- In what ways did the introduction of the Liberal welfare reforms of 1906–14 represent a significant change in the relationship between the state and the individual?

- Why did public expenditure on the social services increase in Britain between 1914 and 1939?
- To what extent did the Beveridge Report and the 'White Paper chase' of 1943–44 lay the foundations of Britain's post-war welfare state?

References

Andrzejewski, S. (1954) *Military Organisation and Society*, Routledge & Kegan Paul, London.

Brewer, J. (1989) *The Sinews of Power: War, Money and the English State, 1688–1783*, Unwin Hyman, London.

Considine, M. and Dukelow, F. (2009) *Irish Social Policy: A Critical Introduction*, Gill & Macmillan, Dublin.

Davin, A. (1996) *Growing Up Poor: Home, School and Street in London 1870–1914*, Rivers Oram Press, London.

Dicey, A.V. (1962) *Lectures on the Relation between Law and Public Opinion in England during the Nineteenth Century*, Macmillan, London (first edition, 1905; second edition first published in 1914).

Edsall, N.C. (1971) *The Anti-Poor Law Movement, 1834–44*, Manchester University Press, Manchester.

Finlayson, G. (1994) *Citizen, State and Social Welfare in Britain 1830–1990*, Oxford University Press, Oxford.

Flinn, M.W. (1965) 'Introduction', in M.W. Flinn (ed.) *Report on the Sanitary Condition of the Labouring Population of Great Britain, by Edwin Chadwick*, Edinburgh University Press, Edinburgh.

Fogel, R.W. (1994) 'Economic growth, population theory, and physiology: the bearing of long-term processes on the making of economic policy', *American Economic Review*, Vol. 84, No. 3, pp. 369–95.

Gilbert, B. (1970) *British Social Policy 1914–39*, Batsford, London.

Hadow, W.H. (1926) *The Education of the Adolescent* (The Hadow Report), The Stationery Office, London.

Harling, P. (1992) 'The power of persuasion: central authority, local bureaucracy and the New Poor Law', *English Historical Review*, Vol. 107, No. 422, pp. 30–53.

Harris, B. (2004) *The Origins of the British Welfare State: Social Welfare in England and Wales, 1800–1945*, Palgrave Macmillan, Basingstoke.

Harris, B. and Bridgen, P. (2007) 'Introduction: the "mixed economy of welfare" and the historiography of welfare provision', in B. Harris and P. Bridgen (eds.) *Charity and Mutual Aid in Europe and North America since 1800*, Routledge, New York.

Harris, J. (1972) *Unemployment and Politics: A Study in English Social Policy 1886–1914*, Clarendon Press, Oxford.

Harris, J. (1977) *William Beveridge: A Biography*, Clarendon Press, Oxford.

Harris, J. (1981) 'Some aspects of social policy in Britain during the Second World War', in W.J. Mommsen (ed.) *The Emergence of the Welfare State in Britain and Germany, 1850–1950*, Croom Helm, London.

Henriques, U. (1979) *Before the Welfare State: Social Administration in Early Industrial Britain*, Longman, London.

Humphries, S. (1981) *Hooligans or Rebels? An Oral History of Working-class Childhood and Youth 1889–1939*, Basil Blackwell, Oxford.

Hurt, J. S. (1979) *Elementary Schooling and the Working Classes 1860–1918*, Routledge & Kegan Paul, London.

Innes, J. (1996) 'The mixed economy of welfare in early-modern England: assessments of the options from Hale to Malthus (c. 1683–1803)', in M. Daunton (ed.) *Charity, Self-interest and Welfare in the English Past*, UCL Press, London.

Jefferys, K. (1987) 'British politics and social policy during the Second World War', *Historical Journal*, Vol. 30, No. 1, pp. 123–44.

Johnson, P. (1996) 'Risk, redistribution and social welfare in Britain from the Poor Law to Beveridge', in M. Danton (ed.) *Charity, Self-interest and Welfare in the English Past*, UCL Press, London.

Jones, K. (1990) *The Making of Social Policy in Britain, 1830–1990*, Athlone, London.

Kidd, A. (1999) *State, Society and the Poor in Nineteenth-century England*, Macmillan, Basingstoke.

Levitt, I. (1988) *Poverty and Welfare in Scotland 1890–1948*, Edinburgh University Press, Edinburgh.

Lewis, J. (1995) *The Voluntary Sector, the State and Social Work in Britain: The Charity Organisation Society/Family Welfare Association since 1869*, Edward Elgar, Aldershot.

Lowe, R. (1990) 'The Second World War, consensus and the foundation of the welfare state', *Twentieth Century British History*, Vol. 1, No. 2, pp. 152–82.

Lowe, R. (2005) *The Welfare State in Britain since 1945*, Palgrave, Basingstoke.

Luddy, M. (1998) 'Religion, philanthropy and the state in late-eighteenth and early-nineteenth century Ireland', in H. Cunningham and J. Innes (eds.) *Charity, Philanthropy and Reform from the 1690s to 1850*, Macmillan, Basingstoke.

Macnicol, J. (1986) 'The effect of the evacuation of schoolchildren on official attitudes to state intervention', in H.L. Smith (ed.) *War and Social Change: British Society in the Second World War*, Manchester University Press, Manchester.

Mitchison, R. (2000) *The Old Poor Law in Scotland: The Experience of Poverty, 1574–1845*, Edinburgh University Press, Edinburgh.

Parliamentary Debates (1908) *Parliamentary Debates*, 4th series, Vol. 190.

Parliamentary Papers (1942) PP 1942-3 Cmd. 6404 vi, 119, *Report by Sir William Beveridge on Social Insurance and Allied Services*.

Parliamentary Papers (1943) PP 1942–3 Cmd. 6458 xi, 21, *Educational Reconstruction*.

Parliamentary Papers (1944a) PP 1943–4 Cmd. 6527 viii, 119, *Employment Policy*.

Parliamentary Papers (1944b) PP 1943–4 Cmd. 6502 viii, 315, Ministry of Health/Department of Health for Scotland, *A National Health Service*.

Pelling, H. (1968) 'The working class and the origins of the welfare state', in H. Pelling, *Popular Politics and Society in Late-Victorian Britain*, Macmillan, London.

Pugh, M. (2002) 'Working-class experience and state social welfare, 1908–1914: old age pensions reconsidered', *Historical Journal*, Vol. 45, No. 4, pp. 775–96.

Roberts, D. (1960) *Victorian Origins of the British Welfare State*, Yale University Press, New Haven, CT.

Roberts, E. (2000) 'The recipients' view of welfare', in J. Bornat, R. Perks, P. Thompson and J. Walmsley (eds.) *Oral History, Health and Welfare*, Routledge, London.

Rose, M. (1966) 'The anti-poor law movement in the north of England', *Northern History*, Vol. 1, pp. 70–91.

Slack, P. (1999) *From Reformation to Improvement: Public Welfare in Early-Modern England*, Clarendon Press, Oxford.

Stevenson, J. and Cook, C. (1994) *Britain in the Depression: Society and Politics 1929–39*, Longman, London.

Szreter, S. (2002a) 'Health, class, place and politics: social capital and collective provision in Britain', *Contemporary British History*, Vol. 16, No. 3, pp. 27–57.

Szreter, S. (2002b) 'A central role for local government? The example of late-Victorian Britain', *History and Policy*, Policy Paper no. 1, available at http://www.historyandpolicy.org/archive/pol-paper-print01.html.

Szreter, S. and Mooney, G. (1998) 'Urbanisation, mortality and the standard of living debate: new estimates of the expectation of life at birth in nineteenth-century British cities', *Economic History Review*, Vol. 51, No. 1, pp. 84–112.

Thane, P. (1982) *The Foundations of the Welfare State*, Longman, London.

Thane, P. (1984) 'The working class and state "welfare" in Britain 1880–1914', *Historical Journal*, Vol. 27, No. 4, pp. 877–900.

Thane, P. (1996) *Foundations of the Welfare State* (2nd edn.), Longman, London.

Titmuss, R.M. (1950) *Problems of Social Policy*, HMSO, London.

Titmuss, R.M. (1987) 'War and social policy', in B. Abel-Smith and K. Titmuss (eds.) *The Philosophy of Welfare: Selected Writings of Richard M. Titmuss*, Allen & Unwin, London.

Welshman, A.J. (1997) 'Evacuation and social policy during the Second World War: myth and reality', *Twentieth Century British History*, Vol. 9, No. 1, pp. 28–53.

Williams, K. (1981) *From Pauperism to Poverty*, Routledge, London.

Further reading

Finlayson, G. (1994) *Citizen, State and Social Welfare in Britain 1830–1990*, Oxford University Press, Oxford. The current chapter has focused on the growth of state welfare provision between 1800 and 1945; this book explores the same issues from the point of view of changes in the voluntary sector.

Fraser, D. (2009) *The Evolution of the British Welfare State: A History of Social Policy since the Industrial Revolution* (4th edn.), Palgrave, Basingstoke. This is the fourth edition of a text that was first published in 1973, and it continues to provide a highly accessible and readable introduction to the history of British social policy.

Harris, B. (2004) *The Origins of the British Welfare State: Social Welfare in England and Wales, 1800–1945*, Palgrave, Basingstoke. This book is designed to provide a comprehensive account of the development of all aspects of British welfare policy. It includes much of the detailed evidence that forms the basis of this chapter.

Lowe, R. (2005) *The Welfare State in Britain since 1945* (3rd edn.), Macmillan, Basingstoke. This book has become the standard academic work on the history of the welfare state in Britain after 1945.

Thane, P. (1996) *Foundations of the Welfare State* (2nd edn.), Longman, London. The first edition of this book was published in 1982. The second edition was thoroughly revised, with the introduction of new material on the relationship between women and welfare and the contribution of the voluntary sector. A distinguishing feature of both editions was the inclusion of international comparisons.

Useful websites

http://www.workhouses.org.uk/ – for much of the nineteenth and early twentieth centuries, the workhouse was one of the central institutions of British social policy. This website provides a fascinating guide to its buildings, inmates, staff, and administrators, even its poets.

http://medphoto.wellcome.ac.uk/ – this website provides access to a range of historical photographs illustrating aspects of nineteenth- and early twentieth-century hospitals.

http://www.nationalarchives.gov.uk/ – this is the website of the UK's National Archives. The Archives include administrative records covering all aspects of welfare history. An increasing number of records are now being made available online.

http://www.historyandpolicy.org – *History and Policy* was founded by a group of historians in 2002 with the explicit aim of using history to address current issues in public policy. This website provides access to a wide range of papers, covering all aspects of welfare policy.

Appendix 1: Prime Ministers and political complexion of governments

1783	William Pitt the Younger (Tory)
1801	Henry Addington (Tory)
1804	William Pitt the Younger (Tory)
1806	Lord Grenville (Whig)
1807	Duke of Portland (Tory)
1809	Spencer Percival (Tory)
1812	Lord Liverpool (Tory)
1820	Accession of King George IV
1827	George Canning (Tory)
1827	Viscount Goderich (Tory)
1828	Duke of Wellington (Tory)
1830	Accession of King William IV
1830	Earl Grey (Whig)
1834	Viscount Melbourne (Whig)
1834	Sir Robert Peel (Tory)
1835	Viscount Melbourne (Whig)
1837	Accession of Queen Victoria
1841	Sir Robert Peel (Tory)
1846	Earl Russell (Liberal)
1852	Earl of Derby (Tory)
1852	Earl of Aberdeen (Tory)
1855	Viscount Palmerston (Liberal)
1858	Earl of Derby (Conservative)
1859	Viscount Palmerston (Liberal)
1865	Earl Russell (Liberal)
1866	Earl of Derby (Conservative)
1868	Benjamin Disraeli (Conservative)
1868	William Ewart Gladstone (Liberal)
1874	Benjamin Disraeli (Conservative)
1880	William Ewart Gladstone (Liberal)
1885	Marquess of Salisbury (Conservative)
1886	William Ewart Gladstone (Liberal)
1886	Marquess of Salisbury (Conservative)
1892	William Ewart Gladstone (Liberal)
1894	Earl of Rosebery (Liberal)
1895	Marquess of Salisbury (Conservative)
1901	Accession of King Edward VII
1902	Arthur James Balfour (Conservative)
1905	Henry Campbell Bannerman (Liberal)
1908	Herbert Henry Asquith (Liberal)
1910	Accession of King George V
1916	David Lloyd George (Coalition)

1922	Andrew Bonar Law (Conservative)
1923	Stanley Baldwin (Conservative)
1924	James Ramsay MacDonald (Labour)
1924	Stanley Baldwin (Conservative)
1929	James Ramsay MacDonald (Labour)
1931	James Ramsay MacDonald (National Government)
1935	Stanley Baldwin (National Government)
1936	Accession and abdication of King Edward VIII; accession of King George VI
1937	Arthur Neville Chamberlain (National Government)
1940	Winston Leonard Spencer Churchill (Coalition)
1945	Clement Richard Attlee (Labour)

Appendix 2: Significant events in politics and social policy

1793–1815: French Revolutionary Wars

1798	First edition of Thomas Malthus's, *An Essay on the Principle of Population*
1799	Introduction of income tax by William Pitt the Younger

1800: Act of Union between Great Britain and Ireland

1802	Temporary suspension of income tax; Health and Morals of Apprentices Act
1816	Withdrawal of income tax
1819	Factory Act
1825	Factory Act
1831	Establishment of the Board of Commissioners for National Education in Ireland
1832	Parliamentary Reform Act
1832	Appointment of Royal Commission on the Poor Laws
1833	Factory Act; Education Grant
1834	Poor Law Amendment Act; formation of Poor Law Commission
1838	Poor Relief (Ireland) Act
1839	Creation of the Privy Council Committee on Education
1842	Reintroduction of income tax
1845	Poor Law (Scotland) Act

1845–47: Irish Potato Famine

1847	Formation of the Poor Law Board
1847	Irish Poor Relief Extension Act
1848	Public Health Act

1853–54: Crimean War

1866	Sanitary Act
1867	Parliamentary Reform Act
1867	Public Health (Scotland) Act
1867	Creation of the Metropolitan Asylums Board
1868	Artisans' and Labourers' Dwellings Act (Torrens Act)
1870	Elementary Education Act (Forster's Act); creation of school boards
1871	Creation of Local Government Board; publication of LGB Circular 20, launching the 'Crusade against Outdoor Relief'
1872	Education (Scotland) Act
1872	Public Health Act, compelling all county boroughs to appoint Medical Officers of Health
1875	Public Health Act; Artisans' and Labourers' Dwellings Improvement Act (Cross Act)
1880	Elementary Education Act (Mundella's Act), making education compulsory throughout England and Wales
1884	Parliamentary Reform Act
1885	Parliamentary Reform Act
1885	Medical Relief (Disqualifications Removal) Act
1886	Chamberlain Circular, authorising the use of public works to relieve unemployment
1890	Housing of the Working Classes Act
1891	Abolition of fees in public elementary schools in England and Wales
1894	Local Government Act (enabled women and non-property-owners to stand for election to Boards of Poor Law Guardians and extended voting rights to all county council and parliamentary electors)
1894	Appointment of the Royal Commission on the Aged Poor

1899–1902: Boer War

1902	Education Act (Balfour's Act), abolishing school boards in England and Wales and transferring their powers and responsibilities to local education authorities
1906	Education (Provision of Meals) Act
1907	Education (Administrative Provisions) Act, authorising the creation of a school medical service
1908	Children Act; Old Age Pensions Act
1908	Education (Scotland) Act (empowering school boards in Scotland to make arrangements for the medical inspection and feeding of school children)
1909	Housing and Town Planning Act; Development and Road Improvement Fund Act; Labour Exchanges Act; Trade Boards Act; introduction of 'People's Budget'
1911	National Insurance Act
1914	Education (Provision of Meals) (Ireland) Act

1914–18: First World War

1915   Introduction of rent controls (Increase of Rent and Mortgage Interest (War Restrictions) Act)

1918   Representation of the People Act (enabled women over the age of 30 to vote in Parliamentary elections)

1918   Maternity and Child Welfare Act

1919   Creation of Ministry of Health; introduction of subsidised housing through the Housing and Town Planning, etc. Act and the Housing (Additional Powers) Act

1920   Unemployment Insurance Act (extension of original scheme to the majority of manual workers and non-manual workers earning less than £250 per year)

1921   Unemployment Insurance Act (introduction of 'uncovenanted' benefit for workers who had exhausted their right to unemployment benefit under the original scheme); Unemployed Workers' Dependants (Temporary Provisions) Act (introduction of allowances for the dependants of unemployed workers)

1922: Creation of the Irish Free State

1923   Chamberlain Housing Act

1924   Wheatley Housing Act

1925   Widows', Orphans' and Old Age Contributory Pensions Act

1926   Publication of the Hadow Report on *The Education of the Adolescent*

1928   Representation of the People Act (extended voting rights to all women over the age of 21, thereby giving women the same entitlement to vote as men)

1929   Widows', Orphans' and Old Age Contributory Pensions Act; Local Government Act (abolishing Boards of Guardians and transferring their powers to local county or county borough councils)

1929   Local Government Acts passed in England and Wales and in Scotland, transferring Poor Law responsibilities to local councils

1930   Greenwood Housing Act

1931   Introduction of transitional payments scheme for workers who had been unemployed for more than 6 months

1932   Town and Country Planning Act

1933   Abolition of Wheatley Act housing subsidies

1934   Creation of Unemployment Assistance Board

1939–45: Second World War

1942   Report on Social Insurance and Allied Services (the Beveridge Report)

1943   White Paper on Educational Reconstruction

1944   Education Act (the Butler Act); White Papers on A National Health
        Service; Employment Policy; and The Control of Land Use
1945   Education (Scotland) Act
1945   Family Allowances Act
1946   National Insurance Act; National Insurance (Industrial Injuries) Act;
        National Health Service Act
1947   Town and Country Planning Act
1948   National Assistance Act

CHAPTER 7

Conservative Governments and the Welfare State Since 1945

Robert M. Page

Learning objectives

- To provide a brief introduction to key elements of Conservative political and social thought
- To consider the One Nation Conservative approach to the welfare state during the Churchill (1955), Eden (1955–57), Macmillan/ Home (1957–64), and Heath (1970–74) eras
- To review Neo Liberal Conservatism and the welfare state during the Thatcher (1979–90) and Major (1990–97) eras
- To explore the emergence of Progressive Civic Conservatism under David Cameron (2005 to present day) and its impact on the social policy agenda of the Conservative/Liberal Democrat Coalition government

Chapter overview

The Conservative Party dominated British government for much of the second half of the twentieth century, and while the most significant welfare reforms are often seen as associated with the post-war Labour government, there have also been major shifts in the direction of policy under the Conservatives. It is therefore important to consider the attitudes and impact of Conservative thinking over the years. This chapter therefore covers the following topics:

- the nature of conservatism;
- One-Nation Conservatism and its role in the post-war period;
- the emergence of a radical Neo-Liberal Conservatism;
- Conservative social policy during the Thatcher and Major governments;
- Conservative approaches to social policy under David Cameron's leadership.

This chapter explores some of the continuities and changes in the Conservative Party's approach to the welfare state during their periods of office since 1945. Before looking at the various post-war Conservative governments and their approach to the welfare state during this period, it is first useful to provide a brief overview of conservatism. In undertaking this task it is important to note that many self-proclaimed conservatives would contend that they do not have any definitive values or beliefs but only general 'dispositions' (see Letwin, 2008). They emphasise their pragmatic approach to economic and social developments, which they contrast with the overt ideologies of their socialist and liberal rivals.

Conservatism

The term 'conservatism' is usually associated with the protection or preservation of the existing social and political order and a reluctance to embrace radical change. Conservatives tend to become most animated or 'reactionary' when they perceive an unwarranted threat to the established order (see Robin, 2011). This defence of the status quo is underpinned by a belief that institutions and practices that have stood the test of time should not be readily abandoned for untested 'modern' alternatives (Scruton, 2013). To understand conservatism more clearly, it is useful to explore conservatives' understanding of a number of key ideas and concepts.

Human nature, human imperfectability, and 'natural' inequalities

Conservatives tend to adopt what they would describe as 'realistic' or 'common sense' views of human nature. While individuals are seen as having a propensity for rational action and selflessness, conservatives believe that these co-exist with baser impulses, which can give rise to selfish and anti-social forms of conduct. Given inherent human frailty, conservatives recognise that it is important to constrain undesirable conduct through the rule of law and the threat of punishment.

Unlike liberals and socialists, conservatives reject the idea that it is possible, through a process of rational action, to 'improve' either individuals or society over time. As a result, they are sceptical of governments that claim to be able to create a more advanced or 'progressive' society (see Gray, 2009).

Conservatives also believe that there are a wide range of 'natural' differences in human characteristics and capacities. As Willetts (1992, p. 111) explains, there are naturally occurring 'inequalities in looks, in intelligence, in talents and prudence. We are not equally good singers or runners. We have different aptitudes'. Such differences are likely to give rise to very different life experiences, with the most talented or 'blessed' likely to achieve levels of wealth and influence that will be denied to the less talented. For conservatives, these 'natural' differences do not justify ameliorative action on the part of government to compensate those who have not been fortunate enough to secure a winning ticket in life's lottery. Religiously minded conservatives also support non-interference of this kind, and believe that secular interventionism might thwart divine intention. From this perspective, prevailing economic and social hierarchies are seen as a reflection of divine will and should be accepted rather than contested.

Although many conservatives would be concerned if levels of economic inequality in society grew to such an extent that they undermined social cohesion, they believe that as long as inequality is kept within bounds (see Dorey, 2011), it can be the servant of both richer and poorer members of society. Allowing the most 'talented' to rise to the top in the economic and political spheres is seen as the optimal way of maintaining prosperity and good governance. Attempts to stifle the more talented on the basis of a principle of social justice or envy would not enhance society and would lead to despotic action by those government officials charged with enforcing greater equality.

Tradition, hierarchy, order, and social change

Conservatives place great store on tradition, believing that it represents 'the aggregated wisdom of generations' (O'Hara, 2011, p. 26). Values and institutions which have stood the test of time and which have been embedded, for example, within the common law or parliamentary conventions are seen as beneficial for both contemporary and future generations of citizens. Although it is acknowledged that these longstanding institutions and practices may have a number of imperfections, they are seen as innately superior to 'modern' blueprints drawn up by any 'expert' body, however knowledgeable.

Conservatives also attach great importance to the preservation of hierarchies within society. For Edmund Burke (1729–97), who is regarded as the father of modern conservatism, the ruling aristocracy had an inalienable and inherent right to rule by virtue of their natural 'superiority' and their long-standing experience of exercising leadership within society. Indeed, one of the reasons that many conservatives have favoured the retention of a hereditary second chamber within Parliament is to ensure that traditions are upheld and that injudicious attempts to modernise society are rebuffed. While some conservatives would support a degree of 'meritocratic' ascendency into the ruling class, they believe this should be a slow and measured process given the perennial danger of evolutionary change escalating into more disruptive and harmful revolutionary action (see Worsthorne, 1978).

Conservatives attach great importance to the maintenance of social order within society. Social order based on the rule of law is seen as a prerequisite for the exercise of personal freedom. Unlike liberals, who believe that the exercise of authority should be a matter of negotiation between free individuals, conservatives prefer to rely on tried and tested methods in which authority is vested in those adjudged best able, on grounds of long-established status, to exercise power. In short, there is a natural demarcation between those who enforce the rules and those who are expected to abide by them. As Heywood (2007, p. 77) notes, 'In schools authority should be exercised by the teacher, in the workplace by the employer, and in society at large, by government. Conservatives believe that authority is necessary and beneficial as everyone needs the guidance, support and security of knowing "where they stand" and what is expected of them'. Importantly, those whose role it is to receive instructions are deemed to gain as much benefit from this process as those issuing them.

One might assume that conservatives would automatically be opposed to all change. Indeed, the conservative voice often comes to the fore during periods of rapid change or transition, as when Burke counseled against the harmful consequences of the French Revolution in the eighteenth century. However, although conservatives are generally reluctant to embrace change, particularly when it is advocated on ideological grounds, they acknowledge that no society can ever be static and that 'non-harmful' adjustments to the status quo should be regarded as legitimate provided that they reflect the grain of national sentiment. Although such change might result in the loss of some cherished traditions and practices, many conservatives would caution against trying to reinstate the past, believing that the focus should always be on adapting to new circumstances.

CONTROVERSY AND DEBATE

Is conservatism ideological?

Many conservatives contend that their approach to politics and government is essentially pragmatic. They seek to respond to social and economic change in ways that best preserve deeply embedded national values such as personal freedom and that allow the continued flourishing of tried and tested social institutions such as Parliament and the established church.

Do you think that such self-assessments are valid or do they merely serve to deflect attention away from more critical scrutiny of the Conservative Party's underlying 'ideological' approach to social and economic questions?

The individual, society, democracy, and the role of government

Conservatives believe in the freedom of the individual and have opposed attempts by collectivists to impose constraints on the ability of citizens to make meaningful choices and follow a particular life course within the rule of law. They recognise, however, that individuals operate within group contexts and that personal actions are undertaken within an existing social order based on custom and tradition and a complex system of rights and responsibilities. Accordingly, individual action cannot be divorced from the norms and mores of a pre-existing community, which helps to shape personal conduct. Children cannot be expected, for example, to develop their individuality in isolation or without the assistance of their family and their local neighbourhood (see Scruton, 2001).

Conservatives have been highly supportive of the notion of 'society', believing that it amounts to something far more than the statistical aggregation of the individuals within it. Society is seen as a delicate, evolving organism in which all individuals have a unique and vital role to play. It is hardly surprising, therefore, that many conservatives expressed concern when Mrs Thatcher appeared to question whether there was any such thing as society in an interview for *Women's Own* in 1987.

Given their belief in hierarchy, order, and tradition, conservatives have tended to be lukewarm supporters of democracy, fearing that it could give rise to undesirable outcomes. In particular, conservatives fear that democracy might lead to the transfer of power from a wise and knowledgeable elite to an ill-educated, uninformed 'mass'. They have been concerned that any extension of democracy to the 'ordinary' citizen might lead to attempts to redistribute wealth from the responsible rich to the irresponsible poor, or, worse, the 'election' of an authoritarian populist who might be willing to overturn historic freedoms and the rule of law. On the other hand, it has been recognised in some conservative circles that increased democracy can help to forestall social unrest and prevent revolutionary forms of change. By granting 'ordinary' citizens a voice in the political process, conservatives were able to demonstrate that they are responsive to the aspirations of less privileged members of society. Disraeli's (1804–81) decision to accede to working-class demands for greater political representation in the nineteenth century is a case in point (see Blake, 1998; Charmley, 2008).

The conservative approach to the role of government is also highly nuanced. On the one hand, they believe that the government has a positive role to play in society in preserving cherished institutions and upholding tradition as well as protecting the vulnerable and maintaining social order. However, conservatives are always alert to the possibility that governments can over-extend themselves and act in authoritarian ways that threaten ancient liberties and communal bonds. In particular, they fear the prospect of a highly centralised socialist government that might exercise control in ways that threaten the free market, local autonomy, and mutual forms of activity.

Private property and the market

The ability to own and dispose of property is a cherished conservative value. Private property, such as a home or some other possession, is seen as an integral part of an individual's 'character' or 'personality', and is seen as the bedrock of family life. The aspiration to own property is seen as a natural human desire, as is a general willingness to work hard to achieve such rewards. Extensive private ownership is also seen as a way of ensuring that government has limited control over the nation's wealth.

Conservatives accept that disparities in talent, ability, and endeavour will give rise to an unequal distribution of wealth. They see no reason why government should interfere in this 'natural' state of affairs, not least because any proposed remedies will cause more harm than good. Ownership, however, is seen as entailing certain responsibilities and obligations. Someone who inherits an historic estate should see it as their duty to maintain the property and its contents. They should also be mindful that their desire to maximise their personal enjoyment of their property does not result in actions that might have a detrimental impact on their neighbours or on the wider community.

Conservatives have also been highly supportive of the free market, believing that it represents the best means for generating wealth. Markets are seen as being responsive to changes in consumer preferences through price signals, which enable them to adapt to potential gains and losses. Market mechanisms and outcomes are favoured as they reflect mutually beneficial forms of spontaneous activity, rather than constraining forms of collective planning. Market activity can also contribute to social stability by ensuring that workers do not press for unrealistic wage increases because of the prospect of unemployment, while producers will be wary of increasing their prices because of the fear of losing customers. Conservative support for the free market is, however, contingent rather than absolute. It is recognised that market activity needs to be regulated, controlled, and sometimes overridden to ensure that it does not result in detrimental effects on other non-marketable aspects of social life.

While all of these interrelated themes can be said to form part of conservatism, political Conservatives are likely to disagree on the relative weight that they would place on any particular element. Indeed, their emphasis on pragmatism will, it is contested, mean that certain elements of conservatism will be prioritised over others at a particular point in time. Moreover, it should be noted that a conservative may hold an apparently contradictory mixture of libertarian, authoritarian, and paternalistic views on social and economic issues simultaneously (see Green, 2002). This propensity to 'pick and mix' makes it difficult to make definitive judgements about the precise ideological underpinning of any particular post-war Conservative government. However, it is possible to identify particular strands of Conservative thinking in the post-1945 era that have distinctive 'dispositional' combinations (see Table 7.1).

> **STOP AND THINK**
>
> How useful is it to try and categorise conservatism in the way outlined in Table 7.1?

Table 7.1 Post 1945 'strands' of British Conservatism

Themes	One Nation Conservatives	Neo-liberal Conservatives	Progressive Civic Conservatives
Approach	Pragmatic 'accommodation'	(Counter)-revolutionary	'Enterprising'
Representative figures	Butler, Macleod, Macmillan, Gilmour	Powell, Joseph, Thatcher, Redwood	Cameron, Letwin, Willetts
Role of the state	Pragmatic	Limited	Enabling/funding
Economic interventionism	Contingent support	Minimum possible	Minimum possible
Social expenditure/ welfare state	Contingent support	Tightly controlled/ opposed	Tightly controlled/ sceptical
Economic inequality	Bounded	Unbounded	Unbounded
Role of civil society/ voluntarism	Integral	Supportive	Pivotal
Primacy of individual or society	Society	Individual	Individual and society
Approach to tradition/ hierarchy	Supportive	Case by case basis	Contingent support
Maintenance of social order	Strong	Pivotal	Strong
Lifestyles and family relationships	Traditional	Traditional	Liberal
Commitment to One Nation ethos	Pivotal	Contingent	Strong
Duty to be prioritised over rights?	Yes	Yes	Yes

Conservative governments and the welfare state since 1945

A number of authors have attempted to identify distinctive 'ideological' strands in post-1945 Conservatism (see Hickson, 2005; Garnett and Hickson, 2009; Dorey, 2011). For the purposes of this chapter, the discussion will focus, initially, on One Nation Conservatism (ONC) that held sway during the Churchill (1951–55), Eden (1955–56), and Macmillan/Home (1957–64) governments, and to a lesser extent during the Heath government (1970–74). The Thatcher (1979–90) and Major (1990–97) governments pursued what can be described as a Neo-Liberal Conservative (NLC) path, while the current Conservative-led coalition government of David Cameron (2010 to present) developed a 'Progressive Civic Conservative' (PCC) approach in opposition but found it difficult to apply this strategy once in government.

'One Nation' Conservatism and the welfare state, 1951–64

The failure of the Conservatives to win the 1945 general election despite having the wartime leader Winston Churchill at the helm provided modernisers such as Hailsham and Butler with convincing evidence that the Party must cast off its image as a movement associated with appeasement, privilege, and *laissez-faire*. They attempted to persuade Churchill, who continued to lead the Conservatives until 1955, to provide a clearer statement of the Party's principles and aims so that the Party could return to government at the earliest opportunity. Churchill responded by appointing an industrial committee under R.A. Butler (who had successfully introduced the wartime Education Act in 1944). The Committee published *The Industrial Charter* in 1947 (Conservative and Unionist Central Office, 1947). The Charter attempted to convince potential voters that the Conservatives were no longer to be regarded as old-fashioned economic liberals, but rather as pragmatic modernisers who acknowledged that judicious forms of government economic interventionism could bolster rather than undermine a 'free enterprise' economy. Crucially, the Charter also emphasised the Party's determination to maintain positive relations with the trade unions. This latter theme was underlined in a pre-election publication, *The Right Road for Britain*, in 1949 (Conservative and Unionist Central Office, 1949), as was another equally important notion, namely, that the Conservatives were fully supportive of the 'new social services' introduced by Labour.

A second, albeit much narrower, defeat in the 1950 general election persuaded nine newly elected Conservative backbench MPs (including future luminaries such as Iain Macleod, Enoch Powell, and Edward Heath) to establish the One Nation Group in an effort to press on with the Party's modernising agenda (see Walsha, 2000, 2003). One of the first tasks of the group was to provide a clearer understanding of the Conservative approach to social policy for the Conservative Political Centre. The resulting pamphlet, *One*

Nation: A Tory Approach to Social Problems (Macleod and Maude, 1950), was supportive of a minimal state safety net for all citizens, but remained opposed to Labour's promotion of standardised welfare provision for all citizens (universalism), which they deemed to be too expensive, poorly targeted, and a threat to the virtues of thrift and personal responsibility.

The One Nation Group used this pamphlet to illustrate their distinctive approach to social policy. This included, for example, the greater involvement of the private sector in providing homes for rent or purchase. They also stressed the importance of cost containment in the NHS by the use of rigorous need assessments and by the greater use of charging for certain services.

Before examining the development of One Nation Conservatism in practice between 1951 and 1964, it is useful to distinguish between the One Nation *Group* and One Nation *Conservatism* (see Seawright, 2005, 2010). The former was comprised of a diverse range of politicians whose enthusiasm for state intervention and the welfare state ranged from the sceptical to the pragmatic to the positive. Among its members were politicians who were to become more closely associated with neo-liberal ideas such as Enoch Powell, Geoffrey Howe, and Keith Joseph. These politicians were keen to ensure that increased forms of state activity did not undermine traditional Conservative commitments to a stable currency, increased efficiency, low taxation, thrift, self-reliance, voluntarism or charitable activity. In contrast, the term One Nation *Conservatism* is associated with members of the One Nation Group, such as Butler, Macleod, and Macmillan, who were more enthusiastic about the role that government action could play in post-war Britain and who believed that Conservative governments should intervene to secure full employment and protect the welfare state. The Macmillan-led governments from 1957 to 1963 tend to be regarded as exemplars of One Nation Conservatism, although the short-lived Eden administration was also sympathetic to this approach. The initial shift towards One Nation Conservatism during the Churchill government of 1951–55 could, however, be said to have occurred despite the lack of any notable enthusiasm by the then Prime Minister.

Modern One Nation Conservatism in practice

The depth of the Conservative commitment to the welfare state was quickly tested following their narrow election victory in 1951, which left them with an overall majority of just 17 seats. Faced with a substantial balance of payments deficit that had triggered international speculation against the pound, the incoming Chancellor, R.A. Butler, decided to cut imports, tighten monetary policy, and review public expenditure commitments (Boxer, 1996). Although a number of cost-containment measures were introduced, such as the introduction of NHS charges and a reduction in the school building programme, Butler's commitment to One Nation Conservatism dissuaded him from making any draconian cuts in the welfare budget (Bridgen and Lowe, 1998).

The appointment of more interventionist ministers in areas such as health (Macleod, 1952–55) and education (Eccles, 1954–57) served to confirm the ascendency of One Nation Conservatism during the administrations of both Churchill and Eden. Over time, a distinctive One Nation approach towards the welfare state, involving targeting, tighter spending controls, and increased reliance on charging (Raison, 1990) gradually took shape. In particular, One Nation Conservatives were keen to distance themselves from Labour's 'socialist' agenda. The establishment of the Phillips Committee (1953) on the Economic and Financial Problems of Provision for Old Age and the Guillebaud enquiry into the costs of the NHS (Guillebaud, 1953) were prompted by a desire of One Nation Conservatives to distance themselves from Labour's 'profligate' and egalitarian approach to the welfare state. Although they wanted to reassure the electorate that they had no covert plans to dismantle the welfare state, they were equally determined to show that they would not follow Labour's socialist agenda. This was made clear in the Party's general election manifesto of 1955.

We denounce the Labour Party's desire to use the social services, which we all helped to create, as an instrument for levelling down. We regard social security, not as a substitute for family thrift, but as a necessary basis or supplement to it. We think of the National Health Service as a means, not of preventing anyone from paying anything for any service, but of ensuring that proper attention and treatment are denied to no one. We believe that equality of opportunity is to be achieved, not by sending every boy and girl to exactly the same kind of school, but by seeing that every child gets the schooling most suited to his or her aptitudes. We see a sensible housing policy in terms, not of one hopeless Council waiting list, but of adequate and appropriate provision both for letting and for sale.

(Conservative Party, 1955)

Implementation of a One Nation Conservative social policy from 1951 to 1964 involved fulfilling a commitment to speed up the construction of new homes (over 300,000 houses were built in 1954), cutting out wasteful expenditure, introducing charges for some NHS services, whilse protecting vulnerable groups such as pensioners (the basic retirement pension rose by 50 per cent in real terms between 1951 and 1964). Balancing traditional Conservative concerns such as low taxes and price stability with social imperatives, such as the maintenance of full employment and support for the welfare state, proved difficult for One Nation ministers, not least given persistent Treasury demands to reduce social expenditure. The Macmillan government's One Nation credentials were regularly put to the test, not least when the Chancellor, Peter Thorneycroft, demanded welfare cuts of £153 million in 1958 to stem inflationary pressures and restore international confidence in the pound. The Cabinet's rejection of this request led to the resignation of the Chancellor and two of his junior cabinet colleagues (Enoch Powell and Nigel Birch). A subsequent sterling crisis in 1961 led the Treasury once again to demand cuts in welfare expenditure. An internal Party review entitled *The Future of the Social Services* (1961–63) suggested that the universal state pension should be withdrawn and that fees for state schooling should be introduced to ease growing financial pressures. Although these proposals were rejected on the grounds that they would compromise the One Nation credentials of the Macmillan government, alternative cost-cutting measures, such as higher health and social security contributions and increased council house rents were introduced (see Bridgen and Lowe, 1998).

Macmillan's resignation as Prime Minister on health grounds in 1963 signalled the end of the high point of One Nation Conservatism. The Party's defeat in the subsequent general election under the leadership of Alec Douglas-Home led to a reappraisal of the One Nation strategy. By the time the Conservatives were next in government in 1970, there were clear signs that the Party was becoming more receptive to neo-liberal ideas in an era of increased economic and social turbulence.

Tiptoeing towards neo-liberalism? The 'One Nation' Conservative government of Edward Heath, 1970–74

Although Edward Heath's personal sympathies were clearly those of a One Nation Conservative, he was willing to consider the selective introduction of neo-liberal forms of economic and social policy on the grounds that these might prove more effective and efficient in the next stage of the modernisation of British society.

The clearest indication that the Conservative Party was becoming more receptive to neo-liberal ideas relating to economic and social policy came at a pre-election Party conference held at the Selsdon Park Hotel in south-east London in 1970. A range of 'neo-liberal' measures were considered, including tax cuts, curbs on trade union powers, reduced government support for failing industries, and the end to prices and incomes policies. On the welfare front, the need for increased targeting of resources was suggested, as was the imposition of charges for non-medical NHS provision such as food and accommodation. This prospective change of direction led the Labour leader, Harold Wilson, to coin the phrase 'Selsdon man' in an effort to portray the Conservatives as the Neanderthal, hard-hearted, enemies of full employment, the welfare state, and economic interventionism.

After securing victory in the 1970 general election, Heath was able to experiment with a neo-liberal economic agenda. This included a pledge by the new Minister of Trade and Industry, John Davies, to put a stop to the use of taxpayers' money to bail out 'lame-duck' industries, and attempts to tackle 'excessive' trade union power by the introduction of industrial relations courts in an attempt to regulate strike action by enforcing ballots and mandatory cooling-off periods. However, in the face of inflationary pressures, rising unemployment, and the possibility of bankruptcy at both Rolls Royce and

Upper Clyde shipbuilders, Heath performed his famous 'U' turn and reverted to an interventionist strategy more in keeping with One Nation Conservatism.

In terms of social policy there was no unilateral shift to an explicitly neo-liberal approach. However, neo-liberal influences were coming to the fore. In the field of social security, the Secretary of State, Keith Joseph, abandoned plans, for example, to increase the level of universal family allowances, opting instead to introduce a targeted means-tested benefit to boost the incomes of low-paid workers – family income supplement. In housing, rent subsidies were targeted at poorer tenants in both the privately and publicly rented sectors, rather than, as previously, being used by local authorities to subsidise the rents of all council house tenants (the 1972 Housing Finance Act). Set against this, a number of Conservative reforms in this era were more in keeping with a One Nation approach. In health, for example, the Conservatives embarked on a costly administrative reform that was intended to bring about greater unification within the NHS (The National Health Service Reorganisation Act, 1973). The Education Secretary, Margaret Thatcher, pressed ahead with an interventionist agenda, presiding as she did over a £132 million investment in primary school buildings, the raising of the school leaving age to 16, the expansion of comprehensive schooling, and the introduction of the Open University.

> **STOP AND THINK**
>
> Did the Heath government of 1970–74 continue along a One Nation Conservative path in relation to social policy?

Consecutive general election defeats for Edward Heath in February and October 1974 served to strengthen the neo-liberal voice within the Conservative Party. One of the key protagonists was Keith Joseph, who had once been regarded as a One Nation Conservative. By the mid 1970s, however, he had pinned his colours firmly to the neo-liberal mast, famously declaring that he had only recently discovered what true Conservatism entailed (see Denham and Garnett, 2002). He established a think tank – the Centre for Policy Studies – in 1974 with the support of Alfred Sherman, Nigel Vinson, and Margaret Thatcher, and made a series of influential speeches in Upminster, Preston, and Birmingham, in which he drew attention to the need for a non-interventionist economic policy based on the free market economy and a focus on the control of inflation rather than the level of unemployment (see Sherman, 2007). In terms of social policy, Joseph questioned the effectiveness of the welfare state, believing that its continuing 'generosity' was giving rise to what came to be known as a 'dependency' culture. He was also highly critical of the so-called permissive society, which, he argued, was leading to a to a growth in 'dysfunctional' single motherhood within working-class communities.

When Heath decided to seek re-election as leader of the Conservative Party in 1975, Joseph was expected to stand against him on an anti-collectivist platform. However, he eventually decided against this course of action, in part because of adverse publicity surrounding a speech he gave in Birmingham, in which he appeared to condone the compulsory sterilisation of 'unfit' adolescent working-class mothers, leaving the way open for Margaret Thatcher to take up the neo-liberal mantle. After defeating Heath in the first ballot for the Conservative leadership, Thatcher saw off challenges from Whitelaw, Howe, Prior, and Peyton in the second round of the contest to become leader of the Conservative Party, and subsequently Prime Minister at the May 1979 general election winning a 43 seat majority.

Neo-liberal Conservatism takes hold: the Thatcher governments and the welfare state, 1979–90

During the 11½ years of her premiership, Margaret Thatcher pursued a broadly neo-liberal economic and social agenda. Although some influential neo-liberals remained critical of her cautious, almost 'Fabian' style approach during her Downing Street years, it is generally accepted that Thatcher succeeded in overhauling the post-war welfare state 'settlement', paving the way for greater private and voluntary sector involvement in service provision and lowered public expectations about the role and capacity of state collectivism.

In her first two terms (1979–83 and 1983–87), Thatcher's focus was primarily on the regeneration of the British economy along neo-liberal lines. In practice, this took the form of bringing inflation under control through 'proper monetary discipline', reducing direct state involvement in industry through closures and privatisation, curbing trade union powers and privileges, and reducing personal taxes.

Although Thatcher did not embark on an all-out attack on the welfare state in her first two terms, it would be misleading to underestimate the importance of the policy changes that were introduced in this era. There was a continuous drive to curb social expenditure. In the area of social security, for example, the earnings-related elements of unemployment and sickness benefits were abolished in Thatcher's first term and benefits to striking workers were reduced. This was followed up by a major second term review (the so-called Fowler Reviews) of social security expenditure in the areas of pensions, housing benefit, supplementary benefits, and provision for children and young people. The aim was to ensure that spending was controlled and targeted on those in greatest need. Although this review and subsequent legislation (the 1986 Social Security Act) did not generate significant short-term savings for the Treasury, the changes (such as the introduction of a less generous State Earnings Related Pension Scheme) did at least curb the *rate* of expenditure growth.

Thatcher proceeded more cautiously in terms of health reforms given its deep-rooted public support. First term changes included the abolition of the Health Services Board, which the previous Labour government had created to phase out NHS pay beds and to regulate private hospitals. Private health care was also to be boosted by restoring tax relief for occupational medical insurance schemes. During the second term, more business-like measures began to be introduced into the NHS. Health authorities were given annual efficiency savings targets, and performance indicators were introduced so that they could cross-compare their performance in relation to length of hospital stays, treatment costs, and waiting times. Competitive tendering processes were introduced for some non-medical services such as cleaning, catering, and laundry with the intention of driving down costs. Following an enquiry by Roy Griffiths (the then Managing Director of the Sainsbury's supermarket chain), private sector management structures were also introduced into the operation of the service in 1983. It was envisaged that a new breed of public sector managers, who would focus more sharply on efficiency and effectiveness, would drive the service forward. These managers would concentrate on the needs of service users, who were now to be regarded as demanding customers rather than passive patients.

It was in housing, arguably, that the most overt form of neo-liberal social policy emerged. The sale of council housing was undertaken with the clear intention of halting the post-war collectivist advance. Under the 1980 Housing Act, council house tenants of at least three years' standing were given the right to buy their home at a discounted price. Not surprisingly, the scheme proved popular with those tenants who could afford to buy their own home. Those who remained as tenants were faced, however, with rising rents as central government subsidies were gradually withdrawn.

Given Keith Joseph's tenure as Secretary of State for Education for the majority of the first two terms of the Thatcher governments (1981–86), one might have expected equally dramatic changes in this area of social policy. Although his predecessor, Mark Carlisle, had introduced an assisted places scheme that allowed 'bright children from modest backgrounds' to study at an independent (private) school on a subsidised basis, Joseph found it difficult to devise administratively workable and politically acceptable school and university reforms of a neo-liberal kind, such as school vouchers (which would enable parents to exercise greater choice in selecting a secondary school for their child) or student loans. Indeed, Joseph's attempt to secure savings of £39 million by requiring high earning parents to contribute towards their children's university tuition had to be withdrawn in the face of vociferous parental and backbench opposition. In addition, Joseph's desire to improve educational standards through the greater use of teacher appraisals and school inspections brought him into persistent conflict with the teaching unions.

Margaret Thatcher (1995) considered her Party's general election manifesto of 1987 to be the finest the Conservatives had ever produced, even though it only hinted at the more extensive welfare reform agenda that would be pursued in government. Soon after the election, constant post-election criticism about ward closures and cancelled operations in NHS hospitals prompted Thatcher to establish an NHS review team consisting of herself, four other ministers (John Moore, Tony Newton, Nigel Lawson, and John Major), three deputy secretaries, and a number of policy unit advisors. The idea that the service should be dismantled was rejected, not least because the Chancellor still believed it to be highly effective in terms of containing health care costs (see Lawson, 1992). Accordingly, it was decided to create an internal market within the NHS that would aim to constrain costs by means of competitive pressures. In the future, hospitals and other providers would need to deliver competitively priced, high-quality services if they were to secure contracts from purchasers such as District Health Authorities and GP fund holders. Although these proposals were opposed by both the Labour opposition and the British Medical Association, the Health Secretary, Kenneth Clarke, pressed ahead with the implementation of the National Health Service and Community Care Act 1990 without making any significant concessions.

The community care reforms contained in this Act were also highly significant in pressing ahead with the government's neo-liberal agenda in the field of social policy (see also Chapter 13). Following influential reports from the Audit Commission (1986) and Roy Griffiths (1988), which had examined the rapid increase in social security spending on residential care (the costs had increased from £10 million in 1979 to some £2 billion by 1991), it was decided to transfer budgetary responsibility for the care of older people from the social security system to local authorities in an effort to contain costs. Crucially, the provider role of local authorities was to be supplanted by 'non-state' providers. The Act stipulated that while local authorities would be required to assess the needs of elderly people and prepare community care plans, they would be obliged to contract out the provision of services to private and voluntary organisations. As Glennerster (2007, p. 191) points out, 'the reform of community care thus fitted into what was now emerging as the common pattern of social policy reforms in the Thatcher period – continued state funding but a variety of forms of private and public providers'.

The education reforms that had been trailed in the manifesto were implemented with the passage of the Education Reform Act (1988). One of the main rationales for the change was to shift power away from local authorities and teachers towards parents. A ten-subject National Curriculum was introduced for all state schools. In addition, national testing for all pupils aged 7, 11, 14, and 16 was introduced to determine the extent to which attainment levels (knowledge, skills, and understanding) had been achieved. These test results were widely publicised so that parents could readily compare the performance of individual schools. The Act also enabled schools to apply for 'grant-maintained' status. Such grant-maintained schools could opt out of local authority control (after a parental ballot), receiving their funds directly from the Department of Education. Non-grant-maintained schools were also to be granted greater autonomy. Under a local management of schools initiative, head teachers and governors were to be given greater control over expenditure and staff appointments. Privately sponsored (but largely state-funded) city technology colleges were also to be set up in an effort to create centres of educational excellence in educationally disadvantaged neighbourhoods.

Third term developments in the areas of social security and housing were less dramatic. Given that many of the previous reforms in social security introduced by Norman Fowler during the second term needed time to take root, there were no major policy changes. However, the policy direction of the new Secretary of State, John Moore, remained firmly neo-liberal. He attacked the growth of the 'dependency' culture by compelling 16- and 17-year-olds to undertake youth training rather than subsist on income support. His preference for selectivity rather than universalism was reflected in his decision to freeze the level of child benefit (a universal benefit) for three consecutive years (1988–91).

In housing, the desire to reduce the state's role in construction, ownership, administration, and regulation remained paramount. Under the 1988 Housing Act, private landlords or Housing Associations were permitted to take over the running of council housing in a given locality, if supported by existing tenants by means of a ballot. Housing Action Trusts were encouraged, rent controls were abolished, and landlords were able to let property on an 'assured' or shorthold basis. Tenants ineligible for housing benefit faced steep rises in rents as a result of the withdrawal of central government subsidies and the prohibition of local authority rent subsidies. In practice, these reforms had only limited success with, for example, only five Housing Action Trusts having been established by 1994, and although some council stock passed from local authorities to alternative landlords, this was rarely the result of so-called 'Tenants' Choice'.

Consolidating the revolution: the Major governments and the welfare state, 1990–97

Margaret Thatcher's position as Prime Minister and leader of the Conservative Party appeared unassailable after her third successive victory in the 1987 general election. Within three years, however, she had been forced out of both positions as a result of a growing internal unease occasioned by an economic downturn, the highly unpopular poll tax (which had replaced the household rating system by an individual tax), and ministerial resignations including Michael Heseltine, Leon Brittan, Norman Tebbit, Nigel Lawson, Norman Fowler, Peter Walker, Nicholas Ridley and, finally, her longest serving minister, Geoffrey Howe (after yet another anti-European speech by the Prime Minister, for which she was becoming renowned). Following a 'stalking horse' leadership challenge from Sir Anthony Meyer in 1989, which she won easily, Thatcher only achieved a relatively narrow victory over Michael Heseltine in a subsequent contest (Thatcher polled 204 votes to Heseltine's 152). Acknowledging that she had lost the support of her 'friends and allies' in the Party (Thatcher, 1995, p. 885), she resigned.

STOP AND THINK

Did Mrs Thatcher modernise or dismantle the welfare state?

After succeeding Thatcher in November 1990, John Major was faced with the unenviable task of trying to secure a fourth consecutive electoral victory for his Party within just two years, having inherited an array of policy dilemmas. He decided to focus on three key issues. First, he attempted to revive the economy. Although his new Chancellor, Norman Lamont, managed to lower both inflation and interest rates, unemployment remained persistently high. Second, he sought to placate the so-called 'Eurosceptics' in his Party by securing an EU 'opt out' for Britain in relation to some areas of social policy (the Social Chapter), minimum wage regulation, and the exchange rate mechanism. Third, the poll tax dilemma was resolved by Major's new environment secretary, Michael Heseltine, who drew up plans to introduce a new, 'fairer', eight-banded property-based tax to take effect from 1993. In the interim, the adverse financial impact on poll tax payers was mitigated by means of a £4.5 billion injection of Treasury funds.

During his first period of office (1990–92), Major also attempted to enhance the welfare state through the introduction of the Citizens' Charter in 1991. Under this initiative, service providers were required to devise independently monitored performance targets and respond more effectively to user complaints and provide redress where appropriate (see Lowe, 2005).

Major's success in steadying the Conservative ship by the time of the 1992 general election did not involve, however, any decisive shift away from the neo-liberal agenda of his predecessor. The Party promised a renewed commitment to the pursuit of price stability, public expenditure restraint, prudent tax reductions, balanced budgets, further privatisation and deregulation, and unequivocal support for the free market (Conservative Party, 1992, p. 5). While Major was fully supportive of Thatcher's neo-liberal welfare reforms, he recognised the importance of reassuring the public that the NHS would continue to be properly funded and that child benefit would continue to be paid to families on a universal basis.

Despite widespread predictions that the Conservatives would lose the 1992 general election, Major achieved his short-term objective of securing a further general election victory for his Party. He achieved more votes than any party had hitherto achieved, although this only gave him an overall majority of 21 seats.

The main objective of the new Major administration was to consolidate the third term reforms. This proved difficult given the gloomy economic prognosis. The Chancellor, Norman Lamont, had to grapple with the fallout from the British withdrawal from the exchange rate mechanism on 'Black Wednesday' (16 September 1992), when costly, but ultimately futile attempts were made to prop up the value of the pound. Lamont was also faced with a projected budgetary deficit of £50 billion in 1993.

The deteriorating state of the public finances led to significant pressure to reduce the social security budget. Responding to a Treasury review of welfare spending in 1993, which identified areas where the government might target resources more effectively or even withdraw funding completely, the Social Security Secretary, Peter Lilley (1992–97) introduced a number of reforms that were intended to bring spending under control. The eligibility criteria for a number of benefits were tightened or changed. For example, a new incapacity benefit was introduced in 1993. It included a more stringent 'work test', which, it was hoped, would secure a 7 per cent reduction in claimant numbers. Tougher benefit rules were introduced for asylum seekers and a less generous housing benefit scheme was developed. The value of the State Earnings Related Pension Scheme (SERPS) was reduced, and it was agreed to raise the pension age for women to 65 (from 60) with effect from 2010. Lone parent benefit rates were also frozen in 1996 (Timmins, 2001). Arguably, the most significant change made by Lilley was the introduction of the jobseeker's allowance in 1996, which 'halved the entitlement to non-means-tested benefit from twelve months to six and merged it with income support for the unemployed' (Timmins, 2001, p. 528). In order to encourage more rapid returns to the job market, those seeking this form of assistance were required to clearly demonstrate that they were actively seeking work.

Major's emphasis on consolidation was far from straightforward. The Education Reform Act of 1988 had, for example, elements of both decentralisation and centralisation. In terms of the former, schools were encouraged to become more autonomous by opting for grant-maintained status, as discussed above. Those that decided to remain under local education authority control were also to be given greater budgetary discretion under the Local Management of Schools (LMS) initiative. In the case of the latter, the government introduced a national curriculum, the systematic testing of pupils, 'performance' league tables, and an enhanced inspection system. Teachers were sceptical of the merits of all of these proposals. For example, after a protracted dispute with the government a compromise agreement was drawn up by the new head of a School Curriculum and Assessment Authority, Sir Ron Dearing, who recommended a reduction in the national curriculum and more limited forms of testing. The grant-maintained initiative for primary and secondary schools also proved problematic. Despite financial incentives, only around 4 per cent of all schools had acquired grant-maintained status by the time of the 1997 general election.

There were fewer 'consolidation' problems in the sphere of housing. A further 300,000 council houses were sold off in this period, while some 170,000 tenants acquired a new landlord under the large-scale voluntary transfer of council housing. Housing Associations became firmly established as the largest providers of 'social' housing, while 'deregulation' appeared to boost the supply of privately rented housing. By 1996, around 2.1 million households were renting privately, compared with 1.7 million in 1988 (Timmins, 2001).

Major's desire to return to more traditional 'common sense' approaches to the remedying of contemporary social problems led him to launch an ill-fated 'back to basics' campaign in October 1993, which aimed to challenge some of the allegedly unworldly forms of left-wing theorising that professionals were applying in areas such as criminal justice, health, education, and social work. In practice, much to Major's dismay, the media interpreted this initiative as an attempt to restore greater personal morality in society. The highly publicised failings of his ministers to provide moral leadership of this kind left Major's initiative in tatters and raised doubts about his ability to control the news agenda. He was also finding it difficult to restrain the Eurosceptic wing of his Party. Faced with constant attacks on his leadership, Major opted to stand for re-election as Party leader in June 1995. Although he secured a comfortable victory over his only rival, John Redwood, this did little to shore up his position. With declining popular support and the arrival of a vibrant 'New' Labour leader, Tony Blair, Major suffered a resounding defeat in the

1997 general election. The Conservatives lost 182 seats and could only muster 31 per cent of the popular vote.

Following Major's defeat in the 1997 general election, the Conservatives spent over a decade in the political wilderness. They seemed unable to readjust to the post-Thatcher era, and not least New Labour's determination to hold on to the 'centre' or 'common' ground of British politics. Following successive general election defeats in 1997, 2001, and 2005 and a brisk trade in Party leaders (William Hague, Iain Duncan Smith, and Michael Howard), it was the arrival of David Cameron as Party leader in 2005 that restored the Party's electoral fortunes.

A Progressive Civic Conservatism? David Cameron and the Conservative-led Coalition government, 2010

As can be seen from Table 7.1, David Cameron attempted to deal with the electorally 'toxic' legacy of the Thatcher era by developing a progressive civic form of Conservatism that attempted to combine a neo-liberal economic approach with a modern, compassionate social agenda, which emphasised the role of civil society. The social agenda of Progressive Civic Conservatives had three key features. First, it was accepted that modern Conservatives must demonstrate greater acceptance of diverse lifestyles. The assumption, for example, that lone parents lacked social responsibility and preferred a life on benefits rather than economic independence was firmly rejected. In addition, condemnatory attitudes within the Party towards gay lifestyles, which had been much to the fore during the so-called Section 28 debate (in which local authorities were prohibited from 'promoting' gay lifestyles to young people; see McManus, 2010), were deemed to be outmoded. More positive messages towards civil partnerships and gay marriage were now the order of the day. Second, while Progressive Civic Conservatism accepted that Conservatives must remain vigilant about the intrusiveness of the state, it was recognised that benevolent forms of government action were needed to protect the poor and disadvantaged. It was hoped that that this more compassionate direction would help to dispel the idea that Conservatives were uncaring. Third, Progressive Civic Conservatives sought to foster and develop what they have termed the 'Big Society' (see Letwin, 2008; Blond, 2010; Norman, 2010; see also Harris, 2011). This involves the promotion and expansion of the various institutions, associations, and activities that lie in the spaces between individuals and families, the market, and the central and local state. The focus is very much on what Ishkanian and Szreter (2012, p. 4) have termed 'individual citizen-volunteers doing good in their community, organizing themselves and taking responsibility for sorting out their locality's needs', as well as philanthropic and charitable endeavour, self-help groups, social enterprises, and non-governmental organisations. In this way, Cameron hoped to ensure that the Conservative Party would come to be regarded as both a modern *and* progressive force in British politics. Cameron made determined efforts to ensure that his conceptual narrative, which relied mainly on non-state initiatives, would drown out the social democratic narrative, which rested on state-funded, egalitarian provision. The aim was to create a stable, contented, opportunity-rich, unequal society in which significant differences in economic outcomes were regarded as both necessary and legitimate (provided the successful paid their fair share of taxes and participated in their local community) and where conditional state support would be provided for those who fall by the wayside. This embrace of both civic engagement and social justice allowed Cameron to distance himself from his neo-liberal Conservative predecessors, who seemed to have little interest in dealing with some of the casualties of free market economic policies or the promotion of civil society.

SPOTLIGHT

The Big Society

The creation of a 'Big' society has been one of the distinctive features of David Cameron's Progressive Civic Conservatism. Encouraging individuals to work together in their local communities to resolve the problems they face is deemed to be more likely to give rise to effective remedies than costly, state-funded initiatives formulated by remote policy-makers in London. By liberalising planning laws it is hoped that local communities will take over the running of parks, libraries, and other services. Crucially, government is seen as having a significant role in this process by offering support and guidance to innovative activists and entrepreneurs who are willing to tackle seemingly intractable problems in their communities. It is recognised that it would be counter-productive for government to compel citizens to become active citizens. Instead, they hope to use more covert 'nudging' techniques (see Thaler and Sunstein, 2009), which have been developed by social psychologists and behavioural economists to gently coax citizens into acting in pro-social ways. This approach is very much in keeping with the pragmatic forms of adaptation that Conservatives favour, as opposed to ideological forms of economic and social engineering.

The title of the Party's 2010 manifesto, *Invitation to Join the Government of Britain* (Conservative Party, 2010), was intended to convey the message that government action alone could not resolve the multitude of issues and problems facing the nation. Active partnerships between individuals, communities, and the government were deemed to be the way forward.

The failure of the Conservative Party to secure an outright governing majority in the inconclusive 2010 general election led Cameron to form a post-election coalition government (Cabinet Office, 2010) with 'orange-leaning' Liberal Democrats (see Laws and Marshall, 2004), in the hope that this would provide the best opportunity of his Progressive Civic Conservatism taking root.

During the initial phase of the Coalition government, there were signs that a Progressive Civic Conservative agenda was being followed in certain areas of policy. For example, Cameron pressed ahead with plans to allow gay people to marry despite significant opposition among his own backbenchers. However, the reversal of the Conservatives' pledge, made when in opposition, to match Labour's spending plans in response to the financial crisis of 2008, seems to have been the catalyst for a reversion to a more overtly neo-liberal social policy agenda in government. Indeed, it could be argued that in areas such as health, education, and social security, the Conservatives seized the opportunity created by the economic downturn to press ahead with the unfinished neo-liberal policy agenda of the Thatcher and Major governments.

At the Department for Education, Michael Gove moved swiftly to accelerate the ending of a social democratic education policy centred on comprehensive schools, which has long been a cherished objective of neo-liberals (see also Chapter 12). This involved allowing all state schools, not just 'under-performing' institutions in disadvantaged areas, to apply for so-called 'academy status'. While still publicly funded, these schools (first introduced by New Labour, albeit with a pro-poor emphasis) enjoy considerable autonomy in determining the pay and conditions of staff, the curriculum, and the length of the school day, although they are not permitted to select pupils on academic grounds unless (as in the case of a selective grammar school) they were previously doing so. In addition, parents, teachers, charities, and businesses were encouraged to set up so-called 'free schools', which draw on developments in the United States (charter schools) and Sweden (Hultin, 2009). These newly created state-funded, all-ability, non-profit-making schools can, with the authorisation of the Secretary of State, be set up in locations that are deemed to lack sufficient 'good' local schools. Over time it seems likely that there will be a highly diverse range of primary and secondary schools with growing numbers of private sector providers and much less local authority provision or oversight. In September 2012, Gove announced that he was proposing to replace GCSE examinations with more demanding English Baccalaureate certificates. Although he was forced to modify this proposal in the light of administrative difficulties and objections from teaching professionals in early 2013, he remained committed to the introduction of a more exacting GCSE syllabus, which would be assessed by formal final examinations. Separate AS level qualifications are also scheduled to be phased out in favour of final year A level examinations.

Despite a promise in the Coalition agreement that there would be an end to the 'top-down reorganisations of the NHS' (Cabinet Office, 2010, p. 24), it was clear from accompanying statements that there was to be a major overhaul of the NHS. Although the service was to remain free at the point of use for all citizens on the basis of medical need, with a 'protected' budget (a real terms spending increase of just over 0.1 per cent over four years), the major changes in the organisation and delivery of the service outlined in the White Paper *Equity and Excellence: Liberating the NHS* (Department of Health, 2010) and subsequently enacted after a lengthy parliamentary process (see

Timmins, 2012), had a clear neo-liberal provenance (see also Chapter 16). For example, the major proportion of the NHS budget was handed over to GP-led consortia, which are subject to limited democratic oversight. In addition, all hospitals were expected to become competitive, non-profit-making foundation trusts, to be scrutinised by a new 'economic' regulator – Monitor. In addition, the groundwork was effectively laid for more NHS work to be delivered by private and social enterprise organisations. One example of the latter is Central Surrey Health. Established in 2006 by two health practitioners, Central Surrey Health now operates with 700 co-owner/practitioners who deliver community therapeutic and nursing services to around 280,000 residents in central Surrey. Co-ownership of this kind is seen as a spur to innovative and efficient provision, as is the opportunity for providers to retain surpluses for service improvements.

In the area of social security, a neo-liberal policy direction can be seen in the introduction of a benefits cap in April 2013, under which couples will not be able to receive more than £500 per week in benefits (including housing costs). It is estimated that 67,000 households will lose £83 per week on average as a result of this measure in 2013–14. The uprating of a number of means-tested benefits was also capped at 1 per cent per annum for three years from 2013. Some universal benefits for better off citizens were also withdrawn. Child tax credits were no longer provided to families with incomes exceeding £26,000 per year in 2013 (the previous limit was £41,300), and families in which there was one higher rate taxpayer lost their entitlement to child benefit. In addition, there are likely to be substantial numbers of claimants who will be worse off under government plans to reform the social security system. A new benefit, *universal credit*, to replace income support, income-based jobseeker's allowance, income-related employment and support allowance, housing benefit, child tax credit and working tax credit, was due to be phased in from 2013. Some other benefits, such as attendance allowance, cold weather payments, pension credits, child benefit, and carer's allowance will be retained, although the eligibility criteria are likely to be 'modified' in ways that will see some claimants losing income. These changes are intended to encourage as many claimants as possible, with the exception of those who are severely disabled, to undertake some paid work and become economically independent. The growing involvement of independent contractors in designing and delivering parts of the Department of Work and Pensions' Work Programme (which aims to help claimants return to paid work) is also compatible with a neo-liberal Conservative approach. These organisations are being funded on a 'payment by results' basis (higher sums being paid to those who are able to demonstrate that their 'customers' have succeeded in finding and remaining in work for the greatest length of time).

Finally, the attempt to create a 'Big Society', by empowering local citizens to organise and run community services such as parks and libraries, and by encouraging charities, social enterprises, cooperatives, and small businesses to operate public services, appears to have been simply an attempt to reduce public spending rather than the rejuvenation of civil society.

Conclusion

Given its 'dispositional' rather than 'doctrinal' reputation, it is difficult to offer a definitive view of what constitutes the British Conservative approach to the welfare state in the post-1945 era. Nevertheless, a case can be made for the proposition that two distinctive forms of Conservatism held sway during the periods when the Party was in office during this period (1951–64 and 1970–74). The governments of Churchill, Eden, Macmillan, Home, and Heath recognised the importance of adapting pragmatically to broader economic and social change while remaining true to core Conservative values such as inequality, low taxes, and personal freedom. In terms of the welfare state, a pragmatic accord took root. This involved an acceptance that the welfare state was providing basic forms of security against unemployment and ill health that appealed to large swathes of the British public. Accordingly, a modernising One Nation approach to the welfare state was crafted. This did not entail a wholesale acceptance of what was regarded as Labour's over-ambitious, costly, universal, egalitarian-inspired vision of state welfare. Instead, a more selective, pared down version was developed with the intention of complementing, rather than undermining, the values noted above.

By the 1970s, this One Nation approach began to unravel in the face of a poorly performing economy, industrial unrest, the rise of the 'permissive' society, and the persistence of poverty and disadvantage despite growing social expenditure. This provided fertile ground for a resurgent neo-liberal Conservatism. Under the Thatcher and Major governments, there were concerted attempts to regenerate the economy along free market lines and to reform the welfare state so that it could no longer act as a fetter on individual aspiration or economic advance. Although the dismantling of the welfare state was eschewed for practical and political reasons, a radical restructuring was undertaken. This involved populist measures such as the selling off of council houses, as well as contracting out services to the private sector and instilling a more commercial mindset into those charged with managing public services. Although overall levels of public spending were not markedly reduced during these neo-liberal administrations, it became apparent that the social democratic features of the welfare state such as egalitarianism and solidarity were being whittled away with the result that the public were starting to view state welfare provision as an individual consumer good rather than as collectively organised citizen services.

Following a lengthy period in opposition, the Conservatives under the leadership of David Cameron sought to forge a new Progressive Civic Conservatism that attempted to retain a broadly neo-liberal economic stance while simultaneously adopting a more sympathetic approach to minorities and disadvantaged groups in society. This would involve enhancing the rights of gay citizens (by permitting them to marry) and by accepting that many lone parents were capable of bringing up their families successfully with appropriate support. Emphasis was placed on social justice and the need to tackle the root 'causes' of poverty. However, it proved difficult for the Coalition government to pursue a distinctive Progressive Civic Conservatism policy, and the provisional conclusion offered here is that the pursuit of neo-liberal economic policies inevitably leads to the development of a neo-liberal social agenda.

Summary

This chapter has considered the nature of conservatism and the changing approaches of the Conservative Party to social policy since 1945. It has shown that:

- Conservatism is both flexible and pragmatic in nature.
- Following the Second World War and Labour's 1945 general election victory, One Nation Conservatism emerged as a major influence within the Party.
- By the early 1970s, neo-liberal ideas were becoming more influential in the Conservative Party.
- During the Thatcher and Major governments, there were significant changes to the welfare state, particularly during Thatcher's third term as Prime Minister, based largely on a neo-liberal economic and social agenda.
- Following their 1997 general election defeat, the Conservatives made little headway in developing a post-Thatcher approach to social policy until Cameron's attempts to develop a new Progressive Civic Conservatism, although this did not sit easily with a neo-liberal economic agenda.

Discussion and review

- How did the One Nation approach to social policy differ from the neo-liberal Conservative approach that followed?
- Was Mrs Thatcher's approach to social policy neo-liberal rather than conservative?
- Is David Cameron pursuing a Progressive Civil Conservative approach to social policy as leader of the Coalition government?

References

Audit Commission (1986) *Making a Reality of Community Care*, HMSO, London.

Blake, R. (1998) *The Conservative Party from Peel to Major*, Arrow, London.

Blond, P. (2010) *Red Tory*, Faber & Faber, London.

Boxer, A. (1996) *The Conservative Governments 1951–64*, Longmans, London.

Bridgen, P. and Lowe, R. (1998) *Welfare Policy Under the Conservatives 1951–1964*, Public Records Office, London.

Cabinet Office (2010) *The Coalition: Our Programme for Government*, Cabinet Office, London.

Charmley, J. (2008) *A History of Conservative Politics Since 1830*, Palgrave Macmillan, Basingstoke.

Conservative Party (1955) *United for Peace and Progress, the Conservative and Unionist Party's General Election Manifesto* (reprinted in Dale, 2000, p. 119).

Conservative Party (1992) *The Best Future for Britain: The Conservative Manifesto 1992*, Conservative Party, London.

Conservative Party (2010) *Invitation to Join the Government of Britain: Conservative Manifesto 2010*, Conservative Party, London.

Conservative and Unionist Central Office (1947) *The Industrial Charter*, Conservative and Unionist Central Office, London.

Conservative and Unionist Central Office (1949) *The Right Road for Britain*, Conservative and Unionist Central Office, London.

Dale, I. (ed.) (2000) *Conservative Party General Election Manifestos, 1900–1997*, Routledge, London.

Denham, A. and Garnett, M. (2002) *Keith Joseph*, Acumen, London.

Department of Health (2010) *Equity and Excellence: Liberating the NHS*, Cm 7881, HMSO, London.

Dorey, P. (2011) *British Conservatism*, I.B. Tauris, London.

Garnett, M. and Hickson, K. (2009) *Conservative Thinkers*, Manchester University Press, Manchester.

Glennerster, H. (2007) *British Social Policy Since 1945*, Blackwell, Oxford.

Gray, J. (2009) *Gray's Anatomy*, Allen Lane, London.

Green, E.H. (2002) *Ideologies of Conservatism*, Oxford University Press, Oxford.

Griffiths, R. (1988) *Community Care: Agenda for Action* (The Griffiths Report), HMSO, London.

Guillebaud, C.W. (1953) *Report of the Committee of Enquiry into the Cost of the National Health Service* (The Guillebaud Report), Cmd. 9663, HMSO, London.

Harris, R. (2011) *The Conservatives – A History*, Bantam, London.

Heywood, A. (2007) *Political Ideologies: An Introduction*, Basingstoke, Palgrave Macmillan.

Hickson, K. (ed.) (2005) *The Political Thought of the Conservative Party Since 1945*, Palgrave Macmillan, Basingstoke.

Hultin, A. (2009) 'Profit is the key to success in "Swedish schools" ', *The Spectator*, 3 October, p. 17.

Ishkanian, A. and Szreter, S. (2012) *The Big Society Debate: A New Agenda for Social Policy?*, Edward Elgar, Cheltenham.

Laws, D. and Marshall, P. (2004) *The Orange Book*, Profile, London.

Lawson, N. (1992) *The View From No. 11*, Bantam, London.

Letwin, O. (2008) 'From economic revolution to social revolution', *Soundings*, No. 40, pp. 112–22.

Lowe, R. (2005) *The Welfare State in Britain Since 1945*, Palgrave Macmillan, Basingstoke.

Macleod, I. and Maude, A. (eds.) (1950) *One Nation: A Tory Approach to Social Problems*, Conservative Political Centre, London.

McManus, M. (2010) *Tory Pride and Prejudice: The Conservative Party and Homosexual Law Reform*, Biteback, London.

Norman, J. (2010) *The Big Society*, University of Buckingham Press, Buckingham.

O'Hara, K. (2011) *Conservatism*, Reaktion, London.

Phillips Committee (1953) *Report of the Committee on the Economic and Financial Problems of Provision for Old Age*, Cmd. 9333, HMSO, London.

Raison, T. (1990) *Tories and the Welfare State*, Macmillan, Basingstoke.

Robin, C. (2011) *The Reactionary Mind*, Oxford University Press, Oxford.

Scruton, R. (2001) *The Meaning of Conservatism*, Palgrave Macmillan, Basingstoke.

Scruton, R. (2013) 'Postmodern Tories', *Prospect*, March, pp. 34–6.

Seawright, D. (2005) 'One Nation', in K. Hickson (ed.) *The Political Thought of the Conservative Party Since 1945*, Palgrave Macmillan, Basingstoke.

Seawright, D. (2010) *The British Conservative Party and One Nation Politics*, Continuum, London.

Sherman, A. (2007) *Paradoxes of Power*, Imprint Academic, Exeter.

Thaler, R.H. and Sunstein, C.R. (2009) *Nudge*, Penguin, London.

Thatcher, M. (1995) *The Path to Power*, HarperCollins, London.

Timmins, N. (2001) *The Five Giants* (revised and updated edn.), HarperCollins, London.

Timmins, N. (2012) *Never Again? The Story of the Health and Social Care Act 2012*, Institute for Government/King's Fund, London.

Walsha, R. (2000) 'The One Nation Group: a Tory approach to backbench politics and organization, 1950–55', *Twentieth Century British History*, Vol. 11, No. 2, pp. 183–214.

Walsha, R. (2003) 'The One Nation Group and One Nation Conservatism, 1950–2002', *Contemporary British History*, Vol. 17, No. 2, pp. 69–120.

Willetts, D. (1992) *Modern Conservatism*, London, Penguin.

Worsthorne, P. (1978) 'Too much freedom', in M. Cowling (ed.) *Conservative Essays*, Cassell, London.

Further reading

Bale, T. (2012) *The Conservatives Since 1945: The Drivers of Policy Change*. Oxford University Press, Oxford. This book provides a comprehensive account of changes in Conservative policy and the drivers behind them.

Bochel, H. (ed.) (2011) *The Conservative Party and Social Policy*, Policy Press, Bristol. A collection of work that examines the development of Conservative Party social policy from Thatcher to Cameron, and specific policy areas in the early period of the Coalition government.

Dorey, P. (2011) *British Conservatism*, I.B. Tauris, London. Focusing on conservative attitudes to inequality, this book provides a thorough analysis of Conservative Party ideology and policy.

Green, E.H. (2002) *Ideologies of Conservatism*, Oxford University Press, Oxford. A useful consideration of developments and changes in the nature of conservatism and conservative political thought throughout the twentieth century.

Hickson, K. (ed.) (2005) *The Political Thought of the Conservative Party Since 1945*, Palgrave Macmillan, Basingstoke. An impressive collection of essays that outline the changing political, social, and economic ideas within the Conservative Party since the Second World War.

Raison, T. (1990) *Tories and the Welfare State*, Macmillan, London. Although now out of print, Raison's book provided an excellent overview of the Conservative Party's approach to the welfare state over the first four decades of the post-war era.

Useful websites

http://www.conservatives.com – the website of the Conservative Party provides a range of information, including access to speeches and policy documents.

http://conservativehome.blogs.com – an independent but Conservative supporting site, Conservative Home provides a wide range of information.

In addition, there are a number of right-leaning think tanks whose websites make available a variety of information and publications. These include http://www.adamsmith.org – the Adam Smith Institute; http://www.centreforsocialjustice.org – the Centre for Social Justice, established by the former Conservative leader, Iain Duncan Smith; http://www.civitas.org.uk – Civitas; http://www.cps.org.uk – the Centre for Policy Studies; http://www.iea.org.uk – the Institute for Economic Affairs; http://www.policyexchange.org.uk – Policy Exchange; and http://www.reform.co.uk – Reform.

CHAPTER 8

Labour Governments and the Welfare State Since 1945

Robert M. Page

Learning objectives

- To provide a brief review of Labour's changing ideology
- To explore the Attlee Governments' (1945–51) democratic socialist approach to the welfare state
- To outline the revisionist social democratic approach to the welfare state in the Wilson (1964–70 and 1974–76) and Callaghan (1976–79) eras
- To consider the 'modern' social democratic/third way approach to the welfare state in the New Labour (1997–2010) era

Chapter overview

This chapter begins by considering the nature of the Labour Party's ideological underpinnings, highlighting the ways in which these have changed since 1945. It then highlights the development of the welfare state by the post-1945 Labour governments. Subsequently, it examines the revisionist social democratic stance of the Wilson and Callaghan governments in the 1960s and 1970s, where the welfare state was seen as having a key role to play in the pursuit of greater social equality. It then turns its attention to the New Labour governments from 1997 to 2010.

The chapter considers:

- Labour's changing ideological emphases from 1945 to 2010;
- the key elements of the welfare strategy pursued by the Attlee governments from 1945 to 1951;
- the revisionist social democratic approach of the Wilson and Callaghan governments in the 1960s and 1970s;
- New Labour's approach to the welfare state from 1997 to 2010.

Introduction

This chapter examines the Labour Party's approach to the welfare state since 1945 through the prism of its changing ideology from democratic socialism to revisionist social democracy and finally to its modern social democratic or third way variant. This ideological framework will then be employed to examine Labour's approach to the welfare state from 1945 to 1951 under Attlee, and then the Wilson (1964–70) and Wilson/Callaghan governments (1974–79) in the 1960s and 1970s. Finally, attention will then be focused on the New Labour governments of Blair and Brown from 1997 to 2010.

Labour's changing ideology

Democratic socialism

Since its formation in 1900, the Labour Party has 'incorporated' a wide range of ideological influences, including Marxism, ethical socialism, Fabianism, and syndicalism (see Bevir, 2011). As such, it can be argued that the Party's ideology is fluid rather than fixed, and that, as a consequence, there will be continuing discussion and debate about what constitutes Labour's 'soul' (Shaw, 2007). Over time the Party has had to consider whether it should, for example, reflect the views and interests of trade unionists, the broader working class, the nation, or the opinion of particular theorists or factions. Some continue to argue that the Party should focus more on ethical concerns, the promotion of fellowship, and the reinvigoration of civil society (see Stears, 2006), while others believe the emphasis should be on public ownership and concerted state action to remedy the injustices and inequities that arise within a capitalist society. This latter perspective was emphasised in the Party's democratic socialist constitution (drafted by the leading Fabian, Sidney

Webb, in 1918), which reflected the importance of collective state action to ensure more equitable forms of ownership, production, and distribution.

Democratic socialists have always been critical of capitalism on the grounds that it encourages impersonal human interactions in which individuals are driven towards exploitative contacts based on personal gain, rather than the pursuit of more meaningful human relationships based on respect, trust, cooperation, and mutual support. The recognition that capitalism was inherently inefficient and gave rise to poverty and unemployment also led to concerted attempts to create a socialist society through peaceful, parliamentary means. This has proved difficult to achieve in practice because of the adaptability of capitalism and lukewarm public support for some of the measures needed to bring about radical change, such as public ownership and a planned economy. Nevertheless, Labour's democratic socialists promoted various measures throughout the twentieth century in an effort to create a more egalitarian and solidaristic society. The state, at both national and local level, is accorded a major role in relation to economic direction and in protecting citizens from the adverse economic and social impacts that arise from unemployment, ill health, homelessness or old age. Another key characteristic of democratic socialists is their determination to improve opportunities for all citizens, especially in the area of education.

CONTROVERSY AND DEBATE

▢ Do you consider it to be a strength or weakness that the Labour Party's ideology has been modified in the light of economic and social change and the infusion of new ideas and perspectives?

▢ Would the UK be a more equal and socially just society with a flourishing welfare state if Labour had consistently followed democratic socialist principles when in government?

Revisionist social democracy

Towards the end of the second post-war Attlee administration (1950–51), it became clear that the Labour Party was uncertain about its future plans for transforming British society. Fundamentalists, such as Bevan, argued for increased forms of public ownership and social expenditure, while consolidators, such as Morrison and Gaitskell, believed that it was necessary to take stock of the first phase of post-war change before embarking on a further round of reform (see Jones, 1996). The revisionists were concerned that issues such as nationalisation, workers control, and increased taxation of the rich, were alienating aspiring middle-class voters (see Fielding, 1997). Labour's defeat in the 1951 general election intensified this debate. During a lengthy period in opposition (1951–64), a revisionist social democratic ideology became more influential within the Party.

This reformist approach owed much to Anthony Crosland's influential text, *The Future of Socialism* (1956). Crosland (1956, p. 57) argued that post-war Britain was no longer an 'unreconstructed capitalist society'. Instead, capitalist power and control had been diluted by the advance of democracy and trade unionism, purposeful state intervention, and the emergence of a more autonomous, socially responsive managerial class. In these new conditions, it was now deemed possible to use the power of the state to check the worst excesses of capitalism while harvesting the fruits of its inherent dynamism and capacity for innovation for the public good. Accordingly, there was no longer any imperative to nationalise private companies to create a more egalitarian society. Although Crosland acknowledged that greater economic equality was required, especially in the distribution of wealth, he contended that Labour should now focus on *social* equality.

> The socialist seeks a distribution of rewards, status, and privileges egalitarian enough to minimise social resentment, to secure justice between individuals, and to equalise opportunities; and he seeks to weaken the existing deep-seated class stratification, with its concomitant feelings of envy and inferiority, and its barriers to uninhibited mingling between the classes.
>
> (Crosland, 1956, p. 113)

For Crosland, increased social expenditure on high-quality state welfare services in spheres such as health care, housing, and education would enhance the wellbeing of all citizens, especially the disadvantaged. Crucially, though, improvements of this kind were now deemed to be dependent on sustained economic growth. Faltering economic performance would hinder progress on the social front. During the Wilson (1964–70) and Wilson and Callaghan (1974–79) eras, a revisionist social democratic strategy of this kind underpinned Labour's approach to economic and social policy.

STOP AND THINK

In the light of subsequent developments, do you think that Crosland's assessment of the changing nature of capitalism was far too optimistic?

'Modern' social democracy/the 'third way'

A subsequent lengthy period in the political wilderness (1979–97) led Labour strategists to consider whether a further ideological 'readjustment' was needed if the Party was to return to government. Under the leadership of Neil Kinnock (1983–92) and, subsequently, John Smith (1992–94), Labour repositioned itself in an attempt to persuade the public that the Party was now more in tune with contemporary public attitudes and broader economic and social developments. According to Shaw (1996, pp. 184–5), this re-orientation involved substantial policy revisions including a retreat from public ownership, a 'rapprochement with industry', a firm commitment to 'fiscal and monetary orthodoxy', the retention of Conservative curbs on trade unionism, a revamped welfare agenda, and the abandonment of nuclear unilateralism. This was complemented by organisational reforms, which gave the Party's parliamentary leadership rather than the trade unions greater power and control over the direction of policy. The revisionism of Kinnock, and to a lesser extent Smith, provided the platform for Tony Blair (who was to lead the Party from 1994 to 2005) and a number of influential modernisers, such as Philip Gould (1998), Peter Mandelson (see Mandelson and Liddle, 1996), and the sociologist Anthony Giddens (1998, 2000), who popularised the notion of the 'third way' to remould the ideology of the Labour Party. According to these self-proclaimed 'modernisers', revisionist social democracy had become outmoded in a period that had seen the demise of communism, the growth of global markets, changing work and family patterns, and more diverse forms of personal and cultural identity. They believed that 'New' Labour needed to discard its romantic attachment to socialism and, instead, seek ways of providing support for market activity *and* the promotion of social justice. To emphasise this change, the Labour leader, Tony Blair, managed (unlike his predecessor Hugh Gaitskell in 1959) to persuade the Party at a special conference held in April 1995 to abandon its constitutional commitment to the common ownership of the means of production (Clause 4, section four) and replace it with a broader statement of aims (Jones, 1996; Garnett, 2006).

One of the reasons that this was deemed necessary was to convince the nation that the Party had modernised and was now willing to embrace the market and respond positively to the demands of globalisation. The role of government would now be to assist firms to become more entrepreneurial and efficient so that they could develop innovative products and secure a greater market share in both developed and emerging economies. Efforts would also be made to improve education and training so that workers would have the necessary skills to allow them to find employment in an increasingly flexible and competitive marketplace. This embrace of the market was accompanied by a more relaxed approach to income and wealth inequalities. While equal opportunity policies were deemed to be of continuing importance, greater equality of outcome was no longer an aspiration. The modern social democrats were also less enamoured of the welfare state, believing that it needed to be reformed to reflect new economic and social circumstances. For 'new' Labour, a modern welfare state should be designed to encourage those of working age to recognise their obligations to remain in the labour market rather than depend on out-of-work benefits. Although the principle of public funding would be retained, more diverse, consumer-focused non-state organisations would be encouraged to provide welfare services. Moreover, the choice between universal and selective provision would no longer be based on socialist principles but rather on pragmatic evidence about 'what works' – that is, the particular mix of services that is judged to best meet the needs of both service users and taxpayers.

Table 8.1 Ideologies of post-1945 Labour governments

Traditions	Democratic socialists	Revisionist social democrats	'Modern' social democratic/third way
Approach to the free market	Negative	Reformist	Positive
Representative figures	Attlee, Bevan	Crosland, Jenkins	Blair, Brown
Role of the state	Pivotal	Pivotal	Strategic
State intervention in the economy	Extensive	Extensive	Strategic
Social expenditure/welfare state	Strongly supportive	Pivotal	Contingent
Commitment to economic/social/ gender equality	Strong/strong/ moderate	Moderate/ strong/strong	Weak/strong/ strong
Role of civil society/voluntarism	Limited	Limited	Integral
Primacy of individual or society	Society	Society and individual	Individual
Approach to tradition/hierarchy	Generally supportive	Reformist	Pragmatic
Maintenance of social order	Strong	Pragmatic	Strong
Lifestyles and family relationships	Traditional	Reformist	Contingent reformist
Commitment to socialism	Pivotal	Strong	Weak
Obligations or rights of citizens to be prioritised?	Duty	Rights	Rights and duties

This ideological framework is used below to chart the social policy developments of the various post-1945 Labour governments.

The Attlee governments, 1945–51: establishing a democratic socialist welfare state

After a resounding victory in the 1945 general election, in which they secured 393 seats out of a possible 604, the post-war Labour government was provided with a clear mandate to fulfil the pledge contained in its election manifesto, *Let Us Face the Future*, to create a 'Socialist Commonwealth of Great Britain – free, democratic, efficient, progressive, public-spirited, its material resources organised in the service of the British people' (Labour Party, 1945, p. 6). For Labour, the pursuit of a democratic socialist strategy involved the creation of an egalitarian and solidaristic society through gradual, constitutional means, rather than just a more humane version of a capitalist society. The first phase of this transformation would involve the nationalisation of key industries, state regulation of the economy, progressive taxation, and the introduction of an egalitarian welfare state. It is this latter objective that is discussed here.

Towards a democratic socialist welfare state

There is still much debate as to whether the incoming Labour government 'created' the welfare state, or merely built on the foundations laid down by pre war governments and Churchill's coalition administration (Addison, 1975; Hennessy, 1992; Pearce, 1994; Francis, 1997). While it cannot be denied, for instance, that there were significant welfare measures introduced by the Liberal government of 1906–14 and by Conservative-led administrations in the inter-war period, as well as during the Second World War, a strong case can be mounted for the notion that it was the post-war Labour government that 'created' the British welfare state (Jefferys, 1992; Francis, 1997). Labour's democratic socialist approach to social welfare was best exemplified in the areas of social security and health care.

Social security

Labour's scheme for social security was closely modelled on its own internal plans (1942) and on William Beveridge's (1942) influential wartime *Report on Social Insurance and Allied Services*. During the Attlee era, a number of landmark measures were introduced. Under the Industrial Injuries Act of 1946, for example, the state, rather than employers and private insurers, was to assume responsibility for compensating those injured at work. The National Insurance Act of 1946 was the cornerstone of Labour's social security programme, entitling all those within the scheme to a range of flat-rate benefits (unemployment benefit, sickness benefit, dependants' allowances, maternity payments, retirement pensions, and a death grant)at time of need. The final element in Labour's social security programme was the National Assistance Act of 1948, which provided means-tested payments for those who were ineligible for National Insurance benefits. These safety net benefits were to be administered by a newly established National Assistance Board rather than local authority Public Assistance Committees.

Although the Beveridge-style scheme that Labour introduced was less egalitarian than a progressive, tax-funded programme, it was recognised that the simplicity, affordability, and apparent fairness of social insurance had captured the public mood. In practice, however, the basic nature of this scheme made it difficult to resolve the problem of poverty. Indeed, when Labour announced their National Insurance benefit rates in 1946 [42 shillings (£2.10) for a couple and 26 shillings (£1.30) for a single person], doubts were expressed as to whether those having to subsist solely on such payments would be able to avoid 'poverty', particularly if they had above-average housing costs. Indeed, by 1948 some 675,000 recipients of National Insurance were claiming additional means-tested National Assistance benefits (which included a full rent allowance) in order to maintain a basic living standard.

The retention of an 'inferior' means-tested safety net benefit for the very poorest could be interpreted as a failure on the part of the Labour government to remove the lingering stigma of the Poor Law. However, Labour believed that the abolition of both the workhouse and the household means test (under which the incomes of individual claimants as well as other household members, including children and lodgers, were taken into account to determine eligibility) by the wartime coalition government had helped to tackle the problem of stigma. The retention of a residual *individual* means-tested scheme, administered in a humane way, was deemed unlikely to stigmatise claimants.

In providing citizens with protection against the 'most abject destitution of the 1930s' (Jefferys, 1992, p. 21), Labour's social security reforms represented a major step forward. It was acknowledged that further modifications in both the design and operation of the system were needed before a fully fledged democratic socialist social security was established, including less rigid eligibility criteria, higher benefit levels, and more comprehensive support for all those outside the labour market.

Finally, it should be noted that Labour's new social security measures formed part of a broader anti-poverty strategy that included the introduction of family allowances (which had been brought onto the statute book by the wartime coalition government; see Macnicol, 1980) and full employment.

SPOTLIGHT

Central or local welfare?

One of the major issues that Labour has had to wrestle with in the recent past is whether the Party should support more localised forms of welfare delivery rather than nationally directed services. One of the reasons why Aneurin Bevan, Labour's post-war Minister of Health and Housing, favoured the introduction of a *national* health service was because he believed that there was no difference between the medical needs of citizens living in Cardiff, Belfast, Edinburgh or London. He believed it would be inequitable if someone received a superior or inferior service due to the accident of geographical location. However, the introduction of devolved administrations in Scotland (which has its own parliament) and Northern Ireland and Wales (which have separate assemblies) coupled with growing demands for increased levels of local autonomy have created a dilemma for Labour. Should it support 'localism' on communitarian and democratic grounds even if it results in less equality in service provision?

The National Health Service

The National Health Service is often regarded as the finest achievement of the Attlee governments (Webster, 2002). Before 1948, medical care had been restricted to the better off and those workers who were covered by the National Insurance scheme of 1911 or through trade union or friendly society membership. Around 20 million workers (although, importantly, not their dependants) were covered by the National Insurance scheme, which provided basic financial protection during periods of ill health, the services of a general practitioner selected from a designated list (the panel system), and a limited degree of specialist provision. However, there was no unified hospital system, which meant that 'the privately run voluntary and publicly run municipal institutions operated side by side, with no semblance of co-ordination' (Brooke, 1992, p. 134).

Labour's new Minister of Health, Aneurin Bevan, was determined to establish a National Health Service in which high standard comprehensive care was to be made freely available to all citizens. His decision to nationalise the hospitals represented a major departure from the wartime coalition government's health strategy. To achieve this objective, Bevan acknowledged that he would have to secure the cooperation of hospital consultants. He achieved this by offering them generous salaries as well as additional merit awards in recognition of their loss of private earnings and their high levels of expertise (Webster, 2002, p. 26). Bevan also upheld their right to engage in private work (pay beds were to be permitted in NHS hospitals) and ensured that they were properly represented within the new NHS administrative structures.

General medical practitioners, who were highly influential within the British Medical Association, were less enamoured by Bevan's proposals. They objected to the possibility that they might become salaried state employees rather than independent contractors, and voiced concerns about the prohibition on the sale of medical practices. They were also uneasy about the 'oppressive' administrative arrangements of the new service that would permit medical personnel to be 'directed' to work in locations with a shortage of qualified staff. It was not until a few weeks before the service was due to come into effect in July 1948 that the GPs finally agreed, after long and protracted negotiations, to participate in the new service.

The concessions that Bevan made to the doctors have been criticised by some commentators on the grounds that it was too high a price to pay for the establishment of a National Health Service (see Campbell, 1994; Stewart, 1999). Others, in contrast, contend that the compromises Bevan made were vital in order to secure a major improvement in health care provision, not least for the poorest members of society. As Francis (1997, pp. 113–14) concludes, the

> new medical service which Bevan had helped to establish had been moulded in accordance with a number of priorities which he understood to be distinctly socialist. The NHS fulfilled the principles of universalism, comprehensiveness, and funding from central taxation. It had also sought to establish that health care should be seen as an inalienable right, rather than a commodity whose provision was dependent on the vagaries of the market.

Labour's achievements in the spheres of housing and education were not so dramatic.

Housing

Labour's manifesto pledge to provide a good standard of accommodation for all proved over-ambitious. In the first place, the post-war housing stock was inadequate for the level of need. It was estimated that some 200,000 houses had been destroyed during the war, while a further 250,000 had been made uninhabitable. Moreover, even the habitable stock required urgent repairs of various kinds (Jones and Lowe, 2002). Second, there was an upsurge in demand for housing from the millions of servicemen and women who returned home after the war. Third, there was a shortage of both building materials (much of which had to be imported) and skilled construction workers.

Bevan (whose ministerial responsibilities included housing as well as health) was convinced that centrally subsidised, local authority house building for rent represented the optimal way of meeting the growing demand for housing in post-war Britain. Although Bevan recognised the importance of increasing the supply of new homes, he was not prepared to sacrifice quality for quantity, believing that working people had as much right as the middle classes to live in spacious, well-built homes (see Francis, 1997).

Bevan has been the subject of much criticism for his housing strategy. It was argued that his 'ideological' opposition to the construction of private homes for sale (Campbell, 1994), and neglect of the privately rented sector, was misplaced. Crucially, though, it was his failure to ensure that sufficient homes were built that attracted the most opprobrium. Only 1 million houses had been built by 1951 instead of the 4–5 million new homes projected. However, as Campbell (1994, p. 153) notes, 'there was in truth no way that any Minister, in the economic conditions prevailing after 1945, could have met in full either the real housing need which the war had left behind or the inflated expectations which Labour had aroused during the General Election'.

One other feature of Labour's post-war housing policy is worthy of note, as it also reflected the government's desire to improve the overall living conditions of the British people. An ambitious New Town programme, which was to become 'one of the great successes of post-war planning' (Timmins, 2001, p. 147), was introduced in 1946. Fourteen new towns development corporations were established, from Crawley in Sussex to East Kilbride in Scotland (Hennessy, 1992).

Education

Labour members of Churchill's coalition government, most notably Chuter-Ede, played a significant role in securing the passage of the 1944 Education Act (Bailey, 1995). The post-war Labour government regarded this wartime reform as a significant step forward. Accordingly, there was deemed to be no urgent need for a more 'distinctive' democratic socialist education policy. For both of Attlee's education ministers, Ellen Wilkinson (1945–47) and George Tomlinson (1947–51), adherence to the principle of equality of educational opportunity, and universal, free secondary education were the key components of a democratic socialist education policy. They did not object, for example, to the competitive academic selection procedures favoured by the grammar schools provided that working-class children had a similar chance of entry as their middle- and upper-class counterparts. Similarly, they supported a 'differentiated', tripartite schooling system (grammar, technical, and modern) provided that pupils were admitted to such schools on the basis of their skills and aptitude *not* their social background. Although pupils would receive different forms of education, it was envisaged that there would be parity of esteem between the three kinds of school. In the more solidaristic and integrated society that Labour was seeking to create, it was envisaged that the technician and the craftsman would eventually enjoy equal status with the doctor and the lawyer (Francis, 1997).

Implementing the Education Act of 1944 and raising the school leaving age from 14 to 15 years proved no easy task for either Wilkinson or Tomlinson. The former had, for example, to persuade Cabinet colleagues such as Cripps and Morrison to release the resources for the additional teachers and new buildings required to extend the school leaving age to 15 by 1947 (see Morgan, 1984).

While Labour's efforts to ensure that all children, regardless of means, should be able to continue in full-time education until the age of 15 were important, their failure to grasp the deep-rooted impact of class factors in determining the type of school that pupils attended, or the socially divisive impact of a tripartite system of schooling, have come to be seen as significant oversights.

There were two spheres in education in which one might have expected Labour to pursue a more overtly democratic socialist approach. First, they could have given more support to the establishment of multilateral or comprehensive schools, not least in the light of growing criticisms about middle-class capture of the grammar schools and the deficiencies in secondary modern education, where pupils were denied the opportunity of sitting external examinations. Although both Wilkinson and Tomlinson were willing to see the setting up of experimental comprehensive *schools*, they had no desire to press for a 'national comprehensive *system*' (Francis, 1997, pp. 144–5). Second, Labour had proved reluctant to tackle the privileged position of the independent (private) school sector. The fact that a number of influential Cabinet Ministers had favourable personal experiences of 'elite' schooling of this kind was one factor why there was limited enthusiasm for reform in this area (see Beckett, 2000). In addition, it was believed that any direct attempt to abolish private schools would prove counter-productive, given limited public appetite for such reform. Rapid improvement in the quality of state education was seen as the best way to challenge the pre-eminence of the private schools.

STOP AND THINK

- How significant was Labour's failure to overhaul the private education system during its period in office from 1945 to 1951 in terms of perpetuating educational inequalities?

- How different would our education system look today if Labour had taken 'bolder' action at this time?

The unity that had been such a feature of Labour's first term in office began to evaporate during their second term in government (1950–51), most notably when Bevan, Wilson, and Freeman resigned following Attlee's decision to support his Chancellor (Gaitskell) over the question of welfare cuts to finance hefty defence commitments following the Korean War. Although there was still much to be done to create a fairer society, as the Party's 1951 general election manifesto made clear, there seemed to be little idea as to how this was to be achieved (Labour Party, 1951). While Labour obtained a higher proportion of the popular vote than the Conservatives, they still lost the 1951 election.

Labour's success in establishing the post-war welfare state was remarkable bearing in mind the perilous state of the post-war economy. Britain had incurred wartime debts of £3000 million and was heavily dependent on US financial support in the form of Lease Lend, which ended abruptly following the Japanese surrender in 1945 (see Morgan, 1984). Exports stood at just one-third of their pre- war level and 40 per cent of overseas markets had been lost. Although Labour was forced to introduce a more 'austere' welfare programme than they would have wished, this still represented a significant advance in terms of both security and opportunity for British citizens (Tomlinson, 1998).

Revisionist social democracy: Labour governments in the 1960s and 70s

By the time Labour returned to power in 1964 a 'revisionist' social democratic doctrine had begun to take root within the Party (see Table 8.1), with the result that social policy took centre stage in the Party's egalitarian strategy. In pursuing a more overtly social democratic approach, the incoming Prime Minister, Harold Wilson (who had become Party leader following the sudden death of Gaitskell in 1963), made a concerted attempt to reassure fundamentalists within the Party that the state would still have a major role to play in the modernisation of British society. Strategic forms of public ownership and central planning as well as an increased reliance on skilled workers, technicians and scientists (rather than 'aristocratic' owners and managers) was seen as vital to bring about the scientific and technological 'revolution' deemed necessary for Britain's future prosperity (see Sandbrook, 2006).

The Wilson governments and the welfare state, 1964–70

Improved economic performance was seen as the key to ensuring that the welfare state would be 'fit for the 1960s and 1970s'. As the Party's 1964 general election manifesto, *Let's Go with Labour for the New Britain,* made clear,

> this will not be achieved all at once: but, as economic expansion increases our national wealth we shall see to it that the needs of the community are increasingly met. *For the children*, this will mean better education; *for the family*, decent houses at prices that people can afford; *for the sick*, the care of a modernised health service; *for the old people and widows*, a guaranteed share in rising national prosperity.
>
> (Labour Party, 1964, p. 13)

A number of specific welfare pledges were put forward. In education, Labour promised to reduce class sizes, reorganise secondary education 'on comprehensive lines', increase the school leaving age to 16, and oversee a 'massive expansion in higher, further and university education' (Labour Party, 1964, pp. 13–14). Labour also vowed to 'reconstruct the social security system' by increasing National Insurance benefits (and subsequently linking them with the rise in average earnings) and introducing a non-stigmatised Income Guarantee for pensioners and widows.

In health care, prescription charges were to be abolished as a first step towards the restoration of 'a completely free Health Service' (Labour Party, 1964, p. 17). A properly funded hospital plan was to be put in place and the numbers of qualified medical staff increased.

Labour's narrow victory in the 1964 general election, followed by a more impressive success in 1966, provided a gilt-edged opportunity for the Party to put its new social democratic welfare strategy into effect. However, serious economic difficulties hindered this process. It proved difficult to stimulate growth and investment, maintain the value of sterling, avoid deflation, control wages, modernise the economy, avoid 'stop–go' economic policies (Tomlinson, 2004), and retain international confidence in the harsher economic circumstances of the time. In addition, various 'white heat' innovations, such as the Department of Economic Affairs and the Ministry of Technology failed to ignite the economy (Jones, 1996; Sandbrook, 2006). Significantly, protecting the value of the pound in order to 'preserve Britain's role as a world banker and to keep sterling as a major reserve currency' (Morgan, 1992, p. 269) was given priority over the maintenance of high employment, growth, and social expenditure.

Not surprisingly, Labour found it difficult to meet some of its welfare objectives because of such economic turmoil. For example, prescription charges, which had been abolished in 1964 in fulfilment of a manifesto commitment, were restored in 1968 as part of a round of expenditure cuts. The decision to delay the raising of the school leaving age from 15 to 16 or press ahead with an innovative national superannuation scheme (see Thornton, 2009) were also linked to the need to limit public expenditure. Although some 2 million new homes were built under Labour's housing drive (1965–70), the quality (system built) and design (high rise) of these dwellings was the subject of much criticism.

Despite these economic problems, Labour made progress in a number of areas. Although their commitment to provide pensioners with a non means-tested income guarantee proved difficult to implement (Timmins, 2001), efforts were made to ensure that the incomes of the elderly poor were improved. Structural reform (the creation of the Supplementary Benefits Commission), more sensitive benefit procedures (a less stigmatised 'rights-based' service), and a more generous and flexible payment system (see Page, 1984, pp. 44–5) led to real improvements in the living standards of many poorer pensioners. The government also introduced earnings-related unem-ployment and sickness benefits, increased National Insurance benefit levels, and abolished the earnings rule for widows. Other initiatives included the introduction of a means-tested rate and rent rebate system and a redundancy pay scheme (see Hill, 1993).

Progress was also made in the area of state education. Under arguably the most famous and effective advisory circular in the history of social policy (10/65), local authorities were requested to submit plans to the Department of Education for the development of non-selective, comprehensive secondary schools. As Timmins (2001, p. 242) notes, 'by 1970 the proportion of pupils in schools that at least in name were comprehensive had risen from 10 to 32 per cent, and by the time Labour left office only eight authorities were actively refusing to submit plans'. Labour also built on previous Conservative attempts to increase the number of higher education places. This was achieved by allowing colleges of advanced technology to become universities, and by the expansion of separate, though nominally equal, local authority-controlled polytechnics, which would specialise in more vocationally oriented programmes that better met the needs of industry. The needs of non-traditional students such as those 'already in work' or 'at home bringing up children' (Glennerster, 2000, p. 127) were to be met by the introduction of the Open University's distance learning courses (Hall, 1975).

During the Wilson years, there was also a concerted attempt to extend personal liberty in areas such as penal reform, homosexuality, divorce, censor-ship, and capital punishment (Brooke, 2011). Although a number of these measures came onto the statute book as a result of Private Members' Bills, few would take issue with Marquand's (2004) assessment that it was 'the courageous and buoyant liberalism' of Labour's Home Secretary Roy Jenkins (1965–67) that was decisive in ensuring the passage of this legislation. Labour also sought to improve community harmony through the introduction of race relations legislation in 1965 and 1968 and the establishment of the Community Relations Commission in 1968. However, its 'two-pronged policy' (Marwick, 2003, p. 133), under which increased protection for migrants who were legally settled in Britain was counterbalanced by restrictions on those seeking residence, such as the Commonwealth Immigrants Act of 1968 (which was hurriedly intro-duced to prevent the sizeable migration of the Asian community from East Africa), proved more controversial (see Foot, 1965; Glennerster, 2000).

Although Labour's record on both public spending and redistribution (of income, if not wealth – see Shaw, 1996) was respectable during the period from 1964 to 1970 (Beckerman, 1972), it failed to inspire either its own supporters or the general public in the way that the Attlee government had managed. In terms of the former, it was noticeable how some members of the so-called 'Titmuss group' (see Ellison, 1994) at the London School of Economics were beginning to express doubts about the limited egalitarian impact of Labour's social policy. Such was the level of scepticism that the Labour government even had to counter a claim made by the Child Poverty Action Group during the 1970 general election campaign that the poor had become even poorer under Labour (McCarthy, 1986; on the validity of this claim, see Tomlinson, 2004). As Ellison (2000, p. 435) concludes, 'the abiding image' of the 1964–70 Labour government was 'of a party beset by criticism from within and without, in many ways doing its best to maintain the welfare state that it had created but, owing to constant economic difficulties, failing to live up to the egalitarian hopes of its supporters'. The 1970s were to prove no less challenging.

The Wilson and Callaghan governments, 1974–79

Labour's defeat in the 1970 general election led to renewed questioning about the revisionist social democratic approach that the party had been pursuing. In particular, concerns were raised about Labour's accommodation with capitalism in an era marked by the rise of the multinational corporation (Holland, 1975). It was contended that 'the private sector of the economy was no longer responsive to persuasion and incentives offered by government, and that a major extension of public ownership into the private manufacturing sector was required if a reforming government was to deliver its economic policy objectives' (Tomlinson, 2000, p. 63). The establishment of a National Enterprise Board, which would take a stake in some leading companies in order to promote improved performance, was seen as a key way of overcoming this difficulty. It was also recognised that Labour's emphasis on the 'social' wage required a new concordat with the trade unions. A Social Contract was proposed, which would commit the trade unions to wage restraint in exchange for government commitments to pursue full employment policies and maintain high levels of public spending.

Although Labour's February 1974 manifesto was 'appreciably more left-wing than in 1964' (Timmins, 2001, p. 314), including as it did a promise to 'bring about a fundamental and irreversible shift in the balance of power and wealth in favour of working people and their families' (Labour Party, 1974, p. 15), this did not signify the jettisoning of a revisionist social democratic approach. Following their narrow victory, Wilson's minority government was unwilling to commit itself to the more radical economic programme favoured by the new Industry Secretary, Tony Benn (who was moved to the Department of Energy in 1975) or his deputy, Eric Heffer. Indeed, both the Wilson (1974–76) and Callaghan (1976–79) administrations found it increasingly difficult to pursue even a modest social democratic agenda. Sluggish growth, high inflation, and rising unemployment continued to dominate the political agenda. As early as the spring of 1975, the then Chancellor, Dennis Healey, was forced to seek Cabinet approval for social expenditure cuts in order to stabilise the economy. Further cuts were agreed to by the Cabinet in 1976 as part of an International Monetary Fund rescue package (Thorpe, 2001). These measures gave the economy a much-needed boost. Growing North Sea oil revenues and an upturn in international trade bolstered the British economy to such an extent that Labour entertained the possibility that they would be able to win the next general election scheduled for 1979. Such optimism proved short-lived as the latest phase of Labour's pay policy unravelled in 1978. As Tomlinson (2000, p. 67) notes, the decision to 'enforce a five per cent pay norm when inflation was several points higher was too much for workers and unions'. Although the impact of the subsequent industrial action (the so-called 'winter of discontent'; see Jefferys, 2002; Lipsey, 2011) was not as extreme as has often been portrayed (see Tomlinson, 2000), it undoubtedly contributed to Labour's electoral defeat in 1979.

The economic challenges faced by the 1974–79 Labour government restricted its room for manoeuvre in the area of social policy. Nevertheless, a number of initiatives were implemented. In the case of social security, the government fulfilled its manifesto commitment to increase the level of pensions and uprate the value of this and other long-term benefits (except those for the unemployed) according to the annual rise in prices or earnings (whichever was the higher). This latter measure helped to ensure that pensioners would be able to share in future prosperity. The government also introduced a State Earnings Related Pension Scheme (SERPS) in 1975 based on an individual's best 20 years of earnings. This was particularly beneficial to those whose earnings peaked at the beginning of their career, female carers, and those with interrupted work records. A number of other benefits were also introduced, including child benefit (albeit after protracted debate; see Field, 1982), mobility allowance, invalid care allowance, and a non-contributory invalidity pension.

In addition, it was decided to abolish direct grant schools in October 1975 and phase out pay beds in the NHS. The impact of both these measures proved disappointing to many egalitarians, since they resulted in an expansion, rather than a reduction in private provision. The vast majority of direct grant schools opted to rejoin the private sector rather than accept comprehensive status, while the lengthy phasing out period for pay beds did little damage to the long-term prospects of private medicine. As Timmins (2001, p. 338) notes, 'just as abolishing direct grant schools had expanded the private education sector, so phasing out pay beds . . . helped the private medical sector to grow. By an awful irony, Barbara Castle had become the patron saint of private medicine'.

Although there was less progress in the area of housing, Labour did freeze council rents on its return to office in 1974 and introduced a Housing (Homeless Person's) Act in 1977, which underlined the importance of improving the housing rights of vulnerable groups such as lone parents and victims of domestic violence.

Persistent economic difficulties during this period led to more wide-ranging critiques of Keynesianism and to suggestions that the welfare state was approaching a crisis point (O'Connor, 1973). Greater credence was being given to the notion that the rising cost of the welfare state might be having an adverse impact on Britain's economic performance (see Bacon and Eltis, 1976; Hickson, 2004). It was not just the rising cost of social expenditure that was seen as problematic, but also the 'rationale' for such spending. In the case of state education, for example, it was suggested that too great an emphasis was being placed on the inculcation of citizenship values rather than on employment-driven competencies and skills that were more likely to have a beneficial impact on future economic prosperity (Lowe, 2004).

When a general election was finally called in 1979, there were few (including Prime Minister Callaghan; see Donoughue, 2003) who thought, correctly as it transpired, that Labour would remain in office. As Seldon and Hickson (2004, p. 1) note, the 1974–79 Labour government was 'attacked for mishandling of the economy, symbolised by the 1976 IMF crisis, for its failure to manage relations with the trade unions, culminating in the "winter of discontent" and for its failure to implement major changes in social policy' (although see Piachaud, 2008).

'Modern' social democracy and the third way: New Labour and the welfare state, 1997–2010

Under New Labour, a third ideological phase, which has been described as modern social democracy, or the 'third way', took centre stage. In examining New Labour's approach to the welfare state, it is useful to adopt a thematic approach. While there were some subtle shifts of emphasis in New Labour's welfare strategy during their period in government from 1997 to 2010, it can be argued that there was significant continuity in its approach during this era.

One of the key reasons for this consistency was New Labour's resolve to act in a pro-market, pro-enterprise way, and to respond positively, rather than negatively, to global economic developments. In practice, this resulted in a continued reluctance to pursue policies that might hinder the entrepreneurial and profit-making activities of the private sector. While it was recognised that this new approach would result in growing forms of income and wealth inequalities, it was concluded that light corporate regulation and a competitive fiscal regime would generate higher tax revenues that could then be used for post-distributional welfare initiatives than more 'direct' pre-distributional policies.

Welfare to work

One of New Labour's defining characteristics was the emphasis given to paid work. They believed that previous Labour governments had been overly concerned with securing citizens' rights to various benefits rather than emphasising their duty to secure paid employment. Using funds from a windfall tax on the excess profits of privatised utility companies, New Labour launched an ambitious Welfare to Work programme in 1998. Under the first phase of this programme, young people under the age of 25, who were unable to find work following initial support and advice, were required to undertake some form of employment, education, training or voluntary work with an environmental task force. The 'conditionality' underpinning this scheme was subsequently applied, albeit initially in a 'milder' form, to other groups of working-age claimants such as lone parents, disabled people, and the over fifties. Claimants in these categories were offered advice and information in the first phase of this scheme. Gradually, more stringent forms of conditionality were applied to all groups of claimants. Following the introduction of the Welfare Reform and Pensions Act in 1999, lone parents were, for example, required to attend an annual review relating to their employment plans. By 2006, lone parents who had been claiming income support for over a year, and whose youngest child was of secondary school age, were required to attend a work-focused interview every three months.

In work benefits, child and pensioner poverty

For New Labour, effective social policy should always complement rather than challenge free market activity. Although New Labour did introduce one noteworthy pre-distributional policy in the shape of the minimum wage in 1998, it placed much greater stress on post-distributional measures, such as an elaborate scheme of tax credits to boost family incomes. A working families tax credit was introduced in October 1999 before being superseded by two separate tax credits, the working tax credit and the child tax credit in April 2003. Both tax credits and the Child Trust Fund (2002) were underpinned by a 'progressive' universal doctrine, which combined wide coverage with variable levels of entitlement, so that those on the lowest incomes received more assistance than those on higher incomes. For example, under the Child Trust Fund, all children were provided with an initial investment of £250 but those living in low-income households received twice as much. This fund aimed to provide a 'nest egg' for children that could be accessed at the age of 18 and used for a designated purpose such as helping to fund continuing education or training (see Nissan and Le Grand, 2003).

New Labour also committed itself to abolishing child poverty, which was blighting the lives of a third of all children in 1999–2000 compared with just 12.6 per cent in 1997 (Department of Social Security, 1997, 2001). In a landmark speech at Toynbee Hall in East London in March 1999, Tony Blair promised to abolish child poverty within 20 years. This was to be achieved by various generic and targeted means including the working families tax credit scheme and increased child benefit and child allowance payments for income support recipients (see Stewart, 2005). Labour was unable to meet either one of its interim poverty reduction targets (a 25 per cent reduction by 2005 and a 50 per cent reduction by 2010). As Toynbee and Walker (2011, p. 198) conclude, 'Aspiration was easier than attainment. Instead of halving the number of poor children by 2010, Labour barely managed to cut it by a sixth'.

Other measures designed to improve the position of children included a national parenting helpline and a new Sure Start programme. Introduced in April 1999, some 250 Sure Start schemes were established in the most deprived neighbourhoods in the UK providing health and support services such as day centres for the under-fours and their parents. Like the pioneering Head Start programme in the USA, it was envisaged that this scheme would enable poorer children to flourish once they started mainstream schooling.

Although New Labour did not set explicit targets for ending pensioner poverty, its decision to increase the basic pension and introduce a means-tested pension credit in 2003 helped to lift a fifth of all pensioner households out of poverty by 2005. Nevertheless, by 2010 it was estimated that some 2 million pensioners were still subsisting on incomes below government guidelines as a result of the complexities of claiming (see Toynbee and Walker, 2011).

Welfare reform

As was noted above, welfare reform was another pivotal feature of New Labour's modernised social democratic approach. It was believed that significant changes were needed in terms of the organisation and performance of the welfare state to cope with citizens' changing needs and a more challenging external environment. Change was deemed of particular importance in the areas of education and health care. It is useful to look at each of these in turn.

EDUCATION

Education reform was a priority policy area for New Labour. Having first decided which of the previous Conservative government's reforms to retain (the National Curriculum, national testing, regular inspections) and which to abolish (the assisted places scheme, which provided subsidised places in private schools, and grant-maintained schools, which were returned to local authority 'control' as foundation schools), the first Blair government attempted to improve educational outcomes. The underperformance of working-class children in what Adonis (2012) has described as poorly performing 'secondary modern comprehensives' was a particular concern. A new Standards and Effectiveness Unit was set up in the Department of Education to oversee these changes. Early initiatives included the introduction of compulsory daily literacy (1998) and numeracy (1999) hours in primary schools and the creation of 73 Education Action Zones in 1999 and 2000, which would foster partnerships between two or three designated secondary schools, their 'feeder' primary schools, and local businesses and community groups. The educational maintenance allowance was also introduced in 1999 to encourage children from low-income households to remain in full-time education after the age of 16.

New Labour had quickly come to the conclusion that drastic action was needed to reform both poorly performing schools and failing local education authorities (LEAs). Under the School Standards and Education Act (1998), it became possible to close poorly performing schools and to dispatch 'improvement' teams to 'under achieving' LEAs. A 'Fresh Start' scheme was also put in place under which a 'failing' school could be closed and then re-opened under the direction of a new head teacher and governors. The best performing schools were awarded 'Beacon' status to signify both their capacity to deliver high-quality education and their willingness to support less successful schools.

New Labour believed that the creation of more diverse, non-selective, independent, state-funded secondary schools, in which head teachers and governors would have the autonomy to pursue educational excellence, was the key to improved educational outcomes. Academy schools became the vehicle for such change. A number of experimental 'city academy' schools were set up following the introduction of the Learning and Skills Act in 2000. Comprehensive schools that remained within the local authority sector were also encouraged to pursue a similar path to these experimental academies by applying for 'specialist' status. By 2005, most of these schools (90 per cent) had acquired specialist status, which meant that in addition to following the National Curriculum they would excel in one or two subjects. These schools were to have 'a strong ethos, high quality leadership, good discipline (including school uniforms), setting by ability and high-quality facilities as the norm' (Labour Party, 2005 p. 35). The Education Act of 2006 also allowed for a more diverse secondary schooling when public funding was extended to a wider range of faith-based schools. The 'success' of Labour's academy programme in terms of improving the academic attainment of pupils in poorly performing schools (see Barber, 2008; Adonis, 2012) led the subsequent Conservative-led Coalition government to encourage all LEA maintained schools to opt for academy status, with the inevitable fragmentation of the comprehensive system of education.

New Labour was also determined to increase the numbers of young people in higher education with a participation rate of 50 per cent remaining the long-term goal. The shift from an elite to a 'mass' higher education system created a funding dilemma for New Labour. To meet the rising costs of higher student numbers it was decided, in line with one of the recommendations of the Dearing Report on *Higher Education in a Learning Society* (1997), to introduce student tuition fees (the Teacher and Higher Education Act of 1998). The initial method of recouping fee income was eventually modified from an unpopular up-front system to a post-graduation repayment scheme. Although New Labour attempted to deflect criticism of its proposals by offering support for students from poorer families with reduced fee and maintenance grant packages, the policy remained unpopular. It became a significant issue in the 2010 general election, when the Liberal Democrats declared

> **STOP AND THINK**
>
> What have been the long-term consequences for the welfare state of New Labour's decision to abandon democratic socialism and traditional social democratic ideology?

that they would abolish all tuition fees (a policy they eventually reneged on when they became members of the Conservative-led Coalition government).

Health care

Upon returning to government in 1997, New Labour declared its opposition to creeping marketisation within the National Health Service, which had gathered pace under previous Conservative administrations. Gradually, however, they came to the conclusion that market-style mechanisms could improve the efficiency within the NHS. Although they acknowledged that public spending on the NHS needed to increase in order to match comparable Western European nations, they remained firmly committed to the idea that higher expenditure should always be linked to greater efficiency, service reform, and improved patient outcomes.

To allay public concerns about delays in accessing health services, New Labour introduced a number of ambitious targets and patient guarantees. By the time they left office in 2010, there had been significant reductions in the time that patients had to wait for an operation following a referral from their GP. To speed up this process, those patients with non-urgent complaints were given the opportunity to choose from a wider range of both NHS and non-NHS providers at a time and location that best suited them. Patients with chronic conditions were also encouraged to take much greater control over their own treatment plans. Several innovative services were also introduced. These included NHS Direct (a telephone advice service which was dealing with 6.4 million calls in 2004), NHS Online (a website which had 6.5 million 'hits' by 2004), and over 40 NHS walk-in centres (Toynbee and Walker, 2005).

While service improvements of this kind were broadly welcomed, concerns were expressed about the increased involvement of the private sector in the NHS (Pollock, 2004; Player and Leys, 2011). For example, although they were formerly critical of the Private Financial Initiative introduced by the previous Conservative government, New Labour embarked on a number of public–private partnerships (PPP), under which commercial contractors financed and built new health facilities which they then leased back to the NHS. While such schemes meant that the government could avoid high initial construction payments, and avoid the risk of cost overruns, these short-term savings had to be set against the higher long-term repayments, which are now undermining the viability of some hospitals. In addition, New Labour also entered into a number of agreements or concordats with private health care providers. In 2000, for example, the then Health Secretary, Alan Milburn, entered into an arrangement with the Independent Health Care Association, which guaranteed private health providers a share of NHS funding for routine procedures (Toynbee and Walker, 2001).

In addition, many NHS providers were granted much greater autonomy following the introduction of the Health and Social Care Act of 2003. Under this Act, for example, an NHS hospital could become a Foundation Trust, providing it with greater freedom in relation to setting pay levels and conditions, entering into agreements with private providers, borrowing on the private market, and setting its own medical priorities. Although such hospitals were not permitted to charge NHS patients or increase their current fee income from private patients, such moves were seen as fragmenting the NHS and undermining cooperative working practices (Pollock, 2004).

In keeping with their ideological approach, New Labour placed great emphasis on setting targets for welfare providers in order to enhance outcomes. The traditional Labour view that public-spirited welfare professionals could be relied upon to develop high-quality, cost-efficient services without external monitoring was treated with scepticism (see Le Grand, 2007).

Performance targets

Public Service Agreements, with accompanying SMART (Specific, Measurable, Achievable, Relevant, Timed) targets, were put in place. Some of New Labour's targets related to highly specific objectives such as reducing deaths from cancer and heart disease, raising literacy and numeracy levels, and cutting street crime and rough sleeping. Others measures were introduced to monitor the performance of public bodies such as local authorities. During New Labour's second term, the Audit Commission was charged with constructing Comprehensive Performance Assessments, ranging from excellent to poor, for all local councils in England and Wales on the basis of existing reports and performance indicators (Travers, 2005).

Although New Labour's commitment to targets and performance management was maintained throughout the Brown and Blair era, these measures were adjusted in the light of experience. Local Public Service Agreements and Local Area Agreements were introduced, for example, in recognition of the fact that the achievement of national targets often requires collaboration between councils, health authorities, businesses, and the voluntary sector at the local level.

Evaluating New Labour

Conflicting assessments have been put forward in relation to New Labour's 'welfare' record. Those on the 'positive' end of the spectrum have tended to focus on its economic competence (which was only called into question following the financial crisis of 2008), which provided the resources necessary to spend on hospitals and schools and invest in Sure Start and a range of other 'progressive' initiatives. Although New Labour found it difficult, given global circumstances, to reduce levels of inequality, it can be argued that they succeeded in keeping a lid on the growth of such disparities while also making significant improvements in areas such as child and pensioner poverty. While many commentators acknowledged that more needed to be done in terms of reducing health and educational inequalities, they have commended New Labour for bringing about meaningful improvements in the quality of provision in both these areas, particularly for more disadvantaged groups (see Hills and Stewart, 2005; Pearce and Paxton, 2005; Giddens, 2007). In contrast, those more sceptical of New Labour's social democratic approach (see Page, 2007; Faucher-King and Le Gales, 2010) have raised concerns about the 'cultural' impact of their decision to strike an accord with the free market and their desire to distance themselves from collective action by the state. New Labour's suspicions about the motivations of welfare professionals and those living in poverty led them to favour greater 'managerial' control over both these groups. Indeed, it could be argued that in seeking reform of the welfare state New Labour always preferred to impose its will on its opponents rather than seeking compromise or agreement. This alienated many public sector workers and led vulnerable citizens (and the general public) to view parts of the welfare state as a malign force rather than as a supportive 'friend' providing security and opportunity.

The general election result of 2010, under the leadership of Gordon Brown, was a clear indication that New Labour had lost significant popular support. Clearly, the fallout from the economic crisis of 2008 played a significant part in Labour's loss. However, Conservative 'success' in linking this crisis with profligate forms of social expenditure by the outgoing government left the welfare state vulnerable to attack from the incoming Conservative-led Coalition government.

Conclusions

This chapter has traced the changing ideological approaches of Labour governments from 1945 until the present day and their impact on the welfare strategies adopted. It can be argued that the deep-rooted democratic socialist ideology of the Attlee government enabled it to press ahead with the creation of the welfare state despite adverse economic circumstances. In contrast, the revisionist social democratic ideology of the Wilson and Callaghan governments of the 1960s and 1970s unravelled when prospective social advances had to be postponed or abandoned in the face of chill economic winds. New Labour's modernised social democratic approach was more suited to the accommodation they had made with the free market. The task of social policy was now to work with the grain of the market rather than against it. While New Labour was able to press ahead with a number of modest welfare initiatives during a period of exceptional economic stability, it can be argued that their abandonment of a transformative social vision left them bereft of public affection or support when the economic tide turned.

Summary

This chapter has outlined the main strands in Labour thinking and the approaches and policies to the welfare state adopted by Labour since 1945. It has argued that:

- The dominant ideological positions within the Labour Party have changed significantly over the period.

- The Attlee governments of 1945–51 created the post-war welfare state on the basis of democratic socialist ideas that emphasised equality and a major role for the state in the economy and the provision of welfare.

- By the time Labour returned to power in 1964, a 'revisionist' approach had taken hold within the Party, grounded in a social democratic belief that capitalism could be managed in the interests of society as a whole and that socialists should focus on achieving social equality.

- The economic difficulties of the 1960s and 1970s meant that the Labour governments of the time found it difficult to fulfil their promises in social policy, although they did introduce a number of reforms that significantly advanced personal freedom.

- Following a series of electoral defeats from 1979 to 1992, Labour leaders sought to 'modernise' the Party. Ultimately, under Tony Blair, the rebranded 'New' Labour won the 1997 general election and the Blair and Brown governments reflected a new support for the market alongside a commitment to social justice.

Discussion and review

- Despite significant changes in ideology, Labour governments have remained remarkably consistent in their approach to the welfare state since 1945. What arguments could you put forward in support of this proposition?

- Have the social policy achievements of the 1964–70 Labour government been under-estimated?

- To what extent can it be argued that New Labour followed a welfare agenda that had largely been set by the previous Conservative governments of Thatcher and Major?

References

Addison, P. (1975) *The Road to 1945*, Jonathan Cape, London.

Adonis, A. (2012) *Education, Education, Education*, Biteback, London.

Bacon, R. and Eltis, W. (1976) *Britain's Economic Problems: Too Few Producers*, Macmillan, London.

Bailey, B. (1995) 'James Chuter Ede and the 1944 Education Act', *History of Education*, Vol. 23, No. 3, pp. 209–20.

Barber, M. (2008) *Instruction to Deliver*, Methuen, London.

Beckerman, W. (ed.) (1972) *The Labour Government's Economic Record 1964–1970*, Duckworth, London.

Beckett, F. (2000) *Clem Attlee*, Politicos, London.

Beveridge, W. (1942) *Social Insurance and Allied Services* (The Beveridge Report), Cmd. 6404, The Stationery Office, London.

Bevir, M. (2011) *The Making of British Socialism*, Princeton University Press, Princeton, NJ.

Brooke, S. (1992) *Labour's War: The Labour Party During the Second World War*, Clarendon Press, Oxford.

Brooke, S. (2011) *Sexual Politics*, Oxford University Press, Oxford.

Campbell, J. (1994) *Nye Bevan: A Biography*, Hodder & Stoughton, London.

Crosland, C.A.R. (1956) *The Future of Socialism*, Jonathan Cape, London.

Dearing, R. (1997) *Higher Education in a Learning Society* (The Dearing Report), HMSO, Norwich.

Department of Social Security (1997) *Households Below Average Incomes*, The Stationery Office, London.

Department of Social Security (2001) *Households Below Average Incomes*, The Stationery Office, London.

Donoughue, B. (2003) *The Heat of the Kitchen*, Politicos, London.

Ellison, N. (1994) *Egalitarian Thought and Labour Politics*, Routledge, London.

Ellison, N. (2000) 'Labour and welfare politics', in B. Brivati and R. Heffernan (eds.) *The Labour Party: A Centenary History*, Macmillan: Basingstoke.

Faucher-King, F. and Le Gales, P. (2010) *The New Labour Experiment: Change and Reform Under Blair and Brown*, Stanford University Press, Stanford, CA.

Field, F. (1982) *Poverty and Politics*, Heinemann, London.

Fielding, S. (1997) *The Labour Party*, Palgrave Macmillan, Basingstoke.

Foot, P. (1965) *Immigration and Race in British Politics*, Harmondsworth, Penguin.

Francis, M. (1997) *Ideas and Policies Under Labour 1945–1951*, Manchester University Press, Manchester.

Garnett, M. (2006) *Principles and Politics in Contemporary Britain*, Imprint Academic, Exeter.

Giddens, A. (1998) *The Third Way*, Polity, Cambridge.

Giddens, A. (2000) *The Third Way and Its Critics*, Polity, Cambridge.

Giddens, A. (2007) *Over to You Mr Brown*, Polity, Cambridge.

Glennerster, H. (2000) *British Social Policy since 1945*, Blackwell, Oxford.

Gould, P. (1998) *The Unfinished Revolution*, Little, Brown & Co., London.

Hall, P. (1975) 'Creating the Open University', in P. Hall, H. Land, R. Parker and A. Webb, *Change, Choice and Conflict in Social Policy*, Heinemann, London.

Hennessy, P. (1992) *Never Again: Britain 1945–1951*, Vintage, London.

Hickson, K. (2004) 'Economic thought', in A. Seldon and K. Hickson (eds.) *New Labour, Old Labour: The Wilson and Callaghan Governments, 1974–9*, Routledge, London.

Hill, M. (1993) *The Welfare State in Britain*, Edward Elgar, Aldershot.

Hills, J. and Stewart, K. (eds.) (2005) *A More Equal Society? New Labour, Poverty, Inequality and Exclusion*, Policy Press, Bristol.

Holland, S. (1975) *The Socialist Challenge*, Quartet, London.

Jefferys, K. (1992) *The Attlee Governments 1945–1951*, Longman, London.

Jefferys, K. (2002) *Finest & Darkest Hours*, Atlantic, London.

Jones, M. and Lowe, R. (2002) *From Beveridge to Blair*, Manchester University Press, Manchester.

Jones, T. (1996) *Remaking the Labour Party: From Gaitskell to Blair*, Routledge, London.

Labour Party (1945) *Let Us Face the Future: A Declaration of Labour Policy for the Consideration of the Nation*, London, Labour Party.

Labour Party (1951) *Labour Party Election Manifesto*, Labour Party, London.

Labour Party (1964) *Let's Go with Labour for the New Britain*, The Labour Party's Manifesto for the 1964 General Election, Labour Party, London.

Labour Party (1974) *Britain Will Win with Labour*, The Labour Party's Manifesto for the 1974 General Election, Labour Party, London.

Labour Party (2005) *Britain Forward Not Back*, The Labour Party's Manifesto for the 2005 General Election, Labour Party, London.

Le Grand, J. (2007) *The Other Invisible Hand*, Princeton University Press, Princeton, NJ.

Lipsey, D. (2012) *In The Corridors of Power*, Biteback, London.

Lowe, R. (2004) 'Education policy', in A. Seldon and K. Hickson (eds.) *New Labour, Old Labour: The Wilson and Callaghan Governments, 1974–9*, Routledge, London.

Macnicol, J. (1980) *The Movement for Family Allowances, 1918–45: A Study in Social Policy Development*, Heinemann, London.

Mandelson, P. and Liddle, R. (1996) *The Blair Revolution*, Faber, London.

Marquand, D. (2004) *Decline of the Public*, Polity, Cambridge.

Marwick, A. (2003) *British Society Since 1945*, Penguin, London.

McCarthy, M. (1986) *Campaigning for the Poor*, Croom Helm, Beckenham.

Morgan, K.O. (1984) *Labour in Power 1945–1951*, Clarendon Press, Oxford.

Morgan, K.O. (1992) *The People's Peace*, Oxford University Press, Oxford.

Nissan, D. and Le Grand, J. (2003) *A Capital Idea: Start-Up Grants for Young People*, Fabian Society, London.

O'Connor, J. (1973) *The Fiscal Crisis of the State*, St. Martin's Press, New York.

Page, R.M. (1984) *Stigma*, Routledge & Kegan Paul, London.

Page, R.M. (2007) 'Without a song in their heart: New Labour, the welfare state and the retreat from democratic socialism', *Journal of Social Policy*, Vol. 36, No. 1, pp. 19–38.

Pearce, N. and Paxton, W. (2005) *Social Justice: Building a Fairer Britain*, Politicos, London.

Pearce, R. (1994) *Attlee's Labour Governments 1945–51*, Routledge, London.

Piachaud, D. (2008) 'Poverty and inequality: Labour in the 1970s', *Benefits*, Vol. 16, No. 2, pp. 147–56.

Player, S. and Leys, C. (2011) *The Plot Against the NHS*, Merlin, London.

Pollock, A.M. (2004) *NHS plc*, Verso, London.

Sandbrook, D. (2006) *White Heat: A History of Britain in the Swinging Sixties*, Little, Brown & Co., London.

Seldon, A. and Hickson, K. (2004) 'Introduction', in A. Seldon and K. Hickson (eds.) *New Labour, Old Labour: The Wilson and Callaghan Governments, 1974–9*, Routledge, London.

Shaw, E. (1996) *The Labour Party Since 1945*, Blackwell, Oxford.

Shaw, E. (2007) *Losing Labour's Soul?*, Routledge, London.

Stears, M. (2006) *Progressives, Pluralists and the Problem of the State*, Oxford University Press, Oxford.

Stewart, J. (1999) *The Battle in Health: A Political History of the Socialist Medical Association*, Ashgate, Aldershot.

Stewart, K. (2005) 'Towards an equal start? Addressing childhood poverty and deprivation', in J. Hills and K. Stewart (eds.) *A More Equal Society? New Labour, Poverty, Inequality and Exclusion*, Policy Press, Bristol.

Thornton, S. (2009) *Richard Crossman and the Welfare State*, I.B. Tauris, London.

Thorpe, A. (2001) *A History of the British Labour Party*, Palgrave, Basingstoke.

Timmins, N. (2001) *The Five Giants*, London, HarperCollins.

Tomlinson, J. (1998) 'Why so austere? The British welfare state of the 1940s', *Journal of Social Policy*, Vol. 27, No. 1, pp. 63–77.

Tomlinson, J. (2000) 'Labour and the economy', in D. Tanner, P. Thane and N. Tiratsoo (eds.) *Labour's First Century*, Cambridge University Press, Cambridge.

Tomlinson, J. (2004) *The Labour Governments 1964–1970, Vol. 3: Economic Policy*, Manchester University Press, Manchester.

Toynbee, P. and Walker, D. (2001) *Did Things Get Better?*, Penguin, Harmondsworth.

Toynbee, P. and Walker, D. (2005) *Better or Worse? Has Labour Delivered?*, Bloomsbury, London.

Toynbee, P. and Walker, D. (2011) *The Verdict: Did Labour Change Britain for the Better?*, Granta, London.

Travers, T. (2005) 'Local and central government', in A. Seldon and D. Kavanagh (eds.) *The Blair Effect 2001–5*, Cambridge University Press, Cambridge.

Webster, C. (2002) *The National Health Service*, Oxford University Press, Oxford.

Further reading

Bevir, M. (2011) *The Making of British Socialism*, Princeton University Press, Princeton, NJ. This book examines the mixture of ideas and other influences that lay behind the emergence of British socialism in the late nineteenth century.

Crosland, C.A.R. (1956) *The Future of Socialism*, Jonathan Cape, London (reprinted by Constable, London in 2006). The classic 'revisionist' work, and greatly influenced Labour in the 1960s.

Driver, S. and Martell, L. (2006) *New Labour*, Polity, Cambridge. This work examines the emergence of New Labour and considers the Labour government's record.

Ellison, N. (1994) *Egalitarian Thought and Labour Politics*, Routledge, London. This book examines the different understandings of equality that have impacted upon the Labour Party from the 1930s.

Francis, M. (1997) *Ideas and Policies Under Labour 1945–1951*, Manchester University Press, Manchester. A lively account of the relationship between political ideas and policies under the Attlee governments.

Useful websites

http://www.labour.org.uk – the Labour Party's website provides information on the Party and its policies, and access to a variety of other materials (see also http://www.scottishlabour.org.uk – the Scottish Labour Party – and http://www.welshlabour.org.uk – the Welsh Labour Party).

http://www.fabians.org.uk – an influence on thinking from before the Labour Party's creation, the Fabian Society's web pages give access to its research and publications.

http://www.ippr.org – the Institute for Public Policy Research was a major source of ideas for the 1997–2010 Labour governments. Information about the work of the IPPR, its research and its publications are available here.

http://www.policy-network.net – Policy Network is a left leaning think tank that produces a variety of research and publications.

http://www.compassonline.org.uk – Compass is a pressure group which favours greater equality and which wishes to see Labour working with other progressive organisations. Its website provides a range of information and ideas.

PART 3
THEMES AND ISSUES

- PENSIONS, INCOME MAINTENANCE, AND TAXATION

- WORK AND EMPLOYMENT POLICY

- EDUCATION

- ADULT HEALTH AND SOCIAL CARE

- CHILDREN AND FAMILIES

- DEBATING THE UPS AND DOWNS OF YOUTH JUSTICE

- HEALTH POLICY

- HOUSING POLICY

- 'RACE', ETHNICITY, AND SOCIAL POLICY

- DISABILITY AND SOCIAL POLICY

- OLDER PEOPLE, POPULATION AGEING, AND POLICY RESPONSES

- AN ALTERNATIVE PERSPECTIVE: GREEN SOCIAL POLICY

- EXPLORING THE BOUNDARIES OF SOCIAL POLICY

CHAPTER 9

Pensions, Income Maintenance, and Taxation

Stephen McKay and Karen Rowlingson

Learning objectives

- To outline the roles of taxation and social security in the United Kingdom
- To consider the levels of social security and taxation
- To examine public attitudes towards taxation and social security systems
- To note how these systems have recently developed, and current plans for reform

Chapter overview

The austerity policies pursued by the Coalition government following the economic crisis of 2008 placed great emphasis on the role of the state – including the level of public spending (much of which goes on the welfare state areas of social security, education, and health) and the rates of taxation needed. This chapter examines perceptions of taxes and benefits – and looks at the reality of both systems. It also notes the increasingly negative attitudes taken towards those receiving social security, itself a way of attempting to constrain spending in that area. It:

- summarises the roles of taxation and social security in the UK – these are the main, but not the only, ways in which money is redistributed between individuals, via the state;
- discusses the size and role of social security spending – in 2011–12, over £200 billion was spent on social security benefits;
- considers the size and role of taxation;
- outlines public attitudes towards both systems;
- describes how these systems have recently developed, and current plans for reform.

CONTROVERSY AND DEBATE

The political significance of Inheritance Tax?

Between June 2007 (when Brown became Labour Prime Minister) and October 2007 (Party conferences), the Conservatives' average poll rating was 34 per cent. After the conferences, featuring a proposed significant increase in the allowance for inheritance tax by the Conservative Party, their poll rating averaged 40 per cent between October and December 2007. Other factors also changed, but this may have been a significant moment in tax policy and underlines the potential popularity of an agenda to cut inheritance taxes.

Introduction

The social security and taxation systems can, to some extent, be seen as two sides of the same coin. One collects money for government, the other distributes it to people – sometimes straight back to the same people, sometimes to the same people at a later time (for example, paying National Insurance, and receiving a pension on reaching the appropriate age), and quite often to other people (from richer to poorer). Virtually all of us will, at one time or another, receive money from the social security system and pay money in the form of various taxes.

This chapter compares and contrasts the social security and tax systems. It begins by setting out the dominant – although by no means the only – discourse on social security and taxation. Within this neo-liberal discourse, taxation is seen as a burden while social security is a waste of money, a price paid for failure. In his speech to the Labour Party Conference in 1996, Tony

Blair was committed to reducing 'the welfare bills of social failure' (cited in Brewer *et al.*, 2002, p. 8). The dominance of this discourse explains why governments of all political persuasions have, in recent decades, tried to maintain or reduce levels of taxation and social security expenditure. Neo-liberalist discourse also explains why 'tax expenditures' (tax breaks) have generally received such little attention, and why benefit fraud is treated far more severely than tax fraud. We, however, put forward a more collectivist discourse, arguing that the tax and social security systems can be seen as a means of securing social justice by reducing levels of inequality. Within this overarching framework, we define the social security and tax systems, discuss their aims, describe the size and structure of the two systems, and speculate on how the two systems are likely to change in the future.

It is worth noting that over the last two decades, the term 'social security' has increasingly been replaced by the language of welfare benefits, or simply 'welfare'. This tends to place the emphasis on those with lower incomes, and perhaps also of working age. However, a key aspect of social security is that the majority of spending is received by older people, and primarily in the form of contributory state pensions.

Cultural assumptions about tax and social security

Debates about each major political party's commitments to tax levels have figured strongly in recent elections, from allegations of 'tax bombshells' and gaps in funding tax cuts, through commitments not to raise income tax levels, to the concept of 'stealth taxes'. The main political discussions over social security would appear to concern how punitive the government should be in tackling fraud and reducing spending on the unemployed and some other vulnerable groups.

Cultural assumptions form a crucial underpinning of the current systems of social security and taxation. These assumptions play a powerful role in setting the political agenda for the reform of social security and taxation. It is all too easy to portray spending on benefits as a 'burden', and to regard tax cuts as giving back people '*their* money'. Only rarely does the system of tax exemptions and its high value figure in discussion.

Public attitudes to government spending and taxation are complex and often ambiguous, with people generally supporting higher taxes (so long as someone else is paying them) and also supporting higher spending on 'deserving' groups such as pensioners (Orton and Rowlingson, 2007). Hedges and Bromley (2001) found that people's responses to the tax system were based on ignorance about the system along with strong emotions. The public generally believed that the level of taxation was constantly increasing and was far higher than that in the rest of Europe. The vision of the tax system as a 'burden' or even 'highway robbery' as one respondent termed it (Bromley, 2001, p. 8), illustrates the deeply negative attitudes towards taxation. People generally saw tax as a penalty rather than as a payment for services. They did not feel that they gained value for money from their payment of taxes and they were generally very confused by the complexity of the system.

When respondents were told that most tax revenue was spent on social security benefits, they were particularly annoyed and felt that this confirmed their view that much of 'their' money was being wasted – on 'scroungers' and the 'workshy'. Respondents assumed that most social security expenditure went on the unemployed, but when they were informed that most of the social security budget was spent on pensioners, they were happier to have 'their' money spent on pensioners than other groups. This attitude towards social security expenditure is confirmed by successive waves of the British Social Attitudes Survey, which have asked respondents about the acceptability of spending more on different groups of social security recipients. Pensioners are generally seen as far more 'deserving' than other groups. This notion of 'deserving' and 'undeserving' groups is another prevailing cultural assumption surrounding the benefit system.

The idea that taxation is a burden, and that social security is a waste of money, fits in with a free market or neo-liberal economic philosophy. This philosophy, stemming from the work of the eighteenth-century thinker Adam Smith (1976), and championed in the twentieth century by Hayek (1976) and Nozick (1974) among others, is that state intervention should be minimal. Nozick (1974, p. 169) famously declared that 'Taxation of earnings from labor is on a par with forced labor'. It is argued that taxes and benefits should be kept very low because if they are set too high people will face disincentives to work. Underlying this philosophy is the idea that people who engage in paid work are 'independent', while those who receive social security benefits are 'dependent'. Wages from paid work constitute an individual's own money, to which they have an inalienable right. Such a philosophy suggests that those who put individual effort into earning wages should therefore be able to keep as much of 'their' money as possible.

These cultural assumptions are very strong in the United States. They are also very strong in the United Kingdom. The Conservative governments from 1979 to 1997 broke the tentative post-war consensus over the welfare state. Thatcherism sought to 'roll back the frontiers of the state' and allow the market to flourish unhindered by regulation and taxation. After successive defeats at the ballot box, 'New' Labour distinguished itself from 'Old' Labour precisely on this point of philosophy. The Coalition government has been able to benefit from New Labour's generally limited arguments concerning redistribution, and move towards quite severe cuts in spending on social security.

An alternative way of looking at tax and social security stems from what might be called a social solidarity or collectivist philosophy. Underpinning this philosophy is the idea that the role of the state is a positive one, as it creates the conditions under which people can flourish and social justice can be achieved. People are not divided into those who are 'dependent' and those who are 'independent'; all are seen as interdependent on each other. This emphasis on social inclusion, interdependency, and solidarity rather than individual freedom is the main difference between this philosophy and that of

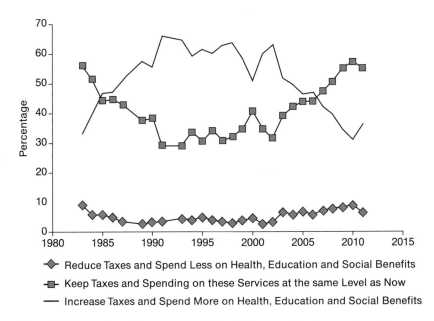

Figure 9.1 Views about what governments should do regarding taxes and benefits
Source: Authors' analysis of British Social Attitudes, 1983–2011

free market neo-liberalism. This broad philosophical approach encompasses elements of socialism and social democracy (see, for example, Tawney, 1921, 1931; Miliband, 1994).

Although neo-liberalism appears the most common way of seeing tax and social security, evidence from the British Social Attitudes Surveys has shown very low support (less than 10 per cent) for the idea that taxes should be cut alongside cuts in social spending (see Figure 9.1). In 1983, the balance of opinion was to maintain levels of tax and spending. Between 1985 and 2006, there were more who favoured increases in both taxes and spending, the former to pay for the latter. After 2007 (which happens to be when power moved from Blair to Brown), however, we see a return to the overall views of the early 1980s, with a preference for retaining taxation levels and benefits (education, health, and social benefits) at their current levels. This view in favour of no change has been a rising trend since 2002.

The importance of social security and taxation

Since the Second World War, spending on social security has risen almost continuously. There has been a tenfold increase over the period, with only occasional dips generally associated with times of falling unemployment. This illustrates the manner in which social security has come to take on roles not anticipated in the post-war Beveridge plan, such as the demands arising from growing levels of economic inactivity (for example, rising spending on disability benefits), increases in life expectancy (affecting pensions spending), and changes in family forms (such as more lone parents receiving benefits in their own right). Until the 1980s, benefit rates also tended to increase more rapidly than price inflation, more closely matching growth in the economy as a whole.

Table 9.1 lists some of the largest benefits in monetary terms. The total of around £200 billion is, in fact, spent to a great degree on older people and on disabled people (including older disabled people). In particular, the £60 billion spent on the main retirement pension is the single largest item of government spending. Housing benefit (some of which goes to older people who rent) is among the largest of the other benefits – at around £23 billion – and has therefore been subject to a number of recent reforms aimed at stemming its growth. By contrast, amounts spent on the unemployed are much less in the context of this volume of spending.

The number of people paying direct taxation has also increased to some 30 million, compared with fewer than 5 million before the Second World War (Figure 9.2). Income tax used to be paid only by higher earners, but is now paid by most people working (both employees and the self-employed). In the last few years, the number paying income tax has been falling, the result of both recession (lower earnings) and rises in the threshold from which people start to pay income tax, a strong policy of the Coalition government.

The combined effects of taxes and benefits include providing some degree of equalisation of income between rich and poor in any given year. The incomes from employment, self-employment, and investments of the best-off 10 per cent were nearly 30 times as great as those of the worst-off 10 per cent in 2010–11. However, if we include the benefits provided by the state in kind (health, education, housing subsidies), as well as the money paid in social security benefits, then the disparity falls to five-to-one (see Figure 9.3).

Table 9.1 Cost of selected social security benefits, 2011–12

Social security benefits	Value
Basic state pension	£58 billion
Additional state pension	£16 billion
Pension credit	£8 billion
Winter fuel payment	£2 billion
Housing benefit	£23 billion
Child tax credit	£22 billion
Disability living allowance	£13 billion
Child benefit	£12 billion
Income support	£7 billion
Attendance allowance	£5 billion
Incapacity benefit	£5 billion
Jobseeker's allowance	£5 billion

Source: Department of Work and Pension Benefit Expenditure Tables (http://statistics.dwp.gov.uk/asd/asd4/index.php?page=expenditure)

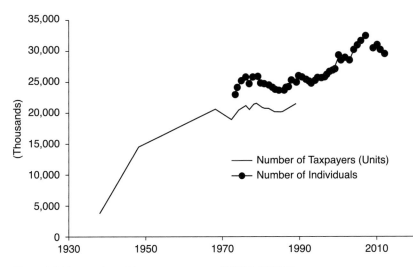

Figure 9.2 The number of income tax payers, 1938/39–2012/13

Source: HMRC tax receipt statistics (http://www.hmrc.gov.uk/statistics/taxpayers.htm)

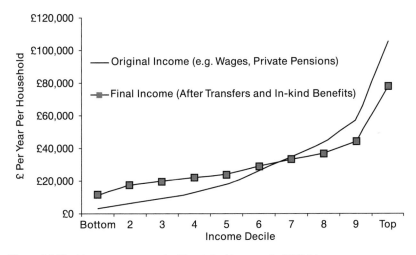

Figure 9.3 Final incomes compared with original incomes in 2010–11

Source: Office for National Statistics (2012)

Defining 'social security' and taxation

Social security and taxation clearly play a central role in people's lives. But what is meant by these terms? There is no universally accepted neat definition of 'social security' or 'taxation', so this section discusses possible definitions.

Social security

Starting with the very widest definition, 'social security' is sometimes used to refer to all the ways by which people organise their lives to ensure access to an adequate income. This wide concept includes securing income from all sources, such as earnings from employers and self-employment, financial help from charities, money from a family member, and cash benefits from the state. So in the area of welfare related to maintaining income there are different means by which this may be achieved. Of foremost importance is the private sector, for example earnings from employment and profits from self-employment are the chief source of income for most people of working age, and pensions in retirement are often based on such earnings.

A slightly narrower definition of social security would include all types of financial support, except those provide by the market system. In this way, reliance on the immediate or extended family would still be classed as helping to achieve social security. However, it is increasingly usual to adopt an even narrower definition, and to regard social security as those sources of immediate financial support provided by the state.

The definition of 'social security' as the system of cash benefits paid by the government to different individuals appears to be fairly simple and unproblematic. But it is inadequate or, at least, does not include the same range of activities that most people would regard as being social security. This is because some 'benefits' are not paid for by the state, or need not be. Statutory sick pay used to be paid by government but, while it remains a legal entitlement, it is now mostly a cost met by employers. There are also occupational schemes for sickness, widowhood, and retirement that are similar to state benefits, and which have a similar function, but which are organised by employers. One could also envisage the government finding ways to 'privatise' what are currently state benefits, or instigating new compulsory private provision, perhaps for pensions. So, both voluntary employer schemes and some programmes mandated by government may also be classed as social security – neither of which neatly fit the above definition.

Taxation

Taxation can be defined as the different sources of government revenue. This definition is quite wide and includes not only those sources known specifically as 'taxes', but also those sources known as insurance 'contributions', as well as 'duties', 'royalties', 'levies', and so on. Revenue from interest and dividends can also be included in a very wide definition of taxation and we employ such a definition for this chapter.

The British tax system is an individualised system whereby people within a couple are treated independently (for example, in having their own personal allowances and not having their income combined for tax purposes). The social security system treats couples as couples, operating a couple-based means test for income-related benefits and allowing additions for 'dependents' in the case of contributory benefits. In general, income tax liabilities are based on annual gross incomes. What payments are due depends on income over the whole tax year. By contrast, many means-tested benefits are based on income over a relatively short period – if you have no money in a particular week, it is important you receive payment promptly. Income tax bills – and rebates – may be considered at a more leisurely place.

Tax expenditures

Most forms of taxation have systems of allowances, reliefs, credits, deductions, and so on, which comprise exemptions from the general applicability of the tax. For example, some income is exempt from taxation – such as gross income spent on private pension contributions, and interest received on special savings accounts, currently called Individual Savings Accounts (ISAs). It may be argued that tax allowances are similar to subsidies and so should properly be seen as public expenditure, rather than deductions from tax. Why should direct payments to pensioners appear as a cost, while tax concessions for private pensions show up – if at all – simply as lower tax? For this reason, the term 'tax expenditures' has been coined for such exemptions, although in popular parlance the term 'loophole' might be equally apt. The existence of such exemptions is one means of pursuing tax avoidance – legal ways of reducing tax liability.

The value of tax expenditures seems to vary widely across OECD countries (Greve, 1994) and often to the benefit of better-off families. Many poorer families are not subject to tax measures attracting such exemptions, and hence cannot gain from certain tax expenditures. Conversely, some specific tax expenditures are said to be targeted at poorer households – such as a lower rate of value-added tax (VAT) on domestic fuel and on children's clothes than on most other goods and services. However, since richer families spend more on these items than poorer households, the cash gain is actually smaller for poorer families than for the rich – although the proportionate gain for poorer households may be greater.

Tax expenditures remain an important part of government policy, although the value of some of them has been reduced, including removal of income tax reliefs for married couples and for mortgage interest payments. The costs of tax allowances and exemptions are only periodically subject to close scrutiny, although regular figures on their size are produced in government reports – if one gets through enough of the annexes! The cost of a tax exemption is inevitably an estimate, since people might behave differently if the exemption

STOP AND THINK

Until 2012, Starbucks, Amazon, and Google all paid very little corporation tax in the UK.

- Do companies have any moral duty to pay more in tax than the law can force them to?

- Should consumers take action to boycott or campaign against such organisations?

- With global companies so easily avoiding tax, does this mean that UK governments should aim to be low-tax regimes for companies, and instead tax people and less mobile objects?

Table 9.2 Value of selected tax expenditures, 2012–13

Tax expenditure	Value
Tax relief for registered pension schemes	£21.6 billion
Capital gains tax: exemption of gains from main residence	£9.9 billion
National Insurance contracted-out rebate for occupational schemes	£9.2 billion
VAT zero-rating of domestic passenger transport	£3.5 billion
Inheritance tax: exemption of transfers on death to surviving spouses	£2.6 billion
ISAs	£1.8 billion
Exemption of first £30,000 of payments on termination of employment	£0.8 billion

Source: HMRC

were removed. The estimated value of tax expenditures is vast. Estimates of the value of some particular tax exemptions by Her Majesty's Revenue and Customs are shown in Table 9.2 (up-to-date estimates are available from http://www.hmrc.gov.uk/stats/tax_expenditures/menu.htm).

The aims of social security and taxation

Having defined taxation and social security, we now ask what are the aims of these systems? The answer is complex. Like elsewhere, the system in Britain has evolved over time and so is not necessarily what would be designed if policy-makers were now starting from scratch. Furthermore, different parts of the system have different aims and so it is not possible to identify one aim, and it is even arguable as to what the main aim of the system is. With these reservations in mind, the Spotlight below lists some of the possible objectives of social security.

SPOTLIGHT

Possible aims of social security

- To insure against the risks of particular events in life, such as unemployment and short-term sickness.
- To relieve poverty or low income.
- To redistribute resources across people's life cycles, especially from working age to retirement.
- To redistribute resources from rich to poor.
- To 'compensate' for some types of extra cost (e.g. children, disability).
- To provide financial support when 'traditional' families break down.

Within these general aims, the British social security system has been designed to achieve the following:

- to maintain incentives for self-provision (such as through earning and saving);
- to keep non-take-up of benefits low;
- to counter possible fraud;
- to ensure that administrative costs are low.

The policies of the Department for Work and Pensions, and more widely across government, are aimed at ending child poverty. The goal is to end child poverty by 2020. The Child Poverty Act 2010 set out four main measures of child poverty by which to judge progress (relative low income; combined low income and material deprivation; absolute low income; persistent poverty). The Coalition government has continued this emphasis. They are strong supporters of the movement into paid work as the primary route out of family poverty, with the added benefit of reducing children living in workless households. Not all movements into paid work may immediately move a family out of poverty, but at least such moves tackle worklessness, which remains much higher in the UK than in comparable countries.

The aims of the British system have traditionally been more limited than those of systems in Europe, if wider than in some parts of the rest of the English-speaking world. The importance of relieving poverty in the British system explains the considerable reliance on means testing in the United Kingdom. Receipt of means-tested benefits depends on a person or family having resources (typically income, and perhaps savings) below a certain level in order to receive benefits. Means testing is also common in America, New Zealand, and Australia, but much less common elsewhere, especially in Continental Europe where social security tends to be less centralised and more concerned with income maintenance and compensation.

Throughout history, one of the main reasons for taxation was to raise money for war. With the growth of the welfare state, however, the tax system has taken on rather different aims, such as enabling/compelling people to save money in case they experience unemployment, sickness or retirement. Taxes are also used to pay money to people who do not have sufficient to live on. The tax system also aims to raise money for local and central government services such as health and education. A rather different possible aim of the tax system might be to reduce people's consumption of particular goods. For example, tobacco is generally considered to be harmful and so it is argued that high taxes on tobacco will reduce people's consumption of this substance. Similarly, taxes on petrol may reduce the number of car journeys, which are detrimental to the environment.

A final possible aim of the tax system is to redistribute income and/or wealth from rich to poor. If the rich are most heavily taxed and most of the money then given out either in cash or services to poorer groups, then the tax system is performing a 'Robin Hood' function. But the extent to which this occurs in practice is debatable, as the poor pay a large proportion of their income in taxes (such as VAT) and wealthier groups actually take a great deal of advantage of welfare state services (for example, education and pensions – because they stay in education for longer and they live longer, thus receiving more in pensions).

A tax system that takes a higher proportion of tax from the income of richer than poorer people is known as a progressive system. Under a regressive system, the poor pay a higher proportion of their income in taxes than do the rich. Generally speaking, direct taxes on income tend to be progressive, while indirect taxes tend to be regressive – partly because poorer groups spend a higher proportion of their incomes and partly because spending on some taxed goods does not rise much with income. Those who argue for greater emphasis on direct taxation often do so from a collectivist perspective, since direct taxation tends to be more progressive than indirect taxation.

SPOTLIGHT

Possible aims of taxation

- To raise money for war and defence.
- To enable people to save against future risks.
- To pay money to people on very low incomes.
- To pay for local or central services.
- To reduce people's consumption of certain goods.
- To redistribute income/wealth.

An overview of the current systems

Social security

The social security system today is highly complex, having evolved over time. Very few people understand it in all its detail. For every possible generalisation about the system, there are myriad caveats. It is therefore difficult to give a brief overview without over-simplifying the system and therefore possibly misleading (for further details, see McKay and Rowlingson, 1999; Millar, 2003). Nevertheless, this section attempts to provide such an overview. There are various ways of classifying the different benefits in the UK system. For example, benefits can be categorised into two dichotomies: universal versus means-tested; contributory versus non-contributory. If we use the rules of entitlement as our yardstick, social security can be divided into three main components: contributory benefits (benefits which rely upon having paid contributions); means-tested benefits and tax credits (benefits which depend upon income); and contingent benefits (benefits which depend upon your position or category), as follows:

Contributory benefits

The root for the current social security system lies in the Beveridge Report, published in the early 1940s, although insurance-based and other benefits had been introduced well before this time. At the heart of the Beveridge approach – of contributory benefits or 'social insurance' – is the idea that people face a range of risks that might lead to severe reductions in living standards. These include the risk of unemployment, being incapacitated and unable to work, retiring, or losing the main income-earner in a family. Some risks are rather uncommon, and relatively unrelated to economic circumstances, such as widowhood. Other risks, such as retirement, are much more widespread and predictable.

Social insurance benefits have entitlement based on having paid National Insurance contributions, and being affected by a risk covered by these benefits (such as unemployment or retirement). These benefits are individualised in that the earnings of a partner do not generally affect entitlement. The main benefit in this group is the state retirement pension. Other benefits are the contributory parts of employment and support allowance (formerly incapacity benefit) and the contribution-based jobseeker's allowance. The payment period of jobseeker's allowance was reduced compared with the preceding unemployment benefit, and similarly contributory employment and support allowance is time-limited for those capable of some work-related activity (to one year) compared with the unlimited duration of incapacity benefit (while of working age).

> **STOP AND THINK**
>
> **Social insurance benefits**
> The main issues that arise with social insurance include:
>
> - Why should the state provide this service, rather than private insurance? What relationship should there then be between state and private insurance?
>
> - What risks should be covered?
>
> - On what basis should contributions be made, or be deemed to be made?

Means-tested benefits/tax credits

Entitlement to means-tested benefits depends on the level of 'family' resources, particularly income and savings. The four main examples in the British system are income support, the working families tax credit, housing benefit, and council tax benefit.

The system of benefits based on means testing, particularly for those on low incomes, is sometimes known as 'social assistance'. In Britain, social assistance is almost synonymous with the benefit income support, and income-based jobseeker's allowance for unemployed people. These benefits are paid to those whose income and savings are below defined levels, taking into account the size and type of family.

Countries differ a great deal in the extent of this type of provision. In Australia and New Zealand, almost all benefits include an element of 'means testing'. This does not mean that only the poorest may receive benefits – in some instances, the aim is to exclude the richest rather than to include only the poorest. In much of Northern Europe, social assistance plays a much smaller role, picking up those not covered by the main social insurance system. In addition, it is often administered locally, with local organisations having some discretion about the precise rules of entitlement.

Additional conditions are often attached to receiving social assistance. People of working age, without sole responsibility for caring for children or disabled adults, must be able to work, available for work, and actively seeking work. In past times, they may have had to enter a workhouse to qualify.

From 2013, in a process expected to take four or five years, a new universal credit will replace many of the key means-tested benefits and tax credits into a single structure for people of working age (see below).

CONTINGENT BENEFITS

These are sometimes referred to as categorical benefits, or as non-means-tested and non-contributory. Entitlement depends on the existence of certain circumstances (or contingencies), such as having a child (child benefit), being disabled (disability living allowance, severe disablement allowance) or, in the past at least, being a lone parent (one parent benefit). However, these benefits are being rolled back. For those of working age, the disability living allowance is being replaced by a new personal independence payment, for which it is anticipated fewer people will qualify. From 2013, child benefit was no longer paid to families where one person earns in excess of £60,000 per year, and starts to be withdrawn at individual earnings of more than £50,000. This new measure has proved controversial, partly because of ending the universal principle in child benefit, but also because it has been seen to be unfair. A couple on £100,000 between them are allowed to retain child benefit (if they each earn half of that figure), while it is denied to a household where £60,000 comes from just one person. It also seems to break the long-standing divide that benefits are at a household level with income tax based only on individual earnings.

It is worth emphasising that this division into three groups is something of a simplification of differences between benefits. Means-tested benefits do not just depend on financial resources; they tend also to rely on some combination of being in a particular situation or a particular family type. For example, able-bodied single people may only claim income support if they meet conditions relating to being unemployed. And it is possible for certain sources of income to affect contributory benefits; for example, jobseeker's allowance and employment support allowance (both with contribution-based elements) can be reduced if a person receives income from a personal or occupational pension.

UNIVERSAL CREDIT

While New Labour introduced a number of benefits and tax credits (family credit, working families tax credit, and then working tax credit), the set of welfare reforms introduced by the Coalition government is more 'root and branch', and replaces several payments with the new universal credit. The new universal credit will be the main form of support for lower income families with children, and will ensure that work pays more than benefits, whatever the hours of work under consideration. This advantage of work over not working will also be clear through other measures, such as the cap on the total benefits received by those not in paid work. Already in place is the Work Programme, which provides a set of support measures (personalised) to assist those capable of working into paid work.

Taxation

The tax system is often divided into 'direct taxes', such as income tax and National Insurance contributions, and 'indirect taxes', such as value-added tax (VAT), which applies to most goods and service, and duties, such as those on petrol, alcohol, and tobacco. But government revenue is more complex than that and we offer a different categorisation, as follows:

- Direct taxes on income
- Capital taxes
- Other indirect taxes
- Corporation taxes
- Council tax
- Other sources of revenue.

Table 9.3 shows that income tax is the largest single source of government revenue but this most prominent form of tax still only accounts for just over a quarter of revenue. National Insurance contributions are the second most important source of government income followed by VAT and then corporation taxes.

Table 9.3 Main and other sources of government revenue, 2011–12

Source	Amount
Income tax	£152.7 billion
National Insurance contributions	£101.6 billion
VAT	£98.1 billion
Corporation tax	£43.1 billion
Fuel duties	£26.8 billion
Council tax	£26.0 billion
Tobacco duties	£9.9 billion
Capital gains tax	£4.3 billion
Insurance premium tax	£3.0 billion
Inheritance tax	£2.9 billion

Source: HM Treasury, *Budget Report, 2013*

Direct taxes on income

'Direct taxes' include both income tax and National Insurance contributions. Income tax is, perhaps, the most politically sensitive.

Not all income is subject to income tax. The main sources of income that are taxed include earnings from employment and self-employment, pension payments during retirement, and some social security benefits (such as retirement pensions). People do not pay tax on all of their income from these sources. They each have a personal allowance and if their income (from taxable sources) falls below this personal allowance, they pay no income tax at all.

Until April 2000, married couples had an extra allowance. This was often used by the man in the couple, particularly if the woman stayed at home to look after children. The Labour government abolished this married couples' allowance for all but those born before 1935. The Labour government's main aim was to redistribute from married couples (who may or may not have children) to people with children (who may or may not be married) and the reform was criticised by the Conservative opposition as penalising marriage.

National Insurance contributions (NICs) may be considered as another form of direct taxation. They were initially introduced in the early part of the twentieth century to pay for unemployment insurance (and for health), before being extended to their main current purpose, retirement pensions, during the 1920s. National Insurance contributions are sometimes portrayed as different from taxation because they are supposed to be contributions to one's own pension or other insurance benefits. However, the revenue from this source has never been invested in the way that private pension contributions are invested. Instead, today's NICs are paying towards the benefits of today's recipients.

The vast majority of revenue from NICs comes from 'Class 1' contributions. These are paid by employees as a tax on their earnings and by employers as secondary contributions on those they employ.

Capital taxes

There are three main capital taxes: capital gains tax, inheritance tax, and stamp duties of various kind. Capital gains tax is levied on gains made from selling assets by individuals or trustees. Inheritance tax is paid when people receive an asset on or shortly before someone's death. Stamp duty is paid on transfers of stocks and shares, land, and property. All transfers of stocks and shares are taxed, but there are different rates depending on the value of land/property, and exemptions for properties in some deprived areas.

Value-added tax

Value-added tax can be divided into four categories, as follows:

- A standard rate of 20 per cent on most goods and services.

- A reduced rate of 5 per cent on a range of products including domestic fuel and power, women's sanitary products, and children's car seats (accounting for 3 per cent of consumers' expenditure).

- Exempt goods have no VAT levied on the final good sold to the consumer but firms cannot reclaim VAT paid on inputs.

- Zero-rated goods (including food, construction of new homes, public transport, children's clothing, books, medicines on prescription) have no VAT levied upon the final good or upon the inputs used in its creation.

Other indirect taxes

Duty on petrol sparked an explosive protest in the late 1990s, when protestors blockaded the movement of petrol and the pumps began to dry up. The existence of high duties on petrol, alcohol, and tobacco can provide incentives to evade taxes. People may cross the Channel to stock up on tobacco and alcohol – that is perfectly legal for personal consumption, but it is illegal to buy such goods with the intention of selling them on.

Vehicle excise duty (often referred to as 'road tax') is another indirect tax in this category. So too are insurance premium tax, air passenger duty, landfill tax, climate change levy, and betting and gaming duties, and so on.

Corporation taxes

Corporation taxes are charges on profits made by UK companies.

Council Tax

The system of local taxation was a major problem area for government in the 1980s, leading to the introduction of the hated poll tax (or community charge as it was officially known). In 1993, the council tax was introduced, based on property price levels rather than on individuals. Properties are put into one of eight bands depending on their value and then individual councils set the amount of tax to be paid by people living in each of the properties. Council tax provides about 20 per cent of local authority revenue (Adam and Frayne, 2001).

Other sources of revenue

Other sources of revenue include the taxation of income from savings. Certain forms of savings have received more favourable treatment under the tax system than others. For example, personal and occupational pensions received tax relief on contributions and no tax on fund income. These reliefs were introduced to encourage people to save in such schemes, but wealthier groups were much more likely to take advantage of these schemes than poorer people and so the tax system had an in-built advantage towards better-off groups. In recent years, various tax-privileged schemes have been introduced (such as ISAs) to benefit people with varying levels of income. These ISAs, however, have mostly been taken up by wealthy people and so government is piloting new schemes, such as the Saving Gateway, which will only be available to working-age people on relatively low incomes.

Tackling fraud in social security and taxation

STOP AND THINK

There are about 30 prosecutions each year for those seeking to avoid paying taxes, which involves in excess of £5 billion. Conversely, there are around 9,000 prosecutions for benefit fraud, which costs around £1 billion (Brooks, 2013: 12).

- Why is there much greater enthusiasm for taking benefit fraudsters to court?

- Does this seem fair?

- Are these different kinds of offence or, as Dee Cook (1989) argued, similar in their effects?

A key issue in relation to the administration of tax and benefits is the extent and nature of fraud. Cook (1989) was one of the first to point to the considerable differences between the treatment of benefit fraud and tax fraud. Benefit fraud has traditionally received much more attention from the state, and investigators, prosecutors, and sentencers have treated much more harshly those suspected of committing benefit fraud. These differences relate back to the prevailing assumptions about tax and social security. For example, those committing tax fraud are generally seen to be merely trying to keep hold of 'their' money, whereas benefit fraudsters are seen as receiving even more money than they should be entitled to. A collectivist perspective might be more sympathetic to benefit fraudsters, as it would consider the very low incomes of people on benefit (and most benefit fraudsters) compared with the very high incomes of tax fraudsters.

Recent reforms and future prospects

Despite substantial increases in spending on health and education, social security remains by far the largest area of spending on the 'five giants' of social welfare. It also retains something of a reputation for being a complex area, with limited public knowledge and discussion. Tax remains a key political battleground. After a decade during which New Labour failed to argue the case for redistribution through higher taxes, the Coalition government has found it easier to take away a range of benefits.

Various reforms to the pension system have been introduced, including: increasing the state pension age for future cohorts; restoring the link between pensions and earnings; and introducing new 'opt-out' personal accounts for those without private pensions. The effects of these will take many years to discern, and we discuss some of the key changes forthcoming.

Pension reform

The reviews of the Pensions Commission during the mid 2000s argued that the UK pension system was very complex (the most complex in the world) and had generated a problem of under-saving for many people. Without reform, pensioners would get poorer (unless taxes rose, savings increased, or people worked longer). The proposals contained in the later reports sought to make a number of proposals, in particular changes to state pensions and the introduction of a new pension product that included auto-enrolment.

First, within state pensions, is the introduction of a single-tier pension. This means a movement away from an earnings-related second pension (S2P and previously SERPS) towards a larger flat-rate state pension, for those making sufficient contributions. At present, the level of the (contributory) basic state pension is below that of (means-tested) pension credit. That means that having entitlement to the full basic state pension does not take someone clear of means testing. One of the aims of the new single-tier pension is that the contributory entitlement will exceed the pension credit level so that more pensioners will be clear of means testing. In turn, that will mean avoiding the current situation, where small amounts of private saving may be seen to be futile as they simply cancel out pension credit entitlement. While there is a savings credit element to pension credit that is capable of rewarding (say) a small personal pension, it is still often the perception and indeed the reality that savings for those on a low pension income may not be rewarded. This point particularly applies to those self-employed workers without a second pension.

The future value of the state pension is also currently protected by the 'triple lock' element where pensions increase at the highest of wage growth, inflation or 2.5 per cent.

A further set of changes within the state system concern moving more quickly to the equalisation of men's and women's state pension ages, and the introduction of higher state pension ages more rapidly over time. Higher state pension ages will reflect increasing longevity and improved health. At the same time, the removal of forced retirement ages will mean greater opportunities to continue in paid work.

The other key reform is the recent introduction of NEST (the National Employment Savings Trust), on a rolling basis. This is accompanied by a reform process incorporating automatic enrolment into either NEST or a suitable alternative pension scheme. This is designed to increase the level of pension savings, given that under-saving for retirement has been identified as a particular issue (for

STOP AND THINK

Many of the new cuts to social security benefits do not apply to older people – they are not affected by changes to rules about housing benefit for tenants, not affected by universal credit, and retain benefits including winter fuel payments and bus passes, without any kind of means-testing.

- Why are pensioners receiving such different treatment from those of working age?

- To what extent do state pensions seem to be part of the same welfare system as benefits for lone parents or the unemployed?

- Are these policies sustainable or desirable?

example, by the Pensions Commission). Indeed, many people only start planning and saving for retirement relatively late in their working lives, from the age of perhaps 45 or 50.

There are also more recent suggestions of ways to try to prevent the decline of occupational pensions. Decline has been evident since 1967 when occupational pension coverage was at its height. Drops in coverage have been particularly acute in terms of the closure of defined benefit schemes to new workers in most companies. One response from the Department of Work and Pensions has been the concept of 'Defined Ambition', which seeks to go beyond the binary defined contribution/defined benefit (DC/DB) divide, in particular for employers wanting to do more than the minimum but cautious about taking on considerable extra risks. That would aim to provide greater certainty for workers about the outcomes (greater than current DC arrangements), but also to expose employers to lower cost risks than under DB schemes.

Reforms to working-age social security

One of the key changes is the introduction of the universal credit, replacing many of the existing means-tested benefits (such as income support and housing benefit) and tax credits (such as child tax credit). This has generally been welcomed in principle – with probable gains in consistency, and transparency – but concern has been raised about some of the details of reform. So, housing benefit will generally be paid to claimants rather than to landlords, and the period of payment will move to monthly – in both cases there will be greater need for budgeting resources than at present.

An important symbolic change is that the total benefits paid to families will be capped at a maximum level of £500 for couples and £350 for lone parents (and single people). Although few people are affected, because those in work and receiving particular disability benefits are exempt, this is seen as emphasising that workers should generally be better off than non-workers (the principle of 'less eligibility' originally enshrined in workhouses; see Chapter 6).

In 2013 and subsequent years, increases in most benefits will be capped at a maximum of 1 per cent per year. In the past they tended to rise in line with inflation, so as to maintain their real value. Again this change has been justified in terms of the limited wage increases in recent times for those in paid work. Child benefit had already been subject to a cash freeze.

Another controversial element of reform has been linking housing benefit for social tenants to the size of the family rather than the size of the property. In the past, housing benefit would pay for the rent on the dwelling, even if the property was somewhat under-occupied (for example, a single person in a two-bedroom house). This reform has been dubbed the 'bedroom tax' by opponents, and the removal of the 'spare room subsidy' by proponents. Critics have pointed out the limited options for people to move property (to downsize) within the social rented sector. Private tenants had already been subject to changes, meaning that their rents needed to be in the bottom third of those in the area, rather than the bottom half, for full housing benefit.

SPOTLIGHT

Restricting the level of housing benefit

Before recent reforms, private tenants could generally have their rent paid as long as it was at or below the 'median' for the local rental area, for a property with an appropriate number of bedrooms. In the press it was possible to report families who received housing benefit of around £100,000 per year, by living in the most expensive areas of the country, such as Kensington and Chelsea. In fact, the numbers doing so are tiny, but they were subject to strong publicity (e.g. http://www.dailymail.co.uk/news/article-1351537/The-10-families-costing-1m-state-handouts.html). The key policy changes in this area were an overall cap on amounts being paid – a reduction from £2,000 to £400 per week, and a stipulation that the rent must be in the bottom 30 per cent rather than bottom 50 per cent of rents in the local area.

With spending on housing benefit having risen to £23 billion by 2011–12 and with 5 million recipients, there was a strong appetite for reform, although that increase resulted from increases in private rents and more people renting privately rather than social housing (a declining sector). London mayor Boris Johnson initially expressed concern that the effects of the policy might lead to 'Kosovo style' social cleansing of the capital (http://www.bbc.co.uk/news/uk-politics-11643440).

Conclusions

Most of what government does is funded by taxation. Commitments to spend must generally be backed by tax revenue. This places an onus on government to find ways to raise taxes that have the least effect on behaviour, unless behaviour change is an objective (such as with 'green taxes'), and to ensure a 'fair' apportionment of who pays tax. The largest area of spending remains social security benefits.

Both tax and social security benefits play an important role in reducing the inequality generated through market incomes. Before looking at transfers, the best-off 10 per cent have incomes about 30 times greater than the poorest 10 per cent. After transfers, the remaining inequality is still very high – a ratio of 5 to 1 – but clearly much reduced. It is an important social policy question as to just how much redistribution is politically feasible. Social security benefits are quite effective at redistributing income from rich to poor; many aspects of the tax system are progressive in this way (such as income tax) but other aspects are regressive (such as taxes on spending). The more hidden world of 'tax expenditures' generally acts to favour the better off.

Policy within social security has been increasingly changed under New Labour and the Coalition government to give even greater emphasis to returning people to work. It has become a work-based system, for most adults of working age. The new universal credit represents a very large reform to the structure of social security. Older people have been largely unaffected, with the new single-tier pension likely to benefit tomorrow's lower income pensioners.

Summary

This chapter has outlined a variety of features of the tax and social security systems in the United Kingdom. It has suggested that:

- The social security and tax systems can seen as two sides of the same coin.
- Notions of the 'deserving' and 'undeserving' poor continue to affect attitudes towards the benefits system.
- Attitudes towards state spending on welfare hardened after 2006, according to British Social Attitudes Surveys.
- Income tax used to be paid by only higher earners, but is now paid by most people in paid work.
- The incomes of the best-off 10 per cent are nearly 30 times as great as those of the worst-off 10 per cent. After taking into account taxes and benefits, they are 'merely' five times better off.
- Tax expenditures ('tax breaks') are also important, but their costs are only periodically subject to close scrutiny.
- There are three main types of social security benefit: contributory, means-tested benefits, and contingent. The importance of relieving poverty in the British system explains the strong reliance on means testing in Britain.

Discussion and review

- Is it inevitable that social security (welfare) spending will be cut, or are there strategies to defend against cuts? Why has the 'them and us' approach proved so easy to introduce with limited objections?
- Only a small minority (under 10 per cent) of estates pay inheritance tax. So, why are proposals to abolish it (or make it affect even fewer people) so popular compared with other taxes?
- Why is the social security system in the UK so complex? Is this complexity justified?

References

Adam, S. and Frayne, C. (2001) *A Survey of the UK Tax System*, Briefing Note No. 9, Institute for Fiscal Studies, London.

Brewer, M., Clark, T. and Wakefield, M. (2002) *Five Years of Social Security Reforms in the UK*, Working Paper W02/12, Institute for Fiscal Studies, London.

Brooks, R. (1989) *The Great Tax Robbery: How Britain became a Tax Haven for Fat Cats and Big Business*, Oneworld Publications, London.

Cook, D. (1989) *Rich Law, Poor Law: Different Responses to Tax and Supplementary Benefit Fraud*, Open University Press, Milton Keynes.

Greve, B. (1994) 'The hidden welfare state, tax expenditure and social policy: a comparative overview', *International Journal of Social Welfare*, Vol. 3, No. 4, pp. 203–11.

Hayek, F. (1976) *The Constitution of Liberty*, Routledge & Kegan Paul, London.

Hedges, A. and Bromley, C. (2001) *Public Attitudes towards Taxation*, Fabian Society, London.

McKay, S. and Rowlingson, K. (1999) *Social Security in Britain*, Macmillan, London.

Miliband, R. (1994) *Socialism for a Sceptical Age*, Polity, Cambridge.

Millar, J. (ed.) (2003) *Understanding Social Security*, Policy Press, Bristol.

Nozick, R. (1974) *Anarchy, State and Utopia*, Basil Blackwell, Oxford.

Office for National Statistics (2012) *The Effects of Taxes and Benefits on Household Income, 2010/11 – Reference Tables*, ONS, London.

Orton, M. and Rowlingson, K. (2007) *Public Attitudes to Economic Inequality*, Joseph Rowntree Foundation, York.

Smith, A. (1976) *The Theory of Modern Sentiments*, Liberty Fund, Indianapolis, IN.

Tawney, R.H. (1921) *The Acquisitive Society*, G. Bell, London.

Tawney, R.H. (1931) *Equality*, Unwin Books, London.

Further reading

Browne, J. and Hood, A. (2012) *A Survey of the UK Benefits System*, Institute for Fiscal Studies Briefing Note No. 13, Institute for Fiscal Studies, London. Outlines the benefit systems and trends and levels of spending on social security.

Browne, J. and Roantree, B. (2012) *A Survey of the UK Tax System*, Institute for Fiscal Studies Briefing Note No. 9, Institute for Fiscal Studies, London. This paper provides a useful overview of the tax system, describing each of the main taxes, how they work, and estimating how much they raise.

McKay, S. and Rowlingson, K. (1999) *Social Security in Britain*, Macmillan, Basingstoke. The authors provide a clear and comprehensive coverage of the social security system.

Millar, J. (ed.) (2009) *Understanding Social Security* (2nd edn.), Policy Press, Bristol. This book provides a good review which takes account of reforms to the social security system up to the time of its writing.

Useful websites

http://www.gov.uk/government/organisations/department-for-work-pensions – the Department for Work and Pensions publishes regular research reports and press releases.

http://www.hmrc.gov.uk – the website of HM Revenue and Customs provides a range of information, including figures on taxation and tax credits.

http://www.ifs.org.uk – the Institute for Fiscal Studies produces timely commentaries on tax and benefit reform, from an economic perspective.

http://www.policypress.co.uk/journals_jpsj.asp – those wanting to keep up to date should read the *Journal of Poverty and Social Justice*.

CHAPTER 10

Work and Employment Policy

Edwin Griggs

Learning objectives

- To explore the nature and purposes of employment policy, and the role of employment policy in relation to the pursuit of social welfare
- To consider the relationship between employment policy and other areas of social and public policy
- To review trends in the British labour market since the 1970s
- To examine the development of 'active labour market policy' in the United Kingdom since the 1980s

Chapter overview

The purpose of this chapter is to provide an introduction to issues of work and employment, considered mainly from the perspective of their impacts on and interrelationships with welfare, in both a broad and a narrow sense. This view – that work, employment, and social policy must be considered together in a comprehensive and universal approach to welfare – was first clearly articulated by William Beveridge in his report on social insurance in 1942. Welfare and work are interrelated; work is a source of welfare and its absence may be problematic, but work may in various ways threaten welfare, in a broad sense. Issues of remuneration, working conditions, equality, discrimination, and exclusion can be considered under this heading. A key issue is that of unemployment – involuntary exclusion from work – and how policy has evolved to deal with it; in particular, attention is focused on the slow emergence of what is known as 'active labour market policy' in the UK since the 1980s.

Introduction: Why work? The connection between work and welfare

The world of work is not something distinguishable from or separate from the world of social welfare and social policy. Issues of employment and employment policy have some relationship to social welfare, broadly conceived. The integration of employment policy and social policy, however explicit in the post-war Beveridgean welfare 'consensus', was made even more explicit after 1997 and the election of the 'New' Labour government, which emphasised work as a source of welfare and as the most appropriate route out of poverty. This view is generally accepted in the European Union and more generally among members of the OECD group of countries, where the commitment has in recent years shifted decisively in the direction of what are called labour market 'activation' policies – roughly speaking, getting unemployed people off welfare and into work (Finn, 2003, p. 114; Bailey, 2006, p. 163; Kenworthy, 2010).

The argument is not simply about poverty and the value of work in overcoming this. Evidence suggests that there is a connection between involvement in work and general wellbeing: 'Overall, the beneficial effects of work outweigh the risks of work, and are greater than the harmful effects of long term unemployment or prolonged sickness absence. Work is generally good for health and well-being' (Waddell and Burton, 2006, p. 32; Kenworthy, 2010, p. 437). In this sense, therefore, a policy to enable or encourage people to engage in work is a welfare policy.

Concepts and definitions

We can distinguish two dimensions of employment policy. *Primary* employment policy is concerned with employment and unemployment, with reducing the latter and creating the conditions that underpin high levels of employment, assisting job search and placement, paying cash benefits to the unemployed, and – via links with the education and training sector – ensuring that there is an appropriately skilled workforce. *Secondary* employment policy involves various kinds of labour market 'regulation'. Workplace health and safety, limitations on hours of work, the pursuit of equal treatment and equal opportunities within employment, in relation to, for example, gender, race and disability, legislation for equal pay and minimum wages are all examples of the state's attempt to regulate the labour market in the pursuit of social objectives. The quality of working life is an aspect of 'secondary' policy, which concerns the 'quality' of jobs – whether they are satisfying and fulfilling, or boring, repetitive, and so on – participation and opportunities for employees' 'voice' to be heard in crucial decisions, employees' degree of autonomy and control over work processes and hours of work, opportunities for training and development, and employees' sense of security and self-worth (Brinkley *et al.*, 2007, pp. 4, 59).

Two concepts used in official statistics and official and academic discussions of employment policy are 'economically active' and 'economically inactive'. The economically active are a combination of the employed and the unemployed – all people who are in some sense 'in' the labour market. The economically inactive are those who, for various reasons, are outside the labour market, and include, for example, all those engaged in full-time education, people who are permanently retired, and those who are engaged in unremunerated caring responsibilities for family members.

Concepts like employment and unemployment are open to interpretation (Whiteside, 1991, pp. 11–13, 126–30). The definition now used in the UK is that of the International Labour Organisation (ILO), a branch of the United Nations, which counts as unemployed 'those aged 16 and over who are without a job, are available to start work in the next two weeks, who have been seeking a job in the last four weeks or are out of work and waiting to start a job already obtained in the next two weeks' (Office for National Statistics, 2006, p. 51). As a definition, however, this is just as artificial as any other. A small child or an old person past retirement age, willing to work and looking for it, but unable to find it, will not be classified as 'unemployed' for official purposes (Glynn, 1991, p. 14). Another example is the argument over the employment status of women, and the circumstances in which they may be defined officially as 'unemployed' – that is, looking for, and available for, work. Policy-makers for much of the twentieth century were remarkably unwilling to afford women, especially married women, the status of being 'unemployed' (Whiteside, 1991, pp. 11–12). Counting the numbers of unemployed people has also been something open to political manipulation; governments have sought to reduce the apparent numbers of unemployed by adopting narrower definitions.

> ### STOP AND THINK
>
> Why do you think policy-makers might have had difficulty with the idea of allowing married women to be classified as 'unemployed'?

It is important to distinguish between long-term and short-term unemployment. In any reasonably dynamic economy, there will be, at any given moment, a proportion of economically active people who are between jobs and therefore 'unemployed'. People are continually moving from one job to another and in and out of unemployment. This is not a problem. Long-term unemployment, on the other hand, is.

Theories of employment and unemployment

Contemporary policies for employment and unemployment should be related to changing theories about the factors influencing employment and unemployment. We can distinguish between 'economic', 'behavioural', and 'institutional' theories of the causes of unemployment (Bryson, 2003, pp. 79–81).

- Economic theories are of two types – demand theories and supply theories. *Demand theories* emphasise changes in the demand for labour as influencing levels of employment and unemployment. Unemployment is due to a lack of demand for labour brought about by lack of 'effective' demand in the economy. This is the kind of unemployment that occurs in an economic recession. (Another term for this kind of unemployment is 'cyclical' unemployment.) Demand theories fell out of fashion after the 1970s but have undergone a revival recently, to some extent as a result of the post-2008 recession and the pursuit of 'austerity' by Western governments, especially, perhaps, the present UK Coalition government. *Supply theories*, which became fashionable as 'demand' theories became less popular, draw attention to the characteristics and quality of the workforce, in terms of skill levels, and emphasise policy instruments such as subsidies, training, 'make work' schemes, or ways of improving the number of job offers individuals receive. Other supply-side factors include economic restructuring, involving the decline of manufacturing and the rise of the service economy, globalisation and the accompanying intensified international competition in the traded sector of the economy (Bryson, 2003, pp. 79–80). (Such unemployment is also known as 'structural' unemployment.)
- Behavioural theories of unemployment emphasise either individual shortcomings – people's unwillingness to look for work or keep it – or the demoralising effects of long-term unemployment on the unemployed and their motivation to seek work.
- Institutional theories, finally, stress the impact of institutions such as the welfare state itself, which place emphasis on unconditional entitlement to benefits, rather than making benefits conditional on appropriate job search behaviour – 'rights' without 'responsibilities' (Bryson, 2003, pp. 80–81).

Of course, these theories of unemployment are not mutually exclusive, and policy may be underpinned by more than one view about causal factors and influences. In fact, contemporary policy towards unemployment in the UK is probably a mixture of all three.

The economic policy of 'inflation targeting', for example, pursued informally from 1993 to 1997 and formally thereafter, has as one of its objectives the creation of a stable economic environment in which demand for labour is buoyant. Policies of removing barriers to freedom of trade, investment and (in a more limited way) movement of labour, associated with the UK's EU membership and involvement in the World Trade Organisation, are also in part designed to create conditions in which business and enterprise can flourish and employers are willing to hire. Trade union reform, carried out by the Conservatives in the 1980s and largely accepted and retained by subsequent Labour governments, was designed to create a more 'flexible' labour market and remove barriers to employer's rights to hire and fire. Changes in the administration of job search and placement services and the administration of benefits for the unemployed, associated for example with Labour's 'New Deals' and the creation of 'Jobcentre Plus', have been designed to ensure that benefit recipients engage with the labour market and that unemployed individuals accept some responsibility for seeking and retaining work, or at least seeking to acquire work-relevant skills by engaging in training.

Trends in employment and unemployment

Since the 1970s, there have been significant changes in the British labour market. One long-term trend has been the rise in the economically active population. Another has been the continuing shift away from employment in manufacturing industry and towards employment in services, coinciding with a shift away from manual and towards white-collar employment (Brinkley *et al.*, 2007, p. 12). Other trends include the relative decline in full-time male employment and the rise in women's employment.

Women and work

A fundamental change in the post-war UK labour market has been the growth of women's employment. Since the 1960s, there has been a growing demand for equality of access to the labour market and equality of treatment within the workplace. Figure 10.1 shows the rise in women's employment over a 40-year period in the UK. The convergence between male and female employment rates is especially marked between the 1970s and 1990s, brought about as much or more by declines in male employment as rises in female employment.

The treatment of women workers and the interplay of work and family responsibilities for men and women have become serious issues. Policy began to address questions of equality of reward, equal treatment in the workplace, and pensions provision in a system that had been based upon the out-dated notion of full male employment. Early forays into equal opportunities were the Equal Pay Act (1970) and Sex Discrimination Act (1976), both passed by Labour governments. In addition, the increasingly complex relationship between work and family where both parents (assuming a two-parent family) are in work, began to pose new questions (see Chapter 14).

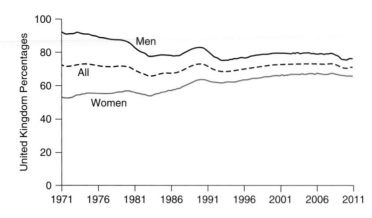

Figure 10.1 Employment rates by sex, 1971–2011. The headline employment rate is the number of people aged 16–64 in employment divided by the population aged 16–64

Source: Office for National Statistics *Labour Force Survey*

Economic activity and unemployment

Figure 10.2 shows long-term trends in economic activity and unemployment rates from 1971 to 2011. The difference between the 'economically active' and the 'in employment' lines is, of course, the unemployment rate, the dashed line at the bottom of the graph. As one might expect, the lines for the employed and the unemployed populations are almost mirror images. Both the 'economically active' and the 'economically inactive' populations grew over the period 1971–2005 (the *percentages* shown in the graph are approximately stable, but absolute population *numbers* have grown over the period). The economically active population is now around 30 million. The trend in employment broadly reflects that in the economically active population. The main factors influencing the rise in the economically active population include

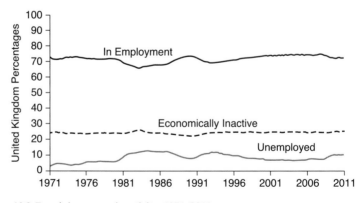

Figure 10.2 Trends in economic activity, 1971–2011

Source: Office for National Statistics *Labour Force Survey*

an increasing UK population arising from natural increase and immigration, and increases in the numbers of women entering the labour market. The growth in the economically inactive population reflects rises in the numbers of retired persons – people living longer and retiring earlier – and expansion in the numbers of people continuing in full-time education. It can be seen that the graphs of all these trends are not smooth, but exhibit fluctuations and discontinuities. Thus there are dips in the numbers of employed and economically active persons in the first half of the 1980s and 1990s, periods of high unemployment, as shown by the lowest, dashed, line.

Figure 10.3, with its exaggerated vertical axis compared with Figure 10.2, gives a rather clearer picture of trends in unemployment over the same period, broken down by sex. (The dashed line for 'all' is simply a spikier version of the 'unemployed' line in Figure 10.2.) Overall unemployment tripled between 1971 and the early 1980s, when it rose to over 3 million, and halved between 1993 and 2005 to about 1.5 million. The sharp increases in both male and female unemployment in the early 1980s and early 1990s are clearly shown. The unemployment experience for men was slightly worse, and that for women rather better, in the early 1990s than they had been in the early 1980s. These differences reflect the concentration of men in manufacturing industry, much more seriously affected by the economic downturns in these periods than were the service industries in which women are more likely to work.

STOP AND THINK

Unemployed men consistently outnumber unemployed women in the UK. The unemployment *rate* for men is higher than that for women in the UK. What do you think might explain these differences between men's and women's unemployment?

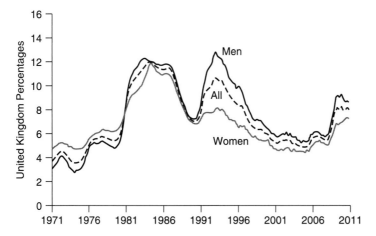

Figure 10.3 Unemployment trends by sex, 1971–2005. The unemployment rate is the number of unemployed people (aged 16 and over) divided by the economically active population (aged 16 and over). The economically active population is defined as those in employment plus those who are unemployed. Data are seasonally adjusted
Source: Office for National Statistics *Labour Force Survey*

The favourable employment record of the UK economy after the end of the recession in 1993 came to an end in 2008. Between the first quarters of 2008 and 2010, the overall unemployment rate increased from 5.2 to 8 per cent – a lower rise than in previous recessions.

Employment disadvantage

What looks like a relatively good UK employment performance in recent years, until the late 2000s, should not lead to an assumption that all is well. There is arguably a good deal of hidden unemployment in the UK among groups not formally labelled as unemployed, such as people on incapacity benefits, lone parents, and older people, as well as among groups experiencing particular disadvantage, such as members of Black and minority ethnic groups.

An examination of unemployment by ethnic group in the UK shows clear patterns of employment disadvantage among minority ethnic groups. All minority ethnic groups have higher levels of unemployment than the 'White British' group and there are differences among ethnic groups. The male unemployment rate is highest among the Black Caribbean population, at around 15 per cent. The female rate is highest for women of Pakistani origin, at around 20 per cent (that for Bangladeshi women is not shown, but is assumed to be comparable with that for Pakistani women). Those of Indian origin had the lowest unemployment rates among non-White groups. These differences between groups and between them and the majority White population reflect varying legacies, of concentration in declining industrial sectors and regions, and continuing experience of discrimination, both direct and indirect. Many non-White ethnic groups, heavily concentrated in traditional manufacturing employment in particular regions and urban areas, have suffered disproportionately from the effects of industrial and employment 'restructuring' and resulting unemployment in the UK since the 1970s, and have subsequently failed to share to the same extent as White groups in the economic recovery that has taken place. Relatively high levels of minority ethnic unemployment have also co-existed, paradoxically, with strong demand for labour in the economy since the mid 1990s and historically high levels of immigration responding to that demand.

Since the 1990s, there has been some improvement in the employment situation of disadvantaged groups. The employment rate for disabled people increased from 38.3 to 46.6 per cent between 1998 and 2009, narrowing the gap between this group and the non-disabled. A similar improvement has been noted for lone parents, whose employment rate increased from 44.6 to 57.3 per cent between 1997 and 2009, substantially narrowing the gap between lone parents and other family types. For minority ethnic groups, the employment rate increased a little from 57.2 to 59.6 per cent, accompanying a slight decline in the employment rate of White groups, thereby narrowing the gap somewhat (Spence, 2011, p. 10). The overall picture, however, remains one of relative employment disadvantage for these groups.

Political responses: employment policy from the beginnings to Thatcher

There is probably no earlier period of British history when governments have not sought to regulate the labour market in some way, whether through the Poor Law, apprenticeship laws or laws governing wages. Even the mid Victorian liberal heyday was in reality characterised by a degree of state intervention. Factory legislation, for example, dates from 1800, and there were subsequently many other legislative interventions relating to employment in mines, factories, and workshops, limiting hours of work, regulating the employment of juveniles and women, and other aspects of working conditions.

Governments hardly recognised, however, any responsibility for influencing the *level* of unemployment. Free market liberal ideas were dominant in economics and among policy-makers, who believed that the economy was a self-regulating mechanism that tended towards 'equilibrium', a state in which all 'factors of production', including human ones, would be employed at an appropriate price (wages in the case of labour). Unemployment could only be a temporary phenomenon (see Chapter 10). The Poor Law, which had existed since 1601, was, after its reform in 1834, reconfigured as a work-focused system of social security, designed to encourage engagement with the labour market and to ensure that support for out-of-work individuals did not discourage them from seeking work by being too generous (Harris, 1972, pp. 1–2).

> ### STOP AND THINK
>
> In terms of the three theories of unemployment described in an earlier section – 'economic', 'behavioural', and 'institutional' – what theory or theories do you think underlie the view of unemployment described in the previous paragraph?

Policy began to change in the early years of the twentieth century. Legislation passed by a Liberal government in 1909 created 'labour exchanges' – the forerunners of today's Jobcentres – providing basic job search and placement services, designed to aid the unemployed to find work, and employers to find workers. Another innovation in this period was the introduction of minimum wages in some low-paid sectors of the economy. A further innovation was the introduction in 1911 of unemployment benefit, a social insurance-based cash benefit, outside the ambit of the Poor Law, for certain limited classes of insured persons.

The optimistic free market view of labour markets as always tending naturally towards full employment equilibrium was dealt a fatal blow by the inter-war experience of high and persistent unemployment. A major redefinition of employment policy took place in the 1940s, under the influence of the ideas of economists like John Maynard Keynes. Unemployment was seen as resulting less from labour market inefficiencies and imperfections, than from the workings of the economy, and in particular, from a deficiency of aggregate 'effective demand'.

The Beveridge Report of 1942 took as one of its basic assumptions the creation and maintenance of high and stable levels of employment (Harris, 1997; Lowe, 2005, pp. 118–19). The wartime Churchill-led Coalition government's 1944 White Paper on employment policy demonstrated Keynesian influence and marked a change in elite opinion about the nature, causes, and remedies for unemployment. Its view of the issue was to become a 'consensual' one in post-war British politics. Governments on both sides of the political divide sought to ensure steady growth, increasing prosperity, and full employment along with low inflation. Unemployment rates remained low, at around 2–3 per cent, from the 1940s to the 1960s.

The economic environment became much less favourable in the 1970s for the British economy, which from the 1960s onwards seemed to become less competitive and to fall behind those of other, especially European, countries in terms of productivity and innovation. Britain became known as 'the sick man of Europe' (Gamble, 1985). The Conservative government of 1970–74 under Edward Heath was the last to try to operate an old-style 'demand management' policy, pursuing expansionary policies at a time when both inflation and unemployment were rising. This went disastrously wrong, and both inflation and unemployment rose sharply.

The succeeding Labour governments under Harold Wilson (1974–76) and James Callaghan (1976–79) fought simultaneously to control inflation, check the rise in unemployment, and promote economic growth. These efforts were modestly successful; unemployment was stabilised at a little above 1 million and inflation was steadily reduced. These policies nevertheless represented a partial departure from those which constituted what has come to be called the post-war 'consensus' (Kavanagh, 1987, ch. 5).

The Thatcher governments, the unemployment crisis, and employment policy in the 1980s

The election of a Conservative government in May 1979 brought about new approaches to the management of the economy, to employment and industrial relations (Kavanagh, 1987, pp. 204–7; Gamble, 1988, ch. 3). 'Monetarism', an approach to economic policy adopted by the first Thatcher government, is a short-hand term for an approach that emphasised the control of inflation as the prime economic objective.

The early years of the Thatcher government were a time of severe economic recession. Unemployment rose from 1.25 million in 1979, doubling within 18 months; by 1985 it had reached 3 million. The government adopted a robust attitude, Margaret Thatcher stating famously that 'there is no alternative'. Policies worsened the effect of the recession. A strongly deflationary monetary and fiscal policy brought down inflation, but at a high cost in business failures and redundancies, especially in manufacturing industry, which was, in international terms, uncompetitive. The experiment failed, not only because of the extremely high financial and social costs imposed by high unemployment, but because inflation was only temporarily and incompletely conquered, and took off again in the late 1980s (Kavanagh, 1987, ch. 8; Gamble, 1988, ch. 4; Smith, 1993).

For critics of the Thatcher government, unemployment constituted a major policy failure, as well as marking the end of the post-war full employment 'consensus'. Critics lamented that the Thatcher government had changed the agenda of politics so that unemployment no longer mattered for electoral success and failure; the Conservatives won subsequent elections in 1983, 1987, and 1992. Although Conservative governments did not formally commit themselves to achieving some particular target rate of unemployment, they did not, contrary to received wisdom, succeed in changing the agenda of politics in such a way that unemployment no longer mattered. Conservative thinking in this period involved a reformulation of the means, rather than the ends, of employment policy.

> **STOP AND THINK**
>
> What do you feel about the status of unemployment as a voting issue? For you, is it high up the agenda or not in terms of which party to support in an election? Will levels of unemployment make a difference to people's voting intentions in the next general election?

One task the new Conservative government set itself in 1979 was the deregulation of the labour market to make it more 'flexible', so that employment, and unemployment, could reach their 'natural' market levels. The Conservative Chancellor of the Exchequer from 1983 to 1989, Nigel Lawson, sketched out an employment agenda for government in his Mais lecture of 1984. In his view, unemployment was a micro-economic, not a macro-economic, problem. Macro-economic policy was concerned with creating economic stability and controlling inflation; it had nothing *directly* to do with employment and unemployment. Unemployment must be tackled through micro-economic policy interventions to improve the workings of the labour market and the quality of the workforce, so that employers would be more willing to invest and hire. This was the obverse of what had come to be understood as the 'Keynesian' position (Smith, 1987, pp. 118–19; Keegan, 1989, pp. 136–7).

The Conservative governments of Thatcher (1979–90) and Major (1990–97) engaged in some presentational manipulation by changing the basis for counting the unemployed, for instance by removing the unemployed who were near to retirement (1981) and school leavers (1983). Altogether, the Conservatives made 31 changes to the method of calculating unemployment. The effect of these was to artificially reduce the number of officially unemployed and to disguise the rate of dependency on unemployment benefits (Lowe, 2005, p. 498, footnote 6).

Youth unemployment was the focus of concern in the early 1980s. Measures were introduced intended to tackle it, building on the previous Labour government's Youth Opportunities Programme (YOP). A variety of schemes were introduced, including the Youth Training Scheme (YTS), the Community Programme for the long-term unemployed, the Enterprise Allowance Scheme, which paid people unemployment benefit while setting up in business on their own.

Unemployed youngsters aged between 18 and 24 were offered a job training scheme which gave an allowance of £10 above benefit levels if the unemployed person participated in recognised training. Another direct subsidy scheme, the Jobstart allowance, offered unemployed 18-year-olds an allowance, for 6 months only, if they accepted work below a given wages ceiling. Such schemes sought to fill a perceived gap between the skills and training provided by compulsory education and those required by employers. There were also policies aimed at encouraging employers to take on unemployed workers, for example, the New Workers' Scheme, which paid employers an allowance for each unemployed worker they took on at a rate under a given wage ceiling. This amounted to a direct wage subsidy.

STOP AND THINK

Why do you think policy-makers were so concerned about the unemployment of younger people?

The older and long-term unemployed, those 'shaken out' and made redundant, mostly from manufacturing industry in the severe recession of 1980–83, received less attention at first. Between 1982 and 1986, the government suspended the requirement that the unemployed should look for work as a condition of receiving unemployment benefits. Policy changed in 1986 with the introduction of the Restart programme for the long-term unemployed, which involved compulsory job search interviews for anyone out of work for more than 6 months (Finn, 2003, p. 112). In 1989, the unemployed were required to actively seek work and the grounds for refusing job offers were restricted. An Employment Service was created at the same time, integrating jobcentres and unemployment benefit offices. The role of the Employment Service was to develop in the direction of strengthening work incentives and monitoring job search behaviour. The Employment Service also became involved in promoting the take-up of in-work benefits, such as the family credit, introduced in 1988, as a way of making low-paid work an attractive option. By 1996, some 600,000 families were in receipt of this benefit (Finn, 2003, p. 113). At the other end of the age scale, government favoured the promotion of early retirement above the retraining of the older unemployed.

The Conservatives also modified social security policies to encourage the long-term unemployed to seek work. The duration of contribution-based unemployment benefit was reduced from 12 to 6 months in 1996. At the same time, unemployment benefit was renamed jobseeker's allowance, and intended only for those 'actively seeking work'. The stricter job search regime accompanying the introduction of the jobseeker's allowance helped to reduce the number of claimants by between 100,000 and 200,000 (Finn, 2003, p. 113).

The later 1980s was a period of economic recovery and the resumption of growth, accompanied by falling unemployment. Monetary policy had been relaxed; 'monetarism' had been abandoned by about 1985 as unworkable (Smith, 1987; Keegan, 1989, ch. 9; Johnson, 1991). Policy became too relaxed and inflation took off once more. From 1990 to 1992, a period that coincided with Britain's brief membership of the exchange rate mechanism of the European Monetary Union, a forerunner of the Euro, the economy lapsed into recession again and unemployment rose (Smith, 1993; Stephens, 1997). The UK's forced exit from the exchange rate mechanism in September 1992 – this was effectively a devaluation of the pound – gave an immediate boost to the economy through lower interest rates and export prices, bringing about sustained growth and falling unemployment, which continued until the recession which began in 2008.

Evaluating Conservative policies

Conservative policies for employment and unemployment should probably be viewed a failure, at least until the latter years of the Major government. Macro-economic policy was unstable for much of the period, leading to economic fluctuations and severe fluctuations in unemployment, as governments searched for an appropriate set of rules for the conduct of policy. The social and fiscal costs of this were high. The Conservative period is nevertheless one of considerable policy activism and innovation. We can trace the emergence of an active labour market policy to this period, and much of the Conservative legacy was to be an inheritance developed by the Labour government elected in 1997.

From 'old' to 'new' Labour: employment policy 1997–2010

New Labour's approach to employment policy, work, and welfare had its origins in the 'modernisation' of the Party's ideology. Labour Party modernisers were sympathetic to the Thatcher–Major 'flexible' employment approach (Whiteside, 1998, p. 104). The focus on work also formed part of their new 'social inclusion' agenda. The modernisers were able to draw on ideas and proposals on the relationship between work and welfare put forward by its semi-formal inquiry, the Commission on Social Justice, whose approach emphasised that welfare and labour market interventions are forms of 'investment' that promote economic success, as well as being desirable on social justice grounds (Commission on Social Justice, 1994, pp. 96–8). These were themes reiterated by such 'third way' commentators as Anthony Giddens (see Giddens, 1998, ch. 4).

This work-focused welfare philosophy was criticised by some observers on the left as uncomfortably reminiscent of American approaches to the poor and unemployed, in which the emphasis seemed to be on re-moralising or re-socialising the unemployed. Such American commentators as Charles Murray and Lawrence Mead take the view that unemployment is a behavioural or cultural rather than a structural issue (Mead, 1997). The social inclusion agenda was criticised by observers who claimed to detect just such a moralising strain in its social philosophy (Levitas, 2005); compulsion in the Welfare to Work strategy violated, it was argued, a Marshallian 'social rights' perspective on benefits that had underpinned the welfare state since the 1940s (King, 1999). Critics also argued that a policy emphasis on paid work devalues other activities such as caring.

As well as American influence there was, however, a European (EU) influence on work and employment policy, close to the social 'investment' approach of the Commission on Social Justice (King and Wickham-Jones, 1999; Annesley, 2003).

> **STOP AND THINK**
>
> Was New Labour right to emphasise the importance of work as a principal component of its welfare strategy? Are there any dangers in such an emphasis?

The Welfare to Work strategy and the 'New Deals'

The new government's welfare policy, labelled 'Welfare to Work', promised to get 250,000 young people off benefit and into work. The 'New Deal', as it was called, made available £3.15 billion to be spent over a 5-year period on employment schemes. Different schemes were proposed, the main one being for 18- to 24-year-olds unemployed for 6 months or more. Another scheme provided for long-term unemployed people in other age groups out of work for two years or more and a separate scheme catered for lone parents.

The New Deal 'Gateway' prepared people for the labour market, providing intensive job search with a personal adviser, and involved a combination of wage subsidies, training allowances, help with childcare, and access to material support from the Employment Service. Tailored advice would be available from personal advisers, followed by a move into an unsubsidised job or one of four options: 6 months in a subsidised job, with subsidy of £60 per week to the employer; 6 months with a voluntary sector organisation; 6 months with an environmental task force; or education and training. There would be no 'fifth option' of staying at home. Those refusing to cooperate faced loss of benefit. In line with New Labour ideology, the programme appeared to involve a 'third way'-ist linking of 'citizenship' responsibilities with rights. The Employment Service and the Benefits Agency were replaced by a 'Jobcentre Plus' executive agency, which integrated job search support and benefit payments (Finn, 2003, pp. 111–12, 122).

The approach of the earlier New Deals was extended further in the 2000s to other groups of the economically inactive, in particular those on incapacity benefits, lone parents, and older people (Department for Work and Pensions, 2006; Hall and Taylor, 2006). A target employment rate – of 80% – replaced a target unemployment rate (Department for Work and Pensions, 2005, p. 22; Brinkley *et al.*, 2007, p. 16). This required substantial numbers of claimants to be moved off benefits and into work: 300,000 lone parents, 1 million people on incapacity benefits, and an increase of a million in the numbers of older people working (Department for Work and Pensions, 2006, p. 3, para. 9).

An independent review of Welfare to Work provision by the banker David Freud concluded that the private sector should play a much larger role in getting long-term unemployed people off benefits and into work, and be paid by results for doing so (Freud, 2007). This bore fruit in a White Paper that led to the final phase of New Labour's 'New Deal', the so-called Flexible New Deal, essentially a modernisation and upgrading of the existing New Deals, which largely accepted Freud's analysis regarding the role of the private sector (Department for Work and Pensions, 2007). Particular attention focused on 'harder to reach' groups, in particular lone parents and those on incapacity benefit. Employment and skills provision were to be integrated. Employment and support allowance was to replace incapacity benefit for new claimants.

The minimum wage

New Labour's 1997 election manifesto promised to introduce a minimum wage for all occupations and industries (Labour Party, 1997, p. 17). The minimum wage was a constituent part of the government's work-focused, anti-poverty, social inclusion strategy, an aspect of its attempt to 'make work pay', in the same way that the new in-work benefits were to make work pay. Trade unions favoured the minimum wage, while employers argued that the minimum wage would have adverse effects on employment, and that it would in fact increase unemployment, by 'pricing workers out of jobs' (Lal, 1995). After 1999, minimum wage rates rose substantially from what was perceived to be a low base. The current rates (2012) are £6.19 for people aged 21 and over and £4.98 for those aged to 18–20.

> **STOP AND THINK**
>
> - How should the level of the minimum wage be decided?
> - What factors should the Low Pay Commission, and the government, take into account in deciding by how much the minimum wage should be increased every year?

The 'living wage' campaign

The debate about work, low pay, in-work poverty, and living standards has recently advanced beyond a concern with the minimum, with the launch of a campaign for a so-called 'living wage' in 2001. The campaign has been supported by political figures such as Boris Johnson, the London Mayor, and been implemented by the Greater London Authority. Although it has no statutory basis and is entirely unofficial, a number of firms and local authorities are paying or have committed themselves to paying it and it is now Labour

STOP AND THINK

Minimum wage or 'living wage'? Many workers have foregone wage increases in recent years as a way of holding on to jobs which might be threatened, given the current economic situation and levels of unemployment. Is the living wage therefore an affordable idea for the UK economy as a whole at present?

Party policy (Press Association, 2012). The current living wage (2012) is £8.55 in London and £7.45 in the rest of the country. The campaign should probably be regarded in a contemporary context simply as a demand for a higher minimum wage, one that is more closely aligned to needs. The present minimum wage is inadequate for this. Left-of-centre think tanks have recently argued that although the living wage would impose higher costs on businesses and public sector employers, the Treasury would benefit substantially from higher tax receipts and National Insurance contributions and savings on tax credits (Helm, 2012; Warrell, 2012).

Work–life balance and 'family-friendly' policies

The family was a focus of attention for New Labour, which was able to present itself as a 'pro-family' party. The ideal of 'work–life' balance might be thought of as an attempt to rebalance work and home life and to mitigate the culture of excessive working hours characteristic of Anglo-Saxon capitalism, but it is as much to do with the expansion of work opportunities for women and an encouragement of men's greater participation in family life and sharing of domestic responsibilities.

These policies are as much about recognising a changed reality as about influencing it. There have been dramatic changes in women's employment experience in the post-war period and policies can be regarded as an acknowledgement of this. Policies included the expansion of state-subsidised nursery provision.

Evaluating New Labour's employment policy

Evaluation of Labour's policies is difficult, because of the changing state of the economy and the demand for labour. Some of the decline in unemployment that took place would have occurred anyway, regardless of the particular employment policies pursued, because the demand for labour has been buoyant, as the immigration influx since the mid 1990s shows. In this sense, the context for employment policy was quite different from that of the 1980s and early 1990s. Some evaluations concluded that the net effect was positive. By 2004, according to one reported study, programmes had raised employment by 17,000 a year, and that the social cost per job was outweighed by the social benefit (McKnight, 2005, pp. 32–3).

In contrast, critics of the programmes argued that there was a relatively high failure rate in terms of job placement and retention. Significant minorities of young NDYP (New Deal for Young People) participants returned to unemployment or failed to retain it for 13 weeks. There were particular problems for ethnic minority unemployed young people and people living in economically depressed urban and regional areas where labour markets are weak, resulting in people being recycled and 'churned' through programmes (Finn, 2003, pp. 124–5).

Recent developments: economic crisis and austerity

The benign economic climate of the period since the early 1990s changed decisively in 2008 with the onset of recession, which largely continues. This had been heralded a year earlier by the beginnings of an international banking and credit crisis, the so-called 'credit crunch', originating in the USA, which saw bank near-collapses (a run on the Northern Rock Bank, the first such event in the UK since 1866). The financial crisis intensified in 2008 and its effects reverberated throughout the 'real' economy, in Europe and elsewhere, with the collapse of US investment banks such as Lehman Brothers and threats to the solvency of UK banks such as HBOS, RBS, and Northern Rock, resulting in their partial or total nationalisation, or takeover (in the case of HBOS) by other banks. An additional problem, stemming from the banking and financial crisis, has been the Eurozone crisis, which began in 2009 and which has further promoted Europe-wide economic instability (Smith, 2010; Darling, 2012; Peston and Knight, 2012). The effects of all this as far as UK employment policy is concerned included a rise in unemployment, stagnating or falling employment incomes, and declines in national income. The UK economy, which had appeared to perform so well since the recession of the early 1990s, became unstable. The then Labour Chancellor of the Exchequer, Alistair Darling, declared in 2008 that the UK faced its most serious economic crisis for 60 years (Darling, 2012, pp. 99–106).

In a sense, this has been the only real employment policy story in recent years. The policy context for any government is now less favourable, and the range of programmes launched by New Labour, described above, and its successors, to boost employment levels – all of which are essentially micro-economic interventions in the labour market – now operate in a changed and more difficult macro-environment.

Recent data from the Office for National Statistics show that by the autumn of 2012, 7.8 per cent of the economically active population (2.51 million people) was without work, while 29.6 million people were in work, a rise of 40,000 from the previous quarter (Elliott, 2012). The average unemployment rate from 1997 to 2007 was 5.5 per cent (Sinclair, 2007, p. 188). The UK's unemployment record in recent years has, curiously, not been quite as bad as some observers feared and employment has held up reasonably well, considering the decline in GDP since 2008 (Brittan, 2012). Jobs have been lost in the public sector as the Coalition's public spending cuts have taken effect, but this has been offset to some extent by growth in private sector employment (Elliott, 2012).

The Coalition government's policies

The general election in May 2010 produced a confused and indecisive result, in which no party gained a clear majority; it was evident, however, that Labour had not won. After some days of negotiation, a Coalition government of the Conservative and Liberal Democrat Parties was formed. The Coalition published a prospectus of agreed policies, which included employment policies (Cabinet Office, 2010). The section on employment in this document seems much closer to that in the Conservative election manifesto than to that in the Liberal Democrat one, and in fact largely derives from a Conservative policy document published a year earlier, which offered a detailed critique of existing policy (Conservative Party, 2009; Cabinet Office, 2010, p. 23; Conservative Party, 2010, pp. 15–16). The Coalition moved swiftly to implement changes in the employment policy regime inherited from Labour, scrapping the Flexible New Deal and other programmes and replacing it with their own scheme, the Work Programme, which was launched in the middle of 2011 (Department for Work and Pensions, 2011). There was little or nothing in the way of consultation in the process leading to the Work Programme, presumably because the Conservatives had already produced a detailed blueprint in their 2009 statement. The new policy is really an incremental rather than substantial departure from the old (Conservative Party, 2009, chs. 3 and 4). In fact David Freud, the banker who had produced the report for the Labour government in 2007 described above, is now a junior minister in the Department for Work and Pensions, with responsibility for employment issues, and the Work Programme reflects much of the thinking embodied in his 2007 report.

The Coalition retained other components of Labour's policies, including the minimum wage, acknowledging the support it gives to low-paid workers and the incentive it provides to take paid work (Cabinet Office, 2010, p. 23).

The Work Programme

The Work Programme involved the replacement of the Flexible New Deal and other Labour programmes by a single programme. The Conservatives, and the Coalition, complained that the previous regime was fragmented and that provider incentives were poorly aligned for achieving results. Jobcentre Plus remains a benefit delivery agency as well as assisting with routine early stages job search. Beyond that the Programme involves a greater emphasis on the use of private sector providers, both for-profit and non-profit, to place long-term unemployed people in work than the previous Labour government had envisaged. Provider remuneration is outcome-based, depending mainly on the results achieved in placing people in sustained work. Payments are higher for placing individuals for whom it is more 'difficult' to find work – those 'further' from the labour market. There are various components of provider remuneration, one of which can consist of 'sustainment' payments, where a client remains in work for a given period (Department for Work and Pensions, 2011, p. 4).

Implementation of the new scheme was rapid, compared with the introduction of previous schemes, and was unpiloted. After a tendering process beginning in 2010, the Department for Work and Pensions (DWP) appointed 18 'prime' contractors, holding 40 contracts, to deliver the scheme. Most of these are in the private sector; a few are non-profit, voluntary or public sector. The prime contractors in turn employ around 800 subcontractors who work directly with clients; about half of these are in the voluntary sector. The scheme therefore exemplifies a privatisation or market-based model of service delivery to some extent (there is supposed to be an element of competition among providers).

There is some novelty in the funding of the Work Programme, involving a departure from standard Treasury public spending rules. The savings on benefit payments generated from placing people in work can be deployed to fund the Programme. Hitherto the two components of DWP spending on the unemployed – funding work programmes on the one hand via Departmental Expenditure Limits (DEL), and cash benefit payments on the other, which come under Annually Managed Expenditure (AME) – were in rigidly separate spending categories. The Department for Work and Pensions is now able to anticipate AME savings, using money up-front to pay providers. The Department estimates that the programme will find work for 36 per cent of people referred, compared with 25 per cent on previous schemes, will cost £3–5 billion and help 3.3 million people find work over five years, and save £1.95 for every pound spent on the programme.

> **STOP AND THINK**
>
> In terms of the three theories of unemployment described in an earlier section – 'economic', 'behavioural', and 'institutional' – what theory or theories do you think underlie the Coalition government's policies on unemployment described in the previous paragraph?

Assessing the Work Programme

The Work Programme, introduced in mid 2011, has been running for only a short time, so evaluation is difficult. Some early evaluations pointed out that meeting the Programme's targets would be extremely challenging in the present economic climate (National Audit Office, 2012). Chris Grayling, the then Employment Minister in the Coalition, rebutted the National Audit Office's suggestion that the target of getting 36 per cent of clients into sustained work over the life of the programme was overly ambitious (the NAO suggested a figure of 26 per cent was more likely). The figures he presented showed that 24 per cent of clients had not claimed benefits for 13 weeks. He implied that the real figure was nearer 30 per cent and dismissed the views of critics who claimed that these apparently good results had only been achieved because private sector providers had creamed off the easiest-to-help groups (Ramesh, 2012). Shortly after this, the Department revised downwards the number of people it expected would be helped by the Programme, from 2.6 million to 1.4 million, giving rise to Opposition charges that the scheme was in chaos (Watt, 2012).

Some other problems with the scheme seem to have emerged. In 2012, fraud charges were levelled against one of the scheme's primary contractors, A4E, resulting in a police investigation and the arrest of four of the firm's employees, and the firm's chair, Emma Harrison, was obliged to step down (Neville and O'Murchu, 2012). Some of the smaller charities acting as subcontractors to the primary providers have also faced difficulties. Eco Actif, a community interest company that subcontracted to A4E, went into liquidation in July 2012. A fall-off in numbers referred to the scheme by JobCentre Plus at around the same time threatened the viability of the main providers and their subcontractors, it was claimed (Plimmer *et al.*, 2012).

The success or failure of the Work Programme is to some extent dependent on and cannot be detached from the success or failure of the Coalition government's overall economic strategy. The government itself would not claim that the Work programme and other measures are, or could be, a solution to the present unemployment problem. The present policy context is that of relatively high levels of unemployment, by contrast with the period 1993–2008. As with Labour's policies from 1997 to 2010, assessment is difficult in the absence of a comprehensive view of policy.

Conclusion

It has been proposed in this chapter that issues of work and employment cannot easily be separated from what we normally think of as issues of social welfare. Governments have pursued policies for the labour market, at least since the Second World War, which have been intended to enhance welfare. The broad view of social policy and its institutionalisation in what later became known as the welfare state, involving policies for employment as well as more conventional areas of social policy, first clearly articulated by Beveridge in 1942, has continued to inform policy since, however attenuated that commitment may have become on occasion.

Summary

In summary, any examination of work and employment policy, as has been presented in this chapter, needs to take account of:

- the nature and purposes of employment policy, and the role of employment policy in relation to the pursuit of social welfare;
- the relation between employment policy and other areas of social and public policy;
- an exploration of trends in the British labour market since the 1970s;

- the gradual development of 'active labour market policy' in the UK since the 1980s, a policy pursued by the main governing parties.

Discussion and review

- Should citizens of working age be expected to 'work' in order to receive benefits? Why might such a social policy be attractive to government and, conversely, what problems can you see with such a social policy?

- And, as we see younger, economically inactive adults being increasingly excluded from welfare entitlements, at what age do you think 'working age' should commence and, therefore, entitlements to state welfare support be available to the young unemployed?

- Finally, can or should governments of the future guarantee full employment for their 'economically active' (working age) population? To what extent does your response emphasise demand- or supply-side solutions and/or behavioural or intuitional explanations of unemployment?

References

Annesley, C. (2003) 'Americanised and Europeanised: UK social policy since 1997', *British Journal of Politics and International Relations*, Vol. 5, No. 2, pp. 143–65.

Bailey, N. (2006) 'Does work pay? Employment, poverty and exclusion from social relations', in C. Pantazis, D. Gordon and R. Levitas (eds.) *Poverty and Social Exclusion in Britain: The Millennium Survey*, Policy Press, Bristol.

Beveridge, W. (1942) *Social Insurance and Allied Services* (The Beveridge Report), Cmd. 6404, The Stationery Office, London.

Brinkley, I., Coats, D. and Overell, S. (2007) *7 out of 10: Labour Under Labour 1997–2007*, Work Foundation, London.

Brittan, S. (2012) 'Explanation for Britain's economic puzzle', *Financial Times*, 25 October.

Bryson, A. (2003) 'From welfare to workfare', in J. Millar (ed.) *Understanding Social Security: Issues for Policy and Practice*, Policy Press, Bristol.

Cabinet Office (2010) *The Coalition: Our Programme for Government*, Cabinet Office, London.

Commission on Social Justice (1994) *Social Justice: Strategies for National Renewal* (The Borrie Commission Report), Viking, London.

Conservative Party (2009) *Get Britain Working*, Conservative Party, London.

Conservative Party (2010) *Invitation to Join the Government of Britain: The Conservative Manifesto 2010*, Conservative Party, London.

Darling, A. (2012) *Back from the Brink*, Atlantic Books, London.

Department for Work and Pensions (2005) *Five Year Strategy: Opportunity and Security Throughout Life*, Cm 6447, TSO, London.

Department for Work and Pensions (2006) *A New Deal for Welfare: Empowering People to Work*, Cm 6730, TSO, London.

Department for Work and Pensions (2007) *Ready for Work: Full Employment in Our Generation*, Cm 7290, TSO, London.

Department for Work and Pensions (2011) *The Work Programme*, Department for Work and Pensions, London.

Elliott, L. (2012) 'UK unemployment falls as private sector jobs hit all-time high', *Guardian*, 12 December.

Finn, D. (2003) 'Employment policy', in N. Ellison and C. Pierson (eds.) *Developments in British Social Policy 2*, Palgrave Macmillan, Basingstoke.

Freud, D. (2007) *Reducing Dependency, Increasing Opportunity: Options for the Future of Welfare to Work*, An independent report to the Department for Work and Pensions, CDS, Leeds.

Gamble, A. (1985) *Britain in Decline*, Macmillan, Basingstoke.

Gamble, A. (1988) *The Free Economy and the Strong State*, Macmillan, Basingstoke.

Giddens, A. (1998) *The Third Way: The Renewal of Social Democracy*, Polity, Cambridge.

Glynn, S. (1991) *No Alternative? Unemployment in Britain*, Faber, London.

Hall, B. and Taylor, A. (2006) 'Ministers set targets to reduce welfare claimants', *Financial Times*, 24 January.

Harris, J. (1972) *Unemployment and Politics: A Study in English Social Policy 1886–1914*, Clarendon Press, Oxford.

Harris, J. (1997) *William Beveridge: A Biography*, Oxford University Press, Oxford.

Helm, T. (2012) 'Milibands unite to urge "living wage" for millions', *The Observer*, 3 November.

Johnson, C. (1991) *The Economy Under Mrs Thatcher 1979–1990*, Penguin, Harmondsworth.

Kavanagh, D. (1987) *Thatcherism and British Politics: The End of Consensus?*, Oxford University Press, Oxford.

Keegan, W. (1989) *Mr Lawson's Gamble*, Hodder & Stoughton, London.

Kenworthy, L. (2010) 'Labour market activation', in F.G. Castles, S. Leibfried, J. Lewis, H. Obinger and C. Pierson (eds.) *The Oxford Handbook of the Welfare State*, Oxford University Press, Oxford.

King, D. and Wickham-Jones, M. (1999) 'Bridging the Atlantic: the Democratic (Party) origins of Welfare to Work', in M. Powell (ed.) *New Labour, New Welfare State?*, Policy Press, Bristol.

King, D.S. (1999) *In the Name of Liberalism: Illiberal Social Policy in the United States and Britain*, Oxford University Press, Oxford.

Labour Party (1997) *New Labour: Because Britain Deserves Better*, Labour Party, London.

Lal, D. (1995) *The Minimum Wage: No Way to Help the Poor*, Institute of Economic Affairs, London.

Levitas, R. (2005) *The Inclusive Society? Social Exclusion and New Labour*, Palgrave Macmillan, Basingstoke.

Lowe, R. (2005) *The Welfare State in Britain since 1945*, Palgrave, Basingstoke.

McKnight, A. (2005) 'Employment: tackling poverty through "work for those who can"', in J. Hills and K. Stewart (eds.) *A More Equal Society? New Labour, Poverty, Inequality and Exclusion*, Policy Press, Bristol.

Mead, L.M. (1997) *From Welfare to Work: Lessons from America* (A. Deacon, ed.), Institute for Economic Affairs, London.

National Audit Office (2012) *The Introduction of the Work Programme*, Report by the Comptroller and Auditor General, HC 1701 Session 2010–2012, Stationery Office, London.

Neville, S. and O'Murchu, C. (2012) 'Founder of A4e steps down as chairman', *Financial Times*, 24 February.

Office for National Statistics (ONS) (2006) *Social Trends 36*, Palgrave Macmillan, Basingstoke.

Peston, R. and Knight, L. (2012) *How Do We Fix This Mess?*, Hodder & Stoughton, London.

Plimmer, G., Neville, S. and Stacey, K. (2012) 'Welfare-to-work "descending into chaos"', *Financial Times*, 18 October.

Press Association (2012) 'Boris Johnson announces rise in London living wage', *The Guardian*, 5 November.

Ramesh, R. (2012) 'Work programme is successful, ministers claim', *The Guardian*, 9 July.

Sinclair, P. (2007) 'The Treasury and economic policy', in A. Seldon (ed.) *Blair's Britain 1997–2007*, Cambridge University Press, Cambridge.

Smith, D. (1987) *The Rise and Fall of Monetarism: The Theory and Politics of an Economic Experiment*, Penguin, Harmondsworth.

Smith, D. (1993) *From Boom to Bust: Trial and Error in British Economic Policy*, Penguin, Harmondsworth.

Smith, D. (2010) *The Age of Instability*, Profile Books, London.

Spence, A. (2011) 'Labour market', in J. Beaumont (ed.) *Social Trends 41*, Office for National Statistics, London.

Stephens, P. (1997) *Politics and the Pound: The Tories, the Economy and Europe*, Macmillan, London.

Waddell, G. and Burton, A.K. (2006) *Is Work Good for Your Health and Well-being?*, TSO, London.

Warrell, H. (2012) '"Living wage" would save money, says study', *Financial Times*, 28 December.

Watt, N. (2012) 'Labour attacks work programme "chaos" after forecasts revised', *The Guardian*, 15 July.

Whiteside, N. (1991) *Bad Times: Unemployment in British Social and Political History*, Faber, London.

Whiteside, N. (1998) 'Employment policy', in N. Ellison and C. Pierson (eds.) *Developments in British Social Policy*, Macmillan, Basingstoke.

Further reading

On employment policy, see chapter 5 in Rodney Lowe's *The Welfare State in Britain since 1945* (Palgrave, Basingstoke, 2005). A useful short book on unemployment and unemployment policy that deals with the subject historically is Noel Whiteside's *Bad Times: Unemployment in British Social and Political History* (Faber, London, 1991). For a statement on employment issues that has helped to inform policy since the 1990s, see chapter 5 of the Report of the Commission on Social Justice, *Social Justice: Strategies for National Renewal* (Viking, London, 1994).

Think tanks such as the Work Foundation, the Institute for Public Policy Research, and Policy Exchange publish useful comments on employment policy. The House of Commons Work and Pensions Committee carries out inquiries into aspects of employment and unemployment. See also publications by the National Audit Office, a parliamentary body that carries out evaluations of government policy on behalf of the Public Accounts Committee of the House of Commons. All these organisations have websites.

Useful websites

National policy development relating to work and employment is led and
    developed in the main by two UK Government departments:
http://www.bis.gov.uk
http://www.dwp.gov.uk
There are various think tanks, pressure and policy groups whose work focuses
    on employment and work including:
http://www.ippr.org – The Institute for Public Policy Research Policy
    Exchange.
http://www.polictexchange.org – The Work Foundation.

CHAPTER 11

Education

Hugh Bochel and Guy Daly

Learning objectives

- To outline the development of education provision
- To consider recent policy developments in preschool, school-age, and post compulsory education
- To highlight contradictions and tensions in policy, including around attempts to devolve decision-making and responsibility and, simultaneously, greater direction from the centre
- To explore factors such as class, 'race', and the role of the private sector in educational inequalities

Chapter overview

Education has long been viewed as a key feature of social policy, whether for its role in enabling individuals to fulfil their potential, as an influence on equality and inequality, or through its importance in providing an appropriate workforce to meet the economic and other needs of the country. Both the Labour governments from 1997 to 2010 and the Conservative-Liberal Democrat Coalition government that followed them saw education as central to their agendas. Yet, education has always raised difficult questions for governments, and as this chapter makes clear, this continues to be the case, with debates focusing on:

- the level of resources available to schools, colleges, and universities, including how higher education, in particular, should be funded;

- how to measure and improve levels of performance, both of educational institutions and of individuals;

- the best means of providing education and the relative roles of governmental organisations and individuals in creating frameworks and exercising choice;

- the relationship between inequality and education, and the role of education in reducing or mitigating inequality.

CONTROVERSY AND DEBATE

As the number of free schools multiplies, the debate about them rages on. The DfE makes a lot of noise about the wonders of autonomy, but it's Whitehall that oversees the schools, leading to accusations of a decentralising policy that actually pushes in the opposite direction. Given that Gove's department is poised to begin compulsory spelling tests and grammar lessons, it might seem odd that he is green-lighting so many schools with wildly different approaches and no obligation to follow the national curriculum (this also applies to academies). And there are questions as to whether funding agreements drawn up between the DfE and a host of private organisations allow any kind of transparency or accountability. In the midst of all this, only one thing is incontestable: that all human life is here, fully paid for out of our taxes. (John Harris, *The Guardian*, 4 January 2013)

This extract from a longer article highlights some of the key debates around the future of school-age education, particularly in England.

Introduction

The development of 'free schools', highlighted above, is one of several recent examples (others include parents being prepared to move house to be in the catchment area for a 'good' school, arguments over the sponsorship of schools such as academies by private businesses and faith groups, and the introduction of tuition fees for higher education) of the importance of education in contemporary society. One of the concerns of this chapter is to identify some of the reasons why education has been such a major topic in social policy.

Chapter 6 set out the broad context within which social policy, including education, developed in the nineteenth and the first half of the twentieth century. However, given the importance of education, it is worth examining the ways in which provision grew over time, and this chapter outlines recent governments' policies from preschool to tertiary levels. While this chapter focuses primarily on England, education is an area where there have been, and remain, significant differences between the constituent parts of the United Kingdom, and it is important to understand these (see also Chapter 4).

Pre-war education provision

During the nineteenth century, education developed in a rather piecemeal fashion. From the 1830s, the government started providing some assistance with funding, which in turn led to the establishment of a Schools Inspectorate in 1839 to monitor the effectiveness of state-funded schooling. However, by the second half of the nineteenth century education was largely restricted to those sections of the middle and upper classes who were able and willing to pay for the limited provision that was available through church, private, and voluntary schools, although concern was growing over the lack of education for poorer elements of the population. This was in part due to the greater appreciation of the need for an educated workforce associated with industrialisation and, in part, due to worries that with the expansion of the franchise many new voters would not be sufficiently well informed to exercise their vote properly. In 1870, the Elementary Education Act created elected School Boards to establish non-compulsory education for 5- to 13-year-olds, funded from the rates, where existing provision was inadequate [in Scotland, where by the mid nineteenth century a considerable proportion of the population was literate, through the provision of schools by large towns, societies, and individuals, the Education (Scotland) Act of 1872 similarly made education the responsibility of School Boards], and this was followed by further rapid change. The 1880 Education Act saw compulsory education introduced for children aged 5–10 years, fees for elementary education for most children were abolished in 1891, and the school leaving age was raised to 11 in 1893 and to 12 in 1899. In 1902, the Education Act made local authorities responsible for schools, including church schools. Then, in 1918, the school leaving age was raised to 14 (this had happened in Scotland in 1901). During this period the bulk of the population was therefore receiving an elementary education around the 'three Rs' – reading, writing, and arithmetic – with teaching based on traditional methods of rote learning and most children were leaving school with no qualifications. Following the First World War, attempts were made to increase the school leaving age to 16, but public expenditure cuts in the 1920s and the economic recession and depression of the 1930s meant that this did not happen, and that true secondary education for all did not become a reality until after the Second World War. It is also important to note that while the role of the state in education was developing gradually over this period, private education, in the form of the independent public schools, was largely left untouched.

The post-war education settlement

During the Second World War, with the widespread recognition that the education system did not meet many of the country's needs, and was largely serving to reinforce privilege, the Coalition government set out to plan for reform, and in 1941 the Conservative, R.A. (Rab) Butler, was appointed Minister for Education. It was envisaged that central government would oversee primary and secondary education, in that the Treasury would provide a significant proportion of the funding while the Ministry of Education would take the policy lead, while local government would be responsible for strategic oversight and management of educational provision (including primary, secondary, and further education) in their areas. The 1944 Education Act saw the creation of a tripartite settlement:

- grammar schools, to cater for academic 'high-fliers', who might be expected to progress to university, or to enter professional careers, business or management;
- technical schools, for children who might go on to work in engineering or crafts;
- secondary modern schools, which would take those children who did not appear to fall into either the 'academic' or 'applied' categories.

The tripartite structure was to cater for children from 11 to the new school leaving age of 15, whereby entry to these schools would be through one common examination, the eleven-plus. The Act proposed raising the leaving age to 16 as soon as possible, but this did not actually happen until 1972. Higher education, in the form of universities, was not affected by these changes, although in the 1960s, when polytechnics were created, local authorities did take responsibility for them.

Despite its radical nature, the Butler Act was criticised for failing to tackle a number of issues. In particular, it left the private 'public schools' untouched, and according to some, actually further institutionalised privilege through the creation of state grammar schools and the use of the eleven-plus for the selection of pupils. The Act also institutionalised the role of religion (that is, Christian and Jewish faiths) and the Church within state education. And, despite Butler's hopes, the Act failed to raise the profile of technical education in Britain, as local authorities tended to focus on academic education through grammar schools, and 'practical' education through secondary moderns, often seeing technical education as something to be addressed by employers through the system of apprenticeships.

There was, however, following the 1944 Act, a period of relative consensus and consolidation of the education system. The main area of conflict was over the eleven-plus examination and grammar schools. Supporters of the system argued that it provided academic excellence and allowed able working-class children to progress to grammar schools on merit, and that the higher level of resourcing for those schools was appropriate in order to enable the most able to develop to their full potential. For opponents, the eleven-plus created a division between those who 'passed' and progressed to grammar schools, and those who 'failed' and went to secondary modern schools, a view given greater credence by the lack of development of technical schools and the lower level of funding given to secondary moderns compared with grammar schools. In addition, evidence tended to show that there was a significant relationship between social class and success in the eleven-plus, raising questions about whether it was really about merit, and this became an important part of the debate about equality and inequality in the 1960s and 1970s.

The Labour Party increasingly saw the existence of grammar schools as being inequitable and divisive, and took the view that a move towards a system of comprehensive schooling, which had already been adopted by some local authorities, would be beneficial. Despite that, it was not until the 1976 Education Act that the government sought to use legislation to ensure the reorganisation of education on comprehensive lines, while also restricting funding to grammar schools, so that many converted to comprehensive schools, moved into the private sector or closed. However, like the Butler Act before it, the 1976 Act did not significantly address the role and position of private education. In Scotland a very different direction was taken, with all state schools becoming comprehensive by the mid 1970s, while the same was true of Wales, although there the shift to entirely comprehensive education was more gradual and took place over a longer period of time.

STOP AND THINK

- Do you think that children should attend their local school, or the one that they and their parents choose for them?

- Was it important for you and your family what school you attended, or to which you sent your children?

One area of consensus was around the expansion of higher education. During the 1950s, the Conservatives established a number of new universities, creating some from scratch and upgrading others from University College to University status. However, the proportion of school leavers entering higher education remained small, with the majority coming from upper- and middle-class families. The government established the Robbins Committee (1963) on Higher Education, which recommended a doubling of student numbers. With the election of the Labour governments of the 1960s, concern over higher education was reinforced by anxiety over Britain's perceived failure to keep up with the rest of the world in industry and innovation. The government sought to develop a new, more vocational, and technologically oriented form of higher education delivered through new 'polytechnics', which were intended to provide degree-level programmes in practical and technical subjects, rather than the arts subjects, which had previously dominated university education. As with schools and further education colleges, the polytechnics were placed under the control of local education authorities, which then had a strategic overview from nursery through primary and secondary schools, and through to higher education within their areas. The other major development in higher education under Labour in the 1960s was the creation of the Open University, with the aim of providing degree-level education to adults who had missed that opportunity earlier in life. This education was radically different from the existing model, being followed by students studying independently at home, supported by well-resourced, good-quality teaching materials supplemented by television and radio programmes.

By the mid 1970s, education had returned to the policy agenda as a significant issue, in part again due to concern over the UK lagging behind its competitors in terms of economic performance, and the view that this was associated with a failure of the UK to produce a sufficiently skilled workforce, with the technical expansion of the previous decade seeming to have had little effect, but also with the emergence of a new issue, in the form of evidence of high levels of illiteracy and innumeracy among school leavers. Some critics sought to blame this on the creation of comprehensive schools and the bias against grammar school education, and argued that these had driven down standards of education for all children. The Labour Prime Minister of the time, Jim Callaghan, encapsulated these concerns in a speech in 1978, in which he suggested that the education system was not equipping school leavers with the education and training needed to take up jobs in the modern age (Riley, 1998).

1979–97: the end of consensus

In some respects, Callaghan's encapsulation of concerns over standards in education foreshadowed those of the Thatcher governments of the 1980s. Those governments placed at least part of the blame for Britain's economic and educational ills on 'trendy' and 'progressive' teachers and local authorities. They therefore wished to wrest control of education policy and provision from the teaching profession and trade unions and left-leaning local authorities, and, in line with their emphasis on individual choice and markets, to use such mechanisms to empower parents and schools and to raise academic standards. The Education Act 1980 removed the requirement on local authorities to purse comprehensive education and introduced the Assisted Places Scheme to allow parents of 'bright' children to apply for their children to be educated in fee-paying private schools.

However, the key piece of legislation during the 1980s affecting schools was the 1988 Education Reform Act, which involved the radical reform of education. This Act allowed for the creation of grant-maintained schools if a majority of parents voted to 'opt out' of local authority control and to receive their budget directly from the Department for Education and Science. A grant-maintained school would be governed by its governing body and managed more directly by the head teacher and senior staff. The Conservatives claimed that such a move would allow schools to develop their own policies, including on entry and selection. Other schools were also to be given more control over their budgets, including salaries and staffing costs, equipment and books, and internal maintenance, through the local management of schools, although local education authorities would retain control over capital funding and local authority-wide services, such as curriculum advisors, educational psychologists, and careers services. Using grant-maintained schools and locally managed schools, the Conservatives hoped to create a 'quasi-market' in primary and secondary education, with schools competing for pupil numbers. Schools would have an incentive to perform well to attract pupils and would be rewarded for that, while less successful schools would have to improve to retain pupils and income and thus remain viable.

To further develop market mechanisms and enable parental choice, the government encouraged the production of 'league tables' of school performance, which allowed comparisons of schools, including in particular areas. However, despite these being widely publicised in the media, critics argued that they largely reflected the social class backgrounds of children attending different schools, and said little or nothing about the extent to which the schools themselves made a difference to their pupils' achievements.

Source: http://www.CartoonStock.com

The government also introduced the National Curriculum across England and Wales, as another part of the response to criticisms that standards of basic literacy and numeracy were falling and that children were leaving school unable to read, write or do basic arithmetic. The National Curriculum prescribed a set of subjects and content. The Secretary of State was given the power to determine what subjects would be taught, as well as the amount of time each week that would be allocated to them, although in practice this responsibility was largely given over to the National Curriculum Council. The intention was for there to be an emphasis on mathematics, English, science, languages, history, and geography, together with a requirement for daily worship of a 'Christian nature'. There were a variety of criticisms of this innovation, including the danger of reducing the time available for other subjects, such as drama, music, and physical education, as well as the appropriateness of a 'national curriculum' in a multicultural and multi-faith society. Indeed, the first version of the National Curriculum was revised in 1995, giving schools greater discretion over non-core subjects, and allowing schools more flexibility over options for 14- to 16-year-olds to encourage more vocational routes for some students.

The Education Reform Act also introduced Standardised Attainment Tests (SATs) to be applied across a range of subjects at various stages in a child's school life, with the original proposal being for tests at ages 7, 11, 14, and 16, although the latter proposals was dropped. Supporters argued that, combined with the National Curriculum, SATs would demonstrate a return to traditional values and provide information to help parents to choose a school for their children. Critics pointed out that it could make children feel like 'failures' from an early age, while instead of empowering parents schools became preoccupied with how their pupils were performing in national tests at the expense of broader educational aims.

The 1988 Act also introduced changes to higher education, allowing polytechnics to gain independence from local education authorities and become freestanding corporations. In 1990, the Education (Student Loans) Act meant that students could receive loans rather than grants. A further significant reform came with the 1992 Further and Higher Education Act, which allowed the polytechnics to take on the title of 'university' and gave them the powers to award their own degrees. A new body in each of the UK's four countries was allocated responsibility for funding higher education. Another important feature of higher education policy under the Conservatives was a commitment to growth in the number of students, with the Further and Higher Education Act setting a target of a 30 per cent participation rate in higher education. The numbers in full-time undergraduate education rose from 473,000 in 1980–81 to 664,000 in 1990–91 and to 1,052,000 in 1997–98, although this was accompanied by a significant reduction in the level of resource paid to each university for each student.

Also, following the 1990 Further and Higher Education Act, from 1992 further education colleges followed the path of incorporation taken by the polytechnics, becoming independent of local education authorities and responsible for their own management and finance. Prior to that the Conservatives had already made some significant changes to post-16 education and training. During the early 1980s, when there was a significant increase in levels of unemployment, including among young people, the Youth Opportunities Scheme, later renamed the Youth Training Scheme, was introduced to provide training for 16- to 17-year-olds (later 16- to 18-year-olds) who would otherwise have been unemployed. In the mid 1980s, National Vocational Qualifications (NVQs) were introduced, with the aim of ensuring that each sector would have the skilled workers it required, and that the country would have a skilled workforce more generally. Shortly after, Training and Enterprise Councils (TECs) were established, taking over responsibility from local education authorities for the planning and funding of post-16 vocational training.

Under Margaret Thatcher's successor as Prime Minister, John Major, the Conservatives continued to develop both consumerist and quality control approaches to education. The 1992 Education (Schools) Act abolished Her Majesty's Inspectorate of Schools and created the Office for Standards in Education (Ofsted), with the remit of improving standards and achievement through regular inspection, advice, and public reporting. Ofsted became a major, if sometimes controversial, force in monitoring and influencing school-age education.

However, despite the Conservatives' claims to be undertaking change to improve education and raise standards, others have argued that they were at least as concerned with reducing the power of teaching professionals and local authorities, and that the attempts to create markets in education were driven as much by ideology as by educational reasons. This view is buttressed by the fact that many of the government's actions in education mirrored those taken in other areas of public provision, such as health care and social care, with an emphasis on the consumer and accountability through the market, rather than the traditional pattern of services accountable to the public through elected representatives.

1997–2010: Education, education, education?

In 1997, Labour returned to government to the echoes of Tony Blair's commitment to 'Education, education, education' and the promise of the Party's general election manifesto that, 'Over the five years of a Labour government . . . Education will be our number one priority, and we will increase the share of national income spent on education' (Labour Party, 1997, p. 5). This was not simply due to the importance of education on its own, but because it was seen as important to several of Labour's other flagship policy areas. Education was seen as vital to tackling social exclusion and creating an opportunity society, and the government therefore sought to emphasise the provision of basic skills, including literacy and numeracy. Similarly, education was seen as an important element in relation to policies such as the New Deal, which aimed to provide every adult with the opportunity to find employment, and Sure Start, which was intended to improve outcomes for children in disadvantaged areas.

In Labour's first term, the focus was arguably primarily on education standards, while in the second and third terms the concentration on systems and structures (including types of schools) was greater. Where expenditure on education was concerned, after a period of fluctuation and decline under the Conservatives, falling to 4.5 per cent of GDP in 1996–97, spending began to grow again, reaching 6.0 per cent in 2009–10, the highest level since the 1970s.

Pre-school provision

Britain has often been differentiated from many other countries by the commencement of compulsory education at the age of five, rather than six or seven in some other states. In the past, it has also had relatively sparse pre-school provision, so that in 1970–71, for example, only 21 per cent of 3- and 4-year-olds were in such settings. Levels of provision grew somewhat during the 1990s and shortly before their general election defeat in 1997, the Conservatives had introduced a voucher system that parents could use to purchase provision from the public or private sector.

The Labour government saw pre-school provision as central to two broad policy imperatives: first, providing children with a satisfactory start in life; and second, as a means of supporting parents, not least in enabling them to work. Labour therefore funded, through nursery vouchers and tax credits, a significant growth in pre-school provision for 3- and 4-year-old children to meet its promises of places for all 4-year-olds and two-thirds of 3-year-olds. During their second term, Labour undertook to provide free nursery places for all who wanted one by September 2004. As a result, 65 per cent of 3- and 4-year-olds were making use of pre-school provision by 2004–5. However, while there was a substantial increase in pre-school provision under Labour, there was no significant change in the nature of the provision, with a mixture of child minders, private nurseries, public sector nurseries, and nursery classes and reception classes in primary schools, and with no major reform of the early years workforce, although, from September 2001, Ofsted was made responsible for inspecting all early years childcare and education in England.

A related major initiative under Labour was the introduction of the Sure Start programme, intended to help tackle social exclusion by working across government departments to ensure that families in disadvantaged areas had access to services, opportunities and help for young children. Sure Start was intended to involve both parents and a range of agencies in a variety of initiatives designed to give children in disadvantaged areas a better start in life, including by increasing the number of childcare places and a number of other programmes associated with education.

Primary and secondary education

The demand for schooling clearly changes over time, reflecting demographic changes, while government policies on levels of resourcing for education and types of school also change significantly. Prior to the 1997 general election, class sizes were widely seen as too large, based at least part on the view that larger class sizes hinder pupils' learning. Labour had therefore promised to increase funding for teachers and other staff and to ensure that as a result no child would be taught in a class of more than 30 pupils. Significant progress was made so that by January 2010 under 2 per cent of Key Stage 1 classes exceeded 30, although 15 per cent of Key Stage 2 classes did so, while the average class size in primary schools was 26.4 (Department for Education, 2010).

Where the primary curriculum was concerned, with continuing concerns about educational standards, Labour maintained the emphasis on 'standards' and 'performance'. The government introduced a National Literacy Strategy and a National Numeracy Strategy, which directed both *what* would be taught and *how* it would be taught. Labour was able to claim considerable improvement among primary pupils, especially at Key Stage 2 (Table 11.1), although in the years running up to the 2010 general election there was a levelling off in the improvement rate.

> **STOP AND THINK**
>
> - Why might it be useful to test school children's numeracy and literacy abilities?
>
> - What might be some of the problems associated with testing school children's numeracy and literacy?
>
> - What might the problems be in constructing school 'league tables' on the basis of pupil performance?
>
> - How would you measure pupil performance?

Table 11.1 Pupils reaching or exceeding expected standards through teacher assessment in England, by Key Stage and sex

	1997		2010	
	Boys	**Girls**	**Boys**	**Girls**
Key Stage 1				
English				
Reading	75	85	81	89
Writing	72	83	76	87
Mathematics	82	86	88	91
Science	84	86	87	90
Key Stage 2				
English	57	70	76	86
Mathematics	63	65	81	82
Science	68	70	84	86
Key Stage 3				
English	52	70	73	86
Mathematics	62	65	79	81
Science	60	63	79	82

Source: Self and Zealey (2008, Table 3.12), Barnes (2011, Table 3)

Of course, as with the use of many other targets, the improvements may, at least in part, arise from those being measured altering their behaviour in order to meet the target, with children being increasingly 'coached' by teachers to perform well in the test. Indeed, there has long been some disquiet about the appropriateness and robustness of testing in schools, and this continued to be reflected during the Coalition government from 2010.

Secondary education

Concern with standards was also reflected in Labour's approach to secondary education, with a variety of approaches being used by the government. Like the Conservatives, Labour used Ofsted to identify schools, or even entire local education authorities, that were 'failing', and further increased the use of targets for national as well as schools' educational performance. However, unlike the Labour government of 1974–79, it did not seek to end grammar schools, leaving it to parents locally to vote on whether they wanted to retain existing grammar schools. Instead, it argued for specialisation among comprehensive schools, to create 'a diverse system where schools differ markedly from each other in the particular contribution they choose to make but are equally excellent in giving their students a broad curriculum' (Department for Education and Skills, 2001).

Secondary comprehensive schools were therefore able to apply to become 'specialist' schools, for example in the arts, languages, maths, sciences or sports. Specialist schools were allowed to select up to 10 per cent of their pupils on 'aptitude'. However, diversification extended beyond this, to include faith-based schools, and enabling external sponsors to take over 'underperforming' schools on fixed-term contracts, and, through Labour's other major policy initiative in relation to secondary education, the promotion of 'academies'. Academies were independent of local education authorities, and were generally established in areas with 'failing' or 'underperforming' schools. They were often newly built or substantially refurbished, and often had an element of financial support from external investors (some being faith-based, with others including successful 'responsible capitalists'), in return for which the investors had a major say in how the school should be run. As the academies were outside the control of the local education authorities, they were able to select their own head teacher and other staff, set their own pay and conditions, appoint the majority of the governing body, and have some latitude over the requirements of the National Curriculum. Unsurprisingly, the

STOP AND THINK

- Why might a government want to encourage the involvement of private sector and other interests in the establishment and running of academies?

- What problems might you envisage in the encouragement of such interests in the state provision of primary or secondary education?

- What are some of the difficulties you might encounter when trying to measure the effectiveness of academies compared with other schools in a particular locality?

development of academies was contentious, with certain sponsors being controversial, while many commentators questioned whether performance was any better than those of the schools they tended to replace, particularly given the extra investment that they received.

One development under Labour of a very different nature was the introduction of the Educational Maintenance Allowance (EMA), in 2004, which provided weekly payments for young people who remained in post-compulsory education and who came from families with an income of less than £30,000 a year.

Further education and training

Where further education was concerned, from 1997 Labour saw it as both contributing to the economy through improving the skills base of the workforce, and contributing to social inclusion through integrating people into the labour force, and indeed into society more generally. Critics, however, have questioned the value to individuals, particularly those who might otherwise not be in employment, education or training (NEETS), and suggested that the financial and social benefits are at best limited, with many getting relatively low-level qualifications.

In 1993, the Conservatives had created Modern Apprenticeships to try to address skills shortages in key areas, and in 2002 Labour announced a target of one-quarter of school-leavers entering apprenticeships, although that level was never achieved. Labour also introduced the Train to Gain programme in 2006, which sought to encourage adults in employment to get NVQ Level 2 qualifications, including by providing some subsidy for training.

Labour also abolished the Training and Enterprise Councils and the Further Education Funding Council and replaced them in 2001 with the Learning and Skills Council (LSC), which was given responsibility for funding for 16- to 19-year-old learners. However, the LSC was widely criticised for problems with its college-building programme and was itself closed down in early 2010.

Higher education

New Labour saw higher education as a key driver in the development of a 'knowledge-based economy' – that is, an economy that is increasingly concerned with high-value products and services, which it saw as beneficial in the face of globalisation that would make it increasingly difficult for developed countries to compete with developing countries in traditional industries due to the marked differences in labour costs. Labour therefore sought to expand higher education provision, including seeking to widen participation from particular groups, such as those from lower socio-economic backgrounds and those who lived in more deprived areas.

However, the twin aims of raising participation and maintaining and increasing the quality of higher education meant that financing became a significant issue, and the Labour government introduced tuition fees for all new undergraduates from the 1998–99 academic year. By the time of Labour's second term, finance remained an issue, with some universities suggesting that they would like to charge fees of up to £15,000 per year and, despite significant opposition both within universities and in Parliament, fees of £3,000 per year were introduced in England from 2006. Nevertheless, the issue of financing higher education remained a problem for the government, with many universities calling for higher fees. At the same time, Labour-led administrations in Scotland and Wales had both reversed some parts of this policy by 2002, and in 2007 the SNP-led Scottish Government abolished the Graduate Endowment Fee that Scottish students had been required to pay on completion of their course (around £2,300 in 2006–07).

The Conservative–Liberal Democrat Coalition

Early in his leadership of the Conservative Party, David Cameron showed a concern with education policy, initially appointing David Willetts as Shadow Education Secretary, with Michael Gove later taking that role and Willetts moving to be Shadow Secretary for Innovation, Universities and Skills. In the years before the 2010 general election, Cameron, Gove, and Willetts significantly changed Conservative rhetoric on education (Exley and Ball, 2010). In some respects, the Conservatives sought to use Labour's own ideas against them, highlighting poverty, educational inequality, and a lack of social mobility. However, alongside the language of compassionate Conservatism remained longstanding Conservative interests, such as 'freedom' for individuals, families, and schools, a shifting of responsibility away from the state, and increased accountability through market mechanisms. It was unsurprising, therefore, that the Conservatives' general election manifesto in 2010 emphasised closing the attainment gap between the richest and poorest, improving the quality of teaching and having tougher discipline in schools, creating a more rigorous curriculum and exam system, and giving parents greater choice of schools through giving every school the opportunity to become an academy (Conservative Party, 2010).

Interestingly, despite the importance of education as a policy concern, *The Orange Book: Reclaiming Liberalism*, published by a group of influential Liberal Democrats (Marshall and Laws, 2004), barely touched upon the issue, although a chapter by Vince Cable, who became Secretary of State for Business, Innovation and Skills in the Coalition government, recognised the desirability of a plurality of providers and considered different ways in which choice could be exercised, with education being used as one of the examples. By the time of the 2010 general election, despite the Liberal Democrats' promise to cut class sizes for both primary and secondary schools, and to create a 'pupil premium', with more money for disadvantaged pupils being directed into schools' budgets, much attention was instead focused upon the Party's promise (which had been reinforced by 400 of its MPs and candidates signing a National Union of Students pledge to oppose an increase in tuition fees) to 'scrap unfair university tuition fees for all students taking their first degree' (Liberal Democrat Party, 2010, p. 39).

Primary and secondary education

One of the first pieces of legislation to be introduced by the Coalition government was the Academies Act, introduced to Parliament only 14 days after the formation of the Coalition itself. The Act enabled not just secondary schools but also primary and special schools that were classed as 'outstanding' to become academies. In many respects, this could be seen as an extension of Labour's use of academies, with such schools being independent from local authority control and having the freedom to set their own pay and conditions for staff, greater freedom around the delivery of the curriculum, and the ability to alter the length of the school day and even of terms. However, as outlined earlier in this chapter, while under Labour academies tended to replace 'failing' or struggling schools and were often newly built or substantially refurbished, under the Coalition the invitation to all schools to become academies was initially underpinned by the potential for schools to increase their budget by up to 10 per cent, as in addition to the standard pupil funding, they received the proportion that would have been held back by the local authority, including to provide central support. For many schools, therefore, there was a financial incentive to convert early to academy status. In addition to funding, the greater independence granted to academies was also likely to appeal to some schools, although this resulted in a shift in accountability away from local education authorities, even if schools remained ultimately accountable to the Secretary of State. There are approximately 20,000 state schools in England, of which roughly 17,000 are primary and 3,000 are secondary schools. When the Coalition government came to power in May 2010, there were only 200 academies in England. By March 2013, approximately 3,000 primary and secondary schools in England had academy status. Of these, less than 10 per cent of all primary but approximately half of all secondary schools had become academies.

Another change to education early in the Coalition was support for 'free' schools; drawing loosely, and for critics, selectively, from 'free' schools in Sweden. These were strongly supported by Michael Gove, the Secretary of State for Education. Free schools are independent, non-profit-making schools, funded by the state. They are intended to be established as a response to local demand for greater variety of schooling. Like academies, they have greater freedom from regulation and, in addition, they are not required to have qualified teachers. Free schools were a controversial initiative, with many claiming that they would simply replicate existing provision, that there was little demand for them, and that they could damage existing schools by competing with them for pupils. It was also pointed out that the Conservatives' 'borrowing' from the Swedish model was problematic, in that free schools in Sweden may actually have contributed to increasing segregation and inequity, including by drawing in children from educated, urban, middle-class families (see, for example, Exley and Ball, 2010). The first group of 24 free schools in England opened in September 2011, with a further 55 following in September 2012. Initial evidence suggested that many were significantly undersubscribed in terms of pupil numbers and that some (all be it, a minority) of them were situated in areas of existing over-supply of school places. However, the government remained clearly committed to them.

SPOTLIGHT

Types of state school

Faith schools
Faith schools can be different kinds of schools (e.g. voluntary aided schools, free schools, academies), but are associated with a particular religion. Faith schools are mostly run like other state schools. They have to follow the National Curriculum except for religious studies, where they are free to only teach about their own religion. The admissions criteria and staffing policies may be different too, although anyone can apply for a place.

Free schools
Free schools are funded by the government but aren't run by the local council. They have more control over how they do things. They are 'all-ability' schools, so can't use academic selection processes like a grammar school. Free schools can set their own pay and conditions for staff, and alter the length of school terms and the school day. They don't have to follow the National Curriculum. Free schools are run on a not-for-profit basis, and can be set up by groups that include:

- charities
- universities
- independent schools
- community and faith groups
- teachers
- parents
- businesses.

Academies
Some academies get funding from sponsors from business, faith or voluntary groups. They also get money direct from the government, not the local

council. Academies are run by a governing body, which employs the staff. Academies don't have to follow the National Curriculum and can select pupils based on academic ability.

University technical colleges
University technical colleges specialise in subjects like engineering and construction – and teach these subjects along with business skills and using IT. Pupils study academic subjects as well as practical subjects leading to technical qualifications. The curriculum is designed by employers, who also provide work experience for students. University technical colleges are sponsored by:

- universities
- employers
- further education colleges.

Studio schools
Studio schools are small schools – typically with around 300 pupils – delivering mainstream qualifications through project-based learning. This means working in realistic situations as well as learning academic subjects. Students work with local employers and a personal coach, and follow a curriculum designed to give them the skills and qualifications they need in work, or to take up further education.

City technology colleges
City technology colleges are independent schools in urban areas that are free to go to. They're owned and funded by companies as well as central government (not the local council). They have a particular emphasis on technological and practical skills.

Source: https://www.gov.uk/types-of-school [accessed 30 March 2013].

What might supporters and opponents of a diversity of types of school make of the position in England in 2013?

Another early action by the Coalition was the scrapping of the Education Maintenance Allowance. Critics pointed out that the removal of the Education Maintenance Allowance was likely to harm social mobility and inclusion. However, the new government followed up manifesto promises by both the Conservatives and Liberal Democrats to introduce a 'pupil premium', to increase support for disadvantaged pupils. The pupil premium, introduced in April 2011, focuses on pupils who are eligible for free school meals, or those who have been 'looked after' (in care) for a continuous period of six months or more. In most cases, the money goes directly to schools and the government intends it to be used by them to help reduce inequalities between those groups and those from higher-income backgrounds. In 2011–12, the amount of funding was £488 per pupil, but this was to rise to £600 in 2012–13. At the same time, the range of pupils for which this funding was available was extended to those who had been eligible for free school meals at any stage during the previous six years. However, a report by Ofsted in September 2012, based on a survey of school leaders, suggested that few schools claimed that the pupil premium had made a significant difference to pupils' performance, and that while more than half believed that it had made some positive difference to performance, they were at that stage unable to provide any evidence to support the belief (Ofsted, 2012). Indeed, in many schools the pupil premium was not disaggregated from the main school budget, and was being used to support or extend existing activities, rather than to undertake new ones. Among Ofsted's recommendations were that schools should be clear about how the budget was being used and that if it was not to be used effectively, the government should consider changing the way it is paid, for example by ring fencing the funding or payments by outcomes.

In addition to seeking to change the accountability, governance, and funding arrangements for schools, another key concern of the Coalition government, and in particular of Michael Gove, the Secretary of State, was standards of learning and qualifications in England. Therefore, the Coalition government has also looked to review and change aspects of the National Curriculum, the curriculum followed by state schools (though there is greater freedom over what is taught in academies and free schools). The Coalition's main proposals for change have been in terms of what is taught. Therefore, the structure of the National Curriculum (when subjects are taught) generally remains as it has since the 1988 Education Reform Act – that is, there remain four key stages of learning:

- Key Stage 1 (ages 5–7);
- Key Stage 2 (ages 7–11);
- Key Stage 3 (ages 11–14);
- Key Stage 4 (ages 14–16).

Across these four key stages, pupils are taught three core subjects along with foundation subjects. The core subjects (English, mathematics, and science) are compulsory at all four key stages, whereas the foundation subjects are taught at various stages:

- art and design (Key Stages 1–3);
- citizenship (Key Stages 3 and 4);
- design and technology (Key Stages 1–3);
- geography (Key Stages 1–3);
- history (Key Stages 1–3);
- computing (Key Stages 1–4);
- music (Key Stages 1–3);
- modern foreign languages (Key Stages 2–3);
- physical education (Key Stages 1–4).

The two main controversies with the Coalition's proposed changes to the National Curriculum relate, first, to its content and, second, to which schools it applies. Regarding its content, there is a move back to tradition; for example, in mathematics, there would be an increased focus on multiplication and mental arithmetic more generally; in English, there would be a greater emphasis on grammar, punctuation, and spelling; in literature, on pre-twentieth-century literature; and in history, on a clear chronology of British and world events. And only certain state schools – that is, academies and free schools – are not required to follow the National Curriculum.

One of the biggest changes proposed in many years occurred in September 2012 when the Coalition government announced that GCSEs would be abolished and replaced by a new English Baccalaureate ('EBacc'). However, after a period of review including pressure from the Liberal Democrats within the Coalition not to change GCSEs (in name at least), Michael Gove did a U-turn of sorts. Consequently, in March 2013, the Coalition proposed that GCSEs would remain the qualification that all school pupils would take at Key Stage 4. However, they would be much reformed, not least with a greater emphasis on end-of-year and course exams as opposed to modular assessments. Therefore, English and maths would be assessed by examination rather than coursework, although in science some coursework would be retained to take account of the importance of work in laboratories.

The government also stated that there would be changes to the GCSE exam syllabi. This would be implemented in two phases. First, from 2015 pupils would be taught new syllabi in English, maths, and science, with the new exam for these subjects being sat for the first time in the summer of 2017. (There would also be 'extension papers' in maths and science for brighter pupils.) Second, from 2016 pupils would be taught new syllabi in geography, history, and modern foreign languages, with new exams in the summer of 2018, although there would still be assessed field trips in geography and some flexibility on oral exams for languages. Gove acknowledged that the changes would result in a significant proportion of students leaving school with no qualifications, and suggested that students who found the new syllabi 'difficult' would be given a detailed record of their achievement by their schools, and would be encouraged to sit the exams aged 17–18 in further education colleges. Unsurprisingly, many viewed with concern the likelihood of more pupils leaving school with no qualifications. Also, teachers, employers, and others who were associated with subjects that were perceived to be being marginalized such as physical education and health, and culture and the arts raised concerns about what this would mean for children, the subjects, and indeed for society in general.

A further change proposed by the Coalition was over how overall secondary school performance was to be judged. Schools would be measured by using pupil performance in the newly reformed GCSEs. Therefore, rather than schools reporting the percentage of pupils achieving five GCSEs (A* to C grades), in the future schools would be expected to report performance in eight subjects, including English, maths, and science. Pupils' and schools' performance would be assessed on average performance rather than emphasizing the proportion of Grade Cs or above achieved, the intention being that schools would not focus on 'mediocrity' but would instead look to ensure that all pupils, including the brightest ones, achieved their potential.

Further education and training

The Programme for Government (Cabinet Office, 2010), set out by the two Coalition parties in May 2010, had relatively little to say about further education and training, other than a general commitment to 'set colleges free from state control and abolish many of the further education quangos', with the aim that funding should follow the student, to the creation of apprenticeships and other forms of training to enable people to get back into work. However, at the same time there were significant cuts to the further education budget as part of the government's approach to reducing the budget deficit.

As with schools, further education colleges were affected by the ending of the Educational Maintenance Allowance. There were also proposals within the government, announced in 2010 but not progressed at that time, to withdraw financial support for students aged over 24 who study for A-level equivalent courses and to replace this with loans on the lines of those previously introduced in higher education. Critics feared that this would lead to increases in fees and a significant drop in the number taking such courses.

Labour's Train to Gain scheme was scrapped at the end of 2010 and was replaced with a smaller-scale and more targeted initiative aimed at helping small employers train low-skilled staff. However, the government also announced that it planned to increase by 75,000 the number of places on adult apprenticeships, so that by 2014–15 200,000 people per year were expected to be in such training. Indeed, in some respects the Coalition government's apprenticeship policy saw early success, with significant and rapid growth, so that 255,600 people (52,000 more than the government's target) started adult apprenticeships in the 2010–11 academic year. However, the growth was most rapid among people aged over 25, who had not traditionally been the main targets of apprenticeship schemes, while the increase was much slower among young people. In addition, according to a National Audit Office report, around one in five apprenticeships lasted for only six months. The report concluded that while apprenticeships were generally good value for public money, the government could do more to target resources more effectively, and to confirm that the training provided through an apprenticeship was additional to that which would have been provided without public support.

Higher education

The funding of higher education continued to be an issue, and the Coalition government drew on the findings of the Independent Review of Higher

Education Funding and Student Finance (IRHEFSF) chaired by Lord Browne, which had been established by the Labour government prior to the general election. By the time of the publication of the report in October 2010, the financial crisis of 2007–08 and its aftermath, and the new government's commitment to reducing the deficit through unprecedented cuts in public expenditure, meant that the broader environment had altered substantially. The report 's major recommendations included:

- the withdrawal of most government funding for teaching for undergraduate courses, although with some support continuing for science, technology, engineering, and mathematics courses;
- the cap on tuition fees should be removed, although higher education institutions charging over £6,000 per year should be subject to a levy that would go towards a national system of financial support for students;
- full-time students should continue to receive loans to pay for tuition fees, and for the first time this should be extended to part-time students;
- the point at which graduates would start to repay loans would increase from earnings of £15,000 to £21,000, and any outstanding debt should be wiped out after 30 years.

These recommendations clearly sought to create something of a market in higher education by increasing competition among higher education institutions through the introduction of different levels of fees, while also allowing new providers, including further education colleges and private bodies, to enter the market. They also sought to shift almost the entire funding of higher education undergraduate teaching from the state to individual students, although the government would shift its support from teaching grants to student loans.

The government, perhaps unsurprisingly, accepted some of the report's recommendations but rejected others. For example, while it accepted the proposals to reduce financial support for teaching, to extend tuition fee loans to part-time undergraduates, and to alter the earning threshold for payments and the period after which debt is written off, it rejected the lifting of the cap on tuition fees, choosing instead to set a limit of £9,000. However, while the government had expected the average tuition fee to be £7,500, it was more than £8,300 for 2012–13 and £8,500 by 2013–14.

In 2011, the government published a White Paper, *Higher Education: Students at the Heart of the System*, which introduced a 'core and margin' system (Department for Business, Innovation and Skills, 2011). Higher education institutions were to be allowed to recruit as many students as they wished who achieved the equivalent of AAB or above at A level (extended to students with ABB or above from 2013–14), while 20,000 places were set aside for institutions whose average fee (after fee waivers) was £7,500 or less. However, initially at least, this approach did not appear to work in the way that many had anticipated, with a whole range of higher education institutions, including many in the Russell Group, being unable to fill places.

Clearly, the Coalition government has been seeking to further marketise higher education, but it is not clear how successful the reforms are likely to be in creating a competitive market or in improving the experience of students. For example, with capped tuition fees and limited student numbers competition is likely to be limited while, if institutions charge fees that are too low, quality may fall rather than rise (see, for example, Callender, 2012). Similarly, social mobility may be damaged, rather than enhanced, if low-income students are deterred from entering higher education.

Private education

Although the bulk of this chapter has been concerned with the role of the state, it is important to recognise that the private sector is involved in the provision of education at every level, from pre-school to higher education. At the pre-school level, the major expansion of places under Labour, noted earlier in this chapter, was founded on a mixed economy, with providers from the public, private, and not-for-profit sectors. There is also a significant role played by the private sector in school-age education, with so-called 'public schools' taking students largely on the basis of their own selection criteria and the ability to pay the requisite fees. Around 7 per cent of pupils attend private schools. Many of these schools have shown high levels of attainment in examinations (for example, they make up around 15 per cent of A level examination entrants), although there is disagreement over the reasons for this. The requirement to pay fees means that private schools take the bulk of their pupils from the upper and middle classes, and their consequent higher levels of funding than state schools allows them to have smaller classes, better facilities, and to pay higher salaries to teachers.

The examination performance of private schools also feeds into controversies over selection entry to universities, with evidence that the acceptance rate for 'elite' universities, including Oxford and Cambridge, is much higher for pupils from private schools than it is for those who attend state schools.

Where higher education is concerned, the United Kingdom has for some time had one private university, the University of Buckingham, which was created during the 1970s. However, in England and Wales, degree awarding powers can be granted to private organisations, with the approval of the Quality Assurance Agency for Higher Education, and in 2007 the government awarded BPP College, part of the company BPP Professional Education, the power to award honours and masters degrees in law. Having previously been seen as keen to expand the role of the private sector in higher education, in the summer of 2012 the Coalition government dropped a proposed higher education bill that would have made it easier to establish new private universities, meaning that further radical reform was likely to have to wait until after the next general election.

Class, gender, and 'race'

Despite 13 years of Labour governments apparently committed to reducing social exclusion, in 2010 significant inequalities in educational opportunities and provision continued to exist. Not only did the private sector continue to thrive, but even within the state sector competition to obtain places in 'good' primary and secondary schools could be intense, as well as for grammar schools where they continued to exist, faith schools, specialist schools, and for some of the new academies.

Inequalities in education frequently mirror others in society, including those associated with class, gender, and 'race'. Where income (and arguably social class) are concerned, pupils who are eligible for free school meals tend to achieve lower levels of development than others, while in 2008–09 39 per cent of pupils in the most deprived 10 per cent of areas in England achieved a good level of development at Early Years Foundation Stage profile compared with 67 per cent of those from the least deprived 10 per cent of areas.

In terms of gender, for a considerable period girls have been outperforming boys with differences clear as young as 5 (Equality and Human Rights Commission, 2011) and remaining throughout primary and secondary school, as illustrated by 73 per cent of girls achieving five or more GCSEs at grades A* to C in 2008–09, compared with 65 per cent of boys (Barnes, 2011). This trend has worked through to higher education, so that in 2008–09 there were around 1.5 million women in higher education compared with 1.1 million men.

Where 'race' and ethnicity are concerned, there are significant differences across ethnic groups, so that in the Early Years Foundation Stage profile in 2008–09, White British pupils and pupils from a mixed White and Asian background achieved above the national average for a good level of development, but pupils from Black and Pakistani ethnic groups performed less well. For all ethnic groups, girls significantly outperformed boys (Equality and Human Rights Commission, 2011).

The Equality and Human Rights Commission (2011) have argued that while schools may aim to provide equal opportunities for all children, in practice different groups have varying experiences of the system and that these affect their chances, so that some groups not only perform less well in school, but are also more likely to be excluded, especially Gypsy and Traveller children, looked-after children, children with special educational needs, and asylum-seeking children.

Given the persistence of such inequalities, it is perhaps unsurprising that prior to the 2010 general election, the then Conservative Shadow Secretary of State for Education, Michael Gove, repeatedly criticised Labour for its failure to reduce inequalities, including in the publication *A Failed Generation: Educational Inequality Under Labour* (Gove, 2008). While Gove was in turn criticised for a partial and selective use of data, it did appear that educational inequality was a concern for the Conservatives. However, as discussed above, critics of the

Coalition government have argued that their policies are unlikely to reduce inequalities and some, such as free schools, are likely to exacerbate them.

Devolution

As noted at the start of this chapter, there have always been some differences in the education systems of England, Northern Ireland, Wales, and particularly Scotland, and these have arguably become more obvious and accentuated over the past two decades (see also Chapter 4). As with some other areas of social policy, responsibility for education policy has become even more fragmented with devolution, with the administrations of Northern Ireland, Scotland, and Wales having responsibility for some or all parts of their own systems, whereas in England, following the 2010 general election, while schools were the responsibility of the Department for Education, higher education was part of the remit of the Department for Business, Innovation and Skills.

Some of the differences in approaches to education between England and Scotland have been longstanding, with Scotland's examination system having been based upon 'Highers', and school students having typically taken five subjects at the age of 17, although recent years have seen a shift towards greater depth of study. Similarly, Scotland took a much more uniform move towards comprehensive education in the 1970s than did England. In addition, in Scotland a General Teaching Council was created in 1966, 35 years before those for England and Wales. At degree level, Scotland's universities have awarded honours degrees after four years of study, rather than after three as in the rest of the United Kingdom. Even after four successive Conservative governments in the 1980s and 1990s, Scotland retained significant differences, with no National Curriculum and no development of specialist schools.

The period since 1999 has seen further differences emerging across the United Kingdom, with some of the most apparent and most significant being the approaches to tuition fees for undergraduate students, even when Labour was simultaneously in power in Westminster, Cardiff, and Edinburgh. The result of different decisions being made was that for the 2013–14 academic year, Scottish students studying in Scotland did not have to pay tuition fees, Northern Irish student studying in Northern Ireland had to pay fees of up to £3,575, while Welsh students studying anywhere in the UK would receive a tuition fee loan of £3,575, plus a tuition fee grant of up to £5,425 to make up the balance of any tuition fee up to £9,000. The Northern Ireland and Scottish Governments also stopped publication of school league tables, while Wales moved towards a system of five bands.

Clearly, with the degree of difference that existed even before devolution, and with the varying policies being adopted by the different governments within the United Kingdom, it seems likely that the education systems of the four administrations will continue to demonstrate further diversity, although perhaps also the opportunity for policy learning from each other.

Conclusions

This chapter has outlined the historical development and some of the most significant recent changes in education. There have clearly been a number of tensions in the education policy of successive governments, both in terms of aims, such as attempting to foster parental choice while working towards reducing inequalities, and in terms of approach, with both Labour and the Coalition government combining attempts to devolve decision-making with simultaneous exercise of power from the centre. At the levels of both further and higher education, the desires to widen participation and to create a flexible workforce have not sat easily with the consequent needs for higher levels of funding, and have seen a shift away from education paid for and provided collectively through the state, towards individuals funding their own education. Many of these tensions and contradictions have been apparent during the Coalition government, including over the funding of higher education, and through Michael Gove's support for greater independence of 'free' schools and academies while at the same time making top-down decisions about the nature of secondary qualifications.

Summary

Education has long been problematic for governments, not least because it is seen as fulfilling a variety of roles in relation to economic and social needs of individuals, families, communities, and society. Reflecting over the period since 1979:

- The introduction of devolution has reinforced the different approaches taken by the constituent parts of the United Kingdom, with diverse policies at every level from pre-school to higher education.

- In England, there has been a steady shift towards the marketisation and diversification of school-age education, with the Labour governments of 1997–2010 accepting the broad direction of many of the reforms previously made by the Conservatives, while the Coalition government has pushed these further.

- The issue of 'standards' and 'quality' has been at the fore of governments' attempts to reform education for all age groups.

- While governments have sought to use education to create a flexible labour force that will be able to meet the demands of the economy, they have continued to face considerable difficulties in implementing such policies.

- There has been increasing pressure on the resources available to higher education, and this, together with attempts to increase the level of participation in higher education, has led to major and continuing debates about how it should be funded, with the different approaches across the United Kingdom reflecting the difficulties of reaching consensus on this issue.

- Despite the attention paid to education by Conservative, Labour, and Coalition governments, private education, and particularly private schools, have largely remained unaffected.

Discussion and review

- How successful have governments been in raising standards in school-age education since 1979?
- What are the main arguments for and against selectivity in education?
- Why is education so central to government's concerns?
- What role should the private sector play in the provision of education?

References

Barnes, L. (2011) 'Education and training', in J. Beaumont (ed.) *Social Trends 41*, Office for National Statistics, London.

Cabinet Office (2010) *The Coalition: Our Programme for Government*, Cabinet Office, London.

Callender, C. (2010) 'The 2012/13 reforms of higher education in England', in M. Kilkey, G. Rabia and K. Farnsworth (eds.) *Social Policy Review 24*, Policy Press, Bristol.

Conservative Party (2010) *Invitation to Join the Government of Britain*, Conservative Party, London.

Department for Business, Innovation and Skills (2011) *Higher Education: Students at the Heart of the System*, The Stationery Office, London.

Department for Education (2010) *Statistical First Release: Schools, Pupils and Their Characteristics*, January (provisional), Department for Education, London.

Department for Education and Skills (2001) *Schools Achieving Success*, The Stationery Office, London.

Equality and Human Rights Commission (2011) *How Fair is Britain? Equality, Human Rights and Good Relations in 2010*, Equality and Human Rights Commission, London.

Exley, S. and Ball, S.J. (2010) 'Something old, something new: understanding Conservative education policy', in H. Bochel (ed.) *The Conservative Party and Social Policy*, Policy Press, Bristol.

Gove, M. (2008) *A Failed Generation: Educational Inequality under Labour*, Conservative Party, London.

Labour Party (1997) *New Labour: Because Britain Deserves Better*, Labour Party, London.

Liberal Democrat Party (2010) *Liberal Democrat Manifesto 2010: Change that Works for You*, Liberal Democrat Party, London.

Marshall, P. and Laws, D. (eds.) (2004) *The Orange Book: Reclaiming Liberalism*, Profile Books, London.

Riley, K. (1998) *Whose School is it Anyway?*, Routledge, London.

Robbins, Lord (1963) *Report on Higher Education* (The Robbins Report), HMSO, London.

Self, A. and Zealey, L. (eds.) (2008) *Social Trends 38*, Office for National Statistics, London.

Ofsted (2012) *The Pupil Premium*, Ofsted, London.

Further reading

Adonis, A. (2012) *Education, Education, Education: Reforming England's Schools*, Biteback Publishing, London. One of the architects of New Labour's education policies sets out his arguments for education reform, including the development of academies.

Ball, S.J. (2013) *The Education Debate*, Policy Press, Bristol. This book covers policy initiatives over the past two decades and considers the ways in which governments have sought to use education to address a range of issues and challenges.

Chitty, C. (2009) *Education Policy in Britain*, Palgrave Macmillan, Basingstoke. Looking at the development of education policy from 1945, this book provides a useful overview.

Woods, P. (2011) *Transforming Education Policy: Shaping a Democratic Future*, Policy Press, Bristol. This book argues for education policy to be underpinned by democratic values and approaches.

Useful websites

http://www.education.gov.uk and http://www.gov.uk/government/organisations/department-for-business-innovation-skills – the sites of the Department for Education and the Department for Business, Innovation and Skills contain and have links to a great deal of government information, including publications and statistics from pre-school provision to higher education.

http://www.education.guardian.co.uk – *Education Guardian* – together with the two *Times* sites below, provides ready access to contemporary debates and an archive of past articles.

http://www.tes.co.uk – *Times Education Supplement* – concerned with school age and further education, this site contains much to interest students, including news and analysis.

http://www.timeshighereducation.co.uk – *Times Higher Education* – covers higher education in a fashion similar to its sister site above.

http://www.scotland.gov.uk – the Scottish Government – makes available a significant amount of information on current developments in education in Scotland, together with some useful historical background.

http://www.wales.gov.uk – the Welsh Government – through this site it is possible to access information on education and training in Wales.

http://www.northernireland.gov.uk – the Northern Ireland Government – through this site it is possible to access information on the education system in Northern Ireland

CHAPTER 12

Adult Health and Social Care

Jon Glasby and Guy Daly

Learning objectives

- To summarise the origins of current health and adult social care services
- To explore key themes and potential tensions in health and adult social care policy
- To highlight the importance, as well as the difficulty, of delivering more integrated care for people with complex needs
- To consider options for future reform

Chapter overview

Many social policy textbooks provide separate chapters on the National Health Service (NHS) and on social care. In contrast, this edited collection includes a standalone chapter on health care (see Chapter 15 by Martin Powell), but also recognises the importance of a more integrated approach. While the UK welfare state has tended to split health and social care into different legal, organisational, and financial silos, most service users do not see the world in these terms. When asked, most people simply want services that are flexible, of high quality, and responsive – and that try their best to help them live their everyday lives.

In recognition of this, successive governments have stressed the importance of health and social care partnerships, from New Labour's emphasis on 'joined-up solutions to joined-up problems' to the Coalition's focus on 'integrated care' (see below for further discussion). This has acquired even greater significance in a period of major financial challenges, with single agencies increasingly unable to discharge their responsibilities without working jointly with a range of partners. Of course, the irony here is that financial pressures can often make people concentrate even more on their own internal 'must dos', and partnership working could become even more important but even harder to achieve in a difficult policy and financial environment.

With all this in mind, this chapter (briefly) describes the origins and evolution of health and social care services for a range of adult service user groups (particularly older people, people with learning difficulties, people with mental health problems, and people with physical disabilities). It then highlights a series of key challenges for current services and considers the extent to which a number of current policy agendas may offer a potential solution. However, to put these more abstract debates in context, the 'Controversy and debate' box below focuses on two high-profile BBC *Panorama* investigations into the distressing events that took place at 'Winterbourne View'.

CONTROVERSY AND DEBATE

Winterbourne View

In 2011, the BBC documentary *Panorama* broadcast shocking undercover footage of adults with learning disabilities being systematically bullied and abused at a private hospital in South Gloucestershire ('Winterbourne View'). Despite a national commitment to caring for people in community-based settings, the unit was based on an industrial estate near the M4, and the documentary makers described residents as 'out of sight, out of mind'. After the story broke, a national review found evidence of deep-seated failings in other services for people with learning disabilities across the country, with half of the services inspected failing to meet essential standards. In a press release, the Chair of the health and social care regulator said (Care Quality Commission, 2012):

'Although many of the services we inspected were intended to be hospitals or places where people's needs were assessed, we found that some people were in these services for too long, with not enough being done to help them move on to appropriate community-based care. All too often, inspection teams found that people using services were at risk of being restrained inappropriately because staff often did not understand what actions count as restraint, and when restraint happened there was inadequate review of these putting people at risk of harm or abuse.

While the findings published today highlight serious concerns about the nature of services for people with learning disabilities, we can offer some reassurance. There is no evidence that points to abuse on the scale which was uncovered at Winterbourne View Hospital. However every single case of poor care that we have found tells a human story and there is plenty of room for improvement to help a group of people whose circumstances make them particularly vulnerable.'

Winterbourne View subsequently closed, the residents moved elsewhere, and a number of care staff were sent to prison. However, in 2012 a second *Panorama* programme ('The Hospital that Stopped Caring') told the broader stories of some of the people abused at Winterbourne View, revealing a catalogue of negative experiences, poor care, and mistreatment in other parts of the system. Previously unseen footage also seemed to suggest that the trainer showing new staff how to restrain residents advised them to hit patients in the groin if they were too big to get to the floor any other way. If questioned, they were to claim that they feared for their life and had no choice but to respond as they did.

Although this is a very distressing – and hopefully untypical – example, it nevertheless reveals a lot about the origins, evolution, and challenges of health and adult social care. Despite significant changes over time, many of our current services began in buildings-based, institutional settings, and care scandals such as Winterbourne View have a long history (see, for example, Robb, 1967; Martin, 1984). Despite the closure of many long-stay hospitals and the development of more community-based approaches, this historical legacy still influences current provision – and much of the thinking that led to such services in the first place is arguably more prevalent than many would like to admit.

- What do you think helped to bring about circumstances such as that at Winterbourne View?
- How likely are current policies to stop something like this happening again?
- What would you do in response if you were Secretary of State?
- When a scandal occurs, we often promise that it will be the last – and yet it seldom is. Can we ever stop such incidents from taking place and what might be needed to genuinely resolve such problems for the long-term?

The origins of current services

While Chapter 15 provides an overview of the history and development of health services, the section below explores the origins of current services for older people, for people with mental health problems, for people with learning difficulties, and for people with physical disabilities. These are often described together in terms of 'community care' (for an overview of these services, see Means and Smith, 1998; Means *et al.*, 2002, 2008; Glasby, 2012) – and this section of the chapter focuses more on the development of social care (given that a corresponding history of the NHS is provided in Chapter 15). Sometimes seen as low-status, 'Cinderella' services, they tend to enjoy less prestige and are less well funded and understood than some of the more mainstream services provided by the NHS (for example, some of medical and surgical services provided in acute hospitals). Indeed, the bulk of the health and social care system has historically been focused on providing resource-intensive, buildings-based, crisis support for people in an emergency or with very substantial needs (in a hospital for health needs and in residential and nursing care for people with social care needs). This is despite the fact that most of these user groups spend most of their time at home and in the community – and need support to stay well and independent (not just emergency support once a crisis occurs and/or needs become very severe). Even following the end of the Poor Law, the closure of many long-stay hospitals, and the emphasis on community care in the second half of the twentieth century, the current health and social care system still feels dominated by institutional forms of provision (and the case study of Winterbourne View above is a good example). Even when services are meant to be community based and tailored to the needs of the individual, they can still feel institutional in their design and ethos (for recent concerns about the quality of home care services, see Equality and Human Rights Commission, 2011).

Although community care services have a low profile, they actually form the bulk of the work of both health and social care. Contrary to what the general public and the media may sometimes think, the NHS spends a significant proportion of its time and budget on people it describes as having multiple 'long-term conditions' or 'chronic diseases'. According to the Department of Health, one in three of the population have a long-term condition, and this accounts for 70 per cent of the primary and acute care budget. Another way of viewing this is that around one-third of the population accounts for over two-thirds of health spending (see http://www.dh.gov.uk/en/Healthcare/Longtermconditions/tenthingsyouneedtoknow/index.htm for these and other statistics). While high-quality hospital services are crucial in an emergency, many people with long-term conditions rely primarily on support at home and manage their own condition. If there are 8,760 hours in a year, the average person with a long-term condition in the UK spends no more than three or four hours a year with a health professional – less than 0.05 per cent of the year (Hannan, 2010, cited in Alakeson, 2011, p. 10). In adult social care, there are around 400,000 older people living in a care home at any one time (for a summary of key issues facing older people with high support needs, see Blood, 2010). However, the vast majority of people live independently, and some 6 million carers play a key role (family members, friends, and neighbours who provide unpaid support). If this support were quantified, it would come to £119 billion per year – more than the entire NHS budget (Buckner and Yeandle, 2011).

The Poor Laws

Depending on how far one chooses to go back, of course, most commentators would regard social care provision as having its origins in the charitable voluntarism of the 1601 Elizabethan Poor Law. Two hundred years later, and the Poor Law Amendment Act of 1834, the emphasis on the 'deserving' and 'undeserving' poor remained – with deserving individuals being able to receive charitable assistance from Victorian philanthropy and charity as opposed to the 'undeserving' individuals, judged to be responsible for their own plight and not, therefore, deemed to warrant others' charitable support. To encourage people to be as independent as possible, those deemed undeserving were subjected to the harsh regime of the workhouse (known as 'the workhouse test' and designed so that only the most desperate people would seek 'support', with anyone with any positive choice making their own arrangements). The residue of this distinction between the 'deserving' and 'undeserving' poor arguably remains with us to this day when we consider what society's response should be to those who require support and assistance, whether in relation to social care or housing, health care or income support. While our approaches to eligibility have changed, the legacy of the 'workhouse test' and deterring all but the most needy from seeking support can still be seen in some of our current systems.

The first Poor Law in Elizabethan times stemmed from the recognition that there was a need for a national set of arrangements to deal with the problems of the poor within a context of increasing movement in populations, more people living in towns, developments in agricultural processes, and the enlargement

STOP AND THINK

The role of carers

Many accounts of health and social care focus on formal services that are funded, organised, and/or provided by the state. However, the vast majority of care is provided not by paid workers, but by family members, friends, and neighbours on an unpaid basis. While caring for someone can be very emotionally rewarding, it can also be a very negative experience if people feel they have no choice but to care and do not receive enough support.

Look at the websites of some of the key carers' organisations (see 'Useful websites' at the end of the chapter):

- What are some of the positives and negatives of caring?

- What impact can it have on people if they do not feel there is enough support?

- How meaningful is it to identify one person in a family as a 'service user' and another as a 'carer'?

- A term often used is 'informal carer'. Does this help to distinguish paid care workers from unpaid family members and friends, or does it minimise the role of family carers (implying that the 'proper' care is done by someone else)?

- Which way round should we view the role of carers? Do you see them as having a key role in supporting formal services, or should a key role of formal services be to support carers?

of towns and cities. Under such circumstances the charitable and voluntary, often church-based arrangements that had existed up until then needed to be augmented. The response, the first Poor Law, gave parishes the responsibility for 'their own' poor and, if necessary, this meant the returning (resettlement) of poor people to their parishes of origin where they would be provided with relief. Such poor relief was to be funded by a local tax on properties – a property rate. While these arrangements worked, after a fashion, for the best part of 250 years, by the beginning of the nineteenth century it was recognised that they needed to be amended. By this time, the process of industrialisation was impacting significantly on cities, towns, and villages. People were increasingly moving into urban areas. The processes of industrialisation and urbanisation were creating their own problems, for example poor public health and impoverishment. The 1834 Poor Law Amendment Act was thus an attempt to respond to this changing context. Among other things, it established the 'workhouses' (though many already existed) where those unable to support themselves would be sent for 'indoor relief'. Underpinning these arrangements was the notion of 'eligibility', mentioned above (i.e. those 'sent to' the workhouse were judged to be more badly off and destitute than anyone in receipt of outdoor relief – that is, the least eligible).

> **STOP AND THINK**
>
> **The deserving and undeserving?**
>
> ▢ How useful is it to distinguish between those people who deserve state care support and those who do not?
>
> ▢ What is problematic about such a distinction?

Twentieth-century reforms

In the early twentieth century, the Liberal government of 1906–14 was responsible at the time for significant social policy legislation, not least the non-contributory and means-tested 1908 Old Age Pensions Act and the contributory but non-means-tested 1911 National Insurance Act for those working who became unemployed or sick (but not their families). Under the 1929 Local Government Act, local authorities inherited responsibility for the old workhouses. Although many of these would pass to the health service as part of the creation of the NHS in 1948, post-war local government continued to have a public health role as well as increased responsibilities for the care and welfare of children, young people, and adults. However, two pieces of post-war legislation set out a significant demarcation between health care and social care: the National Health Service Act 1946 and the National Assistance Act 1948. The National Health Service Act 1946 (as Chapter 15 explores in full) enabled the provision of health care to everyone, free at the point of delivery, irrespective of their ability to pay, on a universal, and uniform, national basis. On the other hand, the National Assistance Act 1948 constructed social care (of older people who needed sheltered or residential care) as local provision, subject to means testing and local variance. Therefore, from the start of the post-war welfare state, a wedge was inserted between means-tested social care and free health care.

In the late 1960s and early 1970s, with the 1970 Local Government Act for England and Wales and the 1968 Social Work (Scotland) Act in Scotland, previously separate Children's Departments and Personal Social Services Departments were merged. In addition and more specifically, the 1970 Chronically Sick and Disabled Persons Act placed a responsibility on local authorities to assist disabled people. At the same time, local authorities expanded their support for older people in terms of the provision of residential care homes, day care, and home care. However, the statutory duty of much of this 'long-term social care' provision was uncertain. At the same time, adult social care has been subject to a number of policy imperatives, particularly since the mid 1980s. These have included a desire to:

- deinstitutionalise social care provision and provide it in more community-like settings;
- promote service users' independence and responsibility;
- promote service user 'choice', not least via quasi-markets;
- reconstruct long-term care as social care rather than health care;
- contain the overall level of expenditure on community social care.

Arguably the key reform was the passage of the 1990 NHS and Community Care Act (fully implemented in 1993), which sought to control rapidly rising social security payments for older people in independent sector care homes by transferring responsibility for assessing and meeting such needs to local government. While money was transferred from the social security budget accordingly, a key aim of the reforms seems to have been to bring an out-of-control budget back in balance and so longer-term financial pressures were inevitable. Critics have also described this as 'the only thing Margaret Thatcher ever gave local government' – and balancing the books and papering over the cracks it inherited is a major unsung achievement of local government at this time. Despite a series of New Labour policies to 'modernise' adult social care, the NHS Community Care Act remains the key underpinning legislation for the adult social care system – and the tensions inherent in the 1990s reforms have not gone away.

Current challenges and policy responses

In the early twenty-first century, the health and social care system faces a series of challenges. Chief among these are a series of demographic changes that mean that formal services have to work with a much larger number of older people and with many more people with very significant needs. This includes a growing number of younger people with very complex physical impairments, who might previously have died but are now surviving into adulthood thanks to rapid advances in medical technology. Changes in family make-up may also mean that older people have less access to informal support at local level, and broader social and technological changes mean that the general public have higher and higher expectations of services. Put all this together, and the current system could be unviable – indeed, Glasby *et al.* (2010) estimate that if we do nothing, the cost of the social care system alone could double within 20 years (and this is for existing services, which are increasingly being criticised as being of insufficient quality). This statistic was also produced before more recent cuts in public spending by the Coalition, which have led one council leader to describe the current situation as 'the end of local government as we know it' (quoted in Dudman, 2012).

While these challenges will place significant strain on existing services, the media and some policy-makers often fall into the trap of seeing many of these issues as evidence of the growing 'burden' being placed on the system. This is very negative language and disguises the fact that many people would see some of the developments above as positive. For example, the growing number of older people and younger disabled people are people who would previously have died – and the fact that they are living for much longer is surely a major success and something to be celebrated. Equally, we might see rising public expectations as a sign of underlying success, with many services providing quality care and prompting the public to want and expect even better in future. In this sense, health and social services might be seen as 'victims of their own success', improving what they do and offering new responses to need over time but raising expectations exponentially in the process. Even the current cuts agenda will be interesting to watch. While it could have a devastating effect on services, necessity is sometimes the mother of invention and it will be intriguing to see if the level of financial constraint is such that health and social care are forced to challenge some of their existing practices and adopt very different approaches in future. In this sense, austerity could force us to grasp some nettles that would never have been possible in an era of relative plenty (see below for discussion of 'care closer to home').

In response to such challenges, the health and social care system is developing a series of new approaches (and/or trying to tackle some long-standing issues with renewed energy). Alongside the key themes identified by Martin Powell (see Chapter 15), this section of the chapter focuses on four key issues:

- care closer to home
- personalisation

STOP AND THINK

Current challenges

- What are the key challenges faced by health and social services, and would you identify the same themes and issues explored in this chapter?

- Is an ageing population a reason for celebration or a potential burden on a system that is already struggling?

- Do the public expect too much from health and social care, or do services have a duty to offer the highest quality care to all?

- Will the financial crisis force services to take fundamentally different approaches than in the past, and would this be a good or a bad thing?

- integrated care
- future funding of long-term care.

Care closer to home

As suggested above, the NHS has tended to be dominated by acute hospitals providing one-off crisis support and episodic care to people in an emergency. These services have often been well resourced compared with other parts of the system and are very highly visible and popular with local people. While this makes perfect sense historically, it is arguably out of keeping with the changing nature of health needs in the wider population. Over time, many services that once had to be provided in hospital have been transferred to the community (or at least are capable of being delivered safely in the community), while specialist, tertiary services have tended to be provided in larger, regional centres. Although the latter trend has often been portrayed as the product of 'cuts', it is arguably more about trying to improve quality and safety by creating even more specialist and expert services. Of course, this has raised ongoing questions about the desirability and viability of some local district general hospitals. There are also particular issues in parts of the country such as London, where cynics (albeit overstating the issue) have suggested there is a world-class hospital on almost every street corner. If designing a system from scratch in an era of long-term conditions, few people would start from where we currently are, and major changes might be needed in future.

In response, successive governments have attempted to develop more community-based responses (often described as a form of 'care closer to home'). While this might make sense logically, actually achieving it in practice is a different matter (see the 'Stop and think' exercise below). Typically, any attempt to change the structure of local hospital services (particularly if it involves the loss of a maternity unit or the downgrading of an accident and emergency department) is seen by local people as a loss – rather than as an attempt to promote more effective services closer to home on the one hand and to concentrate specialist services where they can have maximum effect on the other. According to one former government advisor, the NHS in England may need to close (or radically change) around 40 hospitals – or find an extra £8 billion if not prepared to take such apparently drastic

STOP AND THINK

Acute care reconfiguration

Hospitals provide crucial services and are often much loved by local communities. However, some commentators claim we have too many hospitals in some parts of the country, and that many need to close in order to free up resources for care closer to home. Imagine this was your local hospital:

- How would you feel?
- Would you be in favour or would you oppose such a closure?
- How would you know if this was a positive move to improve care or simply the result of damaging cuts?
- If you were a politician or senior manager responsible for taking and implementing such a decision, how would you go about the task in order to maximise your chances of making the right judgement and bringing local people with you?
- How likely would closure be in practice – even if you felt this was the right decision for most local people, do you think you could actually achieve it?

action (Corrigan and Mitchell, 2011). Recent attempts to concentrate specialist services such as paediatric heart surgery in a smaller number of centres of excellence (NHS Specialised Services, 2010) have also been challenged legally by local services and by protest groups alike. Whatever the official rhetoric, it remains to be seen whether anyone has enough political will to more fundamentally alter the current balance of services towards a system based on care closer to home (and the example of Winterbourne View at the beginning of this chapter is a good example of the enduring nature of institutional forms of service provision). Of course, the bulk of this debate has tended to focus on the design of current NHS services, but also has an impact on community-based health and social care. Often, attempts to reduce the number of emergency hospital admissions and to promote community alternatives to acute care depend upon investing upfront in more integrated health and social care (see below for further debates about the concept of integration).

Personalisation

Of all the topics in this chapter, the advent of the personalisation agenda is by far the most contested and controversial (see 'Spotlight' below on 'Citizenship or privatisation by the backdoor?'). Developed initially by groups of disabled people, the concept of direct payments began in the United States and Canada in the 1970s and spread slowly to parts of the UK in the mind-1980s, with small groups of disabled people campaigning for greater choice and control over their care funding. This way of working was eventually rolled out more generally under the 1996 Community Care (Direct Payments) Act, enabling a range of community care user groups to receive the cash equivalent of directly provided services in order to design their own services and, potentially, to hire their own personal assistants (for an overview of these policy changes, see Glasby and Littlechild, 2009). This has since been supplemented by the broader concept of personal budgets or self-directed support, where the system is clear with the person upfront on how much is available to spend on meeting their needs and allows them greater say over how the money is spent. This could be via public services, via private services, via voluntary services – or via things that do not look like traditional services at all. Options for how the money is managed can range from the local authority or social worker managing the money on someone's behalf (as a form of notional or virtual budget) right the way through to taking the full amount as a direct payment. Other options in between might include a friend or family member managing the money on your behalf, working with an advocate, setting up an independent trust to manage the budget, or giving it to a trusted service provider and negotiating your care with them direct. One of the key innovations here is that by being clear about the money upfront, we allow the person and the worker to have a sense of how much they have to play with in meeting need and enable them to be more creative and innovative.

To date, these have proved very powerful ways of working for some people, enabling them to use scarce public resources much more effectively than in the past and to meet their needs much more fully (see Poll *et al.*, 2006; Glendinning *et al.*, 2008; for an overview, see Glasby and Littlechild, 2009). However, some have questioned whether personal budgets or self-directed support are the best way to promote personalisation for all social care users (Beresford, 2008, 2009; Woolham and Benton, 2012). For example, in the Individual Budgets pilots (the forerunner to Personal Budgets), older people obtained less benefit than other service user groups (Glendinning *et al.*, 2008; Orellana, 2010) and people with mental health problems faced significant barriers to their take-up (Glendinning *et al.*, 2008). Whether this is something inherent in the concept of individual budgets or whether it is more to do with the history and culture of some user group settings is hotly debated. In addition, it has been suggested by some that personal budgets might be more expensive than other forms of social care because of the transactional (i.e. administrative) costs associated with them (Slasberg *et al.*, 2012), although others feel that this need not be the case if we can create systems that are sufficiently simple and proportionate to risk. There is also a concern that we might see a withering away of collective provision – or privatisation by stealth (Ali, 2009) (see 'Spotlight' below on 'Citizenship or privatisation by the backdoor?'). Therefore, the Association of Directors of Adult Social Services recently suggested that we should be less occupied about who provides and more occupied about the what and when of social care provision (see ADASS, 2012; Daly, 2012).

> For many older people the choices they want are not so much about who provides, but what is available [and] when [as well as] . . . whether they feel they have a rapport and relationship with that particular care worker (ADASS, 2012).

The concepts of personalisation and self-directed support have also been piloted in children's services and in health care, raising the possibility that such approaches could form more of a cross-cutting approach to welfare reform. As but one example, it is not difficult to imagine how the service model and 'care' provided by Winterbourne View might have been very different with a much more personalised approach. Indeed, some commentators have gone so far as to describe these concepts as potentially representing a new form of 'Beveridge report for the twenty-first century', suggesting that if privatisation was the mantra of the 1980s, then personalisation could be a key feature of the 2000s and beyond (for an example of these debates in a health care context, see Alakeson, 2011).

Different underlying motives and value bases influence much of the literature and the policy debates around direct payments and personal budgets. On the one hand, some people see these ways of working as a key element of a citizenship agenda, giving people a right to greater choice and control over their services and hence over their lives. This approach is heavily associated with the independent living movement – organisations of disabled people campaigning for civil rights and for social change (in much the same way that key campaigners fought for these things with regards to ethnicity and gender).

On the other hand, others see direct payments and personal budgets as a way of rolling back the boundaries of the welfare state and of undermining public sector services and ethos. If we are not careful, this could just be a cost-cutting exercise that simply passes off risk and cuts onto individual disabled people and allows the state to wash its hands of the problem.

What do you think? If you were receiving formal social care or some health services, would you want a directly provided service or would you consider a direct payment or personal budget? What information would help you make this decision and what support would you need? Is this way of working a radical and powerful way of promoting citizenship and greater entitlement, or is it the end of public services as we know them (or something else in between)?

For further debate on these and other issues, see Ali (2009), Beresford (2008), Daly (2012), Ferguson (2007), Glasby and Littlechild (2009), Needham (2011), Rummery (2006), Scourfield (2007), Slasberg et al. (2012), Spandler (2004), Woolham and Benton (2012).

Integrated care

Alongside the personalisation agenda, successive governments have sought to promote more effective partnerships (between health and social care) and more integrated care (between different parts of the health system as well as between the NHS and other services). While this has long been a policy aspiration (dating back at least as far as some of the Joint Consultative Committees, joint finance and joint planning of the 1960s and 1970s), the emphasis on partnership working acquired increased impetus under New Labour (with its mantra of 'joined-up solutions to joined-up problems'). In an oft-quoted passage, the rationale for this approach was set out forcefully in a government discussion document of 1998, *Partnership in Action* (Department of Health, 1998, p. 3):

All too often when people have complex needs spanning both health and social care good quality services are sacrificed for sterile arguments about boundaries. When this happens people, often the most vulnerable in our society . . . and those who care for them find themselves in the no man's land between health and social services. This is not what people want or need. It places the needs of the organisation above the needs of the people they are there to serve. It is poor organisation, poor practice, poor use of taxpayers' money – it is unacceptable.

Under the Coalition, there has been even greater emphasis on delivering integrated care (NHS Future Forum, 2012), although this language seemed to develop part way through acrimonious debates around the Health and Social Care Act 2012 in an attempt to persuade opponents of these reforms that collaboration as well as competition would be an important element of a new system (for a fascinating account of the passage of the Act, see Timmins, 2012). However, delivering integrated care in a system not necessarily designed with joint working in mind is challenging (see the 'Stop and think' exercise below). Different health and social care organisations have different budgets, obey different legal frameworks, make decisions in different ways, have different cultures, use separate IT systems, cover different geographical boundaries, and have historically been held to account for their performance in different ways. As the Winterbourne View case study at the start of this chapter suggests, it remains all too easy for the care of people with complex needs to break down – often resulting in a crisis-based response that can be very expensive and not always of the highest quality. However, designing more proactive, integrated responses that prevent such situations from occurring remains elusive.

Future funding of long-term care

One of the key differences between health and adult social is that the former is typically provided free at the point of delivery, while the latter is means-tested. This means that people needing social care support often contribute towards the cost of their care – and in the case of residential care the contribution can be

STOP AND THINK

Health and social care partnerships
Doing some things together makes more sense intuitively than doing them separately. However, what does the current evidence say? Do partnerships deliver better outcomes and value for money than single agency ways of working? If so, when, how, and for whom?

For further debate, see key reviews by Cameron and Lart (2003), Cameron *et al.* (2012), Dickinson (2008), Dowling *et al.* (2004), Perkins *et al.* (2010).

STOP AND THINK

Delivering integrated care in practice
Different parts of the health and social care systems have been designed in isolation from each other and have evolved in different directions over time. There are also a series of legal, financial, and cultural barriers to more effective joint working – leading one commentator to describe this agenda as in terms of being asked to interrogate a 'square peg into a round hole' (Leutz, 1999).

Think about a situation where two or more agencies have had to work together (this could be an example from health and social care, but could equally be a situation from everyday life – such as trying to organise a house move, coordinating tradespeople helping to fit different parts of a new kitchen, or putting together a new sports team):

- What factors helped and hindered your attempts to achieve a coordinated approach?
- Despite your best efforts, did you really manage to ensure all parties were working effectively together and the whole was greater than the sum of its parts?
- How easy or difficult was it?
- How did it feel to be on the receiving end of services or individuals who did not necessarily work together as effectively as you hoped they might?

Now, apply these thoughts/lessons to an inter-agency health and social care situation. However difficult or frustrating your experiences were with a new kitchen or moving house, how much more important would these issues be if you were receiving multiple health and social care services? How much more serious could it be if things were not joined up?

substantial. As a practical example, an older person living in a care home might pay many hundreds of pounds a week for their care. If they have more than £23,250 in income, savings or capital, they will automatically receive no financial support at all from the social care system (and this includes the potential cost of the person's home if it were sold). For more specialist services, the costs can be immense (as in the case of services such as those provided by Winterbourne View at the start of this chapter – albeit residents here were probably funded via other routes).

For many older people who thought that the state would provide for them from the cradle to the grave, the sudden realisation that this is not the case (and of the high costs involved) can feel like a major betrayal. Over time, there have been a number of policy initiatives designed to review this system and propose a better way forward (see 'Spotlight' below). Despite several attempts, none of the recommendations made have been implemented in full, and the impression remains of a political system not sufficiently mature to be able to debate these issues openly and generate a genuine, cross-party, long-term solution. Of course, part of the reason for this is that the issues at stake are genuinely difficult – and there seem few easy answers (see the 'Discuss and do' exercise below). Until this issue is resolved, however, it is unlikely that we will make sufficient progress around many of the other policy issues discussed in this chapter – care closer to home, personalisation or integrated care.

Conclusion

Although health and adult social care are often treated separately in social policy textbooks, they are inextricably linked and need to be seen as two sides of the same coin. This has probably always been an artificial divide, but the current system is becoming increasingly difficult to justify given ongoing demographic changes and the growth in the number of people with multiple long-term conditions. As the nature of health and social care need shifts over time, the historical pattern of acute-dominated services no longer seems fit for purpose, and major changes may be needed. Whether or not current financial challenges make it harder to contemplate more fundamental reform – or whether lack of funding forces us to do something radically different – remains to be seen.

SPOTLIGHT

Debates about future funding

Over time, different reviews of long-term care funding have proposed different approaches:

- In 1999, the Royal Commission on Long Term Care suggested breaking down current costs into those related to personal care (the cost of being looked after arising out of frailty or disability), housing costs, and living costs. Whereas housing and living costs would be means-tested as at present, the Commission proposed that personal care should be provided free of charge. This was rejected in England but implemented in Scotland (see Bell and Bowes, 2006).

- In 2006, an unofficial review by Sir Derek Wanless (who had previously reviewed NHS spending for the government) proposed a 'partnership model' in which the costs of long-term care were shared between the state and the individual (with the state guaranteeing a basic minimum, set at perhaps 66 per cent of total care costs, and matching any individual contributions beyond this pound for pound, to an agreed limit).

- In the run up to the 2010 general election, a series of official policy papers proposed the creation of a new system of care and support (dubbed a 'national care service') with various debates around: whether it is feasible to provide free personal care in the community for older people with the highest needs; the possibility of levying a one-off charge on all older people to spread the potential risk of needing significant care; or the scope to place a charge on people's estates after they die (HM Government, 2008, 2009, 2010). Critics at the time felt that some of these measures were rushed and poorly thought through – perhaps influenced by the upcoming election rather than the result of a careful and sustained attempt to build the political consensus needed to achieve a lasting solution. In response, the then Opposition labelled some of the options being considered as a form of 'death tax' – thus lowering the tone of political debate yet further.

Against this backdrop, policy-makers have been seeking to promote a system based on care closer to home, more personalised responses to need, and greater integration. They have also had several abortive attempts at confronting the thorny issue of long-term care funding, although successive governments have subsequently backed away when their official reviews have reported and/

STOP AND THINK

Future funding

- How would you fund long-term care if you were the Secretary of State?

- Is it fair that older people who have paid tax and National Insurance all their working lives have to sell their homes to pay for their care?

- Equally, should older people with relatively generous pensions and who may own their own houses receive government money to fund their care? Would this seem fair to a young generation facing widespread unemployment, higher education tuition fees, high housing prices, and uncertain pension rights?

- What about some older owner-occupiers who have little money but own potentially valuable houses (i.e. who are cash poor but asset rich?)

- If health care is funded from general taxation, should social care be funded in a similar way?

- What are the key challenges faced by health and social services?

- Is an ageing population a reason for celebration or a potential burden on a system that is already struggling?

- Do the public expect too much from health and social care, or do services have a duty to offer the highest quality care to all?

- Will the financial crisis force services to take fundamentally different approaches than in the past – and would this be a good or a bad thing?

or left this issue unaddressed. Whatever happens next, it is likely that a funding solution will require a long-term commitment and cross-party consensus – and both of these have proved difficult in the past (particularly in the run-up to elections when the funding issue has become more openly party political). Whether the other agendas highlighted in this chapter can be addressed in full without a way forward on the funding is not clear. However, personalising care, integrating support, and delivering care closer to home certainly all feel extremely challenging unless there is underlying agreement around the perverse incentives created by different approaches to health and social care funding. For many people, services like those described at the start of this chapter should not need to exist, and the quality of 'care' they deliver should be immeasurably better than the abuse that took place at Winterbourne View. A key challenge for both health and social care will to ensure that such a situation can never occur again – but the history of UK welfare services suggests that we have had similar aspirations in the past and not been able to prevent them from happening again in practice.

Summary

This chapter has outlined developments in adult health and social care policy, historically and contemporaneously. This has included an examination and consideration of:

- the origins of current health and adult social care services;

- key themes and potential tensions in health and adult social care policy, including highlighting the importance – but also the difficulty – of delivering more integrated care for people with complex needs or 'co-morbidities' (that is, multiple 'long-term conditions' or 'chronic diseases');

- future options for reform, including funding reform, in which the state might recognise to a greater extent that, as people live longer with a variety of care needs, there is an inextricable link between how we provide social care and how we provide health care.

Discussion and review

▪ Is the health and social care divide sustainable or should we move to a situation where the welfare state meets citizens' social care needs based on need irrespective of ability to pay in the same way as UK state health care is predicated?

▪ Is an increased emphasis on personalised care and choice for either social care or health care sustainable within a context of increased need and reductions in state funding?

▪ Or, within the context of 'austerity', is the answer increasingly to expect citizens other than the poorest to self-fund?

References

Alakeson, V. (2011) *The Active Patient: The Case for Self-determination in Healthcare*, Health Services Management Centre/Centre for Welfare Reform, Birmingham.

Ali, A.M. (2009) 'The personalisation of the British National Health Service: empowering patients or exacerbating inequality?', *International Journal of Clinical Practice*, Vol. 63, No. 10, pp. 1416–18.

Association of Directors of Adult Social Services (ADASS) (2012) *The Case for Tomorrow: Facing the Beyond*, ADASS, London.

Bell, D. and Bowes, A. (2006) *Financial Care Models in Scotland and the UK: A Review of the Introduction of Free Personal Care for Older People in Scotland*, Joseph Rowntree Foundation, York.

Beresford, P. (2008) 'Time to get real about personalisation', *Journal of Integrated Care*, Vol. 16, No. 2, pp. 2–4.

Beresford, P. (2009) 'Whose personalisation?', *Soundings*, No. 40, pp. 8–17.

Blood, I. (2010) *Older People with High Support Needs: How can We Empower Them to Enjoy a Better Life?*, Joseph Rowntree Foundation, York.

Buckner, L. and Yeandle, S. (2011) *Valuing Carers 2011: Calculating the Value of Carers' Support*, Carers UK, London.

Cameron, A. and Lart, R. (2003) 'Factors promoting and obstacles hindering joint working: a systematic review of the research evidence', *Journal of Integrated Care*, Vol. 11, No. 2, pp. 9–17.

Cameron, A., Lart, R., Bostock, L. and Coomber, C. (2012) *Factors that Promote and Hinder Joint and Integrated Working between Health and Social Care Services*, SCIE, London.

Care Quality Commission (CQC) (2012) 'National report finds half of learning disability services did not meet standards', CQC press release, 25 June, available at http://www.cqc.org.uk/media/national-report-finds-half-learning-disability-services-did-not-meet-standards [accessed 1 November 2012].

Corrigan, P. and Mitchell, C. (2011) *The Hospital is Dead, Long Live the Hospital*, Reform, London.

Daly, G. (2012) 'Citizenship, choice and care: an examination of the promotion of choice in the provision of adult social care', *Research Policy and Planning*, Vol. 29, No. 3, pp. 179–90.

Department of Health (1998) *Partnership in Action: New Opportunities for Joint Working between Health and Social Services – A Discussion Document*, Department of Health, London.

Dickinson, H. (2008) *Evaluating Outcomes in Health and Social Care*, Policy Press, Bristol.

Dilnot, A. (2011) *Fairer Care Funding: The Report of the Commission on Funding of Care and Support* (The Dilnot Review), available at https://www.wp.dh.gov.uk/carecommission/files/2011/07/Fairer-Care-Funding-Report.pdf [accessed 25 November 2011].

Dowling, B., Powell, M. and Glendinning, C. (2004) 'Conceptualising successful partnerships', *Health and Social Care in the Community*, Vol. 12, No. 4, pp. 309–17.

Dudman, J. (2012) 'The end of local government?', *The Guardian*, 30 October, available at http://www.guardian.co.uk/society/2012/oct/30/end-of-local-government [accessed 22 November 2012].

Equality and Human Rights Commission (2011) 'Inquiry reveals failure to protect the rights of older people receiving care at home', EHRC press release, 20 June, Equality and Human Rights Commission, London.

Ferguson, I. (2007) 'Increasing user choice or privatizing risk? The antinomies of personalization', *British Journal of Social Work*, Vol. 37, No. 3, pp. 387–403.

Glasby, J. (2012) *Understanding Health and Social Care* (2nd edn.), Policy Press, Bristol.

Glasby, J. and Littlechild, R. (2009) *Direct Payments and Personal Budgets: Putting Personalisation into Practice* (2nd edn.), Policy Press, Bristol.

Glasby, J., Ham, C., Littlechild, R. and McKay, S. (2010) *The Case for Social Care Reform: The Wider Economic and Social Benefits* (for the Department of Health/Downing Street), Health Services Management Centre/Institute of Applied Social Studies, Birmingham.

Glendinning, C., Challis, D., Fernandez, J., Jacobs, S., Jones, K., Knapp, M. et al. (2008) *Evaluation of the Individual Budgets Pilot Programme*, Social Policy Research Unit, York.

Hannan, A. (2010) 'Real-time digital medicine', Presentation to the International Quality Improvement Exchange, Loch Lomond, 4–6 March.

HM Government (2008) *The Case for Change: Why England Needs a New Care and Support System*, Department of Health, London.

HM Government (2009) *Shaping the Future of Care Together*, TSO, London.

HM Government (2010) *Building the National Care Service*, TSO, London.

Leutz, W. (1999) 'Five laws for integrating medical and social services: lessons from the United States and the United Kingdom', *Milbank Memorial Fund Quarterly*, Vol. 77, No. 1, pp. 77–110.

Martin, J.P. (1984) *Hospitals in Trouble*, Basil Blackwell, Oxford.

Means, R. and Smith, R. (1998) *From Poor Law to Community Care*, Macmillan, Basingstoke.

Means, R., Morbey, H. and Smith, R. (2002) *From Community Care to Market Care? The Development of Welfare Services for Older People*, Policy Press, Bristol.

Means, R., Richards, S. and Smith, R. (2008) *Community Care: Policy and Practice* (4th edn.), Palgrave, Basingstoke.

Needham, C. (2011) *Personalising Public Services: Understanding the Personalisation Narrative*, Policy Press, Bristol.

NHS Future Forum (2012) *Integration – A Report from the NHS Future Forum*, NHS Future Forum, London.

NHS Specialised Services (2010) *Safe and Sustainable: A New Vision for Children's Congenital Heart Services in England – Consultation Document*, NHS Specialised Services, London.

Orellana, K. (2010) Personalisation in Practice: Lessons from Experience. Making Personal Budgets, Support Planning and Brokerage Work for Older People in Later Life, Age UK, London.

Perkins, N., Smith, K., Hunter, D.J., Bambra, C. and Joyce, K. (2010) '"What counts is what works?" New Labour and partnerships in public health', *Policy and Politics*, Vol. 38, No. 1, pp. 101–17.

Poll, C., Duffy, S., Hatton, C., Sanderson, H. and Routledge, M. (2006) *A Report on in Control's First Phase, 2003–2005*, in Control Publications, London.

Robb, B. (1967) *Sans Everything: A Case to Answer*, Nelson, London.

Royal Commission on Long Term Care (1999) *With Respect to Old Age: Long Term Care – Rights and Responsibilities*, TSO, London.

Rummery, K. (2006) 'Disabled citizens and social exclusion: the role of direct payments', *Policy and Politics*, Vol. 34, No. 4, pp. 633–50.

Scourfield, P. (2007) 'Social care and the modern citizen: client, consumer, service user, manager and entrepreneur', *British Journal of Social Work*, Vol. 37, No. 1, pp. 107–22.

Slasberg, C., Beresford, P. and Schofield, P. (2012) 'How self directed support is failing to deliver personal budgets and personalisation', *Research Policy and Planning*, Vol. 29, No. 3, pp. 161–78.

Spandler, H. (2004) 'Friend or foe? Towards a critical assessment of direct payments', *Critical Social Policy*, Vol. 24, No. 2, pp. 187–209.

Timmins, N. (2012) *Never Again? The Story of the Health and Social Care Act 2012*, King's Fund, London.

Wanless, D. (2006) *Securing Good Care for Older People: Taking a Long-term View*, King's Fund, London.

Woolham, J. and Benton, C. (2012) 'The costs and benefits of personal budgets for older people: evidence from a single local authority', *British Journal of Social Work*, DOI: 10.1093/bjsw/bcs086.

Further reading

For an overview of health policy and practice, the following textbooks offer excellent summaries:

Baggott, R. (2004) *Health and Health Care in Britain* (3rd edn.), Palgrave, Basingstoke.
Greener, I. (2009) *Healthcare in the UK: Understanding Continuity and Change*, Policy Press, Bristol.
Ham, C. (2009) *Health Policy in Britain* (6th edn.), Palgrave, Basingstoke.
Klein, R. (2010) *The New Politics of the NHS: From Creation to Reinvention* (6th edn.), Radcliffe Medical Press, Oxford.

For an overview of social care services for key community care groups, see:

Glasby, J. (2012) *Understanding Health and Social Care* (2nd edn.), Policy Press, Bristol.
McDonald, A. (2006) *Understanding Community Care: A Guide for Social Workers*, Palgrave, Basingstoke.
Means, R., Richards, S. and Smith, R. (2008) *Community Care: Policy and Practice* (4th edn.), Palgrave, Basingstoke.
Payne, M. (2005) *The Origins of Social Work: Continuity and Change*, Palgrave, Basingstoke.

For discussion of inter-agency health and social care, see:

Barratt, G., Sellman, D. and Thomas, J. (eds.) (2005) *Interprofessional Working in Health and Social Care*, Palgrave, Basingstoke.
Glendinning, C., Powell, M. and Rummery, K. (eds.) (2002) *Partnerships, New Labour and the Governance of Welfare*, Policy Press, Bristol.
Palgrave's 'Inter-agency Collaboration' series (with books on children's services, disability, learning disability, and mental health).
The Policy Press's 'Better Partnership Working' series.

For a fascinating account of the passage of the 2012 Health and Social Care Act, see:

Timmins, N. (2012) *Never Again? The Story of the Health and Social Care Act 2012*, King's Fund, London.

Useful websites (very selected)

For regular updates on health and social care policy and practice, see:

http://www.communitycare.co.uk – *Community Care* – a free online resource for social workers and people interested in social care.
http://www.hsj.co.uk – *Health Services Journal* – the website of the weekly magazine (access is via subscription only).

Other key sites include:

http://www.dh.gov.uk – Department of Health – government department with regular news items, consultations, and access to key policy documents. Over time, details of developments in the NHS will pass increasingly to the NHS Commissioning Board (http://www.commissioningboard.nhs.uk).

http://www.nhsconfed.org – NHS Confederation – key membership organisation for NHS providers and commissioners, with a series of policy papers, briefings, and news items.

http://www.scie.org.uk – Social Care Institute for Excellence (SCIE) – national body identifying and disseminating what works in social care in England, Wales, and Northern Ireland, with a series of research reviews, guides, film footage, and free online resources.

Helpful insights are also provided by various national voluntary organisations, including:

http://www.ageuk.org.uk – Age UK
http://www.carers.org – The Carers Trust
http://www.carersuk.org – Carers UK
http://www.disabilityrightsuk.org – Disability Rights UK
http://www.mencap.org.uk – Mencap
http://www.mind.org.uk – Mind

CHAPTER 13

Children and Families

Paul Daniel

Learning objectives

- To introduce the concept of family policy
- To examine the UK's historical non-interventionist approach to family policy and to locate this within an international comparative framework
- To assess the extent of diversity of family types experienced by children in contemporary British society
- To discuss New Labour's 'revolutionary' approach to family policy, in particular the primary focus on children within its social and economic strategy
- To outline the direction of the Coalition government's approach to policy on children and families

Chapter overview

Children and families are at the heart of UK social policy as never before. The aim of this chapter is to examine the transformation of family policy since the 1990s. Historically, the UK approach to state intervention in the family has been categorised as 'reluctant and minimal', with a primary focus on child protection. However, it is argued that increasing anxiety over the state of childhood and the role of families, together with the emphasis that New Labour placed upon 'investing' in children, ensured that childhood became a key site for government intervention in the first decade of the new millennium. The suggestion that this constitutes a permanent and revolutionary shift in UK family policy needs, nevertheless, to be treated with a degree of caution in the light of changes in emphasis apparent in the early stages of the Coalition government elected in 2010.

This chapter discusses:

- the idea of 'family policy';
- the extent of demographic change and family diversity;
- New Labour's approaches to children and families and their policy initiatives;
- the changes in emphasis under the Coalition government.

CONTROVERSY AND DEBATE

'[D]espite evidence clearly demonstrating the importance of stable, healthy and, in particular, married families, current policy does not reflect this. The Government has instead focused entirely on the child, rather than the family as a whole and up until recently had refused to acknowledge that children of married parents do better across a wide range of indicators than those with co-habiting or lone parents . . . All the evidence shows that government in the UK has become indifferent to the institution of marriage and in doing so has damaged society.' (Centre for Social Justice, 2010, p. 4)

'Does the left "get" family values? No. And if it means believing that two-parent families are the moral foundation of a good society, nor should it. A more progressive view is to recognise that many kinds of family structures can provide love, care and support. This is confirmed by research which shows that the quality of family relationships matters far more than whether there are two parents.' (Pickett and Wilkinson, 2011)

How useful are these different perspectives in understanding approaches to family policy in the UK?

Introduction

It is difficult to draw boundaries around what we mean by family policy. Almost all social policies either directly impact upon families or are informed by assumptions about the role and responsibilities that families are expected to fulfil, especially in relation to the care of children. In this broad sense, we could include within family policy aspects of health, housing, and especially education policy. However, for the purposes of this chapter we will concentrate more narrowly on what Daly (2004, p. 136) refers to as 'welfare state support for families': 'Policies covering cash support to families, provisions for working parents, services for families with children, and benefits and services for higher need families'.

Although a diverse and disparate range of policies, they have in common the fact that they are targeted specifically at families and are designed 'to have an impact on family resources and, ultimately, on family structure' (Hantrais, 2004, p. 132). We should also stress at the outset that although policy on children and families follows a similar trajectory throughout the individual countries that make up the United Kingdom, there are different emphases and approaches and, in Scotland in particular, separate legislation in relation to many aspects of family policy. This has become more pronounced since devolution in 1999. Unless otherwise stated, this chapter describes policy as it relates to England. For a more detailed discussion of family policy in Scotland, see Tisdall and Hill (2011), and on Wales, Hill (2008) and Ball (2013).

The relationship between the state and the family has long been a delicate and contentious issue in UK social policy. Even measures that might seem relatively straightforward on the surface, such as the introduction of school meals in 1906 and family allowances (the forerunner of child benefit) in 1945, were accompanied by widespread concern that such state provision would undermine the responsibility of parents to care for their own children. This theme of parental responsibility and family privacy has been a strong and perennial theme in UK social policy.

Historically, UK governments have treated the family as a private domain, outside the reach of state intervention. A number of international comparative studies have reached broadly similar conclusions in this respect. Kamerman and Kahn (1978), for example, reviewed family policy in 14 countries and concluded that the UK was among a small group whose approach to family support was 'minimal and reluctant'. Subsequently, Gauthier (1996) analysed 22 advanced welfare states and produced a classification based upon their approach to family policy. Here again the UK was among those countries which she labelled as 'pro-family and non-interventionist'. In other words, the traditional family is strongly supported ideologically and rhetorically, but benefits and services, such as childcare, are limited to those in need. A similar conclusion was reached by Hantrais following her assessment of the 25 countries in the EU in terms of the extent to which they use social policy to minimise individuals' reliance on their families. Here the UK was classified, along with Ireland, Germany, Austria, and the Netherlands, as 'partially de-familialised'. In all five countries, Hantrais (2004, p. 202) suggested, 'government rhetoric is supportive of families but policy actors are reluctant to intervene in family life . . . they all expect families to bear the main responsibility for organising care for children and older people'.

Demographic change and the family

Any reference to 'family' or 'childhood' obscures the diversity and complexity of social relationships within UK households. Children experience many different types of childhood in a variety of family situations (see Table 13.1 and Figure 13.1). Bradshaw (2011, p. 24) provides an excellent overview of the main demographic developments and concludes that:

> Delayed fertility, falling birth rates and the relative instability of new family forms is giving rise to very different experiences of childhood both within and between peer groups. Children of the 21st century have a higher probability of experiencing parental separation, lone parenting, step families, visiting families, half siblings and being an only child than children of any previous period of time.

Table 13.1 Changing family structures, 1997–2009 (millions)

	1997	2001	2005	2008	2009
No. of dependent children by family type					
Married couple[3]	9.6	9.0	8.6	8.3	8.3
Cohabiting couple[4]	1.0	1.3	1.5	1.7	1.7
Female lone parent	2.5	2.7	2.8	2.8	2.9
Male lone parent	0.2	0.2	0.3	0.2	0.3
No. of families with dependent children					
Married couple[3]	5.1	4.8	4.7	4.6	4.6
Cohabiting couple[4]	0.6	0.8	0.9	1.0	1.0
Female lone parent	1.5	1.6	1.7	1.7	1.8
Male lone parent	0.2	0.2	0.2	0.2	0.2

1. Children aged under 16 and those aged 16–18 who have never married or who are in full-time education. See Appendix, Part 2: Families.
2. Data are at Q2 (April–June) each year and are not necessarily adjusted. See Appendix, Part 4: Labour Force Survey.
3. Data for 2008 onwards include civil partnerships.
4. Data for 2008 onwards include same-sex couples.

Source: Office for National Statistics, *Labour Force Survey*

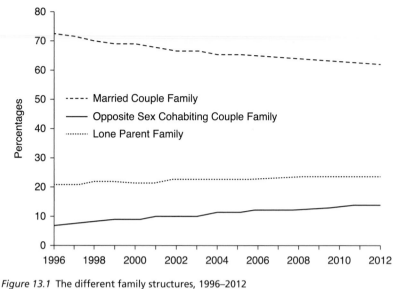

Figure 13.1 The different family structures, 1996–2012

Source: Office for National Statistics, *Families and Households 2012*

In fact, the demographic data, based as they are on cross-sectional and static views of family life, do not give the full picture of the way family changes impact on individual children. In this respect, the Millennium Cohort Study, a longitudinal study of nearly 19,000 children born between 2000 and 2002, gives us a much richer picture. Using these data, Panico *et al.* (2010) have shown that during the first five years of life, about 20 per cent of children experienced one change in their family structure, while 7.5 per cent experienced more than one change. Children born to lone parents were the most likely to experience at least one change in their family by age five (see Table 13.2). However, while these data highlight a growing diversity and fluidity in the living arrangements of young children, the authors stress that it also indicates continued stability among certain groups. 'Three quarters of all children did not experience any changes at all over the first five years of life. Over 90% of children born to married parents and over 80% of those born to cohabiting parents were still living with two parents by age five' (Panico *et al.*, 2010, p. 11).

In the literature on the diversity of family life, the views of children themselves have been very under-represented. However, more recently work by Morrow (2009), Brannen *et al.* (2000), and Mayall (2002) has gone some way to address this imbalance. In general terms, this work seems to suggest that children, particularly the older ones, are quite phlegmatic about family change and their definitions of what constitutes a family are quite elastic, based more upon the quality of relationships rather than legal form. So that while parental conflict undoubtedly has a deleterious impact upon children, this is balanced to some extent by the benefits from living in complex families, in terms of expanded networks of social support (Morrow, 2009).

Table 13.2 Change and stability in family structures over time, compositional change (percentages)

Relationship status at:	9 months	3 years	5 years
Married at birth			
Married (no change)	98.5	93.4	90.8
Cohabiting	0.2	0.8	1.7
Lone parent	1.2	4.8	7.2
Cohabiting at birth			
Married	7.1	27.9	27.1
Cohabiting (no change)	85.7	56.1	53.7
Lone parent	6.6	15.2	18.7
Not living with father at birth			
Married	5.6	13.1	14.7
Cohabiting	17.5	25.9	27.6
Lone parent (no change)	75.3	60.0	57.5

Note: Unweighted sample (cases with complete longitudinal data), 13,234. Shaded rows represent groups that did not experience a change in family structure.

New Labour: children and families

With the election of the Blair government in 1997 came a radical transformation of policy relating to children and families. Childhood replaced the family as the central focus of policy. Indeed, children became pivotal to the New Labour project of political and social reform and in particular two of its key concepts, social investment and social exclusion. Taking social investment first, the idea that spending on children could be seen as a valuable 'investment in the future of the nation' was far from new. For example, Eleanor Rathbone, the pioneering campaigner for family allowances had argued: 'Children are not simply a private luxury. They are an asset to the community and the community can no longer afford to leave the provision of their welfare solely to the accident of individual income' (Eleanor Rathbone, 1940). Similar sentiments have been expressed on behalf of children by numerous campaigners, as well as social reformers going back to the Boer war (Hendrick, 2003). Most notably, the Beveridge Report, which provided the foundation for the post Second World War welfare state, was motivated to a large extent by a concern 'to ensure the adequate continuance of the British race' (Beveridge, 1942, para. 114).

So an emphasis on children as investment is a common theme in social policy. However, what was new and different about New Labour's approach was the fact that this theme was so central to its economic and social policy. Informed by the work of Giddens, and facing an increasingly globalised knowledge-based economy, the Blair government set out to transform the welfare state from one that compensated for dis-welfares to one that more actively intervened to improve skills and competitiveness. The prime focus of

STOP AND THINK

- Do you agree that family policy in the UK 'has become indifferent to the institution of marriage'?

- What are the arguments for and against using tax incentives to promote marriage?

this overhauled 'social investment state' lay within child and family policies. Blair made this very clear in his 1999 Beveridge lecture, when he argued that 'if the knowledge economy is an aim then work, skill and above all investing in children become essential aims of welfare . . . we have made children our top priority' (Blair, 1999).

The second key concept underlying New Labour's social policy was 'social exclusion'. Again this was not an idea that was exclusive or original to the Blair government, but certainly one that became ubiquitous in its approach to children and families. An early attempt to define social exclusion by Labour's newly created Social Exclusion Unit reads as follows: 'a short-hand term for what can happen when people or areas suffer from a combination of linked problems such as unemployment, poor skills, low incomes, poor housing, high crime environment, bad health and family breakdown' (Social Exclusion Unit/DSS, 1999, p. 23).

This gives some sense of the elastic and imprecise nature of the concept. It encompasses, as Levitas (2005) has pointed out, structural explanations of exclusion (poverty, poor housing) as well as what she terms 'the moral under-class' discourse of criminal behaviour, dysfunctional families, and so on. What is striking about Labour's approach to 'social exclusion' is that, as with 'social investment', children were at the heart of government policy. A glance at the Social Exclusion Unit's agenda indicates that truancy, school exclusions, and teenage pregnancy were among its early priorities. This focus on childhood can, in part, be explained, Hendrick (2003) suggests, by the profound impact that the James Bulger murder had on New Labour at a time when it was formulating its political identity. This case, involving as it did the murder of a 2-year-old (James Bulger) by two 10-year-old boys, Jon Venables and Robert Thompson, in a deprived area of Merseyside, provoked a degree of soul searching and national debate that is hard to overestimate looking back. Amidst the outpouring of national and international media attention, not to mention the academic and political analysis about the state of contemporary childhood, Labour drew the following lesson, according to Hendrick (2003, p. 241):

> For the Bulger killers were, like the child himself, figures of social exclusion par excellence. And this was a key reference for modernisers in the Labour Party, who took from the case a belief that the excluded posed real dangers to the wider social fabric . . . The reality of life among the socially excluded became an important issue in the reassessments of childhood, welfare and progressivism (at least the remnants of it).

Just as with 'social investment', the emphasis given to childhood within the 'social exclusion' discourse rests heavily on the idea of the child as future adult.

The main justification for intervening in childhood, primarily, as we will see, in the very early years, is the fact that this will prevent the emergence of an adult 'underclass'. This was made clear in a report to the Office of the Deputy Prime Minister in 2004: 'Tackling social exclusion in childhood is crucial in part because of its longer term consequences . . . So getting it right in the early years is seen as crucial' (Office of the Deputy Prime Minister, 2004).

This instrumental view of the child as an 'adult in waiting' has been pervasive in social policy, and was a particularly powerful theme of the New Labour years. This view of children as 'human becomings' rather than as 'human beings' has been widely critiqued (Daniel and Ivatts, 1998; Fawcett *et al.*, 2004). Specifically in relation to social exclusion, Ridge (2002, p. 6) has pointed out that 'while the effects of poverty and social exclusion undoubtedly reverberate from childhood into adulthood, children experience social exclusion within the immediacy of childhood'.

New Labour and early years policy

New Labour's two overriding social policy priorities of 'social investment' and 'social inclusion' came together in the emphasis given to early years intervention. Drawing heavily on much quoted evidence from the American Perry Pre-School Project, which had indicated that for every dollar invested in the early years, seven dollars was saved in terms of reduced state intervention in later life (Schweinhart *et al.*, 1993; Commission on Social Justice, 1994), Labour placed early years intervention at the top of its policy agenda.

The introduction of the National Childcare Strategy in 1998 was something of a breakthrough in British social policy in that it represented the first time that childcare was seen as a public and not simply a private responsibility. Labour inherited a very fragmented set of early years services, with public provision limited in most areas to children considered to be at risk of harm. Through its National Childcare Strategy (with a parallel development in Scotland), subsequently updated in the Ten Year Strategy (HM Treasury, 2005), Labour committed itself to 'a longer term vision of the childcare market in which every parent can access affordable, good quality childcare' (Ashton, 2002).

Labour's strategy was wide-ranging and included a multiplicity of initiatives, but two stand out. First, there was an attempt to support parents with the cost of childcare, most specifically with the introduction of the childcare tax credit. Second, there was an expansion of the supply of daycare places. Particularly significant here was the launch of the Sure Start initiative. Described as 'the jewel in the crown' of Labour's support for children and families, the first Sure Start projects were opened in the 250 most deprived areas of the country (rising to 350 by 2002). The aim of the centres was to offer a range of services, including family support, health, education and childcare, and despite having a range of targets that were fixed centrally they also aimed to involve local communities. In contrast to previous approaches to childcare and family support (for example, in the 1989 Children Act and its equivalent, the Children Act 1995 in Scotland), Sure Start services were not restricted to children in need. Within their catchment areas they were universal services, open to all. This inevitably led to the criticism that most poor families were geographically excluded – it was estimated that only 30 per cent of poor families were within the Sure Start catchment areas (La Valle and Smith, 2009) – and also prompted accusations of a 'middle-class' takeover of some Sure Start local projects. It is unsurprising, then, that the Labour government attempted to capitalise on the popular brand in 2004 by announcing plans to develop 3,500 Sure Start Children's Centres by 2010. These were placed upon a statutory footing by the Childcare Act 2006, but in giving local authorities responsibility for developing and managing Children's Centres, the essence of the original Sure Start was arguably lost. As Haux (2012, p.6) has observed: 'What had started as a localised programme for parents living in poor areas with a high level of voluntary sector involvement evolved into centres run by local authorities that were focusing much more on childcare in order to get more parents into work'. The same point is echoed by one of Sure Start's principal authors and the lead civil servant for the project, Norman Glass, who claimed:

> the early Sure Start documents make very little reference to childcare in the sense of somewhere children can be looked after to enable their parents to work; it was all about child development . . . However Sure Start, originally a child-centred programme, became embroiled in the childcare agenda and the need to roll out as many places as possible to support maternal employment.
>
> (Glass, 2005)

Whether or not it is the case that Labour's early years policy was ultimately driven more by the welfare to work agenda and the needs of working mothers than those of children, it is certainly true that many early years specialists were highly critical of the lack of a child-centred perspective in much of what was achieved (Moss, 2004). This was particularly so in debates around the introduction of the Early Years Curriculum, with its heavy emphasis on children's cognitive skills and on 'children as learners'/future workers rather than on play, and what Peter Moss (2004, p. 21) has dubbed 'children's spaces'. By contrast, there was a much more overt emphasis on play-based learning in the early years stage of the Scottish Curriculum for Excellence.

Nevertheless, for all the criticisms, there is little argument that the Blair government instigated a radical departure in early years policy. It invested around £21 billion between 1997 and 2006 and doubled the number of childcare places over the same period (HM Government, 2007). Daly (2010) has described this as the 'discovery of something of a new policy domain' in the UK and Lister (2003) as a 'breakthrough in British social policy'. However, for all that there was a clear acceptance by Labour, for the first time in British social policy history, that childcare was a public responsibility, Daly suggests that there remained as many points of continuity as change in their approach. In particular the reliance upon, and indeed the encouragement of, markets for childcare provision. As Ball and Vincent (2006, p. 563) claim: 'for most families childcare is still treated as a private good, something individual parents find for themselves and purchase. As in other areas of education and welfare, New Labour's emphasis is on the individualisation of responsibility'. Even after the substantial level of investment and a plethora of policy initiatives, Labour left office without the 'universal, publicly funded, integrated and equitable child care system' that would indeed have constituted a paradigm change, according to Daly (2010, p. 440).

Tackling child poverty

If we are looking for the clearest indication that social policy priorities during the New Labour years shifted towards children, then it must lie in the commitment to tackle child poverty. When Tony Blair pledged in his Beveridge memorial lecture in 1999 to 'end child poverty forever' within 20 years, it was as historic as it was unexpected. What was arguably the most significant and defining aspect of the Blair/Brown governments, at least in the social policy field, was not flagged up in the 1997 manifesto, nor had there been any hint of it in the first year in office. There is no doubt that during the 1980s children bore the brunt of the suffering caused by the social and economic changes, including policies of the Conservative government led by Margaret Thatcher (Bradshaw, 1990; Daniel and Ivatts, 1998). During this period, the number of children living in poverty doubled, so that by the end of the twentieth century children in Britain were some of the poorest in Europe and the developed world (Ridge, 2002).

Tackling child poverty fits squarely with Labour's twin preoccupations with social investment and social inclusion. In a report for the Joseph Rowntree Foundation, Hirsch estimated the social costs of child poverty, and therefore the potential 'social investment' returns on its elimination. Hirsch (2008, p. 1) concluded that:

> Child poverty costs the country at least £25 billion a year, including £17 billion that could accrue to the Exchequer if child poverty were eradicated. Moving all families above the poverty line would not instantly produce this sum. But in the long term, huge amounts would be saved from not having to pick up the pieces of child poverty and associated social ills.

Labour employed a twin strategy to help reduce child poverty (defined as children living in households with up to 60 per cent of median household income). The first part of this was to reduce the number of children in workless households. The New Deal for Lone Parents, working tax credits, the national minimum wage, and increased availability of childcare were all part of a process of 'welfare to work'/'making work pay' that helped to raise the proportion of lone parents in work. About 54 per cent of children of lone parents were living in households with no work in 1997. This fell to 44 per cent by 2005 (Dickens, 2011). But equally important in tackling child poverty was the significant increase in the rate (and range) of benefits for children – child benefit principally, but also including new benefits such as the educational maintenance allowance and child trust funds.

In aiming to eliminate child poverty in 20 years, Labour set interim targets to cut the numbers by a quarter by 2004–05 and by half by 2010–11. Neither of these targets was met. If we take the data for 2011–12, for example, the number of children living below the official poverty measure was 2.3 million or 18 per cent of the child population (DWP, 2012). This compares with 3.4 million or 27 per cent of the child population in 1996–97 when Labour entered office. However, it can be argued that this 1.1 million reduction understates Labour's achievement since, as the Institute for Fiscal Studies has shown, if the tax benefit system that Labour inherited in 1997–98 had simply been uprated for price inflation there would have been 4.3 million children below the poverty line in 2010–11 (Brewer *et al.*, 2010). For a greater sense of perspective, we should add that the scale and rate of this reduction in child poverty was historically unprecedented in the UK and compares favourably with child poverty trends in other developed countries during this period.

Although this was a significant achievement, Labour's approach to tackling child poverty preserved an historic distinction in UK social policy between 'the deserving' and the 'undeserving poor' (see Chapter 6), to the extent that children whose parents fell into the latter category were excluded from receiving financial support. The most egregious example of this was the policy on asylum-seeking children, which consistently viewed such children as 'asylum seekers first' and 'children second' (Giner, 2007).

THE CHILD POVERTY ACT 2010

Perhaps the most notable legacy of the Labour government, in relation to child poverty, was the fact that before leaving office it managed to achieve consensus between the three main parties to pass the Child Poverty Act 2010. This set out a number of duties for future governments, including most significantly the target of reducing the proportion of children in poverty (measured as 60 per cent of median income) by 2020–21 to no more than 10 per cent. It also required government to produce an annual child poverty strategy. Subsequently, however, in its first such strategy document, the Coalition government that succeeded Labour in 2010, while not reneging on the central target, appeared to muddy the waters by suggesting that Labour's focus on income-based measures of child poverty had been

STOP AND THINK

- What is the best measure of child poverty?

- Do you think that the Coalition government's proposals to widen the range of indicators used to measure child poverty help us to understand and address the problem or are they a way of confusing the debate?

too narrow (DWP/DfE, 2011). Launching a consultation in autumn 2012, the Coalition government suggested that a wide range of other indicators, such as educational participation, early health inequalities, teenage pregnancies, and children in workless households, might be included in any child poverty measure. Despite government protestations to the contrary, this appeared to be an attempt on the part of the Coalition to move away from a monetary measure of poverty towards one that focuses on behavioural features. This came at a time when the Institute for Fiscal Studies was predicting that welfare benefit cuts were likely to lead to an increase of 300,000 in relative child poverty by 2014–15 (Brewer *et al.*, 2011).

Every Child Matters

If the commitment to eliminate child poverty was the most radical and unexpected of all Labour's policies on children and families, it was perhaps the *Every Child Matters* agenda (DfES, 2004) that was the most emblematic development, and the one that best captured the essence of the Blair government's approach to children. Ostensibly its origins lay in that most traditional of concerns, child protection. The death of Victoria Climbié in February 2000, and the subsequent inquiry report by Lord Laming in 2003, highlighted a series of familiar failings in the child protection system, including the lack of communication between the various agencies involved and the failure to ensure that the child was always the central concern. Similar concerns had been raised in earlier cases such as Maria Colwell (1973) and Jasmine Beckford (1984). What was different in Labour's response to the Laming Report was that it set out a much more wide-ranging and holistic approach to child protection, setting it within a framework of concern for the wellbeing of all children. This followed on from the 2002 Spending Review, which examined services for children, and the suggestion by Blair that the government should publish a Green Paper on 'children at risk'. In the event, *Every Child Matters*, which was signed by no fewer than 16 ministers from 13 separate government departments, provided an all-embracing umbrella for all the services and programmes that Labour were developing for children and families. As Frost and Parton (2009, p. 37) have pointed out, it starts from the premise 'that any child, at some point in their life, could be seen as vulnerable to some form of risk. The government therefore deemed it necessary that *all children* should be covered by its proposals'. It was based upon the twin themes of early intervention and better integration of services, or 'joined up' government. The aim was to improve the welfare of all children, based on a set of five outcomes: being healthy, staying safe, enjoying and achieving, making a positive contribution, and achieving economic wellbeing. It is true that one or two of these 'outcomes' were rather narrowly defined. For example, 'enjoying and achieving' was to be measured in terms of school attendance and attainment, while 'making a positive contribution' was perceived rather negatively in terms of a reduction in offending, school exclusions, and anti-social behaviour. This prompted Williams (2004), for example, to dismiss *Every Child*

Matters as a 'dreary vision of childhood based on a work ethic of academic achievement and social conformity'.

CHILDREN ACT 2004

To carry forward many of the aims of *Every Child Matters* in England and Wales [Scotland established a similar programme under the title *Getting it Right for Every Child* (Scottish Executive, 2006)], Labour introduced legislation that changed the governance and administration of children's services in a number of significant ways. The Children Act 2004 established new Children's Departments, which integrated social services and education at local authority level, mirroring the creation of the Department for Children, Schools and Families and the newly appointed Minister for Children within central government. The most controversial aspect of the new legislation, however, was the proposal to introduce a national database of all children to aid information-sharing between professionals. After much debate and concern over the civil liberties implications, a modified form of the database, called ContactPoint, was launched in 2007, only to be scrapped by the Coalition government in 2010.

There is no doubt that *Every Child Matters* and the Children Act 2004 between them constituted a 'significant shift in the relationships between children, parents, professionals and the state' (Frost and Parton, 2009). Indeed, Kirby has gone so far as to suggest it amounted to 'the nationalisation of childhood' (Kirby, 2006). Certainly, the shift in emphasis away from a narrow, reactive stance on child protection towards a more universal and inclusive approach that was concerned with the wellbeing of all children.

Support for families

Parenting support has been described as 'a creature of the New Labour era' (Henricson, 2012, p. 30). We have already suggested that UK governments have historically taken a low profile when it comes to intervention in families, especially compared with other European countries. Before the 1990s, state involvement with family life in the UK was largely confined to 'problem' families where children were at risk. However, as Henricson (2012, p. 36) has suggested:

> the distinctiveness of the New Labour project was to establish a population-wide parenting support network where one had not existed . . . In summary, by the time New Labour left office family policy had changed from a relatively insubstantial function of government in the 1980s to one of its most substantial.

Labour's Green Paper, *Supporting Families* (Home Office, 1998), set the tone for this shift by suggesting that seeking advice should be seen as 'a sign of responsible parenting rather than an admission of failure'. Over the next few years, the government proceeded to establish the National Family and Parenting Institute, a national helpline, Parentline, and a host of initiatives at local authority level that have been well mapped by Henricson and colleagues (Henricson *et al.*, 2001). Although the Green Paper paid lip service to support for marriage as the best arrangement for raising children, there is no doubt that Labour adopted a rather pragmatic approach to family support, and Lewis's claim that the main preoccupation was not the unity of the couple, or even the permanence of relationships, 'but the need to secure stable arrangements for children' (Lewis, 2001, p. 178), is apt. The married couple tax allowance was abolished in favour of increased child benefit and family law was reformed to place more emphasis on improving support for children in the event of relationship breakdown and less on patching up failed marriages.

The fact that support for families was delivered on a universal, and non-stigmatising basis, through Sure Start centres and increasingly via schools (Churchill, 2011) meant that, on the whole, there was a relatively high level of popular support for the programme. However, some of the more intrusive and controlling aspects of family intervention such as Parenting Orders and Home–School Contracts were more controversial. There was criticism, too, from a feminist perspective that an emphasis on 'parenting' implicitly led to a focus on mothers (Fawcett *et al.*, 2004). To counter this the Home Office funded projects involving work with fathers from 1999 to 2004, and a helpline, Fathers Direct, was established. Engaging with fathers, however, remained a problematic issue for agencies working in the field (Lloyd *et al.*, 2003).

Within this framework of universal support for families, there was a more targeted approach aimed at families with multiple problems. The most notable example of the schemes that were introduced to tackle anti-social or dysfunctional family behaviour was the Family Intervention Project (FIP) programme (originating in a small Scottish project, the Dundee Family Project set up in 1996). Extended across the UK in 2006–07 with a relatively modest budget of £15 million, the FIP is a home-based intensive family support service led by a key worker, usually lasting for a year and often accompanied by sanctions (such as loss of social housing) for non-compliance. Speaking at the 2009 Labour Party Conference, the Prime Minister Gordon Brown announced that 'starting now and right across the next Parliament every one of the 50,000 most chaotic families will be part of a family intervention project – with clear rules, and clear punishments if they don't stick to them' (Brown, 2009).

Looked-after children

The group of children whose lives are most dependent on the policy and practice of the state are also the most overlooked. Although a relatively small proportion of the child population, looked-after children, or children in care, attracted considerable policy interest in the New Labour years. They occupied a central place within the social exclusion agenda. Indeed, all three of the initial reports of the Social Exclusion Unit, established by the Blair government, identified looked-after children as a group who were especially vulnerable to social exclusion (the reports covered truancy/school exclusion, homelessness/rough sleeping, and teenage pregnancy). What made action on looked-after children a particularly pressing government priority, though, was the evidence that emerged throughout the 1990s of widespread physical and sexual abuse of children in local authority care. A series of inquiry reports by Utting (1991, 1997) and Waterhouse (2000) had provided a powerful and authoritative critique of the care system and in particular the failings of residential care.

Historically, the care system has suffered from 'the long shadow of the Poor Law, which made the provision that state welfare should be "less eligible", or, in other words, of a lower standard than life in the community' (Frost and Parton, 2009, p. 96). Although the 1989 Children Act attempted to remove the stigma of care by presenting it as part of the package of services offered to support families with children in need (replacing the term 'in care' with 'looked after' or 'accommodated'), nevertheless accommodation of children, especially in a residential placement, continued to be seen as 'the darkened door at the end of the line' (Department of Health, 1998). Both Utting and Waterhouse painted a picture of a service (residential care) that was, in the 1980s and early 1990s, demoralised and underfunded, with poorly trained staff and inadequate management.

Against this background, Labour's response was in many ways typical of its reform and modernisation agenda across the whole of the public sector. Its approach was increased managerialism, using performance indicators, inspection regimes, and enhanced audit systems on the one hand, and an expansion of private market provision on the other. The result was a plethora of initiatives such as Quality Protects, the Care Standards Act 2000, the establishment of a Performance Assessment Framework (PAF) in 1999, and *Care Matters: Time for Change* (DfES, 2007). The latter pledged to 'looked-after children' that they 'should expect from a good corporate parent, everything that a good parent would provide and more' (para. 1.20). In short, there is no doubting Labour's energy and commitment to improving life for looked-after children. However, it has been suggested that Labour substituted 'confidence in *management systems* for trust in individual social workers' *professional practice*' (Frost and Parton, 2009, p. 161).

Children's rights and the United Nations Convention on the Rights of the Child, 1989

A notable feature of policy in relation to children during this period is the extent to which children's rights continued to play only a very marginal role. Attitudes on the part of the government at Westminster (this is an area of policy where devolution has led to significant differences within the UK, as we will see later) to the United Nations Convention on the Rights of the Child (UNCRC), 1989, in particular, have been at best lukewarm. When the Major government ratified the Convention in 1991, it committed the UK to 'undertake all appropriate legislative, administrative and other measures for the implementation of the rights recognised in the present Convention' (Article 4, UNCRC). In practice, no change was felt necessary. Moreover, the Conservative government showed little inclination to enter into the spirit – or for that matter the letter – of the Convention by failing to promote awareness and debate on the issue of children's rights, or to engage meaningfully with the process established to monitor its implementation. The UK government's first Report to the Committee on the Rights of the Child has been described as 'complacent' and 'superficial' (Fortin, 2009, p. 48).

In comparison to what had gone before, the Second Report to the UNCRC (and the first to be produced under New Labour) was more self-critical and based on input from a broader range of voluntary organisations representing children – although it still did not involve children themselves. However, by the time of the combined Third/Fourth Reports (amalgamated because of slippage in the United Nations Committee's timetable), there was a degree of structural change in the governance of childhood, including the appointment of a Minister for Children (2007) and Commissioners for Children in Wales (2001), Northern Ireland (2003), Scotland (2004), and England (2005). For the first time, the Third/Fourth Reports included a separate submission by children and young people, coordinated by the Children's Rights Alliance for England (CRAE, 2008). Despite these important structural changes, there is a good deal of evidence that the Labour government was not comfortable with the discourse of children's rights and, indeed, actively resisted a number of attempts to incorporate a rights framework into its social policy relating to children. For example, the wording of the terms of reference for the English Commissioner, a hotly contested issue at the time, studiously avoids any mention of 'rights'. More strikingly, the *Every Child Matters* Green Paper makes no reference to the UNCRC whatsoever. Attitudes within the devolved authorities have been rather more positive, especially in Wales, which in 2011 passed the Rights of Children and Young Persons Measure. This requires (from May 2012) all ministers in the Welsh Assembly to have due regard to the UNCRC in all legislation.

The argument that Labour's policy on children, and in particular the *Every Child Matters* programme, simply maps on to the UNCRC, with almost identical aims and outcomes, has been challenged by David Archard (2009). As he points out, a rights perspective embodies a very different view of children and childhood, and one that challenges the 'children as future adults' perspective that was so dominant in Labour's approach to policy. Perhaps the issue that most clearly demonstrates the failure of the government to embrace children's rights and a commitment to the UNCRC was its stance on smacking. Forced to confront this issue by a legal challenge at the European Court of Human Rights (*A v United Kingdom*, 1998), the government came under pressure to abolish the defence of 'reasonable chastisement', which allowed parents to use corporal punishment with impunity. The United Nations Committee on the

STOP AND THINK

'There is no good reason why children are the only people in the UK who can still be lawfully hit . . . By not changing the legislation, we continue to send out confusing messages to parents about the acceptable use of violence across society.' (Children's Commissioner for England, Al Aynsley-Green, *The Guardian*, 25 October 2007)

'It is up to parents to determine the way they want to help their children navigate boundaries and how they define right and wrong, it is not for the state to define that for them,' he said. 'The state is not there on the 15th floor of a tower block, where there may be drug dealers and violence and families may be struggling.' (David Lammy, MP for Tottenham, *The Guardian*, 29 January 2012)

Do you think that disciplining of children should be a private matter of parental judgement or is the state justified in legislating to prevent the smacking of children?

Rights of the Child (in all three of its responses to the UK's Reports) and a strong coalition of children's organisations all urged a straightforward ban on smacking, but in the event the 2004 Children Act fell well short of this.

The Labour years: conclusion

There is some disagreement among commentators as to whether the 13 years of Labour government radically changed the relationship between the state and the family. Certainly it is possible to stress the continuities rather than the change as Daly has done: 'While New Labour legitimised a more explicit and broader role for the state in regard to the family, the UK continues as a market oriented, family policy model' (Daly, 2010, p. 442). As Daly points out, in relation to early years childcare, for example, there is still an assumption that this is an individual family responsibility within a largely private market context. Indeed, there are a number of areas where the responsibility of parents has expanded. This is particularly the case in relation to schools, where parental involvement in children's education, through a range of practices such as home–school contracts and homework diaries, has become the norm. This leads Daly to conclude that there has been no paradigm change in UK family policy

On the other hand, Labour's highly interventionist agenda in relation to families, and children in particular, has been described as a 'Revolution in Family Policy' (Henricson, 2012), and a 'remarkably aggressive attempt to re-position family life as a public rather than a private concern' (Gillies, 2011, p. 4), while Churchill is confident that the New Labour years 'will have an enduring legacy' (Churchill, 2011, p. 3).

The Coalition government and family policy

Compared with the wide-ranging and high-profile nature of family policy under the Blair/Brown governments, the Conservative and Liberal Democrat coalition that resulted from the 2010 general election has approached this area of policy in a more low-key fashion. It is true that in the lead up to the election there was a fair degree of congruence in the three main parties' manifestos on key areas such as tackling child poverty, investment in early years provision, and support for family-friendly working arrangements. It is not surprising, then, that Churchill concluded, as we have just seen, that Labour's agenda would continue more or less unchanged.

In reality, however, there have been important shifts in emphasis. Perhaps the most significant of these is a retreat from universal support for children and families and the increased level of state intervention, which was outlined earlier in this chapter. This has been replaced by a targeted approach, focusing on more disadvantaged families, together with a greater emphasis on personal, family, and community responsibility. Of course, the fact that the Coalition government has made the reduction of the budget deficit its overriding imperative ensured that spending on children and families would be in the firing line. The Coalition government has, for example, calculated that the cost of tax credits alone stood at £150 billion between 2004 and 2011 (HM Government, 2011). The Children's Plan of 2007, which consists of over 60 programmes aimed at improving children's lives, was estimated to cost £5 billion per year (Burkard and Clelford, 2010).

There is little doubt, though, that ideological reasons also underpinned the Conservative wing of the Coalition's support for scaling back state intervention in family life. Indeed, one of the major themes that framed Conservative thinking during the run up to the 2010 general election was the 'Big Society'. This was an idea that David Cameron first aired at a public lecture in November 2009, in which he outlined his ambition to take power and responsibility from the state and give it to individuals, neighbourhoods, and voluntary organisations. It is true that the idea of the 'Big Society' was given much less prominence once in government and did not translate easily into actual policy – the introduction of a National Citizen Service for 16- to 19-year-olds being one of its very few tangible results. Nevertheless, with its stress on individual, family, and community, rather than state, responsibility, it did put down a clear marker of more traditional Conservative values.

A second significant theme informing the Conservative family policy agenda before May 2010 was that of 'Broken Britain'. A series of reports by the influential Centre for Social Justice, a policy think tank headed by Iain Duncan Smith, ex-leader of the party and Minister for Work and Pensions within the Coalition government, developed the idea that Britain was experiencing serious social breakdown. Somewhat in the face of evidence that, at least as far as children were concerned, a wide range of indicators suggested that wellbeing had been moving steadily in the right direction since 1997 (Bradshaw, 2011, p. 265), the Centre for Social Justice painted a near apocalyptic picture of family life. By choosing to focus so selectively on families with multiple problems (variously estimated at between 120,000 and 140,000 in number), the Conservative Party signalled that its policy concern in relation to families was to be much more limited in scope than Labour's had been. Not only this, but in its *Green Paper on the Family*, the Centre for Social Justice had claimed, as we have seen at the beginning of this chapter, that the problem of family breakdown was, in part, a consequence of the fact that Labour's approach to the family, in its focus on the child, had 'become indifferent to the institution of marriage' (Centre for Social Justice, 2010, p. 5). On this basis, the Conservative Party had made financial support for marriage one of its central family policy objectives during the 2010 election campaign. Despite widespread scepticism about this among policy commentators (Toynbee, 2010), and more importantly within the Liberal Democrat ranks, it was included in the Coalition Agreement that the new government forged in the aftermath of the election. Moreover, the shift in focus towards 'dysfunctional' or 'problem' families, given a further boost by the riots of August 2011, led David Cameron to declare that 'we have got to get out there and make a positive difference to the way families work, the way people bring up their children and we've got to be less sensitive to the charge that this is about interfering or nannying' (David Cameron speech in Witney, 15 August 2011). The government therefore announced an increase in targeted policy aimed at the most troublesome families, specifically, through Family Intervention Projects.

This shift away from a wide-ranging and universal approach to family and child support was marked very clearly the day after the 2010 election when the Department for Children, Schools and Families was re-branded as the Department for Education. Ofsted's new inspection framework removed those aspects that dealt with schools' responsibility for children's social and emotional wellbeing in favour of a much narrower focus on pupil achievement and teaching quality. The *Every Child Matters* agenda, although never subject to a formal announcement by the Coalition government, was quietly dropped and its website removed and archived. This same shift away from universalism can be seen in relation to another of Labour's flagship services, Sure Start. The Coalition Agreement announced that 'we will take Sure Start back to its original purpose of early intervention and increase its focus on the neediest families' (Cabinet Officet, 2010, p. 19). Further doubts about the continuing viability of Sure Start were raised when it emerged that the Coalition government's policy of extending free nursery education to 2-year-olds was to be funded, in part, by raiding the budget allocated by local authorities for Sure Start Centres (*The Guardian*, 27 September 2012).

Conclusion

The New Labour years (1997–2010) can justifiably be seen as marking a significant shift in terms of family policy. From being a relatively neglected, if not alien, function of government, support for children and families became one of the most substantial policy programmes. As Henricson (2012, p. 11) has argued, 'Family Policy exemplified the major tenets of New Labour philosophy and the aspiration was enormous, addressing the whole social fabric', and nothing exemplified this more clearly than the target of eliminating child poverty by 2020.

Whether Labour's conceptual shift will result in a lasting legacy in terms of the role of the state in supporting families is more difficult to assess. Despite the apparent political consensus which produced the Child Poverty Act 2010, as well as a good deal of 'continuity in policy themes, priorities and programmes' (Churchill, 2011, p. 3) within the 2010 manifestos of the three main parties, the Coalition government showed early signs of rowing back from Labour's universalist and interventionist approach to family support, illustrated in the shelving of the *Every Child Matters* agenda and the changes made to Sure Start, and instead moving towards greater selectivity of 'dsyfunctional families'.

Summary

This chapter has explored the increasing importance given to family policy under New Labour from 1997 to 2010, including its centrality to Labour's economic and social priorities. It has also considered the changing emphasis under the Conservative-Liberal Democrat Coalition government since 2010. It has suggested that:

- The extent of demographic change and increasing family diversity challenged a model of family policy built around a model of heterosexual marriage, leading to Labour's more pragmatic support for children rather than for the 'traditional family'.
- Labour made significant changes in a range of areas, including child poverty, early years provision, and looked-after children.
- However, there remained a variety of tensions within Labour's approach, including in relation to increasing support for parents while at the same time placing greater responsibility on parents (including the Family Intervention Project).
- Since 2010, the influence of Iain Duncan Smith and the Centre for Social Justice has ensured that marriage has become more pivotal in Coalition family policy, and the theme of 'Broken Britain', with its emphasis on dysfunctional families, has led to an increased focus on identifying and intervening in a small number of 'problem families' rather than the universal approach to family support pioneered by Labour.

Discussion and review

- To what extent can it be argued that there has been a 'revolution' in UK family policy since 1997?
- Should support for the family mean support for marriage?
- 'The UK may have ratified the United Nations on the Rights of the Child, 1989, but the only way to ensure that it truly observes its obligations under the Convention is to incorporate it within UK law'. How helpful would such an approach be?

- Can Labour's strategy to eliminate child poverty by 2020 be said to have been a success or failure?
- What are the key lessons that can be learned from Labour's approach to child poverty?

References

Archard, D. (2009) 'Every child's rights matter', in K. Broadhurst, C. Grover and J. Jamieson (eds.) *Critical Perspectives on Safeguarding Children*, Wiley-Blackwell, Chichester.

Ashton, Baroness (2002) *Inter-Departmental Childcare Review*, Cabinet Office, London.

Ball, S.J. and Vincent, C. (2005) 'The "childcare champion"? New Labour, social justice and the childcare market', *British Educational Research Journal*, Vol. 31, No. 5, pp. 557–70.

Ball, W. (2013) *Transforming Childcare and Listening to Families: Policy in Wales and Beyond*, University of Wales Press, Cardiff.

Beveridge, W. (1942) *Social Security and Allied Services* (The Beveridge Report), HMSO, London.

Blair, T. (1999) Lecture at Toynbee Hall, 18 March, reprinted as 'Beveridge revisited: a welfare state for the 21st century', in R. Walker (ed.) *Ending Child Poverty: Popular Welfare in the 21 Century*, Policy Press, Bristol.

Bradshaw, J. (1990) *Child Poverty and Deprivation in the UK*, National Children's Bureau, London.

Bradshaw, J. (2011) *The Well Being of Children in the UK*, Policy Press, Bristol.

Brannen, J., Heptinstall, E. and Bhopal, K. (2000) *Connecting Children: Care and Family Life in Later Childhood*, Routledge, London.

Brewer, M., Browne, J., Joyce, R. and Sibieta, L. (2010) *Child Poverty in the UK since 1998–99: Lessons from the Past Decade*, Institute for Fiscal Studies, London.

Brewer, M., Browne, J. and Joyce, R. (2011) *Child and Working-Age Poverty from 2010 to 2020*, Institute for Fiscal Studies, London.

Brown, G. (2009) Speech to Labour Party Conference, available at http://www.labour.org.uk/gordon-brown-speech-conference.

Burkard, T. and Clelford, T. (2010) *Cutting the Children's Plan*, Centre for Policy Studies, London.

Cabinet Office (2010) *The Coalition: Our Programme for Government*, Cabinet Office, London.

Cameron, D. (2011) Speech in Witney, reported in *New Statesman*, 15 August.

Centre for Social Justice (2010) *Green Paper on the Family*, Centre for Social Justice, London.

Children's Rights Alliance for England (CRAE) (2008) *Submission to the United Nations Committee on the Rights of the Child*, CRAE, London, available at http://www.crae.org.uk/under-18s/childrens-human-rights-and-the-uncrc.html.

Churchill, H. (2011) *Parental Rights and Responsibilities: Analysing Social Policy and Lived Experiences*, Policy Press, Bristol.

Commission on Social Justice (1994) *Social Justice: Strategies for National Renewal*, Vintage, London.

Daly, M. (2004) 'Changing conceptions of family and gender relations in European welfare states and the Third Way', in J. Lewis and R. Surrender (eds.) *Welfare State Change: Towards a Third Way?*, Oxford University Press, Oxford.

Daly, M. (2010) 'Shifts in family policy in the UK under New Labour', *Journal of European Social Policy*, Vol. 20, No. 5, pp. 433–43.

Daniel, P. and Ivatts, J. (1998) *Children and Social Policy*, Macmillan, Basingstoke.

Department for Education and Skills (DfES) (2004) *Every Child Matters: Change for Children*, The Stationery Office, London.

Department for Education and Skills (DfES) (2007) *Care Matters: Time for Change*, TSO, London.

Department for Work and Pensions (DWP) (2012) *Households Below Average Income*, available at http://research.dwp.gov.uk/asd/index.php?page=hbai_arc [accessed 18 March 2013].

Department for Work and Pensions/Department for Education (DWP/DfE) (2011) *A New Approach to Child Poverty: Tackling the Causes of Disadvantage and Transforming Families' Lives*, The Stationery Office, London.

Department of Health (1998) *Caring for Children Away from Home*, HMSO, London.

Dickens, R. (2011) 'Child poverty in Britain: past lessons and future prospects', *National Institute Economic Review*, Vol. 218, No. 1, pp. R7–19.

Fawcett, B., Featherstone, B. and Goddard, J. (2004) *Contemporary Child Care Policy and Practice*, Palgrave Macmillan, Basingstoke.

Fortin, J. (2009) *Children's Rights and the Developing Law*, Cambridge University Press, Cambridge.

Frost, N. and Parton, N. (2009) *Understanding Children's Social Care: Politics, Policy and Practice*, Sage, London.

Gauthier, A.H. (1996) *The State and the Family: A Comparative Analysis of Family Policy in Industrialised Countries*, Clarendon Press, Oxford.

Gillies, V. (2011) 'From function to competence: engaging with the new politics of the family', *Sociological Research Online*, available at www.socresonline.org.uk/16/4/11.

Giner, C. (2007) 'The politics of childhood and asylum in the UK', *Children and Society*, Vol. 21, No. 4, pp. 249–60.

Glass, N. (2005) 'Surely some mistake', *The Guardian*, 5 January.

Hantrais, L. (2004) *Family Policy Matters: Responding to Family Change in Europe*, Policy Press, Bristol.

Haux, T. (2012) *Parenting Support Policies in England from 1997 to the Present: An Overview*, available at www.parentingresearch.eu.

Hendrick, H. (2003) *Child Welfare: Historical Dimensions, Contemporary Debate*, Policy Press, Bristol.

Henricson, C. (2012) *A Revolution in Family Policy: Where Should We Go from Here?*, Policy Press, Bristol.

Henricson, C., Katz, I., Mesie, J., Sandison, M. and Tunstill, J. (2001) *National Mapping of Family Services in England and Wales*, National Family and Parenting Institute, London.

Hill, D. (2008) *21 Years of Children and Young People's Policy in Wales*, Action for Children, Cardiff, available at http://www.actionforchildren.org.uk/media/63612/wales.pdf [accessed 15 May 2012].

Hirsch, D. (2008) *What is Needed to End Child Poverty in 2020*, Joseph Rowntree Foundation, York.

HM Government (2007) *Building on Progress: Families*, Cabinet Office, London.

HM Government (2011) *A New Approach to Child Poverty: Tackling the Causes of Disadvantage and Transforming Families' Lives*, Cm. 8061, The Stationery Office, London.

HM Treasury (2005) *Support for Parents: The Best Start for Children*, The Stationery Office, London.

Home Office (1998) *Supporting Families: A Consultation Document*, The Stationery Office, London.

Kamerman, S. and Kahn, A. (eds.) (1978) *Government and Families in Fourteen Countries*, Columbia University Press, New York.

Kirby, J. (2006) *The Nationalisation of Childhood*, Centre for Policy Studies, London.

La Valle, I. and Smith, R. (2009) 'Good quality childcare for all? Progress towards universal provision', *National Institute Economic Review*, Vol. 207, No. 1, pp. 75–82.

Levitas, R. (2005) *The Inclusive Society? Social Exclusion and New Labour*, Palgrave Macmillan, Basingstoke.

Lewis, J. (2001) *The End of Marriage? Individualism and Intimate Relations*, Edward Elgar, Cheltenham.

Lister, R. (2003) 'Investing in the citizen-workers of the future: transformations in citizenship and the state under New Labour', *Social Policy and Administration*, Vol. 37, No. 5, pp. 427–43.

Lloyd, N., O'Brien, M. and Lewis, C. (2003) *Fathers in Sure Start*, National Evaluation of Sure Start (NESS), Birkbeck College, London.

Mayall, B. (2002) *Towards a Sociology for Childhood*, Open University Press, Buckingham.

Morrow, V. (2009) 'Children, young people and their families in the UK', in H. Montgomery and M. Kellett (eds.) *Children and Young People's Worlds*, Policy Press, Bristol.

Moss, P. (2004) 'Setting the scene: a vision of universal children's spaces', in Daycare Trust, *A New Era for Universal Childcare?*, Daycare Trust, London.

Office of the Deputy Prime Minister (2004) *The Drivers of Social Exclusion: A Review of the Literature*, Office of the Deputy Prime Minister, London.

Panico, L., Bartley, M., Kelly, Y., McMunn, A. and Sacker, A. (2010) 'Changes in family structure in early childhood in the Millennium Cohort Study', *Population Trends*, No. 142, pp. 75–89, Office for National Statistics, London.

Pickett, K. and Wilkinson, R. (2011) 'Family breakdown and the riots', *New Statesman*, 22 August.

Rathbone, E. (1940) *The Case for Family Allowances*, Allen & Unwin, London.

Ridge, T. (2002) *Childhood, Poverty and Social Exclusion: From a Child's Perspective*, Policy Press, Bristol.

Schweinhart, L.J., Barnes, H.V. and Weikart, D.P. (1993) *Significant Benefits: The High/Scope Perry Preschool Study through Age 27*, High/Scope Press, Ypsilanti, MI.

Scottish Executive (2006) *Getting it Right for Every Child*, Scottish Executive, Edinburgh.

Social Exclusion Unit/DSS (1999) *Opportunity for All: Tackling Poverty and Social Exclusion*, The Stationery Office, London.

Tisdall, K. and Hill, M. (2011) 'Policy change under devolution: the prism of children's policy', *Social Policy and Society*, Vol. 10, No. 1, pp. 29–40.

Toynbee, P. (2010) 'Family life is a viper's nest politicians should not poke', *The Guardian*, 18 January.

United Nations (1989) *Convention on the Rights of the Child*, United Nations, New York.

Utting, W. (1991) *Children in the Public Care*, The Stationery Office, London.

Utting, W. (1997) *People Like Us: The Report of the Review of the Safeguards for Children Living Away from Home*, The Stationery Office, London.

Waterhouse, R. (2000) *Lost in Care: Summary of the Report*, The Stationery Office, London.

Williams, F. (2004) 'What matters is who works: why every child matters to New Labour', *Critical Social Policy*, Vol. 24, No. 3, pp. 406–27.

Further reading

Bradshaw, J. (2011) *The Well Being of Children in the UK*, Policy Press, Bristol. This volume provides a useful collection of information about the position of children in the United Kingdom.

Churchill, H. (2011) *Parental Rights and Responsibilities: Analysing Social Policy and Lived Experiences*, Policy Press, Bristol. This book considers the rights and responsibilities of parents across a range of policy areas.

Frost, N. and Parton, N. (2009) *Understanding Children's Social Care: Politics, Policy and Practice*, Sage, London. With its overview of children's social care in England following the introduction of *Every Child Matters*, this book provides a critical analysis of child care policy.

Hantrais, L. (2004) *Family Policy Matters: Responding to Family Change in Europe*, Policy Press, Bristol. This book provides a consideration of the relationship between family and public policy in the European Union.

Henricson, C. (2012) *A Revolution in Family Policy: Where Should We Go from Here?*, Policy Press, Bristol. Following the New Labour years, this book examines the shifts in relationships between families and the state and argues for family policy to be developed in its own right, separately from other government agendas.

Useful websites

http://www.centreforsocialjustice.org.uk – the Centre for Social Justice was established by the former Conservative Party leader Iain Duncan Smith. It has produced a variety of reports dealing with families and social breakdown.

http://www.crae.org.uk – the Children's Rights Alliance for England is an alliance of voluntary and statutory organisations that are committed to the full implementation of the United Nations Convention on the Rights of the Child.

http://www.familyandparenting.org – the Family and Parenting Institute is a charity that undertakes research and policy analysis on the wellbeing of children and families.

http://www.jrf.org.uk – the Joseph Rowntree Foundation makes the results of the research that it funds available through its web pages.

http://www.statistics.gov.uk – the Office of National Statistics website is a gateway to a wide range of official statistics and publications.

CHAPTER 14

Debating the Ups and Downs of Youth Justice

Peter Squires

Learning objectives

- To examine the scope and construction of 'criminalisation'
- To explore the 'punitive turn' in criminal justice
- To consider recent changes in youth justice

Chapter overview

In years to come, 2013 may come to represent a critical turning point in criminal justice – a time when the hitherto dominant and expansionist pressures of 'criminalisation' and 'punitiveness' began to wane, and new balances began to be struck between public and social policy in its fullest sense and criminal justice policy in particular (Bateman, 2012). I say 2013 *may* come to represent this turning point because, in both a very real and a rather metaphorical sense, it is fair to say that 'the jury' is still out on this one. Even so there are signs, and we should take them seriously and try to work out what they mean. In that sense, the aims of this chapter are threefold:

- it poses questions about what might be called the 'proper scope' of criminalisation, or, how far the state should rely upon the power to criminalise and to punish? How much criminalisation is consistent with the demands of social justice?;
- it explores how and why this 'explosion' of criminalisation occurred in the first place;
- it considers the extent to which this apparent 'excess of criminalisation' might now be starting to recede, while outlining some of the consequences of its passing.

Introduction

It is important to note, at the outset, how youth crime and criminal justice form an important 'rendezvous point' in the relationships between the fields of criminal justice and of social policy. This is so in a number of senses. First, youth crime, rather more than offending by adults, has historically been understood in terms of its social and familial 'causes' (Utting *et al.*, 1993). Poor parenting, the influence of criminal peers, school failure, and social exclusion were (together with immaturity) uppermost among the explanations of juvenile delinquency. That is, until relatively recently there was widespread agreement that the most effective means for preventing youthful delinquency fell squarely within the field of social policy (Goldson, 2010). Second, in the case of those young people who found themselves 'in trouble with the law', there was for many years substantial agreement, underpinned by 'labelling theory', that either diversion from criminal justice, or the minimum engagement with it, were likely to be the most effective in encouraging desistance from offending. Third, if, in a presumed minority of cases, the prosecution and punishment of children and young people were to be considered, then it was acknowledged that principles of 'welfare' – the best interests of the child – should be uppermost. These three principles ensured that crime and delinquency remained close to – indeed, part of – social policy.

However, over the last 20–30 years, these connections began to break down. A greater inclination to prosecute the young became apparent; to some commentators, the 'best interests of the child' began to sound like an excuse for bad behaviour, or even 'impunity' (Home Office, 1997). The wider social policies that had once played their part in preventing youth offending were restructured, and now offered only increasingly residual services for the very poorest, for whom they began to more and more resemble disciplinary and behavioural management policies. In turn, criminal justice, and especially anti-social behaviour management policies, became the way by which large numbers of young people gained access to these 'welfare' services. And as more young people acquired criminal records, more of them embarked upon adult criminal careers; the fracturing of connections between youth justice and social policy *produced* criminalisation and the prisons began to fill. An examination of the youth justice system over the past two decades provides a vital key for understanding the potential relationships between social policy and criminal justice as a whole. Correctly aligned, crime prevention and social welfare can be the outcomes; wrongly aligned, then growing inequality and criminalisation might result. However, even as this chapter documents the flow and subsequent ebb of a contemporary propensity to punish, it is worth entering one small caution: while criminalisation may represent one particular form of state-inflicted harm, it is not necessarily the only form that such social and policy harms might take. Even as criminalisation and punitiveness themselves might be 'rolled back', what replaces them may still fall short of the demands of social justice.

The politics of youth criminalisation: What goes up . . .?

The year 1993 was a critical turning point in juvenile justice. In February that year, a 2-year-old toddler named James Bulger was abducted from a shopping centre near Liverpool and, over the course of the next few hours, he was subjected to a relentless and brutal assault by two boys, themselves aged only 10 and 11. Finally, they killed him, leaving his body upon a railway track in the hope that passing trains would obscure evidence of the injuries that they had inflicted. The case itself was truly awful, the reactions to it equally so (the two boys were charged in adult court, reporting restrictions were waived, a vigilante mob mentality surrounded the trial, whipped up by tabloid coverage with people physically attacking the prison transports conveying the two young offenders in and out of court). All in all these were dark days for British justice, but, over the course of time, the incident became especially significant for the change of culture and attitude it signalled with respect to juvenile offending and youth crime. John Major, Prime Minister at the time, speaking in reference to the case, commented that such incidents suggested that 'we should understand a little less; and condemn a little more' (Hayden and Scraton, 2000), his words contributing to a marked toughening in attitudes to youth crime. In effect, they launched what some commentators have referred to as a British 'punitive turn' (Muncie, 2008), prompting politicians to assert a new-found faith in prison's effectiveness while scaling up the 'war on crime' that has brought in its wake a marked demonisation of youth and accelerating processes of criminalisation. These issues have become the subject of debate concerning the 'punitive turn' in youth justice (Matthews, 2005; Pitts, 2011) and regarding the more general demonisation and criminalisation of young people, just as they resonate with Cohen's (1972) original work on 'moral panics' and Pearson's (1983) 'history of respectable fears'.

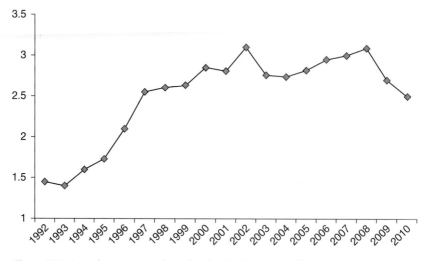

Figure 14.1 Annual average number of under-18s in secure facilities in England and Wales, 1992–2010 (thousands)

Source: Prison Statistics 2000, Youth Justice Statistics 2010–11

For the moment, however, the criminalising and punitive is clearly illustrated in Figure 14.1, beginning in 1992 and depicting the increasing use of custodial disposals for young offenders. Yet, potentially just as significant, is the marked downward turn in youth custody numbers from 2008 onwards.

Underpinning the more recent reductions in the use of custody for young offenders, the total number of 'immediate custody' sentences handed out by the courts for young offenders fell by 10 per cent between 2009–10 and 2010–11. This is in line with an 11 per cent reduction (to 176,511) in 'proven offences' by juveniles between 2009–10 and 2010–11.

In their annual publication of Youth Justice Statistics, the Ministry of Justice (MoJ) and Youth Justice Board (YJB) put a very positive gloss on this emerging new picture of declining youth criminalisation: 'Since 2007–08 there are 55% fewer young people coming into the system, 30% fewer young people in custody and 29% fewer re-offences by young people . . . the rate of re-offending has been fairly stable over the last decade [but] the frequency of re-offending has reduced by 17% since 2000' (YJB/MoJ, 2012, p. 4). Completing this picture of falling youth crime and declining rates of youth criminalisation, The Howard League for Penal Reform reported, in 2012, on research revealing that the number of arrests of young people aged 17 and under had fallen by a third, from 315,000 in 2008 to 206,000 in 2012. The League noted, however, that this still amounted to a child or young person being arrested 'every two and a half minutes' and, specifically, six children of primary school age being arrested by the police every day (Howard League, Press Release, 7 December 2012). Announcing these figures, Frances Crook, Chief Executive of the Howard League, pointed to a cultural and institutional change, similar to that which had prompted the upsurge in youth criminalisation and custody in the early 1990s: 'Under the last government, police success was measured by the number of arrests and children proved a seductive way to make up the numbers. The fact that the number of child arrests has fallen by a third since 2008 is a testament to a change of culture, more focused on public safety than targets' (Howard League, Press Release, 7 December 2012).

A punitive transformation?

But how do we explain the tendency to arrest and incarcerate more young people in the first place? David Garland focused his answer upon the political culture that necessitated, justified, and sustained an expansion of criminalisation throughout the final decades of the twentieth century. His book, *The Culture of Control,* was published in 2001. In it he described what he referred to as a new 'crime complex'.

STOP AND THINK

How should we explain the rise and fall in the numbers of young offenders arrested and sentenced to youth custody? How might changes in arrest and sentencing rates be influenced by wider social, political, and economic changes?

How much crime is committed by young people (i.e. those under 18)? Is the youth crime rate rising or falling? Why is there such a widespread perception that 'young people today' are more troublesome (more criminal?) than in previous generations?

The crime complex consisted of both a new and popular state of mind, comprising the fears and insecurities, intolerances and expectations of 'justice' that formed the late modern consciousness regarding the problems of crime and disorder. Think, perhaps, of the growing demonisation of young people after the James Bulger murder and the 'construction' of a new type of 'persistent young offender' (Hagell and Newburn, 1994), and of the significant elevation of fears and uncertainties following 9/11.

The crime complex also consisted of a new series of criminal justice institutions, new laws and policies, and new relationships between them – the patterns of enforcement, methods of control, systems of security and discipline. We might consider, among the latter, the increasing numbers of private security personnel on our streets from the early 1980s onwards (Button, 2002; Jones and Newburn, 2002); and from the early 1990s onwards, the extensive networks of public CCTV and ANPR surveillance and offender tagging (Whitfield, 1997; Goold, 2004), sexual and violent offender registers (Thomas, 2008); by the late 1990s, the Youth Justice Board, Crime and Disorder Reduction partnerships, local Youth Offending Teams [collectively described by Goldson as the 'new' youth justice (Goldson, 2000)], and later, the National Offender Management Service. Arguably, however, trumping all of these developments for both its reach and significance and its impact upon popular attitudes and expectations was the 'invention' of anti-social behaviour (Burney, 2005; Squires and Stephen, 2005).

In describing and defining this new crime complex, there is little doubt that Garland was attempting to define a shift in the politics of law and order that was no less significant, in its own ways, than the transformations described by writers such as Foucault (1977) and Weiner (1990), which ushered in a new legal order, comprising a formal uniformed policing, a national prison system, a sentencing system and the staple 'prison sentence', in the first few decades of the nineteenth century. Garland's own aim, to describe the contours of a new, late-twentieth-century crime complex, is no less ambitious or significant. In the first chapter of his book, he provides a compelling synopsis of the most significant social, political, and economic changes impacting upon the criminal justice arena and ushering forth the new era. Most significantly of all, he describes two underlying social forces as being in the driving seat of social change. The first involved the series of social changes and the 'distinctive forms of social organisation of late modernity' involving globalisation, the media and culture, rising mobility, and increasing inequality. The second involved the rising influence, from the late 1970s, of neo-liberal economic – 'free market' but socially conservative – politics, and the marketisation and commodification they entailed; the increasing 'privatisation' of social provision (the rolling back of the welfare state) and the establishment of a culture of exclusive and competitive self-reliance in place of a public service model of social inclusion (Young, 1999).

In the wake of these broad social changes, gathering pace since the late 1970s and early 1980s, we see, according to Garland, a series of consequential shifts in the politics and discourses of 'Law and Order'. One of the first shifts he detects is a declining commitment to – or faith in – offender rehabilitation. The post-war optimism for social reform (of ex-offenders) begins to fade just as the empirical conditions in which rehabilitation is meant to be accomplished (an affluent society of opportunities, housing, and full employment) also begins to turn for the worse. However, the failure of individual offenders to reform is understood as their *own* failing, a sign of misplaced tolerance and an over-indulgent welfare system. The gentle way in rehabilitation is seen not just as failing, but as part of the problem, and those who will not, apparently, help themselves, need a different kind of message. The door is thereby opened for the return of a more punitive politics. Garland detects what he terms changes in the 'emotional tone' of criminal justice policies, as if one of Cohen's 'moral panics' (Cohen, 1972) were starting up; or a 'deviancy amplification spiral' (Young, 1971) were being shifted into a higher gear.

For Garland, part of the changing emotional tone of criminal justice comprised the call for more 'expressive' criminal justice responses. These might encapsulate any number of recent 'tough justice' rhetorics from recurring calls to bring back corporal punishment ('the birch'), or capital punishment, to arming the police. While such appeals are generally more obvious in the tabloid headlines, they also make their way into political and policy-making arenas, for example, as calls to bring back the 'short, sharp, shock' for young offenders; to introduce 'truth in sentencing' (or, versions of 'three strikes and you're out' laws); or appeals to 'name and shame' offenders as is evidenced by the high-visibility orange vests that offenders undertaking 'community payback' schemes are now required to wear. An interesting variant of this expressive aspect of recent justice was the way in which some commentators referred to the application of anti-social behaviour orders

(ASBOs). ASBOs were intended to be relatively swift, and somewhat more informal, orders to allow authorities to quickly bring an end to behaviour causing, in the language of the legislation, 'harassment, alarm, and distress' to members of the community. These very features were a part of what many legal commentators found unacceptable about the ASBO, but they were also what led many people to refer to the process of 'slapping' an ASBO on trouble-makers. The expressive, sudden, and implied physicality of this process was precisely what appealed to many people.

Another shift that Garland identifies in the formation of the new 'crime complex' also entails its expressive elements; this concerns what Garland calls the return of the victim, the place and significance of victims within criminal justice procedures and, specifically, the opportunities provided to victims to prepare 'victim impact statements' for courts at the sentencing stage. This innovation allows victims of crime to express something of the effect of a given crime upon them, but also, effectively, bring the experiential dimension of harm, suffering, and trauma to the courtroom's legal process.

This experiential dimension of victimhood has subsequently been taken further into the policy-making arena. For example, Sara Payne, mother of a murdered 8-year-old girl has been active as a focal point in campaigns for new laws to manage sex offenders (the Sarah's Law campaign); Brooke Kinsella (sister of a stabbing victim) was commissioned by the Home Secretary to lead a review of projects to tackle knife crime (Kinsella, 2011); and the campaign group Mothers Against Guns (mothers of gun crime victims) were significant in the 'Connected Campaign', which the Home Office established to tackle gang-related violence after 2003. This victim-centred criminal justice policy is also, for Garland, part of a wider populist turn in criminal justice policy-making that included 'engaging communities in fighting crime' (Casey, 2008). Chapter two of Casey's report was entitled 'putting victims, witnesses and other law abiding citizens first', a proposal which carried further the hard Blairite distinction (Blair, 2004) between 'innocent victims' and 'guilty offenders', and giving effect to the 're-balancing' of criminal justice that the Prime Minister had proposed (Tonry, 2010). Many commentators similarly read the introduction of Police and Crime Commissioners, first elected in November 2012, as a further step towards the politicisation of local law and order issues (although the very low turnouts in the PCC elections told, perhaps, another story).

These initiatives also relate to what Garland referred to as the expansion of the 'crime control' and community safety infrastructure. An obvious aspect of this involved the extensive investment in public area CCTV surveillance over the decade starting in the mid 1990s. Goold (2004) has reported that, during this decade, some 75 per cent of the entire Home Office crime prevention budget was invested in the relatively untried potential of surveillance cameras to cut crime. Subsequent evaluations have tended to confirm that scepticism was probably an appropriate response (Gill and Spriggs, 2005; Squires, 2010). Just as dramatic was the wave of anti-social behaviour enforcement – especially that targeted at young people and involving new principles of enforcement; new agents of enforcement; new and often rather subjective, standards of disapproval of behaviour; and new mechanisms of enforcement which some commentators came to argue, culminated in the 'criminalisation of nuisance' (Squires, 2008). Furthermore, just as new surveillance technologies allowed the entry of commercial security companies into the domestic law and order market (Coleman, 2004a), so we have witnessed a number of further developments, including privatisations (of selected prison establishments, prisoner escort duties, police custody staffs, offender electronic monitoring) and the creation of new mixed economies, purchaser and provider contracting, in the community justice and National Offender Monitoring 'markets', which have so significantly re-shaped the probation field after the Offender Management Act of 2007.

Following Garland, Bell (2011, p. 189) has argued that these developments have ushered in an increasing 'commodification of crime control', which, slowly but surely, adopting new management styles and working practices, have come to reorient crime control priorities around private sector and market interests. Criminalisation may be costly, but for security, correctional, and custodial service agencies it is also profitable. What Garland calls the 'reinvention of the prison' is also deeply implicated in this process, this idea being best reflected in the resurgent faith that, according to a former Home Secretary, 'prison works' (Burnett and Maruna, 2004; Hough *et al.*, 2008). As Figure 14.1 shows, the 1990s were a decade in which custodial sentencing of the under-18s rapidly increased, just as it did for adult offenders. Even as crime began to fall from the later 1990s onwards, more custodial sentences were applied and average sentence lengths grew. Ultimately, the prison population grew by around a third during the 1990s.

Many of the transformations discussed by Garland and briefly sketched in the paragraphs above, informed as they were by newer, trans-Atlantic, populist, and neo-liberal strands of thinking, laid the foundations of a revived neo-conservative criminology, which had profound consequences for academic criminology in Britain. These issues are encapsulated in Garland's final two themes: first, the transformation of criminological thought and, second, the perpetual sense of 'crisis' that this occasioned. One sign of this crisis is undoubtedly a diminished criminological confidence, that however much policy-makers might assert their support for 'evidence-based' policy-making (Naughton, 2005; Goldson, 2010), something else was happening.

With crime as a – if not *the* – leading social problem, it became everybody's business, and populist debates saw politicians, the media, the public, criminal justice professionals such as the police (often, still, the 'primary definers' of the problem), and victims all shouting louder and more pointedly than criminologists. Emotion often trumps evidence; measured social democratic reformism is out-manoeuvred by tough talking, as politicians compete for the decisive 'party of law and order' label. One sign of this 'crisis' is undoubtedly the renewed, and not altogether successful, quest for a 'public criminology' (Loader and Sparks, 2010), which speaks to popular fears and concerns while also raising the level of debate. Of late, criminology has also become rather besieged by the more practical 'crime sciences' and the application of criminalistic technique (undoubtedly influenced by the popularisation of – both fictional and reality – 'forensic' TV), which, as Wacquant (2009) has argued, in its worst-case scenario, descends into a voyeuristic 'pornography' of law and order, where crime, punishment, and justice are ultimately commodified as entertainment. And for Garland, the end-point of this process and of the foregoing changes in the subject matter of criminology, crime, and justice, is that criminology and criminological understanding are not sacrosanct areas of knowledge, they do not control their own destiny; they are merely, as Foucault (1977) argued, fields of quasi-science where differing ideas and competing discourses battle for dominance. This led Garland to perhaps the most fundamental insight with which criminologists have to deal: 'Crime control strategies and criminological ideas' he says, 'are *not* adopted because they are known to solve problems' (Garland, 2001, p. 26).

> ## STOP AND THINK
>
> The obvious question that Garland's comment leaves us with is: If 'crime control strategies' are *not* adopted because of their effectiveness, then what reasons can we provide for *why* they *are* adopted?
>
> What kinds of factors, groups or ideas influence the ways in which 'delinquent youth' are defined and understood? Similarly, what kinds of influences are brought to bear on what we think needs to be done about youthful delinquents?

Youth justice U-turns

The increased criminalisation of youth and the punitive shift in sentencing practice was not confined to the routine decision-making of criminal justice agencies, it was also reflected in an abrupt U-turn in thinking about youth justice. Neither criminological research nor evidence were responsible for these sharp changes in policy direction, instead they have their roots in politics, institutions, assumptions, and practices. The scale of the changes and the changing political tone of the youth justice debate are reflected in four key government policy documents that fell either side of 1993 and the Bulger case. The documents consist of a Home Office Green Paper from 1988, *Punishment, Custody and the Community* (Home Office, 1988), and the 1991 Morgan Report (Home Office, 1991), which outlined an entirely new approach to community safety policy-making, both of which were then swept unceremoniously aside by a more hard-headed Audit Commission Report (1996), *Misspent Youth*, which sought to curb the growing expense of the youth justice system. Finally, there was Labour's White Paper, *No more Excuses* (Home Office, 1997), which went forward to implement some of the key ideas of the Audit Commission's efficiency drive while laying the foundations for the new youth justice and anti-social behaviour strategies contained in the 1998 Crime and Disorder Act.

The first document, a Conservative Green Paper, had argued, in terms that no labelling theorist could find objectionable, that:

> most young offenders grow out of crime as they become more mature and responsible. They need encouragement and help to become law-abiding. Even a short period in custody is quite likely to confirm them as criminals, particularly as they acquire new criminal skills from more sophisticated offenders. They find themselves labelled as offenders and behave accordingly.
>
> (Home Office, 1988, p. 6)

Three years later, the Morgan Report on Community Safety took up the same theme. Young offenders were generally responsible for minor offending, 'behaviour which is rowdy or anti-social rather than strictly criminal', while 'most young people grow out of delinquency as they move through adolescence' (Home Office, 1991, p. 24).

However, only five years later and, significantly, three years after the Bulger case, *Misspent Youth*, the Audit Commission report of 1996, rounded upon the liberal orthodoxy that had held sway before. Things were now apparently quite different, and young people seemed no longer to mature out of crime. Thus, 'young males are not growing out of offending as they used to' (Audit Commission, 1996, p. 12). A year later the new Home Secretary, drawing a line under the dangerous liberal complacency that had gone before, with the apparent endorsement of the criminological establishment, introduced his youth justice White Paper, *No More Excuses*, in the following no-nonsense terms:

> For too long we have assumed that young offenders will grow out of their offending if left to themselves . . . today's young offenders can easily become tomorrow's hardened criminals. As a society, we do ourselves no favours by failing to break the link between juvenile crime and disorder and the serial burglar of the future.
>
> (Home Office, 1997)

Persistent young offenders, or 'pre-pubescent super predators', were the new focus of concern; later it would become youth gangs and the 'weaponisation' of youth violence (Squires, 2011). Rolling out this new strategy against a range of troublesome youth behaviours – from anti-social behaviour to youth crime – now seen as a continuum, involved intervening earlier, scrutinising youthful misdemeanours more closely than ever, looking for the seeds of future delinquency in once innocuous youthful street socialising behaviours (Corrigan, 1979; Measor and Squires, 2000), anticipating future signs of crime tomorrow in nuisance behaviour today, and what became known as 'nipping crime in the bud'.

As Figure 14.1 reveals, a direct consequence of these changed perceptions about youth crime and young offenders was an 85 per cent increase in the total number of children and young people (aged 10–17) sentenced to secure accommodation or youth custody. Garside and Solomon (2008) noted that, between 2001 and 2008, youth custody numbers seldom fell below 2,800, with the Youth Justice Board continually failing to meet its own custody reduction targets; concern was expressed that, overall, performance here was deteriorating. The growth in the numbers of under-15s held in secure facilities had been a particular area of concern, rising by an incredible 800 per cent in the five years after 1998 (Bateman, 2003).

Yet, even as populist understandings of youth crime and disorder appeared to justify the ramping up of enforcement practice and custodial sentencing, the predominant *criminological* messages about youth crime remained fairly constant. First, youthful delinquency was seen as a relatively normal feature of teenage development; second, youth crime trends were themselves fairly stable (and by no means an explanation for the youthful 'punitive turn'); third, forms of minimum intervention or youth diversion projects were generally more effective – as well as being cheaper; fourth, universal forms of youth provision, holistic services, and 'de-criminalising' interventions tended to do the least harm to young people's future prospects; while fifth, youth custody, as a punishment, tended to be the most expensive, least effective, and most damaging way of dealing with young offenders (Pitts, 2003; Squires and Stephen, 2005; Goldson, 2010). Furthermore, as Muncie (2008) has argued, even though the international norms of youth justice (such as the Beijing Rules) have tended to reflect these existing understandings of youth offending, policy and practice began to take a more punitive turn. The age of criminal responsibility was lowered to ten (although 'acceptable behaviour contracts' could be applied in the cases of children as young as eight), important elements of 'due process' were side-stepped in anti-social behaviour enforcement proceedings that were governed by the civil (rather than criminal) burden of proof – the 'balance of probabilities' – and dispersal orders conferred more powers upon the police (Crawford and Lister, 2007).

In one sense, we might say that the new anti-social behaviour enforcement powers became a veritable 'Trojan horse' for the new youth justice. They were premised upon a perceived need to tackle the 'culture of impunity' (Campbell, 2002) that was alleged to have grown up around young offenders, 'apparently confident that neither the police, nor the rest of the youth justice system, could touch them' (Squires and Stephen, 2005, p. 4). What sustained these new ideas were a series of widening social divisions between poorer and better-off residential areas. The 1990s had seen the resurgence of concerns (undoubtedly fanned by American commentators; see Lister, 1996) about a supposedly new British 'underclass'; a group so, apparently, removed from mainstream opportunities and aspirations that they lived their entire lives in the shadowy inner-cities and sink estates of post-welfare Britain (Morris, 1994). Although this idea was profoundly disputed by British social scientists, it resonated with contemporary concerns about welfare dependency, teenage parenthood, educational under-achievement, the virtual collapse of youth labour markets, the decline of social mobility, the 'death' of community (anticipating more recent 'Broken Society' narratives), and the concentration of victimisation in Britain's poorest neighbourhoods (Hope, 2001) where the presence of street socialising young people was invariably taken as a visible sign of all that was wrong and threatening.

For a decade this perception of 'disorder' would find its echo in repeated British Crime Surveys, respondents consistently identifying 'young people hanging about' (Bottoms, 2006) as the most obvious indicator of anti-social behaviour. In time, another American concept, 'disconnected youth' (MacDonald and Marsh, 2005), came to be applied to these young people of the underclass, although later, it was less their apparent disconnections *from* their communities and more their alleged connections *to* criminality and gangs that signalled the major concerns. In turn, as the language used to describe young people changed to 'feral youth' (Jeffs and Smith, 1996), 'chavs' (Hayward and Yar, 2006), and 'gangsters' (Goldson, 2011), public policy for young people increasingly came to take the form of pest control. Academic commentators began to refer to the 'demonisation' of youth in media and political discourses (Pitts, 2003; Scraton, 2007; Deuchar, 2009). In an effort to combat social exclusion, halt community decline and the resulting disorder, and thereby reassure neighbourhoods, policy-makers turned against its most visible, street-socialising manifestation – young people. American criminologist Michael Tonry, commenting upon the politics behind Britain's investment in tackling delinquency and anti-social behaviour, and having noted the extent to which the British policies drew upon doubtful experiments in 'zero tolerance' policing in the USA, remarked: 'by making anti-social behaviour into a major social policy problem, and giving it sustained high visibility attention, Labour made a small problem larger, thereby making people more aware of it (Tonry, 2004, p. 57). He referred to this as a 'high risk' strategy. Tonry was referring to the political risk of inflating public expectations about containing youth crime, yet failing to deliver on this promise, but the real risks of criminalisation fell upon young people themselves.

The more intensive and earlier targeting of youth (Muncie, 1999), outlined already, was also reflected in a shift in academic orientations to 'problem youth'. Along with the notion of 'disconnected youth' came the idea that disadvantaged and marginalised young people were 'at risk'. No new body of pathbreaking research evidence really justified this substantial change in focus; indeed, the complaint of many social scientists concerned just how little impact they were having upon the policy process (Muncie, 2000; Faulkner, 2001). Instead, one academic paradigm on youth delinquency simply overtook another: risk analysis simply eclipsed causation. All the, by now, familiar elements of delinquency explanation – deprived social environments, dysfunctional families, poor education, criminal peer groups, and a lack of opportunities – remained in place, fashioned into perfect order through a series of studies by Utting *et al.* (1993), Graham and Bowling (1995), and Farrington (2002); the only difference was that these were no longer regarded as 'causes of delinquency' to be eliminated, but merely risks associated with delinquent choices. The focus was to be on the delinquent making the choices rather than improving the environments in which they were made. To go back to the 'broken windows' thinking, there was still no-one fixing the windows, and indeed, a profound scepticism had grown up about *whether* the windows could be fixed; instead, public and social policy was concentrating upon the young people throwing the stones.

In *Criminalising Social Policy* (2007), Rodger neatly contrasts the alternative discourses, or languages, in which these different takes on the question of youth crime and disorder were constructed. In the first place, he says, there is a welfare discourse that comprehends the problem of youth crime and disorder through the language of needs, rights, wellbeing, opportunities, and social justice and inclusion. This way of thinking, he argues, has been replaced by a new language focusing upon risk, culpability, prevention, discipline, control, and exclusion. Effectively, individuals and their behaviour became foregrounded; solving social problems, addressing inequalities, and creating opportunities became the windows that no-one could fix (Pitts, 2003). In turn, mobilising social and public policy around individual delinquency, family dysfunction, and peer group influence necessitated earlier intervention and a stronger focus upon personal responsibility. These features became key to the criminalisation strategy rolled out from the mid 1990s onwards.

> **STOP AND THINK**
>
> The policy debate about dealing with youth offending has, in recent years, turned upon a difference between 'tackling causes' and 'addressing risks'. What difference do you think this makes?
>
> When dealing with the problem of youth offending, what is the difference between 'tackling causes' and 'addressing risks', and what policy approaches might be adopted in either case? What consequences might follow from the adoption of different policies? How might the 'success' of the different policy approaches be judged?

Enhancing the capacity to criminalise

The process of 'expanded' criminalisation – a process closely allied to Young's (1971) notion of 'deviancy amplification' – took a number of forms: first and foremost, it entailed a significant expansion of areas of behaviour over which forms of 'summary justice' prevailed. These new measures included, in order of their numerical significance, penalty notices for disorder, fixed penalty notices, cannabis warnings, and ASBOs. The ASBO also illustrated a particular feature of this expanded criminalisation: the creation of hybrid civil/criminal powers. The ASBO carried the force of an injunction, stipulating a series of behaviours, places or associates that named persons had to avoid, or curfew hours they had to abide by. In turn, breach of the conditions of the civil order (the need for which was originally to be proven to the civil standard – the 'balance of probabilities') would be a criminal offence. Subsequently, the 2002 Police Reform Act allowed for the introduction of 'interim' ASBOs that could be imposed immediately on application to the clerk of the court. They were intended to provide communities with immediate relief from troublesome behaviour, but they could even be imposed 'without notice of proceedings being given to the defendant'. Simester and Von Hirsch (2006) have described these measures as a form of 'bespoke two-step criminalisation', which involved identifying a particular class of troubling individuals and then applying *distinct* and specific enforcement powers against them.

Both developments here also relate to a greater 'enabling' of street-level policing. Police powers ('robust reassurance') were also developed in respect of policing 'dispersal zones', confiscating alcohol, and including stop and search powers under, for example, 'Operation Blunt' (tackling knife crime) and regarding anti-terrorism policing. The police practice of 'containment' (sometimes known as 'kettling') also became subject to controversy. There was also, as a number of commentators (Pantazis, 2008; Squires, 2008) have noted, a significant degree of 'mission drift' about the ways in which anti-social behaviour and crime and disorder powers were developed and extended throughout the Labour administrations of 1997–2010. These tendencies continued under the Conservative-led Coalition after 2010, which proposed replacing ASBOs with a further series of orders, injunctions, notices, and 'police directions'.

Taken together, the new anti-social behaviour powers clearly delivered 'early intervention', with 'Acceptable Behaviour Contracts' (ABCs) made available for children as young as eight. ABCs, parenting orders, child safety orders, and curfews reinforced a growing conception of 'pre-delinquency' or 'pre-crime', an idea with more than a little hint of science fiction about it (Fox, 2002; Pantazis, 2008). Squires and Stephen (2005, 2010) argue that such interventions often amounted to a form of 'precautionary criminalisation' where rights and principles of justice were sacrificed for those deemed to be 'at risk' in order to preserve order for others. This was justified more broadly in governmental terms by what was referred to as the 're-balancing of criminal justice' in favour of the so-called 'law-abiding majority' (Blair, 2004) and, by definition, *against* those deemed to be causing the problems. Ignoring evidence on the distribution of victimisation in society, that offenders are themselves often the most frequent victims of crime (Hope, 2001), and certainly the most disadvantaged, talk of the 'law-abiding majority' erected a sharp, although misleading, distinction between 'good' and 'bad', 'us' and 'them', while justifying the use of tougher powers against those who (supposedly) only 'had themselves to blame' (Tonry, 2010). As Phoenix (2012) has argued, such an approach can have quite perverse consequences, for example where victimised young people, bullied or coerced into either gang membership or sexual exploitation, are themselves treated as criminals (see also Pitts, 2007).

A further dimension of the criminalisation we have experienced relates to the phenomenon of 'net-widening', as described by Cohen (1985). Three features of this net-widening process are worthy of note. First, the idea simply describes the way in which the criminal justice system expands, drawing more people into its net. In this sense, the expansion of the range of 'regulated behaviours' to include 'anti-social' rather than simply *criminal* activities is an obvious case in point. Second, the lowering of the age of criminal responsibility to ten and the availability of early intervention powers for even young children is also important. However, it is not just the size of the net – the narrowness of the mesh, or the intensity of the scrutiny, is also important (Austin and Krisberg, 1981). Here we should note the inclusion of the range of pre-criminal and pre-delinquent behaviours that will attract discipline. The third aspect of this net-widening, for Cohen, concerned the ways in which whole new groups of the population became either (or both) givers and receivers of discipline and surveillance. Teachers, youth workers, housing officers, neighbourhood wardens (and social workers obviously) became part of the new networks of behaviour management, monitoring and recording the behaviour of young people. To continue the nets and fishing metaphor, not only were there bigger nets with a tighter mesh, there were also more people out fishing now. Even parents (and implicitly whole families) were incorporated into this network of monitoring and responsibilisation, reinforced by 'parenting orders' (Holt, 2009, 2010) – usually targeted at mothers – where compliance was not readily forthcoming.

There is another aspect to the net-widening, taking us right back to the original concept of 'deviancy amplification' referred to earlier. This entails the wider deployment of police surveillance and intelligence-gathering powers and relates to the familiar practice of police agencies 'defining up' deviancy. Thus, young people congregating in public space become 'anti-social troublemakers'; young people in groups committing offences become 'gangs'; in turn, 'gangs' become the supposed accelerators of 'gang-related' violence. The government even suggested that gangs were a major cause of the 2011 English riots (HM Givernment, 2011), but later changed tack, the Centre for Social Justice (2012) identifying 'gang culture' when it became clear that only a small proportion of the rioters and looters arrested were actually 'gang-affiliated'. Hallsworth and Young (2008) have cautioned against this 'talking up' of the gang problem, pointing out that the label 'gang' carries its own ideological baggage and, typically, serves to justify more heavy-handed police responses. Research by Smithson *et al.* (2013) has confirmed how the use of gang labels has tended to further 'marginalize and isolate ethnic minority communities' (p. 113).

Two final instances of this 'criminalisation as net-widening' relate, first, to the use of 'gang injunctions' (sometimes called gang ASBOs) against supposed gang-involved or gang-affiliated young people. The measures are designed to regulate the social interactions of young people but, as Hallsworth and Young (2008) have noted, everything here depends precisely upon the prior definition of the 'gang'. Critics have argued that gang injunctions simply criminalise poor communities (Lavender, 2011). Even more controversial is the practice of 'joint enterprise' prosecution, by which police arrest and the CPS seek to prosecute *every* member of a given gang as 'accessories' when one or more gang members commit offences. Joint enterprise raises a number of dilemmas relating to criminal liability and has already been subject to a critical report by the House of Commons Justice Select Committee (2012). Joint enterprise prosecutions widen the scope of criminalisation by extending culpability for criminal acts to entire groups of young people, especially supposed gang members (Abbott, 2010; Campbell, 2012).

In many ways, the net-widening principle also relates to the extended surveillance capacities of modern security systems, especially public area CCTV systems. The fact that surveillance systems have proliferated beyond the architecture of the 'panopticon' to our city centres and traffic networks adds significantly to policing capacity. But where this surveillance capacity extends also to the power to exclude: which is to say, where the panopticon becomes the BAN-opticon (Hempel and Töpfer, 2009), and here one thinks of young people wearing 'hoodies' prohibited from entering shopping malls or subjected to surveillance and stop and search when 'out of place' in high-value shopping precincts (Coleman, 2004a, 2004b).

A final dimension of extended criminalisation completes the cycle begun by 'pre-criminalisation' and refers to 'post-criminalisation' processes whereby offenders continue to be subject to 'offender management' processes even after an initial sentence has been undergone. These interventions might be most familiar in relation to sexual and violent offender registration requirements, but they have been supplemented by other orders and post-sentence requirements such as ASBOs 'on conviction' (an ASBO attached to a criminal conviction), and their consequences can extend for young people into wider areas of public and social policy such as (exclusion from) education, training and employability, and housing.

And down again?

The extended criminalisation (of youth) just described is sometimes equated with a 'punitive turn' in British penal policy, a reflection of the more dramatic rise of mass incarceration described at length in the USA by Wacquant (2009) and others (see Garland, 2001), and further evidenced by the rising prison population in the UK. Figure 14.1, with which this chapter commenced, might also be seen as evidence of a tougher youth justice system emerging as the twenty-first century approached, except that one of the chief aims of the Blair government's youth justice reforms had been to reduce the cost and improve the effectiveness of the youth justice system. Incarcerating young people was expensive, custody consumed fully 75 per cent of the youth justice budget (Smith, 2003); reducing the cost of custody was intended to play a vital role in redirecting resources to crime prevention although, for the best part of a decade, youth custody rates continued their stubborn climb, prompting criticism of the Youth Justice Board (Lakhani, 2008; Lepper, 2008). And then, in 2008, custody rates began to fall; more than that, as the Howard League research has suggested; juvenile arrests were falling too.

So how might we account for the fact that, in the wake of nearly two decades of enhanced criminalisation, net-widening, earlier interventions, and full-scale youth demonisation and, on the back of rising concern about gangs, the 'crisis of youth' (Goldson, 2011) and even a 'knife crime moral panic' (Squires, 2009, 2011) not to mention widespread rioting, lower numbers of young people are now being arrested and fewer of these appear to be finding their way into custody?

CONTROVERSY AND DEBATE

Despite falling crime and declining rates of criminalisation, weapon carrying and rioting seem to buck the trend and still attract tough custodial sentences. For example, the government changed the law so that young people arrested for carrying an offensive weapon, such as a knife, should expect to receive a custodial sentence. Yet almost every survey on the subject reports that young people say that they carry weapons 'for protection'. How should the courts respond?

The sentences handed down to the August 2011 rioters and looters raise similar questions:

- Ursula Nevin, a mother of two was asleep when the Manchester riots were raging, but was sent to prison for six months because she accepted a pair of looted shorts from a friend.

- Nicholas Robinson was sentenced to spend six months in prison for taking a £3.50 case of water from a smashed-up Lidl in Brixton.

- Jordan Blackshaw and Perry Sutcliffe-Keenan received four years each for using Facebook to incite a riot that never took place.

All were in their early twenties and none had previous convictions.

The Liberal Democrats' home affairs spokesman Tom Brake argued, 'There have been some cases where people who have committed petty offences have received sentences which, if they had committed the same offence the day before the riots, they would not have received a sentence of that nature' (Baggini, 2011). What sentences should such offences attract?

As Bateman (2012, p. 45) notes, 'the substantial fall in child imprisonment inevitably raises questions for analyses of youth justice that have drawn on the notion of punitivism'. The answers to such questions involve a number of related issues, including: underlying rates of youth crime, 'austerity' policies and public expenditure constraints, and policy alternatives and diversions.

Recent preoccupations with gangs, weapons, and violent youth crime have tended to obscure the fact that youth crime, overall, has been falling for some years. For example, there were 137,335 proven offences by young people in 2011–12, down 47 per cent over the decade (YJB/MoJ, 2013). The numbers of young people entering the youth justice system for the first time have fallen markedly over the past five years. The number of repeat offenders aged under 18 has likewise fallen by almost a third over the same period. Of course, the number of young people entering the criminal justice system is itself a 'constructed' consequence of the ways in which young people are dealt with by the youth justice system. For example, penalty notices for disorder are not counted as 'entry to the criminal justice system' and, from 2007–08, the much criticised police performance indicator 'sanction detection', which had pushed the police towards a problematic strategy of results-oriented over-criminalisation of young people was abandoned. Instead, a new key perform-ance indicator was installed prioritising *reducing* the numbers of first time entrants to the youth justice system.

Whether by accident, design or pragmatism, the youth justice system has rediscovered the potential of 'diversion' and 'alternatives' to custody. Of course, preventing young people entering the criminal justice system is a sure-fire way of ensuring they do not re-enter it, still less progress through it to find themselves locked up (Bateman, 2010). As Figure 14.2 shows, the fall in youth criminalisation was as dramatic as the increases had been almost two decades earlier. In recent years, a number of secure establishments for young offenders have even been closed. Diversions and alternatives have taken a number of forms, however; for example, the numbers of ASBOs handed out in respect of young people fell by around half and, subsequently, the Home Secretary announced they would be replaced. Reprimands, final warnings, and referral orders have similarly had a significant impact on the numbers of young people sentenced by the Youth Courts. More recently, these include newer 'early intervention' strategies – the *Troubled Families Programme* in particular (Department for Communities and Local Government, 2012). This initiative was first announced in the UK Government gang strategy document *Ending Gang and Youth Violence* and aims to work with 120,000 'troubled and dysfunctional families' (HM Government, 2011) which are seen as the environments driving many disadvantaged, abused or neglected young people into the arms of gangs or persistent criminal careers.

But there is little doubt that, in the wake of the 2008 'credit crunch' and the Conservative-led Coalition government's austerity measures, falling rates of reported youth crime are also being shaped by the diminishing budgets of

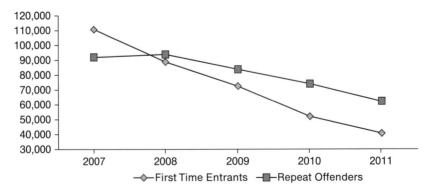

Figure 14.2 First-time entrants and repeat offenders in the criminal justice system, 2007–11

Source: CIVITAS Crime Fact Sheet (2011) Youth Crime in England and Wales

the police and the youth justice system. Significant restrictions on criminal justice spending, including cuts to front-line policing, will further impact upon the capacity of the criminal justice system. In one sense, this might be a positive outcome; we might even argue that key aspects of criminal justice early intervention have become 'de-criminalised', were it not for the fact that 'crime control' functions and responsibilities have become attached to more and more areas of social and public policy. These include education (exclusions), housing (evictions), welfare benefits (entitlement restrictions), parenting (contracts and orders), the continuing role played by anti-social behaviour management policies, and the new Troubled Families Programme. Little substantially new government expenditure was earmarked for this programme, even though it entailed a significant range of supposedly 'joined-up' activities to supervise the risky journeys through life taken by the children of Britain's poorest families. The new programme and the new powers carry many of the hallmarks of the original anti-social behaviour programme; the reason they were attractive to Blairite modernisers in the first place. They are low-intensity/high-utility: swift, local, visible, cheap, responsibility oriented, and 'entry-level'. Such interventions, whether *diversions from* or *alternatives to* criminal justice, facilitate control and containment without involving the consequences of criminalisation or imprisonment. They represent alternative forms of 'criminal justice' activism whilst sidestepping the symbolism of crime or the expensive requirements of justice.

It is debateable also how far these policies actually deliver justice, for, as Rodger (2007) has argued, social policies no longer correspond to a language of social justice, opportunity or inclusion. Rather, as austerity-driven inequalities widen, the recognition that most crime is intra-communal (the poorest victimising one another) *and* under-reported, the imperative for the state to address it becomes diminished while containment displaces problem-solving. There is often little justice, either, for the 'usual suspects' who do, from time to time, find themselves within the criminal justice system. In 2011–12, twenty young people died while under Youth Offending Team supervision and three died in custody, while there were over 3,000 assaults by young people within custody and a 21 per cent year on year increase (to 1725) in incidents of self-harm in custody (YJB/MoJ, 2013).

Conclusion

There have been significant changes in perceptions of the 'problem' of youth crime over recent decades. From the early 1990s there was a shift towards an increasing demonisation of young people and a parallel process of increasing criminalisation and the use of a range of new powers to tackle the perceived problem. However, despite these developments, recent years have seen the use of a variety of alternatives that seek to divert people away from custody, together with the greater use of 'early intervention' initiatives, most notably Family Intervention Projects and the Troubled Families Programme. Whether for those or other reasons, we have seen a decline in the number of offences committed by young people and the numbers entering the youth justice system. But whether the new regimes of 'decriminalised' management of youthful behaviour represent a fairer society (or a greater degree of social justice) remains an open question.

Summary

This chapter has explored the reasons for the sharp upturn in youth criminalisation during the 1990s and an equally sharp decline in youthful criminalisation after 2007–08. It has:

- Used Garland's argument that many factors quite unconnected with policy effectiveness are often responsible for policy choices to consider the range of social influences responsible for changing youth custody trends over the past two decades.
- Drawn attention to a shift from 'causality' to 'risk' in policy discourse and how this has focused policy interventions on dangerous individuals.
- Posed questions about the appropriate scope of criminalisation, exploring the consequences of criminalisation and asking how much criminalisation is consistent with the demands of social justice?
- And has begun to examine the ways in which 'diversions from' and 'alternatives to' custodial sentencing are (except in more serious cases – weapon carrying and rioting) impacting upon rates of youth criminalisation.

Discussion and review

- To what extent have changes in debates over law and order been driven by broader socio-political debates?
- Why was there an increased criminalisation of youth from the early 1990s?
- What did the 'net-widening' process in the criminal justice system entail?
- Why might the Coalition government's austerity measures be associated with falling numbers of young people entering the criminal justice system?

References

Abbott, D. (2010) 'Time to review police use of "joint enterprise" ', *The Guardian*, 29 July.

Audit Commission (1996) *Misspent Youth*, Audit Commission, London.

Austin, B. and Krisberg, J. (1981) 'Wider, stronger and different nets', *Journal of Research in Crime and Delinquency*, Vol. 18, No. 1, pp. 165–96.

Baggini, J. (2011) 'England riots: are harsh sentences for offenders justified?', *The Guardian*, 17 August.

Bateman, T. (2003) 'A state of affairs that shames us all', *Safer Society*, Autumn, reprinted in No. 35, Winter 2007/08.

Bateman, T. (2010) 'The number of "first time entrants" to the youth justice system in England falls; as does the population of the secure estate for children and young people', *Youth Justice*, Vol. 10, No. 1, pp. 84–95.

Bateman, T. (2012) 'Who pulled the plug? Towards an explanation of the fall of child imprisonment in England and Wales', *Youth Justice*, Vol. 12, No. 1, pp. 36–52.

Bell, E. (2011) *Criminal Justice and Neo-Liberalism*, Palgrave Macmillan, Basingstoke.

Blair, T. (2004) 'A new consensus on law and order', Prime Minister's speech at the launch of the Home Office and Criminal Justice System strategic plans, 19 July, available at http://www.labour.org.uk/news/tbcrimespeech.

Bottoms, A.E. (2006) 'Incivilities, offence and social order in residential communities', in A. von Hirsch and A.P. Simester (eds.) *Incivilities: Regulating Offensive Behaviour*, Hart Publishing, Oxford.

Burnett, R. and Maruna, S. (2004) 'So "prison works", does it? The criminal careers of 130 men released from prison', *Howard Journal of Criminal Justice*, Vol. 43, No. 4, pp. 390–404.

Burney, E. (2005) *Making People Behave: Anti-social Behaviour, Politics and Policy: The Creation and Enforcement of Anti-social Behaviour Policy*, Willan Publishing, Cullompton.

Button, M. (2002) *Private Policing*, Willan Publishing, Cullompton.

Campbell, D. (2012) 'When should one gang member take responsibility for the actions of others?', *The Guardian*, 18 January.

Campbell, S. (2002) *A Review of Anti-Social Behaviour Orders*, Home Office Research Study 236, Home Office, London.

Casey, L. (2008) *Engaging Communities in Fighting Crime: A Review* (The Casey Report), Cabinet Office, London.

Centre for Social Justice (2012) *Time to Wake Up: Tackling Gangs One Year After the Riots*, Centre for Social Justice, London.

Cohen, S. (1972) *Folk Devils and Moral Panics*, Routledge, London.

Cohen, S. (1985) *Visions of Social Control*, Polity, Cambridge.

Coleman, R. (2004a) *Reclaiming the Streets: Surveillance, Social Control and the City*, Willan Publishing, Cullompton.

Coleman, R. (2004b) 'Watching the degenerate: street camera surveillance and urban regeneration', *Local Economy*, Vol. 19, No. 3, pp. 199–211.

Corrigan, P. (1979) *Schooling the Smash Street Kids*, Macmillan, Basingstoke.

Crawford, A. and Lister, S. (2007) *The Use and Impact of Dispersal Orders: Sticking Plasters and Wake-up Calls*, Policy Press, Bristol.

Department for Communities and Local Government (2012) *Working with Troubled Families*, The Stationery Office, London.

Deuchar, R. (2009) *Gangs, Marginalised Youth and Social Capital*, Trentham Books, London.

Farrington, D.P. (2002) Developmental criminology and risk-focussed prevention, in M. Maguire, R. Morgan and R. Reiner (eds.) *Oxford Handbook of Criminology* (3rd edn.), Oxford University Press, Oxford.

Faulkner, D. (2001) *Crime, State and Citizen*, Waterside Press, Winchester.

Foucault, M. (1977) *Discipline and Punish: The Birth of the Prison*, Allen Lane, London.

Fox, C. (2002) 'The real life pre-crime officers', *Safer Society Magazine*, No. 15, pp. 9–19.

Garland, D. (2001) *The Culture of Control*, Oxford University Press, Oxford.

Garside, R. and Solomon, E. (2008) *Ten Years of New Labour's Youth Justice Reforms: An Independent Audit*, Centre for Crime and Justice Studies, London.

Gill, M. and Spriggs, A. (2005) *Assessing the Impact of CCTV*, Home Office Research Study No. 292, Home Office Development and Statistics Directorate, London.

Goldson, B. (ed.) (2000) *The New Youth Justice*, Russell House Publishing, Lyme Regis.

Goldson, B. (2010) 'The sleep of (criminological) reason: knowledge–policy rupture and New Labour's youth justice legacy', *Criminology and Criminal Justice*, Vol. 10, No. 2, pp. 155–78.

Goldson, B. (ed.) (2011) *Youth in Crisis: 'Gangs', Territoriality and Violence*, Routledge, London.

Goold, B. (2004) *CCTV and Policing: Public Area Surveillance and Police Practices in Britain*, Oxford University Press, Oxford.

Graham, J. and Bowling, B. (1995) *Young People and Crime*, Home Office Research Study 145, Home Office, London.

Hagell, A. and Newburn, T. (1994) *Persistent Young Offenders*, Policy Studies Institute, London.

Hallsworth, S. and Young, T. (2008) 'Gang talk and gang talkers: a critique', *Crime, Media, Culture*, Vol. 4, No. 2, pp. 175–95.

HM Government (2011) *Ending Gang and Youth Violence: A Cross-Government Report*, The Stationery Office, London.

Hayden, D. and Scraton, P. (2000) " 'Condemn a little more, understand a little less": the political context and rights' implications of the domestic and European rulings in the Venables–Thompson case', *Journal of Law and Society*, Vol. 27, No. 3, pp. 416–48.

Hayward, K.J and Yar, M. (2006) 'The 'Chav' phenomenon: consumption, media and the construction of a new underclass', *Crime, Media, Culture*, Vol. 2, No. 1, pp. 9–28.

Hempel, L. and Töpfer, E. (2009) 'The surveillance consensus: reviewing the politics of CCTV in three European countries', *European Journal of Criminology*, Vol. 6, No. 1, pp. 157–77.

Holt, A. (2009) '(En)gendering responsibilities: experiences of parenting a 'young offender', *Howard Journal of Criminal Justice*, Vol. 48, No. 4, pp. 344–56.

Holt, A. (2010) 'Disciplining "problem parents" in the youth court: between regulation and resistance', *Social Policy and Society*, Vol. 9, No. 1, pp. 89–99.

Home Office (1988) *Punishment, Custody and the Community*, HMSO, London.

Home Office (1991) *Safer Communities* (The Morgan Report), The Stationery Office, London.

Home Office (1997) *No More Excuses*, The Stationery Office, London.

Hope, T. (2001) 'Crime victimisation and inequality in risk society', in R. Matthews and J. Pitts (eds.) *Crime, Disorder and Community Safety*, Routledge, London.

Hough, M., Allen, R. and Solomon, E. (2008) *Tackling Prison Overcrowding: Build More Prisons? Sentence Fewer Offenders?*, Policy Press, Bristol.

Jeffs, T. and Smith, M. (1996) " 'Getting the dirtbags off the streets" – curfews and other solutions to juvenile crime', *Youth and Policy*, Vol. 52, No. 1, pp. 1–14.

Jones, T. and Newburn, T. (2002) 'The transformation of policing? Understanding current trends in policing systems', *British Journal of Criminology*, Vol. 42, No. 1, pp. 129–46.

Justice Select Committee (2012) *Joint Enterprise: Eleventh Report of Session 2010–12*, The Stationery Office, London.

Kinsella, B. (2011) *Tackling Knife Crime Together: A Review of Local Anti-Knife Crime Projects*, Home Office, London, available at http://www.homeoffice.gov.uk/publications/crime/tackling-knife-crime-together/tackling-knife-crime-report?view=Binary.

Lakhani, N. (2008) 'Youth Justice Board's future in doubt over failure to reduce crime', *The Independent*, 6 July.

Lavender, G. (2011) 'Gang injunctions just criminalise poor communities', *The Guardian*, 1 February.

Lepper, J. (2008) 'Critics attack YJB as the target to reduce youth custody is dropped', *Children and Young People Now*, 15 October.

Lister, R. (ed.) (1996) *Charles Murray and the Underclass: The Developing Debate*, IEA Health and Welfare Unit, London.

Loader, I. and Sparks, R. (2010) *Public Criminology?*, Routledge, London.

MacDonald, R. and Marsh, J. (2005) *Disconnected Youth? Growing Up in Britain's Poor Neighbourhoods*, Palgrave Macmillan, Basingstoke.

Matthews, R. (2005) 'The myth of punitiveness', *Theoretical Criminology*, Vol. 9, No. 2, pp. 175–201.

Measor, L. and Squires, P. (2000) *Young People and Community Safety: Inclusion, Risk, Tolerance and Disorder*, Ashgate, Aldershot.

Morris, L. (1994) *Dangerous Classes: The Underclass and Social Citizenship*, London, Routledge.

Muncie, J. (1999) 'Institutionalised intolerance: youth crime and the 1998 Crime and Disorder Act', *Critical Social Policy*, Vol. 19, No. 2, pp. 147–75.

Muncie, J. (2000) 'Pragmatic realism: searching for criminology in the new youth justice', in B. Goldson (ed.) *The New Youth Justice*, Russell House Publishing, Lyme Regis.

Muncie, J. (2008) " 'The punitive turn" in juvenile justice: cultures of control and rights compliance in Western Europe and the USA', *Youth Justice*, Vol. 8, No. 2, pp. 107–21.

Naughton, M. (2005) " 'Evidence-based policy" and the government of the criminal justice system – only if the evidence fits!', *Critical Social Policy*, Vol. 25, No. 1, pp. 47–69.

Pantazis, C. (2008) 'The problem with criminalisation', *Criminal Justice Matters,* Vol. 74, No. 1, pp. 10–12.

Pearson, G. (1983) *Hooligan: A History of Respectable Fears*, Macmillan, Basingstoke.

Phoenix, J. (2012) *Out of Place: The Policing and Criminalisation of Sexually Exploited Girls and Young Women*, Howard League for Penal Reform, London.

Pitts, J. (2003) *The New Politics of Youth Crime: Discipline or Solidarity*, Russell House Publishing, Lyme Regis.

Pitts, J. (2007) *Reluctant Gangsters*, Willan Publishing, Cullompton.

Pitts, J. (2011) 'The third time as farce: whatever happened to the penal state?', in P. Squires and J. Lea (eds.) *Criminalisation and Advanced Marginality*, Policy Press, Bristol.

Rodger, J. (2007) *Criminalising Social Policy: Anti-social Behaviour and Welfare in a De-civilised Society*, Willan Publishing, Cullompton.

Scraton, P. (2007) *Power, Conflict and Criminalisation*, Routledge, London.

Simester, A.P. and Von Hirsch, A. (2006) 'Regulating offensive behaviour through two-step prohibitions', in A. von Hirsch and A.P. Simester (eds.) *Incivilities: Regulating Offensive Behaviour*, Hart Publishing, Oxford.

Smith, R. (2003) *Youth Justice: Ideas, Policies, Practice*, Willan Publishing, Cullompton.

Smithson, H., Ralphs, R. and Williams, P. (2013) 'Used and abused: the problematic usage of gang terminology in the United Kingdom and its implications for ethnic minority youth'. *British Journal of Criminology*, Vol. 53, No. 1, pp. 113–28.

Squires, P. (ed.) (2008) *ASBO Nation: The Criminalisation of Nuisance*, Policy Press, Bristol.

Squires, P. (2009) 'The knife crime "epidemic" and British politics', *British Politics*, Vol. 4, No. 1, pp. 127–57.

Squires, P. (2010) Evaluating CCTV: lessons from a surveillance culture, *European Forum for Urban Safety: Citizens, Cities and Video-Surveillance*, Programme and EFUS CCTV Charter launched in Rotterdam, May, available at http://www.fesu.org/.

Squires, P. (2011) 'Young people and "weaponisation" ', in B. Goldson (ed.) *Youth in Crisis: 'Gangs', Territoriality and Violence*, Routledge, London.

Squires, P. and Stephen, D.E. (2005) *Rougher Justice: Young People and Anti-social Behaviour*, Willan Publishing, Cullompton.

Squires, P. and Stephen, D.E. (2010) 'Pre-crime and precautionary criminalisation', *Criminal Justice Matters,* Vol. 81, No. 1, pp. 28–9.

Thomas, T. (2008) 'The sex offender register: a case study of function creep', *Howard Journal of Criminal Justice*, Vol. 47, No. 3, pp. 227–37.

Tonry, M. (2004) *Punishment and Politics: Evidence and Emulation in the Making of English Crime Control Policy*, Willan Publishing, Cullompton.

Tonry, M. (2010) 'The costly consequences of populist posturing: ASBOs, victims, 'rebalancing' and diminution in support for civil liberties', *Punishment and Society*, Vol. 12, No. 4, pp. 287–314.

Utting, D., Bright, J. and Henricson, C. (1993) *Crime and the Family: Improving Child-rearing and Preventing Delinquency*, Family Policy Studies Centre, London.

Wacquant, L. (2009) *Punishing the Poor: The Neo-liberal Government of Social Insecurity*, Duke University Press, Durham, NC.

Weiner, M.J. (1990) *Reconstructing the Criminal: Culture Law and Policy 1830–1914*, Cambridge University Press, Cambridge.

Whitfield, D. (1997) *Tackling the Tag: The Electronic Monitoring of Offenders*, Waterside Press, Winchester.

Young, J. (1971) *The Drugtakers: The Social Meaning of Drug Use*, Judson, McGibbon & Kee, London.

Young, J. (1999) *The Exclusive Society*, Sage, London.

Youth Justice Board/Ministry of Justice (2012) *Youth Justice Statistics 2010/11: England and Wales*, available at https://www.gov.uk/government/uploads/system/uploads/attachment_data/file/218557/yjb-statistics-10-11.pdf.

Youth Justice Board/Ministry of Justice (2013) *Youth Justice Statistics 2011/12: England and Wales*, available at http://www.justice.gov.uk/downloads/statistics/youth-justice/yjb-stats-2011-12.pdf.

Further reading

Garland, D. (2001) *The Culture of Control*, Oxford University Press, Oxford. This book examines changes in crime control and criminal justice in the UK and USA and explains them through a consideration of the organisation of contemporary society and political and cultural change.

Knepper, P. (2007) *Criminology and Social Policy*, Sage, London. Explores the relationship between the two disciplines and assesses the role of criminology in addressing social problems and the role of social policy in tackling crime.

Newburn, T. (2012) *Criminology*, Routledge, London. This is a comprehensive, readable textbook that includes developments in criminological theory as well as criminal justice practice.

Rodger, J. (2007) *Criminalising Social Policy*, Willan Publishing, Cullompton. Takes the issue of antisocial behaviour in its broad socio-economic context and looks at attempts to manage and prevent it.

Squires, P. (ed.) (2008) *ASBO Nation: The Criminalisation of Nuisance*, Policy Press, Bristol. This book examines the notion of antisocial behaviour, considers governmental responses, and analyses the problems of policy and implementation.

Useful websites

http://www.crimeandjustice.org.uk – the website of the Centre for Crime and Justice Studies, which has links to other excellent sources of information and analysis.

http://www.howardleague.org – the Howard League for Penal Reform campaigns on a wide range of topics. Its web pages provide a variety of information about its work and key issues.

https://www.gov.uk/government/organisations/home-office and http://www.justice.gov.uk – these are important source of information about current government policy, and their websites have links to policy documents and to research.

http://www.nacro.org.uk – NACRO is a charity that aims to reduce crime. The NACRO website provides information on the work of the organisation and access to its publications.

CHAPTER 15

Health Policy

Martin Powell

Learning objectives

- To provide a chronological discussion of the development of the NHS in terms of the main events: (1) in the period before the NHS; (2) in the 'classic' consensual period of the NHS; and (3) the Conservative (1979–97), New Labour (1997–2010), and Coalition (2010–) periods of government
- To explore issues that have raged over the 60 years since its inception, including finance, structure, and the principles of the NHS
- To present an evaluation of the effectiveness of the NHS: (1) temporally (is the NHS getting better over time?), (2) intrinsically (is it delivering its aims, or being consistent with its principles?), and (3) extrinsically/comparatively (how does it compare with other health systems?)

Chapter overview

The British National Health Service (NHS) is sometimes regarded as the crowning glory of the welfare state. This means that debates over the service tend to be high profile and particularly polarised. It is important to note that the NHS is part of wider health policy, and that there are many different ways of ensuring that populations are healthy and have access to health care.

Introduction

Health policy comprises all factors that have a significant effect on health. In the extreme, all public policy is health policy because issues such as poverty, unemployment, housing, and pollution all have effects on health. However, it might be said that Britain has a policy for health services but no health policy. Although curative health services are the most visible symbols of health policy, their contribution to the nation's health has been questioned, and the earliest legislation on health policy was not concerned with individual health care but with collective or population public health (Powell, 1997, p. 13). In 2007, over 11,000 readers of the *British Medical Journal* chose the 'sanitary revolution' (the introduction of clean water and sewage disposal) as the most important medical milestone since 1840 (when the *British Medical Journal* was first published). This was closely followed by: antibiotics, anaesthesia, vaccines, and the discovery of the structure of DNA (*British Medical Journal*, 2007).

STOP AND THINK

Given that 'prevention is better than cure', why do we continue to devote the vast majority of health resources towards curative health care?

According to Hunter (2008, p. 141), one of the curious ironies of most health systems is that few pay much attention to health, focusing instead on ill health and disease. Using the analogy of a garage (cf. Klein, 2010), the health care system is a breakdown service that focuses on 'repair', with little stress on both regular (e.g. checking tyre pressures) and annual servicing. To use another analogy, health care systems are like a lifeguard saving people from drowning in a river ('downstream' measures or 'medical model') but rarely trying to prevent them from falling into the water in the first place ('upstream' measures or 'social model'; see Hunter, 2008, ch. 6).

An assessment or evaluation of the NHS is difficult (see Powell, 1997) partly due to polarised ideological positions. For some, the NHS is the best in the world, while others consider that it is among the worst in the world. Some commentators believe that the NHS needs to change radically, while others denounce any change as breaking the principles of the NHS, leading to the 'end of the NHS', which is due to supine governments acting on behalf of international capitalism. This is largely an account of the English NHS. Although there have always been some differences between the health systems of England, Scotland, Wales, and Northern Ireland, these were amplified after 'political devolution' in 1999 (see Ham, 2009, ch. 7).

Origins and development

The industrial revolution of the nineteenth century led to rapid population increase in new industrial cities. High death rates were associated largely with infectious diseases. These issues were documented in Edwin Chadwick's famous 'Report on the Sanitary Condition of the Labouring Population of

Great Britain' of 1842, which has been termed 'perhaps the greatest of the nineteenth century Blue Books' (Fraser, 1984, p. 62). The solution to the problem of insanitary housing and deficient sewerage and water supply was 'sanitary reform' in the form of the Public Health Act of 1848, 'a great landmark in social reform' (Fraser 1984, p. 70).

The poor health of the population was seen most clearly by government in times of war. The state of health of many recruits for the Boer War led to the establishment of the 'Interdepartmental Committee on Physical Deterioration'. Its report in 1904 led to measures aimed at improving the health of children through school meals and school medical inspection. For one commentator, these measures 'marked the beginning of the welfare state' (Gilbert, 1966, p. 102).

Many people found it difficult to afford primary care doctors (today's general practitioners). Many working men belonged to friendly societies; mutual aid that provided the services of a doctor and sick pay in return for weekly contributions. David Lloyd George, Chancellor in the Liberal government, effectively nationalised this arrangement for lower paid workers in his National Health Insurance (NHI) scheme of 1911. Despite its name, it was effectively aimed at poverty rather than health issues, as it covered the (male) breadwinner of the family rather than women and children, with the objective of enabling the breadwinner to return to work as soon as possible with sick pay to tide the family over in the meantime.

Voluntary hospitals, which provided services for the poor, were financed by the philanthropy of the rich. However, shortage of finance led many hospitals to raise money from their patients through contributory schemes and means testing. Rudimentary health care for sick paupers was provided through the Poor Law in workhouses. The 1929 Local Government Act allowed local authorities to 'break up the poor law', transferring services to their public health committees, which enabled a service to be provided for all local citizens. However, both voluntary and municipal provision varied widely in quantity and quality, which led to a situation similar to the modern term of the 'post code lottery'.

The National Health Service

The NHS was launched in 1948 by the 1945–51 Labour government that won office at the end of the Second World War. The Minister of Health, Aneurin Bevan, created a NHS that was comprehensive in two senses – in scope (covering all possible treatments) and in being universal (covering everybody) – financed largely by national taxation, and delivering care based on medical need that was free at the point of delivery. In short, it was designed to be an island based on Marx's Communist notion of 'from each according to their ability; to each according to their need' within a capitalist sea.

STOP AND THINK

As food is essential to health, should we have a 'National Food Service' that distributes food on the basis of need and free at the point of delivery?

Bevan created a 'tri-partite' structure of hospitals governed by local appointed boards, family practitioner services (GPs, dentists, opticians, pharmacists) governed by different appointed boards, and elected local authorities that ran a range of domiciliary and environmental health services. Bevan's most significant contribution was to nationalise the hospitals, but he was forced by the medical profession to concede on issues such as private practice (pay beds) within NHS hospitals, generous 'merit awards' for hospital consultants, and a large degree of medical representation on NHS bodies.

The basic organisational structure endured for many years, until the first major reorganisation of the NHS of 1974. This created some 90 area health authorities, which included the formerly independent teaching hospitals, and community nursing services, which were transferred from local government. It also created community health councils, which were designed to be a 'watchdog' to represent the local community.

However, financial issues were much less stable than organisational structures. The original financial estimates for NHS spending were quickly seen to be flawed. The Labour government was concerned that the NHS was out of financial control, and legislated to allow charges for dental and optical work, and for prescriptions. This was one of the issues on which Bevan resigned from the government. In the 1950s, the (1951–64) Conservative government appointed the Guillebaud Committee to examine the cost of the service. However, its report in 1956 pointed out the need for more, rather than less, NHS expenditure.

The Hospital Plan of 1962 was the first real attempt to direct resources from the pattern inherited by the NHS. Many of the inherited hospitals were old and out-dated, and some parts of the country had more hospital beds per thousand population than others. Minister of Health Enoch Powell set out a series of planning norms, such as 3.3 acute beds per 1,000 population, and aimed to achieve this through a series of new 'district general hospitals' of between 600 and 800 beds serving some 100,000 to 150,000 people. In addition, following the development of new drugs and treatments, it was intended that mental illness would be treated in future in the 'community' and in general hospitals rather than the old, large Victorian asylums.

Despite the growing economic difficulties of the 1970s, it was this period that saw a significant effort to respond to equity issues in the NHS. A series of scandals in long-stay hospitals forced some reactive 'crisis management' measures by Labour and Conservative Secretaries of State, Richard Crossman and Sir Keith Joseph. Crossman set up an inspectorate of the 'Hospital Advisory Service', and both attempted to divert some resources to the 'Cinderella' or 'priority' groups such as people with mental illness and mental handicap. However, implementation of this strategy was difficult in the face of powerful local clinical priorities of the more 'visible' and 'popular' medical specialties. The 1974–79 Labour government set up a 'Resource Allocation Working Party', which attempted to allocate geographical resources according to need. This meant redistributing money from London and the south to the north and midlands. Finally, in 1976 the Labour government set up a group to examine inequalities in health. Its report pointed to significant social class gradients in health that showed that professional and managerial workers had lower mortality rates than unskilled manual workers. The report recommended a significant increase in public expenditure and a redistribution of income in favour of the poorest groups. However, the group had taken so long to report that by 1980 the political world had changed.

Conservative health policy (1979–97)

The NHS did not feature heavily in the early years of the Conservative government of Margaret Thatcher. The NHS was reorganised in 1982 whereby the area health authorities, which lasted only eight years, were swept away, with some 200 district health authorities becoming the main NHS local bodies. Although expenditure on the NHS continued to rise in real terms, critics complained that the NHS was under-funded. The government attempted to increase the efficiency of the NHS by squeezing more 'output' from the input of expenditure. Its general assumption was that the private sector was more efficient than the public sector, and so it introduced some elements of private sector management in the NHS. This efficiency drive included the introduction of 'contracting out' in 1983 where the government required the NHS to put its 'hotel services' such as catering, cleaning, and laundry out to private tender, and the 'in house' suppliers were forced to compete with private sector firms to win the contracts. A rather different element of the efficiency drive involved the introduction of performance indicators within a system of central performance management. Hospitals were judged on simplistic indicators such as 'length of stay' rather than more complex measures such as the impact of that hospital stay on the patient's health. In 1983, the government asked the managing director of Sainsbury, Roy Griffiths, to look into the NHS. The 'Griffiths Report' consisted of a 24 page letter that was termed 'the most important single change to the NHS since 1948' (Timmins, 1996, p. 409). It recommended the introduction of 'general managers' along the lines of the private sector who would be responsible for performance.

However, a more important change to the NHS was seen in the 1989 White Paper, *Working for Patients* (Department of Health, 1989), which formed part of the 1990 National Health Service and Community Care Act. This introduced an 'internal' or 'quasi' market into the NHS. In the 'purchaser/ provider split', district health authorities became purchasers or commissioners of care, while hospitals became providers. In a similar fashion to the hotel services, providers competed for contracts from the commissioners. Some GPs were allowed to become 'general practitioner fund holders' (GPFH) where they were given a budget to commission selected treatments for their patients. Supporters of the reforms argued that these GPFHs tended to get their patients treated more quickly by providers, but critics argued that this constituted a 'two-tier service' that undermined the equity principle of the NHS. Finally, in 1995 an experimental scheme of 'Total Purchasing Pilots' (TPPs) was introduced, where fund holders could purchase virtually the entire package of NHS services on behalf of their health authorities (see Klein, 2010, pp. 174–6).

However, the level of market operation was unclear. Most of the contracts can be seen as wholesale/internal contracts (Powell, 2003) as they were placed as 'block' contracts by commissioning managers rather than by individual patients, and stimulated competition largely within the NHS rather than between the NHS and the private sector. Indeed, despite the aim of the reform to 'increase choice', individual patients largely saw reduced choice as most GPs lost the (theoretical) right to refer to any NHS provider. Rather than the objective of 'money following the patients', patients largely followed the money. The exceptions to this were that GPFHs could refer to any provider, and there were a limited number of 'extra contractual referrals' (Timmins, 2012). Klein (2010, p. 184) stresses a 'managed market' with the emphasis on contestability rather than competition. Alain Enthoven, the American academic often credited with the idea behind the reforms, claimed that, ranking market forces on a scale of zero (complete central planning) to 10 (the regulated but relatively free American commercial economy), the NHS got to between 2 and 3 for a year or two but then fell back (Enthoven, 1999, p. 58, cited in Powell, 2003).

Despite the stress on markets, other modes such as hierarchy and networks had not disappeared. Indeed, Klein (2010, pp. 170–1) points to 'a new hierarchy of command' that displayed 'another cycle in the NHS's oscillating progress between devolution and centralisation, and back again, which had characterised the service ever since 1948'. Moreover, talk of 'markets' was toned down by later Conservative Secretaries of State (e.g. Ham, 2009, pp. 49–50). It is generally claimed that the impact of the reforms did not produce the degree of measurable change predicted by proponents and feared by opponents (Mays *et al.*, 2011), or disappointed their advocates and opponents alike, producing neither a transformation nor catastrophe (Klein, 2010, p. 179), as the incentives were too weak and the constraints were too strong (Le Grand *et al.*, 1998, p. 130, cited in Mays *et al.*, 2011, p. 49; see also Ham, 2009, pp. 43–5).

CONTROVERSY AND DEBATE

Some commentators have argued that the NHS contains a mix of 'governance' types such as markets (competition between organisations), networks (coordination or collaboration between clinicians or organisations) or hierarchy (top down 'command and control' orders and targets from the centre) (cf. Harrison and McDonald, 2008, pp. 80–93). What are the advantages and disadvantages of each type?

The publication of *The Health of the Nation* White Paper (Department of Health, 1992) is said to have marked a significant shift in public policy (Klein,

2010, p. 167). There was certainly a rhetorical commitment to health as opposed to health care, and the document contained some 25 specific targets. However, critics pointed out that the targets appeared to be largely extrapolations of existing trends, and issues such as government action on structural issues such as unemployment and poverty, along with discussion of health inequalities, were missing.

New Labour health policy (1997–2010)

It has been noted that the incoming New Labour government was 'clearer about what it was opposed to – the fragmentation of the NHS market – than what it was for' (Ham, 2009, p. 51). The 'third way' term that broadly described New Labour's social policy (Powell, 1999) was applied to the NHS:

> In paving the way for the new NHS the Government is committed to building on what has worked but discarding what has failed. There will be no return to the old centralised command and control system of the 1970s . . . But nor will there be a continuation of the divisive internal market system of the 1990s . . . Instead there will be a 'third way' of running the NHS – a system based on partnership and driven by performance.
>
> (Department of Health, 1997, p. 10)

Labour's objective of 'abolishing the internal market' was problematic in a number of ways. First, there were some doubts over their chronological narrative of moves from hierarchy to market to network. It was unclear to what extent the NHS had seen 'ideal type' command and control hierarchies or competitive markets, and New Labour's partnerships or networks were also to prove somewhat elusive. Timmins (2012, p. 18) writes that if the 1990s was a mix of two steps forward, one step back and then some reinvigoration of the market-like mechanisms, the arrival of the 'traditional' or 'Old Labour' Frank Dobson as Health Secretary was a distinct step away from them. His tenure between 1997 and 1999 saw the most determined effort in NHS history to run the service by 'command and control' from Whitehall. Moreover, Dobson strongly discouraged what limited use the NHS was making of private hospitals.

Second, New Labour claimed to abolish the market but kept the purchaser/provider split. This was part of its commitment to 'renew the NHS as a genuinely national service'. It abolished GPFH in order to eliminate the 'two-tier service' and increase equity, but attempted to universalise the responsiveness of GPFH to all through creating primary care commissioning (about 500 primary care groups, with average populations of about 100,000; later to become primary care trusts, which were reduced to about 100 in 2003; Klein 2010: 242). As Klein (2010, p. 193) puts it, while fundholding was abolished the role of primary commissioning was expanded: in effect, fundholding was universalised. New Labour also introduced the National Institute of Clinical Excellence (NICE) and National Service Frameworks (NSF) to increase the 'national-ness' of the NHS. NICE would decide whether new treatments and drugs were cost-effective, and so should be available to all within the NHS, or not cost-effective, in which case they would not be available to anyone. The NSF aimed to lay down more common ways of working to ensure that best practice was universal. Finally, New Labour introduced the Commission for Health Improvement, which was essentially an inspectorate/regulator to oversee performance.

In an attempt to rid itself of its 'tax and spend' image, New Labour promised that it would not raise income tax and would stick to Conservative spending plans. However, it was clear that the financial pressure on the NHS was continuing. In an echo of Mrs Thatcher's announcement on her 1989 review of the NHS on a TV programme, Tony Blair announced a significant rise in NHS spending, with a commitment to bring it to the average of the European Union, on breakfast TV in January 2000.

However, this investment would need to be matched by reform, which was unveiled in July 2000 in *The NHS Plan* (Department of Health, 2000). Thus the ten-year plan (Department of Health, 1997) gave way to another ten-year plan (Department of Health, 2000) only three years later. The NHS super-tanker was about to change course under the command of the new modernising Secretary of State, Alan Milburn. The NHS Plan was a curious mixture of commitments without an overall clear narrative. However, it laid the foundations for a new architecture of the NHS, or perhaps a revival and extension of the Conservative market architecture (Ham, 2009, p. 64; Mays *et al.*, 2011, p. 1; Timmins, 2012, p. 17). Klein (2010, pp. 218–19) notes a change in direction, or perhaps a tectonic shift following *Delivering the NHS Plan* of 2002, where patients not GPs (as in the 1997 model) were to be in the driving seat (Klein, 2010, p. 218). Greener (2009, p. 220) claims that the biggest turnaround in Labour policy since 1997 was the revival of the marketplace for care in the NHS.

> **STOP AND THINK**
>
> ■ How much choice do you want in health care?
>
> ■ Do you think it is important to be able to have a say in the choice of hospital, clinician or treatment?

One important difference from the Conservative market was that Labour introduced a fixed price tariff for procedures rather than the variable price that resulted from contract negotiations between purchaser and provider in the earlier period. This 'transactional' reform was misleadingly termed 'payment by results', as payment was by volume or activity rather than results. Moreover, as late as 2009–10, only £26 billion of English NHS activity of a total of £105 billion was paid for under payment by results (House of Commons Health Committee, 2010).

New Labour gradually rolled out greater choice for patients, culminating in a total 'free choice' (which included private hospitals) from 2008. The government increased the plurality or diversity of supply. NHS foundation trusts were set up as public benefit corporations – a sort of half-way house between the public and private sectors – and they also received additional freedoms such as being able to set their own pay rates, and to make surpluses and losses so long as those surpluses were spent to the benefit of NHS patients. However, they remained subject to oversight by a regulator known as Monitor, which had extensive powers to intervene, replacing boards and chief executives where necessary. Foundation trust status was rolled out gradually, encouraged but not imposed (Timmins, 2012, pp. 18–19). New Labour 'crossed the Rubicon' by ending Old Labour's class war with private medicine. It signed a 'concordat' for private hospitals to carry out NHS work (Klein, 2010, pp. 236–8). Moreover, the private sector was invited to run 'independent surgical treatment centres'. These 'surgical factories' had a threefold role: first to increase capacity to help cut NHS waiting times; second, to provide NHS hospitals with an element of competition; and third, to undercut the UK's indigenous private hospitals, which frequently charged 30–50 per cent above the tariff (Timmins, 2012, p. 19).

Timmins (2012, p. 20) notes that there was heady talk that 15 per cent or more of NHS waiting-list type treatments could one day be provided by the private sector, although the proportion in fact has yet to reach 5 per cent.

In 2005, in another example of a step forward following a step back, there was a 'resurrection' of GPFH as 'practice-based commissioning', which allowed GPs to take full control of the entire local budget, although primary care rusts would remain responsible for signing the cheques (Klein, 2010, p. 233). Like GPFH, the scheme was voluntary, and relatively few primary care trusts took it up. In October, David Colin-Thomé, the health department's lead doctor on primary care, declared it to be a 'corpse', which he judged was 'not for resuscitation' (cited in Timmins, 2012, p. 20). The critical view of practice-based commissioning was part of a broader view that commissioning as a whole had not lived up to its promise in the two decades since *Working for Patients*, with critical reports from bodies such as the Commons Health Select Committee, the King's Fund, and the Audit Commission (see Klein, 2010; Mays *et al.*, 2011; Timmins, 2012).

Great stress was placed on the role of regulation, which resulted in several institutional and title changes (Commission for Health Improvement to Healthcare Commission to Care Quality Commission). Some commentators claim that regulation or performance management was the dominant instrument for New Labour until about 2002. This consisted of a series of targets (e.g. reductions in waiting time for treatments, and hospital infection rates such as MRSA) and 'star ratings', with the best ('three star') performers rewarded with a degree of 'earned autonomy'. This agenda was shaped significantly by 'events'. Klein (2010, pp. 198–200) points to an inquiry by the General Medical Council on the Bristol Royal Infirmary, which had a high mortality rate for small children undergoing cardiac surgery. Two doctors were

> ## STOP AND THINK
>
> Does it matter whether 'NHS patients' are treated in a state (NHS) or private hospital so long as the treatment is of high quality and is free at the point of use?

struck off the Medical Register, but the broader focus was that the medical profession was on trial, with the system of professional self-regulation found 'guilty'. An investigation by Sir Ian Kennedy produced 198 recommendations (Klein, 2010, p. 230). This led to the government's promise to place 'quality at the heart of the new NHS' (a promise largely forgotten, only to be recycled by Lord Darzi a decade later; see below). Warm words about quality could not prevent future scandals at institutions such as Stafford and Winterbourne (see Chapter 12). A number of investigations into 'excess mortality' at Stafford Hospital uncovered 'a catalogue of appalling management and failures at every level' where 'the quality police had been caught napping' (Klein, 2010, pp. 269–71). The Francis Report of the Mid Staffordshire NHS Foundation Trust Public Inquiry (2013) pointed to serious and systemic failures within the organisation and in the wider 'checks and balances' of the 'plethora of agencies, scrutiny groups, commissioners, regulators and professional bodies' in the wider NHS system, and produced 290 recommendations. There was an element of history repeating itself as some of the major issues such as the culture of the organisation, leadership failures, 'duty of candour', and a failure to put patients first were clearly highlighted in the Kennedy Report some 12 years earlier (see above).

> **STOP AND THINK**
>
> The Kennedy and Francis Reports together produced nearly 500 recommendations. What would be your top five recommendations to prevent another 'Bristol' or 'Stafford'?

This complex system was summarised in the 'Next Steps' document (Department of Health, 2005) as a 'coherent and mutually supporting set of reforms' composed of four elements: supply side (more diverse providers, e.g. private, independent sector treatment centres, foundation trusts); demand side (choice, voice, commissioning); transactional (money following the patient; payment by results); and system reform (system management and regulation). However, it can be argued that the reforms were unbalanced rather than being mutually reinforcing, with the centre of gravity being more on the supply than on the demand side (Mays *et al.*, 2011; Powell *et al.*, 2011).

One controversial 'supply side' reform not discussed in the document was the 'Private Finance Initiative' (PFI). The Conservatives introduced the PFI as a way of encouraging the private sector to undertake infrastructure projects such as building new roads and schools. The private sector builds and runs facilities, and the state leases them typically over 30–40 years, paying for them with 'mortgage payments'. It was little used in the NHS, and condemned by the Labour opposition as 'privatisation'. However, the Labour government soon embraced PFI for projects including the NHS, not least as it allowed new facilities to be built while keeping the finance off the 'public books' (i.e. not appearing in national accounts). Soon PFI became 'the only game in town'; in other words, the only way to build a new hospital was through PFI. This led to the largest building programme in NHS history, although critics pointed out the long-term payments of 'mortgage' and running costs were very expensive (e.g. Greener, 2009, pp. 216–19; Ham, 2009, pp. 86–7; Klein, 2010, p. 238).

With Gordon Brown replacing Tony Blair as Prime Minister in June 2007, there was some uncertainty about the direction of health policy. On the one hand, there were some steps away from markets, with a scaling back of the independent sector treatment centre (ISTC) programme; and the later scheme of NHS as 'preferred provider', where NHS organisations were to be given a first and then a second chance to improve before their services were put out to tender.

Moreover, the 'Next Steps' led to the 'Next Stage' with the production of reports from Lord Ara Darzi, a surgeon who had been appointed a Labour Health Minister. Darzi's major themes were quality and clinical engagement (e.g. Ham, 2009, pp. 71–2; Klein, 2010, pp. 256–9).

The impact of the New Labour reforms have been heavily debated (Ham, 2009, pp. 72–5; Klein, 2010, pp. 247–8; Mays *et al.*, 2011). According to Julian Le Grand, Blair's health policy advisor, it would be hard to resist the impression that on balance the reforms have worked (cited in Mays *et al.*, 2011, p. xiii). However, Ham (2009, pp. 72–5) writes that early broadly positive assessments gave way to more cautious and critical judgements. There were certainly major gains in issues such as the large reduction in hospital waiting times, but it is difficult to say whether these are associated more with reform mechanisms or increased investment. However, comparisons between England and other parts of the UK, which tended not to use market mechanisms, suggest that increased investment alone may not have had a significant impact (e.g. Mays *et al.*, 2011). Issues over investment became more important, as with the financial crisis the NHS years of feast turned to famine. In the summer of 2009, the NHS Chief Executive, David Nicholson, warned that the NHS would have to make 'efficiency savings' of £20 billion, or about 20 per cent of the 2009–10 budget by 2013–14 (Klein, 2010, p. 261). It was difficult to see how the so-called 'Nicholson challenge' could be met without job losses in such a labour-intensive sector as health care.

Initially, at least, New Labour took significant interest in wider public health issues (see Harrison and McDonald, 2008, pp. 163–6; Hunter, 2008; Ham, 2009). It established the Acheson Committee to update the findings of the Black Report. Acheson stressed similar 'structural' issues to Black, and produced 39 recommendations (the so-called 39 steps), of which all but three focused outside the NHS. New Labour's 1998 Green Paper on public health, *Our Healthier Nation*, stressed a third-way approach. It stated that 'the Government is setting out a third way between the old extremes of individual victim blaming on the one hand and nanny state engineering on the other hand . . . Our third way is a national contract for better health' (Department of Health, 1998, p. 5). Its aim was to improve the health of the population as a whole, but to improve the health of the worst off in society more so as to narrow the health gap. However, although the document led to the first Minister for Public Health and the setting up of health improvement programmes at local levels, it did not set national health inequality targets. These broad themes were continued in the White Paper of the following year, *Saving Lives* (Department of Health, 1999) The first national health inequality targets were set out in 2001 (Klein, 2010, p. 245). These involved reducing health inequalities by social class and by area by 10 per cent, although these ambitious targets have not been met. Hunter (2008, p. 142) writes that the growing embrace of market-style thinking and neoliberal principles from around 2002 onwards, stressing individual lifestyle issues and downplaying structural determinants of health and the role of government in tackling them, can be seen in the second public health White Paper of 2004, *Choosing Health*.

This may be a little pessimistic. Ham (2009, p. 93) sees more continuity: following the commitments included in *Choosing Health* (Department of Health, 2004), the government created powers in the Health Act of 2006 to implement a ban on smoking in public places from July 2007. Moreover, Sir Michael Marmot was invited in 2008 to set out the most effective evidence-based strategies for reducing health inequalities in England (Marmot, 2010). However, much of the report echoed the earlier Black and Acheson Reports. For example, it is stated that social gradients in health exist, and that reducing health inequalities is a matter of fairness and social justice. Reducing health inequalities will require action on six policy objectives, which include giving every child the best start in life, creating fair employment and good work for all, ensuring a healthy standard of living for all, and strengthening the role and impact of ill health prevention. It was unlikely that yet another rehearsal of the evidence would result in a radically new policy direction.

According to Ham (2009, pp. 95–6), progress in implementing public health policies under Labour shows a mixed picture. He considers that although there has been a long-term improvement in the health of the population, and that the most important public health measure was arguably the use of legislation to ban smoking in public places, significant challenges, such as continuing health inequalities and tackling new risks like obesity, remain. On the other hand, Hunter (2008, ch. 6) paints a more pessimistic picture, pointing to some modest gains, but also to a worsening trend of health inequality.

Coalition health policy (2010–)

The centrepiece of the health policy of the Conservative-Liberal Democrat Coalition government of 2010 is the Health and Social Care Act 2012, which has been seen as by far the most controversial piece of NHS legislation in more than two decades, and is widely regarded as a 'car crash' of both politics and policy-making (Timmins, 2012).

The manifestoes of all three major parties focused heavily on cutting management costs (or 'red tape') and achieving efficiency gains. All endorsed at least a degree of choice, competition, and use of the private sector in the provision of NHS care. The Liberal Democrat manifesto included a pledge to scrap strategic health authorities, and to replace primary care trusts with elected local health boards – promises that were eventually to have a big impact on Coalition plans (Timmins, 2012, p. 41)

The 2010 general election produced a Conservative-Liberal Democrat Coalition government. As Timmins (2012) points out, the 2012 Act is uniquely identified with the Conservative Secretary of State for Health, Andrew Lansley, but without the Liberal Democrats it would have been a very different bill. Timmins points out that the Coalition's now partly forgotten 'programme for government' – cooked up purely by the politicians in Downing Street over 12 days immediately after the election in May 2010 – radically reshaped the Health Secretary's plans.

The Coalition attempted to 'square the circle' between the different approaches of markets (Conservative) and democracy (Liberal Democrats). The result was a synthesis of the two parties' opposing philosophies (markets versus democracy); or (less kindly) a 'policy fudge', a 'half horse/half donkey', or a 'a cut and shut' job (the process where the good back half of a crashed car is welded to the good front half of another wreck to produce a vehicle that may look roadworthy but is in fact potentially lethal). The document also contained the 'pledge that had gone missing in the Tory manifesto' of no more 'top-down reorganisations' (Timmins, 2012, pp. 47–8).

However, back in the department, the programme for government was regarded quite simply as 'a disaster'. Lansley essentially ignored the document, and attempted to find a way around it. This involved the abolition of primary care trusts, and therefore strategic health authorities, with their role of overseeing the PCT commissioning role, and overseeing NHS trusts, as all hospitals were intended to become foundation trusts.

The White Paper, *Liberating the NHS* (Department of Health, 2010a), produced far faster than any previous health white paper, in a record 60 days after the Coalition government was formed – announced that family doctors were to take over the commissioning of NHS care. Their work was to be overseen by a new national commissioning board. The entire existing superstructure of the NHS (the 10 regional health authorities and 152 primary care trusts) was to be abolished. A new economic regulator was planned to oversee choice and competition, both of which were to be extended. From the private and voluntary sectors, 'any willing provider' was to be allowed to supply NHS care at agreed NHS prices. The existing public health body, the Health Protection Agency, was to be absorbed into the health department, but with an appreciable chunk of the public health budget transferred to local authorities. Health and Wellbeing Boards were to be created in local government to join up the commissioning of NHS services, social care and prevention. Finally, a new patient's voice organisation, 'Healthwatch', was to be created.

The resulting Health and Social Care Bill was vast – more than 280 clauses plus 22 schedules, some 550 pages in all – three times the size of the 1946 Act that founded the service. The opposition to the White Paper and subsequent Bill over the next 20 months forced the government onto the back foot. For example, in early March Lansley finally announced that he would table amendments to the Bill including to rule out price competition (Timmins, 2012, p. 88). In an unprecedented 'pause' and 'listening' exercise, the government set up the independent 'Future Forum'. The government accepted just about every one of its recommendations. These included Monitor becoming not just a competition regulator but also being charged with promoting 'integrated care'. Instead of 'promoting competition', its task was to be tackling 'anti-competitive practices'. A token hospital doctor and nurse were to be put on each Clinical Commissioning Group, with the idea of pure GP consortia now consigned to history (Timmins, 2012, p. 99). There were more concessions on issues such as the 'private patient cap', with the government effectively capping a trust's income from private patients at 49 per cent in an attempt to offset the charge of 'privatisation' and to try to constrain the application of EU competition law (Timmins, 2012, p. 105).

As the Bill headed back to the Commons for its final approval, some 2,000 amendments had been made, although the overwhelming majority were technical, such as name changes. Timmins (2012, p. 118) notes that 50 days of debate in Parliament had produced a piece of legislation even longer, more complex, and in some areas appreciably less clear than the original huge edifice. He continues that there were perhaps three new elements to the original plan: the insistence that all GPs had to be in a GP consortium – now a clinical commissioning group; the extent to which Lansley wanted to turn the NHS into a version of a regulated industry, creating a form of self-improving machine that required minimal ministerial oversight; and his determination to legislate for all this in such a way that it would take further legislation to change the key building blocks in the new dispensation. Added to that were speed and the complete dismantling of the primary care trusts and strategic health authorities – a by-product of coalition politics. It was the combination of those five factors that turned evolution into something that can be seen as revolution.

The Coalition's public health White Paper, *Healthy Lives, Healthy People* (Department of Health, 2010b), promised a radical shift in the way we tackle public health challenges, and a 'new era for public health'. It stated that localism would be at the heart of this system, with local government and local communities central to improving health and wellbeing for their populations and tackling inequalities. A dedicated new public health service, Public Health England, was to be set up, and there would be ring-fenced public health funding from within the overall NHS budget. It is far from clear what impact this would have. The revived role of local authorities is potentially very significant, but a greater stress on localism broadly tends to increase inequalities between areas. Moreover, the claim in the 'Foreword' by Andrew Lansley that 'it is simply not possible to promote healthier lifestyles through Whitehall diktat and nannying about the way people should live', and 'we need a new approach that empowers individuals to make healthy choices and gives communities the tools to address their own, particular needs' has clear resonances of New Labour's 'third way' (Blair, 1998) and *Choosing Health* (Department of Health, 2004) documents.

It is clearly too early to provide much rigorous evaluation of the Coalition government's health policy. According to the Secretary of State's Annual Report (2012), the health service performed well during 2011–12. It maintained or improved performance against a range of quality indicators set out in the NHS Operating Framework, while meeting the financial challenge. It claimed that waiting times remained low and stable in 2011–12. Over 90 per cent of admitted and 95 per cent of non-admitted patients were treated within 18 weeks of referral. On infection control, the NHS made significant improvements over that year, with MRSA bloodstream infections and *C. difficile* infections at their lowest levels since mandatory surveillance for each was introduced. However, the document continued that, 'Whilst the 2011/12 performance data has undoubtedly been positive', we face a number of significant challenges. Compared with other countries, we continue to lag on performance on some key outcomes including life expectancy for women, cancer survival, and conditions related to obesity. Similarly, the Chief Medical Officer's Report (Davies, 2012) drew attention to a number of key issues including liver disease, which is the only major cause of mortality and morbidity that is on the increase in England while decreasing among our European neighbours. According to the King's Fund 'mid term' assessment, despite the pressures on the NHS budget, waiting times for hospital services generally remained steady, with median waits for hospital services at the end of 2011, including inpatients, outpatients and diagnostics, very close to the levels recorded in 2009, although waiting times for treatment in accident and emergency (A&E) departments had risen. In short, it appears that the performance of the NHS is holding up despite financial pressures and the disruption of reforms. However, cracks are emerging – for example, with deterioration in waiting times in A&E, and significant variations remaining by geography and socio-economic status in access to care, health outcomes, and the quality of care received (Gregory *et al.*, 2012, p. 56).

However, it is also important to focus on more qualitative aspects of care. A series of reports have drawn attention to concerns over aspects of the quality of care. For example, the Patients' Association (2012) published its fourth consecutive annual collection of some of the worst stories from their Helpline. In reaction to this document, NHS Confederation Chief Executive Mike Farrar commented that, 'We should never excuse poor standards of care and we need to take bold and decisive action when we see what is happening' (http://www.publicservice.co.uk/news_story?id21522). However, he did not explain what this 'bold and decisive' action would be, or why it has not been taken in the past.

The Care Quality Commission (2012, pp. 40–1) reported that in 2012 some 27 per cent of services that the CQC had inspected were not meeting at least one standard on 31 March 2012. Some 10 per cent of NHS hospitals did not meet the standard on treating people with respect and dignity, and involving them in their care. These issues are not 'new' (see the hospital scandals in the 1960s, and Bristol and Stafford hospitals, above), but they do give an important 'human' dimension to 'dry' statistics.

Discussion

Debates over issues such as finance, structure, and the principles of the NHS have raged for over 60 years. Over much of the period there were claims that the NHS was 'under-funded' even though determining the correct level of funding was problematic. This issue largely went away for a brief period from about 2000 to 2009 during New Labour's significant increase in NHS expenditure, only to return with the new austerity associated with the financial crisis.

Timmins (2012, p. 13) notes that after a period of marked stability between 1948 and 1974 which saw no material change, the service has since been subjected to something like 20 reorganisations, depending on precisely how you count them, which is on average around one every two years. This appears to result from the belief that there is a 'perfect' structure out there waiting to be implemented, and that an 'organisational fix' of 'one more push' would find it. However, the perfect structure remains elusive (cf. Hunter, 2011). This may be partly due to many of the changes such as GP fundholding and foundation trusts being gradual and voluntary. As Timmins (2012, p. 16) puts it, Clarke's proposals for NHS trusts and for GP fundholding, while revolutionary in concept, were evolutionary in implementation. In principle, this provides a 'laboratory' or 'natural experiment' that can evaluate impact. However, this was undermined by the second factor of a continuous process of hyperactivity of change, where evaluators often found that the policy being evaluated changed or disappeared before the end of the evaluation. This might be seen like an oscillating pendulum that changes back and forth between centralisation and devolution or large and small health organisations (cf. Klein, 2010, pp. 170–1). However, perhaps re-inventing the wheel due to a lack of organisational memory is a better description. For example, Timmins (2012, p. 16) notes that the Conservatives' Total Purchasing Pilots (TPP) 'look remarkably like the GP consortia that Andrew Lansley proposed in his white paper', with the crucial difference that they did not directly control the cheque book.

As Timmins (2012, p. 34) points out, few of the elements of New Labour's revived market such as foundation trusts, independent sector treatment centres, and the search for a failure regime were seen through consistently, as ministers chopped and changed and policy was battered by events. According to Lansley (cited in Timmins, 2012, pp. 34–5):

> There was never a consistent programme of reform carried through over a period of time . . . What I set out to do was entrench a consistent and coherent structure of reforms so that the NHS would be able to take a more autonomous long-term view of their own role . . . [knowing] that things would not change just at the behest of a change of secretary of state, or even more a change of government.

Timmins (2012, p. 125) concludes that this might, after all – and despite the current consensus view among commentators, analysts, and many senior figures in the NHS – prove over the long run to be not only the most successful piece of NHS legislation since the founding act in 1946, but its last major structural reorganisation, at least for many years.

However, despite many twists and turns, and steps forwards and back-wards, the direction of travel over the past 30 years or so is fairly clear. Some commentators claim that there is a great deal of continuity between Conservative, New Labour, and Coalition health policy (Hunter, 2011; Timmins, 2012, p. 123). As the former Conservative Health Secretary, Kenneth Clarke put it in 2008 (cited in Timmins, 2012, p. 6):

> Labour secretaries of state have got away with introducing private sector providers into the NHS on a scale which would have led the Labour Party onto the streets in demonstration if a Conservative government had ever tried it. In the late 1980s I would have said it is politically impossible to do what we are now doing. I strongly approve.

Assessment

There are a number of possible evaluation templates (see Powell, 1997; Ham, 2009; Klein, 2010: Mays *et al.*, 2011): temporal (is the NHS getting better over time?); intrinsic (is it delivering its aims, or being consistent with its principles?); and extrinsic/comparative (how does it compare with other health systems?).

The NHS generally scores well on temporal evaluation. Health has clearly increased over the past 60 years or so, although how much of that is due to changes in medical science such as new drugs and treatment, or environmental factors outside the NHS is difficult to say. Moreover, there are clearly new health challenges such as obesity, with the UK being the most obese nation in Western Europe (Department of Health, 2010b; see also Davies, 2012; Secretary of State for Health, 2012).

Evaluations of the NHS or changing NHS policies depend on a number of factors, including which evaluation criterion (such as efficiency or equity) is chosen (Powell, 1997; Boyne *et al.*, 2003; Mays *et al.*, 2011). For example, according to the King's Fund (Gregory *et al.*, 2012), there are nine dimensions of care that makes an effective health care system: access, patient safety, promoting health, managing long-term conditions, clinical effectiveness, patient experience, equity, efficiency, and accountability. There are often some tensions between the different criteria of the 'balanced score-card' (cf. Ham, 2009, ch. 10; Klein, 2010, pp. 271–3, ch. 10). Debates about the principles of the NHS are most problematic. There is often a tendency to 'over-read' changes. Timmins (2012, p. 15) notes that critics were warning

> ### STOP AND THINK
>
> - How should health resources be rationed – for example, between young and old people, and different parts of the country?
>
> - Who should decide – politicians, clinicians, the public?
>
> - Should very elderly people be entitled to expensive treatments?
>
> - Should resources be directed away from those who some say may have contributed to their own unhealthy position, for example through the use of alcohol, illegal drugs, etc.?

that the Conservative changes marked 'the end of the NHS as we know it', taking it down a road towards US-style privatised care. Among the first to 'cry wolf', predicting 'the end of the NHS', was Bevan in about 1952, and yet over 60 years later it is still around. There is also a tendency to point to a perfect imagined past, forgetting scandals such as at some long-stay hospitals in the 1960s and 1970s. It may be unfair to judge the NHS on what it gets things wrong rather than what it does right, but a series of scandals such as Ely, Bristol, Shipman, Alder Hey, Stafford, Winterbourne, and so on show that every period of the NHS has experienced some serious deficiencies.

Finally, the NHS can be compared with other health systems (Hunter, 2008, pp. 27–31; Ham, 2009, chs. 7, 12; Klein, 2010). First, the English NHS can be compared with other systems within the UK. There is some evidence that England has demonstrated greater improvement on some indicators, particularly reducing waiting lists, than other countries, although some commentators have attributed this more to 'command and control' rather than market mechanisms (see, for example, Mays *et al.*, 2011, pp. 131–2). Second, the English NHS can be compared with health systems outside the UK. Different studies at different times stressing different measures have produced rather different results. A World Health Organisation (WHO) study in 2000 ranked the NHS 18th out of 191 countries. However, this study is dated and its methodology has been heavily criticised. The NHS was ranked first among six countries in the annual Commonwealth Fund study in 2007, and above average in the 'Eurobarometer' survey in 2007 of public attitudes to health care systems. The most recent survey (Commonwealth Fund, 2010) placed the NHS in second place overall behind the Netherlands, but ranked first on the criteria of effective care, cost-related access, and efficiency. Although there have been improvements in recent years, the NHS does less well on some indicators such as life expectancy, avoidable mortality, cancer survival rates, and MRSA infection rates in hospitals (see, for example, Davies, 2012; Secretary of State for Health, 2012). For example, it was ranked six out of seven (with the USA in last place) in terms of 'long, healthy, productive lives' (Commonwealth Fund, 2010).

Conclusions

Health policy has changed significantly since the foundation of the NHS over 60 years ago, and changed rapidly in the last 30 years or so. However, despite the policy froth, rhetorical differences between political parties, and some steps forwards and backwards, there appears to be a clear direction of travel (cf. Baggott, 2011; Timmins, 2012). There has been an increasing emphasis on market mechanisms of choice and competition, with moves from a largely internal/wholesale administration towards a more external/retail market (Powell, 2003). Within public health, there has been a similar broad move towards greater 'individual responsibility' of making 'healthy choices'. However, it is also important to stress broad continuities within health policy.

First, 'health policy' continues to be dominated by 'health care policy', with more stress on curative health care and less on prevention and care. Second, while means or mechanisms may have changed, ends or principles have seen greater continuity, albeit under greater strain and with some changing emphases. The NHS still delivers a largely comprehensive service that remains largely free at the point of use. At the time of writing, the NHS is under increasing pressure and there has been some deterioration in aspects such as increased waiting times and rationing of procedures. It is less clear whether these are linked more with financial pressures, changing mechanisms or the disruption of change. However, whatever level of continuity or change, it can be said with some certainty than debates over the future of the NHS (e.g. Hunter, 2008, ch. 7; Ham, 2009, ch. 13; Klein, 2010, ch. 10; Mays *et al.*, 2011, ch. 10) will continue.

Summary

This chapter has outlined the development of health policy in Britain, examining some of the major issues around health and health care, including:

- The continuing dominance of 'health policy' by 'health care policy', with more stress on curative health care and less on prevention and care.
- The rapid changes in health policy over the last 30 years or so, but with a fairly clear broad direction of travel.
- A changing mix of means or mechanisms of markets, hierarchies, and networks, with an increasing emphasis on market mechanisms of choice and competition.
- Greater continuity of stated ends or principles, albeit under greater strain and with some changing emphases, with the NHS still delivering a largely comprehensive service that remains largely free at the point of use.
- The difficulty of a clear assessment or evaluation, due to differing ideological positions, criteria, and problematic data.

References

Baggott, R. (2011) 'Conservative health policy', in H. Bochel (ed.) *The Conservative Party and Social Policy*, Policy Press, Bristol.

Blair, T (1998) *The Third Way: New Politics for The New Century*, Fabian Society, London.

Boyne, G., Farrell, C., Law, J., Powell, M. and Walker, R. (2003) *Evaluating Public Management Reforms*, Open University Press, Buckingham.

British Medical Journal (2007) 'BMJ readers chose the "sanitary revolution" as greatest medical advance since 1840', *British Medical Journal*, Vol. 334, No. 7585, p. 111.

Care Quality Commission (2012) *The State of Health Care and Adult Social Care in England in 2011/12*, The Stationery Office, London.

Commonwealth Fund (2010) *US ranks last among seven countries on health system performance based on measures of quality, efficiency, access, equity, and healthy lives*, available at http://www.commonwealthfund.org/~/media/Files/News/News%20Releases/2010/Jun/Mirror%20Mirror/Mirror%20Mirror%20Release%20FINAL%20%2061410%20rev3%20v2%202.pdf

Davies, S.C (2012) *Annual Report of the Chief Medical Officer, Volume One, 2011, On the State of the Public's Health*, Department of Health, London.

Department of Health (1989) *Working for Patients*, Department of Health, London.

Department of Health (1992) *The Health of the Nation*, HMSO, London.

Department of Health (1997) *The New NHS: Modern, Dependable*, The Stationery Office, London.

Department of Health (1998) *Our Healthier Nation: A Contract for Health*, The Stationery Office, London.

Department of Health (1999) *Saving Lives: Our Healthier Nation*, The Stationery Office, London.

Department of Health (2000) *The NHS Plan: A Plan for Investment, A Plan for Reform*, The Stationery Office, London.

Department of Health (2004) *Choosing Health: Making Healthy Choices Easier*, The Stationery Office, London.

Department of Health (2005) *Health Reform in England: Update and Next Steps*, The Stationery Office, London.

Department of Health (2010a) *Equity and Excellence: Liberating the NHS*, The Stationery Office, London.

Department of Health (2010b) *Healthy Lives, Healthy People*, The Stationery Office, London.

Francis, R. (Chair) (2013) *Report of the Mid Staffordshire NHS Foundation Trust Public Inquiry: Executive Summary*, HC 947, The Stationery Office, London.

Fraser, D. (1984) *The Evolution of the British Welfare State*, Macmillan, Basingstoke.

Gilbert, B.B. (1966) *The Evolution of National Insurance in Great Britain*, Michael Joseph, London.

Greener, I. (2009) *Healthcare in the UK*, Policy Press, Bristol.

Gregory, S., Dixon, A. and Ham, C. (eds.) (2012) *Health Policy Under the Coalition Government: A Mid-term Assessment*, King's Fund, London.

Griffiths, R. (Chair) (1983) *NHS Management Inquiry*, HMSO, London, available at http://www.sochealth.co.uk/history/griffiths.htm.

Ham, C. (2009) *Health Policy in Britain* (6th edn.), Palgrave Macmillan, Basingstoke.

Harrison, S. and McDonald, R. (2008) *The Politics of Healthcare in Britain*, Sage, London.

House of Commons Health Committee (2010) *Public Expenditure of Health and Personal Social Services 2009*, HC 269-1, The Stationery Office, London.

Hunter, D. (2008) *The Health Debate*, Policy Press, Bristol.

Hunter, D. (2011) 'Change of government: one more big bang health care reform in England's National Health Service', *International Journal of Health Services*, Vol. 41, No. 1, pp. 159–74.

Klein, R. (2010) *The New Politics of the NHS* (6th edn.), Radcliffe Publishing, Abingdon.

Marmot, M. (2010) *Fair Society, Healthy Lives*, The Stationery Office, London.

Mays, N., Dixon, A. and Jones, L. (eds.) (2011) *Understanding New Labour's Market Reforms of the English NHS*, King's Fund, London.

Patients' Association (2012) *Stories from the Present, Lessons for the Future*, Patients' Association, London.

Powell, M. (1997) *Evaluating the National Health Service*, Open University Press, Buckingham.

Powell, M. (ed.) (1999) *New Labour, New Welfare State?*, Policy Press, Bristol.

Powell, M. (2003) 'Quasi-markets in British health policy: a longue durée perspective', *Social Policy and Administration*, Vol. 37, No. 7, pp. 725–41.

Powell, M., Millar, R., Mulla, A., Brown, H., Fewtrell, C., McLeod, H. *et al.* (2011) *Comparative Case Studies of Health Reform in England*, Report submitted to the Department of Health Policy Research Programme (PRP), available at http://hrep.lshtm.ac.uk/publications/Comparative_powell.pdf.

Secretary of State for Health (2012) *The National Health Service and Public Health Service in England: Secretary of State's Annual Report 2011/2012*, The Stationery Office, London.

Timmins, N. (1996) *The Five Giants*, HarperCollins, London.

Timmins, N. (2012) *Never Again?*, Institute for Government/ King's Fund, London.

Further Reading

There are a number of texts on the NHS that have seen multiple editions. The most up to date (at the time of writing) and most readable is Rudolf Klein (2013) *The New Politics of the NHS* (Oxford: Radcliffe Medical, 7th edn. 2013). Chris Ham provides the best focus on the policy process in *Health Policy in Britain* (6th edn. 2009, Basingstoke: Palgrave Macmillan). A strong analytical focus is given in Steve Harrison and Ruth McDonald *The Politics of Healthcare in Britain* (London: Sage, 2008), and Ian Greener *Healthcare in the UK* (2008, Bristol: Policy Press). Perhaps the best coverage of wider public health can be found in David Hunter *The Health Debate* (2008, Bristol: Policy Press) and Rob Baggott, *Public Health: Policy and Politics* (2010, 2nd edn. Basingstoke: Palgrave Macmillian). The relationship between health and social care is explored in Chapter 8, and by the same author in Jon Glasby, *Understanding Health and Social Care* (2012, 2nd edn. Bristol: Policy Press).

A (now dated) evaluative focus is provided by Martin Powell, *Evaluating the National Health Service* (1997, Buckingham: Open University Press). Evaluations of recent governments health policy can be found in Nicholas

Mays et al.'s *Understanding New Labour's Market Reforms of the English NHS*, (eds, 2011, London: King's Fund); Ruth Thorlby and Jo Maybin, *A High-Performing NHS? A Review of Progress, 1997—2010* (eds, 2010, London: Kings Fund); and Sarah Gregory et al., *Health policy under the coalition government. A mid-term assessment*, (eds, 2012, London: King's Fund).

An excellent and readable account of the Coalition governments' major NHS reform is given by Nicholas Timmins, *Never Again?* (2012, Institute for Government/King's Fund: London). The annual *Social Policy Review* (Bristol: Policy Press) usually has a chapter reviewing developments in health policy.

Useful websites

http://www.kingsfund.org.uk/ and http://www.nuffieldtrust.org.uk/ – two health 'think tanks' that present blogs; talks; publications (including those in 'Further Reading); and data.

http://www.nhshistory.net/cvrivett.htm – NHS history by Geoffrey Rivett, covers the period from 1948 to date, with very useful sources and links.

http://www.hscic.gov.uk/ – Health & Social Care Information Centre, contains data on the NHS.

http://www.nhs.uk/Pages/HomePage.aspx – NHS Choices includes 'services near you' and health news.

CHAPTER 16

Housing Policy

Guy Daly and Kevin Gulliver

▌ Learning objectives

▨ To outline the development of state involvement in the provision of housing

▨ To examine the development of different housing sectors – private rental, public rental, and owner occupation

▨ To consider the Conservative New Right's housing policy of 1979–97, including:

  ▨ the residualisation of council housing

  ▨ the development and operation of the private housing market – and the aspiration to promote a 'property-owning democracy'

▨ To consider New Labour's housing policy, including:

  ▨ the re-fashioning of the public rented (social housing) sector

  ▨ the continued promotion of the private housing market

  ▨ the support for homeless and other vulnerable individuals and groups

▨ To explore the emerging policy of the Conservative-Liberal Democrat Coalition government housing strategy and its effects

Chapter overview

Housing is a crucial aspect of people's welfare. Having inadequate housing or being homeless is a terrible predicament in which to find oneself, as can be seen from the newspaper article below (Booth, 2007) about Ed Mitchell, who had previously been a successful television journalist for ITN until debts and alcohol problems impacted on him and his family.

SPOTLIGHT

ITN man once interviewed the influential, now he sleeps rough

Journalist homeless for 10 months after losing job and going through divorce

Robert Booth, *The Guardian*, 15 December 2007

He was the ITN broadcaster who interviewed Margaret Thatcher, John Major and Tony Blair. But not for Ed Mitchell the knighthoods, celebrity and bestselling books that have come to other leading broadcasters. Mitchell said yesterday he had been homeless for the last 10 months, sleeping on a bench next to a nightclub on the windblown seafront at Hove, Sussex.

'It's a bit bleak,' the 54-year-old said as he surveyed his view across the Channel. 'But at night the constellation of Orion rises clearly over there above the Babylon Lounge.'

It was one poetic thought in an otherwise desperate story of increasing credit card debt and alcoholism that has taken Mitchell from his status as a broadcaster earning £100,000 a year with a wife and two children, to divorce, bankruptcy and homelessness.

He admitted yesterday that his decline has left Frederick, 22, and Alexandra, 24, ashamed of him, and his 83-year-old mother unable to understand how her son's 'fall from grace should be so sharp and steep'.

He told how he sleeps fitfully in fear of attack, shaves in public toilets and tries to survive on just £52 a week in jobseeker's allowance . . . Now, he wants to get back to work and find housing. 'I know so much about the pain of being homeless, I want to give back through volunteer organisations my time and expertise.'

Introduction

This chapter examines the development of housing policy since the creation of the British welfare state. Housing has increasingly come to be seen as the 'wobbly pillar' (Harloe, 1995; Malpass, 2003) of welfare state provision in that while state health and education provision have been constructed as universal (that is, provision for all), housing policy has been focused on (a) public provision for the most needy and (b) the promotion of the private market for the majority (for example, through mortgage income tax relief, the promotion of the 'right to buy' for council tenants, and the promotion of the notion of a 'property-owning democracy'). This chapter therefore provides an overview of British housing policy, initially via an account of the historical background and then by exploring more recent trends of home ownership and rented provision.

> **STOP AND THINK**
>
> ▪ Why is housing so crucial to an individual or a family's welfare?
>
> ▪ What do you think are the consequences of being homeless or inadequately housed?

Historical background

Historically, the question of housing policy was one of the last areas of social provision to attract the attention of a nascent and developing welfare state. It was not until the years of the First World War that the question of housing for the working classes received serious attention on the British political agenda when the protests of workers against the profiteering of their landlords, in sensitive industrial areas, such as munitions and shipbuilding in and around Glasgow, forced the Lloyd-George government to act. Initially, the political response was to subsidise rents to buy industrial peace and it was not until the years following the war that the state's interest in the construction and management of public housing projects began in earnest. Even then the response was short-lived, as public expenditure restrictions in the early years of the 1920s restricted the ability of local municipal authorities (councils) to finance house building.

As Malpass and Murie (1990) indicate, before 1914 there was barely a recognisable housing policy. However, the years of the First World War (1914–18), during which housing production fell, meant that by 1918 there existed a severe housing shortage that the private building sector was unable to address. During the inter-war years, housing policy developed on two fronts: the control of rents in the private rented sector and the subsidy of local authority building, partly prompted by the various programmes of slum clearance, particularly after 1930. Emphasis, however, remained with the private building sector, which alone constructed 100,000 dwellings every year from 1925 to over 250,000 annually between 1934 and 1938, with local authorities averaging only 25,000 completions annually during the same period (Malpass and Murie, 1990). Thus housing policy as a part of the formative welfare state remained hardly recognisable, but there was nonetheless a shift in the pattern of tenure as private ownership began to take over from private rentals as the preferred option – herein, arguably, lay the roots of Britain's 'property-owning democracy'.

Public housing at this time, therefore, was very much a minority undertaking with many local authorities reluctant to enter the property development market. But those that did, especially those controlled by Labour councillors, sought to show that workers' housing needed no longer to be slums, and in so doing mirrored works undertaken by the cooperative and trades union movements. They sought instead to instal the range and type of facilities that they considered were the best that could be bought, and the space available in many early public housing projects was generous. These councillors were keen to show that a future Labour government could construct and successfully manage quality homes for their working-class constituents at affordable rents. However, the building costs of those early projects were high as authorities sought to maintain high quality but at the same time were forced to pay high labour costs to attract skilled building workers away from the private sector (Malpass and Murie, 1990).

This general picture remained largely unaltered during the inter-war years as the majority of newly built houses were, as we have seen, in the privately owned sector. Government interest in housing instead focused on the question of inner-city congestion and slum clearance. It was only really as a result of the Second World War (1939–45), and the effects of civilian bombing together with the desire to fulfil the promises of the 'khaki election' to build homes for heroes, that housing policy was placed more centrally on the policy stage. The programmes of slum clearance continued, although priorities began to change as building standards were gradually lowered in an attempt to accelerate the building programme. Urban planning, as a result, became chaotic as towns began to spread as new suburbs sprang up and the back-to-back terraces of the town centres disappeared. Local authorities were, as Malpass and Murie (1990) indicate, fulfilling a residual role at this time, as they sought to rehouse those people displaced by slum clearance, while for those who had the resources and opportunity, a privately owned suburban semi-detached became a realisable dream.

The early years of the 1940s were witness to a radical shift in housing priorities for the policy-makers of the post-war years. By 1945, some 3.5 million dwellings were either wholly destroyed or substantially damaged by air raids and the slum clearance programmes, which had temporarily halted, could renew apace. The housing crisis facing this generation's set of returning war heroes was thus far more severe than that seen in 1918–19 and the incoming government was required to act quickly and moreover to build quickly. Both the major political parties (Labour and Conservative) promised rapid completion rates in house building to replace those properties damaged or destroyed and to allow slum clearance to resume. However, there was a difference in emphasis, with Labour favouring public building projects and municipal management of new estates, while the Conservatives retained their traditional loyalty to the private building industry and adopted the new slogan that promised the creation of a 'property-owning democracy'. We are thus, from these rather different ideological stances, able to identify clear periods in the development of post-war housing policy and priorities:

- 1945 to 1953 saw a rapid growth in municipal housing developments
- the mid 1950s to mid 1960s was a period of growth in private sector developments
- the mid 1960s onwards saw an emphasis on improvement to existing housing stock
- the 1980s into the 1990s was a time when public housing was no longer seen to be effective
- the late 1990s into the 2010s has seen public or social housing become a residual sector, the political consensus one of home ownership as the aspiration for most households, and the vast majority of households being housed privately.

Housing, then, at least as an identifiable area of government policy, is almost exclusively confined to the post-1945 era and may be characterised by an air of euphoria, at least on the part of the housing bureaucracy, as successive construction targets were reached. However, dramatic failure, particularly in municipal projects, was always just around the corner, and in the 1980s the ground was laid bare for a revolution in property ownership and the large-scale disposal of council-owned property. The dominant policy rhetoric by the early to mid 1980s was that local authority run municipal housing had by now come to embody inefficient, ineffective, and unpopular provision – that is, not very dissimilar to the privately rented stock it had been designed to replace. Local authority housing departments were perceived to be as inflexible as any private landlord in their regulation of tenants. Local authorities were charged, not always unfairly, with replacing the inner-city slums with newer suburban or high-rise slums. These council houses and estates were increasingly regarded as poorly built, poorly maintained, inefficiently managed, and/or used as dumping grounds for the local authorities' most troublesome tenants. On the other hand, after 1975 local authorities may justifiably point to increased central control over their finances, which restricted their ability to act, for instance in controlling how capital from council house sales could be used. Even so, by the 1980s local authority council housing was increasingly seen by politicians and other policy-makers to be no longer part of the solution to housing those in need but instead a significant part of the problem.

The 1980s was to witness radical changes to British housing policy. The 1979 general election returned a 'New Right' Conservative government, under Margaret Thatcher's leadership, which among other things promised to give council tenants the opportunity to join the property-owning democracy by giving them the 'right to buy' their council house or flat. Indeed, though already permissible, the sale of council houses at a discount was one of the central planks of the Conservatives' election victory in 1979.

Housing policy under the New Right – residualised state involvement and the promotion of the market

It is often tempting to begin a review of contemporary housing policy trends with the 1979 general election and the manifesto promises of the first Thatcher administration. But we can detect the beginnings of policy change within the final years of the previous Labour government. However, the 1979 election victory for Margaret Thatcher heralded something of a revolution. The next 18 years would be a period in which home ownership was promoted as the preferred form of tenure, alongside the 'dismantling of the public rented sector' and the 'deregulation of private renting', by which process housing would be regarded less and less as a public or merit good and the provision of a decent home no longer considered part of government's basic responsibility, and instead came to be regarded increasingly as a private good with the government's role one of market regulation (Linneman and Megbolugbe, 1994; Malpass, 1996). The period of New Right Conservative rule began almost triumphantly as the 1980 Housing Act introduced the right of council tenants to purchase their homes at substantial discounts. This was made easier for these would-be home owners by the subsequent deregulation of the financial markets, which made the obtaining of a mortgage far easier. Local authorities would then be left to provide what was frequently referred to as 'residual housing', for the poorest of tenants.

Public housing under the Conservatives

The right to buy was substantially buoyed by the economic boom of the mid 1980s and the general availability of low-cost credit. However, the picture changed rapidly and dramatically at the end of the 1980s as the economic boom turned to recession and the economy, controlled largely by interest rates, seriously undermined the efficacy of the burgeoning housing market. Mortgage default, negative equity, and even repossession were experienced by millions of home-owners in the 1990s. In the private rented sector, the government sought to revitalise the market by deregulating and creating incentives for private landlords, while at the same time attempting to force the transfer of local authority housing stock into the hands of alternative landlords in the form of 'tenants' choice' and encouraging other social housing providers, particularly housing associations (see below). Perhaps most fundamentally, the 1980s heralded a shift in housing finance away from the subsidy of supply (i.e. house building) towards one built more around the subsidising of demand – via means-tested housing benefit in the rental sector and mortgage interest relief for owner-occupiers.

Throughout much of the 1980s and particularly between 1983 and 1989, both the economy and in turn the housing market enjoyed an unprecedented boom, during which time over one million council houses were transferred from state to private ownership; with tenants being encouraged both by continually rising rents and increasingly more generous discounts on sale price during this period. Government opted to use the mechanism of council house sales, first to individual tenants who were to be encouraged by a discounted price compared with the market value of the property and determined by the length of their tenancy (the maximum would eventually be a 70 per cent discount), and by the right to obtain a mortgage. Second, and later in the decade, sales to other landlords were encouraged either at the instigation of the local authority itself or at the initiative of the tenants.

Figure 16.1 illustrates the scale of the privatisation of public sector housing via the right to buy and indicates that between 1980 and 2011 (that is, continuing under the New Labour government) the ownership of almost two million public sector dwellings was transferred to tenants. Despite the 'right to buy' scheme, however, local authorities continued to provide the majority of rental sector housing in the 1990s with council house sales appearing to reach something of an impasse (Whitehead, 1993; Linneman and Megbolugbe, 1994) in the 1990s. To overcome this stalling, first the Conservatives between 1990 and 1997 and then the Labour government from 1997 to 2010 endeavoured to use 'stock transfer' (see discussion of this later in the chapter) as a means of accelerating and perpetuating the residualisation of council housing. More recently, the Conservative-Liberal Democrat Coalition government sought to reinvigorate the sale of council housing to tenants in 2011 and 2012.

Therefore, the story of council housing in the 1980s and early 1990s only explains part of the picture of public rental housing in Britain. A significant

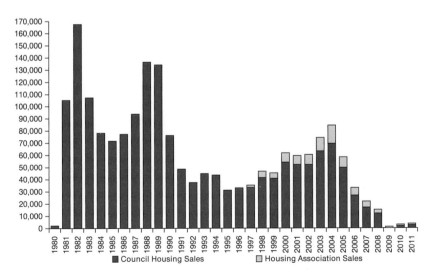

Figure 16.1 Social sector right-to-buy sales, 1980–2011

Source: DCLG (2013)

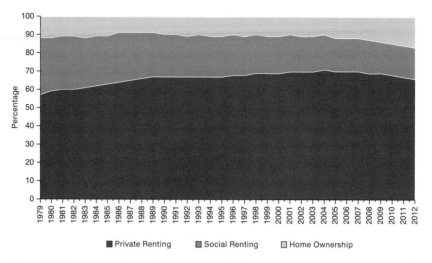

Figure 16.2 Percentage change in tenure in England, 1979–2012

Source: DCLG Live Tables (2013)

and growing, though still proportionately small, number of dwellings were and are available to rent within housing association control (sometimes described as registered social landlords or RSLs), which are non-profit organisations and remain, largely at least, publically funded. Indeed, of council house transfers over the period 1984–94, some 155,000 council houses in England were transferred to the control of housing associations, and therefore remained within the public rental sector. Over the decade of the 1980s and into the 1990s, the Conservative government sought to expand significantly the role of housing associations within the housing sector, not least the number of housing association (RSL) properties. This included encouragement and legislative recognition of those schemes, which, usually at the initiative of local councils, effected the transfer of housing to association control. But, as part of this change of role, associations saw their revenue support from public funds fall as they were encouraged to seek private sources of finance to supplement public funds. As a result, and to encourage private investment, housing association rents rose to a market level in order to offer better rates of return to private investors. The key tenure trends shown in Figure 16.2 show the residualistion of social housing (council and housing association) and the growth of owner-occupation (although owner-occupation fell back later with private renting resurgent).

Home ownership

The availability of cheap credit and loans secured against homes ensured that the house market expanded and house prices rose rapidly during the 1980s and early 1990s, reaching a peak during 1988–89. However, the end of the 1980s brought with it economic recession, increases in unemployment, high rates of inflation, high interest rates, and negative equity. All of this, in turn, led to significant increases in the repossession of homes by banks and building societies, a trend that reached a peak of over 75,000 repossessions in 1991. Even so, the decade of the 1980s had established, ideologically and politically, home ownership as the most desirable form of housing tenure (Doling, 1993), which, as we have already witnessed, was encouraged by government policies that enforced the sale of public-owned and rented properties and forced rapid rent increases across the public rental sector. Allied to these policies, deregulation in British financial markets had made mortgages, and loans secured against property, increasingly attractive.

By the time New Labour was elected into government in 1997, it had recognised and fully accepted the consensus of home ownership as the dominant form of tenure. When elected back into power, Labour simply promised to manage the housing market better than the Conservatives by ameliorating the worst of the economic fluctuations affecting the housing market and reducing the boom–bust housing cycle. However, as we will see shortly, Labour's period of office coincided with a further boom in the home ownership housing market.

The private rental sector

The private rental sector was, over the course of the twentieth century, arguably in a state of decline. Governments over the years, particularly in the years after 1945, promoted either public rented council housing or private ownership (the property-owning democracy, which became in the 1980s firmly rooted in the popular imagination). Governments sought to revitalise the private rented sector, whether to fill gaps in housing policy that were not met by other sectors or to promote private entrepreneurship and landlordship; or sought to regulate what they perceived to be a firmly established relationship of exploitation, especially where the sector provided low-income tenancies. The Conservative government in the 1980s recognised that there was still a demand for rented accommodation by people perhaps more mobile in their employment. Government therefore sought to develop strategies that would revive the private rental sector by making the development of rental accommodation a more attractive investment. Despite this, there was little impact in terms of increasing available rented stock, as Figure 16.2 illustrates, and the number of rental units available in the private sector changed little over the ten years between 1984 and 1993 (and, indeed, since then). As a percentage of total available stock, the private rented sector continued to decline and while housing association lets increased, this had not been enough to replace those units lost in the process of council house sales and the overall quantity of rented accommodation also declined.

Homelessness

Much of the 1980s and 1990s was characterised by what has been termed an affordability crisis in British housing (Bramley, 1994). Policies aimed at widening the base of home ownership, such as council house sales and financial deregulation, had been largely successful, but arguably at a price. The stock of affordable rented accommodation continued to decline, and the low rent sector developed into low-quality housing for the poorest of tenants. Councils were left with stock that proved the most difficult to maintain successfully in a climate of continued financial restrictions. Housing associations were unable to fill the gap left in the provision of social housing. Similarly, as we have seen above, private landlords did not significantly expand provision as the government had hoped in the early 1990s. Against this background we must now turn to what was one of the hallmarks of the housing scene in the 1980s and early 1990s (and has continued to be a persistent challenge for housing policy) – the rise in homelessness, and most visibly youth homelessness.

The rise in the homeless can be identified in a number of related areas. The economic downturn of the 1980s, as we have noted, severely curtailed the revolution in home ownership of the early years of that decade. Unemployment led to a rapid rise in mortgage arrears and ultimately repossessions. Dwindling stocks of low rent accommodation, paralleled by rising rents in that sector, took rented accommodation beyond the reach of many poorer families. Most importantly, perhaps, changes in benefit regulations for young people virtually ended the possibility of young people obtaining rented accommodation until they reached their mid twenties. The situation was exacerbated because single people were no longer regarded as a priority by local authorities when accepting claims for help.

These individuals also represented a demographic change in Britain as we entered a period in which more young people were entering the housing market and the desire for living singly continued to increase as people chose to marry later in life. Unemployment together with a lack of access to cheap, low-quality accommodation and benefit reductions continued therefore to contribute to increasing numbers of homeless individuals in the Thatcher and Major periods of office (Bramley, 1994) and persisted under New Labour (as the newspaper story at the beginning of this chapter on the television broadcaster, Ed Mitchell, demonstrates). It is probably fair to say that by the end of the Conservative government's term of office in 1997, housing had become a key social policy issue not least in terms of affordable home ownership, an adequate supply of good quality social housing, and the persistent incidence of homelessness.

New Labour's housing policy

By the time that Labour was elected back into government in May 1997, it was thus faced with a number of housing policy challenges, not least:

- what to do about a private housing market that had resulted in negative equity and significant levels of repossessions for some individuals and families;
- how to respond to the lack of supply of private housing and an associated increasing unaffordability for significant sections of the population unable to enter the housing market;
- a residual local authority housing sector that had divested itself of its better properties via the right to buy and stock transfer schemes;
- a private rented sector that remained a significant but proportionally small part of the housing scene;
- the persistent problem of homelessness.

Labour's housing policy developed fitfully during its time in office as a response to these problems, with relatively little policy development in its first term (1997–2001) but becoming more active from 2000 onwards. As with other parts of New Labour's social policy, its housing policy was based on an acceptance of the market, an advocacy of choice, and an evocation of duty.

It is perhaps unsurprising that despite the policy challenges it faced on election in 1997 and thereafter, New Labour's housing policy has been fairly consistent with the preceding approach of the New Right governments of Margaret Thatcher and John Major, in as much as it has been possible to discern a thought-through housing policy under New Labour (Lund, 2006; Stephens and Quilgars, 2006). There was little mention of housing in its election manifesto in 1997 or in initial policy documents on returning to government (Mullins and Murie, 2006; Murie, 2007). However, since 2000 Labour did focus on housing to a greater extent. This could be seen initially by the publication of its first Housing Green Paper *Quality and Choice – A Decent Home for All* (DETR, 2000) since its election in 1997, which concerned itself with the quality of housing and the promotion of choice. Subsequent policy initiatives included the Treasury commissioned Barker Report (Barker, 2004) on the supply of housing and the government commissioned Hills review of the role of social housing (Hills, 2007) as well as the 2007 Housing Green Paper *Homes for the Future: More Affordable, More Sustainable* (DCLG, 2007). In addition, latterly Gordon Brown's Premiership pursued a more active housing policy (Summers, 2007). As such, Labour's housing policy developed in terms of:

- the promotion of non-local authority social housing and the continued residualisation of council housing during its first two terms of office;
- its promotion of home ownership and an associated drive to increase the supply of housing, including affordable housing;
- the support of the private rented sector;
- policy initiatives to support provision for homeless and other vulnerable individuals and groups.

For writers such as Lund (2006) and Malpass and Cairncross (2006), Labour's approach prefaced a new phase – a belief in an ample housing supply. Historically, British housing policy had been concerned with public health, then adequate housing supply, followed by state control over production and consumption, and then the Conservative's belief in market solutions in the 1980s and 1990s. Labour's approach was described by Lund (2006, p. 222) as being 'characterized by a recognition that an ample housing supply is vital . . . and hence a state requirement to ensure that supply is more responsive to demand; consensus on the virtues of home ownership; the selective use of state resources to supply the infrastructure for sustainable housing both in low-demand and high-demand areas; promoting social inclusion', whether that be in relation to homelessness or anti-social behaviour. This section of the chapter has described how Labour's housing policy evolved and emerged in relation to public housing, home ownership, the private rental sector, homelessness, and other vulnerable households.

Public housing under New Labour

Labour's approach to public or social housing focused initially on the quality of public housing stock, on providing tenant choice, and on housing associations as the preferred vehicle for new build and the ongoing management of social housing stock. Its 2000 housing Green Paper *Quality and Choice* (DETR, 2000) concentrated on the poor quality of social housing, particularly council housing stock. Here it acknowledged the underinvestment in social housing and, as a consequence, its unpopularity. New Labour therefore chose to concentrate on improving the quality of the stock and providing greater opportunities for choice for social housing tenants. Regarding housing stock quality, it set a target that by 2010 all social housing would have to meet a 'decent homes' standard, a stiff target when one considers that in 2001 nearly half, that is 43 per cent, of council housing could not meet the decent homes standard. In the 2007 Housing Green Paper *Homes for the Future* (DCLG, 2007), the government adjusted the target to 95 per cent of homes meeting the decent homes standard by 2010. In 2000, it had estimated that there was a catalogue of outstanding repairs and underinvestment to the value of some £10 billion. Many local authorities judged that the government was reluctant simply to provide the funding to facilitate improvements, and so local government looked for other sources of funding. As such, local authorities had three main options open to them. First, they could transfer their housing stock ('stock transfer') to a registered social landlord (RSL) such as a housing association that could then borrow money commercially. Second, under the Private Finance Initiative, a local authority could enter into an agreement with a private company whereby that company provided capital funding in return for a contract to mange the housing stock for a considerable period, typically 25 years. Third, local authorities could set up Arms Length Management Organisations (ALMOs) that would manage their housing stock and, in so doing, be permitted to borrow additional funds. Of these three options, only stock transfer (a policy initially introduced by the Conservative government) manifested itself to any significant extent and it is this option that the Labour government continued to pursue enthusiastically (Daly *et al.*, 2005). In its 2000 Housing Green Paper, the government argued for significant levels of stock transfer, aiming for 'the transfer of up to 200,000 homes each year from local authorities to registered landlords' (DETR, 2000, p. 11). This was to be the main means by which local authorities could lever in housing investment, that is, private (and, therefore, 'off balance sheet') funding.

Some local authorities, trades unions, and tenants groups (not least the Defend Council Housing pressure group) continued to press (unsuccessfully) for a 'fourth option' – whereby local authorities would be allowed to borrow funds directly themselves and be provided with Treasury assistance in paying off outstanding debts. However, the government continued to resist these demands even when expressed repeatedly by members of the Labour Party at the Annual Labour Party Conference. In part, this was because of the government's desire to restructure the governance of public housing. As such, New Labour can be seen to be as antipathetic as the previous Conservative governments to local authorities as significant suppliers of social housing. Stock transfer has, therefore, not only been used as a mechanism to lever in private finance but also as a means by which local authorities are increasingly being regarded no longer as direct providers but instead as strategic enablers of the provision of housing in their areas.

Stock transfer therefore continued steadily since transfers began in earnest in the mid 1980s under the Conservatives. However, by the mid 2000s, more than half of council housing stock remained with local authorities (Malpass and Cairncross, 2006), although the number of transfers grew significantly after the election of New Labour in 1997 and particularly since 2000. As one can see from Figure 16.1, stock transfer ('large-scale voluntary transfer') rose significantly in the years 2000–02, averaging out at over 100,000 properties per year – although this was considerably fewer properties than the 200,000 per year aimed for by the government. Where stock transfer did occur, it was frequently transferred to, and therefore created an expansion in, housing association provision.

Housing associations also continued to be the preferred source of new build and management arrangement for public housing under Labour (Murie, 2007). Housing associations saw their provision increase from 1,147,000 units in 1997 (4.6 per cent of all housing stock in the UK) to 2,001,000 (7.7 per cent of housing stock) in 2004 (ODPM, 2005b). As we have seen above, this was partly through stock transfer but was also due to housing associations being encouraged by government to build new stock. Housing associations saw significant numbers of new build completions each year during Labour's rule from 1997, with 28,554 new build completions in its first year of office (1997–98) and 22,682 more recently (2004–05). And yet, neither of these years compared favourably with the numbers of new build completions under the previous Conservative government, which, for example, saw 30,951 completions in its last year of government (1996–97) (Office of the Deputy Prime Minister, 2005b). Nor were such completion rates adequate by the Labour government's own target, which stated that there needed to be an increase of new builds of 17,000 per year, a virtual doubling of rates (Malpass, 2005). New Labour recognised in its 2007 Housing Green Paper *Homes for the Future* (DCLG, 2007) the need to increase the amount of social housing new builds. Indeed, it set itself and the social housing sector significant targets for social housing new builds but did not realise them.

Labour's social housing policy also strove to promote 'choice' for public housing tenants. It sought to do this via three main policy reforms: 'choice-based lettings', 'market-based rents', and reforms to housing benefit. Choice-based lettings was a scheme the Labour government expected all local authority housing providers to have adopted by 2010. Traditionally, social housing had been allocated broadly according to need, with applicants typically being awarded points depending on their circumstances. For example, homeless applicants had been treated as some of the neediest applicants. Other criteria included the awarding of points for the length of time an applicant had been on the waiting list, for how many children they had, whether their living conditions were overcrowded, and so forth. Once an applicant had enough points they would be offered a suitable property when one became available. Labour housing policy endeavoured to move to a situation where applicants were consumers who would be offered a choice of properties. Therefore, under choice-based lettings housing vacancies were to be advertised such that would-be tenants could apply for a property that they would like. However, critics of this quasi-market, consumerist approach argued that it would not necessarily result in a demand for properties in less popular areas, whereas in popular areas and for popular types of property demand would remain greater than the supply. Therefore, instead of properties being allocated according to need, they would be allocated to those applicants willing to wait the longest (Stephens and Quilgars, 2006).

Market-based rents were the second facet of Labour's choice agenda in social housing policy. As part of its 2000 Green Paper (DETR, 2000), the Labour government proposed to restructure social housing rents. Labour believed that rents should reflect more closely the size, quality, and location of homes, taking account of local property values so that tenants would pay a comparable rent for a comparable property. However, property values would not be the only consideration such that rent calculations could take account of other factors, such as regional earnings and running costs. Paraphrasing the government's own words, it was proposed that social housing rents should be both 'affordable and fair'.

The third aspect of the Labour government's housing policy choice agenda were their proposals to reform housing benefit with the intention that it reflected the rent that a household would typically have to pay in a particular region, in much the same way that market rents would take account of context. In this way, it was intended that recipients of housing benefit could make choices about their housing costs, for example whether they wished to add to their housing benefit in order to access more expensive housing or, instead, to rent something cheaper and to retain the difference in cost to spend on other priorities. This initiative fitted in with the Labour government's advocacy of welfare choice (White and Wintour, 2005), since the government believed that tenants would be able to choose the quantity and quality of their housing (Stephens and Quilgars, 2006). However, there were two weaknesses with the policy. First, it assumed that social housing consumers had surplus income that they could use to supplement their housing benefit if they wanted to consume more housing, arguably an unlikely scenario particularly for citizens in receipt of benefits. Second, the policy assumed that there was sufficient supply of social (and/or privately rented) housing at a variety of prices and of various stock types from which housing consumers could choose. This second matter, that of housing supply, also relates to the next area of the Labour government's housing policy – home ownership – to which we now turn.

Home ownership under Labour

On entering office, New Labour continued with the previous Conservative government's commitment to promoting home ownership as the main type of housing tenure. It confirmed this commitment in both its 2000 housing Green Paper (DETR, 2000) and again in its 2007 Green Paper (DCLG, 2007) where it declared its intent to increase home ownership to some 75 per cent of households. According to *Social Trends* (Summerfield and Gill, 2005), by the end of New Labour's second term, that is 'in 2003/04, 70 per cent of dwellings (18 million) in Great Britain were owner-occupied. This was an increase of 45 per cent from 12 million in 1981'. But, 'Tenure . . . varies regionally. In 2003/04 owner-occupation was highest in the South East, East Midlands and East (75 per cent) and lowest in London (58 per cent) and Scotland (67 per cent)' (Summerfield and Gill, 2005). These trends have since intensified as shown in Figure 16.3; by 2012, home ownership had declined except in the South East and South West. Social housing had declined as a proportion of the total housing stock in all regions. Private renting began to rise again in the early 2000s, reaching a new height in 2012 of more than 17 per cent of total dwellings, especially in London (at 26 per cent).

In its first term of office, the Labour government concerned itself mostly with ensuring that home owners did not suffer from the high interest rates that had jeopardised mortgage repayments for many homeowners during the latter part of the previous Conservative government. Early in its first term, New Labour hived off responsibility for determining interest rates to the Bank of England Monetary Policy Committee (MPC). Meanwhile, the Treasury saw its role as being to ensure low inflation and economic growth and stability

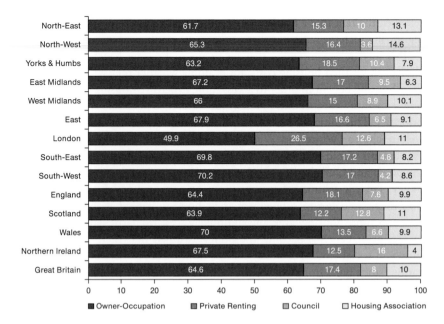

Figure 16.3 Percentage tenure in UK by region, 2012

Source: DCLG Live Tables (2013)

to ensure that low interest rates would not be threatened. However, the low interest rates perversely assisted the boom in house prices, whereby the average house price increased from £70,000 in 1997 to £195,000 in 2007 (Collinson, 2007). Within these increases were significant regional differences, such that the increases in the South East were more marked than in the Midlands and the North.

In addition, house price increases also meant both a reduction in the numbers of first-time buyers and an increase in the average age of first-time buyers, indicating increased difficulty in particular for young people to enter the housing market (Murie, 2007). The government hoped that the increase in demand for home ownership would lead to a corresponding increase in supply by the house building industry but this did not materialise sufficiently to stabilise house prices or cope with demand and need. It was in part because of the dislocation between demand and supply and associated house price inflation that led the Treasury to establish the Barker Review into housing supply. The Barker Review (Barker, 2004) concluded that the lack of supply of new homes was a major cause of high house prices, that the demand for housing was outstripping supply and, as a consequence, this was driving UK house prices ever higher. The lack of supply was due, in part, to fewer homes being built in Britain in the mid 2000s than at any time since the early 1970s (see Figure 16.4) and subsequently fell further after the credit crunch of 2008.

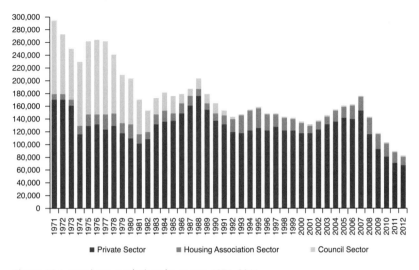

Figure 16.4 Housing completions by sector, 1971–2011

Source: DCLG Live Tables (2013)

The other main reason for the mismatch between supply and demand in housing provision was the impact of the demographic changes in the number and types of households. For example, in 1991 there were just over 19 million households in England (of which 11.7 million were married couples or co-habittees, 1 million were lone-parent, and 5.1 million were one-person households) whereas in 2006 it was estimated that there were nearly 22 million households (of which 11.8 million were married couples or co-habittees, 1.3 million were lone-parent, and 8.5 million were one-person households). The overall number of households in England was estimated to increase by a further one million by 2016 (Office of the Deputy Prime Minister, 2005a). As a consequence, the Barker Review recommended that Britain needed to build up to 140,000 extra new homes a year in order for housing supply to match demand. The government's response to the Barker Report was to commit itself to an even more exacting target of 200,000 new properties per year over a 10-year period, that is 2 million new homes by 2016 and 3 million by 2020, mostly provided by the private sector (Office of the Deputy Prime Minister, 2003, 2005a; DCLG, 2007). As can be seen in Figure 16.4, neither this annual target nor overall aggregate target were met and are not likely to be met in the foreseeable future.

The private rental sector

The private rental sector continued to remain static as a proportion of housing tenure, remaining fairly constant at 10–11 per cent of overall housing provision while Labour was in government (Office of the Deputy Prime Minister,

2005a; Lund, 2006; Murie, 2007). However, the Labour government tried to promote the private rental sector, seeing it as a key provider for those individuals not wanting, or not able, to become owner-occupiers; as well as providing accessible and flexible housing, particularly attractive to younger people (DETR, 2000). As such, the government had distanced itself from the Labour Party's previous antipathy to this part of the housing sector. In so doing, the government attempted to assure private landlords that it did not intend to make any changes to the structure of assured tenancies or assured shorthold tenancies (terminated after six months) and it would not re-introduce rent controls. This Labour government therefore saw the private rental sector as an integral part of housing provision.

What one did see during Labour's period of office was an increase in the numbers of 'buy-to-let' providers. According to Lund (2006), in the period from 1998 to 2004 there was an 18-fold increase in the number of mortgage loans on buy-to-let properties, with approximately half a million outstanding loans in 2004. This was partly as a result of low interest rates as well as due to the availability of 100 per cent mortgages, which made it easier for more people to buy up properties to rent out. (This does, consequently, act as a further pressure on supply and helps fuel house price inflation.) Indeed, an aspect peculiar to British housing provision is its reliance on small-scale landlords (Stephens and Quilgars, 2006). Rather than large-scale business conglomerates being the financiers and managers of private rental stock, much is owned and managed by individual landlords who own a few properties; the average number of properties owned by a landlord in the 2000s was four (Lund, 2006). This made the sector liable to volatility and meant that the individual tenant might normally only be likely to enter into short-term tenancies.

Many of the issues traditionally associated with the private rented sector persisted under Labour in the 2000s, whether in terms of rents, the demographic spread of tenants, length of tenancies, or the quality of rental property (Office of the Deputy Prime Minister, 2004, 2005a; Lund, 2006). First, rents remained significantly higher than in the social housing sector – the average rent in 2004–05 in the private rented sector was £523 per month as against an average social housing rent of £293 per month and an average council tenant rent of £255 per month (Office of the Deputy Prime Minister, 2005b). Second, unlike in the social housing sector, a significant majority of tenants continued to be employed and were often young professionals. Third, private tenants tended to rent a property for a relatively short period of time, often less than a year. Finally, the quality of the private rented sector continued to be below that of the other housing sectors when measured against the Labour government's 'decent homes standard' – with 17 per cent of private rented stock falling below the standard compared with 8 per cent of owner-occupied stock, 9 per cent of local authority stock, and 5 per cent of housing association properties. Accordingly, the private rental sector was not without its issues and arguably remained a marginal, though significant, part of housing provision.

Homeless and other vulnerable individuals and households

In exploring Labour's housing policy in relation to homelessness, the first thing to note is that any examination of statistics on homelessness is problematic not least because of the difficulties of definition. The definition of homelessness has been liable to frequent change. For example, in the 1977 Housing (Homeless Persons) Act, a homeless person was someone who did not have a legal right to occupy a dwelling. The Act then went further by distinguishing between those who were and were not intentionally homeless as well as those in priority need. The 1986 Housing and Planning Act widened the definition of homelessness to include those people living in unfit accommodation, while the 1996 Housing Act altered things so that local authorities were only obliged to provide temporary accommodation to homeless people. The 2002 Homeless Act expanded the category of priority need to include those leaving care, prison or the armed forces, or those who were vulnerable because of domestic violence or the threat of domestic violence. Therefore, attempts to analyse the levels of homelessness are difficult since the definition of homelessness has been and remains subject to change.

Two measures typically used to compare changes in the levels of homelessness during the New Labour period of office were the number of households judged to be unintentionally homeless per year and in priority need, and the numbers of households in temporary accommodation. Using the first set of statistics – households judged to be unintentionally homeless and in priority need – the numbers of homeless increased during Labour's rule, and almost returned to the numbers experienced in the early 1990s. Thus, not long after Labour returned to power in 1997–98, the numbers of unintentionally homeless in priority need amounted to some 102,400 households. By 2004–05, this had increased to 120,860 (Office of the Deputy Prime Minister, 2005b). The second measure of homelessness – households in temporary accommodation – also saw significant increases year on year from 1997; indeed, there was a doubling in the numbers during Labour's first two terms of office – from 41,000 in 1997 to 97,000 households in 2004, and of these the numbers being accommodated in 'bed and breakfast' accommodation increased from 4,000 in 1997 to 7,000 in 2004 (ODPM, 2005b). However, the Labour government's more liberal definition of homelessness helped to explain, in part at least, the increase in the numbers of homeless during their time in office; for example, as was noted above, in 2002 the definition of 'unintentionally homeless and in priority need' was extended to include additional priority needs such as young homeless people and people who were homeless who had been 'in care'.

As a response, the Labour government undertook a number of initiatives during its time in office to address the problems of homelessness. The 2002 Homelessness Act was an attempt to coordinate provision for homeless people, not least those leaving care, prison or the armed forces, or vulnerable because of domestic violence or the threat of domestic violence. Local authorities were required to have in place a homelessness strategy to tackle the problems of homelessness, including pro-active preventative measures used to tackle the problem of people sleeping rough and the overuse of bed and breakfast as temporary accommodation. The government's 'Sustainable Communities' plan (Office of the Deputy Prime Minister, 2003) and *Homes for All* (Office of the Deputy Prime Minister, 2005a) included proposals to reduce homelessness, not least by halving the number of households in insecure temporary accommodation by 2010. As such, the government provided additional funding to increase the supply of new social housing and to expand preventative services (National Audit Office, 2005). In 2005, the National Audit Office judged that the Labour government had made good progress in addressing the problems of homelessness.

New Labour also focused its housing policy on 'rough sleepers', that is, individuals sleeping outdoors. In 1998, it was estimated that there were 1850 rough sleepers in England (National Audit Office, 2005). The government's Social Exclusion Unit (1998) stated that many rough sleepers had troubled personal backgrounds, such as difficulties with leaving care, the armed forces or prison, or personal difficulties that caused them to leave home. Indeed, the example of Ed Mitchell at the beginning of the chapter illustrates the detrimental impact of such personal difficulties on an individual's housing situation. The government's approach included providing three sorts of accommodation for rough sleepers: initial hostels and shelters, specialist hostels and shelters to meet particular needs, and more permanent accommodation once an individual was able to manage this. By 2004, in part because of these initiatives, the numbers of rough sleepers in England had been reduced to just over 500. Even so, there remained an issue of rough sleeping in London, where half of England's rough sleepers were to be found.

One further significant area of housing policy was the development of provision for other 'vulnerable people' such as the 'Supporting People' initiative, which aimed to provide support to vulnerable people (older people, people escaping from domestic violence, people with learning difficulties or mental health problems) to continue to live independently in their own homes. This initiative enabled over 1.2 million people to continue to live independently.

A final area of policy pursued by New Labour was its approach to dealing with the perceived problem of anti-social behaviour, arguably an area related as much to criminal justice policy as to housing policy. Even so, anti-social behaviour was believed to have a detrimental effect on the reputation of a locality and the desirability of people to live there. Labour's housing and wider policy therefore sought to emphasise the renewal of local environments, for example through its 'New Deal for Communities' neighbourhood renewal initiative and the 'Respect' agenda (Home Office, 2006) rather than solely the repair of housing stock or the demolition of whole estates. The government linked its neighbourhood renewal strategy to that of tackling anti-social behaviour. Managing anti-social behaviour therefore presented local authorities, the police, and the criminal justice system generally with challenges. Even though local authorities had long had powers to evict 'troublesome' tenants, this was often difficult as it required statements from witnesses and getting a court conviction. However, in 1998 the Labour government passed the Crime and Disorder Act, which included the power for local authorities and the police to place an anti-social behaviour order (ASBO) on any individual, aged ten or older, who was judged in a civil court to be a violent threat. The law was strengthened in 2003 with the Anti-Social Behaviour Act, which gave the police and local authorities the powers to disperse individuals from particular neighbourhoods or move them back into a particular area. It also gave RSLs the power to prohibit anti-social behaviour by its tenants, through placing restrictions on the tenancy and removing from the tenant the 'right to buy'. However, views on the merits and effectiveness of ASBOs were mixed. On the one hand, some writers suggest that they improved the quality of life of communities blighted by anti-social behaviour, while on the other, ASBOs were also seen to be part of an anti-civil liberties enforcement agenda (Stephens and Quilgars, 2006) that was actually counter-productive, as it was as likely to provide young people on whom an ASBO was placed with local notoriety rather than make them curb their behaviour.

Overall, what one can conclude form New Labour's period of office was that home ownership remained the dominant policy preference, though limited investment in (non-local authority council housing) social housing did occur, in terms of increases in stock volume and improvements in the quality of social housing. In addition, approaches to support vulnerable individuals and groups were developed with a degree of success, not least for homeless people. However, the lack of supply of affordable and accessible housing remained in place by the time that the Coalition government took over the reins of power in 2010, exacerbated as it was by the 2008 credit crunch.

The 'credit crunch' and housing under the Coalition government

When the credit crunch hit in early 2008, Gordon Brown had just become Prime Minister, succeeding Tony Blair the year before. The long boom that began in the mid 1990s had come to an end with a crash in commodity prices, linked partially to the sale of packaged sub-prime mortgages in the USA to banks around the world, particularly British banks. The result was an international financial crash with governments in the major industrial economies, including in the UK, having to rescue their banking systems. The credit crunch, as it came to be known, followed, whereby banks' lending to businesses and the housing market pushed the world into great recession and resulted in an explosion in public debt (in which the UK's national debt increased from 35 per cent of GDP in 2007 to 66 per cent in 2010).

Social housing under the Coalition

The Coalition between the Conservatives and the Liberal Democrats, formed in May 2010, was based upon a negotiated agreement for a governing programme. Central to the agreement was the reduction of the so-called structural deficit of £80 billion (that is, the deficit created by 'overspending' by the previous Labour government beyond the capacity for the economy to repay through resumed economic growth). The Coalition commenced its debt reduction programme via 'austerity economics' that sought to reduce the structural deficit by 2015 (although subsequently this target was extended to 2018 mainly because the austerity approach adopted by the Coalition government created an economy with very little economic growth between 2010 and 2013).

The response of the Coalition to the effects of the credit crunch for the UK's housing system were profound in two main respects. First, the Coalition reduced (capital) support for the building of new homes and, second, it reduced the levels of rent support to social housing tenants and introduced tougher eligibility criteria for those requiring social housing. The Coalition government's emergency budget in the summer of 2010 sought to cut two-thirds of the capital budget for social housing. Therefore, spending on social housing was replaced by the Affordable Housing Programme, which included a greater input from private finance in the financing of new social housing stock. Second, squeezes were applied to rental support such that housing associations were expected to set their rents at 80 per cent of market rents. In addition, changes embodied in the Coalition's 2012 Welfare Reform Act (see Chapter 9) included the introduction of a 'bedroom tax' for those deemed to be under-occupying social housing. Between 600,000 and 700,000 social tenants of working age were judged to be affected by the bedroom tax, equating to between 14 and 22 per cent of all social housing tenants and between 25 and 35 per cent of those of working age. In addition, and also part of the Welfare Reform Act, the Coalition introduced a benefit cap that sought to create a benefit ceiling of £26,000 for families and £18,200 for single people in total benefits they could claim, including housing benefit. These benefit changes, along with changes to council tax benefits, the decision not to increase benefits in line with inflation, and the impact of the introduction of the universal credit, were estimated to affect at least two-thirds of social tenants with losers probably outweighing winners. Overall, therefore, the Coalition's austerity drive both dampened social housing supply and impoverished social housing tenants (Gulliver and Smith, 2013).

At the same time as reducing capital support and rental support, the Coalition did enable councils to take greater financial responsibility for their own housing stock, with the aim of supporting councils to build new homes for the first time since the early 1980s. Local councils were also granted the freedom to allocate stock in the way that they saw fit, including prioritising working households rather than general need. In addition, councils were no longer obliged to have open waiting lists. Furthermore, the Localism Act aimed to reform social housing by creating a housing sector that used social housing as a 'springboard' for social mobility, for example with the introduction of HomeSwap Direct, a scheme designed to enable social tenants to manage moving house themselves. Overall, though, the Coalition's approach to social housing has arguably been to further marginalise and residualise social housing as a tenure option, such as average new tenancies being granted for only five years, and tenancies of between two and five years being allocated in 'exceptional circumstances'. After that, such tenants were expected to have made their own housing arrangements.

The promotion of home ownership under the Coalition

The second part of the Coalition's housing policy strategy since May 2010 has been its desire to address a decline in home ownership. Since 1979, government has wished to spread home ownership ever more widely. As discussed above, the primary mechanisms for this have been the right to buy scheme and by recalibrating social housing development programmes away from renting to a range of low-cost home-ownership initiatives. The historically low rate of housing development (and, therefore, housing supply) and the growing availability of mortgage credit in the last two decades created housing market bubbles that were key drivers of both household debt and the credit crunch. This resulted in massive increases in house prices and problems of affordability. Even though housing sales collapsed following the credit crunch, house prices and unaffordability have stayed relatively high because housing supply has been choked off (see Figure 16.5). Home ownership under the Coalition

Figure 16.5 Average house prices and house sales volume, April 1995 to April 2011

Source: Land Registry (2011)

has, therefore, remained beyond the reach of many individuals and families. The ratio of median income to median house price reached a peak in 2007 at 7.2 but has only fallen back marginally since then to 6.7 because of stagnant household incomes, stubbornly high house prices, and low levels of housing construction.

The limited social housing development over the last 30 years is part of the reason why the levels of housing needs in the UK have remained entrenched. Therefore, housing waiting lists have remained high since the 1990s and homelessness increased by 20 per cent between 2010 and 2012. Overcrowding and poor housing conditions continued to persist in all tenures, but especially at the low end of the home ownership and private rented sectors. The costs of these housing needs to the UK economy have been estimated by the National Housing Federation to run at £6 billion per annum in terms of the costs to the NHS, criminal justice system, and low educational attainment. At the same time, geographical mobility in social housing has collapsed (Gulliver, 2011).

So by 2011, the government was facing a housing crisis with growing housing needs and waiting lists and low levels of housing development. At the same time, home ownership had fallen back from its high point of 70 per cent in 2005 to 65 per cent in 2012. The Coalition government's response was to promote home ownership, as set out in *Laying the Foundations* (DCLG, 2011). It wished to promote choice, flexibility, and affordability and to 'get the housing market moving again'. Unveiling the strategy, David Cameron said it would 'unlock the housing market, get Britain building again, and give many more people the satisfaction and security that comes from stepping over their own threshold'. He claimed that the plans were 'ambitious', but that the government was determined to deliver.

On housing development, the government promised to invest an extra £400 million in new development through supporting small and medium-sized builders. The mortgage indemnity scheme designed with the Home Builders Federation and Council of Mortgage Lenders offered 95 per cent loans to value mortgages for new build properties in England, to support 100,000 households. The strategy promised to free-up public sector land with 'build now, pay later' deals for developers, releasing enough land to build 100,000 new homes and creating up to 200,000 new jobs in the construction industry. A new £500 million Growing Places fund was also established to support infrastructure development.

Further support was provided in the hope of stimulating owner-occupation. This included a new push on the 'right to buy' of social housing, with new right-to-buy owners offered a discount of as much as half the value of their homes. The government did promise, though, that homes sold through right to buy would be replaced by new homes developed for social rent, although there was considerable doubt about whether this was feasible. In addition, the Coalition earmarked £400 million for First Buy, a scheme designed to help over 10,000 first-time buyers via an equity loan that could be up to 20 per cent of the value of the property. This programme was later extended in the 2013 budget through the help to buy scheme. The help to buy scheme proposed to offer two forms of support: first, purchasers would be able to take up an interest-free loan from the government and, second, government would act as a guarantor for a proportion of a borrower's debt. The help to buy scheme could be used by any prospective purchaser, irrespective of their income, and could be used to buy properties up to £600,000 in value. The Coalition hoped that the £3.5 billion scheme would help up to 74,000 purchasers. However, criticism of the scheme emerged almost immediately following its announcement in the 2013 budget, not least because it was argued by commentators that the scheme might do little more than subsidise demand, resulting in property values being inflated artificially. Critics also argued that the Coalition would have been wiser to have used the funding simply to subsidise supply through assisting in the building of new properties, and thus decrease demand and price.

Overall, the Coalition's policies have been ineffective in stimulating or promoting the provision of either social or private housing. The private sector has yet to recover sufficiently from the dampening of demand due to the credit crisis and has received little support from the Coalition in terms of promoting supply. The Coalition's focus on promoting private demand might be counter-productive. At the same time, social housing has, arguably, continued to be residualised both through a lack of capital support for new build and through the impact of the Coalition's welfare reforms, which may well result in the further impoverishment of social housing tenants.

> ## STOP AND THINK
>
> ▪ Do you think government should assist people to buy a home, for example through 'right-to-buy' discounts, interest-free loans, mortgage tax relief or by acting as a mortgage guarantor?
>
> ▪ What might be some of the unintended consequences of such a policy?
>
> ▪ Why might subsidising supply, for example through assisting with the building of new social housing or subsidising private house building, be a better policy?

Conclusion

What, then, are we able to conclude from this review of changing housing policy over the last 70 years and, in particular, over the last 35 years? We can see that there was a rise and then more recently a decline in the prominence of housing policy. We will return to this alleged decline in housing policy shortly. As this chapter has explored, what, arguably, we have witnessed in Britain over the last 70 years is:

- a fairly constant and persistent increase in the numbers of households year on year;
- a significant increase in the supply of housing, though not sufficient to meet demand and, since the credit crunch in 2008, housing construction has gone into recession;
- an increase in the quality of housing for most people whereby 90 per cent of households could be judged as living in adequate housing as opposed to

80 per cent of households living in either overcrowded, substandard or unfit accommodation in 1951;

- a shift in the patterns of tenure, from a small minority of people living in owner-occupied households (10 per cent in 1910) to a majority of the population being so housed today (up to 70 per cent in 2005 but declining to 65 per cent by 2012) and the general acceptance of owner occupation as the preferred type of tenure;

- a consensus across all the major political parties in the support of owner occupation as the main form of tenure;

- an associated shift from local authority rented housing as being the dominant form within the rented sector to one where council housing decreased from 30 per cent to around 10 per cent of tenures over the last 35 years;

- a corresponding (though not proportionate) increase in social housing being provided by registered social landlords (e.g. housing associations) from just over 2 per cent to 10 per cent of all tenures over the last 35 years;

- the decline of the private rented sector to a fairly constant 10 per cent of stock over the last 35 years.

Therefore, the picture of housing in Britain is somewhat mixed, one in which there have been winners and losers. As such, there remains a need for government to have a clear housing policy. Borrowing from Malpass and Cairncross (2006), it is possible to conclude that:

- affordability remains a barrier to decent housing for significant sections of the population, particularly in the South East of England;

- while parts of the country experience over-demand, such as the South East, other areas and regions – for example, parts of the Midlands and the North, and South Wales – suffer from insufficient demand;

- lack of supply remains a key problem, with predictions of the need for 200,000 new homes per year over the next 10 years;

- social housing remains residualised, as a result of successive governments' lack of adequate investment and support;

- as a consequence, many communities where social housing is dominant or prevalent continue to experience social disadvantage and exclusion.

Thus, although the housing problems now experienced by many British citizens are not as acute as they were at the end of the Second World War, housing policy should continue to be, or return to being, an aspect of British social policy and government activity. Governments should continue to attend to the matter of housing because issues of affordability, lack of supply, homelessness, and poor quality of provision, all continue to persist. Therefore, while housing policy has been described as the 'wobbly pillar' of the British welfare state, it should remain an important part of British social policy and government attention.

Summary

This chapter has outlined developments in housing policy, examining some of the major issues around how the state and civil society should support people's housing needs. This has included an examination and consideration of:

- the development of state involvement in the provision of housing;
- the evolution of different housing sectors – private rental, public rental, and owner-occupation;
- the response of the Conservative New Right's housing policy of 1979–97, in which council housing was 'residualised' and the expansion of home ownership was promoted;
- New Labour's 'third way' housing policy response in which the public rented (social housing) sector was re-fashioned but the promotion of the private housing market continued, entrenching the dominant paradigm of owner-occupation as being the preferred choice of both individuals and the state;
- emerging Conservative-Liberal Democrat Coalition government policy; a response that sits within the 'austerity discourse' such that state support for building new homes (in both the private and public sectors) has been reduced, as has support for social housing tenants through cuts in welfare benefits, not least the 'bedroom tax' and its effects but, paradoxically, an increase in 'state support' of private demand through the 'help to buy' scheme.

Discussion and review

- To what extent do you think housing is a public or social good as well as being a private one?
- Should the state assist in the provision of housing at all and, if so, should it support supply (the building and availability of housing) or demand (through providing subsidies, cash incentives, discounts to purchasers or tenants)?

References

Barker, K. (2004) *Review of Housing Supply: Final Report*, HM Treasury, London.

BBC (2007) 'Crisis warning over house prices', BBC Website, 27 November, available at http://www.bbc.co.uk.

Booth, R. (2007) 'ITN man once interviewed the influential, now he sleeps rough', *The Guardian*, 15 December.

Bramley, G. (1994) 'An affordability crisis in British housing: dimensions, causes and policy impact', *Housing Studies*, Vol. 9, No. 1, pp. 103–24.

Cole, I. and Furbey, R. (1994) *The Eclipse of Council Housing*, Routledge, London.

Collinson, P. (2007) 'Hackney predicted to be a winner before the Games – house price growth in UK towns and cities', *The Guardian*, 29 December.

Daly, G., Mooney, G., Poole, L. and Davis, H. (2005) 'Housing stock transfer in Birmingham and Glasgow: the contrasting experiences of two UK cities', *European Journal of Housing Policy*, Vol. 5, No. 3, pp. 327–41.

Department for Communities and Local Government (DCLG) (2007) *Homes for the Future: More Affordable, More Sustainable*, The Stationery Office, London.

Department for Communities and Local Government (DCLG) (2011) *Laying the Foundations: A New Housing Strategy for England*, The Stationery Office, London.

Department of the Environment, Transport and the Regions (DETR) (2000) *Quality and Choice – A Decent Home for All*, DETR, London.

Doling, J. (1993) 'British housing policy: 1984–1993', *Regional Studies*, Vol. 27, No. 6, pp. 583–8.

Gulliver, K. and Smith, P. (2013) *All in it Together? The Effects of Housing Strategy, Austerity and Welfare Reform on Vulnerable Groups Living in Social Housing*, Human City Institute, Birmingham.

Harloe, M. (1995) *The People's Home? Social Rented Housing in Europe and America*, Blackwell, Oxford.

Hills, J. (2007) *Ends and Means: The Future Roles of Social Housing in England*, LSE, London.

Home Office (2006) *Respect Agenda*, Home Office, London.

Linneman, P.D. and Megbolugbe, I.F. (1994) 'Privatisation and housing policy', *Urban Studies*, Vol. 31, No. 4/5, pp. 635–51.

Lund, B. (2006) *Understanding Housing Policy*, Policy Press, Bristol.

Malpass, P. (1996) 'The unravelling of housing policy in Britain', *Housing Studies*, Vol. 11, No. 3, pp. 459–70.

Malpass, P. (2003) 'The wobbly pillar? Housing and the British postwar welfare state', *Journal of Social Policy*, Vol. 32, No. 4, pp. 589–606

Malpass, P. (2005) *Housing and the Welfare State*, Palgrave, Basingstoke.

Malpass, P. and Cairncross, L. (2006) 'Introduction', in P. Malpass and L. Cairncross (eds.) *Building on the Past: Visions of Housing Futures*, Policy Press, Bristol.

Malpass, P. and Means, R. (eds.) (1993) *Implementing Housing Policy*, Open University Press, Buckingham.

Malpass, P. and Murie, A. (1990) *Housing Policy and Practice* (3rd edn.), Macmillan, London.

Mullins, D. and Murie, A. (2006) *Housing Policy in the UK*, Palgrave Macmillan, Basingstoke.

Murie, A. (2007) 'Housing policy, housing tenure and the housing market', in K. Clarke, T. Maltby and K. Kennett (eds.) *Social Policy Review 19*, Policy Press, Bristol.

National Audit Office (2005) *More than a Roof: Progress in Tackling Homelessness*, The Stationery Office, London.

Office of the Deputy Prime Minister (2003) *Sustainable Communities: Building for the Future*, ODPM, London.

Office of the Deputy Prime Minister (2004) *Annual Report*, ODPM, London.

Office of the Deputy Prime Minister (2005a) *Sustainable Communities: Homes for All. A Five Year Plan from the Office of the Deputy Prime Minister*, ODPM, London.

Office of the Deputy Prime Minister (2005b) *Housing Statistics*, ODPM, London.

Social Exclusion Unit (1998) *Bringing Britain Together: A National Strategy for Neighbourhood Renewal*, The Stationery Office, London.

Stephens, M. and Quilgars, D. (2006) 'Strategic pragmatism? The state of housing policy', in L. Bauld, K. Clarke and T. Maltby (eds.) *Social Policy Review 18*, Policy Press, Bristol.

Summerfield, C. and Gill, B. (eds.) (2005) *Social Trends 35*, The Stationery Office, London.

Summers, D. (2007) 'Brown outlines legislative programme', *The Guardian*, 11 July.

White, M. and Wintour, P. (2005), 'Choice is a "tidal wave" that Labour must not ignore', *The Guardian*, 11 February.

Whitehead, C.M.E. (1993) 'Privatising housing: an assessment of UK experience', *Housing Policy Debate*, Vol. 4, No. 1, pp. 101–39.

Further reading

Perhaps the most useful and enduring overview of British housing policy is the volume by Malpass and Murie, *Housing Policy and Practice* (Macmillan, Basingstoke, 1999, 5th edn.). Also useful is the text by Malpass and Means (eds.), *Implementing Housing Policy* (Open University Press, Buckingham, 1993). For an account of the decline of (municipal) public sector housing, see Cole and Furbey's *The Eclipse of Council Housing: Housing and the Welfare State* (Routledge, London, 1993). Books that provide general overviews include that by Brian Lund, *Understanding Housing Policy* (Policy Press, Bristol, 2006), and the one by Mullins and Murie, *Housing Policy in the UK* (Palgrave Macmillan, Basingstoke, 2006). An interesting discussion of the place of housing policy and state involvement in housing provision is provided by Malpass (2003) in his article 'The wobbly pillar? Housing and the British postwar welfare state', *Journal of Social Policy*. Indeed, to obtain up-to-date accounts of housing policy developments, it is useful to refer to the general social policy journals such as *Critical Social Policy, Journal of Social Policy, Social Policy and Society, Journal of Public Policy, Journal of Public Administration*, and *Social Policy and Administration*. In addition, the more specific academic housing journals such as *Housing Studies* and the *European Journal of Housing Studies* are useful sources, as are other journals such as *Local Economy* and *Urban Studies*. The 'trade' journal *Inside Housing* provides useful contemporary commentary and analysis of developments in housing policy and practice.

Annotated reading

Perhaps the most useful and enduring overview of British housing policy is the volume by Malpass and Murie, *Housing Policy and Practice*. Also useful is the text by Malpass and Means, *Implementing Housing Policy*. For an account of the decline of (municipal) public sector housing see Cole and Furbey's (1994) *Eclipse of Council Housing*. Books that provide general overviews include that by Brian Lund (2006) *Understanding Housing Policy* and the one by Mullins and Murie (2006) *Housing Policy in the UK*. An interesting discussion of the place of housing policy and state involvement in housing provision is provided by Malpass (2003) in his article 'The Wobbly Pillar? Housing and the British Postwar Welfare State', *Journal of Social Policy*. A very interesting personal account of living on council estates that also applies sociological, historical and socio-political perspectives is Lynsey Hanley's *Estates* (2012).

To obtain up-to-date accounts of housing policy developments, it is useful to refer to the general social policy journals such as the *Critical Social Policy, Journal of Social Policy, Social Policy and Society, Journal of Public Policy*, the *Journal of Public Administration* and the *Social Policy and Administration* journal. In addition, the more specific academic housing journals such as *Housing Studies* and the *European Journal of Housing Studies* are useful sources as are other journals such as *Local Economy* and *Urban Studies*. The 'trade' journal *Inside Housing* provides useful contemporary commentary and analysis of developments in housing policy and practice.

Useful websites

http://www.dclg.gov.uk – National housing policy development is led and developed in the main by the Department for Communities and Local Government.

http://www.local.gov.uk – whilst the view of local government can be found on the Local Government Association's website.

There are a variety of housing related policy research centres including:

http://www.humancity.org.uk – The Human City Institute

http://www.shu.ac.uk/research/cresr – Centre for Regional Economic and Social Research

http://www.york.ac.uk/chp – Centre for Housing Studies

http://www.st-andrews.ac.uk/chr – Centre for Housing Research

Two of the key websites maintained for and by housing professionals including:

http://www.chi.org – Chartered Institute of Housing

http://www.housing.org – National Housing Federation

A useful site for latest developments in social housing is the weekly publication Inside Housing – http://www.insidehousing.co.uk

CHAPTER 17

'Race', Ethnicity, and Social Policy

Norman Ginsburg

Learning objectives

- To clarify the key concepts – 'race', ethnicity, and racism – and their use in and application to social policy analysis
- To map out the development of Britain as a multicultural, multi-ethnic, and multi-racial society
- To discuss how both direct and institutional racism have been inscribed in and resisted within British social policy
- To consider how, in several major fields of social policy, ethnic inequalities and injustices are both reinforced and ameliorated, using material on policy-making and its impact on minority ethnic communities, as well as reflecting on communities' experiences

Chapter overview

Issues around 'race' and ethnicity have become pervasive within social policy in Britain as society has increasingly become multi-racial and multi-ethnic since the Second World War. This chapter examines some of the most prominent aspects of recent discourse and policy-making by:

- reviewing the meaning and use of the terms 'race', ethnicity, and racism in the context of British social policy;

- examining the shift from a 'race relations' policy discourse inaugurated in the 1960s to an 'ethnic integration' discourse in the 2000s/2010s;

- considering data on the ethnic composition of the population and the ethnic categories used by policy-makers;

- discussing possibly the most important field for this topic – immigration and refugee policy, because it essentially involves racialised barriers to accessing the welfare state;

- complementing this with consideration of anti-discrimination measures;

- considering four major areas of social policy in which issues of racism and anti-racism have been prominent – employment/income, policing, schooling, and housing.

CONTROVERSY AND DEBATE

A new phase in policy against racial discrimination began in the wake of the Macpherson Inquiry (1999) into the death of Stephen Lawrence, the victim of a racist murder in 1993 (see below). The performance of the police was understood as the outcome of institutional racism, which Macpherson (1999, para. 6.34) defined as:

> 'The collective failure of an organisation to provide an appropriate and professional service to people because of their colour, culture, or ethnic origin. It can be seen or detected in processes, attitudes and behaviour which amount to discrimination through unwitting prejudice, ignorance, thoughtlessness and racist stereotyping which disadvantage minority ethnic people'.

This is a distinct and controversial definition of institutional racism, because in the second sentence it focuses on individual behaviour rather than the policies of an organisation and the accompanying managerial and workplace cultures. The notion of 'unwitting prejudice' is particularly confusing because it seems to absolve individuals, but only partially (see Rattansi, 2007, pp. 132–40). In the wake of public concern about the Stephen Lawrence case, not least from the Black community, the government, somewhat hesitantly, enacted the Race Relations (Amendment) Act 2000 Act, which required most publicly funded services, not just local authorities, to produce Race Equality Plans covering both users and employees in order to challenge institutional racism. This inaugurated the 'Macpherson process' across the welfare state and the public services, involving much more ethnic monitoring of employment within and of use of services, and the setting of targets for specific improvements. As yet, no adequate assessment of the impact of race equality planning has been done, and the process seems to have remained a largely bureaucratic, managerial exercise, as the political force behind the Macpherson Inquiry has waned.

'Race', ethnicity, and racism

It is essential to examine briefly a few of the key concepts involved both in the public discourse and in social scientific understanding of this topic. Here we are obviously and immediately confronted by a huge conundrum. 'Race' does not exist as an essential difference among human beings, yet it continues to be widely used to denote differences in physical appearance – differences of 'skin, hair, and bone'. Over the centuries, white Europeans used notions of racial hierarchy and superiority to bolster their imperialist ambitions and regimes. This means that the moment we use notions of 'race' and 'anti-racism' we are unavoidably embracing ideas of essential difference and hierarchy. To distance themselves from that embrace, social scientists in recent years have often put the word 'race' in inverted commas, to signify that it is a social construction, which must be continuously subject to critical reflection. The terms 'ethnicity' and 'ethnic group' came to the fore in the second half of the twentieth century, as the idea of 'race' was discredited by its exposure as scientifically bogus and by its role in Nazi ideology. Membership of an ethnic group suggests an identity socially constructed around descent and/or culture. Obviously in everyday usage there is much blurring and inconsistency in the use of the terms 'race' and 'ethnicity'. Prejudice and discrimination on the basis of ethnic identity is commonly described as racism or racial discrimination, because there is no such word as 'ethnicism', which is particularly confusing. Hence 'race relations' legislation in the UK has included discrimination on 'grounds of race, colour, nationality (including citizenship), or ethnic or national origin' and has been successfully used by members of the UK's old, national ethnicities (Scots, Welsh, Irish, English). The legislation steers clear of defining 'race' and ethnicity, but the mere fact that such a wide range of identities are covered by 'race relations' indicates the enduring, if constantly shifting, ambit of the idea of 'race' in social policy. In contemporary British discourse, the phrase 'ethnic minorities' is most commonly used as a coded term to describe non-whites. Social scientists refer to 'minority ethnic groups' to point up that there is a white 'ethnic majority'. Public services sometimes use the category 'Black and Minority Ethnic' (BME) in recognition of Black identity as a political and cultural force. 'Black' is used to describe people of Black African and African-Caribbean descent, while 'black' is often used as a generic term for non-white people or people of colour.

Explicit operationalisation of the ideas of 'race' and ethnicity in British social policy emerged in the second half of the twentieth century in the wake of the great post-colonial migration, initially predominantly from the Asian subcontinent and the Caribbean. But it was embedded in the origins of the modern welfare state as it developed out of the Poor Law. The first immigration legislation (the Aliens Order 1905, which sought to exclude Jews fleeing ethnic cleansing in Eastern Europe) went alongside the development of national insurance and public education, health care and family welfare services for the indigenous population. This occurred amidst a panic about the unfitness of British troops fighting Dutch farmers and Africans for control of southern Africa. This was the era of 'social imperialism', when it was felt that the world's foremost imperial power had to attend to the breeding, education, and welfare of its own people not only to survive, but to cement their sense of collective superiority over others. The linkage between welfare policy and national ethnic identity was strengthened after the First World War with the promise of 'homes fit for heroes to live in' (council housing) and, again, after the Second World War, with the construction of a more fully fledged national welfare state and social rights of citizenship (see Chapters 6, 7, and 8). Eligibility for these rights was founded on membership of the national community, a British ethnic identity that was strongest during and after the Second World War. Both the British and English ethnic identity (which the English have often largely seen as synonymous) embrace a peculiarly insular and disdainful attitude towards 'bloody foreigners' as a whole, laced with ethnic and racial stereotypes as appropriate (Winder, 2004). This is reflected in continuing and widespread hostility towards asylum seekers, refugees, immigrants, and even the EU, which is, in turn, reflected in social policy.

The watershed 'event' in shaping the complex relationship between 'race', ethnicity, and social policy in contemporary Britain was the great post-colonial migration from the late 1940s to early 1970s, coinciding with the flowering of the classic welfare state. The latter was part of the post-war 'class settlement', but it was never established to what extent, if at all, it should be accessible to immigrants, particularly social housing. Hence there began a long and continuing struggle to establish the social rights of the then 'new' minority ethnic groups in the face of direct and institutionalised racism. There was a particular ambiguity towards the Black and Asian post-colonial migrants in British social policy. It formally bestowed British citizenship on them under the British Nationality Act 1948, and actively recruited staff for the public services in the former colonies, while in practice often making them second-class citizens and deterring family settlement. Governments in the 1950s and 1960s tried to juggle the needs of the economy for migrant workers, including the welfare state itself (most notably doctors, nurses, and ancillary workers for the NHS), with virulent hostility to their presence in many quarters. The boom–bust economy from the late 1950s generated bouts of unemployment, which contributed to the spread of explicit racism into mainstream politics, Labour as well as Conservative. This 'movement' is often known as Powellism (Weight, 2003; Rattansi, 2007), after the maverick Conservative politician Enoch Powell, who advocated forced repatriation of post-colonial migrants to prevent 'rivers of blood'. Thus 'race relations' came onto the policy agenda.

From 'race relations' to 'community cohesion' and integrationism

'Race relations' (or 'community relations'), as it emerged in the 1960s, has had a rich meaning in British social policy. It has been explicitly two-sided – racialised immigration control combined with measures to integrate settled minorities. Hence it was about the managed exclusion of racialised others and the management of those who had 'got under the wire', as it were. The former was achieved with a series of racist immigration acts from 1962 to 1971, which all but prevented migration by people of colour from the former colonies. The latter, the management of settlers, was encapsulated in the words of the Labour Home Secretary in 1966, Roy Jenkins, as 'equal opportunity accompanied by cultural diversity in an atmosphere of mutual tolerance'. In policy terms, this 'liberal' consensus generated fairly soft anti-discrimination legislation to deter more explicit forms of racism, and a *laissez-faire* approach to cultural diversity, an arms-length multiculturalism. In 1971, a Conservative Home Secretary, Reginald Maudling (1971) outlined the policy consensus very bluntly:

> The main purpose of immigration policy . . . is a contribution to peace and harmony . . . If we are to get progress in community relations, we must give assurance to the people, who were already here before the large wave of immigration, that this will be the end and that there will be no further large-scale immigration. Unless we can give that assurance, we cannot effectively set about improving community relations.

This two-sided policy consensus has been sorely tested over the decades by pressure from many and varied quarters. In the late 1970s, the far right and Powellites made a big push for repatriation of Black and Asian settlers, accompanied by increased police harassment and violence, particularly against Black and Asian young people. This was fiercely resisted on the streets and in local politics. Very high levels of youth unemployment and more police brutality contributed to the inner-city uprisings of 1981. The policy response was to tone down quietly some of the pressure on minority communities. The ten years or so from the late 1970s to the late 1980s saw a turning of the tide against exclusionary and segregationist sentiment, and the emergence of Black British and British Asian as respected identities. Above all, this established firmly in the minds of the white majority that Black British and British Asian people were here to stay and that Britain had become a permanently multi-racial society.

Another big moment came in the early 2000s, when the far right coordinated attacks on Pakistani communities in some northern towns in the run up to the May 2001 general election, which provoked strong resistance. Politicians and the media rushed to blame the Pakistani community, hundreds of whom were subsequently convicted of violent offences, unlike any of their white foes. 9/11 and the 7/7 London bombings in July 2005 added significantly to anti-Muslim feeling, directed inevitably towards people of Pakistani and Bangladeshi heritage, who form the great majority of Muslims in Britain. Quite suddenly in the wake of these events, politicians, intellectuals, and policy-makers across the mainstream identified these communities as self-segregated, as living 'parallel lives', and as having failed to integrate into British society. This became most explicit in September 2005 when Trevor Phillips, New Labour's race relations guru and head of the Commission for Racial Equality, suggested that Britain was 'sleepwalking to segregation' (see Finney and Simpson, 2009).

The truth is to some considerable extent the exact opposite – it was local segregationist policy-making in housing and education, accompanied by 'white flight' from urban neighbourhoods and industrial decline, which contributed substantially to the social exclusion of the Muslim communities of the northern towns over several decades. Kundnani (2007) argues that the aftermath of 2001 has led to 'the end of tolerance' and of liberal, arms-length multiculturalism, with the move towards a more authoritarian integrationism directed at Muslim communities across the land. It is certainly true that 'the Muslim community' has effectively become 'an ethnicity rather than a group sharing a religion' (Kundnani, 2007, p. 126) and that a new discourse in local policy-making has rapidly emerged built upon the idea of 'community cohesion'.

The concepts of 'parallel lives' and 'community cohesion' first came to prominence in a report by Cantle (2001) for the government on the events in the northern towns in 2001. The view of Cantle (2005), shared by New Labour, was that central and local government should pursue a much more interventionist, normative strategy towards the integration of those minorities leading 'parallel lives', obviously a coded reference to Muslim communities. This view has been endorsed by the Coalition government. In 2011, the Prime Minister, David Cameron, called for a 'muscular liberalism' to replace the old-style arms-length multiculturalism. But what does this mean in policy terms? The New Labour government's Commission on Integration and Cohesion (CIC, 2007) came up with a large number of policy recommendations, including more funding for voluntary groups promoting integration and for classes in English for non-English speakers, restricting the translation of council documents into foreign languages, and, most controversially, an end to funding for voluntary organisations representing a single ethnic or religious identity. The government accepted most of the recommendations, but implementation has been patchy and resisted. Funds for civic integration programmes have dried up, while the effort to limit funding to mono-ethnic/faith has proved illegal and impractical, not least because it completely contradicts government support for faith schools. Integrationist policy has also been undermined by the anti-terrorist strategy PREVENT, which has covertly funded voluntary activity opposed to radical Islamist mobilisation. According to Kundnani (2009), this has been experienced as a divisive form of surveillance, involving a simplistic political conditionality in accessing resources. 'Integration policy' is likely to remain a discourse and a practice generating complex controversies and community resistance, based as it is on a 'flawed paradigm' of community cohesion (Ratcliffe, 2012) that focuses on cultural difference rather than socio-economic divisions.

Ethnic categorisation and growing ethnic diversity

One of the effects of the 'settlement' of the 1980s was the recognition of the social significance of the minority ethnic communities by social policy-makers, symbolised by the inclusion of a question about ethnic identity in the 1991 population census. If the 'equal opportunities' element of the liberal consensus was to have any credibility, then ethnic inequalities and the particular needs of different ethnic communities had to be officially quantified. The ethnic classification in the census had been shaped by the post-colonial migration and the labels most commonly used by the 'host community'. Hence, in the 2011 census for England and Wales the proportions for the major five ethnic categories were: White (86.0 per cent), Mixed/Multiple Ethnic (2.2 per cent), Asian/Asian British (7.5 per cent), Black/African/Caribbean (3.3 per cent), and Other (1.0 per cent). The proportion of people identifying as non-white increased from 5.9 per cent in 1991 and 8.7 per cent in 2001 to 14.0 per cent in 2011.

From the detailed ethnic breakdown in Table 17.1 the most striking developments are the proportionate growth of all the groups, except the Irish and Black Caribbeans. This reflects the emergence of what has been called 'superdiversity' in Britain, linked to a range of phenomena including the 'new' economic migration particularly from Central Europe, the relative ageing of the white British group, and the wider acceptance of mixed parenting (for some of the implications for future social policy, see Vertovec, 2007).

Immigration and refugee policy

Control of immigration lies at the heart of social policy in the UK, because it is the means by which the state discriminates as to who has the right to be resident, even temporarily, within its borders. This inevitably has racial and ethnic dimensions, because many, if not most, of the people wanting to reside in Britain are not of white European origin, whether they are economic migrants or refugees/asylum seekers. Hence immigration controls can be described as an example of structural racism, a consequence of the global

STOP AND THINK

- Why was there a panic in 2005 about England sleepwalking its way to segregation?

- How is and should segregation be measured?

- What are the positives (if any) of residential segregation?

- How does the housing 'system' shape residential patterns based on ethnicity?

Table 17.1 Ethnic minority groups in England and Wales, 2001 and 2011, percentages

		2011 (%)	2001 (%)
White			
	White British	80.5	87.5
	Irish	0.9	1.2
	Gypsy or Irish Traveller[1]	0.1	—
	Other White	4.4	2.6
Mixed/multiple ethnic groups			
	White and Black Caribbean	0.8	0.5
	White and Asian	0.6	0.4
	White and Black African	0.3	0.2
	Other Mixed	0.5	0.3
Asian/Asian British			
	Indian	2.5	2.0
	Pakistani	2.0	1.4
	Bangladeshi	0.8	0.5
	Chinese[a]	0.7	0.4
	Other Asian[a]	1.5	0.5
Black/African/Caribbean/Black British			
	African	1.8	0.9
	Caribbean	1.1	1.1
	Other Black	0.5	0.2
Other ethnic group			
	Arab[2]	0.4	—
	Any other ethnic group[3]	0.6	0.4

[1] No comparable data exist for these ethnic groups in the 2001 census.
[2] Comparability issues exist between these ethnic groups for the 2001 and 2011 censuses.
[3] No comparable data exist for these ethnic groups in the 2001 census.
Source: ONS (2012a)

structure of inequality between the predominantly white, rich countries and the predominantly non-white, poor countries. But they can also be conceived as an example of institutional racism (institutionalised within the state itself) whereby people of colour and distinct ethnic difference are treated adversely compared with Whites. By the early 1970s, Britain had closed the door to non-white economic migrants from the former colonies, except for spouses and relatives of those already settled, itself a major site of conflict ever since. It would be difficult to underestimate the impact and the message conveyed by the 1962–71 immigration legislation; it officially recognised and legitimated Powellite racism, and it made non-white post-colonial migrants and their families settled in Britain feel permanently insecure and of second-class status.

Britain's economic stagnation and recurrent high levels of unemployment through to the mid 1990s meant that economic migration remained at a low level. Up to around 1993 very few of the growing numbers of asylum seekers and refugees arriving in Western Europe were allowed to enter the UK. Both of these situations changed in the mid 1990s – an economic boom lasting into the late 2000s produced an unprecedented demand for labour and Britain could no longer sustain its rejection of asylum seekers in the face of EU and human rights pressures.

Issues surrounding asylum seekers and undocumented migrants dominated the policy discourse from the mid 1990s to mid 2000s as the government busily responded to xenophobic and racist hostility to them across wide swathes of British society, nourished by the print media. Paralleling in some ways the development of immigration control in the 1960s, no less than eight Acts of Parliament between 1993 and 2009 ratcheted up the legal and administrative means to deter refugees from seeking asylum in the UK, to deny those already here access to employment and the welfare state, and to incarcerate them prior to deportation as quickly as possible. Much of the hostility to asylum seekers has been couched in terms of their real motives being to scrounge off the welfare state, 'a never-evidenced "pull factor" of "generous" social provision' (Mulvey, 2011, p. 1480). Hence legislation has steadily sought to deny them the social rights that the welfare state proclaims as universal. The 1993 Asylum and Immigration Appeals Act withdrew asylum seekers' access to social rented housing tenancy. The 1996 Immigration and Asylum Act ended their right to social security benefits unless they had children, and replaced them with vouchers. The 1999 Asylum and Immigration Act created a separate welfare regime for asylum seekers and their families, run by a new agency – the National Asylum Support Service (NASS) providing voucher support at levels significantly less than the official poverty line. The 1999 Act also introduced compulsory dispersal, which took people away from the informal support of their ethnic communities and often left them isolated on bleak housing estates in hostile, poor white communities. These features of the 1999 Act were an unmitigated disaster, creating destitution and desperation, and exposure to racist violence, which was in a few cases murderous. Dispersal continues to cause severe problems for asylum seekers, notably pregnant women who cannot get access to antenatal care (Feldman, 2013). The 2002 Nationality, Immigration and Asylum Act partially abandoned dispersal and vouchers in favour of warehousing in prison-like residential centres with their own education and health care provisions. This signalled a move towards physically excluding asylum seekers from normal life in the community. Asylum Acts in 2004 and 2006 further tightened the monitoring of asylum seekers and speeded detention and removal by the withdrawal of legal rights. Throughout, these measures have been challenged in the courts (sometimes successfully) with refugee organisations, other NGOs, and minority communities themselves leading the resistance and trying to fill the gap left by the withdrawal of the welfare state. Riots, serious fires, and mass escapes at detention centres have exemplified a different form of resistance. After peaking in 2002 at almost 85,000, the number of asylum applications fell dramatically to under 25,000 a year in the second half of the 2000s, as measures to deter applications and to process them 'off shore' bit hard.

While asylum seekers and refugees were the focus of most media attention and policy-making in the late 1990s and early 2000s, at the same time there took place another important shift in policy on migrant workers and 'economic migration'. The New Labour government proclaimed a shift towards 'managed migration' in the context of growing shortages of labour across almost all occupations from dentists, teachers, and social workers to farming, catering, hotels, elder and child care, and construction. The management of labour migration is not new in itself; the post-colonial migration of the 1950s and 1960s was managed covertly as employers (both public and private) were permitted to recruit in the former colonies under government surveillance. Although primary immigration was formally ended from the 1970s through the 1990s, there were government schemes and quotas to facilitate recruitment abroad to fill specific niches and to encourage wealthy people to settle in Britain. Nevertheless, the economic boom from the mid 1990s generated a new large-scale inward migration of workers, arriving in very diverse circumstances ranging from the victims of traffickers and unscrupulous gangmasters to skilled, self-organised craftspeople, graduate professional and corporate executives. The key point about this migration in relation to 'race' and ethnicity is that many have been white people from new EU member states in Central Europe.

A glimpse of the impact of recent economic migration policy is given by census data on international migrants in England and Wales. The non-UK born population rose from 9 per cent to 13 per cent between 2001 and 2011, accounting for 71 per cent of the overall population growth of 4 million. The top ten countries of origin for non-UK born residents were (in order of significance): India, Poland, Pakistan, Ireland, Germany, Bangladesh, Nigeria, South Africa, USA, and Jamaica (ONS, 2012b). These numbers include a significant number of higher education students, who contributed an increasingly important proportion of university funding in the 2000s. The ethnic composition suggests that, despite the institutional racism historically built into the 'system', postcolonial non-white migration remains significant, alongside substantial white migration from the northern hemisphere.

So, the era of managed migration has to some extent continued racialised processes. This allowed the New Labour government to be much more open about the benefits of immigration than previous regimes. The unspoken assumption has been that new migrants should not be encouraged to settle. Hence managed migration does not extend to social provision being made for their welfare. Local education, health care, housing, and social services experience extra demands on their limited resources without extra funding, as, inevitably, many of the new migrants have settled on at least a semi-permanent basis. This fuels anti-immigrant sentiment, and increases support for the far right.

STOP AND THINK

- What role did policy play in shaping the post-colonial migration from the 1940s to the 1970s?

- What role did policy play in shaping the 'new migration' of the 1990s and 2000s?

- What are the arguments for and against giving migrants full access to the services and benefits of the welfare state?

Anti-discrimination

The centrepiece of official anti-racist policy is the Equalities Act 2010 (see Hepple, 2010), which incorporates the Race Relations Act 1976 and the Race Relations (Amendment) Act 2000. The 1976 Act enabled individuals to seek legal redress against direct discrimination; it established the Commission for Racial Equality (CRE), now incorporated into the Equality and Human Rights Commission (EHRC), as the public agency promoting anti-discrimination with legal powers to challenge indirect (or institutional) racism; and it obliged local authorities to 'promote good race relations'. The impact of the legislation and the associated measures has been modest, as the data above suggest, but certainly not insignificant. If it did not exist, the situation would undoubtedly be a lot worse.

The Commission for Racial Equality was severely limited by its modest funding and its vulnerability to ridicule by the tabloid media, underpinned by right-wing hostility to the 'race relations industry' as a whole. This was particularly true during the 1980s, when there was a constant threat to its existence under the Thatcher governments. The Commission undertook over 50 'formal investigations' into organisations where systematic, institutionalised discrimination had come to light. Many of these led to the issuing of a 'non-discrimination notice' to try to ensure that the organisation implements the Commission's recommendations. In 1984, a 'non-discrimination notice' was served on the London Borough of Hackney, after a CRE investigation (CRE, 1984) revealed indirect discrimination in the allocation of council housing. This process served as a benchmark for more equitable local authority housing allocation throughout the country thereafter. In 2003, the Commission published a major investigation into the Prison Service, documenting entrenched racism therein (CRE, 2003). The Prison Service agreed to implement an Action Plan under CRE supervision, but in 2005 the Commission announced that 'major questions remain over the effectiveness of this work' (CRE, 2005, p. 11). In such front-line challenges to institutionalised racism the Commission had, and the EHRC now has, limited power to achieve change.

Poverty and the labour market

Perhaps the most pressing racial and ethnic inequalities that should be addressed by social policy are those surrounding incomes and jobs. A thorough review of the data by Platt (2007) found substantially higher than average poverty rates for all the major non-white ethnic groups, particularly among people of Bangladeshi, Pakistani, and Black African origin. These differences have persisted over recent decades and are experienced as much by children as by older people: 'Bangladeshis were identified as having the greatest poverty for most measures. Poverty for this group also appeared to be severer and more long lasting than that experienced by other groups' (Platt, 2007, p. x). While much of this entrenched poverty can be explained in terms of poor education and employment opportunities, the bedrock of social policy in the form of the pensions, benefits, and tax credits system has also differentially failed minority ethnic groups, who 'both experience more limited entitlement to certain benefits (through, for example, interrupted contributions records) and are less likely to claim various forms of benefit to which they are entitled' (Platt, 2007, p. 100).

A simple measure of the position of minority ethnic groups in the labour market is given by the proportion of adults aged 16–64 'not working' (i.e. unemployed or economically inactive). In the second quarter of 2012, the proportion of Whites 'not working' was 29.0 per cent, compared with 32 per cent of Indians, 56.7 per cent of Pakistanis, 58.2 per cent of Bangladeshis, 57.7 per cent of Chinese, and 42.7 per cent of Black Africans/Caribbeans. Another measure is low pay; around a quarter of Whites, Black-Caribbeans, Indians, and Black-Africans earned less than £7 per hour in 2008–10, compared with almost half of Pakistanis and Bangladeshis (ONS *Labour Force Survey*, www.ons.gov.uk). The patchwork of available data clearly suggests that the situation of people of Pakistani and Bangladeshi heritage is particularly difficult both in terms of remuneration in employment and exclusion from the labour market.

There are many complex social, structural, and biographical factors involved in maintaining the persistent disadvantages of minority ethnic groups in the labour market, but direct discrimination by employers and employees is certainly of serious significance. Heath and Cheung (2006, p. 67) concluded from their evidence 'on continued ethnic penalties, on the rates of job refusals reported by members of ethnic minorities, and on the levels of prejudice reported by white managers and employers . . . that discrimination continues to be a major problem and is unlikely to disappear of its own accord without new and effective interventions . . . directed at firms and employers'.

In 2011–12, a total of 4,800 claims of race discrimination were taken up by employment tribunals, but only 140 cases were successful, with a median award of £5,256 (Ministry of Justice, 2012). Complainants are not eligible for legal aid and bringing a case to the tribunal is extremely stressful. Thirty per cent of claims were withdrawn and 36 per cent were settled by negotiation. Compared with the USA, the prospects of individual success in pursuing individual claims of employment discrimination and the level of compensation are much less. The situation in the UK has changed little over many years, contributing to cynicism about the effectiveness of individuals' legal rights to pursue anti-discrimination claims. The Commission for Racial Equality and EHRC have pursued a quiet strategy of behind the scenes negotiation with employers and organisations to persuade and cajole them into adopting more conscious and explicit anti-discrimination measures, as laid out, for example, in their Code of Practice on Employment. The Code is not legally obligatory, but employment tribunals use it to try to bring employers into line.

Policing

From the 1960s to the 1980s, the media and policy 'conversation', and the practice of the police and criminal justice system (PCJS), stereotyped black young men as a particular threat on the streets, which had to be met with a tough law and order response from the police, the courts, and the prisons. When the police response is unjust or disproportionate, as it often has been, the discourse suggested and continues to suggest that it was a price worth paying. There was and is no evidence that black youth are any more criminal than white youth in poor neighbourhoods. Public disorder and protest are fuelled both by police brutality and by police inaction against racist violence. Within the PCJS there has been an attitude of internal colonialist policing, control, and repression in which visible minorities have been treated as particularly threatening and dangerous. This seems to have been embedded within the canteen cultures (the everyday, subcultural assumptions) of the PCJS.

The Stephen Lawrence case and the Macpherson Inquiry (SLMI) exposed these processes to critical, public scrutiny. Stephen, a Black British teenager, was murdered in April 1993; after a collapsed trial in 1996, an inquest took place in February 1997, exposing police incompetence. The *Daily Mail* then named five white youths as the murderers, a cataclysmic event; two of the five were eventually convicted in 2012. In May 1997, the New Labour government was elected, anxious to repay some of their debts to Black and Asian voters. In July 1997, the Macpherson Inquiry was announced, and its report in February 1999 exposed professional incompetence, institutional racism, and 'failure of leadership at senior levels' in the police response to the murder. Institutional racism was exemplified in the lax approach by the police to the investigation, the fobbing off of Stephen's family, and the web of suspicion cast over his companion Duwayne Brooks. There was strong evidence of racial stereotyping. The Macpherson Report made over 70 recommendations, largely concerned with police procedures and accountability, which have formally been implemented. They included: a new, explicit definition of racial incidents; new procedures and practice at serious incidents; improved family liaison and handling of victims and witnesses; much more race awareness training; and the establishment of the Independent Police Complaints Commission and the Metropolitan Police Authority, bringing significantly increased lay scrutiny of policing in London.

A study for the Home Office of the impact of the Stephen Lawrence case and Macpherson on policing conducted in 2002–04 found much activity and anxiety within the police, but also confusion and anger around the notion of institutional racism, widely misunderstood as labelling all police officers as racist. The study (Foster *et al.*, 2005) revealed continuing mistrust and expectation of discrimination among minority ethnic communities, particularly young people. The police have been 'weathering the storm'; the managerial, public face signifies reform and a change of culture, but on the ground the changes are not so dramatic. A review of SLMI by criminologists (Rowe,

2007, p. xvii) concluded that 'while police officers might have stopped being overtly racist, a more widespread understanding of diversity has not been embedded within the service', and that the 'reconstruction of the police as an anti-racist service' has stopped short. SLMI is far from having achieved fundamental institutional change. Racial violence is still far from effectively policed (Burnett, 2012); 'stop and search' continues to be much more likely for visible minorities (EHRC, 2010); the criminal justice system beyond the police remains largely unaffected by SLMI. A government commissioned report (Neyroud, 2011) documented how the police service continues to have a dominant white male profile, estimating it would take over 18 years to achieve 7 per cent minority representation across the service as a whole. Legislation in related areas (freedom of information, refugees and asylum seekers, prevention of terrorism) strengthens institutional racism, so that the processes uncovered during SLMI and prior to that by decades of struggle and of solid sociological research still seem to persist.

Schooling

Two big issues have been recurrently prominent in policy discussion around schooling since the post-colonial migration in the 1950s and 1960s, namely 'underachievement' and 'segregation and multiculturalism'. 'Underachievement' is related to a number of linked issues. Black pupils leave school with lesser qualifications than Whites and Asians; they are much more likely to be suspended or expelled from school; minority ethnic groups are seriously underrepresented in the teaching profession.

Over more than four decades, Black parents have struggled to get their voices heard, sometimes with some impact at the local level, but at the national level, until recently, they have been fobbed off. In 1971, a celebrated pamphlet discussed *How the West Indian Child is Made Educationally Subnormal in the British School System* (Coard, 1971). The subsequent pressure on the Labour government in the late 1970s produced two useful reports by Rampton (1981) and Swann (1985), but by the time they surfaced, the Thatcher government was in power and they were shelved. Rampton and Swann drew particular attention to the problem of teachers' low and stereotyped expectations of Black pupils and the small numbers of Black teachers in schools to act as role models. The advent of New Labour at last brought some purposeful recognition of the issues with the publication of national data and the allocation of grant funding for initiatives in schools to try to remedy the situation.

The widely used parameter for underachievement is the proportion of pupils achieving below 5 or more A*–C grades at GCSE. Figure 17.1 shows that pupils of Chinese, Indian, Irish, and Bangladeshi heritage do better than the average, while pupils of Pakistani and Black Caribbean heritage do worse. The performance of Bangladeshi pupils has improved markedly since the early 1990s when they were the most underachieving of the major ethnic groups.

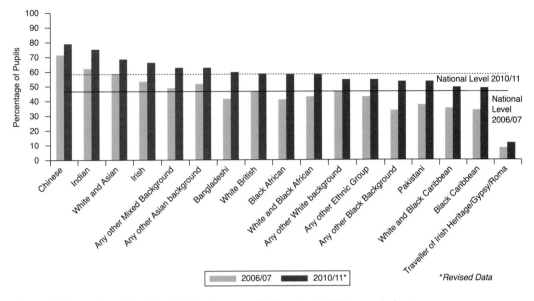

Figure 17.1 Proportion of pupils achieving 5 or more A*–C grades at GCSE or equivalent including English and Mathematics by ethnic group in England, 2006–07 and 2010–11

Source: DCSF (2012a, figure 2)

Pupils of Traveller heritage do much worse than any other ethnic group. For all ethnic groups, girls outperform boys; the gender gap is greatest for Black Caribbean pupils and least for Irish pupils.

GCSE examination teaching is 'tiered' so that students can only attain A/B grades if they are entered for them and taught in the top 'sets'; Black students are underrepresented in the higher tier(s) (Gillborn and Rollock, 2010). There are also very significant 'class' effects at work here; a substantial minority of Indian heritage pupils have professional/managerial family backgrounds; minority ethnic households are differentially underrepresented in professional/managerial ranks, at least until quite recently.

Clearly, there are many economic and cultural factors involved beyond black–white racism, but the situation of Black pupils is exacerbated by their being much more likely to be suspended or excluded from school. The rate of exclusions in England has fallen from a peak in 1997, when Black pupils were six times more likely to be excluded from school, but in 2010–11 the ratio was still two times. Asian pupils were half as likely to be permanently excluded than the average (DCSF, 2012b). According to Gillborn and Rollock (2010, pp. 152–3), 'there is growing evidence that the over-representation of African Caribbean students is the result of harsher treatment by schools rather than simple differences in behaviour of students. Twice in recent years Ofsted found that Black students are treated somewhat more harshly than their peers'. This is despite Ofsted school reports being criticised for rarely commenting on the disproportionality.

In the early 1980s, only 0.2 per cent of teachers were of minority ethnic origin. By 2009 in England, the ethnic breakdown of teachers in local authority maintained schools was 94.0 per cent White, 2.7 per cent Asian/Asian British, and 1.8 per cent Black/Black British (DCSF, 2009). This obviously indicates a continuing significant underrepresentation of teachers with a minority ethnic heritage.

A number of interrelated aspects of multiculturalism in schools have become national policy issues over the decades. In the 1960s, there was much concern about the integration of the children of immigrants into the school system, particularly through language teaching. Some extra resources were allocated to schools with significant numbers of African Caribbean and Asian pupils, and there was some experimentation with 'bussing' secondary school students to prevent 'segregated' schools (i.e. those with a predominance of non-white pupils). In the 1970s and 1980s, there was conflict around shifting the curriculum and school culture away from monocultural, traditional approaches towards having both multicultural and anti-racist content. In 1985 in Bradford, a prominent head teacher, Ray Honeyford, lost his job for staunchly resisting the multicultural and anti-racist momentum. Despite the personal support of Prime Minister Thatcher, he had lost that of the white and Asian parents (Todd, 1991). In Dewsbury in 1987, white parents withdrew their children from a school with an Asian majority, demanding an alternative choice. Eventually in 1992, the High Court ruled that 'local education authorities must comply with parents' wishes to transfer a child to another school, even if the request is motivated by racial factors' (Law, 1996, p. 170). But these events were exceptional, as schools adapted to the development of a consciously multicultural and multi-ethnic society, moving away to some extent from a completely monocultural curriculum and largely avoiding ethnically segregated schools. Across England, attendance at predominantly mono-ethic schools is only the norm for white pupils (Johnston *et al.*, 2004).

STOP AND THINK

- What are the most significant factors and processes invoked to explain minority ethnic underachievement in schools?

- What impact has multiculturalism had on schooling in Britain?

- What role do faith schools play in the recognition of ethnic identity and the maintenance of ethnic division?

The disturbances in some northern towns in 2001 and increased concern about Islamism in the 2000s generated much increased anxiety about the integration of pupils and teachers from Muslim communities of Pakistani and Bangladeshi origin. In some northern towns, some schools were over 90 per cent Asian, while the ethnic mix in the towns as a whole was roughly two-thirds white, one-third Asian. In 2007, the government made it a duty of schools and education authorities to promote 'community cohesion', supported by PREVENT funding (see earlier discussion). Such measures have forced school mergers in Burnley, Blackburn, Leeds, and Oldham, leading to some increased harassment of Muslim pupils and some white hostility to what is perceived as social engineering (Miah, 2012). The 'community cohesion' agenda has translated into a citizenship curriculum for schools, which suggests that integration into British values and culture is something of a one-way process, closer to assimilation (Osler, 2011). At the same time, governments since 1997 have favoured the development of more faith schools, including Muslim state schools, which seems to give rather different signals.

Housing

The post-colonial immigrants of the 1950s and 1960s faced a housing policy regime that often excluded them, while priority was given to the housing needs of the white British in the forms of council housing and subsidies to mortgaged owner-occupation. Racialised minorities were commonly excluded from council housing by institutionalised discrimination in access to waiting lists and in allocation of tenancies. Access to mainstream owner-occupation was limited by conservative, discretionary lending policies of the building societies. Hence they had to fall back on informal borrowing for low-cost ownership or on private renting, often enduring very poor and overcrowded conditions. Access to social rented housing for all minorities was not achieved without much struggle and self-organisation from the 1960s onwards. Efforts to undermine racialised access and allocation polices, institutionalised in both the council and housing association sectors, took many years. From the late 1970s, access to both social housing and mainstream mortgages was opened up.

The contemporary pattern of housing tenure in Figure 17.2 shows some of the diversity of housing experiences across the major ethnic groups. The data show that social housing, rented both from councils and from housing associations, now houses proportionately much more of the Black Caribbean (45 per cent) and Black African (47 per cent) communities than the White community (15 per cent). The data fail to show that around half of the Bangladeshi community are in social housing, much of it in London where the costs of homeownership are prohibitive. Other Asian groups are strongly underrepresented in social housing. All the minorities (25 per cent) are much more likely to be in the private rented sector than Whites (14 per cent), which remains the reception tenure with the poorest housing conditions on average.

Since 1998, the government has published an annual ethnic breakdown of the number of families accepted as homeless by English local authorities (DCLG, 2012). Minority ethnic households are about three times more likely to be officially homeless than the general population. The proportion of non-white households accepted increased steadily from 18 per cent in 1998 to 28 per cent in 2011, of whom about half are Black/Black British, and a quarter Asian/Asian British. It is impossible to say whether this is because services have become more responsive, or whether minority ethnic families have suffered proportionately higher levels of homelessness. The number of officially homeless families fell by more than half between 1998

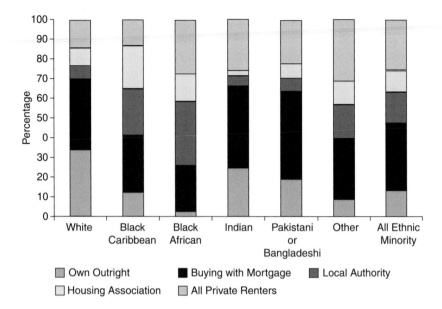

Figure 17.2 Contemporary pattern of housing tenure

and 2010, but by less than 10 per cent for Black/Black British people. Gervais and Rehman (2005) reviewed this topic in depth with policy recommendations that remain highly relevant.

The allocation of social housing and of housing regeneration funds has always raised profoundly difficult issues for local policy-making, just as much in the 2000s and 2010s as in previous decades, and perhaps more so because of more limited public spending on housing. A recent study of the Bangladeshi and white communities in London's East End (Dench *et al.*, 2006) illustrates this very starkly. While recounting the robust survival of the Bangladeshi community against all the odds, it also tells of widespread resentment among white families that their housing needs have, they believe, been given a lower priority than those of the Bangladeshis. The older generation of white people want their sons and daughters to be allocated housing in the neighbourhood to keep kith and kin close together, not least to facilitate informal caring for elders and children. For a number of years the Borough in some neighbourhoods had an allocation policy to match this aspiration, but that was seen to discriminate against Bangladeshis and more recent newcomers who had more pressing housing needs. A sense of injustice among some low-income white families contributes to recent support for the far right in East London, the northern towns, and beyond.

The formation of Black and Minority Ethnic (BME) housing associations to address the pressing need for rented housing, particularly in London, was a very important and positive development in the 1980s and 1990s (Harrison, 2002). The increasingly vocalised demand for social rented housing from minority ethnic communities in the 1980s and 1990s coincided with a sharp decline in the supply of social rented housing, with the end of new council house building and around a third of existing council housing being sold to tenants under the 'right to buy'. So, while racist barriers in access to social housing were coming down, new barriers were being erected in the form of reduced supply, perhaps an example of institutional racism or an ethnic penalty at the level of government policy.

Parallel processes also occurred from the late 1980s in the owner-occupied sector. The phased withdrawal of subsidies to homeowners through mortgage tax relief and of assistance with mortgage costs for homeowners claiming income support coincided with an accelerated growth of mortgaged home-ownership among minority ethnic groups. The withdrawal of these forms of assistance to low-income households has differentially affected minority ethnic groups because of their relatively adverse socio-economic circumstances, and may be considered as another form of institutionalised discrimination or ethnic penalty in housing. Data on the proportion of minority ethnic households experiencing mortgage default, arrears, and repossession are not available, but it is probable that they are significantly higher than average. Direct and indirect discrimination by mortgage lenders and estate agents was exposed in the 1970s and 1980s by social scientists and the Commission for Racial Equality. There is recent evidence (Ratcliffe, 2011) that such processes are continuing in some northern towns, and possibly elsewhere.

SPOTLIGHT

Over recent decades there have been a series of cases of abuse of black patients in psychiatric care, the most notorious perhaps being the case of David 'Rocky' Bennett. He died at a secure psychiatric unit in Norwich in 1998 after being severely restrained for a prolonged period of time. Eventually the health authority commissioned an inquiry chaired by a judge, whose report appeared in 2003 (Blofeld, 2003). He said that there was a 'festering abscess of institutional racism in the NHS' and made a number of important recommendations, including a three minute time limit on pinning patients to the floor and the appointment of an 'ethnicity tsar' to lead reform. Although neither of these recommendations has been implemented, the NHS and the government responded with an unprecedented series of policy responses addressing mental health needs and inequalities faced by minority ethnic communities, which has achieved some modest gains (Craig and Walker, 2012). This is a good illustration of the making and implementation of contemporary British social policy in the field of 'race' and ethnicity. It shows that, under pressure from minority ethnic users, public authority is capable of making a critical and progressive anti-racist response, but that progress is slow and implementation in practice continues to be resisted.

Conclusions

Social policies have played a central role in defining, maintaining, and mitigating the processes involved in defining 'race' and race relations. Despite a variety of policies seeking to control immigration, the growing ethnic diversity of the country has continued to increase. Indeed, the principal challenges to discrimination and differential treatment of minority ethnic groups has been led by the post-colonial migrant communities themselves, which have become increasingly firmly embedded in both the political sphere and the professional and managerial realms of public services.

During the New Labour era there was a wider acceptance and understanding of the notions of indirect discrimination and institutional racism, which led to a managerial, regulatory form of anti-discrimination practice, focused largely on the public services, the impact of which was likely to be quite limited. Indeed, if anything, the racialised dimension of immigration policy has been strengthened by concerns over asylum seekers and new economic migration from Central and Eastern Europe, and has been reflected in hardening rhetoric from the Coalition government. Yet, in the policy areas discussed here – poverty, policing, education, and housing – social science and minority ethnic activism have generated much better evidence and understanding of the complex processes involved. There is therefore the potential for this to contribute to more effective policy and practices for the future.

Summary

This review of policy in a number of key areas suggests that racial and ethnic inequalities and injustices remain a prominent feature of British society and, hence, of its welfare state. It has suggested that:

- The definitions of 'race' and ethnicity in contemporary British social policy have been shaped by the diverse politics (racist, liberal, and anti-racist) generated by the post-colonial migration and more recently by the racialisation of the Muslim community.
- Since the 1960s, racialised immigration control has been legitimated by anti-discrimination measures.
- Since the mid 1990s, policy and legislation on asylum seekers and refugees has ratcheted up their isolation and exclusion within British society, including their access to the welfare state.
- There are persistent ethnic penalties in the labour market, resulting in quantifiable disadvantages in earning power, particularly affecting people of Black Caribbean, Black African, Pakistani, and Bangladeshi origin.

- Liberal anti-discrimination policy and legislation has had some success in mitigating more overt forms of discrimination. It has been strengthened in the 2000s by the use of managerial, regulatory processes in the public services.

- There has been a protracted series of important challenges to institutional racism in the police service, culminating in the post Macpherson processes.

- Black pupils' underachievement in schools remains a prominent issue that central government has finally taken up with the prospect of some success.

- Minority ethnic groups' access to decent, affordable housing has improved compared with earlier decades, but is constrained by the shortage of social rented housing and by racialised income inequalities.

Discussion and review

- How useful is the concept of institutional racism in understanding and challenging processes at work in particular areas of social policy?

- To what extent, if any, has British immigration policy shifted from its racist antecedents in the 1960s?

- How and why are ethnic groups categorised within British social policy?

- What are the strengths and weaknesses of anti-discrimination legislation and policies in the UK?

References

Blofeld, J. (2003) *Independent Inquiry into the Death of David Bennett*, Norfolk, Suffolk and Cambridgeshire Strategic Health Authority, Norwich, available at http://image.guardian.co.uk/sys-files/Society/documents/2004/02/12/Bennett.pdf.

Burnett, J. (2012) 'After Lawrence: racial violence and policing in the UK', *Race and Class*, Vol. 54, No. 1, pp. 91–8.

Cantle, T. (2001) *Community Cohesion: A Report of the Independent Review Team*, Home Office, London.

Cantle, T. (2005) *Community Cohesion: A New Framework for Race and Diversity*, Palgrave Macmillan, Basingstoke.

Coard, B. (1971) *How the West Indian Child Is Made Educationally Subnormal in the British School System*, New Beacon Books, London.

Commission for Racial Equality (CRE) (1984) *Race and Council Housing in Hackney*, CRE, London.

Commission for Racial Equality (CRE) (2003) *Racial Equality in Prisons*, Part 2, CRE, London.

Commission for Racial Equality (CRE) (2005) *CRE Submission to Phase II of the Zahid Mubarek Inquiry*, CRE, London.

Commission on Integration and Cohesion (CIC) (2007) *Our Shared Future*, Commission on Integration and Cohesion, London, available at www.integrationandcohesion.org.uk.

Craig, G. and Walker, R. (2012) '"Race" on the welfare margins: the UK government's Delivering Race Equality mental health programme', *Community Development Journal*, Vol. 47, No. 4, pp. 491–505.

Dench, G., Gavron, H. and Young, M. (2006) *The New East End: Kinship, Race and Conflict*, Profile Books, London.

Department for Children, Schools and Families (DCSF) (2009) *The School Workforce in England, 2009*, DCSF, London.

Department for Children, Schools and Families (DCSF) (2012a) *GCSE Attainment by Pupil Characteristics in England, 2010/11*, DCSF, London.

Department for Children, Schools and Families (DCSF) (2012b) *Exclusions from Schools in England, 2010/11*, DCSF, London.

Department for Communities and Local Government (DCLG) (2011) *English Housing Survey: Household Report 2009–10*, DCLG Publications, London.

Department for Communities and Local Government (DCLG) (2012) *Table 771: Homeless Households Accepted by Local Authorities by Ethnicity, England 1998–2012*, DCLG Publications, London.

Equality and Human Rights Commission (EHRC) (2010) *Stop and Think*, EHRC, London.

Feldman, R. (2013) *When Maternity Doesn't Matter: Dispersing Pregnant Women Seeking Asylum*, Maternity Action/The Refugee Council, London.

Finney, N. and Simpson, L. (2009) *Sleepwalking to Segregation?*, Policy Press, Bristol.

Foster, J., Newburn, T. and Souhami, A. (2005) *Assessing the Impact of the Stephen Lawrence Inquiry*, Home Office Research Study 294, Home Office Research, Development and Statistics Directorate, London.

Gervais, M.-C. and Rehman, H. (2005) *Causes of Homelessness in Ethnic Minority Communities*, Office of the Deputy Prime Minister, London.

Gillborn, D. and Rollock, N. (2010) 'Education', in A. Bloch and J. Solomos (eds.) *Race and Ethnicity in the 21st Century*, Palgrave, Basingstoke.

Harrison, M. (2002) 'Black and minority ethnic housing associations', in P. Somerville and A. Steele (eds.) *'Race', Housing and Social Exclusion*, Jessica Kingsley, London.

Heath, A. and Cheung, S.Y. (2006) *Ethnic Penalties in the Labour Market: Employers and Discrimination*, Department for Work and Pensions Research Report 341, DWP, London.

Hepple, B. (2010) 'The new single equality Act in Britain', *Equal Rights Review*, Vol. 5, pp. 11–24.

Johnston, R., Wilson, D. and Burgess, S. (2004) 'School segregation in multi-ethnic England', *Ethnicities*, Vol. 4, No. 2, pp. 237–65.

Kundnani, A. (2007) *The End of Tolerance: Racism in 21st Century Britain*, Pluto Press, London.

Kundnani, A. (2009) *Spooked! How Not to Prevent Violent Extremism*, Institute of Race Relations, London.

Law, I. (1996) *Racism, Ethnicity and Social Policy*, Prentice-Hall, Hemel Hempstead.

Macpherson Report (1999) *The Stephen Lawrence Inquiry*, The Stationery Office, London, available at www.archive.official-documents.co.uk/document/cm42/4262/4262.htm.

Maudling, R. (1971) *Immigration Bill: 2nd Reading*, Hansard, House of Commons Debates, 8 March, Vol. 813, Cols. 43–4.

Miah, S. (2012) 'School desegregation and the politics of "forced integration"', *Race and Class*, Vol. 54, No. 2, pp. 26–38.

Ministry of Justice (2012) *Employment Tribunals and EAT Statistics 2011–12*, Ministry of Justice, London.

Mulvey, G. (2011) 'Immigration under New Labour: policy and effects', *Journal of Ethnic and Migration Studies*, Vol. 37, No. 9, pp. 1477–93.

Neyroud, P. (2011) *Review of Police Leadership and Training*, Home Office, London.

Office for National Statistics (ONS) (2012a) *Ethnicity and National Identity in England and Wales 2011*, ONS, London.

Office for National Statistics (ONS) (2012b) *International Migrants in England and Wales 2011*, ONS, London.

Osler, A. (2011) 'Education policy, social cohesion and citizenship', in P. Ratcliffe and I. Newman (eds.) *Promoting Social Cohesion*, Policy Press, Bristol.

Platt, L. (2007) *Poverty and Ethnicity in the UK*, Policy Press, Bristol.

Rampton Report (1981) *West Indian Children in Our Schools*, HMSO, London.

Ratcliffe, P. (2011) 'Housing, spatial patterns and social cohesion', in P. Ratcliffe and I. Newman (eds.) *Promoting Social Cohesion*, Policy Press, Bristol.

Ratcliffe, P. (2012) 'Community cohesion: reflections on a flawed paradigm', *Critical Social Policy*, Vol. 32, No. 2, pp. 262–81.

Rattansi, A. (2007) *Racism: A Very Short Introduction*, Oxford University Press, Oxford.

Rowe, M. (2007) 'Introduction: policing and racism in the limelight', in M. Rowe (ed.) *Policing Beyond Macpherson*, Willan Publishing, Cullompton.

Swann Report (1985) *Education for All: The Education of Children from Ethnic Minority Groups*, HMSO, London.

Todd, R. (1991) *Education in a Multicultural Society*, Cassell, London.

Vertovec, S. (2007) 'Super-diversity and its implications', *Ethnic and Racial Studies*, Vol. 30, No. 6, pp. 1024–54.

Weight, R. (2003) *Patriots: National Identity in Britain 1940–2000*, Pan Macmillan, London.

Winder, R. (2004) *Bloody Foreigners: The Story of Immigration to Britain*, Little Brown, London.

Further reading

Bloch, A. and Solomos, J. (eds.) (2010) *Race and Ethnicity in the 21st Century*, Palgrave, Basingstoke. Edited collection of reflexive, original chapters on important policy areas, including housing, education, employment, policing, health, and asylum seekers.

Craig, G., Atkin, K., Chatoo, S. and Flynn, R. (eds.) (2012) *Understanding 'Race' and Ethnicity*, Policy Press, Bristol. Original and accessible chapters covering all the major areas of social policy, including mental health and social care, as well as historical context.

Finney, N. and Simpson, L. (2009) *Sleepwalking to Segregation? Challenging Myths about Race and Migration*, Policy Press, Bristol. Calmly and critically deconstructs populist discourse about immigration numbers, failure to integrate, ghettoization, and so on using solid social science data and research.

Ratcliffe, P. and Newman, I. (eds.) (2011) *Promoting Social Cohesion*, Policy Press, Bristol. Unpicks the dominant policy discourse around integration and community cohesion, and coded responses to post-9/11 panic over Muslim communities; well-grounded material on education, housing, and local situations.

Sales, R. (2007) *Understanding Immigration and Refugee Policy*, Policy Press, Bristol. An accessible yet detailed account of this central issue, giving appropriate attention to both explanations and experiences.

Williams, C. and Johnson, M.D. (2010) *Race and Ethnicity in a Welfare Society*, Open University Press, Maidenhead. Tackles important topics not touched on here, including devolution, the 'Black' voluntary sector, social care, and issues around social welfare practice in an accessible and reflexive approach.

Useful websites

http://www.equalityhumanrights.com – Equality and Human Rights Commission (EHRC), the British government's race equality agency. Informative on anti-discrimination legislation and processes, and publishes important research (for example, on stop and search).

http://www.irr.org.uk – Institute of Race Relations. Invaluable archive of critical analysis, data, commentary, and articles on a wide range of issues – British, European, and global.

http://www.guardian.co.uk/racism – *The Guardian*. Archive of the newspaper's articles on race in Britain.

http://www.runnymedetrust.org – Runnymede Trust. Long-established British think tank, publishes research on a wide range of policy relevant issues together with a regular *Bulletin*.

http://www.migrantsrights.org.uk – Migrants' Rights Network. Campaigning NGO, monitors and publicises the ongoing struggle, particularly on family issues.

http://www.ethnicity.ac.uk – information and links to research material and data from the UK social science community.

CHAPTER 18

Disability and Social Policy

Alan Roulstone

▌ Learning objectives

- ▪ To introduce the concept of disability policy
- ▪ To examine differing approaches to policies affecting disabled people
- ▪ To explore the factors that have led to changes in disability policy
- ▪ To consider recent policy debates and developments

▌ Chapter overview

This chapter aims to explore critically the factors that have shaped changing policies for disabled and chronically sick people. It will provide a policy typology that sums up the changes over time and will then explore post-war developments in substantive policy for disabled people. It argues that although conceptually policy frameworks have become much more progressive, the impact of policy change has been much more limited. It highlights the fact that disability and poverty continue to be familiar realities and that a price being paid for more responsive and self-directed packages seems to be a narrowing of access to and conditionality underpinning disability support. This chapter will:

- explore policy frameworks that help contextualise substantive discussion;
- outline barriers to wholesale improvements in the lives of disabled people;
- consider substantive policy changes in the areas of social care, social welfare, and the transition to adulthood;
- argue that there is still a long way to go in affording enabling and equitable policy solutions for many disabled people.

Background and policy context

The question of policy responses to disability is not a new one. The Poor Laws of 1601 and 1834 had major concerns to draw the line between those who were too sick to work and who could be legitimately (if meagrely) supported, and those deemed unfit by virtue of idleness (Borsay, 2005). This inevitably led to grey areas where the boundaries between disabled and able-bodied became administratively unclear. The preoccupation with 'sturdy beggars', those who wanted to claim what Stone (1984) calls the 'disability category' but who were thought to be able-bodied, was one part of this. As we shall see later, this state concern has not entirely gone away and re-emerges, in particular, at times of economic recession and high unemployment (Garthwaite, 2011). However, throughout the development of the welfare state from the twentieth century there has been an important growth in state provision for disabled people. The following were important and diverse drivers of greater provision for disabled and chronically sick people:

- The two world wars, so that the consequent perception that disablement can be 'caused' by state-sponsored and legitimate factors led to major policy changes from 1914 onwards (Barnes, 1991).
- The realisation that being disabled has often been synonymous with being in poverty – this led to new welfare developments based on both contributory and non-contributory systems that formed what might be dubbed the 'social welfare system' for disabled people (Walker and Walker, 1991).
- The Disabled People's Movement helped foster independent living, direct payments, and policy change from the grassroots level.
- The acknowledgement that families of severely 'disabled' children and adults require packages of support that a market system could not provide led to the development of a 'social care system' for disabled people (Walker, 1982).

Disability policy: a case of non-conformity to policy paradigms?

The factors outlined above led to major developments in the provision of disability services and cash transfers for many disabled people. However, looking back at developments since the Second World War, it seems paradoxical that despite so much policy activity many disabled people remain in poverty, outside of paid employment, and often outside of the mainstream of life. This is worth exploring. Disability and disability policy is a challenging area. Not only is disability a difficult thing to pin down administratively (for example, two people with the same impairment might view themselves as disabled and not-disabled respectively), but disability policy also lacks a neat congruity with wider ideological shifts at the heart of social policy analyses (George and Wilding, 1994). Indeed, the immediate post-war years of the welfare settlement were very lean years for disabled people, especially as the Beveridge blueprint assumed full employment, when many working age disabled people could not work or were not welcomed in the workplace (Humphries and Gordon, 1992). Half a century on, although promoted furiously by a Labour MP, the Chronically Sick and Disabled Person's Act 1970, a sort of blueprint for comprehensive support for disabled people, was resisted by the then Secretary of State for Social Security, Richard Crossman, who staunchly opposed the Bill, stating it was simply unaffordable to provide for community-based disability provisions. The Bill benefited from the sponsor, Alf Morris, winning a Private Member's Bill to push the legislation forward in Parliament. It might never have surfaced had it not been for that stroke of luck. Similarly, the trade unions were not that favourable to disabled people staying in the labour force after the Second World War (Bolderson, 1980), making plain that it would deny able-bodied workers their place in the labour market.

Disability policy has never been a straightforward party political issue. The development of disability living allowance in 1992, a non-means-tested, non-contributory benefit, and its forerunners, the mobility allowance and attendance allowance, in the early 1970s, witnessed major growth and political support under a Conservative government (Drake, 1999; Roulstone and Prideaux, 2012). Similarly, the Disability Discrimination Act 1995, although forged during a Labour period in office, became statute during a Conservative administration (Gooding, 1995). However, the first real reforms amounting to cutbacks in disability benefits took place during the Fowler reforms of income support disability supplements of the mid 1980s. This may seem contradictory given the Conservatives' support for mobility allowance and later disability living allowance, however it does mark the beginnings of a binary approach, increasingly shared by both left and right of British politics, that social care was largely a social good and social welfare a growing liability. As we shall see below, the accession to power of the Coalition of Conservative and Liberal Democrats has witnessed a major attack on both systems for the first time, with a particularly aggressive attempt to pare back the numbers claiming the out-of-work disability benefit, incapacity benefit (recently renamed employment and support allowance) (Roulstone and Prideaux, 2012). Overall, what we can say, and in a way that cuts across the shift from welfare paternalism to choices and rights in adult social care, is that the neoliberal turn since 1979 and more markedly since 1997 (see Chapters 7 and 8) has fundamentally questioned who counts as disabled for the purposes of

British social policy. We will explore in more detail below the unprecedented shifting of the disability category (Piggott and Grover, 2009).

Before we explore in more detail the shape of policy and provision, we need to step back and reflect on just what we mean by and how the state constructs disability. Why are definitions important? Well, as the social philosophers W.I. Thomas and D.S. Thomas (Thomas and Thomas, 1928, p. 572) noted: 'If men define situations as real, they are real in their consequences'. What this means in policy terms is that the way the state constructs the 'disability problem' will profoundly shape the policy frameworks and substantive provision. That is, we cannot have policy without ideas and constructions of social problems, and social issues-policies do not emerge from abstracted debates and ivory-tower musings. On the contrary, policy for disabled people has been based on very worldly principles. However, throughout much of the twentieth century disability was framed as a problem of the individual – their deficits (Barnes, 1991). While this afforded generous provision for some, it was felt that in order to get support one had to emphasise the things a person could not do. Borsay, drawing on Wright-Mills, distinguishes between disability as a personal trouble or a social issue (Borsay, 1986). She argues that for much of the twentieth century disability policy was firmly rooted in a perception of disability as a personal trouble. This was evident in the Chronically Sick and Disabled Persons Act of 1970, with its construction of disability (one derived from Section 29 of the 1948 National Assistance Act), so that a disabled person is a person:

> aged 18 or over who are blind, deaf, or dumb, or who suffer from mental disorder of any description, and other persons aged 18 or over who are substantially and permanently handicapped by illness, injury, congenital deformity or such other disabilities.
>
> (Chronically Sick and Disabled Person's Act 1970, section 1)

Similarly, some 20 years later the NHS and Community Care Act, despite its emphasis on community, continued in the same vein, defining a person's eligibility based on the definition of disability as 'a person may be in need of such as a result of illness, disability or impairment, the local authority has a duty to provide services if the needs are assessed as eligible' (National Health Service and Community Care Act 1990, section 47).

Most recently, the Disability Discrimination Acts (1995 and 2005) have constructed disability as 'impairment that is substantial and long-term and which impacts on day-to-day activities' (EHRC, 2008). Despite the apparent pervasiveness of these constructions, responses from disabled people's organisations and disability writers have, since the 1990s, challenged these ideas with a social model of disability, one which sees the real policy imperative as responding to the barriers that result from a society that is not geared up to the needs of disabled people (Campbell and Oliver, 1996). For Drake, a key writer on disability policy, 'the key question from this perspective was whether a society served the needs of all of its members equally, irrespective of their physical shapes and differing intellects' (Drake, 1999, p. 15).

This then shifts the focus onto society and away from a disabled person's 'problems'. As policy students and writers, we need to be aware of the challenges thrown out by these debates. Finkelstein takes this idea forward by arguing that policy not only has to comprehend a 'disabling society', but to involve disabled people in the process of redefining the disability problem and in shaping social policy provision more generally:

> Control over the shaping and reshaping of social assistance has not only enabled specific social groups to dominate others, but has also enabled them to define what is 'normal' and, in so doing, label all assistance required by other groups as 'special' and 'compensatory' . . . Disabled people in organisations of disabled people (our vehicles for change) have begun to express their human nature by re-defining themselves and inventing their own forms of assistance in this image.
>
> (Finkelstein, 1999, p. 1)

In reality, the solution cannot simply be to turn the focus solely on to social barriers and user-control as we need to focus scarce funding on those who need it most. Indeed, despite the power of Finkelstein's ideas, most disabled people have no connection with disability organisations. Conversely, policy that is only built on personal eligibility could never underpin macro-level changes in transport access and buildings access policy. So we can see that policy design and review ought to be influenced by individual expressions of need alongside a more collective macro-level struggle for environmental, workplace, healthcare, education, and social welfare access. The extent to which these two dynamics converge and support each other is a key policy question. A recent example where they have gone out of kilter is over the future of sheltered employment for disabled people, where the social model emphasis on mainstreaming sits awkwardly with limited opportunities for the former workers to move into the mainstream. Here the relationship between idealism and realism in disability policy raises its head, a point explored later in the chapter. What will also be clear from the above is that the focus of much policy change, legislation, and guidance is on disabled adults. Disabled children have received policy attention, but largely from within the education and institutional care system (Barton, 1997; Abbott *et al.*, 2000), which goes beyond the scope of this chapter. This arguably reflects the powerful construction of all childhoods as periods of social dependency – an idea that sits awkwardly with the focus of the Disabled People's Movement on independence and choice. In reality, disabled people's organisations and parent groups have been less effective or concerned to embrace the issues of choices and rights for disabled children and disabled childhood beyond an institutional model, and have faced parental and professional resistance to change.

Policy frameworks and disabled people

This section explores further the changing policy frameworks that have supported specific disability-related policies of the last hundred or so years. The chapter will then focus on post Second World War welfare settlement policy developments in the transition to adulthood, employment, social care, and social welfare, as these get closest to analysing the economics of disability policy that are so central to debates around poverty, work, choices, and lives in the mainstream. The chapter will end with a reflection on the key developments and challenges of social policy design and implementation for disabled people.

By way of a fuller contextualisation of post Second World War disability policy, it is worth saying a little about the journey to the post-war settlement, and how perceptions of disability and 'right treatment' have changed and continue to change. Drake's (1999) typology of disability policy (non-linear) captures the general direction of travel:

1 Containment and segregation
2 Compensation
3 Welfare provision
4 Rights and citizenship.

Here Drake depicts an image of early policy response as rooted in a *containment* approach to those disabled people who were seen as a *risk to* or *at risk from* society (Wright and Digby, 1996). It is perhaps shocking to look back at the extent of institutional care for disabled people until the 1960s and 1970s. For example, Peter Townsend's survey of institutional care in the early 1960s established that there were 110,767 older, sick, and disabled people living in over 3,000 residential and long-stay contexts (Townsend, 1964). While those with less obvious or 'severe' impairments might avoid institutions and receive what was euphemistically dubbed a 'home cure' (Humphries and Gordon, 1992), many disabled people were placed in such contexts often against the wishes of themselves or their parents and wider families (Humphries and Gordon, 1992) and policy was driven and legitimised largely by medicalised logic (Wright and Digby, 1996), even where active 'treatment' was often rare.

STOP AND THINK

Why might institutional care for so many people have remained in place for so long?

Containment, as many writers note, was often about warehousing people who did not fit with the mainstream as they were seen as delicate, vulnerable or risky (Barnes, 1990). However, we need to understand that impairment-related constructions led to very diverse institutions, with the Mental Deficiency Act 1913 underpinning hospitals for those with what we would now call learning difficulties and certain types of 'mental illness'. On the other hand, people with visual impairments or profound deafness were often accommodated in schools and later workshops, and often received intensive instruction to be as close to productive citizens as possible (Cole, 1989). Indeed, contrary to notions of enforced dependency that were characteristic of asylums, such training approaches often aimed for maximum (and a decidedly harsh) independence from reliance on others (French and Swain, 1997). Either way, segregated institutions inadvertently furthered the social and cultural construction of disabled people as different, while institutional provision, except at time of scandals and exposés, was often unaccountable and a closed book in policy terms.

Erving Goffman (1961) and other commentators managed to lift the lid on the worst aspects of institutional care from the 1960s onwards. Together with changing social sensibilities about difference, embodied in normalisation theory, institutional provision began to be seen as an old and at worst harmful 'solution' to the disability problem. Although the beginnings of community-focused policies can be traced back to the early 1960s, the major shift came with the NHS and Community Care Act 1990. The Act consolidated previous provisions laid out in the 1948 National Assistance Act and the 1970 Chronically Sick and Disabled Persons Act, but most importantly enshrined the link between disability, policy, and community-lives to be lived in the community.

Community-based provision proved a major challenge. Alongside some successes, the absence of real communities for some and the barriers to paid work, leisure, and wider opportunities, led some writers to conclude that much post Second World War policy was simply *compensatory* or stuck within a *welfare model* – that rather than the mainstream be accessible communities, welfare continued to be offered in parallel to the mainstream and in a way that professionals still heavily shaped policy and service implementation. A good example of this is that despite the shift to the community, the provision of social care, welfare benefits, and community equipment were still premised on medical model assumptions and controlled by professional dynamics (Barnes, 1991). Disillusionment with previous policies and the rise of the disabled people's movement did, however, help push forward more person-centred policies for some via the Disabled Person's (Direct Payment) Act 1996. For the first time in UK history, policy for some disabled people has approximated to a *rights-based* approach that offers to place disabled people at the centre of the policy implementation equation. To understand the paradox of greater choices for some and continued barriers for many, we need to reflect briefly on the foundations of the British welfare state.

An edifice of social rights: a foundation of economic citizenship?

The last 70 years have witnessed a seemingly irrevocable shift towards a citizenship- or rights-based model of policy for disabled people. The movement from institutions to community to personalised choice is a momentous one

(Means and Smith, 1998). While many of the earlier provisions were founded within a post-war settlement mindset of combating the roots of what Beveridge called the '5 Giant Evils' (Beveridge, 1942), the assumption behind Beveridge's propsals were that full employment would be achievable and underpin the welfare settlement. Economic and social dynamics would become more congruent within the Beveridge plan. These sentiments were extended to many disabled people, as Tomlinson noted in the cross-governmental report on disabled people and employment barely a year after the Beveridge report:

> In a highly industrialised country such as Britain, the number of separate occupations is so large and their demand on physical activity so varied, that it is possible to find an occupation within the physical capacity of all save a minority of the disabled.
>
> (Tomlinson, 1943, p. 6)

Beveridge largely concurred with this sentiment, and while toying with the idea of partial work capacity, was rather over-optimistic about the scope for the economic integration of disabled people, for example rejecting the idea that blind people of working age could retire early. The economic assumptions of Beveridge and the post-war settlement arguably left untouched the structural and economic exclusion of most disabled people. Indeed, the reality beneath the 'inexorable rise of choices and rights' for some is the continued link between disability and poverty for many (Burchardt, 2003), so that figures from the 2008–09 Households Below Average Income (HBAI) survey discovered that 3.9 million people who live in households with at least one disabled person are living in income poverty (Hansard, 2010). If we factor in the attempt from the 1990s onwards to reduce or ration disability provision in both the social care and welfare systems through increased conditionality, re-testing or redrawn eligibility, then the picture becomes one of rights for some and enforced dependency for many.

If we revisit Drake's typology from our current position, we also need to add the rise of conditionality to his typology (Drake, 1999; Roulstone and Prideaux, 2012). Here we can distinguish between the financial conditionality embodied in the contribution principle for an increasing range of 'funded' support, for example in adult social care, and moral conditionality – the idea that certain behavioural norms have to be adhered to if a disability benefit is to be claimed, for example social welfare benefits (incapacity benefit, employment and support allowance). As Figure 18.1 suggests, the disability category has shifted from that of a protected and non-stigmatised policy area from the 1940s, to one of conditionality, increased 'boundary' scrutiny (i.e. who counts as disabled).

We now need to explore substantive areas of policy change to fully grasp the growing paradox of selective citizenship, rights for some, and conditionality for many disabled people.

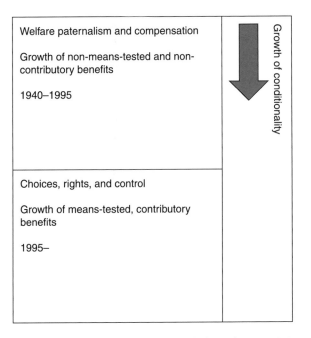

Figure 18.1 Typology of policy for disabled people, post-1940

Source: Roulstone (2012)

The transition to adulthood

A question might reasonably be raised as to why the transition to adulthood features in an introductory chapter on disability policy. However, if we view social policy and social inclusion as intimately linked to economic prosperity, then the efficacy of aiding disabled people's transition to economic and social independence becomes of central concern. In fact, the already high level of economic dislocation of the 16–24 age group in the UK (Nuffield Foundation, 2009) is magnified yet more dramatically for disabled young people. Although comparative data on rates of un/employment are not available by disability and age group, comparative figures for those not in employment, education or training (NEET) at ages 19–21 are 44 per cent for disabled young people and 23 per cent for their non-disabled peers (Labour Force Survey, 2009).

As disabled teenagers grow into their early twenties, the picture becomes yet starker, as Burchardt's (2005) study of disabled 16- to 24-year-olds established. She established that baseline ambitions for 16-year-old physically disabled people were roughly similar to those of their non-disabled peers. Worryingly, by age 24 those ambitions and achievements are markedly reduced. For people with learning difficulties and for those with mental health problems, the un/employment rates are very different to that of their non-disabled peers. Emerson and Hatton's (2008) study suggested that the employment rate of people of working age was as low as 8 per cent, while the figure for people with mental health problems was 20 per cent in 2009 (Labour Force Survey, 2009).

The area of young disabled people has received little discrete policy attention and the issues that confront disabled young people are perhaps best understood in the wider context of economic recession, raised unemployment, and a re-commodification of the education and training infrastructure in the UK. However, mention is made of the cost of disabled young people's exclusion in the cross-governmental *Life Chances* report (Cabinet Office, 2005), *Every Child Matters* (DfES, 2003), and the Nuffield Foundation review of education and training for 14- to 19-year-olds (Nuffield Foundation, 2009). Connexions, the agency tasked with connecting people with education, training and employment, do, of course, have a mandate to identify those with a 'special need' and to offer a personalised transition plan as laid out in the DfES's Special Educational Needs (SEN) Toolkit (e.g. DfES, 2001; Connexions, 2010). This involved holding a 'transition review' before the young person reached year 9, to form the basis of a plan for their future. Connexions, following the precepts of *Every Child Matters*, were tasked to both join up with all other relevant agencies and to have a leading role in challenging the well-documented barriers to education, training, and employment. HM Treasury had helpfully identified the barriers for young disabled people as: 'lack of flexibility around appointment times', 'physical barriers such as shortage of disabled parking spaces', 'language barriers and lack of effective information . . . particularly for ethnic minority groups', and 'transport problems' (HM Treasury, 2007, p. 63; see Yates and Roulstone, 2013). The development of wider welfare to work and intensive support schemes, such as Pathways to Work and the now defunct Workstep (Purvis *et al.*, 2006), seem to have had little impact on disabled younger people; these schemes seem better placed to respond to the needs of people who have been in work or have the education and skills to benefit from a stepping up approach.

So, despite much 'sound and fury' on disabled youth unemployment, the position has actually worsened. The number of disabled young people entering the NEET category rose during the mid to late 2000s so that some five years after the *Life Chances* report was completed, 27 per cent of disabled young people were NEET (Dickinson-Lilley, 2010) compared with 9 per cent of non-disabled young people. The Nuffield review of 14- to 19-year-olds in education and training also paints a rather bleak picture, with 21 per cent of disabled 14- to 19-year-olds having no qualifications compared with 9 per cent of non-disabled 14- to 19-year-olds. Clearly, low expectations play some part in the production of such stark differences. Evidence of refusal of access to vocational and educational options (particularly at or above level 2 education) is cited in the literature, and disabled people are less likely to have reached level 3 education at age 18 (16.4 per cent of disabled young people versus 30 per cent of non-disabled 18-year-olds) (Yates and Roulstone, 2013). Research on the transition process for young adults with complex needs points to continued barriers to joined up, coordinated or personalised transition planning and delivery, and the absence of employment as a consideration (Commission for Social Care Inspection, 2007; Ofsted, 2010, 2011).

While the exact causes of the situation described above are hard to disentangle, we do know that aspirations are worn down by the transition process, poor transition planning, and unresponsive providers of training and education. Increasing marketisation is also a factor here, with more training opportunities offered in-house once a person has already gained a job. The role of education and training policy in shoring up disability and transition policy is then a moot point. The lack of access to employment itself in an increasingly marketised and payments-by-results approach may simply be a shadow variable for poor relative access to training. Indeed, the *Life Chances* report and the social inclusion discourse in which it was embedded can be seen to conflate structural and individual roles in reducing economic exclusion (Levitas, 2005; Roulstone and Prideaux, 2012).

The emphasis upon rights and responsibilities, while unobjectionable in its wider sense, holds real dilemmas for those historically excluded by structural factors (attitudes, workplace/training barriers, low educational expectations). The emphasis on supply-side solutions to high unemployment fostered from the late 1970s was not fundamentally challenged by rights and responsibilities discourses of the third way (see Chapters 7 and 8) as 'responsibilisation' was arguably the centrepiece of welfare to work thinking in New Labour and now Coalition policy. It is noteworthy that during the period of emphasis on rights and responsibilities, the number of disabled people in the NEET category increased (Disability Rights Commission, 2007). The attempt to foster a self-directed active labour approach arguably misreads structural factors that require other more planned and interventionist policies.

CONTROVERSY AND DEBATE

'Scandal-plagued welfare-to-work provider, A4E has managed to get just 3.5 per cent of its jobseekers into long-term roles. Fewer than four out of 100 unemployed people who have gone through the firm have secured jobs that last more than 13 weeks'.

(excerpt from *mailonline*, 28 June 2012)

Private contractors now deliver a great deal of employment support. Are some critics right to challenge this role and to ask for a statutory right to education and training based on personal need and not on payment by results?

Social welfare

The area of social welfare, as noted above, has been a policy area in which stigma and contestation are familiar ideas. Both before the welfare settlement and from the 1980s, disability welfare has been under the spotlight for policy and spending review. The very fluid nature of disability itself affords the state a role in recalibrating just who counts as disabled (Stone, 1984). Unlike the social care arena, where packages of support have tended to go to more obviously disabled people (the majority of disabled people have never been allocated a social worker for example), social welfare, in the form of disability benefits, has been prey to recent regular reviews, and of late an unprecedented reappraisal (Piggott and Grover, 2009). The height of re-stigmatisation of welfare came not, of course, from disability policy, but through broader critiques of welfare recipients from the Conservative government from the late 1970s (Dean and Taylor-Gooby, 1992) and incrementally from the New Labour government from 1997 onwards (Roulstone, 2000). The redoubled attention on the 'waste' of welfare dependency has, of course, been a key facet of Coalition policy (Cabinet Office, 2010).

These re-evaluations of the welfare settlement and the growth of the welfare state (Gamble, 1988) came from both home and abroad. Murray's discussion of the rise and cost of the Western underclass in the 1980s provided a sort of political primer onto which specific policy prescriptions could be built (Murray, 1984). Murray's arguments managed to inveigle their way into the very highest political contexts, and found an audience among key government ministers (Dean and Taylor-Gooby, 1992). There were arguably two levels of analysis to such debates: at a macro-level the state, in allowing a growth in public spending and 'subsidy' of the jobless, had become not simply hypertrophied (overgrown) but also ineffectual (Gamble, 1988; Hall and Jacques, 1983; Brown and Sparks, 1989), and renewed market ideals were offered up by neo-liberal thinkers who were keen to reassert that only the market could link people with equity and opportunity (Loney, 1987); at a more immediate level, out-of work benefits were seen as encouraging perverse behaviours that made being out of work a better option than working. Put simply, the poor were viewed as too well off under this settlement. This of course completely overlooked the rationality of choosing benefits where local labour markets afforded few opportunities and often very low-paid jobs (Fothergill and Wilson, 2007). Interestingly, until the 1990s disabled people had been spared these sorts of discursive constructions by politicians and the media. Although the Fowler reforms did reduce the supplements paid to disabled people in receipt of income support (a mainstream out-of-work benefit), this reform was principally aimed at reforming income support and had little avowed concern to pull back on disability funding through, say, invalidity benefit or mobility/attendance allowance.

The real head-on reform of disability benefits was not attempted until the accession of the Labour government of 1997 (Roulstone, 2000). The growth of incapacity benefits throughout the 1980s and 1990s from 600,000 in 1979 to 1.5 million in 1995 was due in part to post-industrial joblessness and the complex intersection of poor labour opportunities and personal reappraisal of impairment (Beatty et al., 2011). However, there is also evidence, albeit heavily contested, that the Thatcher governments of 1979–92 engineered the movement of over a million jobless people from unemployment to incapacity benefit to reduce the headline unemployment data (Bartholomew, 2006). Certainly, health did not decline for working age people during the period

1979–95 in a way that can explain the growth in incapacity, but incapacity is of course the result of personal, professional, and statutory assessments of work capability (Office for National Statistics, 1998). Building on the spending limits set by the outgoing Conservative government, and drawing on the powerful metaphor of 'rolling back the frontiers of the state' (Gamble, 1988), New Labour for the first time arguably since the Poor Law began to pick away at the defensibility of a growing number of incapacity benefit (formerly invalidity benefit) recipients and claimants of disability living allowance. It did this while drawing on its newly minted idea of rights and responsibilities (see Chapter 8), formulated through the Blairite binary of 'work for those who can, security for those who cannot' (Department of Social Security, 1998, p. 1). This rather simplistic formula of binaries between those disabled people who should work but are not working, and those who require support, was arguably the ideological glue that helped underpin a planned retraction of out-of-work benefits where sick or disabled people were seen as capable or work, and justly better placed there than 'languishing' on benefits. Despite the rhetoric of wasted lives, none of these political characterisations of volitional worklessness were rooted in robust evidence (Garthwaite, 2011).

Despite evidence that the major growth in incapacity benefit claimants was in former industrial areas where jobs were scarce, New Labour began to review claims with the aim of reversing this growth. Recipients of disability living allowance, meanwhile, were selectively invited for reassessment under the Benefits Integrity Project. Both of these reviews were premised on the perception that these benefits had become too easily accessible and too infrequently reviewed. Of note here is the centrality of paid work and the paid labour market as the core answer to many problems: over-spending on welfare, learnt dependency, and 'wasted lives' could all be erased at a stroke by identifying better those that could benefit from the shift from claimant to worker (Department of Social Security, 1998). This argument, however, ignores the evidence from sympathetic but independent reviews of the labour market orientations of some disabled workers, with one think tank referring to the 'missing million' sick and disabled people who would work if suitable accommodations and jobs were available (Stanley and Regan, 2003).

Actually, the profiles of incapacity benefit claimants did change in the 2000s, with the previous preponderance of physical impairments caused in part by industrial impairments giving way to a growth in more female claimants with mental health problems (Beatty et al., 2011). This has since spawned a whole array of debates about the causes and 'reality' of growth in the numbers of disabled people. Some argued that the growth in incapacity benefits was just a rise in hidden unemployment, as claimants sought the shelter under the higher rates of benefit available from incapacity benefit. Others pointed to the realities of living with the social and personal costs of deindustrialisation (Fothergill and Wilson, 2007). In terms of the growth in the number of claimants of disability living allowance, the evidence provides the basis for a thoroughgoing critique of government interpretations. The majority of the growth came from disability living allowance for middle and older (but sub-retirement) claimants, and is arguably a facet of an ageing population. Indeed, impairment and age are heavily correlated (Office for National Statistics, 2008). The Benefits Integrity Project was quickly shelved amid what seemed like a pitch battle between disability organisations and the government. This might have been predicted, as most higher-rate disability living allowance recipients are more obviously disabled and the source of much greater public and activist sympathies (Howard, 2005). However, this backlash did not stop a further and much less public programme, the Right Payments Programme, being rolled out. Long-established policy concerns about major fraud and over-claiming have also arguably provided the climate for the major Coalition review of disability living allowance, as the replacement personal independence payment is rolled out from 2013 to 2016 (Department for Work and Pensions, 2012). Nevertheless, the National Audit Office was forced to 'qualify' DWP accounts on benefit fraud and overspend, and its own figures put fraud at less than 1 per cent of annual spend, a figure exceeded by DWP and Benefits Agency overspending error (National Audit Office, 2009). The battle over disability living allowance and incapacity benefits may have been won in the late 1990s and 2000s, but the war against 'out of control' disability benefit growth continues.

The accession of the Coalition government to power represented a continuity of neo-liberal thinking. Indeed, if one views, as some do, Thatcherism as a failed starting point, the plans on paper of the Coalition might reasonably be seen as the real instigation to substantiate the project. Indeed, it is worth remembering that Thatcherism oversaw a growth in disability living allowance and invalidity benefit/incapacity benefit, as did the majority of New Labour years in office. The firm resolve to tackle 'welfare dependency' and to reduce the 'unsustainable' growth in disability benefits is clear in Coalition policy:

> We share a conviction that the days of big government are over; that centralisation and top-down control have proved a failure. We believe the time has come to disperse power more widely in Britain today.
>
> (Cabinet Office, 2010, p. 7)

The more specific resolve, in this case the determination to reduce the headcount on incapacity benefit (now revamped as employment and support allowance), is evident in the following from the Secretary of State at the Department for Work and Pensions:

> We estimate we will find around 23 per cent of people fit for work immediately, with more needing just a bit of extra support to get to a position where they can look for a job . . . If they refuse to take up work, they will have their benefit cut by up to a third.
>
> (Duncan-Smith, 2010)

There was a unprecedented backlash against the proposed reforms, with a myriad of disabled people's organisations setting up blogs critical of the Coalition government's stance. The following is a typical post, one verified by a BBC report at the same time:

In March 2012 Cecilia Burns had her Employment Support Allowance reduced by £30 a week even though she was still undergoing treatment for breast cancer. Cecilia Burns died this morning. At the time of the decision Ms Burns described the medical test as a 'joke'. The Social Security Agency said everyone who received the benefit must undergo a test for capability to work. Ms Burns was diagnosed with cancer last year and had undergone surgery, chemotherapy and radiotherapy. She said dealing with the side effects of the treatment were bad enough, but she had been angered by the cut in benefit after she went for a medical. 'I know there's other people out there and they're all scared to come forward' she said.

(http://www.yerknowthedance.com/survival-of-the-fittest/; accessed 13 March 2013)

SPOTLIGHT

'Everyone agrees that benefits should be restricted to those who need them. Rather than labelling claimants as scroungers, these posters should focus their energy on solving the problem of too few suitable and flexible jobs. We need investment in people's contributions' (Liz Sayce, Chief Executive, RADAR).

(http://www.radar.org.uk/news/radar-to-osborne-and-treasury-stop-your-spending-challenge-website-spreading-prejudice/)

- To what extent is Liz Sayce's response to anti-fraud campaigns the right response to government concerns about growing disability benefit claimant numbers?
- What are the arguments to support get tough approaches?
- Should disabled people be exempt from such programmes?

Unlike previous reforms, benefit reduction and withdrawal are being undertaken often without independent medical scrutiny and consideration of the economic realities of being taken off a particular benefit. Some recipients of disability living allowance who had once been legitimately deemed disabled for life are now being told they are to be reassessed to determine whether they are still disabled. So the reforms are far reaching and the disability welfare system is arguably in disrepute for government and claimants alike. How this will unravel is difficult to predict. However, a system that was built largely on trust during the post-war settlement is now very much more contested and potentially stigmatising.

Social care

Perhaps the greatest advances in disability policy have taken place in the realm of social care and support, and largely as a result of disabled people's organisations pushing for independent living approaches embodied in the growth of direct payments (Barnes and Mercer, 2006). There has been a dizzying array of rights-based and self-directed forms of transfers from adult social care to eligible disabled people: direct payments, personal budgets, and individual budgets (for a fuller account, see Roulstone and Prideaux, 2012). Here we concentrate on direct payments as they represent the 'purest' interpretation of choice and control at the heart of a rights-based approach. Direct payments to individuals aimed to break the link between entitlement and having to accept social support in the format that local authorities preferred. Prior to direct payments, social care/support was delivered by either social services or an appointed contractor, often unknown to the disabled person. Support was often fragmented, impersonal, and disempowering (Barnes and Mercer, 2006). Direct payments were novel in allowing cash transfers to eligible disabled people which they could use to employ personal assistants and manage the use of the direct payment. The UK Department of Health supported direct payment developments by giving individuals money in lieu of social care services; they are also given greater choice, greater control over their lives, and are empowered to make their own decisions about how their care is delivered (Department of Health, 2007a). In an earlier statement, the Department of Health asserted that direct payments would 'help increase opportunities for independence, social inclusion and enhanced self-esteem' (Department of Health, 2003, p. 3). Developments since the passing of the original statute have aimed to break down budgetary territorialism between health, social care, housing, and employment support in the form of the Individual Budgets pilots (Glendinning *et al.*, 2008), and latterly the Trailblazers pilot (Office for Disability Issues, 2009). In the field of direct payments itself, the payments have been extended to children and older people and the guidance affords direct payment use via an advocate, appointee or the ability to take a mix of cash and directly provided service (personal budgets). This responds to the early limitations to direct payment uptake by frail older people, people with learning difficulties, and people with mental health problems (Riddell *et al.*, 2006). Wider policy shifts towards independence and personalised social policies helped drive home the idea of a disabled person being at the centre of the policy and practice equation (Department of Health, 2005, 2006, 2007b, 2010).

The current period of austerity has resulted in the paradoxical situation that some disabled people are wresting increased levels of choice and control for themselves, but in most local authorities there has been a narrowing of eligibility under the growing misnomer of 'Fair Access to Care' (National Centre for Independent Living, 2008) to 'substantial' and 'critical' needs, so that some local authorities are now only funding critical need. In a policy sense, what we have is a social care and support system that is increasingly residual in terms of the redrawing of eligibility to fewer disabled people. As we will see below, the preventative and planned approach to social care (Department of Health, 2005) and support has arguably reverted back to a crisis model of social support whereby those *in extremis* are likely to gain access to the social support system. The irony of the most progressive models sitting alongside extraordinary amounts of unmet need is very stark. Indeed, some writers have claimed that the headlong shift towards direct payments sits well with a planned retraction or rolling back of the state, although this is heavily contested (Ferguson, 2007). Indeed, there is evidence of policy and linguistic shift from self-direction to the 'self-management of risk' (DoH, 2007b), which rings alarm bells for some commentators (Roulstone and Morgan, 2009).

> ## STOP AND THINK
>
> ☐ Do you think local authorities should still be referring to *personalised* support and self-directed support when increasingly numbers of disabled people are falling out of the eligibility criteria set by local authorities?
>
> ☐ What do you see as the policy alternatives where the number of disabled people exceeds the amount of available funding? What would you do if you had the power to decide?

Although direct payments and wider self-directed support chime with first-wave disability studies' concern for a de-professionalisation of social support, the argument now is that local authorities are externalising risk onto disabled people in handling direct payments, especially where the financial value of a package may reduce over time (Ferguson, 2007). Studies from both disabled people's organisations and statutory bodies themselves point to concerns. The latter would suggest that some local authorities are concerned about the possible impact of central funding cuts (Local Government Association, 2010). This headlong movement towards self-direction and risk management has, perhaps not surprisingly, led to diverse responses from service users with a range of impairments, and clearly one size does not fit all. For example, the take up rate for self-directed approaches had been much higher for younger disabled adults with physical impairments and much lower for older disabled people, people with mental health problems, and those with learning difficulties (Davey *et al.*, 2007). Evidence also suggests something of a lottery of provision of direct payments and some practitioner ambivalence as to how choice can be interpreted. For example, can direct payments be used to fund what for some are seen as dependency-creating day centres, even if this is the choice that a disabled person wants (Roulstone and Morgan, 2009)? Evidence suggests that people with learning difficulties may require additional support in direct payment use via brokerage services, while some applicants are deemed ineligible as they do not meet basic eligibility thresholds (Leece and Bornat, 2006), and it should be recognised that the government is trying to foster such intermediary roles, especially via user-led organisations. However, there is evidence that local authorities are still not adequately procuring the fullest involvement of user-led organisations (Office for Disability Issues, 2009).

Conclusions

Despite the great promise contained in the shift from institutions to community to control and the undoubted increase in independence and choices for some, major paradoxes still abound in disability policy. Personalised models of policy sit alongside increasing rationing of services and the more extensive use of means testing for direct payments and disabled facilities grant. The binary between those 'deserving' support and those who 'need' to enter the work-based welfare system is becoming ever more starkly defined, even though many disabled people do not fit neatly into a policy category. Highly differentiated definitions and eligibility criteria attach to a range of social goods that the same person may have to navigate. The muddle of activity versus inactivity-based benefits remains very real, with the same person having to emphasise what they can do with, say, a direct payment, but having to say what they cannot do in order to get access to the support in the first place.

Recent discussion of a streamlining of the disability welfare system is short on detail. The hard won gains of personalisation and self-direction may be viewed as under threat given the harsh budgetary plans of the Coalition government. For some disabled people needing more intensive support in residential contexts, the future looks yet more uncertain. We can only hope that disabled people and their advocates gain further voice in shaping future policy.

Summary

This chapter has outlined approaches to disability and has considered a number of areas of policy that are important for disabled people. It has shown that:

- Approaches to disability have changed considerably over time, but despite this some concerns have remained fairly constant, including over how to determine who is 'fit for work' and who is deserving of support from the state.

- There were a number of policy advances in the post-war years, in part built upon a shift towards a rights-based model for disabled people.

- The disability movement had a significant impact in arguing for empowerment and choice for disabled people.

- Despite these changes, major paradoxes continue to face disabled people, including pressures to simultaneously demonstrate both abilities and inabilities in order to access resources.

- Economic problems since 2008 and governments' responses to these, including the major cuts in public expenditure by the Coalition government, together with ongoing concerns about welfare dependency, pose a significant threat to some of the gains made in the preceding half century.

Discussion and review

- Why is the question of 'welfare dependency' so significant for policy-makers and disabled people?
- For what reasons has policy in relation to social welfare developed in a different direction from that for social care?
- How useful is Drake's typology for understanding contemporary policy for disabled people?

References

Abbott, D., Morris, J. and Ward, L. (2000) *Disabled Children and Residential Schools: A Survey of Local Authority Policy and Practice*, Norah Fry, Bristol.

Barnes, C. (1990) *Cabbage Syndrome: The Social Construction of Dependence*, Falmer, Lewes.

Barnes, C. (1991) *Disabled People in Britain and Discrimination: A Case for Anti-Discrimination Legislation*, Hurst & Co., London.

Barnes, C. and Mercer, G. (2006) *Independent Futures: Creating User Led Disability Services in a Disabling Society*, Policy Press, Bristol.

Bartholomew, J. (2006) *The Welfare State We're In*, Politico, London.

Barton, L. (1997) 'Inclusive education: romantic, subversive or realistic?', *International Journal of Inclusive Education*, Vol. 1, No. 3 pp. 231–42.

Beatty, C., Fothergill, S., Gore, T. and Powell, R. (2011) *Tackling Worklessness in Britain's Weaker Local Economies*, Centre for Regional Economic and Social Research, Sheffield Hallam University, Sheffield.

Beveridge, W. (1942) *Social Insurance and Allied Services*, HMSO, London.

Borsay, A. (1986) 'Personal trouble or public issue? Towards a model of policy for people with physical and mental disabilities', *Disability, Handicap and Society*, Vol. 1, No. 2, pp. 179–95.

Borsay, A. (2005) *Disability and Social Policy in Britain Since 1750: A History of Exclusion*, Macmillan, Basingstoke.

Brown, P. and Sparks, R. (eds.) (1989) *Beyond Thatcherism*, Open University Press, Milton Keynes.

Burchardt, T. (2003) *Being and Becoming: Social Exclusion and the Onset of Disability*, CASE Report 21, LSE Publications, London.

Burchardt, T. (2005) *The Education and Employment of Disabled Young People: Frustrated Ambition*, Policy Press, Bristol.

Cabinet Office (2005) *Improving the Life Chances of Disabled People*, Cabinet Office, London.

Cabinet Office (2010) *The Coalition: Our Programme for Government*, Cabinet Office, London.

Campbell, J. and Oliver, M. (1996) *Disability Politics: Understanding Our Past, Changing Our Future*, Routledge, London.

Cole, T. (1989) *Apart or A Part: Integration and the Growth of British Special Education*, Open University Press, Milton Keynes.

Commission for Social Care Inspection (2007) *Growing up Matters: Better Transition for Young People with Complex Needs*, Commission for Social Care Inspection, London.

Connexions (2010) *About Connexions and Transition Planning*, Connexions, London.

Davey, V., Fernández, J.L., Knapp, M., Vick, N., Jolly, D., Swift, P. *et al.* (2007) *Direct Payments in the UK: A National Survey of Direct Payments Policy and Practice*, Personal Social Services Research Unit, London School of Economics and Political Science, London.

Dean, H. and Taylor-Gooby, P. (1992) *Dependency Culture: The Explosion of a Myth*, Harvester Wheatsheaf, Hemel Hempstead.

Department for Education and Skills (DfES) (2001) *SEN Toolkit*, DfES, London.

Department for Education and Skills (DfES) (2003) *Every Child Matters*, DfES, London.

Department for Work and Pensions (2012) *Personal Independence Payment: Policy Document*, available at http://www.dwp.gov.uk/policy/disability/personal-independence-payment/ [accessed 6 October 2012].

Department of Health (2003) *Fair Access to Care: Guidance on Eligibility Criteria for Adult Social Care*, The Stationery Office, London.

Department of Health (2005) *Independence, Wellbeing and Choice*, The Stationery Office, London.

Department of Health (2006) *Our Health, Our Care, Our Say*, The Stationery Office, London.

Department of Health (2007a) *Putting People First: A Shared Vision and Commitment to the Transformation of Adult Social Care*, The Stationery Office, London.

Department of Health (2007b) *Independence, Choice and Risk*, The Stationery Office, London.

Department of Health (2010) *Putting People First: A Whole System Approach to Eligibility for Social Care*, The Stationery Office, London.

Department of Social Security (1998) *New Ambitions for Our Country: A New Contract for Welfare*, The Stationery Office, London.

Dickinson-Lilley, J. (2010) *Behaviour and Discipline in Schools – House of Commons Education Committee: Examination of Witnesses*, Questions 176–207, 27 October, The Stationery Office, London.

Disability Rights Commission (2007) *Further Education and Training Bill*, Disability Rights Commission, London.

Drake, R. (1999) *Understanding Disability Policies*, Macmillan, Basingstoke.

Duncan-Smith, I. (2010) 'Reforms will tackle poverty and get Britain working again', Department for Work and Pensions Press Release, 27 May, available at http://www.dwp.gov.uk/newsroom/press-releases/2010/may-2010/dwp070-10-270510.shtml [accessed 6 October 2012].

Emerson, E. and Hatton, C. (2008) *People with Learning Disabilities in England*, CEDR, Lancaster.

Equality and Human Rights Commission (EHRC) (2008) *Disability Discrimination Act: Guidance on Matters to be Taken into Account in Determining Questions Relating to the Definition of Disability*, available at http://www.equalityhumanrights.com/uploaded_files/guidance_on_matters_to_be_taken_into_account_in_determining_questions_relating_to_the_definition_of_disability.pdf [accessed 24 November 2013].

Ferguson, I. (2007) 'Increasing user choice or privatizing risk? The antinomies of personalization', *British Journal of Social Work*, Vol. 37, No. 3 pp. 387–403.

Finkelstein, V. (1999) 'Professions allied to the community', presented at University of Leeds, available at http://www.leeds.ac.uk/disability-studies/archiveuk/finkelstein/pacall.pdf [accessed 6 October 2012].

Fothergill, S. and Wilson, I. (2007) 'A million off Incapacity Benefit: how achievable is Labour's target', *Cambridge Journal of Economics*, Vol. 31, No. 6, pp. 1007–24.

French, S. and Swain, J. (1997) *From a Different Viewpoint: The Lives and Experiences of Visually Impaired People*, Jessica Kingsley, London.

Gamble, A. (1988) *The Free Economy and the Strong State*, Palgrave, Basingstoke.

Garthwaite, K. (2011) 'The language of shirkers and scroungers? Talking about illness, disability and coalition welfare reform', *Disability and Society*, Vol. 26, No. 3, pp. 369–72.

George, V. and Wilding, P. (1994) *Ideology and Social Welfare*, Routledge & Kegan Paul, London.

Glendinning, C., Challis, D., Fernandez, J., Jacobs, S., Jones, K., Knapp, M. *et al.* (2008) *Evaluation of the Individual Budgets Pilot Programme Final Report*, Individual Budgets Evaluation Network (IBSEN Consortium), York.

Goffman, E. (1961) *Asylums: Essays on the Social Situation of Mental Patients and Other Inmates*, Anchor Doubleday, New York.

Gooding, C. (1995) *Disabling Laws, Enabling Acts*, Pluto, London.

Hall, S. and Jacques, M. (1983) *The Politics of Thatcherism*, Lawrence & Wishart, London.

Hansard (2010) *House of Commons Debates*, 4 October, Col. 1342W.

HM Treasury (2007) *Policy Review of Children and Young People*, The Stationery Office, London.

Howard, M. (2005) 'Disability: rights, work and security', *Benefits*, Vol. 13, No. 3, pp. 93–7.

Humphries, S. and Gordon, P. (1992) *Out of Sight: The Experience of Disability 1900–1950*, Northcote, Plymouth.

Labour Force Survey (2009) *Labour Force Survey: Quarterly Bulletin*, Spring 2009, ONS, London.

Leece, J. and Bornat, J. (eds.) (2006) *Developments in Direct Payments*, Policy Press, Bristol.

Levitas, R. (2005) *The Inclusive Society? Social Exclusion and New Labour*, Palgrave Macmillan, Basingstoke.

Local Government Association (LGA) (2010) *Revenue Spending Power 2011/12*, LGA, London.

Loney, M. (ed.) (1987) *The State or the Market? Politics and Welfare in Contemporary Britain*, Sage, London.

Means, R. and Smith, R. (1998) *From Poor Law to Community Care: The Development of Welfare Services for Elderly People 1939–1971*, Policy Press, Bristol.

Murray, C. (1984) *Losing Ground*, Harper Collins, New York.

National Audit Office (2009) *Department for Work and Pensions: Resource Account 2009–10*, National Audit Office, London, available at http://www.nao.org.uk/publications/1011/dwp_account_2009-10.aspx [accessed 6 October 2012].

National Centre for Independent Living (2008) *Review of Adult Social Care*, National Centre for Independent Living, London.

Nuffield Foundation (2009) *Education for All: The Future of Education and Training for 14–19 Year Olds*, Routledge, London.

Office for Disability Issues (2009) *Independent Living: A Cross-government Strategy about Independent Living for Disabled People*, Office for Disability Issues, London.

Office for National Statistics (ONS) (1998) *Health Survey for England, SN4150*, ONS, London, available at http://www.esds.ac.uk/findingData/snDescription.asp?sn=4150 [accessed 4 February 2013].

Office for National Statistics (2008) *Health Survey for England*, ONS, London.

Ofsted (2010) *Improving Progression to Sustainable Unsupported Employment*, Ofsted, London.

Ofsted (2011) *Progression Post-16 for Learners with Learning Difficulties and/or Disabilities*, Ofsted, London.

Piggott, L. and Grover, C. (2009) 'Retrenching Incapacity Benefit: employment support allowance and paid work', *Social Policy and Society*, Vol. 8, No. 2, pp. 159–70.

Purvis, A., Lowrey, J. and Dobbs, L. (2006) *Exploring the Design, Delivery and Performance of the WORKSTEP Programme*, Department for Work and Pensions, Sheffield.

Riddell, S., Priestley, M., Pearson, C., Mercer, G., Barnes, C., Jolly, D. *et al.* (2006) *Disabled People and Direct Payments: A UK Comparative Study*, ESRC Final Report, available at http://www.leeds.ac.uk/disability-studies/projects/UKdirectpayments/UKDPfinal.pdf [accessed 6 October 2012].

Roulstone, A. (2000) 'Disability, dependency and the New Deal for disabled people', *Disability and Society*, Vol. 15, No. 3, pp. 427–43.

Roulstone, A. and Morgan, H. (2009) 'Neo-liberal individualism or self-directed support: are we all speaking the same language on modernising adult social care?', *Social Policy and Society*, Vol. 8, No. 3, pp. 333–45.

Roulstone, A. and Prideaux, S. (2012) *Understanding Disability Policy*, Policy Press, Bristol.

Stanley, K. and Regan, S. (2003) *The Missing Million: Supporting Disabled People into Work*, Institute for Public Policy Research, London.

Stone, D. (1984) *The Disabled State*, Temple University Press, Philadelphia, PA.

Thomas, W.I. and Thomas, D.S. (1928) *The Child in America: Behavior Problems and Programs*, Knopf, New York.

Tomlinson Report (1943) *Report of the Inter-departmental Committee on Rehabilitation and. Resettlement of Disabled Persons*, HMSO, London.

Townsend, P. (1964) *The Last Refuge*, Routledge, London.

Walker, A. (1982) *Community Care: The Family, the State and Social Policy*, Blackwell & Robertson, Oxford.

Walker, A. and Walker, L. (1991) 'Disability and financial need', in G. Dalley (ed.) *Disability and Social Policy*, Policy Studies Institute, London.

Wright, D. and Digby, A. (1996) *From Idiocy to Mental Deficiency: Historical Perspectives on People with Learning Disabilities*, Routledge, London.

Yates, S. and Roulstone, A. (2013) 'Social policy and transitions to training and work for disabled young people in the United Kingdom: neo-liberalism for better and for worse?', *Disability and Society*, Vol. 28, No. 4, pp. 456–70.

Further reading

Barnes, C. and Mercer, G. (2010) *Exploring Disability: A Sociological Introduction* (2nd edn), Polity, Cambridge. This book examines a range of key themes and debates in disability studies.

Borsay, A. (2005) *Disability and Social Policy in Britain Since 1750: A History of Exclusion*, Macmillan, Basingstoke. This book provides an accessible and comprehensive coverage of the treatment of disabled people since the industrial revolution.

Oliver, M. and Barnes, C. (2012) *The New Politics of Disablement*, Palgrave, Basingstoke. This book sets disability policy (and disability studies) in the context of capitalism, globalisation, and cuts in public expenditure.

Roulstone, A. and Prideaux, S. (2012) *Understanding Disability Policy*, Policy Press, Bristol. This book examines the context within which policies are made and considers a range of policies and their implications for disabled people.

Useful websites

http://disability-studies.leeds.ac.uk – the Centre for Disability Studies at the University of Leeds undertakes a variety of research and related activities.

http://disabilitybenefitsconsortium.wordpress.com – this is a coalition of more than 50 charities that campaigns on benefits issues.

http://www.disabilityrightsuk.org – Disability Rights UK is an organisation led by disabled people. Its website provides a wide range of information including publications and advice.

http://www.equalityhumanrights.com – the Equality and Human Rights Commission has a statutory obligation to promote and monitor human rights. It provides access to a variety of information on a range of equality topics.

CHAPTER 19

Older People, Population Ageing, and Policy Responses

Karen West

Learning objectives

- To examine the emergence of the idea of population ageing and its prominence in public discourse and policy debates
- To consider the emergence of the idea of generational fairness and its possible implications for inter-generational relations (in particular in relation to the idea of generational intelligence)
- To explore prominent policy ideas and policies aimed at maintaining older people's independence and active ageing and their implications
- To examine current policy discussions and proposals for older people's pensions and work and their implications for society as a whole

---

Chapter overview

Wherever we currently are in the life cycle, with luck, we will get older. With further luck we will age with our health intact. If we do, we may also be fortunate enough to have supporting families, communities, and friends. We may wish to pursue careers or get involved in voluntary activities. For many older people, though, this kind of quality of life is sadly lacking. There are inequalities in older age groups as there are in any age group: income inequalities, wealth and asset inequalities, and health inequalities. Some will be extremely lonely and others will be overwhelmed with caring responsibilities. Social policies and public services can either smooth out these inequalities or they can compound them. There is currently a common perception that older people have been too politically strident and that their electoral power has secured them unfair advantages relative to other age groups. This perception has, if anything, been reinforced by these turbulent economic times, and coupled with concerns about the increasing number of older people relative to younger people (which we refer to as population, or demographic, ageing), there is a strong feeling that it is time to seriously consider scaling back government expenditure on older age groups. This common sense is ripe for challenge and that is what we are aiming to do in this chapter. Focusing simply on population ageing statistics masks a number of hidden realities. It is also leading us down a dangerous path of ageism. We will examine whether the current solutions proposed to address population ageing in a context of economic uncertainty and austerity are, in fact, the overdue correction to skewed inter-generational transfers that they claim to be, or whether they could, in fact, leave society in general very much worse off.

Introduction

The chapter begins with a discussion of population ageing, adopting a critical stance with respect to the causes and consequences that are claimed in dominant public discourse. It then discusses the idea of generational fairness and its consequences in terms of relations between generations. It then proceeds to critically examine the emergence of the key ideas of older people's independence and active ageing as responses to the ageing population. Finally, it examines how the current problematisation of population ageing, and its associated ideas of generational fairness, independence, and active ageing play out in recent policies with respect to pensions and work for older people. Again, it invites consideration of the broader social consequences of pension reform and the extension of labour market participation into older age.

SPOTLIGHT

Some hidden realities of older age

First, the untold story of inequality in old age (Cann and Dean, 2009). It is true that the current generation of over-50s holds some 85 per cent of the country's wealth (Cann and Dean, 2009), but this very large category contains the likes of Bob Diamond, born in 1951 and former chief executive of Barclays Bank, who in 2008 alone received a £14.8 million bonus (Dorling, 2011), and others of his ilk. It is also the case that three-quarters of those aged 60–70 own their own home (Dorling, 2011). But, the value of these homes will, of course, vary enormously. It is also true that 70 per cent of pensioners (currently defined as anybody over the age of 65) rely on pensions and welfare for at least half their income. Income and wealth inequalities also translate into inequalities in life expectancy and health inequalities. A recent House of Lords report (to which we will return later in the chapter) states that level of wealth is a good 'single predictor of mortality rates' (House of Lords Select Committee, 2013, p. 47). It goes on: 'Poorer people arrive in older age "lacking wealth, in particular, but also with poorer pensions and having accumulated health disadvantage throughout their lives"' (House of Lords Select Committee, 2013, p. 47)

Second, the untold story of loneliness and isolation. Research on loneliness suggests that: 1 million people over the age of 65 in the UK are lonely; 13 per cent of older people do not leave their house because of ill health; 9 per cent feel cut off from society completely; and for half of all people over the age of 65, television is their main company (Campaign to End Loneliness: http://www.campaigntoendloneliness.org.uk/).

Population ageing

It is hard to overstate the extent to which population ageing has come to frame social policy, and not altogether positively as we will shortly explore. Across the advanced capitalist countries, the age of populations has generally been increasing. That is, the ratio of older people to younger people has been steadily increasing. For England, for example, it is estimated that by 2030 there will be 51 per cent more people aged over 65 than in 2010 and 101 per cent more people aged over 85; and the picture for the UK generally looks quite similar (House of Lords Select Committee, 2013). This tends to be framed as a problem because it means that there will be fewer younger people to support the growing number of older people. The impression often given is of an unstoppable trend in which populations will get ever older, and of the needs associated with older age, principally in terms of health and social care and pensions, further draining already overstretched public funds. This is a complex topic, but it is worth looking beyond the somewhat alarmist headlines to examine in greater detail the causes, consequences, and prognosis of population ageing.

STOP AND THINK

In what ways can social policies either ameliorate or exacerbate these realities?

Perhaps the first thing worth noting is that population ageing is, on one level, something we ought to celebrate, for it means that people are not dying at the same rate that they once did. Advances in diet and, in particular, in public health mean that life expectancy has increased dramatically over the last 100 years or so. It may seem strange, but while population ageing is about older people themselves living longer, this is not the whole story. In fact, it is only the end of the story. There are a number of factors at work in population ageing, including birth rates; death rates, and migration. To take the first of these, birth rates have been falling across Europe since the 1960s (Zaidi, 2008). In fact, demographers believe this to be the most crucial factor in population ageing; more important than gains in life expectancy (Mullan, 2002). Migration is another significant factor, but we will not explore that in detail here. Even when it comes to mortality and life expectancy, it is not a simple case of older people living longer. There have been dramatic gains in life expectancy across *all* age groups. Babies no longer die to the extent that they did. Teenagers and middle-aged people live longer and some are lucky enough to live to a ripe and healthy old age. So, given this combination of factors, what then is the prognosis for demographic ageing? Is this an unstoppable trend? Does it mean that people will go on and on living longer? What does it mean for social policy, the welfare state, and public services?

What needs to be separated out here is general, underlying trends and specific cohort effects. The current phenomenon of population ageing is in large measure due to a specific ageing cohort: the so-called baby boom generation (of whom we will here more further in the chapter when we examine the idea of inter-generational relations). This particular generation of people, born between 1945 and 1965, have, *on average* – and this is a term that we need to treat with some caution – benefited enormously from the many years of economic growth and the terrific advances in health care and public health during that same period. After this period came dramatic social change in which women gained more control over their lives, including over decisions about the number of children they would have and the possibility of careers. So from the late 1960s and into the 1970s we see falling levels of fertility. This is skewing what demographers and economists call the older age dependency ratio: the ratio of the (inactive) 65 plus generation on the (active) 16–65 generation. (We will examine the dangers of dividing the population into these two groups further in the chapter.) Fewer younger people means that there are fewer people of working age paying taxes and national insurance, which has implications for the pensions of the current group of retirees and for the financing of public services, on which older people are themselves reliant. Furthermore, changes in rates of economic participation for younger women mean that we cannot necessarily rely on care needs being met within families any longer (Daly and Lewis, 2000). Families are increasingly dependent on state support or private care providers to meet the care needs of elderly relatives.

Given these scenarios, it is not hard to see how we could be lulled into policy nightmares. But there are several factors that surely ought to temper this pessimism. First, we cannot simply assume that population ageing will continue indefinitely. As we have noted, there is a specific baby boom cohort effect, which is expected to disappear around the middle of this century (Mullan, 2002). And, in general, as Hill (2006, p. 242) notes, 'European countries that already had quite a high elderly population in 1960 tend to be expected to experience less growth in the elderly population in the fifty years after 2000'. Second, as rapid as medical advances have been since the turn of the twentieth century, we cannot automatically assume that we will see a continuation of the sort of gains in life expectancy that we have witnessed over the last 50 years. This is not a given, but a matter of considerable debate and controversy (Gee, 2002). Third, we cannot accurately predict the reproductive behaviour of future child-bearing generations. This is highly sensitive to many factors, not least economic ones (Gee, 2002). But these uncertainties do not really feature in current public discourse, which generally tends to present population ageing as an unmitigated and inexorable fact of life, which, if left unaddressed, will lead us to the point of economic collapse. This rather pessimistic turn of mind has clearly been exacerbated by the current financial and economic crisis, but long before that it had been a policy obsession. Some have even suggested that it is 'a policy fetish', which has come to justify welfare retrenchment (Gee, 2002; Mullan, 2002). We will examine some of the policy responses to population ageing in greater detail, focusing in particular on the idea of active ageing and the promotion of older people's independence and pension reform. But first, let us consider questions of generational fairness and what this might mean for relations between generations. The idea of generational fairness is another key idea that is exercising considerable influence on social policy. As population has come to be seen as even more of an urgent problem in a context of recession of austerity, it has become a key evaluative principle in decisions on public spending priorities. It is timely to reflect on the consequences of insisting on generational fairness for longer-term relationships between generations. Will it foster or destroy inter-generational empathy and solidarity?

STOP AND THINK

- What might be some of the problems with dividing the population up into two groups: the active working and the inactive retired?
- Are these meaningful categories?
- In what ways might they be inadequate or misleading?

The UK House of Lords Select Committee on Public Service and Demographic Change Report: 'Reading for Ageing?'

There has been much talk of the implications for public services and social security of an ageing population for many years now, but to date very little meaningful action. Doubtless the more recent economic difficulties will galvanise policy-makers. The UK House of Lords has set up a Select Committee specifically to consider the implications of population for the UK Government.

Its focus is largely on the key areas of health care, social care, and pensions as these are the areas that are most affected by population ageing, for which it argues there will be frightening financial consequences if we do not take immediate action.

The problem we will consider here is that of basing calls for sweeping reforms to social policy on demographic projections. All estimates and scenarios in the report flow from the projection that at some point around 2020 the absolute number of people over the age of 65 will outstrip that of those under the age of 16 (see Figure 19.1). But this is only a projection.

If one takes the trouble to read the various submissions to the Select Committee, the extent of the uncertainty surrounding population predictions (and the consequences that flow from) them is readily apparent. First, we cannot accurately predict future fertility levels since we cannot accurately predict the behaviour of future generations. Second, we do not know the extent to which life expectancy will continue to increase. Third, we are even less certain about the extent to which life expectancy will translate into healthy life expectancy, which, in turn, is crucial to (a) any further projections about how long people can be expected to continue working and, therefore, (b) the extent of dependency of the old on the young; and (c) on the pressures that this may bring to bear on key public services and benefits (in particular health, social care, and pensions). Yet even though the report acknowledges these very crucial uncertainties, it nonetheless proceeds to talk with considerable certainty about the implications for public services and of the absolute imperative for a new social contract between generations (a point to which we will return later in the chapter). The opening chapter of the report concludes with the following statement: 'The doubling by 2030 of the number of people aged 85+ will have a substantial impact on those public services that are particularly important for older people, an impact for which they are worryingly ill-prepared'. The absolute self-evident fact of population ageing and its terrifying consequences would seem to be very much out of step with the tentative projections upon which it is based.

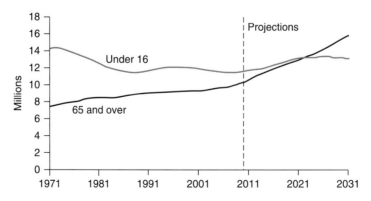

Figure 19.1 Population aged under 16 and aged 65 and over in the UK, 1971–2031

Source: House of Lords Select Committee (2013, p. 20)

The point here is not to suggest that there is no such phenomenon as population ageing or that we would not be wise to consider the implications and needs of an ageing population. (Indeed, the report contains some very useful discussion, particularly on the rather overlooked question of older people's housing needs.) It is, however, to underscore that uncertain demographic projections are dignified in official discourse in a way that other kinds of projections are not. We might, for example, ask ourselves why there is no House of Lords report on, say, 'Ready for Inequality' or 'Ready for Persistently Low Economic Growth' or 'Ready for Climate Change'. We could just as easily extrapolate dire consequences for the public purse from projections on all of these phenomena.

Generational fairness and inter-generational relations

We have all heard of the famous 'generation gap', which captures the idea that older and younger generations are always destined to misunderstand each other. Indeed, relations between the generations are characterised by a kind of necessary ambivalence (Biggs and Lowenstein, 2011). The ideas that we have and the identities we assume are the products of a certain point in time; a certain generation. This is not to say that all people of a certain generation think alike, but that the ways in which they think and act are, to a certain extent, shaped by certain common experiences. We speak of 'the post-war baby boom generation' or 'Thatcher's children' or 'the Facebook generation'. Thatcher's children have a variety of views and opinions, but the idea is that those views and opinions will have been influenced in some way by the social turning point that was Thatcherism. Similarly, 'the Facebook generation' will have grown up immersed in social media in a way that previous generations have not. This is bound to affect the way they think and act. The idea of the necessary ambivalence that characterises one's view of people of a different generation – 'the age other' to use Biggs and Lowenstein's (2011) term – captures the idea that we seek both to protect our generational identities and to achieve some understanding of 'the age other'. Second, and somewhat more controversially as we will explore in the next section of the chapter, the notion of ambivalence captures something of the sheer fact of ageing. As we age we gain experience of life, and we may come to adjust our ambitions and desires in the light of this experience. Our bodies also physically age, which may also affect our ambitions and desires. Again, we will do our best to communicate with 'the age other' but all the while we remain within our ageing bodies and minds.

Biggs and Lowenstein (2011) have coined the term 'generational intelligence' to capture the idea that we can, with effort and tolerance, bridge this generation gap; a gap, moreover, that exists between different generations of what we conveniently label 'older people', as much as it does between young and old. We can try, but never entirely succeed, to place ourselves in the position of 'the age other'. Often, though, they argue, levels of generational intelligence are low. When it comes to public and social policies, we often suffer from low generational intelligence. Too often policies are proposed and developed by the dominant, working age generation immersed in its own generational perspective and ignorant of the feelings and needs of older generations. The promotion of independence and active ageing (as we will come on to discuss) and personalisation (as discussed in Chapter 12) are arguably examples of social policies that have been pursued with low generational intelligence. We too readily fall into the trap of equating everybody's needs and priorities as extensions of our own. On the one hand, there has been considerable recognition of this in social policy among both the academic and practitioner community. Initiatives like the 'Better Government for Older People' programme (Chang *et al.*, 2001) and the involvement of older people as co-participants in social policy research (Barnes and Taylor, 2007) exemplify the potential for a higher generational intelligence. On the other hand, as Biggs and Lowenstein themselves point out, '[i]ntergenerational relations are in a state of transition that is historically unprecedented' (Biggs and Lowenstein, 2011, p. 142). In a climate of austerity and resource scarcity and in which the working age generation are themselves struggling to get by, there is heightened potential for conflict between the generations. This is true not just of the UK, but of all jurisdictions facing the broader economic consequences of the banking crisis. Arguably, we are already witnessing signs of emerging conflict between generations, which is being encouraged in two tendencies: (1) the tendency of media and certain public intellectuals to somewhat simplistically posit the current spending crisis as one of a skewed transfer of resources towards the baby boom generation and away from the current younger generation, and (2) the current problematisation of population ageing.

To take the first of these – media and public intellectual attacks on the baby boom generation – leading up to, and in the aftermath of, the UK Coalition government's first public spending review came a slew of media articles, which were less than veiled in their condemnation of the baby boom generation. One article in the *Daily Mail* and two articles in *The Guardian* newspaper (Ducan, 2011; Inman, 2011; Toynbee, 2011) exemplify this kind of thinking. These coincided with the publication of Higher Education Minister, David Willetts' (2010) floridly titled book *The Pinch: How the Baby Boomers Took Their Children's Future – and Why They Should Give it Back*. Other countries have their own versions of the Willett's narrative (Moulaert and Biggs, 2012). Polly Toynbee's *Guardian* article makes the crucial point that politically it is far easier to address questions of inequality and injustice in inter-generational terms rather than in class terms. Here, it is the specific baby boom generation that is under attack. The unfortunate effect of this though is that the wildly unequal impacts of austerity within generations of older people are skirted over. As Reed and Horton (2010) argued, in a report for the older people's charity Age UK, when public services as well as benefits are taken into account, there are huge disparities in the effect of austerity across different incomes for different older age groups.

On the second issue – the current problematisation of population ageing – there is a further tendency, to regard this as necessitating a fundamental overhaul of the social contract between generations. This is exemplified in the UK House of Lords report (discussed above), which argues unequivocally (and very much with the grain of current thinking in social policy) that there ought to be some better 'balance of fairness between generations and over time' (House of Lords Select Committee, 2013, p. 43). But, this is problematic, because it gives the rather simplistic, but politically comforting, impression that there are distinctive and identifiable winners and losers in this new social settlement – younger winners and older losers. However, when we consider the kinds of policies that are necessary to make this slogan of generational fairness a reality – requiring older people to work longer and to bear more of the financial responsibility (as individuals) for retirement and social care needs (see Chapter 12) – it is clear that all generations will be losers in various ways; because these are unlikely to be temporary measures aimed at the relatively asset-rich baby boom generation, but rather a likely irrevocable shift in social policy away from state-organised collective risk pooling towards individual risk management.

In summary, then, there is always a tendency for generations to misunderstand each other and for social policies to be developed with low generational intelligence. When economic times were good, there was some effort to develop a higher generational intelligence in social and public policy. Now, in a context of austerity, we may be in danger of slipping back. An insistence on generational fairness, while politically popular, may simply divert attention from the far more worrying trend of rising levels of inequality within generations. It may stop us fostering inter-generational solidarity against the more fundamental injustices of austerity. Finally, such developments are clearly detrimental to public perceptions of older people.

STOP AND THINK

- Does the problematisation of generational fairness that is becoming so prominent in social policy debates relate to your own experience within either your family or your community?

- In what ways are inter-generational relations different in those settings?

Promoting independence and active ageing

We discussed in the previous sections how an ageing population has come to be seen as an unbearable burden on societies and economies and how, in a context of recession and austerity, the notion of generational fairness is gaining in importance. What we now want to explore are some of the ways in which social policies of various kinds are responding to this problematisation, and in particular, the ways in which they are coming to redefine older people.

Old age and the older person has, of course, always been, in part, a social construct. The meaning of older age changes in line with social and economic change. There may be a time lag but, over time, policies adjust to new socio-economic realities and older people themselves adjust too. Even as recently as the nineteenth century, the category of older person did not really exist, as people died before they could reach old age (Mullan, 2002). They were born, worked, and died. As we noted above, the fact that we now recognise the category of old age is one of the consequences of human progress (Mullan, 2002). As life expectancy has increased, older people have fought for greater recognition and have acquired greater social rights such as the right to an old age pension and now the right to continue working if they so choose, more of which later in the chapter. Older people have struggled against the idea that they are economically useless and dependent. The question now, though, is whether current policies aimed at encouraging older people to keep active and independent for as long as possible so as to avoid the costs associated with health care, social care, and pensions, empower older people or, in fact, restrict their choices. Before we explore this question, let us first examine what are meant by independence and active ageing.

Independence is a long-standing theme in social policies across the globe (Plath, 2008). The central idea is that maintaining people's capacities to live independently in their own homes for as long possible will prevent the need for intensive and expensive health and social care interventions. In the UK, the themes of prevention and independence have a long provenance, but they were made an explicitly central element of health and social care policy by New Labour in its 2006 report *Our Health, Our Care, Our Say: A New Direction for Community Services* (Department of Health, 2006). Here the aim was to give all people, not just older people, more choice and control over their care and to channel resources away from acute hospital care towards health and social care in communities. In social care, more explicitly, the theme of independence has also been strongly associated with those of individual wellbeing and choice (Barnes *et al.*, 2013), as set out in the White Paper *Independence, Wellbeing and Choice* (Department of Health, 2005). Despite its claim to offer a new direction, all of these themes and objectives have recently been reaffirmed in the Coalition's White Paper, *Caring for our Future: Reforming Care and Support* (HM Government, 2012). So independence (together with its allied concepts of wellbeing, choice, and control) seems to be the guiding theme in health and social care. It is a common policy response to ageing demographics (Barnes *et al.*, 2013). Rather fortuitously it must be said, it seems also to correspond with what people say they want, which in the case of older people, in particular, when faced with often appalling institutional alternatives (see Chapter 12), is perhaps hardly surprising.

If the maintenance of independence is the common policy response to the health and social care implications of an ageing population, then active ageing is the counterpart response to the presumed pensions crisis. As with independence, active ageing is something of a global phenomenon. Moulaert and Biggs (2012) pinpoint its crystallisation as a policy response to population ageing to the 1994 Word Bank report, 'Averting the Old Age Crisis: Policies to Protect the Old and Promote Growth' (World Bank, 1994). This and subsequent reports, 'suggested a change of vision away from seeing ageing as a time of dependency and decline' (Moulaert and Biggs, 2012, p. 27) and an incitement to older people to redefine themselves as active workers until well into their later years. Initially, the idea of active ageing allowed for a rather broad range of active ageing possibilities. The Organisation for Economic Cooperation and Development (OECD) took up the idea and turned it into a rather 'more holisitic vision of participation in society' (Moulaert and Biggs, 2012, p. 6). The World Health Organisation produced another report on the theme in 2002, in which it stated: 'The word "active" refers to continuing participation in social, economic, cultural, spiritual and civic affairs, not just the ability to be physically active or to participate in the labour force' (WHO, 2002, quoted in Moulaert and Biggs, 2012, p. 6). By the mid 2000s, however, WHO's holistic vision of active ageing was abandoned in favour of a narrower vision of the active older worker. As Moulaert and Biggs (2012, p. 6) put it, the 2006 OECD report 'Ageing and Employment Policies: Live Longer, Work Longer' 'boils the argument down succinctly'. We will examine later in the chapter more precisely what this has come to mean for older people in the workplace, but for now we will explore in more general terms what these calls to independence and active ageing might mean for older people.

Originally, the promotion of independence and active ageing for older people was welcomed, both by older people themselves and those working on their behalf. More recently, however, more critical appraisals of what this means for the possibilities, identities, and material conditions of older people have emerged. The arguments are complex, but there are very real concerns that these kinds of policy orientations do not recognise the challenges that many older people face (particularly those who have aged in poverty and with ill health) and the kinds of choices that the kinds of identities they may wish to assume in older age (Estes *et al.*, 2003; Biggs and Lowenstein, 2011; Coole, 2012). Independence can, in the absence of policies to ensure older people's social connectivity, turn into isolation and social exclusion (Plath, 2008). Similarly, active ageing, if it does simply come to mean *work*, is also problematic when choice about whether to continue in work is removed. It may 'condemn older people to hard labour from the cradle to the grave' (Coole, 2012, p. 62), placing those who really are no longer able to work in a residual category of inactive pauper. It may also prevent older people from different identities in later life; identities, moreover, which, because they are not linked to economic productivity, may foster other existential possibilities and values (Biggs and Lowenstein, 2011; Coole, 2012). This is rather an intangible idea, but nonetheless serious. Retirement is often a time of slowing down and taking time to pursue non-economic activities, to nurture and mentor others, to contemplate and reflect, and to bring a different perspective to life. Such values are perhaps more highly prized in other cultures. There is a strong argument that we need more such alternative perspectives in the context of the considerable economic and environmental challenges we face (Coole, 2012).

Let us now consider how all these ideas – population ageing, generational fairness, and active ageing – are being applied in policies. The idea of independence has been discussed elsewhere in the book (notably in Chapter 12).

What we will focus on here is policies on old age pensions and older people in the labour market (work).

Pensions and work

Old age, together with unemployment and disability, is one of the contingencies that welfare states and social security systems have typically provided for (Spicker, 2011). Across the advanced capitalist world, old age pensions account for a relatively high proportion of government spending and expenditure on social security. In Austria, France, and Germany, for example, old age benefits account for some 25 per cent of total government spending (OECD, 2011). Japan spends around 27 per cent, while in Italy the figure is closer to 30 per cent. For the UK, publicly funded retirement pensions account for 12 per cent of government spending, compared with 16 per cent in the USA. For the Netherlands, the figure is a mere 10 per cent. But levels of expenditure as a proportion of government spending do not necessarily tell us how generous pensions are. If we look at the level of public pensions relative to average earnings after tax, we see a different picture (Hill, 2006). Although there has been some recent uprating of the state pension, the UK has one of the least generous public pensions, lower even than that of the USA, while the Netherlands has one of the highest (Hill, 2006). The generosity of Japan's public pension is also relatively low. But, many people will not be solely dependent on the public pension. Many will have a work pension and/or private pension. In a context of an ageing population and declining state fiscal resources, questions of the state's capacity to fund retirement pensions and the appropriate balance between state, work, and private pensions have become preoccupying. Indeed, some have argued that such debates have been driven largely by global policy-makers, specially the World Bank, rather than national ones (Mullan, 2002; Orenstein, 2008; Coole, 2012). This results in a high level of policy convergence between national government policies on retirement, pensions, and work. Before we discuss global pension policy, it is worth briefly setting out the history and current development of pensions in the UK – why have them and how they are funded.

Like many advanced capitalist countries, the UK has what is commonly referred to as a pay-as-you-go pension system. This means that the pensions of current retirees are paid for out of the contributions of current workers. When generations are in balance, this is not at all problematic, but with the mounting concerns about the old age dependency ratio (discussed above), comes concern about the affordability of pay-as-you-go systems. The UK pensions system is also what is known as a contributory, flat rate pension system. This means that so long as people have made their contribution during their working years, they will receive a fixed rate pension that is not related to the level of their earnings on retirement and will remain the same for as long they live (subject to whatever changes in general rates apply). For many years, the age of entitlement to a state pension was 65 for a man and 60 for woman, but this has recently been changed and can be anything from 61 to 68, depending on when someone was born and whether they are a man or a woman. The state pension is one of very few examples of a universal benefit: everybody (who works) pays and everybody benefits. For this reason, it has traditionally enjoyed strong political support. In the current climate of austerity and cuts, much is said about the relative generosity that has been shown to pensioners. The state pension has not been cut and, indeed, its value has been increased, albeit very modestly. While it is true that the position of retirees has been steadily improving for the last 30 years or so (Spicker, 2011), the basic state pension is still hardly enough to live on and has to be supplemented by means-tested pension credit and, as noted above, is one of the least generous in the advanced capitalist world. While it is possible to live on a pension enhanced by pension credit, it is probably fair to say that most people would not choose that life. Nevertheless, there are strong pressures for further retrenchment of the state pension.

The World Bank has been at the forefront of thinking on these issues. Its seminal 1994 report 'Averting the Old Age Crisis: Policies to Protect the Old and Promote Growth', which we have already discussed above, has been extremely influential in steering national policies on pension and work reform. Once again, the 'fact' of demographic ageing is seen as the main driver of policy change. The reasoning is that as there will be more older people spending longer in retirement, state pensions are no longer affordable and, moreover, that it is unfair to expect the current contributing generation, of which there are fewer, to pay for the pensions of the current retired generation. The report argues that governments ought to adopt a three-pillar pensions system consisting of (1) publicly managed, redistributive state pensions funded through taxation; (2) privately managed pension savings accounts; and (3) voluntary occupational (work-based) pensions. The first of these pillars is currently dominant in many advanced capitalist countries, but the report recommends that this be scaled back to become a safety net for the poorest retirees only, with the two other pillars becoming the dominant forms of pension provision. Again, the stated objective is greater generational fairness, but the end result is that all generations are likely to become increasingly subject to the vagaries of financial markets. In the UK, recent reforms will see automatic enrolment in the National Employment Savings Trust (NEST), a scheme for workers whose employers did not have an existing pension scheme. This is an effort to encourage more people to plan for their retirement while in employment instead of relying solely on the state pension, and is a significant step in the direction of the World Bank's recommendations to shift the emphasis towards the two market-based pillars. The arguments for and against moving away from state pension provision are controversial and complex, and full discussion is beyond the scope of this chapter, but as Coole (2012, p. 46) states: 'The new language of pillars implies that a solid, well-supported edifice is being built, but it actually plants pensions on the shifting sands of speculative markets while dismantling more reliable foundations of universal taxation and entitlement'.

DISCUSS AND DO

A recent report by the Organisation for Economic Cooperation and Development, 'Pensions at a Glance' (OECD, 2011), sets out what it calls a 'pensions paradox'. The paradox is that governments have to maintain an adequate retirement income without endangering financial stability. An insufficient level of pension coverage means that governments may end up having to spend money on other means-tested measures to avoid pensioner poverty. It sees three basic solutions to this paradox: (1) to compel people to work longer either by setting higher pension ages or by setting an automatic link between pensions ages and average life expectancy; (2) to concentrate the state pension on the lowest income groups only; (3) to encourage people to save for their retirement.

Do you agree with this assessment of the pensions paradox? Are these the only solutions available to governments? If so, which are preferable and why?

In parallel with debates on the future of state pensions are debates on the future of older people and the labour market. The European Union's Lisbon Strategy for Growth sets out targets for increasing the labour participation of older people (Coole, 2012). In the UK, for example, the age at which one is entitled to draw a pension has also been the age at which one is expected to retire from the labour market. In the UK, however, that has changed recently. The retirement age is no longer the same as the state pension age and older people now have the right to request to remain in employment with the same rights and working conditions as other employees. This is, of course, one way in which the old age dependency ratio can be reduced. For what matters is not so much the age composition of the active working population as the rate of labour market participation (Hill, 2006). For some older people themselves, this is very welcome legislation. Many want the right to choose to stay on in work that they enjoy. For some, though, this is not entirely a matter of choice. For those with no savings and continued housing costs, work may be a necessity, and any deterioration in the level of state pensions or other benefits to which older people are entitled (for example, winter fuel payments and free bus passes) and/or changes to the rules of entitlement to the state pension would mean that work becomes a necessity for many more older people.

DISCUSS AND DO

The following is a passage from Danny Dorling's (2011) book, *So You Think You Know about Britain*. He states:

We can *all* afford to retire; we can *all* afford to study. We can all afford to do a lot of things in our adult lives that are not simply about making money and giving much of it to others to supposedly make more out of it. We don't need so many people in paid work, unless we allow a few to grow fabulously wealthy at the expense of the rest of us. To perpetuate such an imbalance, retirement age would need to rise and those who couldn't work, or couldn't find work, would need to be on punitively low benefits. I think this would be wicked. Low benefits also perpetuate the imbalance: fewer students would be able to attend university (so the rich need not be taxed for that); more people would be forced into low-paid jobs. Few people cannot become hugely wealthy without millions of others becoming poorer. The profits that generate the wealth have to come from somewhere. (p. 192)

How willing are people to consider the ageing population question as one of inequality rather than generational fairness? What are the objections to this kind of analysis?

The House of Lords report, 'Ready for Ageing','? discussed above, sees encouraging people to work longer and the avoidance of what it calls 'cliff edge retirement' (the setting of a fixed age of retirement) as part of a solution to demographic ageing. It stresses that this is a matter of choice: 'the choice to continue in work must remain entirely with the individual' (House of Lords Select Committee, 2013, p. 32) and paints a picture of tolerant employers who will allow their employees to progress gently from work to cutting down hours to eventual full retirement as well as support for employees with caring responsibilities. It states: 'Employers should demonstrate more flexibility towards the employment of older workers, and help them to adapt, re-skill and gradually move to more suitable roles and hours when they want to so' (House of Lords Select Committee, 2013, p. 33). Yet, in the same report, it is admitted that for many older people facing a financially insecure future, there will be no choice about whether to continue in employment. It quotes Sir Bob Kerslake, head of the Civil Service, who says: 'It is absolutely clear that we will have to work longer' (House of Lords Select Committee, 2013, p. 35). It also states, somewhat alarmingly: 'By employing older workers, employers would benefit from the fruits of older workers' experience, knowledge and wisdom and a substantial implicit wage subsidy from employing people over state pension age, because they may undertake part-time work for a relatively low wage due to enjoying supplementary pension income' (House of Lords Select Committee, 2013, p. 32). These various statements seem to strike different tones: on the one hand, the right to choose to work for caring and sympathetic employers; on the other hand (for some), no choice and, it must be said, a

STOP AND THINK

- If an adequate state pension effectively gives people the right to retire, should it be maintained?

- Are there certain jobs from which older people ought to be retired? If so, at what age and on what criteria?

- What might the broader consequences for society be of removing an effective right to retire?

suggestion that older people are a relatively cheap source of labour because they come with an automatic supplement to low wages in the form of a pension.

What is often overlooked in discussions about older people, pensions, and retirement is the very significant contribution that older people already make to the economy, albeit in forms that are not recognised in official national income statics. The Women's Royal Voluntary Service recently attempted to put a financial value on the contribution that older people make in terms of care (for other older adults and children) and other forms of voluntary work (WRVS, 2011). They estimated that older people currently contribute something of the order of £34 billion in social care; £10 billion in other forms of voluntary work; and a further £10 billion in charitable donations. These are sizeable sums of money and are absolutely vital to what has come to be known as 'the Big Society', itself an increasingly important element of social policy. Compelling, or otherwise incentivising, older people to remain in work for longer may alleviate certain financial pressures associated with pension costs, but if significantly higher numbers of older people remain in work, these very significant additional, and it must be said, probably insufficiently quantified, contributions must also be reckoned with. The report also refers to a whole range of activities in which older people participate, which it characterises as 'social glue': things like neighbourliness and being 'pillars of the community', which are much harder to quantify. There are also, as we have alluded to in the discussion on independence and active ageing above, a number of other benefits which are simply about different ways of being and the different values they bring, which are impossible to quantify, but are no less important for that.

Conclusions

In this chapter, we have seen how any discussion of older people's social needs and their treatment in social policy has become inextricably bound up with (a particular problematisation of) population ageing. In a context of economic recession and austerity, we have seen the strengthening of the idea of generational fairness, in which it is argued that we need a fundamental redistribution of public resources between generations; in short, a new kind of 'social contract' between young and old. We then examined how concerns about population ageing allied to an insistence on generational fairness have given rise to a set of dominant ideas in policy around the need to promote older people's independence and to keep them active in the labour market. We explored how these ideas are being applied in current reforms of pensions provision and older people's participation in the labour market. We have sought to think critically about the implications of these for all generations and society at large. You must, of course, draw your own conclusions, but our own view is that we are in danger of heading down a path of vengeful politics in which the simplistic impression of a fairer deal for younger and middle-age groups diverts us from considering deeper problems associated with escalating levels of inequality in a context of shrinking economic growth. This cannot be solved by compelling some older people to work for relatively low wages, and returning those older people who are unable to access the labour market into pensioner poverty. There is clearly scope to reconsider the necessity of all universal pensioner benefits (subject to adequate consideration of the special difficulties associated with means testing for some age groups) but going too far down this road will, in our view, in the long run, be bad for us all.

Summary

This chapter has outlined developments in social policy as they relate to an ageing population, examining some of the major issues around how the state and civil society are and should respond to these circumstances. This has included an examination and consideration of:

- the emergence of a focus in public and political discourse on population ageing;
- the development of discussions around fairness and inequities between generations, not least the notion that in times of austerity older people may be increasingly constructed as unfairly advantaged in relation to which generations are in receipt of welfare support;
- the possible implications of a focus on generational fairness for inter-generational relations;
- the fact that a focus on perceived generational equity in policy discourse ignores the reality of inequalities within generations;
- the dominant policy focus in relation to older people whereby polices are aimed at maintaining older people's independence and active ageing;
- and, finally, the implications of this for older people's pensions and work expectations and entitlements.

Discussion and review

- To what extent do you think the debate about inter-generational as opposed to intra-generational fairness is warranted and helpful?
- Should older people be expected to work to a certain age? Why has it been suggested that the age of retirement needs to increase, and what do you think the merits are – if any – of such a position?
- How might the state and society support people to ensure that they have as fulfilling lives as possible as they become older?

References

Barnes, M. and Taylor, D. (2007) *Involving Older People in Research: Examples, Purposes and Good Practice*, ERA-AGE European Research Area in Ageing Research.

Barnes, M., Taylor, D. and Ward, L. (2013) 'Being well enough in old age', *Critical Social Policy*, Vol. 33, No. 3, pp. 473–93.

Biggs, S. and Lowenstein, A. (2011) *Generational Intelligence: A Critical Approach to Age Relations*, Routledge, Abingdon.

Cann, P. and Dean, M. (2009) *Unequal Ageing: The Untold Story of Exclusion in Old Age*, Policy Press, Bristol.

Chang, D., Spicer, N., Irving, A., Sparham, I. and Neeve, L. (2001) *Modernising Service Delivery: The Better Government for Older People Prototypes,* Department of Social Security, London.

Coole, D. (2012) 'Reconstructing the elderly: a critical analysis of pensions and population policies in an era of demographic ageing', *Contemporary Political Theory*, Vol. 11, No. 1, pp. 41–67.

Daly, M. and Lewis, J. (2000) 'The concept of care and the analysis of contemporary welfare states', *British Journal of Sociology*, Vol. 51, No. 2, pp. 281–98.

Department of Health (2005) *Independence, Wellbeing and Choice: Our Vision for the Future of Adult Social Care in England*, Cm. 6499, The Stationery Office, London.

Department of Health (2006) *Our Health, Our Care, Our Say: A New Direction for Community Services*, Cm. 6737, The Stationery Office, London.

Dorling, D. (2011) *So You Think You Know about Britain: The Surprising Truth about Modern Britain*, Constable & Robinson, London.

Ducan, H. (2011) 'Pampered pensioners cost taxpayer £16bn', *Daily Mail*, 23 February.

Estes, C., Biggs, S. and Phillipson, C. (2003) *Social Theory, Social Policy and Ageing: A Critical Introduction*, Open University Press, Maidenhead.

Gee, E. (2002) 'Misconceptions and misapprehensions about population ageing', *International Journal of Epidemiology*, Vol. 31, pp. 750–3.

Hill, M. (2006) *Social Policy in the Modern World: A Comparative Text*, Blackwell, Oxford.

HM Government (2012) *Caring for our Future: Reforming Care and Support*, The Stationery Office, Norwich.

House of Lords Select Committee on Public Service and Demographic Change (2013) *Ready for Ageing? Report of Session 2012–13*, The Stationery Office, London.

Inman, P. (2011) 'Baby boomers are Britain's secret millionaires', *The Guardian*, 28 February.

Moulaert, T. and Biggs, S. (2012) 'International and European policy on work and retirement: reinventing critical perspectives on active ageing and mature subjectivity', *Human Relations*, Vol. 66, No. 1, pp. 23–43.

Mullan, P. (2002) *The Imaginary Time Bomb: Why an Ageing Population is Not a Social Problem*, I.B. Taurus, London.

Orenstein, M. (2008) 'Global pensions policy', in N. Yeates (ed.) *Understanding Global Social Policy*, Policy Press, Bristol.

Organisation for Economic Cooperation and Development (OECD) (2006) *Ageing and Employment Policies: Live Longer, Work Longer*, OECD, Paris.

Organisation for Economic Cooperation and Development (OECD) (2011) *Pensions at a Glance: Retirement-income Systems in OECD and G20 Countries*, OECD Publishing, available at http://dx.doi.org/10.1787/pension_glance-2011-30-en.

Plath, D. (2008) 'Independence in old age: the route to social exclusion?', *British Journal of Social Work*, Vol. 38, pp. 1353–69.

Reed, H. and Horton, T. (2010) *How the Government's Planned Cuts will Affect Older People'*, Age UK, London.

Spicker, P. (2011) *How Social Security Works: An Introduction to Benefits in Britain*, Policy Press, Bristol.

Toynbee, P. (2011) 'How sad to live in a country that won't invest in its young', *The Guardian*, 19 August.

Willetts, D. (2010) *The Pinch: How the Baby Boomers Took Their Children's Future – and Why They Should Give it Back*, Atlantic Books, London.

Women's Royal Voluntary Service (WRVS) (2011) *Gold Age Pensioners: Valuing the Socio-Economic Contribution of Older People in the UK*, WRVS, Cardiff.

World Bank (1994) *Averting the Old Age Crisis: Policies to Protect the Old and Promote Growth*, Oxford University Press, New York.

World Health Organisation (WHO) (2002) *Active Ageing: A Policy Framework to the Second United Nations World Assembly on Ageing*, WHO, Madrid.

Zaidi, A. (2008) *Features and Challenges of Population Ageing: The European Perspective*, European Centre for Social Welfare Policy and Research, Vienna.

Annotated further reading

Population ageing

Commentary on population ageing and its implications for social expenditure includes: Mason, A., Lee, R., Tung, A-C., Lai, M-S., Miller, T. 'Population aging and intergenerational transfers: introducing age into national accounts'. NBER working paper series No 12770.2006. http://www.nber.org/papers/w12770; Spijker, J. and MacInnes, J. (2013) 'Population ageing. The time-bomb that isn't' *British Medical Journal*, Nov: pp. 1–5. For commentary in a critical vein, see Lundgren, A.S. and Ljuslinder, K. (2011) ' "The baby boom is over and the ageing shock awaits": populist media imagery in news-press representations of population ageing', *International Journal of Ageing and Later Life*, Vol. 6 No.2:pp. 39–71.

Intergenerational relations

The message of Alan Walker's paper in Ageing and Society in 1990 is as relevant today as it was then: Walker, A. (1990) 'The economic burden of ageing and the prospect of intergenerational conflict' *Ageing and Society* Vol. 10 No.4: pp. 377–396. See also Walker, A. (1996) *The new generational contract*, London: UCL Press. Claudine Attias-Donfut's work in this area is also well worth consulting. See: Attias-Donfut (2000) 'Cultural and economic transfers between generations. One aspect of age integration', *The Gerontologist* Vol.40: pp. 270–272; Attias-Donfut, C., Ogg, J. and Wolff, F. (2005) 'European patterns of intergenerational financial and time transfers, *European Journal of Ageing*, Vol. 2: pp. 161–73. An excellent reference on intergenerational relations in the workplace from a sociological perspective is: Roberts, I. (2006) 'Taking age out of the workplace: putting older workers back in?', *Work, Employment and Society:* Vol. 20 No. 1: pp. 67–86.

Ageing and work

For a succinct analysis of issues in age discrimination see Macnicol, J. (2010) *Ageism and Age* Discrimination: *Some Analytical Issues*, ILC-UK. On attitudes to older people in the work place, see: McNair, S. (2006) 'How different is the older labour market? Attitudes to work and retirement among older people in Britain', *Social Policy and Society:* Vol.5 No.4: pp. 484–494; Walker, A. (2005) 'The Emergence of Age Management in Europe'. *International Journal of Organisational Behaviour.* Vol.10. No.1. pp. 685–697. For a critical analysis of active ageing, see: Moulaert, T. and Biggs, S. (2012) 'International and European policy on work and retirement: Reinventing critical perspectives on active ageing and mature subjectivity', *Human Relations* (DOI: 10.1177/0018726711435180).

Cultural representations of ageing and older people

There are numerous references here, but a selection includes: Biggs, S. (1999) *The mature imagination: Dynamics of identity in midlife and beyond*, Open University Press; Featherstone, M. and Wernick, A. (1995) *Images of* Ageing: Cultural *representations of later life*, London and New York: Routledge; Gillerad, C. and Higgs, P. (2000) *Cultures of ageing: Self, citizen and the body.* Prentice Hall; Gilleard, C. and Higgs, P. (2013) *'Ageing, corporeality and embodiment'* Anthem Press. These are sociological texts, but they also consider the significant impact that cultural representations of ageing have on the kinds of policies that are pursued and how, in turn, policies feed cultural representations of ageing.

Useful websites

National policy development relating to older people is led and developed in the main by three UK Government departments:

http://www.dclg.gov.uk
http://www.dh.gov.uk
http://www.dwp.gov.uk

There are various think tanks, charities, research and pressure groups actively involved in researching and raising the profile on age related issues, including:

http://www.ageuk.org.uk – Age UK is a charity that researches 'later life' as well as providing information and advice for older people.

http://www.cpa.org.uk – Centre for Policy on Ageing promotes the interests of older people through research, policy analysis and the dissemination of information.

http://www.britishgerontology.org – British Society of Gerontology researches aspects of ageing and later life.

http://www.jrf.org.uk – Joseph Rowntree Foundation researches various social policy areas including ageing society.

CHAPTER 20

An Alternative Perspective: Green Social Policy

Michael Cahill

Chapter overview

Although economies and the environment are interlinked, the nature of their crises is different; the economic crisis of 2007–08 was a sudden crash affecting the world economy within days and producing immediate action by the G8 group of rich nations, whereas the environmental crisis, while it has a global impact on world weather patterns and serious and immediate consequences for millions in the poor world hit by more frequent famines and widespread flooding, appears to be more of a slow motion crisis, despite its likely impact being much more severe (indeed, some would say that it will be catastrophic if global temperatures exceed a rise of 2°C). This chapter takes the environment, in the widest sense, as its theme, and introduces some of the new social and environmental thinking, relating it where possible to social policy.

The chapter discusses:

- the environmental crisis and why it matters for social policy;
- consumerism, capitalism, and the consumer society and their impact on environmental destruction;
- responses to the paradox that rising levels of consumption have not led to higher levels of life satisfaction in the UK or the USA;
- examples of how green perspectives show that environmental and social policy can be interlinked;
- arguments from green perspectives, both from the political right as well as the left, relating to the wider aims of social policy, including well-being and quality of life.

Introduction

For many years, environmentalists have been predicting that the rich world would pay serious attention to their warnings of the dangers posed by global warming and climate change if New York, a key centre of contemporary capitalism, was hit by one of the increasing number of hurricanes which rage in the Caribbean. Some even predicted that if Wall Street, the heartland of American capitalism, were affected, then governments would be leant on heavily by insurance firms and finance capital to take effective action on climate change. In autumn 2012, Hurricane Sandy struck New York and the eastern seaboard of the United States in the final fortnight of an American presidential election in which climate change had been barely mentioned. Indeed, critics would argue that leadership from the United States has been singularly lacking in global environmental policy, with the US Government not according the Earth Summit held in Rio de Janeiro in 2012 a high priority, and not ensuring that an agreement was reached in 2009 on a treaty reducing carbon emissions at the Copenhagen conference.

In 2007–08, New York had also been centre-stage when Wall Street witnessed a near collapse of Anglo-American capitalism as the boom years fuelled by consumer debt came crashing to a halt and thousands of financial sector staff found themselves unemployed. These two crises in what one might call the economic and the environmental systems have had global repercussions, and the 'business as usual' response of most governments, with states shoring up a near terminal banking system and the superpowers failing to agree a way forward on international action on climate change, does not disguise the depth of the crises. The two crises have understandably produced numerous books, articles, and television programmes trying to comprehend their nature, some of which stem from what Rowan Williams, the recently retired Archbishop of Canterbury, called in his foreword to one of these books, 'a widespread anxiety about the kind of society we have become' (Williams and Elliott, 2010, p. xi). The economic crisis of 2007–08 was the closest the international capitalist system has come to collapse since the Wall Street crash of 1929. If it showed that Karl Marx was right all along about the tendency of capitalism to self-destruct, there was no coherent alternative policy, but governments believed they had to act quickly to keep the cash machines running and felt they had no alternative other than to bail out the banks. This has been extremely costly: taking together both the bailout and the economic stimulus packages put in place in many countries, the estimated global cost has been upwards of $10 trillion (Dodds *et al.*, 2012, p. 273). Part of the response, in policy discussion and politics, has been many attempts to offer both an explanation as to what went wrong, but more importantly, to develop a credible alternative to the existing model of economic growth and environmental destruction.

The environmental crisis

The connection between the environmental, economic, and social crisis could be seen vividly on our television screens when Hurricane Katrina hit New Orleans in 2005 or Hurricane Sandy New York in 2012, or in the UK when the television news shows graphic images of flooding, its affect on properties, and the disruption to people's lives. However, although UK and US flood victims experience serious and painful upheaval in their lives, millions in areas of the poor world, where problems of poverty and food shortages are exacerbated by the impact of the changing climate, suffer far more serious consequences from drought, flooding, and increasingly violent storms. As a result, the increasing number of severe weather events is producing severe strain on national and international social policy.

> **STOP AND THINK**
>
> The economic development of the world's poorer countries will contribute further to climate change. Yet rising temperatures and increasing extreme weather mean that they are already its greatest victims.

The development of environmental consciousness

The origins of environmental movements and environmental awareness can be traced back to the late eighteenth century, when industrialism began to disrupt the geography, society, and economy of the United Kingdom, heralding the beginnings of a market society. Surprisingly, it was not until well into the post Second World War boom years that the impact of this economic transformation on the natural environment began to be scientifically explored, although the urban–industrial complex had been in existence for almost two centuries. In 1962, a book was published in the USA that was to have a profound impact: *Silent Spring*, by Rachel Carson, provided detailed evidence on the extremely harmful effects that the chemical DDT was having on plant life, insects, and birds in particular, wherever it was used. *Silent Spring* was an early warning of the damage that chemicals were causing to the natural world.

Ten years later, public opinion was confronted with another warning, this time in economics, with the publication of *The Limits to Growth* by Donella Meadows and colleagues in 1972. The authors' case was that the industrial system, and particularly the post-war boom, had been built upon the use of minerals, fossil fuels built up over millennia, which were now being squandered in the pursuit of ever higher rates of economic growth (Meadows *et al.*, 1972). Meadows and her colleagues believed that if the rates of economic and population growth, food production, and mineral extraction of the 1970s continued, then there would be a collapse in the world economy at some point in the ensuing decades when natural resources finally ran out. There has been extensive debate as to whether the model used by the authors was sufficiently comprehensive to include all the necessary inputs, and it has been noted that they took no real account of differential rates of resource use by world region. Economists were quick to point out that Meadows and colleagues ignored the price mechanism, whereby if demand increased price would rise and hence ration the resource (Victor, 2008). Nonetheless, even if the timescale was erroneous, the Meadows thesis foreshadowed the current alarm about 'peak oil', the point when oil production hits its peak and subsequently declines. The idea of limits to human endeavour became part of the 1970s environmental debate, be that in psychology, economics, politics or social science generally. An outstanding contribution was made by Hirsch (1977) in *Social Limits to Growth*, where he highlighted the importance of positional goods, those which are high status and hence only able to be enjoyed by a few: these might be immaterial, such as a ticket to a Buckingham Palace investiture, or material, such as a sports car with a limited production run. When the mass of the population are driving round in cars or going to exotic locations for their holidays, not only are there problems of congestion, on the roads or at airports, it also means the satisfaction derived by each person from these positional goods is reduced (Hirsch, 1977).

E.F. Schumacher's *Small is Beautiful: A Study of Economics as if People Mattered*, posed fundamental ethical questions about the economic system, questioning the whole thrust of economic growth and its attendant attributes, which he claimed did not serve the needs of humanity (Schumacher, 1973). Alongside these texts must be ranked the work of the dissident Roman Catholic priest, Ivan Illich, who in a series of publications analysed the environmental and human consequences of mass schooling, health, and transportation (Illich, 1971, 1974, 1975). All of these books were widely read and discussed, making a major contribution to the deepening of the environmental alternative to mainstream social and economic thought. In UK politics, this flourishing of environmental awareness was, however, largely confined to the fringes of the main parties. The public looked to pressure groups to promote the environmental message, among the best known being Friends of the Earth and Greenpeace. Their message, and that of the nascent Green Party in the 1970s, was that environmental problems could be solved and disaster averted, even though this would entail substantial reforms. Essentially it was a message of hope, and a belief that something could be done to avert the worst-case scenarios outlined by environmental doomsters. At the same time, a section of the environmental movement saw mainstream politics as part of the problem, viewing it as corrupt and incapable of responding adequately to the environmental challenge. And it is only since the 1992 Rio Earth Summit that environmental politics has arguably become part of the UK's political mainstream.

The 1980s saw the environmental debate move on with the popularisation of the term 'sustainable development', which was defined by the Brundtland Commission with this neat formula: development that meets the needs of the present without compromising the ability of future generations to meet their own needs (World Commission on Environment and Development, 1987). Brundtland was a United Nations report and led to the United Nations Rio Earth Summit in 1992, where most of the world's nations signed up to sustainable development as a policy goal. Sustainable development was one way of characterising the response to the environmental crisis, yet its easy acceptance as a concept seemed to owe much to the fact that it could mean different things to different people. Much 'sustainable development' activity was actually no more than putting a green gloss on existing forms of consumption and production. Green consumerism, for example, might result in shoppers choosing products that are less environmentally damaging, as with certain makes of car, but if total car ownership increased, then the environmental benefits are quickly outweighed.

Sustainable development was a policy aspiration within an economic system characterised by consumption. It is important to note how the environmental debate has changed. Until the 1990s, it was possible to agree that major changes in the global climate were likely in the future, that there was a real possibility that oil was going to be a declining resource, and that biodiversity was seriously threatened, but still to argue that it was a future scenario; now, in the twenty-first century, it is fast becoming a reality, with serious consequences for economy and society. Many argue that one of these consequences is that we need to re-examine the organisation of the economy, and in particular the role given to consumption.

Consuming

The dominant version of the good life in the world's richest nations is consumer capitalism, where populations are encouraged to enjoy the cars, domestic appliances, and many other goods that have made lives more convenient, easier, and enjoyable than for the vast majority of humans in previous centuries. Given the reach of the global media, this seductive vision of the good life is seen by millions around the world, many of who are still living in poverty, so that the rapidly industrialising nations are becoming consumers of this way of life. Yet consumption of the world's resources at the rate now being experienced is simply unsustainable, and has led to 'a significant squandering of resources, in many instances relatively scarce, if not irreplaceable natural resources, the production of increasing quantities of waste, various forms of pollution, and perhaps most significantly of all, increasing evidence of global warming' (Smart, 2010, p. 160).

Consumerism can be defined as the ideology of the consumer society, the belief that happiness and self-fulfilment – the good life – is to be found, in large part, through the accumulation of consumer goods and services. This belief became all pervasive in the post Second World War period in the UK, and clearly altered the stance of the main political parties who, in order to win elections, have had to appeal to the motivations, desires, and aspirations of the voting public. The 'good life' in consumer society was to be found in the acquisition of goods and the enjoyment of affluence. This was a break with the past.

In the early British socialist movement, from the late nineteenth century onwards, critics of the distribution of wealth had counterpoised to the conspicuous consumption of the rich an alternative ethic based upon fellowship and equality, commonly known as ethical socialism. For their part, many Liberals and Conservatives believed in moderation and had an antipathy to overt displays of wealth. These perspectives receded over time, particularly with the spread of affluence subsequent to the Second World War, which produced many more ways in which status could be displayed and as consumer goods began to define a lifestyle to which everyone could aspire. Yet, as John Barry has observed, it also produced a narrowing of the self: 'Our primary identity under capitalism is not as parents, lovers or citizens ... but workers and consumers' (Barry, 2012, p. 71).

Consumer culture is appealing because it enables a diversity of styles, opinions, and cultures to flourish without interference. One of the strengths of consumer culture is that it is often able to assimilate its critics. For example, consumer culture lives off street style and makes money out of rebel movements, so that the Virgin empire of Richard Branson was able to package the hippy culture of the late 1960s, which was in many respects anti-consumerist, and embody and sell it in a number of consumer products. Consumption has, in turn, become a major problem for rich world societies now that they are aware of the

> ## STOP AND THINK
>
> 'This $60-billion industry sold 241 billion litres of water in 2008, more than double the amount sold in 2000. Through its global advertising efforts, the industry has helped create the impression that bottled water is healthier, tastier, and more fashionable than publicly supplied water, even as studies have found some bottled water brands to be less safe than public tap water and to cost 240 to 10,000 times as much' (Assadourian, 2010, p. 14).

environmental impact of consumer activity. The engagement with sustainability over the last 20 years has highlighted the growing burdens being placed on the planet by the commitment to economic growth and the consumer society. Indeed, the consumer society has become a global phenomenon, with the USA still the largest consumer nation, but other countries such as China, Russia, Brazil, India, and South Africa rapidly embracing the consumer lifestyle.

Environmentalists argue that the 'good life' predicated upon increasing consumption patterns is unsustainable. On both sides of the Atlantic, evidence has appeared of the human consequences for those caught up in status anxiety and debt produced by the affluent society, or 'affluenza', defined as 'a painful, contagious socially transmitted condition of overload, debt, anxiety, and waste resulting from the dogged pursuit of more' (De Graaf *et al.*, 2005, p. 2; see also James, 2007).

States can promote reduced consumption through a variety of mechanisms. For example, luxury goods can be more highly taxed, while advertising, particularly through the mass media, can be more restricted (see Skidelsky and Skidelsky, 2012). Yet populations who have been weaned on a consumer sensibility arguably need to be offered an alternative that promises life satisfaction and different rewards. It remains to be seen whether a focus on wellbeing and quality of life, as discussed later, will satisfy people's aspirations for a good life.

Responding to the environmental challenge

The problem of economic growth

'Growth' has an undeniably positive ring to it, for children grow, plants grow, and hence it is thought natural that economies should grow. Economic growth is seen by mainstream political parties as the way in which progress will be achieved and a better quality of life ensue. Economic growth has been seen as essential for individual and family prosperity, the increasing wealth of the country, and via state redistribution the functions of government. Nonetheless, this emphasis on economic growth as a concern of government is relatively recent: the first UK government report that included a commitment to economic growth was in 1950 (Victor, 2008, p. 13). Economic growth is regarded as essential not just for neo-liberal policies, but for social democratic and left of centre policies as well. Indeed, in the 1950s, some socialists regarded economic growth as the elixir that would enable social inequalities to be reduced while ensuring that the living standard of the majority of the population remained untouched (see Crosland, 1956; see also Chapter 8). In the 1980s, neo-liberals argued that high taxation and other restrictions on amassing wealth could be dispensed with, as a process of 'trickle-down' would ensure that the poor would, ultimately, enjoy some of this wealth. This has not happened in the UK or the USA where this doctrine was most keenly implemented; indeed, there is strong evidence that tax reductions for the rich and reductions in corporate taxation have been accompanied by an increase in income inequality (Stiglitz, 2012).

Following the 2008 economic crisis, the UK economy has failed to match the growth rates experienced before the credit crunch. With very low growth, or even zero growth, there have been real fears that Britain would decline economically and socially. We can, however, set against this the observation that since the early 1970s, green economists have argued that there were limits to growth and the planet had reached them and that a temperature rise of more than 2°C would produce extreme climate instability, which in turn would inevitably entail a reduction in economic output for rich world countries, and that could well equate to no economic growth. There may therefore be opportunities as well as challenges from the current economic problems.

Ecological modernisation is the economic model favoured by many European governments to reconcile economic growth with environmental protection. This has two main features. One is the idea of dematerialisation: that for each product a progressive reduction in resources can be obtained over time. It is thought that this will lead to a decoupling of economic growth and resource use, meaning that economic growth will not be so dependent on resource use. The second is the 'polluter pays' principle, ensuring that firms build pollution controls into the production process. Some of this technology can be marketed and sold to other businesses and countries (Carter, 2007). The difficulty with this new environmentally aware version of economic growth is whether it is going to work; is it going to reduce emissions to the level where catastrophic climate change is averted? Jackson (2009) has confronted this question in his book *Prosperity without Growth*. His conclusion is that the decoupling of growth from emissions is a myth, in that it is not feasible to think that the necessary technological and environmental efficiencies could be made to achieve the carbon reductions to which the UK and other rich countries are committed. He is, however, not anti-economic growth as such, believing that it is still necessary in the developing world, and that in the rich world there will still need to be growth in sustainable technologies as well as human knowledge. This is typical of many greens who are not anti-growth, but merely certain types of growth. Even those (mainly French) advocates of 'de-growth' do not argue for nil growth and countenance some forms of growth (see, for example, Latouche, 2009).

CONTROVERSY AND DEBATE

What is a steady state economy?

'At its simplest a steady-state economy is an economy that aims to maintain a stable level of resource consumption and a stable population. It's an economy in which material and energy use are kept within ecological limits, and in which the goal of increasing GDP is replaced by the goal of improving quality of life.

'A steady-state economy would require striking a balance between the stock of natural capital and the stock of built capital, with both remaining relatively constant over time. A constant stock of natural capital implies the preservation of wilderness areas and the maintenance of important ecosystem services, such as climate regulation. A constant stock of built capital means maintaining and improving the quality of infrastructure, such as buildings and roads, but not constructing more and more of these over time.

'It's important to distinguish between what's on and what's off the list of things to hold steady in a steady-state economy. Only a few items need to be held steady – the number of people, the stock of artifacts (built capital), and the quantity of material and energy flowing through the economy . . . In contrast the list of items that can change is long. It includes knowledge, technology, information, wisdom, the mix of products, income distribution, and social institutions, among other things. The objective is to have the items on this second list improving over time, so that the economy can develop qualitatively without growing quantitatively.

'In short, a steady-state economy is an economy with *enough* as a goal. It prioritizes well-being above consumption, and long-term health over short-term gains. It focuses on innovation and development instead of growth. The pursuit of endless economic growth, with all of its downsides, is clearly unsustainable in the twenty-first century. A steady-state economy is the sustainable alternative to perpetual economic growth.

From Dietz, R. and O'Neill, D. (2013) *Enough is Enough: Building a Sustainable Economy in a World of Finite Resources*, Routledge, London, pp. 45–6.

Vulnerability

The increasing frequency of environmental crises reveals the vulnerability, that is to say the potential for loss, of human populations, although this vulnerability is much greater in the poor world than in the rich world. This is not to argue that the rich world is invulnerable, for it relies for everyday life on a complex web of systems and infrastructure that when disrupted can lead to societal breakdown. The electricity grid, transportation, and food supply systems are all sophisticated in their organisation, but are not immune to disruption. We can term this 'social vulnerability', when a society becomes vulnerable, which can be distinguished from biophysical vulnerability, which is when society interacts with the biophysical conditions, as in drought or land degradation (Cutter, 2006).

A more environmentally informed social policy takes this vulnerability into account, noting that it is a characteristic of human beings. Babies and small children are extremely vulnerable and highly dependent on others for their welfare, while older children, although less dependent, are still highly vulnerable, as evidence of child sexual abuse attests. Some adults are also vulnerable, possibly because of mental or physical disability, and vulnerability, along with dependence, can increase with old age, with its associated infirmities and sensory loss. The local environment plays an important role in relation to vulnerable groups in the population.

Children's lives and the local environment

For the most part we tend to think of environmental problems as being big global issues, like climate change, that affect everyone on the planet, yet the local environment outside our front door, on the street where we live, has its own environmental problems with social consequences. One only has to think of the increase in traffic over the last half century, from 2 million motor vehicles in 1951 to over 28 million in 2011, to appreciate the environmental problems that this has created: there has been an increase in air pollution and greenhouse gases as a result, but it is arguably the human consequences that have had more of an immediate impact on many people's lives, particularly those of children. For most children, their immediate neighbourhood, the streets where they live, are no longer a play space because of the fear of traffic. There have been too many accidents involving cars and children, resulting in death and serious injury, for parents to allow their offspring to play freely in the streets, as was possible until the 1960s. Yet there is considerable evidence that active play is an important part of children's learning about the world. As the Children's Play Council states in its Charter for Children's Play:

> Play is an essential part of every child's life and vital to processes of human development. It provides the mechanism for children to explore the world around them and the medium through which skills are developed and practised. It is essential for physical, emotional and spiritual growth, intellectual and educational development, and acquiring social and behavioural skills.
>
> (Charter for Children's Play, 1998,
> quoted in Cole-Hamilton et al., 2002)

This is one restriction on children's lives, but there are many others that derive from the priority given to speeding traffic in so many urban and rural neighbourhoods, including travel to see their friends and to amenities such as swimming pools.

The Department of Health recommends that children should spend an hour a day undertaking physical activity, although there is overwhelming evidence that children do not get enough physical exercise in their daily lives. The dangers from traffic, combined with the increasing attractions of screen-based entertainment in the home, have undoubtedly played their part. Reduced physical activity can have worrying health consequences, such as obesity, but also susceptibility to diabetes and other long-term conditions. Cycling is an excellent form of exercise for children, but again fear of traffic means that many children do not use their bikes as a form of transport. Where walking is concerned, studies of children's independent mobility carried out over the period from the early 1970s to 2010 reveal that the major decline in primary school age children walking to school on their own occurred between the 1970s and the 1990s, although there was a further reduction by 2010 (Shaw *et al.*, 2012, pp. 19–20). Clearly, taken together, these developments are highly problematic.

Older people

Just as the local environment is important for children, it is also important for older people, who are more likely than the adult population as a whole to be physically frail, to have sight or hearing problems or a physical disability of some sort. The Department of Health recommends that adults should undertake at least half an hour a day of physical activity, and walking in the local environment is an obvious way to attain this target. Yet in some areas the pavements are in such poor condition that frail older people are reluctant to venture out in case they fall. As Easterbrook *et al.* (2002, p. 3) comment, 'Fear of falling, and the fear of undertaking tasks or activities that might lead to a fall can lead older people to become disempowered, more isolated and with a reduced quality of life'. Speeding traffic in residential areas is another hazard. Older people have a higher fatality rate once injured because of their frailty, and as pedestrians they are more vulnerable because they may be more severely injured and more pedestrians aged 70 and over are killed on the roads than any other age group (Whitelegg, 2012, p. 51; European Commission, 2013).

When there is a collision between a human being and a car, the speed of the vehicle is important. There is sufficient evidence to show that when a car travelling at 40 mph hits a pedestrian there is a very high probability that the pedestrian will die. When the car is being driven at 20 mph, then the pedestrian will, in all likelihood, live. It is evidence such as this that is persuading many local authorities to declare 20 mph zones in urban areas.

Housing can be another hazard for older people, as buildings are often not properly insulated, and as a result heating bills can be high, or some older people may choose not to use their heating so much, and thus run the risk of hypothermia. Policies such as the winter fuel allowance for pensioners may be designed to respond to this, but factors such as the need to apply for it and the triggers for payment mean that some older people do not make use of it.

Given these issues, there would appear to be a linkage between a child-friendly local environment and an older person-friendly environment: for example, both would be designed and organised to reduce car danger and at the same time would enable more people to become physically active in their neighbourhoods. Such challenges also emphasise the fact that policy and planning need to be interlinked, with environmental and social policies working together to create a safer and healthier local environment. There is a related argument here that caring for the local environment is part of an environmental awareness, and that for local people to care for their environment requires the powers to be able to do so, meaning that some power over planning and transport, for instance, needs to be restored to localities.

A conservative perspective on environmental change is that it is only when sufficient numbers of people begin to link environmental awareness and action with their concern for their own home that there will be widespread support for change. Scruton (2012) argues that the core of caring for the environment has to be love of home, or oikophilia. For him oikophilia denotes not only love of the home but the people in it, for this is the place where most men and women live out their lives. Scruton believes that love of the environment will come from respecting the dead, the generations who have gone before and left us a legacy of a beautiful countryside. His policy proposals have an emphasis on restoring the economic and social life of the locality by making the transit of goods more expensive, promoting local cultivation, and reducing household energy consumption.

Quality of life and wellbeing

Environmentalists' concerns with the quality of life can be taken as part of a wider debate that has come to the forefront of public attention in the last decade, and can be summarised as being about why in the world's richest countries there is so much dissatisfaction with the quality of life. That debate started before the financial crisis of 2007–08 but has intensified since, with the financial meltdown adding a clear sense of present danger and urgency to these deliberations, for indebted states in Europe, the USA, and Australasia cannot continue to spend on welfare at the old pre-crash levels.

There has been a long held assumption that increasing the economic wealth of a society via growth would increase overall subjective wellbeing. The evidence suggests that up to a certain point this association holds true, but beyond that point increasing wealth seems to lead to a decrease in subjective wellbeing. This paradox has led to a great deal of discussion and debate as to why this should be the case. Indeed, there is some evidence that increasing wealth beyond a certain point may be associated with a rise in depression and mental illness. It would appear that the reason why some of the negative consequences arise is to do with the ways in which wealth is consumed, obtained, displayed, and organised. That is, it is necessary to examine the role played by wealth in a society, and crucially this includes the disparities between incomes, or the degree of inequality. If we have two societies where the gross domestic product is the same, but society A has very high taxes on wealth holding and on high incomes and luxury goods together with high state spending on health, social services and education, whereas society B has a low overall rate of tax both on incomes and consumption and low levels of spending on health, social services and education, we might find that in society A there are low levels of depression and mental illness while in society B the reverse is true. There is a strong argument that the mechanisms whereby wealth is transmitted through a society seem to be important for the overall subjective wellbeing of people. These mechanisms can include the culture of the country, which in turn embraces the values by which people live. Avner Offer (2006, p. 369) argues that there are two components to high levels of what he terms 'ill being': these are the social stigma associated with low social status, and the lack of 'intimacy, reciprocity and regard'. For him, the transition from a consumerist society to one where material goods are not so highly prized has been made more difficult by the change in values in the UK, which he argues began to occur in the early 1970s, when what he calls the 'culture of restraint' began to weaken. This was wide-ranging, with both the UK and the USA moving away from policies that promoted greater social equality and social inclusion. There was considerable economic restructuring and,

> At a personal level, there was a shift towards a more self-regarding individualism, captured by demographic trends such as more divorce, a lower birth rate, later marriages, out of wedlock births; at the normative level by an increased quest for self-fulfillment and an increased assertion of individual entitlements and rights.
>
> (A. Offer, 2006, p. 365)

In this emerging culture there was a growing emphasis on consumer rights in relation to public services, with individuals being encouraged to think of themselves as consumers of services. The market was seen as a superior way to allocate resources, and quasi-markets were promoted by governments in areas such as health and personal social services from the late 1980s.

CONTROVERSY AND DEBATE

Can we measure happiness?

'Money can't buy you love, nor does it turn out to buy much extra cheer in the world's richer societies. Inspired by that finding, David Cameron has followed the lead of the king of Bhutan and established official measures of wellbeing, so that this can be targeted alongside traditional GDP metrics, as it has been in the Himalayan statelet since the 1970s. If money doesn't matter, the things that do make the difference are company, community and – above all – a sense of purpose. Thus it is, for example, that a new study in the British Journal of Psychiatry suggests that those who successfully quit smoking for 2013 can expect to become significantly less anxious: the immediate calming draw of a cigarette for the addicted would appear to be overwhelmed by the empowering wellbeing that comes with the feeling of having kicked the habit.

'In the face of a stubborn financial depression, one might have thought it would be a great relief to discover that joy stems from non-material roots – it at least creates the possibility that the human heart might flourish through austere times. Sadly, unemployment provides a nasty eudaemonic twist to every economic downturn – the hardships of a squeezed pay packet might be endured with a smile, but the futility of getting up in the morning without something productive to do cannot be shrugged off. The Prince's Trust today published research that revealed an enormous hit to confidence about every aspect of life faced by young people who are stuck without work or college. A return to growth will not guarantee happiness, but in its absence we will likely remain stuck with joblessness – which guarantees the opposite'.

The Guardian, 2 January 2013, available at http://www.guardian.co.uk/commentisfree/2013/jan/02/happiness-index-money-work [accessed 25 March 2013].

How useful are attempts to measure happiness and wellbeing?

Public service

The debates about wellbeing have led to a renewed emphasis on what makes for a good life. It is important to remember that the pioneers of social reform in this country in the late nineteenth and early twentieth century did not envisage a 'welfare state'; they wanted to see an end to poverty and ill health and to give the majority of the population opportunities to improve their lives through education or the labour market, but many of them would have been horrified if they had thought they were creating a bureaucratic 'welfare state' responsible for a large proportion of public expenditure (see Chapter 6).

The institutions that emerged in post-war Britain and which are collectively known as the 'welfare state' can be seen, in part, as emanating from a long tradition of public service, which was created in the late Victorian period by an array of philosophers, social investigators, politicians, and social reformers as an answer to the perceived evils of that society (J. Offer, 2006).

The roots of the belief in public service may be traced back to the philosopher T.H. Green (1836–1882), who translated his philosophical ideas, known as idealism, into a personal commitment to social reform and a belief that those who shared them should dedicate their time to the service of others. Many prominent politicians and social reformers were influenced by this idealism, with probably the best-known and most important for social policy being William Beveridge (see Chapter 6). Idealism was also among the mix of influences that led to the establishment of social administration and social work departments in a number of universities before the First World War. Early social work courses had a curriculum, which, while training students to work with the poor, included the study of economics and the administration of services. There was also substantial attention given to social philosophy, with the study of ethics from ancient Greece to the twentieth century, considering questions such as, 'What is the good life?', 'What does it mean to be a citizen?', and 'How does one practise the virtues?' During the long post-war period of full employment and the expansion of the welfare state, consideration of these questions of social philosophy disappeared from the curriculum of social work training and social administration courses.

At least part of the motivation of the Labour government of 1945–51 in expanding the public sector was a belief that a new society could be created that would offer an alternative ethic to that of capitalism (see also Chapter 8). The accommodation reached between capital and labour in the years between the 1940s and the 1970s was in part mirrored in the rise in affluence and the burgeoning of the welfare state. There were many who, like Richard Titmuss, the UK's first Professor of Social Policy, believed that the values embodied in the welfare state would transform capitalist society in the UK, making it more egalitarian, caring, and united. Titmuss believed that institutions would play a major role in achieving this mixed economy of public and private working together in the common interest. These institutions, whether schools, libraries or social services, would embody the values of the public sector, as opposed to those of private enterprise. There was for many people a pride in working for these institutions, which was often allied to a pride in working for a local authority that reflected the population of a particular area. In the current era of disillusionment with the state, it is difficult to convey the sense of public sector pride that informed the development of the health service, and the education and other departments of local authorities. Since then, of course, in academic work and in the vocabulary of contemporary politics, the bureaucracy of the public sector has been severely criticised – for inefficiency, overstaffing, and for too much producer control. Yet this attachment to *place* is at the centre of a green perspective on the locality, although it takes different forms. One example of these is the transition towns movement, discussed below.

Resilience

Consumer societies rely on copious supplies of energy to sustain them and produce a great deal of waste. If the predictions about peak oil are correct, then within our lifetimes we may be living in a much more energy-constrained world than at present. One response to this has been the transition towns movement, started by Rob Hopkins in Totnes, Devon, and now with numerous transition towns and cities across the UK and spreading across the globe (Hopkins, 2011). The transition towns movement is directed towards surviving in an energy-constrained world and preparing for the consequences of a world where oil is a much more scarce resource. A number of transition towns have produced what they call Energy Descent Plans, which outline how the energy demands of a locality can be reduced and replaced. In addition, there has been a focus on a number of other areas. As transition town members believe that food production should become more local, they encourage food production at the local level in gardens or allotments or on waste ground if need be. An energy-constrained world would also not be able to rely, or indeed want to rely, on supplies of low-cost clothing often produced at low wages by workers thousands of miles away. For this reason, many of the transition towns have begun to teach skills of self-reliance, such as knitting and sewing, growing vegetables, and baking bread. Running through these activities is an emphasis on resilience: the capacity to withstand and recover from, and respond to, difficult, and possibly harmful, circumstances. Barry sees this as a facet of character, close to the idea of fortitude, making the best of things, sometimes seen as an inner toughness or at times the capacity to be adaptable in the face of adversity (Barry, 2012, p. 89).

Resilience can be considered at the personal level, but we can also think of resilience at the level of the town or the city. The great majority of urban areas are not resilient, in that their dependence on energy means that any interruption in energy supply or other form of disruption means that a major social dislocation can occur, such as traffic gridlock or people in outlying areas being unable to get to work. Resilience at the level of urban planning would entail the creation of 'compact cities', where as many people as possible would live close to their place of work and where a high proportion of the population would be able to walk or cycle to work. This kind of resilient urban environment would mean less energy use and an environment that was less vulnerable to disruptions.

Resilience assumes importance in the green vision of society, where consumer goods and material aspirations are not so highly prized. Previous generations in pre-consumer societies, before consumerism took hold of the individual and social psyche, had to cultivate values that enabled them to survive in a society governed by scarcity. In the post-consumer society, the citizen's inner resources will need to be strong in order to flourish in a less bountiful society, and to withstand the shocks that will result from a warming world.

Conclusion

Although environmentalists have been highlighting for many years the dangers of damage to the environment, including global warming and the impacts of climate change, it has taken a considerable period of time for these ideas to enter the political mainstream, and even longer for links to be made with social policy. However, scientific evidence and other factors, such as extreme weather events in recent years, have helped bring these issues to the forefront of attention, and green perspectives have begun to feed into policy agendas.

The economic crisis of 2007–08 helped highlight problems with capitalism and consumerism as they have developed in the post-war years. Increasingly, governments and individuals are being required to consider the implications of continued economic growth in the developed world, including in relation to the environment, but also to broader related factors such as quality of life. There are now significant debates about how to respond to the questions posed by environmental change and by environmentalists.

Summary

This chapter has reviewed some of the key ideas that green thought has brought to the debates about the kind of life, and lifestyle, which we can and should expect to live in a low carbon economy and society. It has shown that:

- The debate is now much more wide-ranging than it used to be, with contributions from the right and left of the political spectrum.
- Linked with this is the realisation that economic growth and consumerism not only fail to satisfy many people's aspirations for a good life but are actually damaging to the environment.
- Social and environmental policy need to be integrated more closely in order to protect those who are most vulnerable.

Discussion and review

- Is consumerism always detrimental for the environment?
- Is economic growth the problem or is it instead the kind of economic growth?
- How might we reduce the vulnerability of sections of the population such as children and older people to environmental threats?
- How might towns and cities become more resilient?

References

Assadourian, E. (2010) The rise and fall of consumer cultures, in *State of the World 2010*, W.W. Norton, New York.

Barry, J. (2012) *The Politics of Actually Existing Unsustainability: Human Flourishing in a Climate-Changed, Carbon Constrained World*, Oxford University Press, Oxford.

Carson, R. (1962) *Silent Spring*, Houghton-Mifflin, Boston, MA.

Carter, N. (2007) *The Politics of the Environment*, Cambridge University Press, Cambridge.

Cole-Hamilton, I., Harrop, A. and Street, C. (2002) *The Value of Children's Play and Children's Play Provision*, New Policy Institute, London.

Crosland, C.A.R. (1956) *The Future of Socialism*, Jonathan Cape, London.

Cutter, S.L. (2006) 'Vulnerability to environmental hazards', in S.L. Cutter (ed.) *Hazards, Vulnerability and Environmental Justice*, Earthscan, London.

De Graaf, J., Wann, D. and Naylor, T.H. (2005) *Affluenza: The All Consuming Epidemic*, Berrett-Koehler, San Francisco, CA.

Dietz, R. and O'Neill, D. (2013) *Enough is Enough: Building a Sustainable Economy in a World of Finite Resources*, Routledge, London

Dodds, F., Strauss, M. and Strong, M. (2012) *Only One Earth: The Long Road via Rio to Sustainable Development*, Earthscan, London.

Easterbrook, L., Horton, K., Arber, S. and Davidson, K. (2002) *International Review of Interventions in Falls among Older People*, Department for Trade and Industry, London.

European Commission (2013) *Mobility and Transport: Pedestrians*, available at http://ec.europa.eu/transport/road_safety/users/pedestrians/index_en.htm

Hirsch, F. (1977) *Social Limits to Growth*, Routledge, London.

Hopkins, R. (2011) *The Transition Companion: Making Your Community More Resilient in Uncertain Times*, Green Books, Totnes.

Illich, I. (1971) *Deschooling Society*, Harper & Row, New York.

Illich, I. (1974) *Energy and Equity*, Harper & Row, New York.

Illich, I. (1975) *Medical Nemesis*, Calder & Boyars, London.

Jackson, T. (2009) *Prosperity without Growth: Economics for a Finite Planet*, Earthscan, London.

James, O. (2007) *Affluenza: How to be Successful and Stay Sane*, Vermilion, London.

Latouche, S. (2009) *Farewell to Growth*, Polity, Cambridge.

Meadows, D., Randers, J., Meadows, D.L. and Behrens, W.W. (1972) *The Limits to Growth: A Report for the Club of Rome's Project on the Predicament of Mankind*, Universe Books, New York.

Offer, A. (2006) *The Challenge of Affluence: Self-Control and Well-Being in the United States and Britain since 1950*, Oxford University Press, Oxford.

Offer, J. (2006) *An Intellectual History of British Social Policy: Idealism versus Non-idealism*, Policy Press, Bristol.

Schumacher, E.F. (1973) *Small is Beautiful: A Study of Economics as if People Mattered*, Blond & Briggs, London.

Scruton, R. (2012) *Green Philosophy*, Atlantic Books, London.

Shaw, B., Watson, B., Frauendienst, B., Redecker, A. and Hillman, M. (2012) *The Erosion of Children's Independent Mobility: A Comparative Study in England and Germany (1971 to 2010)*, Policy Studies Institute, London.

Skidelsky, R. and Skidelsky, E. (2012) *How Much is Enough? The Love of Money, and the Case for the Good Life*, Allen Lane, London.

Smart, B. (2010) *Consumer Society: Critical Issues and Environmental Consequences*, Sage, London.

Stiglitz, J.E. (2012) *The Price of Inequality*, Allen Lane, London.

Victor, P. (2008) *Managing without Growth: Slower by Design, Not Disaster*, Edward Elgar, Cheltenham.

Whitelegg, J. (2012) *Quality of Life and Public Management: Redefining Development in the Local Environment*, Routledge, London.

Williams, R. and Elliott, L. (2010) *Crisis and Recovery: Ethics, Economics and Justice*, Palgrave Macmillan, Basingstoke.

World Commission on Environment and Development (1987) *Our Common Future*, Oxford University Press, Oxford.

Further reading

Barry, J. (2012) *The Politics of Actually Existing Unsustainability: Human Flourishing in a Climate-Changed, Carbon Constrained World*, Oxford University Press, Oxford. This book looks at the causes of unsustainability and seeks to offer a green alternative to economic growth and economic security.

Dietz, R. and O'Neill, D. (2013) *Enough is Enough: Building a Sustainable Economy in a World of Finite Resources*, Routledge, London. The authors of this work seek to present an alternative future where the goal is enough rather than more.

Fitzpatrick, T. (ed.) (2011) *Understanding the Environment and Social Policy*, Policy Press, Bristol. This book explores a range of challenges that environmental thinking poses for social policy. It also considers these in relation to a number of key policy areas.

Jackson, T. (2009) *Prosperity without Growth*, Earthscan, London. Questioning the links between prosperity and economic growth, the author argues against continued growth in the developed nations.

Scruton, R. (2012) *Green Philosophy: How to Think Seriously about the Planet*, Atlantic Books, London. Starting from a conservative perspective, Scruton argues that there is a need to encourage individual responsibility and local decision-making as the best way of caring for the environment.

Useful websites

http://www.neweconomics.org/ – the website of the New Economics Foundation, a 'think and do tank' that provides a stream of interesting policy proposals from a green perspective.

http://www.sd-commission.org.uk/ – the Sustainable Development Commission was created by the Labour government to assess government performance on sustainable development. Although it was abolished by the Coalition, this is an 'archive site' with valuable research and publications.

http://www.transitionnetwork.org – the website of the Transition Towns network provides information and links to resources.

CHAPTER 21

Exploring the Boundaries of Social Policy

Catherine Bochel

Learning objectives

- To consider the relevance of social policy analyses to broader policy areas
- To explore the way in which 'new' areas of social policy such as food, the environment and sustainability, transport and travel, and ICT can create inequalities just as older more traditional areas are seen to do
- To consider policies and approaches that might help minimise inequalities arising from these 'new' social policy areas
- To explore the implications of these for social policy and society

---

Chapter overview

This chapter considers why it is that issues that in the past had not been regarded as being within the domain of social policy have more recently come to be seen as having relevance to social policy issues and concerns. Traditionally, social policy has been concerned with issues such as health, housing, education, income maintenance, and the personal social services, but with changes in society, combined with changes in the development of the subject of social policy, it is now possible to argue that the scope of analysis of social policy can and should be broadened. This chapter therefore:

- examines the development of the subject and the extension of social policy analyses to areas other than traditional concerns;
- focuses upon issues of food, the environment and sustainability, transport and travel, and ICT to illustrate links with key social policy ideas;
- considers the implications of these for social policy and for society.

CONTROVERSY AND DEBATE

Wind farms are seen as one source of renewable energy. They are increasingly being built across the countryside. There is general agreement that, as a society, we need to become less dependent on carbon fuels, such as oil and gas, which are becoming increasingly hard to extract. So, generating electricity in this way might be seen to be a good thing. However, just as with other social policy issues, there are other aspects to this debate, and the health and wellbeing of people who live close to wind farms is one of these.

An e-petition submitted to the National Assembly for Wales in July 2011 urged the Welsh Government 'to pass a statute controlling the noise nuisance from wind turbines during anti-social hours' and 'for the implementation of respite periods during which time turbines would be switched off' (National Assembly for Wales, 2012, p. 7). Such respite periods are common in public health legislation, and are operated in the UK on construction sites, factories, and airport operations. In response to the petition, the Petitions Committee of the National Assembly for Wales decided to ask people for their views on wind turbines. The overwhelming majority of responses concerned the noise generated by wind turbines. *Inter alia*, people reported issues from no longer being able to enjoy sitting out in the garden through to having difficulty or not being able to sleep at night, resulting in mental and physical health problems.

To what extent should the health and wellbeing of citizens take priority over the need to generate renewable sources of energy?

Introduction

Although at one time it was possible to characterise the study of social policy as being largely concerned with five main areas of service delivery – education, health, housing, the personal social services, and social security – the contents of the remainder of this book make clear that this is no longer the case and that the subject has developed significantly (see Chapters 17–20, for example). This chapter demonstrates that the application and relevance of social policy ideas to new areas continues to develop, and that many of the analyses that have developed from social policy are applicable across many aspects of life.

'New' and 'old' social policy concerns

The Spotlight below sets out some of the 'new' social policy concerns and contrasts those with more traditional concerns to illustrate the scope and permeability of the boundaries of social policy. It is important to recognise that these areas of interest are effectively a web of interconnecting policy concerns, impacting not only on one another, but also on issues such as social exclusion, lifestyle, and quality of life, which in turn can be linked to topics such as the role of big business, globalisation, and the world economy (see Chapter 24).

SPOTLIGHT

Late 20th and 21st century concerns	Traditional concerns
Food	Health
Environment and sustainability	Housing
Transport and travel	Education
ICT	Personal social services
Work	Social security
New forms of money	Employment
Leisure	

To illustrate the complexity of this we can consider the role of transport. Good public transport can be important to people without private transport, such as those in isolated rural communities, people on low incomes, and those in cities, in enabling access to work and facilities such as libraries, GP and dental surgeries, crèches, hospitals, and supermarkets. Transport therefore facilitates the workings of the economy in transporting people, goods, and services. Conversely, poor, limited or non-existent public transport may limit possibilities for employment, which in turn can affect the levels of household income (which has the consequent effect of less money to spend on food and other goods), limits the opportunities for leisure and socialising, and restricts access to work and facilities. This is likely to be detrimental for the UK economy, reducing governments' income from taxes and therefore their ability to provide services.

Clearly, social policy analysts also have to recognise that inequalities in these areas may replicate and/or reinforce social divisions. There may also be a role for government in monitoring or seeking solutions to such problems. Therefore, alongside a consideration of the effects of these issues on individuals and families, we also need to examine the wider policy context and consider how governments are responding to these issues. The role of other bodies such as the media and pressure groups (see also Chapter 3) may also be worthy of consideration.

Setting the context: the changing nature of social policy

As outlined clearly elsewhere in this book, the subject of social policy was not always as we know it today, and has developed in a number of different ways and directions over the years. However, it is possible to argue that for a considerable period the study of social policy and administration was based upon the traditional welfare state and tended to focus around subjects such as health, housing, poverty, education, the personal social services, employment, and social security. Much of this was set in the context of the post-war consensus (see Chapters 6–8), over a period stretching from 1945 to the 1970s, when the major political parties were in broad agreement over many aspects of the welfare state, such as the maintenance of full employment, funding of the NHS, and a basic standard of social security provision, despite differences in political ideology.

This consensus came to an end in the mid to late 1970s and rapid change began to take place. A new language of politics and social policy emerged centred around 'Thatcherism'. Emphasis, which had previously been on collective provision, now shifted towards the individual, underpinned by New Right ideology with its desire for reduced state intervention and greater individual responsibility, which in New Right terms justified a cutback in collective provision to tackle concerns around inequality and social exclusion. During this period, significant attempts were made by governments to restructure the welfare state. New terminology appeared, and terms such as choice, participation, cost, efficiency, and effectiveness all became major parts of the language of government. Those who had previously been seen as 'service users' were now viewed as 'consumers', who were to have a say in the operation and delivery of services. This period saw the introduction of privatisation, internal markets such as those in the NHS and education, the use of performance measures and standards, a centralisation of power, and the reform and residualisation of local government.

Change continued after 1997 under the Labour government. The 'third way' was adopted by some as an argument for a mix of market and state provision in welfare, albeit in a very different sense from that of the post-war consensus, and there was arguably a greater recognition of the structural causes of poverty, inequality, and social exclusion, but at the same time individuals were expected to recognise that they had duties and responsibilities to society in return for social rights and services. Under the Coalition government from 2010, the emphasis on individuals, families, and communities as the sources of responsibility and support increased further, while both public expenditure cuts and policy changes meant a smaller role for the state. All of these issues are dealt with in greater depth elsewhere in this book, but all are important in helping emphasise the changing scope of social provision and the study of social policy.

Alongside these developments, changes have also been taking place in the global economy. Food policy, one of the areas with which this chapter is concerned, is no longer just about local or national policy; increasingly, it is about European and global policy. It concerns powerful lobbies, such as the food industry, who use their contacts in government to help shape policy and steer regulations in the direction that food retailers and manufacturers find most beneficial. On the other side are the interests of the consumers, who are usually much less powerful. Multi-national and trans-national companies, and the ways in which they operate, therefore impact on transport, the environment, work, and many of the issues that can be associated with a broader interpretation of social policy.

Inequalities have become further accentuated between those at the top, who are wealthy and highly paid, and those at the bottom, who are not. At the same time, through the media we are constantly bombarded with products and images that we are encouraged to believe we 'need'. Local services and facilities, such as shops, health centres, and various welfare services, are declining in preference to centralised facilities. These tend to require travel, costing money, causing environmental damage, and increasing the risk that those who are poor or who do not have access to a car or good local transport facilities may be excluded. A further consequence of the consumer society that we live in is the massive amount of waste we produce through our consumption (see also Chapter 20).

These areas impact on social policy concerns and therefore need to be taken seriously by governments and consideration given to policies and approaches that might help to minimise any new inequalities that might arise from them. The remainder of this chapter considers a range of very different concerns that reflect the broader boundaries of social policy and which have been the focus of social policy analysts: food, the environment and sustainability, transport and travel, and information and communication technology. Given the potentially huge debates around these issues, the discussion here is inevitably limited and focuses on particular aspects of these debates.

Food

Food is regularly headline news on the television and in the newspapers, be it concerns over the sustainability of our foods, food waste, genetically modified foods, intensive farming methods, the use of fertilisers and pesticides, antibiotics and growth promoting agents, scares over carcinogenic dye in food products, bovine spongiform encephalopathy (BSE), *Listeria* and *Salmonella*, or problems such as the incorrect labelling of food products. The media has helped to create a climate of public awareness and concern, which in turn has helped keep food on the agenda. For example, in recent years, one of the reasons that food has been in the public eye has been because of concern over the growing number of people who are obese. In 2010, 26 per cent of both men and women age 16 or over in England were classified as obese as measured by body mass index (BMI) (Figure 21.1). At the same time, 31 per cent of boys and 29 per cent of girls aged 2–15 were classed as either overweight or obese (NHS Information Centre, 2012). By 2050, obesity is predicted to affect 60 per cent of adult men, 50 per cent of adult women, and 25 per cent of children (Foresight, 2007).

Figure 21.1 suggests that the rise in obesity prevalence appears to be slowing for both sexes. Overall, obesity prevalence remains higher for women, but the gap between men and women appears to have narrowed over time. The National Obesity Observatory describes the prevention of obesity as 'a major public health challenge'. It is associated with health problems including cancer, Type 2 diabetes, and cardiovascular disease. Costs to the NHS are projected to reach £9.7 billion by 2050 and the costs to wider society to reach £49.9 billion per year (Foresight, 2007). Here, food can clearly be seen to impact upon health, and poor health in turn impacts on the economy. This also raises implications for the role of education in tackling the link between poor health and diet, as well as over the food given to school children.

There are other concerns over diet and nutrition. Fewer people than in the past now cook their own meals, instead either using the numerous fast food

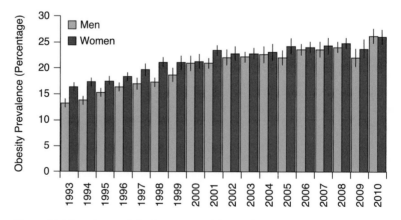

Figure 21.1 Prevalence of obesity among adults aged 16 years and over, 1993–2010. The chart shows 95% confidence limits. Adult (aged 16+ obesity): body mass index ≥ 30 kg/m²

Source: Public Health England (2013) http://www.noo.org.uk/NOO_about_obesity/trends

outlets or relying on the rapidly growing market for ready meals. This means that we have less control over the nutritional content of our food. Ready meals and food from fast food outlets are often high in fats, salt, and sugar. Furthermore, everyday foodstuffs often contain large amounts of additives and flavourings. This leads some to argue that there is a role for government in regulating food manufacturers and retailers to ensure that the food we eat is safe. Others, such as Boris Johnson, the Mayor of London, argue that diet and related issues should remain a matter for individual choice and that governments should not interfere. Johnson famously questioned Jamie Oliver's healthy school meals campaign, asking 'Why shouldn't [parents] push pies through the railings?' (*The Guardian*, 2007, p. 11). However, diet is a public health issue and to suggest that what we eat is purely a matter of personal responsibility merely reinforces existing inequalities in this area. Indeed, research carried out for the British Social Attitudes Survey (Park *et al.*, 2012) on ways to improve public health found that just under one in five people believe that individuals should be left to make their own health choices without interference from government. Furthermore, people on low incomes may not be able to afford fresh fruit and vegetables, they may lack transport facilities to get to good food stores, and are more likely to suffer from diet-related diseases. However, this does not necessarily mean that they have a worse diet than the rest of the population. In fact, findings from a study carried out on behalf of the Food Standards Agency in 2007 found that people on low incomes actually have similar diets to the rest of the population, suggesting that the population as a whole could eat more healthily (Nelson *et al.*, 2007).

Issues associated with diet are arguably compounded by the dominance of the large supermarket chains and major food producers in the supply of food to the consumer, and this has a whole range of social policy impacts. In general, smaller local stores are unable to compete on price or the range of goods available in supermarkets and risk being forced out of the market. The supermarket then becomes the main supplier of food to consumers in the area. By relying on a small number of producers, they are able to influence the choices available to the consumer, but the supermarkets' primary concerns might be about the shelf life or appearance of food, rather than with its taste or quality.

In addition, pricing policies within supermarkets often mean that fresh, 'healthy' food is more expensive than less healthy options. People on low incomes may find supermarkets expensive, and those without a car or those without access to good public transport, perhaps in outlying rural areas, may find that it is difficult to get to them. Thus, as noted above, income affects choice of food and this in turn impacts on diet and health. The dominance of a few large food producers and retailers may therefore create hardship for groups such as low-income families, older people, disabled people, and homeless people. In these ways, food moves on to the social policy agenda alongside some of the more traditional concerns of the subject.

Food interests

In the UK, powerful bodies represent the interests of food manufacturers and retailers, notably the British Retail Consortium and the Food and Drink Federation, which act as pressure groups (see Chapter 3) and which are skilled in lobbying government and shaping the food agenda to promote the interests of the food industry. As governments have sought to improve food safety and related health issues, lobbying has become intense. The Food Standards Agency was set up by the Labour government in 2000 to act as a watchdog for consumer interests and public health in relation to food as a result of concerns that policy-makers were neglecting the interests of consumers in the face of strong interests of producers. The issue of food labelling has been particularly controversial in a number of respects. The Health Select Committee's Report on Obesity (2004) recommended that the government introduce a 'traffic light' system for labelling foods, with red for high energy foods, amber for medium, and green for low, in order for consumers to see more easily what was in food products and to help tackle obesity in the population. The aim was that the food industry would work with the Food Standards Agency and introduce a single standard coding system for consumers to easily determine which foods could contribute to a healthy diet. However, a coalition of major food and drink producers campaigned against this and argued for their own labelling scheme detailing the percentage of 'guideline daily amounts' of fat, salt, and sugar contained in food products, with the result that both labelling systems were introduced and arguably created much confusion for consumers. Almost a decade after the Select Committee's report, the Coalition government announced that consistent front-of-pack food labelling would be introduced in the UK from the summer of 2013. The system will be voluntary but the government claimed to be confident that the food industry is on board. The Public Health Minister, Anna Soubry, said 'by having a consistent system we will all be able to see, at a glance, what is in our food. This will help us all choose healthier options and control our calorie intake' (Campbell, 2012). However, food labelling is not just about being able to select healthier products to eat. In early 2013, it came to light that processed meat products labelled as containing beef in fact contained varying proportions of horsemeat, an ingredient not listed on the packaging. The scandal appeared to be on an international scale and highlighted the complexity of the food chain, supplier networks, and the difficulty that retailers have in monitoring these. This raises issues about the extent to which the public can have confidence in processed food products and over what is or is not on the label.

The interests of the major food and drink producers and TV and advertising industry also came under the media spotlight when, in 2006, as part of the government's drive towards healthier eating, Ofcom announced a ban on junk food advertising around all children's programming that had 'particular appeal' to the under-16s. The major food and drink producers and the TV and advertising industry were concerned about loss of sales and advertising revenue, while health campaigners' concerns were that people have healthy choices of food and know whether they are making healthy choices. While the restrictions do seem to have been adhered to by children's channels and broadcasters, in 2012 Scotland's public health minister drew attention to a loophole 'that allows HFSS (high in fat, sugar and salt) food adverts to feature during programmes with a high child audience such as soaps and talent shows' (BBC News Scotland, 2012) and called for cooperation between the UK and Scottish governments to address this.

Food is clearly a controversial topic. We can see that there are push-and-pull factors at play here. It is important to recognise that there are a number of different interests at work in relation to food production, distribution, and safety. On the one hand, there are the food and drink corporations, who are often able to influence the agenda of governments through effective lobbying; and on the other, there are consumers and health organisations. However, as is the case in many areas of social policy, these groups have differing levels of power and ability to influence the agenda and political decisions, and it is arguable that at present manufacturers and retailers often have more influence than consumers.

Government policy

Following the Second World War, British governments generally sought to increase the amount of food being produced and to keep the costs of food down for consumers. In addition, for much of the post-war period, food safety policy was concerned with ensuring that health legislation and regulations were enforced, rather than with a broader view of the consumer interest or public health. However, following a number of food safety crises, including BSE, the Labour government established a Foods Standards Agency in 2000, and a new Department of the Environment, Food and Rural Affairs in 2001, in an attempt to shift some of the emphasis back to wider food safety issues and to give a greater voice to consumers.

However, food is also important at a more micro level. Until 1992, when the White Paper, *Health of the Nation*, was published (Department of Health, 1992), the Conservative governments had largely pursued an individualistic approach to food policy in which the individual consumer was responsible for their own health and diet through their food choices. This publication marked an important change in government policy so that, as Lang notes, there was 'a shift in policy from the denial of food poverty to an exploration of coping strategies' (Lang, 1997, p. 223). Now the relationship between diet and income was recognised, hailing a shift towards a more structural approach in terms of government policy, and a Nutritional Task Force was established to consider issues such as catering education and school meals. From 1997, the Labour governments aimed to build on this structural approach and to strike 'a new balance – a third way – linking individual and wider action' (Department of Health, 1999, para. 1.27). The White Paper, *Saving Lives: Our Healthier Nation* (Department of Health, 1999), recognised the importance of a combination of physical activity and a balanced healthy diet. The Department of Health therefore sought to focus on matters such as the links between cancer, heart disease, and diet and the health benefits of eating five portions of fruit and vegetables a day. In promoting a structuralist approach, a variety of 'healthy eating' initiatives, such as the National Fruit Scheme aimed at school children, were promoted and a National Healthy Schools Programme was set up.

At roughly the same time, celebrity chef Jamie Oliver ran a campaign in the media highlighting the poor nutritional content of school meals that further acted as a catalyst for policy change. The Labour government agreed to provide £280 million to improve the situation. In addition, in September 2005 the Education Secretary announced that junk food was to be banned in schools including a ban on slot machines selling chocolate bars and fizzy drinks. However, following the 2010 general election. the Coalition government announced that academies did not have to adhere to these regulations, and with the pressure for schools to become academies there were likely to be increasing numbers of schools able to opt out of the ban.

While the Labour government aimed in some respects to take a more structuralist approach towards food, the Coalition government appeared to take a step back from this with a less intrusive approach. The White Paper, *Healthy Lives, Healthy People: Our Strategy for Public Health in England* (Department of Health, 2010), drew on the Nuffield Council on Bioethics Ladder of Interventions and reflected an intention to use the least intrusive approach to achieve the set aim. Figure 21.2 provides examples of the range of possible forms of interventions.

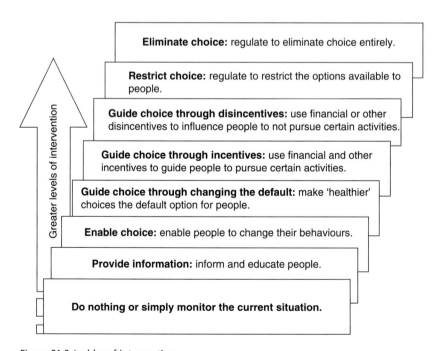

Figure 21.2 Ladder of interventions

Source: Nuffield Council on Bioethics

Alongside this, in March 2011 the Coalition government published *The Public Health Responsibility Deal*, which it claimed 'taps into the potential for businesses and other organisations to improve public health and to tackle health inequalities through their influence over food, physical activity, alcohol, and health in the workplace' (Department of Health, 2011, p. 3). The then Health Secretary, Andrew Lansley, set up five 'responsibility deal' networks with business, co-chaired by ministers, to come up with pledges for action. The emphasis was on a partnership approach with organisations to tackle health inequalities. However, by 2013, and perhaps reflecting the conflicting nature of policy-making in practice and the need to satisfy different interests – the alcohol industry, treasury receipts from sales of alcohol, consumer views, public health – despite the Prime Minister's earlier pledge to stop cheap alcohol being sold in supermarkets, the Coalition had failed to follow the example set by the Scottish Parliament and introduce a minimum price per unit of alcohol (although even in the case of Scotland the alcohol industry had launched a legal challenge to the move).

Overall, the Coalition government's approach to health in relation to food policy demonstrated a preference for voluntary rather than regulatory approaches, and suggested that once again food policy may be left to the market, with the government stepping back from the more interventionist approach adopted by Labour. While the government might claim to have taken actions in relation to food safety, and to some extent in relation to food quality, its critics were still able to argue that this has been insufficient, that the individualistic perspective remains largely dominant, and that the interests of the food producers often dominate at the expense of those of consumers.

SPOTLIGHT

Seven million . . .

. . . the estimated amount of food, in tonnes, that is wasted each year in the UK (DEFRA, 2013). Much of this is fit for human consumption.

The Fareshare impact survey of 2012 reported that 59 per cent of the community projects and charities supplied by Fareshare reported 'a rise in demand for food'. In addition, '42 per cent of charities surveyed are facing funding cuts' and 70 per cent fear that 'demand for food will only increase in the future' (Fareshare, 2012).

In 2011, Fareshare collected 3,600 tonnes of unwanted food and redistributed this to charities and community projects feeding 36,500 people every day.

Fareshare estimate that if 1 per cent of the food that is wasted each year was fit for human consumption, they could use it to provide 70 million meals for those in need.

That people are going hungry in the UK today is a social policy concern. The number of vulnerable people needing meals is growing every day, so what can be done about it?

Some supermarkets and food manufacturers supply surplus food to Fareshare, but there is still plenty of unwanted food that does not get to Fareshare – why? Because there is a market for end-of-line or slightly damaged food. Online retailers can buy this and sell it cheaply. Other competition comes from anaerobic digestion plants that turn waste food into renewable energy.

- At a time when growing numbers of people are in poverty, does the food industry have an ethical duty to ensure that food that is fit for human consumption gets to people who need it?
- How likely is it that government will intervene and regulate the food industry to ensure that this happens?
- Why might governments not wish to intervene?

Food is clearly an important social policy issue. It has impacts on diet and on health. Government and the food industry arguably have a responsibility in enabling individuals to make healthier choices, while government can intervene to regulate food manufacturing and retailing in order to help reduce inequalities in this area. However, governments have often pursued a policy of leaving food to the free market and have been unwilling to challenge the dominance of the food producers and retailers. While the Labour governments of 1997–2010 in some respects pursued a more structural approach, the extent to which the Coalition government might be willing to challenge the major food interests and to force change remains to be seen.

The environment and sustainability

Chapter 20 looks in greater depth at the challenges for social policies posed by environmental change and the arguments of environmentalists. Here the issues are dealt with in the context of the changing boundaries of social policy, and particularly in relation to notions of sustainability.

The Brundtland Commission, established in 1987 by the United Nations Commission on Environment and Development, developed a definition of sustainability that is about 'meeting the needs of the present without compromising the ability of future generations to meet their own needs' (World Commission on Environment and Development, 1987, p. 43). This concern with sustainability has gathered pace in recent years as governments have begun to take on board the importance of 'green' issues and as attention has been paid to their implications for social policy. Neglect of such issues in the past has led to damage to the natural environment, pollution, and land being stripped of its natural resources.

Climate change

Climate change is a serious problem that affects us all. Emissions of greenhouse gases, such as carbon dioxide (CO_2), are changing the world's climate. In fact, DEFRA (2008) stated that 'Carbon Dioxide is the main man-made contributor to global warming'.

But why should any of this be of concern to us, and particularly for social policy? Climate change affects our quality of life in a variety of ways, including pollution of the environment, the quality of the food that we eat, our health – our very existence. However, policies to address environmental issues often have costs attached to them, and these impact differentially on groups in society. If councils limit the number of waste bins they will collect per household, or if people are charged for refrigerator disposal, or vehicle recycling and disposal, then the greater burden falls on the least well off in our society, who are most likely not to be able to afford these costs. Thus, strategies that promote charging or limit the number of waste collection bins per household regardless of the size of the household may serve only to exacerbate and reinforce existing inequalities. This may also lead to increased dumping of waste, which in turn contributes to environmental pollution with consequent impacts on the health of the population.

Source: http://www.CartoonStock.com

It is difficult to be exact about the proportion of CO_2 emissions that come from the actions of individuals in the UK because organisations use different definitions. For example, DEFRA (2008) say that in 2006 total emissions from business accounted for 35 per cent, residential users accounted for 27 per cent, and the transport sector 28 per cent. However, since individuals drive cars, use public transport, go on plane journeys, and may be part of businesses, and such like, then these figures may not be as clear-cut as they appear at first glance. The Carbon Trust take a different approach, and say that 'recreation and leisure, space heating and food and catering are the three consumer needs with the highest carbon emissions. Together they account for almost half of the total UK carbon emissions' (Carbon Trust, 2006, p. 1). Clearly, whichever way we look at this, a significant proportion of CO_2 emissions in the UK come from our actions as individuals, including heating our homes and using electricity to power lighting and appliances, such as washing machines, tumble dryers, computers, televisions, mobile phone chargers, and so on. Driving vehicles and making plane journeys are also a source of individuals' CO_2 emissions.

The UK produces more waste per head of population than many of its European neighbours, with an average of 449 kilograms per year, compared with 406 kilograms for the European average. Much of this waste goes to landfill or is incinerated. While a considerable proportion of this comes from the unnecessary packaging of consumer goods, because producers do not have to take into account the cost of disposal of packing when they set the price of the finished goods, there is no incentive for them to cut down on unnecessary packaging. This is an example of what economists call 'market failure', where prices fail to reflect full social costs.

Figure 21.3 shows municipal waste in the EU in 2007. While only broad comparisons can be made between countries because of different waste management definitions, it shows that the UK landfilled around 15 per cent more municipal waste than the EU27 average (40 per cent). It also had lower recycling and composting rates (34 per cent) than the EU27 average (39 per cent).

The EU Waste Framework Directive requires the UK to recycle, compost or re-use 50 per cent of waste from households by 2020, and while it currently lags behind many of its European neighbours in terms of municipal waste management, it is showing signs of overall improvement. For example, in 2009–10 recycling and composting rates accounted for 39 per cent of household waste, an increase on previous years. There was also a reduction in the amount of non-recycled household waste per person of 8 per cent between 2001 and 2009–10. This is now at the lowest level since estimates were first made in 1983–84. These figures suggest that the UK is moving in the right direction, albeit more slowly than some of its EU partners. But as with other issues highlighted in this chapter, there is a range of different interests at play, and furthermore this needs to be set in a global context, since the actions or inactions of individual nations impact on all nations and their populations.

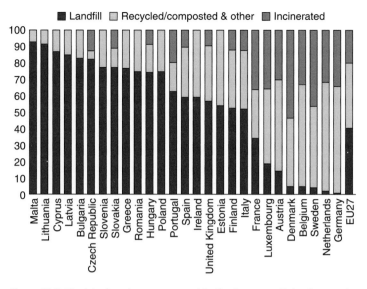

Figure 21.3 Municipal waste management in the European Union by country and EU27, 2007 (percentages)

Source: DEFRA (2012)

In 1994, most countries joined an international treaty – the United Nations Framework Convention on Climate Change (UNFCCC) – to consider what could be done to address global warming. The 1997 Kyoto Protocol on greenhouse emissions was an addition to this treaty approved by a number of nations, including the United Kingdom, although not by the United States, a major polluter, which refused to endorse it and adopted the stance that big business had no responsibility to tackle climate change.

Under the treaty, countries had to meet targets primarily through national measures, but they also had a number of other mechanisms available to them including carbon trading. However, developing countries, including China, India, and Mexico, did not have binding obligations under the treaty, and as the US refused to ratify it, Europe was left as the main market in this area, and global carbon trading moved down the agenda. Instead, governments have been working towards a new climate change treaty aimed at setting emissions cuts for developed and developing states, with the aim of reaching agreement by 2015 and the treaty taking effect from 2020.

Government policy

Domestically, as with the issue of food discussed earlier in this chapter, there is evidence that it is likely to be the least powerful who lose out. Research for the Joseph Rowntree Foundation underlines this, showing that higher income households have the highest overall emissions, with road and air travel accounting for a high proportion of the difference between them and poorer groups (Fahmy *et al.*, 2012) and 'the that social dimensions of vulnerability to climate change have not yet been sufficiently recognised in adaptation policy' (Lindley *et al.*, 2012, p. 1).

We have seen how the UK Government has been involved in the global arena in respect of attempts to reduce the effects of climate change, but what is it doing within the UK to tackle environmental issues and minimise the effects on social policy? The Climate Change Act 2008, introduced by the Labour government, made the UK the first country in the world to have a legally binding long-term framework to cut carbon emissions. It introduced a binding reduction target requiring the UK to reduce its emissions by at least 80 per cent by 2050 against 1990 levels. It also introduced a long-term framework for managing emissions through a series of carbon budgets. Each of the budgets set caps on the total quantity of greenhouse gases permitted in the UK over a five-year period from 2008 to 2012, from 2013 to 2017, and from 2018 to 2022. While, as discussed below, the Coalition government's intentions in this policy area have not always been clear, they have established a Green Investment Bank that has been charged with providing financial solutions in order to promote private sector investment in the green economy. In November 2012, the Coalition government also introduced an Energy Bill to create a 'low carbon economy' and to move the UK's energy production to a mix of energy sources, such as nuclear, wind, and biomass, with less dependence on fossil fuels, but the absence of a target for decarbonising the energy sector by 2030 was seen as a weakness and as potentially undermining investment in renewables. This and other decisions have led to questions being raised about the commitment of the Coalition government to the green agenda. At the Conservative Party conference in 2011 the Chancellor, George Osborne, referred to environmental regulation as an unacceptable burden on British industry and gave the appearance of being critical of the green agenda. In addition, 'the Chancellor has questioned future subsidies for renewables and backed the building of at least 20 gas-fired power plants instead' (Carrell and Harvey, 2012, p. 24). The Labour Leader, Ed Miliband, noted that 'investment in renewable energy had halved between 2009 and 2011' (Carrington, 2012, p. 16). The seeming lack of commitment by the Coalition government led to a hiatus, where firms were unwilling to invest in green technology in the UK because they were unsure of the level of government commitment to it. This is in contrast to Scotland, where many politicians are strongly in favour of wind power, with the result that French nuclear and renewables group, Areva, signed 'an outline agreement with the investment agency Scottish Enterprise to site one of three new European factories in eastern Scotland' (Carrell and Harvey, 2012, p. 24).

Devolution has also enabled the constituent parts of the UK to set their own targets for waste recycling. Scotland has developed a Zero Waste Plan, which sets out a framework to deliver a zero waste Scotland over the next 10 years. The plan argues that such a strategy makes economic and environmental sense. It suggests that 'achieving zero waste could generate over 2,000 jobs in Scotland' (Scottish Government, 2010, p. 7), and notes that:

> Over 2 million tonnes of food waste is produced every year from all sectors in Scotland. If just half of this waste was captured and treated though anaerobic digestion, the electricity generated could power a city the size of Dundee for six months, provide heat for local homes and businesses, and could produce enough fertiliser for ten per cent of Scotland's arable needs.
>
> (Scottish Government, 2010, p. 1)

It sets the target of '70 per cent recycling and maximum 5 per cent to landfill by 2025' (Scottish Government, 2010, p. vi). The Welsh Assembly Government has also set out a waste strategy with two main targets: an intermediate target to significantly reduce waste by around 27 per cent of 2007 levels by 2025; and an overall target 'to achieve zero waste and live within our environmental limits' by 2050 (Welsh Assembly Government, 2010, p. 4).

Clearly, as outlined here and discussed in greater depth in Chapter 20, the environment and sustainability are important issues that governments are now beginning to address, although not to the satisfaction of all. While this is to be welcomed, it is important that the relatively recent emphasis on 'green issues' is not seen in isolation but is integrated into all areas of policy-making at both local and national level, including areas such as transport (see below), food, education, and health, and that policy-makers take account of the potential differential impacts of policies on different social groups.

Transport and travel

Transport has consequences for many areas of relevance to social policy, including the economy, the environment, food, and social life. These in turn impact upon issues such as quality of life, inclusion and exclusion. Good transport systems for passengers and freight are vital for the workings of the economy. Road, rail, water, and air transport are key to transporting goods not only from one part of the country to another but also from destinations around the globe. Globalisation has created new opportunities for business in the opening up of worldwide markets (see Chapter 22). For example, super-markets source their produce from around the globe, enabling the consumer to purchase many types of fruit and vegetables all year round regardless of the season. For individuals, travel to distant destinations provides the opportunity to experience other cultures and broaden our knowledge of the world. This has been aided by the growth in ICT (discussed later in this chapter), which has enabled communication between people on opposite sides of the world to take place at the touch of a button, reducing distances in both time and space.

However, while opportunities may have been created, there are also down-sides to the revolution in transportation and travel. The volume of traffic on our roads has increased, causing pollution, road damage, traffic congestion, noise, increasing the chances of accidents and having consequent effects on the health of people who live on or near busy traffic routes. Many of these are clearly issues of concern to social policy analysts (see also Chapter 20). If we have access to good transport systems, then this has the potential to benefit our work and social lives. However, this is frequently skewed. For example, in 2012, 25 per cent of households in Great Britain did not have access to a car (Mackie *et al.*, 2012). Access to a car is affected by both household income and household type. For example, 'nearly all households with above-average incomes have a car but half of low-income households do not' (see Figure 21.4). In addition, 'nearly all couples have a car, but many singles, both with and without children – do not' (The Poverty Site, undated).

Not surprisingly, not having access to a car increases reliance upon public transport, and certain groups, including people living in the most deprived areas of the country, are forced to rely on public transport. For people who do not own a car, or who do not have access to good public transport, the effects can be damaging. Access to jobs and facilities may be restricted, with conse-quent effects on people's economic and social life. A study undertaken for Greener Journeys found that 'over 50 per cent of students over 16 are frequent bus users' and '30 per cent of those who are dependent on bus services to access their education and training courses live in areas in the top 10 per cent most deprived areas in Great Britain' (Mackie *et al.*, 2012).

So transport is not just about travelling. Poor transport is a contributor to social exclusion, 'it restricts access to activities that enhance people's life chances, such as learning, health care, work, and food shopping' (Social Exclusion Unit, 2003, p. i), and 'deprived communities also suffer the worst effects of road traffic through pollution and pedestrian accidents' (Social

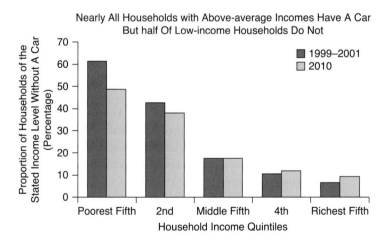

Figure 21.4 Proportions of households without a car by household income quintile, 1999–2001 and 2010. Nearly all households with above-average incomes have a car but half of low-income households do not

Source: The Poverty Site (undated) http://www.poverty.org.uk/75/index.shtml

Exclusion Unit, 2003, p. 13). These are all reasons why transport is of concern to social policy analysts in the twenty-first century and why it is an issue for government to address.

Car manufacturers, road haulage firms, and fuel companies all have a major interest in a transport policy that favours road users. Big businesses, supermarket chains, and others also seek to influence policy in a way that will benefit them. There are also a variety of other pressure groups, such as those that seek to represent pedestrians, and which campaign on environmental concerns and other issues such as health. As with the issues of food and the environment, discussed above, these interest groups have different agendas and varied abilities to lobby government, which is affected by factors such as the amount of power they each wield, public opinion, and the role of the media.

Transport policy

Transport policy is multi-faceted, serving economic, social, and environmental goals. It has the potential to affect social exclusion and inclusion and to impact upon the quality of life in communities. Under the Labour government, the 1998 White Paper *A New Deal for Transport* (DETR, 1998) recognised much of this in setting out a framework to promote healthy lifestyles by encouraging walking and cycling, and in acknowledging the threat to health through accidents, traffic noise, vibration, and pollution. *Transport 2010: The 10 Year Plan* (DETR, 2000) built on the White Paper, setting targets in relation to road safety to reduce the number of people killed or seriously injured in road accidents. It also discussed measures to contribute towards meeting the target from the Kyoto Protocol to reduce greenhouse gas emissions. From this perspective, we can see at least an element of 'joined up' government in the linking of environmental, transport, and health issues. Perhaps one of the biggest question marks over Labour's transport policies was its attitude to the car. In the early years of government, it emphasised an integrated transport policy, but later, perhaps fearing being seen as 'anti-car', played down measures such as road pricing by shifting much of the onus for these onto local authorities.

The Coalition government that came to power in 2010 inherited a transport system dominated by road transport. In its programme for government, it set out its priorities based on a combination of supporting new transport technologies alongside more sustainable and greener initiatives. These included:

- Supporting sustainable travel initiatives including promoting cycling and walking and encouraging joint working between bus operators and local authorities.
- Stopping central government funding for new fixed speed cameras and using technology such as 'drugalyser' to make roads safer.
- Reforming the way decisions are made on transport projects to take into account the benefits of low carbon proposals.

▪ Mandating a national recharging network for electric and plug-in hybrid vehicles.

▪ And establishing a high-speed rail network (adapted from Cabinet Office, 2010, p. 31).

The Coalition government initially agreed to scrap the third runway for Heathrow, but later appeared to be backing down over this and set up the Davies Commission to consider the options for airport expansion. The Commission was to produce an interim report by the end of 2013 and a more detailed report by 2015, to be presented to the incoming government after the next election. The High Speed 2 rail line finally received the go ahead after judicial review in March 2013.

While Coalition and Labour governments shared some of the same aims for transport policy in terms of making transport greener and more affordable and accessible, they differ in a number of respects. Butcher and Keep (2011, p. 7) highlight aviation policy as being one of the main areas where Coalition and Labour policies diverge. For example, the Labour government reformed air passenger duty and, in contrast to the Coalition, was supportive of a third runway at Heathrow. In addition, they highlight different approaches to the delivery of transport policy and to the free market approach being pursued by the Coalition. In respect of plans for the rail network, they note that 'there is a danger of this type of approach delivering unequal outcomes. For example, deprived and rural areas, where there is less public transport and often lower incomes, could well face a higher financial burden and more extensive cuts to services' (Butcher and Keep, 2011, p. 8).

Transport is also one of the areas where policy change in another field can have a significant (and perhaps unintended) impact. For example, the reductions in public expenditure made by the Coalition government have in turn led to cuts in public transport and rising bus and rail fares, which have meant that 'families with children (but not households without children) living in urban areas outside London defined a car as essential' (Davis *et al.*, 2012). On similar lines, the Campaign for Better Transport has (2012) argued that 'a lack of affordable and accessible public transport is having a serious effect on low income households and reducing people's ability to find work'. Indeed, the Campaign for Better Transport went further, arguing for a need for a careful definition of 'transport poverty'. And perhaps most significantly, it argued, reflecting traditional social policy concerns, that 'low income communities tend to have higher exposure to the negative impacts of transport, facing greater risks of being killed or seriously injured on the roads, higher levels of air pollution leading to greater risk of premature death' (Campaign for Better Transport, 2012, p. 1).

Information and communication technology

The growth of new technology has impacted enormously on areas such as work, money, leisure, travel, communication, consumption, and the environment. This has led to a blurring of the boundaries between our public and private lives as the development of digital technology – smartphones, 'apps', social networks, the Internet, and wireless networks – are transforming the ways in which we work and use our leisure time. Access to a huge range of information is available at the press of a button. Through the Internet we can download documents, search for specific information, access market information on customers, and market products to a worldwide audience. As consumers we can search for products and select the supplier that offers a product at the cheapest price, often below the price in shops. With the growth of cable networks, satellite broadcasters, and the Internet, numerous TV channels can be brought into our homes, increasing the choice available to the consumer. We can now select from dedicated channels for films, cartoons, sport, history, cookery, shopping, chat shows, and so on. Technology can also bring social policy issues into people's lives. We can sit at home and watch debates on homelessness or poverty and sometimes participate by using social networks, phoning in or texting. We can choose to watch or listen to programmes that have previously been broadcast, by downloading podcasts or using catch up TV at a time that suits us. We can see debates on programmes such as *Newsnight* on current issues, with professionals, politicians, and others. At the same time, soap operas dramatise social policy issues, such as teenage pregnancy, drug and alcohol addiction, and so on. These may help raise consciousness around social policy issues, and people can learn about what is going on in the world and how the actions of others impact on people's lives. However, they may also stereotype or personalise issues and problems. The use of ICT therefore raises a myriad of possibilities and challenges for social policy.

Modern methods of communication mean that we can be in almost constant contact for work or leisure. We can communicate with customers, family, and friends from across the other side of the world. Recently, it has been argued that social networking has enabled people to mobilise in response to various causes. One example of the use of ICT to mobilise people is the direct action group UK Uncut, which has mobilised thousands of people, including to protest against multinational corporations and businesses such as Starbucks, Vodafone, Topshop, Amazon, and Google, who pay little or no corporation tax in the UK. UK Uncut argues that if they paid the full rate of tax, this could be used to provide welfare services that are being cut by the government in the recession. Even governments have sought to use technology, including, for example, the use of e-petitions to enable members of the public to communicate their views to government.

In the welfare state, technology has the potential to make life easier for both professionals and consumers of services. The Government Digital Service is responsible for overseeing the development of technology within the public sector. 'Digital-by-default' is the idea that each public service should be rebuilt with digital technology at the basis of each service and the assumption that most people will communicate with the government digitally for much of the time. This is clearly a major task since as the

Government's Digital Strategy (Cabinet Office, 2012, p. 2) notes, 'the vast majority (82%) of the UK population is online but most people rarely use online government services'.

Nevertheless, digital-by-default is gradually taking shape with the development of a single government website – http://www.gov.uk (Cabinet Office, 2012; Fink, 2012). The idea behind this is that it should enable people to identify government services more easily. A report for the Policy Exchange think tank has also suggested that the appropriate use of ICTs could help reduce social exclusion, particularly among 'the 1 million young people not in education, employment or training (NEETs), and the 5.4 million people aged 65 and older who have never used the internet' (Fink, 2012, p. 12). The same report makes the recommendation that 'The government should take advantage of modern interactive technology to connect young people struggling with unemployment to helpful, personalised content and advice' (Fink, 2012, p. 10). It suggests focusing on different NEETs and providing them with 'advice and help specific to their interests', whether it be for 'part-time work and child care, CV feedback and an internship, or sustained mentoring' (Fink, 2012, p. 10). The report also recommends 'A new Technology Advocate role . . . to reach out to people who are digitally excluded and mentor them as they start to access digital public services' (Fink, 2012, p. 9). This would mainly be targeted at older people.

There are, however, a range of negative impacts of this revolution in ICT. For example, one of the main contributors to exclusion from this ICT revolution is cost – we have to pay to take advantage of much of this choice. If you can afford a computer and pay for access to the Internet and for the running costs of mobile phones, then you can be part of this growth in new technology and the opportunities it brings. However, those who cannot afford to pay for these things may be disadvantaged and excluded from access to knowledge.

'According to the Office for National Statistics, nearly eight million adults in the UK have never accessed the internet. Of these:

- Just under half have a disability as defined by the Disability Discrimination Act
- Half of those without home internet access belong to DE socio-economic groups.

(Fink, 2012, p. 18)

We have considered above some of the potential that new technologies have to both reduce and widen the digital divide with consequent impacts on social inequality, but what evidence is there to support either view? *Inclusion Through Innovation: Tackling Social Exclusion Through New Technologies* (ODPM, 2005) challenged the view that new technology is widening inequalities. It cites examples such as the NHS Direct Telephone Service, which is available to all regardless of whether they are registered with a GP or not. This facilitates access to health services for people who might normally be excluded from them because they are not registered with a GP. Other examples include homeless people, who by leaving a mobile phone number on job applications avoid the stigma of not having a permanent address. Access to information for people who are socially excluded is vital. Websites such as Homeless UK (http://www.homelessuk.org) and UK refuges online (http://www.ukrefugesonline.org) list hostel, refuge, advice, and support services for homeless people and women experiencing domestic violence across the UK. Such information can now be accessed via a mobile phone or through a computer. Individuals do not need to own a computer, since they are available in a variety of places such as libraries, drop-in centres, community centres, Internet cafés, and so on. The national charity, StartHere (http://www.starthere.org.uk), provides a one-stop-shop electronic information service that is available on PCs, digital TV, kiosks, and mobile phones, providing information on employment, housing, health, and social issues. However, all of the above not only presumes that people have access to new forms of technology, but also that they want to engage with it. With the introduction of universal credit (see Chapter 9), it is expected that most people will not only apply online but also manage their benefits in this way too. This poses challenges for people who rarely use digital services, or who have never been online. The government says that alternative access routes will be provided for those who are unable to use online technology, but it is impossible to know how accessible they will be.

The growth in new technology has also raised other issues. For example, one challenge is associated with the regulation of information – there are issues around balance of coverage, access for independent producers, content, and appropriateness. Another element of these developments has also raised new health concerns, with, for example, mobile phones and masts having been linked by some to concerns over cancer. And there are concerns over data protection, privacy, and civil liberties, with some expressing fears over the amount of data that is collected by the state and other organisations, and the uses to which this may be put. The loss by HM Revenue and Customs in 2007 of discs containing the bank details, addresses, and telephone numbers of 25 million child benefit claimants served to highlight concerns over the security of personal data.

The growth in the use of ICT and the government's digital strategy clearly has the potential to create positive outcomes for many. However, a key issue that remains for social policy is that of access for individuals and groups to this ICT revolution, particularly those on low incomes and other potentially vulnerable groups.

Conclusions

This chapter has demonstrated how the subject of social policy has broadened out beyond the traditional areas such as health, housing, education, and social services to new areas, such as food, the environment and sustainability, transport and travel, and ICT.

In the past it was recognised that inequalities existed in the traditional areas and therefore it was appropriate that governments should intervene to try to address these. However, it is now accepted that inequalities also exist in the new areas and thus it is legitimate for governments to also try to tackle these.

Above all the chapter illustrates the ways in which all these areas impact on one another. The environment impacts on health, which affects quality of life and wellbeing. Transport creates pollution, which in turn affects the environment and health. Poor health affects the ability to participate in society, whether this is contributing to the economy by working or taking part in sport and leisure activities. Good transport also provides access to work and facilities, and can enhance life chances and opportunities, while poor transport links can contribute to isolation and reduced opportunities for work and leisure. Lack of employment may result in financial exclusion, which affects the ability to purchase goods and services. Together, these can create a web of social exclusion.

While individuals can work to ameliorate the impact of the above to some degree, there is also a role for government in helping reduce inequality in these areas and in encouraging big business to take a more socially responsible attitude to the provision of goods and services.

Summary

This chapter has sought to examine and explain the relevance of social policy beyond the traditional boundaries and concerns of the subject. In the chapter, a number of issues have been highlighted:

- The constantly changing and permeable barriers of the subject of social policy, with economic, social, political, and technological developments combining to produce both new areas of study for social policy analysts and new impacts on existing areas of social policy concerns.

- That social policy ideas and analyses continue to be relevant to new economic and social developments, so that each of the topics examined in this chapter – food, the environment and sustainability, transport and travel, and ICT – is amenable to social policy analysis and to considerations of issues such as inequality, equity, exclusion and inclusion, as well as to other social policy concerns such as the appropriate roles of public and private sectors and the means of policy formulation, implementation, and evaluation.

- There is a danger that existing social inequalities and divisions will be replicated and reinforced – the chapter has illustrated that in relation to each of the areas studied there is evidence that groups that have traditionally been the focus of social policy are in danger of losing out and being further excluded by recent developments, and there is a need for analysts and policy-makers to be aware of this and that action, including potentially government intervention, may be necessary to ensure that greater social exclusion does not result.

Discussion and review

- What social policy effects will a less interventionist, more market driven approach towards food be likely to have on different groups in society?
- Why might policies to create a greener more sustainable environment be important for tackling social inequalities?
- How might a good transport system contribute to tackling social exclusion?
- Will the government's increasing emphasis on the use of ICT to deliver services reduce or exacerbate social inequalities?

References

BBC News Scotland (2012) 'Call for pre-watershed ban on junk food advertising', 18 March, available at http://www.bbc.co.uk/news/uk-scotland-17414707 [accessed 11 December 2012].

Butcher, L. and Keep, M. (2011) *Transport Policy in 2011: A New Direction?*, House of Commons Library Research Paper 11/22, House of Commons, London.

Cabinet Office (2010) *The Coalition: Our Programme for Government*, Cabinet Office, London.

Cabinet Office (2012) *Government Digital Strategy*, Cabinet Office, London.

Campaign for Better Transport (2012) *Transport, Accessibility and Social Exclusion*, available at http://www.bettertransport.org.uk/files/Transport-and-social-exclusion-summary.pdf [accessed 4 April 2013].

Campbell, D. (2012) 'All supermarkets to adopt "traffic-light labelling" for nutrition', *The Guardian*, 24 October.

Carbon Trust (2006) *The Carbon Emissions Generated in All that We Consume*, Carbon Trust, London, available at http://www.carbontrust.co.uk/publications/publicationdetail.htm?productid=CTC603 [accessed 24 April 2013].

Carrell, S. and Harvey, F. (2012) 'Turbine factory pledge is coup for Scotland', *The Guardian*, 20 November.

Carrington, D. (2012) 'Miliband presses Coalition on 2030 no-carbon target', *The Guardian*, 23 November.

Davis, A., Hirsch, D., Smith, N., Beckhelling, J. and Padley, M. (2012) *A Minimum Income Standard for the UK in 2012: Keeping up in Hard Times*, Joseph Rowntree Foundation, York.

Department for Environment, Food and Rural Affairs (2008) *UK Climate Change Sustainable Development Indicator: 2006 Greenhouse Gas Emissions*,

Final Figures, Statistical Release 25/08, available at http://webarchive. nationalarchives.gov.uk/20130123162956/http:/www.defra.gov.uk/news/ 2008/080131a.htm [accessed 25 April 2013].

Department for Environment, Food and Rural Affairs (2012) *Municipal Waste Management in the European Union*, available at http://webarchive. nationalarchives.gov.uk/20130123162956/http:/www.defra.gov.uk/statistics/ environment/waste/wrfg08-munec/ [accessed 25 April 2013].

Department for Environment, Food and Rural Affairs (2013) *Policy: Reducing and Managing Waste*, https://www.gov.uk/government/policies/reducing-and-managing-waste/supporting-pages/food-waste [accessed 25 April 2013].

Department of the Environment, Transport and the Regions (1998) *A New Deal for Transport: Better for Everyone: The Government's White Paper on the Future of Transport*, The Stationery Office, London.

Department of the Environment, Transport and the Regions (2000) *Transport 2010: The 10 Year Plan*, The Stationery Office, London.

Department of Health (1992) *The Health of the Nation*, The Stationery Office, London.

Department of Health (1999) *Saving Lives: Our Healthier Nation*, The Stationery Office, London.

Department of Health (2010) *Healthy Lives, Healthy People: Our Strategy for Public Health in England*, The Stationery Office, London.

Department of Health (2011) *The Public Health Responsibility Deal*, Department of Health, London.

Fahmy, E., Thumim, J. and White, V. (2012) *The Distribution of UK Household CO_2 Emissions: Interim Report*, Joseph Rowntree Foundation, York, available at http://www.jrf.org.uk/sites/files/jrf/carbon-reduction-policy-full.pdf [accessed 16 April 2013].

Fareshare (2012) 'FareShare calls on the food industry to act as more people go hungry across the UK', media release, 23 October, available at http:// www.fareshare.org.uk/wordpress/wp-content/uploads/2012/10/ NIS-Media-Release.pdf [accessed 12 November 2012].

Fink, S. (2012) *Simple Things Done Well: Making Practical Progress on Digital Engagement and Inclusion*, Policy Exchange, London.

Foresight (2007) *Tackling Obesities: Future Choices – Summary of Key Messages*, Department of Innovation, Universities and Skills, London.

Health Select Committee (2004) *Obesity*, The Stationery Office, London.

Lang, T. (1997) 'Dividing up the cake: food as social exclusion', in A. Walker and C. Walker (eds.) *Britain Divided: The Growth of Social Exclusion in the 1980s and 1990s*, Child Poverty Action Group, London.

Lindley, S., O'Neill, J., Kandeh, J., Lawson, N., Christian, R. and O'Neill, M. (2012) *Climate Change, Justice and Vulnerability*, Joseph Rowntree Foundation, York, available at http://www.jrf.org.uk/sites/files/jrf/climate-change-social-vulnerability-full.pdf [accessed 16 April 2013].

Mackie, P., Laird, J. and Johnson, D. (2012) *Buses and Economic Growth*, Institute for Transport Studies Report for Greener Journeys, Institute for Transport Studies, University of Leeds, Leeds.

National Assembly for Wales Petitions Committee (2012) *Control of Noise Nuisance from Wind Turbines*, National Assembly for Wales, Cardiff.

Nelson, M., Erens, B., Bates, B., Church, S. and Boshier, T. (2007) *Low Income Diet and Nutrition Survey*, The Stationery Office, London.

NHS Information Centre (2012) *Statistics on Obesity, Physical Activity and Diet: England 2012*, The Health and Social Care Information Centre, London.

Nuffield Council on Bioethics (2010) 'Council cited in White Paper on public health' available at http://www.nuffieldbioethics.org/news/council-cited-white-paper-public-health [accessed 3 March 2013].

Office of the Deputy Prime Minister (ODPM) (2005) *Inclusion Through Innovation: Tackling Social Exclusion Through New Technologies*, ODPM, London.

Park, A., Clery, E., Curtice, J., Phillips, M. and Utting, D. (2012) *British Social Attitudes 29*, National Centre for Social Research, London.

Public Health England (2013) *Trends in Obesity Prevalence*, available at http://www.noo.org.uk/NOO_about_obesity/trends [accessed 25 April 2013].

Scottish Government (2010) *Scotland's Zero Waste Plan*, Scottish Government, Edinburgh.

Social Exclusion Unit (2003) *Making the Connections: Transport and Social Exclusion – Interim Findings from the Social Exclusion Unit*, Social Exclusion Unit, London.

The Guardian (2007) 'Chavs, losers, addicts and frankfurter buses', 17 July, p. 11.

The Poverty Site (undated) 'Ability to travel', available at http://www.poverty.org.uk/75/index.shtml [accessed 12 November 2012].

Welsh Assembly Government (2010) *Towards Zero Waste: One Wales: One Planet*, Welsh Assembly Government, Cardiff.

World Commission on Environment and Development (1987) *Our Common Future*, Oxford University Press, Oxford.

Useful websites

http://www.food.gov.uk – the Food Standards Agency provides advice and information to government, businesses, and consumers about food safety, including nutrition and diet.

https://www.gov.uk – this site is intended to be the central point for government services and information.

https://www.gov.uk/government/organisations/department-for-transport – the Department of Transport's website gives access to government policy and other documents for transport and related issues.

http://www.jrf.org.uk – the Joseph Rowntree Foundation funds a wide variety of research on social policy issues and publishes the results. Its website provides access to much of this work.

PART 4
EUROPEAN AND INTERNATIONAL DEVELOPMENTS

- COMPARATIVE SOCIAL POLICY

- GLOBAL SOCIAL POLICY AND THE POLITICS OF GLOBALISATION

- THE EUROPEAN UNION AND SOCIAL POLICY

- CONCLUSIONS

CHAPTER 22

Comparative Social Policy

Harry Cowen

Learning objectives

- To articulate the main methods for comparing national welfare states
- To evaluate the 'archetypal' welfare state systems
- To compare developments and policies in nations' welfare systems
- To describe and assess the impacts of the 2008 global financial recession
- To compare governments' social policy responses to the global crisis

---

Chapter overview

For a number of years, the growing literature on the field of comparative social policy focused upon discrete nations (Hill, 1995; Sykes and Alcock, 1995). This included comparison of such aspects as economic growth rates, but also the particular approaches between, for example, the UK and Germany with respect to housing assistance or unemployment benefits. Esping-Andersen's (1990) *The Three Worlds of Welfare Capitalism* transformed the whole sphere of comparative study by seeking explanations for the differences and similarities, successes and failures, producing prime categories of welfare states. His research collected and analysed data from 18 advanced industrial economies, leading to his typology of welfare regimes: the corporatist state, the liberal state, and the social democratic state.

In this chapter, we compare welfare states, assuming that the nation state remains an important player in the context of developing globalisation, and discuss the national differences in social policy approach. Clearly, problems arise with such comparisons because of the diverse means of recording information and the very measurement of differences. Into these 'ideal types' were inserted countries that fit best into the appropriate regime. In the first part of this chapter, we look at Esping-Andersen's typology, which suggests three essential regimes of welfare capitalism, utilising a set of criteria for making measured comparisons between different economies. This part of the chapter also discusses the critiques and suggested modifications of the typology, so as to update the shift of capitalist economies under neo-liberalism and the significance of global convergence tendencies. Next, we look at the different welfare regimes (Esping-Andersen's archetypal welfare states: the conservative, the liberal, and the social democratic) focusing upon a wider set of themes, and survey the characteristics and history of social policy in Germany (conservative corporatist), the USA, UK, and smaller Anglo-Saxon economies (liberal regimes), and Sweden, plus other selected Scandinavian economies (social democratic regimes). This analysis is supplemented by a supportive international study relating specifically to comparative measurements of inequality between nations. We then assess the impact of the 2008 crisis and recession on the social environment and personal health of the inhabitants of discrete countries, covering those already discussed as 'archetypal welfare state regimes' but in addition presenting information on the marginalised Mediterranean European countries, and nations from Central Europe. Research data are synthesized on unemployment, income levels, poverty, education, and public expenditure, while we also assess the overall impacts of the austerity programmes imposed in particular on citizens of the Mediterranean countries. Following on from studying the effects of the recession, we compare nation-states' social policy responses to the crisis and recession, including those from Germany, the USA and the UK, smaller liberal states, the Scandinavian welfare states, and the countries of the global south, in addition to those Mediterranean governments too heavily indebted to exercise any meaningful independent social policy of their own. The chapter ends with an overarching set of conclusions. We start by engagement with the methodological issues of comparison.

SPOTLIGHT

The welfare state, typologies, and global change

In the academic study of the modern welfare state, and how to compare the different types, Danish sociologist Esping-Andersen's *The Three Worlds of*

Welfare Capitalism represents the seminal text, in which he formulates a typology of welfare states. This typology, however, has its critics based on the matter of global change:

> 'The welfare state is not just a mechanism that intervenes in, and possibly corrects, the structure of inequality, it is, in its own right, a system of stratification. It is an active force in the ordering of social relations . . . As we survey international variations in social rights and welfare-state stratification, we will find qualitatively different arrangements between state, market and the family. The welfare-state variations we find are therefore not linearly distributed, but clustered by regime types' (Esping-Andersen, 1990, pp. 23, 26).

> 'The changing politics and policies of social welfare . . . raise issues about the values and limitations of typologies of welfare states and welfare regimes . . . One problem (in analysing the US liberal regime) in the Esping-Andersen typology on state/market distinctions emphasize liberal (or neo-liberal) political ideology. Yet some of the key elements of US welfare politics and policy of the last 30 years have been conservative (or neo-conservative) forces . . . [Perhaps] the most significant question is how to link typologies and the dynamics of change' (Clarke, 2001, pp. 147–8).

Comparing welfare states

Esping-Andersen's (1990) path-breaking work identified essentially three types of welfare regime: the corporatist state (e.g. Germany), the liberal state (e.g. USA), and the social democratic state (e.g. Sweden). The corporatist or conservative welfare regimes largely entail 'corporatist' arrangements that reproduce social differences, feature the centrality of the state, and emphasise maintenance of the system and social order. The liberal regime stresses benefits distribution by means testing, and market-oriented social insurance; welfare policies focusing on groups living in poverty; and the promotion of insurance schemes in the private sector. The social democratic welfare regime upholds the principles of equality of social strata through universal provision within a full welfare state; strives for full employment; and accords the market a lower priority than the state.

Esping-Anderson's model of welfare state regimes continued to dominate in comparative social policy studies throughout the 1990s and into the new millennium. Esping-Anderson distinguished between the three types of regime based on specific criteria:

- How much welfare protection was provided by non-market providers, what Esping-Andersen called 'decommodification'?

- The extent to which social class (based on stratification) determined a population's access to welfare.
- The achievement of high employment levels in the economy.

He was careful to state that no modern economy could possibly boast all of the prerequisites needed: a balanced national state budget, a moderate economic equality, and impressive employment levels. Therefore, decisions made by individual nation states in plumping for one or two of the goals have resulted in divergent experiences. However, other sociologists and social policy analysts offered alternative models for accurately portraying welfare regime types. Maurizio Ferrera (1998, cited in Giddens, 2007) proposed a Mediterranean regime, made up of Spain, Portugal, and Greece. In hindsight, this proposal, given the crippling debt from the 2008 financial crisis and the more recent euro crisis (covered in more detail in Chapter 24 on the EU), has become startlingly prescient. Giddens himself suggested a fifth type: the former 'Soviet' regimes that have encountered a host of difficulties in adapting their economies to the Western industrialised nations' welfare state model.

At another level of the 'regime' debate, and clearly important since it raised further issues of a methodological nature, Cochrane *et al.* (2001) suggested that Esping-Andersen's focus upon the decommodification (i.e. the challenge to employers' control over payment to workers) of labour and stratification was too narrow. They believed it was also necessary to broaden the criteria in the assessment of social policy, by encompassing class divisions, gender relations of welfare, ethnicity, age, and disability, while examining those features coursing through all of the above: inequalities in health services, citizenship, and poverty levels. (These criteria are considered later in this chapter when comparing individual nations' social policy 'heritage'.)

STOP AND THINK

How useful is Esping-Andersen's methodology for differentiating between nation states' approach to welfare?

Again, Esping-Andersen's presumption that economies travel in different directions came under attack from other researchers in the policy field. Hemerijck (2002) believed that no evident empirical distinction exists between the various welfare regimes: they have all operated a combination of policies on taxation, employment, and public welfare. Accordingly – and recognised by Esping-Andersen himself (1996), Taylor-Gooby (2004), and others – a policy convergence has materialised closely aligned with the pressures of globalisation and the hegemony of neo-liberalism, rendering unfeasible the post-war goals of sustained economic growth and full employment accompanied by increasing equality. Such convergence has even been observed in Europe's most social democratic welfare states. Each has faced rising unemployment and burgeoning social security bills.

On the other hand, John Clarke (2004) is less than convinced by the ostensibly plausible convergence thesis. In his re-assessment of social policy developments, he investigates changing welfare and new directions in social policy and expresses scepticism towards the convergence idea and the accompanying notion of the termination of the welfare state *per se*. Are we not on shaky ground, he asks, in trying to answer whether this is the end of the welfare state? In fact, he observes, a diversity of welfare states continue to exist, and welfare states remain subject to multiple forces and pressures (to whit, from the 'nation', from the 'state', and from the market), as well as to political and ideological forces. The latter, of course, have been part of globalisation but, according to Clarke, these may be rather exaggerated as against the welter of national welfare differences. Notwithstanding, global neo-liberalism has formed an essential part of the ideological landscape in the international social policy arena since the 1970s. It has acted as the major global/transnational force. Yet its impacts have been uneven, depending upon culture, region of the world, and the particular nation under discussion.

The 'Anglophone' nations, for example – namely, the USA, UK, Australia, Canada, and New Zealand – have tended to be open to global neo-liberalism in the refashioning of their welfare states. Latin American nations have similarly interpreted 'the Washington Consensus' (the ideological emphasis of the Washington-based IMF upon 'free markets' unconstrained by nation state interference) as a positive boost to reconstructing their own state and welfare systems. Alternatively, on the African continent, the IMF and WTO among the global capitalist bodies have pressurised vulnerable economies to accept neo-liberal policies that have culminated in a diminution of public services and privatisation of the service sector. Since 1989, neo-liberalism's impact upon the former Soviet Union's Eastern Bloc's welfare framework was awesome in its very speed of implementation. Neo-liberal strategies represented the seminal contribution to the reform and marketisation of the new Eastern European economies' resources, the collapse of welfare systems, and the increased growth of inequalities. Clarke notes the more equivocal outcomes in East Asian nations, ideologically distancing themselves from stark neo-liberalism with a mix of Confucianism, focus on the family, and state involvement in the economy and social policy. On the other hand, the resistances to neo-liberalism, emanating from both popular-based protest movements or linked to political parties, were more prominent in Northern and Western European welfare states.

One needs, then, a theoretical framework for comparing welfare state performances, the most celebrated of which has been that of Esping-Andersen. State political perspectives are doubtless central in accounting for national differences, but it is wise to make the Esping-Andersen model of typologies more expansive, to widen the criteria of 'performance', and to pay more attention to the obvious convergence that has transpired in an age of neo-liberal hegemony and the domination of the 'Washington Consensus'. The next section examines the essential features of the archetypal welfare states.

The archetypal welfare states

Adopting both the Esping-Andersen typology and the criteria formulated by Cochrane *et al.* (2001), this section describes and evaluates the prime features of those nations fitting most obviously into the identified models of Western capitalist welfare delivery, that is:

- Conservative
  - e.g. Germany
- Liberalist
  - USA
  - UK – liberal rather than liberalist
  - Canada, Australia, and New Zealand
- Social democratic
  - Scandinavian

Germany and the Conservative Regime

Germany (West Germany at the time of Esping-Andersen's analysis) stands as the archetypal conservative model regime as derived by Esping-Andersen. First, its welfare regime is employment-based, centred around social insurance, and hence reiterates status differentials among its citizens. Second, it is corporatist, embracing interest groups in the process of policy-making; this leads to coalition building, incremental change, and the preservation of 'social' stability. Third, it is committed to the principle of subsidiarity, deriving from a Catholic social ethic deeming the family as the prime welfare provider. At the same time, decision-making is devolved to the lowest administrative unit (Poole, 2001).

Social assistance is viewed as distinct from social insurance. As it is discretionary, it means that 'beneficiaries' become dependent. It is important to note that the German state's concept of citizenship has undergone change, in that place of birth has replaced 'blood ties'. Through the decades after the Second World War until the 1970s, there were few redistributive income tax policies, wages were low, and unskilled work predominated. Germany's reliance on the 'traditional family' for the maintenance of social stability has remained. Women's entry into the job market essentially transpired through part-time work, against the continuance of a powerful 'breadwinner' model (not unlike Lord Beveridge's conception in the years of Britain's classic welfare state). In the late twentieth century, female employment gains scarcely compensated for the above model. Welfare in Germany has been 'racialised', particularly through the 'guest worker' system. The latter have been marginalised from work opportunities and 'guest workers' have experienced high levels of poverty.

Throughoujt the period from 1975 to 1999, the West German model of welfare was hit by external, global pressures: recession; the European Union developments; and the rise of unemployment, including that of male unemployment. Since 1990, perhaps the foremost external pressure on the nation's welfare regime was the impact of the unification between East and West Germany (following the dismantling of the Berlin Wall in 1989 as the Soviet Communist empire began to fall apart). A major social consequence has been huge disparities in welfare between East and West Germans: the GDR's (German Democratic Republic) model of welfare (basically the former Soviet model) entailed extensive state provision, coupled with sizeable subsidies for those already in work. In practice, all the measures were centred upon the right to work. For those who were not in work, no system of unemployment insurance or transfers operated. Productivity in the GDR was poor. Although the GDR's political ideology was formerly universalistic, social policy was in fact work-based welfare.

Unification between the 'communist' GDR and the capitalist West Germany has resulted in gaping inequalities between East and West. For example, East German women have witnessed shrinkage in the available range of benefits, increased unemployment, and single mothers experiencing life at the borders of poverty. As unemployment rose in the East, the West initially suffered rising unemployment alien to Germany in the post-war period.

The USA and the liberalist regime

The USA generally fits into Esping-Andersen's characterisation of the liberalist welfare regime, but the reality is more fluid and multi-layered than implied by the model. The idea of welfare here is best located in the 'New Deal' of the 1930s. To manage the mass unemployment, Federal money was mobilised and major public works' projects were implemented, including the celebrated Tennessee Valley Authority scheme. In addition, the government set up a structure of welfare benefits and an insurance contributions scheme aimed at the employed, which represented an 'incentive to work' policy.

The USA's approach to welfare was imbued with three central principles: that social insurance should not be focused on the elimination of all hardships; that workers had to note that high benefits were not to be expected, since benefits were dependent upon their income and insurance contributions; and that the scheme needed to be completely differentiated from public assistance. Benefits were considered a right to be 'earned'. In effect, such provisos added up to a 'semi-welfare' system. Welfare was much to the fore in the 1960s under President L.B. Johnson. However, the evident concern with and support for welfare was overturned in the 1980s under the 'New Right' policies. Neo-liberalism became the policy paradigm for the remaining quarter of the twentieth century and stretching into the new decade of the twenty-first century. The paradigm constituted the reform of state provision of the social public sector, namely through the marketisation and privatisation of health and social services, and an open rejection of this mode of state involvement (as opposed to powerful military spending by the state). The shared transatlantic perspective of Republican President Reagan and the Conservative Prime Minister Thatcher in the UK (similarly fitting into Esping-Andersen's 'liberalist welfare regime') characterised welfare expenditure as growing dependence by a lazy 'underclass' upon state hand-outs (Clarke, 2001).

Inequalities increased through the 1980s and 1990s. The gap between rich and poor grew; race and gender differentials widened, leading to poverty among Black and female Americans. What is undeniable is that these trends were not produced by pragmatic policies; they represented a major ideological challenge to the previous welfare regimes (Clarke, 2001). In the 1990s, reforms were implemented in the USA, constituting an ostensibly viable (and cheaper) alternative to a social welfare system. Originating in Wisconsin, they were then wholeheartedly adopted in the UK by the Blair New Labour governments (for example, their 'Welfare to Work' reforms). This 'welfare to work' alternative suggests that offering employment experience and training improves the chance of obtaining long-term employment, thereby breaking the claimed cycle of dependence (Deacon, 2002). The Wisconsin welfare scheme was based on the ideas of Lawrence Mead, an American academic who carried out fieldwork in the State of Wisconsin, which emphasise the work ethic and require 18- to 24-year-olds claiming jobseekers' allowance to meet up with an employment advisor who helps them find work. Success in this direction, reasoned Mead, reduces total welfare payments and boosts tax-generating income: a positive result for the community as well as the individual. From another perspective, such a strategy simply labels as 'scroungers' many without employment because of the system's inadequacies, rather than their own: a direct refutation of welfare state values.

The UK and the liberal welfare state model

The UK's welfare state also dovetails with Esping-Andersen's 'liberalist regime', achieving prominence in the years immediately after the Second World War, and was termed the 'mixed economy' (a mix of capitalist market principles and welfare collectivism). As a result of the economic and social policies of the Attlee Labour government during the 1940s, its welfare state became a role model of its kind. Keynesianism (after the economist, John Maynard Keynes) promoted the necessity of state expenditure in enhancing economic growth and 'full' employment, in tandem with the nationalisation of key heavy industries. The Beveridge Report of 1942 (Social Insurance and Allied Services; as explored in Chapter 6) became the welfare paradigm equivalent to Keynesian economic policy, charting a comprehensive welfare benefits system providing social insurance for employment, ill health, and old age. The 1944 Education Act brought educational provision basically under the aegis of the state, increasing educational opportunities; the 1946 National Health Service Act did the same for health. But paralleling the USA's liberalist assumptions (with the possible exception of health provision), welfare benefits were not to be understood as interfering with the labour market's fundamental principles: benefits were to be viewed as a 'last resort'; problems of unemployment or sickness were essentially matters for the individual, the family unit or the charitable voluntary sector. The male was considered as the household's 'breadwinner'. Women's rights were thus negligible. Even if working at some point, females' allotted role was as 'dependent'. Citizens applying for the extra 'National Assistance' found themselves subject to a means test also applied to 'family benefit' payments.

From the 1980s, however, the traditional UK welfare statism and Keynesianism was subjected to the 'New Right' policies of Reagan and Thatcher (as mentioned above), whereby the global capitalist ideology of neo-liberalism spread market forces across the world (to eventually encompass the economy of the massive, politically Communist-led Republic of China). Thatcherism attempted a major restructuring of the welfare state, in the first instance by cutting back on public expenditure, which resulted in debilitating knock-on effects upon social welfare services, education, and employment. Across this period of Conservative government (1979–97), economic and social inequalities widened rapidly, along with an unprecedented growth in child poverty. The health, welfare, and education sectors imported business decision-making models as the antidote to 'welfare' professionalism. This strategy plus privatisation of certain welfare services (e.g. old people's homes and the assiduous adoption of the Wisconsin approach to employment policy) was maintained by the 'New Labour' government (1997–2010) throughout its three consecutive terms of office (Clarke and Newman, 1997), deflecting UK social policy far away from the objectives of its post-war liberal welfare state (Clarke *et al.*, 2001).

Canada, Australia, and New Zealand

Canada's liberalist welfare state was born out of the depression years of the 1930s, and was built upon universalist principles and prioritisation of the public sector. Legislation was passed on old age security, universal family allowances and universal health care, unemployment insurance and the Canada Assistance Plan (1966: a consolidated federal-provincial programme to meet needs irrespective of cause of hardship), among other welfare policies. But from the late 1970s the federal state moved in accord with neo-liberalism, and delivered reforms that clearly weakened its traditional welfare state through privatisation of services, deregulation of financial activities and the like, rendering attacks upon universal provision of family allowances, old age security, and abolition of the popular Canada Assistance Plan (Irving, 2007).

Both Australia and New Zealand operated what might be termed minimal formal welfare states compared with their European counterparts. In the 1970s, they made available flat-rate benefits and also distributed child and family benefits. In Australia, a Medibank was formed, basically a public health insurance system, financed from income tax. However, by the 1980s, as in the case of Canada and other liberalist regimes, New Zealand in particular had rapidly adopted the global neo-liberalism of market forces, presaging the transformation and fragmentation of its welfare state. This led to the implementation of a more 'flexible' labour market, the 'liberalisation' of the financial sector, and a relatively limited marketisation in health, education, and pensions. The government oversaw privatisation of a huge proportion of the public sector, far in excess of that pertaining under Margaret Thatcher in the UK at that time. In Australia's case, markets were introduced into the public sector much more gradually (Schwartz, 2000).

The Scandinavian economies and the social democratic regime

The Scandinavian economies have functioned on the basis of substantial state involvement, coupled with a positive redistribution of resources, though operating from within a capitalist economy. Sweden is considered as the archetypal social democratic state; in the 1970s, it devoted a bigger slice of its national income to welfare benefits and services than any other capitalist nation. The largest proportion of the Swedish old age pension emanates from the country's state pension scheme. Furthermore, inequalities in social groups and gender were also less than in all other economies (Wilkinson and Pickett, 2009). Following the Second World War, Sweden's low unemployment levels were without parallel in the West. However, during the 1980s, Sweden, along with other economies, was affected by the global recession and the global capitalist neo-liberal turn towards adaptation of markets, thereby reducing social spending and privatising local services. Inequalities widened and poverty levels increased. This reversal of fortune more or less continued into the 1990s.

Unemployment increased, especially among foreign workers, while unemployment rates were almost identical for men and women, reflecting traditional positive social democratic policies and the related fact that for a number of years women had enjoyed impressive levels of paid employment.

Sweden's ability to at least restrain the growth of unemployment may be attributed to a proactive labour market policy, which included the following measures:

- financial inducements to relocate
- organised training schemes
- wage subsidies for disabled persons
- positive discrimination in favour of women
- unemployment insurance benefits administered by voluntary societies and funded by government, trades unions, and employers.

Yet, with the continuation of global economic pressures, the rules for eligibility have been tightened. The country's gender policies have been on the whole positive, and its state support for single mother families unequalled globally, but traditional attitudes were equivocal (until the 1980s, women were viewed as predominantly child-raisers based in the family home). Since the 1990s, women's employment situation has become more uncertain due to a hesitant labour market.

Up to the 1970s, strong 'immigration control' policies reinforced the traditional antipathy in Scandinavia towards non-white ethnic groups. Later, the Swedish state passed substantial anti-discrimination legislation and encouraged multiculturalism. However, Sweden's strategies of restructuring to deal with global economic problems in the 1990s left minority ethnic communities disadvantaged by welfare state policies and in labour markets (Ginsburg, 2001).

A recent international study, currently considered required reading on national differences in inequality (Wilkinson and Pickett, 2009), investigated measures of equality and inequality in 23 developed capitalist countries, and calculated the Index of Health and Social Problems (IHSP). The findings displayed a clear relationship between inequality and health and social problems. Nations with the least inequality – the Scandinavian nations (Denmark, Finland, Norway, Sweden) and Japan – displayed the highest levels of health. At the other end of the scale, countries with the greatest inequality – Portugal, USA, and the UK – suffered frequently from most health and social problems: fragmentation of community life and social relations; rise in mental illness and drug use; poor physical health and low life expectancy; rapid increase in obesity levels; unequal learning opportunities for young disadvantaged persons in education; high rates of teenage births; high levels of violence; high rates of imprisonment; low social mobility and greatly unequal opportunities.

To summarise, this section on empirical comparisons first described the social policy approaches of Germany, reflecting a corporate conservatism, primarily resting upon the system of work-based social security. The United States, as an archetypal liberal regime, has in fact abandoned most of its welfare state apparatus and ideology through the neo-liberal years, whereas UK governments, similarly in thrall to market principles, have maintained various strands of a welfare state philosophy, akin to some of the smaller Anglo-Saxon economies. What stands out is the continuity of social democratic welfare state egalitarian principles in the Scandinavian economies, despite external global neo-liberal pressures, features accounting for the combination of strong economic performance and social wellbeing, an assessment echoed by Wilkinson and Pickett's (2009) comparative study of the relationship between, on the one hand, the levels of a country's health and, on the other, the levels of social and economic inequality within countries. In the following section, we investigate the manner in which global economic recession, added to the waves of neo-liberal reforms, has opened up an even larger gap between any 'ideal type' of welfare state and the current national attempts at social policy.

> **STOP AND THINK**
>
> What kind of political conclusions may be drawn from the diversity of types of welfare state regime?

Welfare state systems and the impact of the 2008 economic recession

Recently, the economic climate at the global level, with the bursting of the US property boom and sub-prime mortgage lending, has exerted a dramatic and worrying effect upon welfare policies in all of the welfare regimes. Impacts upon jobs have been crushing. The International Labour Organisation (2012) declared:

> The G20 countries would need to create 21 million jobs in 2012 in order to return to pre-crisis employment levels. In 2012, 40 per cent of global jobless were young people. Almost seventy-five million 15–24 year olds were unemployed, a growth of almost four million since 2007.

In Greece, Italy, Slovakia, and the Czech Republic, unemployment due to the financial crisis hit women more than men. In others, including Ireland, Romania, and Lithuania, male unemployment has been considerably higher.

Following a period of ebullient economic growth during the first decade of the twenty-first century, Spain was badly affected by the bursting of its own property bubble. Ireland, with a similar trajectory, had experienced rapid growth in the early 2000s build around a massive property building bubble that also burst in 2008, sending it into bankruptcy. The EU and the IMF bailed out the Irish state for almost 70 billion euros, leaving it with nearly the highest household debt in Europe. In Greece, Italy, and similar economies, the imposed austerity programmes created social dislocation from cuts to pensions, health services, public services, and spending on education, leading to a series of mass protests.

In July 2012, the European Working Conditions Observatory (EWCO) focused on wages and working conditions in the crisis (Eurofound, 2012a), a study undertaken in diverse countries based on individual national reports, compiled from responses to a standard questionnaire. It found that most EU member states had felt severe impacts, including wage de-acceleration, pay freezes, and occasional pay cuts. Vulnerable groups, such as the low-skilled, young people, and migrants, had suffered in particular. Let us now consider the impact of the global economic crisis on two aspects: (1) unemployment rates and (2) falls in wage levels and reductions in working conditions.

Unemployment rates

It was estimated that in 2012 there were 25.5 million (10.5 per cent) men and women unemployed in the EU. But the distribution of unemployment was rather uneven: the highest rates were in Greece (24.4 per cent) and Spain (25.1 per cent), while the lowest were in Austria (4.5 per cent), Luxembourg

(5.2 per cent), the Netherlands (5.3 per cent), and Germany (5.5 per cent). The mass unemployment was directly due to the global financial crisis. Sweden's unemployment levels also increased owing to the crisis, but the rise was scarcely dramatic: the rate grew from 6 to 8 per cent from 2007 to 2009. Whereas in 2008 unemployment had stood at 6.7 per cent in the EU, by 2011 it was 9.7 per cent, the highest since 2000 (when the statistics had first been made available). A key problem, too, was that of long-term unemployment, not just because of the financial and social effects on individuals' personal life, but also because it affects social cohesion and may indeed stymy economic growth. Of those unemployed in 2011, 41 per cent had been unemployed in excess of a year; 2.2 per cent had been out of work for more than two years.

In the USA, unemployment was high in almost every American state. From 2007 to 2010, unemployment almost doubled among all occupational groups, and by the end of 2011 a total of 13 million people were unemployed compared with 6.8 million in 2007. However, Krugman (2012) notes that by applying a broader measure of unemployment (those looking for full-time work but only able to find a part-time job), 24 million were unemployed, virtually twice the equivalent 2007 figure. As elsewhere, the outcomes for young workers were particularly stark. Unemployment for this group doubled in the period imme-diately following the 'credit crunch' (Krugman, 2012).

In the UK, unemployment stood at 2.5 million by the end of 2010. Although it had reached 2.51 million by late 2012, the Central Office of National Statistics revealed a further one million under-employed (i.e. people wanting more hours of employment, such as part-time workers) than in 2008. The number of public sector jobs dropped by almost 400,000 in the 12 months from 2011 to 2012, leaving their proportional significance the lowest since 1999 (when such data were first available).

In the light of its traditional welfare orientation, Australia was relatively less affected. Following the onset of the financial crisis, at its highest unemploy-ment reached 6 per cent, but hidden unemployment was an added factor, in that employment had become predominantly part-time.

A particularly negative employment issue among the EU nations was the precariously high levels of unemployment among young people (Fig. 22.1). A study for Eurofound (2012b) estimated (an educated guess) that the European Union was paying 153 billion euros per year for the 14 million unemployed young people aged 15–29 (forming 15 per cent of the EU's total adult popula-tion). These are now categorised as NEETS (those 'not in employment, education or training'), and their needs have increased by 28 per cent since 2008. In 2007, 1.2 million youths (15.7 per cent) were unemployed in the EU; by 2011, this figure had increased to 5.5 million (21.4 per cent). The explicit social unease regarding this section of the EU's population was that NEETS were more likely to suffer from a set of cumulative disadvantages; they were more likely to experience poor future employment prospects; more likely to pursue dangerous lifestyles; and also more likely to suffer from phys-ical and mental health problems. They also participated less in politics and social activities. In most of the EU member states, the youth unemployment

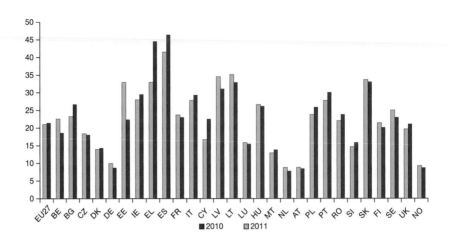

Figure 22.1 Youth unemployment rates in the EU27 countries and Norway, 2010 and 2011 (percentages). BE, Belgium; BG, Bulgaria; CZ, Czech Republic; DK, Denmark; DE, Germany; EE, Estonia; IE, Ireland; EL, Greece; ES, Spain; FR, France; IT, Italy; CY, Cyprus; LV, Latvia; LT, Lithuania; LU, Luxembourg; HU, Hungary; MT, Malta; NL, Netherlands; AT, AUSTRIA; PL, Poland; PT, Portugal; RO, Romania; SI, Slovenia; SK, Slovakia; FI, Finland; SE, Sweden; UK, United Kingdom; NO, Norway

Source: Eurofound (2012c), reproduced with permission

rate had doubled or tripled since 2007. And even 16.7 per cent of those with some tertiary education were unemployed in 2011 (compared with 11.4 per cent in 2007) – the biggest recorded increase. As a solution, the European Commission proposed a new set of integrated guidelines for training schemes to equip young people with a skill relevant to the labour market, plus start-up funding to assist young people in developing their skills.

Falls in wage levels and reductions in working conditions

The global economic crisis has also affected pay in most EU member states, producing wage moderation, pay freezes, and occasional pay cuts, especially affecting vulnerable groups, such as the low-skilled, young people (once again), and migrants. Interestingly, data culled from the five key sectors showed that the crisis had a more pronounced effect on employment than on wages. The Eurofound (2012a) study on wages and working conditions in the crisis, essentially a questionnaire survey, produced the following findings for Greece, Portugal, and Spain. Greece's economic conditions were greatly weakened by externally imposed 'austerity measures' to curb its mounting debt. From 2008 to 2011, Greece's unemployment rate increased from 7.7 per cent to 16.6 per cent, and by 2012 was expected to have exceeded 20 per cent. Wages had either been frozen or had declined, along with a reduction in working conditions. The results led to large demonstrations in Athens. Greece's situation was already dire, but was soon to be intensified by the Eurozone crisis (discussed fully in the next chapter on the European Union).

For Portugal, the survey ran into problems *vis-à-vis* a paucity of studies and statistics for the 2006–2010 period. However, '[it] is increasingly visible', stated the survey report, 'that the current crisis has been impacting upon wages across the country' (Eurofound, 2012a). The imposition of wage freezes and cutbacks was socially punitive, although they were not yet in evidence in the official statistics (most of the available data were for 2009); many of the country's industrial sectors were imposing restrictions upon wages. At the same time, there had been no sign of policies to support insecure groups of workers.

Spain's extensive economic boom of the 2000s suddenly terminated with the 2008 financial crisis. The nation's unemployment rate had soared to 24.4 per cent in 2012, the highest in Europe. Again as with Greece, the 'austerity' measures, affecting Catalonia more than other regions, resulted in mass demonstrations and even threats of secession from the Spanish Republic from pro-independence parties among the Basques and the Catalonians at the regional elections in late October 2012 (*The Guardian*, 2012b). One other effect of the crisis was a strong out-migration of Spain's migrant community returning home to Latin American countries, engendering a huge fall in births (from 519,00 in 2008 to 483,000 in 2011): this meant a cut in Spain's fertility rate (*Economist*, 2012).

No big wage increases were advanced in the United States; indeed, highly educated graduates were forced to accept extremely large pay reductions. Poverty had spread across the country. A 2011 poll revealed that close to 40 per cent of families had suffered from reduced hours, wages or benefits. Lost jobs meant the disappearance of health insurance, the eventual cessation of unemployment benefit for the long-term unemployed, and the surrendering of homes (Krugman, 2012, pp. 8–12).

When the UK went into a period of recession in 2008, it was the most affected of the Western European economies. Considering the close working arrangements between the UK financial sector and that of the USA (where the crisis was initiated), it is understandable that the UK felt the impact of the credit crisis both sooner and harder than many other countries (Farnsworth and Irving, 2011). Similar to the United States, the recession became long-term, and still evident in 2013. The rescue of the banks by nationalisation under New Labour resulted in major national debt. Yet the heaviest burden imposed upon the UK population stemmed from the new Conservative-led Coalition government's strategy to pay off all debt. Thus, its concomitant response to the global crisis was a set of austerity measures from 2010 harsh enough to stymy economic growth for years ahead, and falling disproportionately upon the poorest part of society via the cutbacks in social welfare expenditure. Local government services' budgets were reduced by 40 per cent, cutting away the very fabric of the welfare state. The Institute for Fiscal Studies international investigation into the impact of 'The Great Recession' predicted that the Conservative Chancellor Osborne's strategy 'will cast a very long shadow in the UK' and will 'cut the standard of living of the country's families by more than ten per cent by 2014' (*The Guardian*, 2012a). Germany bore the marks of global financial crisis only marginally. Despite the crisis, its trade balance, contrary to that of the UK, exceeded US$150 billion. Earlier German social policy reforms in health care, old age pensions, social assistance, and parental leave benefits (see the 'Social policy responses' section below) had reduced the price of labour. The retention of a viable manufacturing sector, along with the progress of its services sector, made for a sound balance across its workforce, which also boasted enhanced female participation rates. For all these reasons, Germany, with its relatively smaller financial sector, was able to emerge more protected (though still having suffered socially) from the economic crisis (Farnsworth and Irving, 2011).

Canada, bruised from the crisis due to its historic ties to the US economy, felt the impact even more immediately than during earlier recessions. But because of its well regulated financial sector, the repercussions were less than those in the USA.

Few of the developing countries, unsurprising considering their position outside of global capitalist networks, were worse hit by the crisis in particular. The outcome was nevertheless unacceptable to these nations (and indeed to those elsewhere viewing it as morally reprehensible). An extra 73 million people survived on less than $1.25 a day and another 92 million on below $2 per day. Only a handful of these countries possess a viable income maintenance programme.

CONTROVERSY AND DEBATE

Impacts of global crisis and recession

Farnsworth and Irving (2011) have made the following assessment of the divergent impacts of global crisis, counter-posing 'collectivism' to 'market competitiveness':

'Countries within the social democratic model already benefit form a historically strong sense of togetherness and previous experience . . . There was negligible engagement in the international sub-prime market in Sweden, for example . . .

'Liberal market economies, on the other hand, are least well equipped in both economic buffers and social solidarity to deal with the impact of a crisis in welfare funding because interests are not shared corporately or between classes . . . The long-term consequences of public sector cuts combined with recession have not been fully acknowledged'. (Farnsworth and Irving, 2011, pp. 23–5)

What do you think of this assessment? To what extent is this view aligned to the argument of the national disparities in economic and social inequalities?

To summarise, the recession has seriously dislocated the welfare regimes, but the results have been uneven. Mediterranean European nations have suffered to the point of national bankruptcy, mass unemployment, personal sickness, and financial hardship, whereas Germany's more balanced economy and earlier social policy reforms cushioned the nation from the worst ramifications. Sweden's social democratic framework has also meant steelier resistance, but the liberalist regimes of the USA and the UK, both at the heart of the initial 'credit crisis', have ironically felt the chill winds of unregulated neo-liberalism. The smaller liberal economies have managed to avoid long-term recession. In the next section, we present a more detailed comparison of individual states' social policy responses to the crisis.

Social policy responses to the crisis

The USA's social policy responses to the crisis

In 2009, the incoming Democratic administration of President Obama was faced with increasing economic and financial difficulties. He brought in the ARRA (American Recovery and Reinvestment Act) in 2009 to boost the economy and introduced a spending package of $787 billion, which included financial support for its Unemployment Insurance and Food Stamps Programme; $7 billion were advanced from the Federal Government to the individual American states to give protection to 7 million unemployed and low-wage workers not yet in receipt of unemployment income. Even so, President Obama achieved in 2010 what his Democrat predecessors had failed to do: the reform of health care making health insurance available to millions more (Béland and Waddan, 2011).

Germany's social policy responses to the crisis

Germany's response was less dramatic than that of other economies, given its earlier 'pre-crisis' period of welfare reforms, which, as we noted above, covered more stringent criteria for old age benefits and costlier contributions for health care plus cuts in expenditure, alongside other welfare aspects. Coupled with the fact that the country's financial sector was smaller than those of its Western economic competitors, its immediate policies in the face of crisis were relatively moderate; the government provided 500 billion euros to steady the banks; 50 billion euros to rescue nearly one million jobs; and 50 billion euros for educational infrastructure and improvement of workers' wages. Alternatively, savings on pensions, parental leave and public sector pensions, albeit of a fairly mild nature, were made under Chancellor Merkel's government (Hudson and Kühner, 2011).

Canada and Australia's social policy responses to the crisis

As already observed, the impact of the global crisis on the Canadian nation state was much less than in the United States, because of its better regulated financial sector. The Federal Conservative Government (Canada operates a Federal system of government, with separate provincial governments holding their own budgets) under Premier Stephen Harper, resisted any substantial social policy reform, although the Premier indicated to Parliament that he was prepared to debate the matter! In 2009, employment eligibility for benefits was slightly truncated. The Canadian pension system, traditionally positive in assisting poverty reduction, was revisited. But since many Canadians still rely heavily on personal savings and private pensions, the financial crisis pressured many into delaying retirement and damaged the pension funds. A revised comprehensive social policy did not appear, despite the worsening fiscal conditions in the Provinces (Béland and Waddan, 2011). Australia, aided too by traditional welfare state leanings, was affected only moderately. Employers managed to retain their workers, although this was largely because of the country's shortage of skilled labour. Premier Kevin Rudd's Labour government soon embarked upon a set of stimulus programmes in 2008 and 2009, worth approximately 7 per cent of GDP; substantial income tax cuts for low-income families; bigger pension payments; and subsidies for home buyers. The first stimulus package totalled A$10.4 billion (including A$4.8 billion for pensions and carers' allowance). Low-income families received A$1000 for every child. A Jobs Fund was launched in 2009, as part of the state's labour market policy, additional monies were released for the purpose of case management for job seekers, and the criteria for the receipt of benefits were relaxed.

Developing countries' social policy responses to the crisis

Although not many of the developing countries were hit badly by the crisis in particular, the knock-on effects are nevertheless parlous. However, some Latin American economies (e.g. Mexico and Brazil) have introduced non-contributory pension programmes. Aspects of social assistance appeared in South Africa (child support grants) in the 2000s but it remains doubtful whether these have been sufficient to weather any negative crisis effects (Barrientos, 2011).

European Union Member States' social policy responses to the crisis

The situation of Greece is expounded at greater length in the EU chapter, as its sovereign debt was responsible for the Eurozone crisis. Suffice to state at this point that the Greek Government was in no position to respond to the 2008 global crisis, by dint of the fact that between 1995 and 2008 government spending each year (paying for welfare services) exceeded half of its GDP. The Greek economy was stagnant; its taxation collection system was dysfunctional; its sovereign debt was used to generate liquidity. Hence, unlike other economies' stimulus programmes in 2008, Greece was bereft of an independent social policy response other than the conditions of 'austerity' dictated by the global social policy organisations.

By December 2011, Spain's Conservative government under Mariano Rajoy's Popular Party delivered a further austerity package; the package included the equivalent to $11.5 billion in spending cuts. Spain had to be bailed out, leading to further reductions in the budget. However, the appearance of the country's second recession occasioned Rajoy into accepting an additional bailout of 19 billion euros, following the same route as Greece, by replying with more cutbacks in pensions, benefits, jobs, and salaries (*New York Times*, 2012).

Portugal's results, too, were sobering: the population encountered wage freezes and public service cutbacks with severe human ramifications, especially for the low-waged. In addition, no state or local policies were on hand to aid poorer groups. Furthermore, inequalities along gender and social class lines (according to educational levels) had widened, and in 2012 the national state minimum wage was frozen.

Italian respondents reported a national decline in wages, under the state's 'wage moderation' policy, exacerbated by a marked fall in worked hours. A three-year pay freeze was imposed in 2010 upon the country's public sector

In the Czech Republic, wages stopped growing after 2008; in a number of industrial sectors they actually dropped. Security of employment was weakened. The Republic's government was striving to mitigate the pressures with policies to assist private companies in overcoming pessimistic results without having to dismiss employees or to cut wages.

The Swedish government, through corporate 'crisis agreements', was focusing upon training schemes to support the unemployed. In 2009, 13 per cent of Sweden's GDP was approved for investment in jobs. In keeping with its long-standing welfare state tradition, public expenditure was increased and training opportunities were improved. It was felt that the effects of the crisis had begun to diminish by 2010. Plans were published to protect health care, care for elderly people, and education. Women's wages grew rather faster than those of their male counterparts, although any increases were generally temperate (Starke *et al.*, 2011; Eurofound, 2012a).

> **STOP AND THINK**
>
> What type of conclusion might we make as to the variety of national social policy responses to the 2007–08 global crisis?

The UK's social policy responses to the crisis

The UK's Coalition government social policy strategy in responding to the crisis, under Prime Minister David Cameron and Deputy Nick Clegg, stood in stark contrast to some of the other Western capitalist states discussed above, with its overall retrenchment and growing inequalities. Unemployment levels rose, especially among the younger and Black populations. Incomes remained static or were even reduced. Cutbacks were directed at social benefits, training opportunities, and social services; evidently, few policy measures were put in place for the protection of vulnerable sets of workers. The UK Government has eschewed both protection of welfare services (with the exception of the NHS or pensions to some degree) and economic growth, in favour of repayment of debt (largely due to the necessary nationalisation of ailing banks), requiring austerity budgets leading to reductions of 5 per cent in GDP per annum between 2011 and 2015), and including cutbacks to the welfare sector of an additional £10 billion (announced by the Conservative-Liberal Democrat Coalition in late 2012) (*The Guardian*, 2012b). Nationwide protests took place in 2012, but they tended to be fragmentary in their effectiveness.

In summary, just as the impacts of the crisis, then, were uneven, so the social policy responses have diverged, although the boundaries have been rather blurred: all economies are marked by restraint. The United States of America, under a Democratic Administration, indulged in prodigious extra expenditure (nevertheless inadequate) and added protection for workers. Its reversal of health insurance policy has to be seen as a seminal political moment. The German response is positive, but perhaps misleading, given its earlier neo-liberal reforms. The UK governmental response among the wealthier western capitalist welfare regimes is seemingly atypical in the severity of its austerity measures and the corresponding social inequalities, and in its failure to produce any real economic growth. The smaller liberal nations, calling upon their own welfare state traditions, have managed to stem the early shockwaves of crisis. At the other extreme, given the immense depth of their singular debt crises, the Mediterranean economies have lacked the resources to improve social conditions; indeed, austerity budgets exogenously imposed have worsened conditions for the majority of their citizens. Finally, the Scandinavian response was mitigated because of the traditional welfare state infrastructure, so that it was eventually able to steer these economies away from the direst effects of global crisis.

Conclusion

Having considered these topics in some detail, we may arrive at a set of conclusions. Esping-Andersen's regime model has acted as the methodological standard bearer for enabling comparisons between similar and diverse nation states, although the criteria for comparison have had to be updated in the event of criticisms over what constitutes interventionism in welfare issues, the typology of regimes, and the extent to which neo-liberal reforms have produced a convergence of policy routes among the differing welfare states. One may nevertheless usefully delineate the corporate conservatism of modern Germany, with social insurance as its foundation stone; the archetypal liberalist regime of the USA, whose welfare state orientation had been relegated to the margins since the 1980s; and the archetypal Scandinavian states adopting the social democratic perspective, a set of welfare values and overarching egalitarianism most resistant in the face of global economic downturn and global neo-liberal reform. Indeed, if anything seems to have tested this ostensibly uncomplicated formula for 'typing' nation states in the sphere of social policy, it is the contemporary global economic recession and its attendant social impacts. True, no glaringly obvious pattern is discernible, except that the liberal states, by definition most geared to free and unregulated markets, have been closest to the cause of systemic disaster: they were, arguably, an essential part of the cause! Yet the Mediterranean economies have proved most threatened by the financial disruptions from Wall Street, in contrast to the partially disorientated but stronger Western capitalist economies such as France and Germany. While the social democratic states are, in common with others, affected by global tendencies, they remain sufficiently robust to stave off the direst consequences. Unsurprisingly, the comparative social policy responses to the crisis mirror the intrinsic unevenness of the impacts, so that by the start of 2013 the American and the British policies had barely restored any bearable social prospects for their respective constituencies. Germany has had to modify very little. The smaller but more stable 'liberalist' states of Canada, Australia, and New Zealand have held on to their residual welfare state traditions and soon recovered. In contrast, the Mediterranean regimes' austerity policies are in effect policed by Washington and Frankfurt. Although the traditional social democratic welfarism of the Scandinavian countries was severely bruised by neo-liberal global pressures and right-wing policies in the 1990s, the Swedish welfare state has more or less survived; Sweden is now in the midst of employment training planning. Meanwhile, the UK's continuing social and economic policies of prioritising national debt repayment fundamentally eschew the maintenance of full welfare provision, equality and requisite economic growth.

Summary

In this chapter, you have been introduced to the following topics:

- Esping-Andersen's welfare state regime model, and its critics' suggested modifications.
- Profiles of the archetypal welfare states: corporate conservative, liberal, and social democratic.
- Discrete impacts of the 2008 financial crisis and recession upon archetypal welfare states.
- Comparative social policy responses of nation states to the 2008 financial crisis and recession.

Discussion and review

- To what extent are the differences between national welfare states hidden by the forces of convergence and neo-liberalism?

■ Why do you think the Mediterranean economies appear so vulnerable to economic crisis?

■ What is the significance of inequality in comparing welfare states?

References

Barrientos, A. (2011) 'Poverty, the crisis and social policy responses in developing countries', in K. Farnsworth and Z. Irving (eds.) *Social Policy in Challenging Times: Economic Crisis and Welfare Systems*, Policy Press, Bristol.

Béland, D. and Waddan, A. (2011) 'Social policy and the recent economic crisis in Canada and the United States', in K. Farnsworth and Z. Irving (eds.) *Social Policy in Challenging Times: Economic Crisis and Welfare Systems*, Policy Press, Bristol.

Clarke, J. (2001) 'US welfare: variations on the liberal regime', in A. Cochrane, J. Clarke and S. Gewirtz (eds.) *Comparing Welfare States*, Sage/Open University Press, London.

Clarke, J. (2004) *Changing Welfare, Changing States: New Directions in Social Policy*, Sage, London.

Clarke, J. and Newman, J. (1997) *The Managerialist State*, Sage, London.

Clarke, J., Langan, M. and Williams, F. (2001) 'Remaking welfare: the British welfare regime in the 1980s and 1990s', in A. Cochrane, J. Clarke and S. Gewirtz (eds.) *Comparing Welfare States*, Sage/Open University Press, London.

Deacon, A. (2002) *Perspectives on Welfare: Ideas, Ideologies and Policy Debates*, Open University Press, Buckingham.

Economist (2012) 'Spain in crisis', 30 June.

Esping-Andersen, G. (1990) *The Three Worlds of Welfare Capitalism*, Polity, Cambridge.

Esping-Andersen, G. (ed.) (1996) *Welfare States in Transition: National Adaptations in Global Economies*, Sage, London.

Eurofound (2012a) *Wages and Working Conditions in the Crisis – A Comparative Study*, European Working Conditions Observatory (EWCO), available at http://www.eurofound.europa.eu/docs/ewco/tn1203015s/tn1203015s.pdf.

Eurofound (2012b) *NEETS: Young People Not in Employment, Education or Training: Characteristics, Costs and Policy Responses in Europe*, Publications Office of the European Union, Luxembourg.

Eurofound (2012c) *Industrial Relations and Working Conditions Developments in Europe 2011*, available at http://www.eurofound.europa.eu

Farnsworth, K. and Irving, Z. (2011) 'Varieties of crisis', in K. Farnsworth and Z. Irving (eds.) *Social Policy in Challenging Times: Economic Crisis and Welfare Systems*, Policy Press, Bristol.

Giddens, A. (2007) *Europe in a Global Age*, Polity, Cambridge.

Ginsburg, N. (2001) 'Sweden: the social democratic case', in A. Cochrane, J. Clarke and S. Gewirtz (eds.) *Comparing Welfare States*, Sage/Open University Press, London.

Hemerijck, A. (2002) 'The self-transformation of the European social model(s)', in G. Esping-Andersen (ed.) *Why We Need a New Welfare State*, Oxford University Press, Oxford.

Hill, M. (1995) *Social Policy: A Comparative Analysis*, Prentice-Hall/Harvester Wheatsheaf, London.

Hudson, J. and Kühner, S. (2011) 'Tiptoing through crisis? Re-evaluating the German social model in light of the global recession', in K. Farnsworth and Z. Irving (eds.) *Social Policy in Challenging Times: Economic Crisis and Welfare Systems*, Policy Press, Bristol.

International Labour Organisation (ILO) (2012) *The Youth Employment Crisis: Time for Action*, ILO Conference, Geneva, Switzerland.

Irving, I. (2007) *The State in Canada: Past, Present and Future*, Conference Forum of the Alliance of Seniors, Toronto, Ontario, 6 November.

Krugman, P. (2012) *End This Depression Now!*, Norton, New York.

New York Times (2012) 'Spain in crisis', 1 August, 15 October.

Pierson, C. and Castles, S. (eds.) (2006) *The Welfare State Reader* (2nd edn.), Polity, Cambridge.

Poole, L. (2001) 'Germany: a conservative regime in crisis?', in A. Cochrane, J. Clarke and S. Gewirtz (eds.) *Comparing Welfare States*, Sage/Open University Press, London.

Schwartz, H. (2000) 'Internationalization and two liberal welfare states: Australia and New Zealand', in F. Scharpf and V. Schmidt (eds.) *Welfare and Work in the Open Economy, Vol. 2. Diverse Responses to Common Challenges*, Oxford University Press, Oxford.

Starke, P., Kaasch, A. and van Hooren, F. (2011) 'Comparing social policy responses to global economic crises: constrained partisanship in mature welfare states', Paper presented at ESPAnet Annual Conference, Edinburgh, 6–8 September.

Sykes, R. and Alcock, P. (eds.) (1995) *Developments in European Social Policy: Convergence and Diversity*, Policy Press, Bristol.

Taylor-Gooby, P. (ed.) (2004) *Making a European Welfare State? Convergences and Conflicts Over European Social Policy*, Blackwell, Oxford.

The Guardian (2012) 'George Osborne given stark warning on cuts' impact', 12 September.

The Guardian (2012) 'Catalonia and regional elections', 22 October.

Wilkinson, R. and Pickett, K. (2009) *The Spirit Level: Why More Equal Societies Almost Always Do Better*, Allen Lane, London.

Further reading

Comparative social policy literature is becoming a fertile field for debating the viability of national sovereignty versus the forces of universal convergence.

Esping-Andersen's *Three Worlds of Welfare Capitalism* (Polity, Cambridge, 1990) remains a methodological benchmark. Pierson and Castles' (eds.) *The Welfare State Reader* (Polity, Cambridge, 2006, 2nd edn.) charts the shifts in the welfare state, the impacts of globalisation, and the 'welfare regime' theme. Clarke's essays in *Changing Welfare, Changing States: New Directions in Social Policy* (Sage, London, 2004) are thought-provoking and weigh up the evidence for neo-liberal forces on the one hand and national distinctiveness on the other. Wilkinson and Pickett's *The Spirit Level: Why More Equal Societies Almost Always Do Better* (Allen Lane, London, 2009), measuring equality from country to country, has rapidly become a 'must read', although not without its detractors on grounds of method. Farnsworth and Irving's (eds.) *Social Policy in Challenging Times: Economic Crisis and Welfare Systems* (Policy Press, Bristol, 2011) is an impressive and timely set of articles evaluating social policies in the context of economic crisis, including the USA, Southeast Asia, Ireland, and Scandinavia.

Useful websites

Eurofound (http://www.eurofound.europe.eu)
EU (http://www.Europa.eu)
European Commission (http://www.ec.europa.eu)
IMF (http://www.imf.org/external/index.htm)
World Economic Outlook (WEO) for Data and Statistics (http://www.imf.org/external/data.htm)
United Nations (http://www.un.org)
World Bank (http://www.worldbank.org)
UK Politics/Government (http://www.politics.co.uk)
BBC News (http://www.bbc.co.uk/news/business)
BBC News Europe (http://www.bbc.co.uk/news/Europe)
The Guardian (http://www.guardian.co.uk)
Economist (http://www.Economist.com)

CHAPTER 23

Global Social Policy and the Politics of Globalisation

Harry Cowen

Learning objectives

- To outline the role of the major global social policy institutions, and critiques
- To present the features of global wealth distribution and income inequality
- To identity the activities of transnational corporations and their relationship to global inequalities
- To discuss the competing perspectives on globalisation
- To assess the effects of the global recession upon social welfare and welfare states
- To evaluate the global social policy response to crisis
- To compare selected competing explanations of the global crisis
- To analyse the key developments of the anti-globalisation and 'occupy' movements

Chapter overview

The term 'globalisation' entered into the English language in the past 25 years, although for certain social policy commentators (e.g. Hirst and Thompson, 1999) globalisation is scarcely a new phenomenon, as distinct from the international economy, which operated at the birth of the twentieth century. Globalisation may be defined more for the intensification of supranational connections, and for its penetration into all wakes of life than for its historical novelty. Giddens (2007) views globalisation as a two-way set of procedures, which might most appropriately be characterised by the Internet. George and Wilding (2002, p. 19) define globalisation as: 'the increasing inter-connectedness of the world through the compression of time and space brought about by advances in knowledge and technology as well as by political events and decisions'.

As a result of the growth and faster speed of inter-connections, many aspects of life (economic, social, cultural, personal, urban) have been drawn into the network, whereas its most prominent users are ostensibly the arenas of commerce and industry. For the purposes of this chapter, we are directly concerned with the inter-relationship between globalisation and social policy, and between global industry and social policy issues. In this chapter, then, we outline the ways in which social policy in the modern world is integrally linked to the whole process of globalisation and invariably to its politics. The chapter begins with a discussion of the role of global social and economic institutions, basically those agencies involved in the execution of economic and social policy across national and regional boundaries. This entails scrutiny and critical assessment of those US-based institutions formed at Bretton Woods before the end of the Second World War (the International Monetary Fund and the World Bank), the World Trade Organisation, created much later (1994) as a complement to the Bretton Woods institutions, and the long-standing International Labour Organisation. The section also addresses future alternative proposals for social policy governance. The next section is concerned with the uneven wealth and income distribution between rich and poor, and between the global North and the global South. It investigates the income inequality (usually less dramatic than wealth distribution) and levels of poverty adduced from the UN indices of multiple deprivation. This is followed by an examination of the part played by transnational and multinational corporations in driving the global economy, but also in contributing to the widening of global inequalities. The chapter then proceeds to analyse the contending perspectives on globalisation, drawing upon a range of typologies culled from academic social policy writings, as an aid to interpreting the multiplicity of factual data on global trends (since positivist information is rarely communicated free of values). The next section deals with the global recession of 2008 and its severe effects upon social welfare and the very project of the welfare state, which is followed by an evaluation of the global social policy response to the crisis. The chapter then engages in an assessment of competing explanations of the global crisis and recession, before analysing the collective oppositional responses (stemming from the anti-globalisation movement) to the social policies resulting from the crisis, and the implicit forms of protest. The final section derives a set of conclusions. But we commence with the analysis of global social policy.

SPOTLIGHT

The purpose and accountability of global institutions

Key issues in the study of global social policy relate to the stated goals of the major world institutions, what they have achieved, and how they may be brought to account. Hence, it is instructive to juxtapose official statements with those of their critics.

'The IMF provides loans to countries that have trouble making their international payments and cannot otherwise find sufficient financing on affordable terms . . . The IMF also provides concessional loans to low-income countries to help them develop their economies and reduce poverty.' (International Monetary Fund – Statement of Aims)

'The main purpose of the formation of the World Bank was to reduce poverty across the globe. The bank grants loans to developing countries.' (World Bank – Statement of Aims)

'Sometimes the IMF program left the country just as impoverished but with more debt and an even richer ruling elite.' (Stiglitz, 2002, p. 52)

'It is not easy to give a definitive answer as to what is Bank social policy . . . (But) (nowhere) have we found evidence of the Bank using the language and analytical frameworks of European social democracy or the democratic class struggle.' (Deacon, 2007, p. 37)

'The problem is . . . the release from globalization which both economic agents and nation states have been able to negotiate. They have been able to operate so freely because the people of the world have no global means of restraining them. Our task surely is not to overthrow globalization, but to capture it, and to use it as a vehicle for humanity's first global democratic revolution.' (Monbiot, 2003, p. 23)

Global social policy and institutions

Deacon (1997, 2007) suggests that in the light of the forces and pressures of globalisation, one should concentrate more upon global social policy and its attendant institutions than upon individual national state policies.

The main global agencies responsible for economic and social policy-related delivery are:

- *The International Monetary Fund* (IMF), set up in 1944 at Bretton Woods, is orientated towards economic growth, and indeed has championed the framework of neo-liberalism, but tenders scant social policy advice. It provided assistance after 1989 to a number of economies in Central and Eastern Europe in instituting their social security schemes, given the huge and sudden rise in unemployment in those newly 'market-oriented' nations freed from the domination of the Soviet Union.

- *The World Bank*, also based in Washington, DC, is more overt in its mission to enable social development in struggling economies so as to defeat poverty, acting as a kind of safety net for the poor.

- *The Organisation for Economic Co-operation and Development* (OECD), comprising the richest Western capitalist nations, proposes welfare less as a burden and more as an investment, and its origins lay in encouraging European economic growth. Its contemporary goals are to contribute to social and economic welfare; to match social policy objectives to budgetary constraints; to facilitate the nurturing of human potential; to organise the combination of public with private responsibilities; and to achieve greater policy coherence.

Deacon has interpreted these 'new pathways' as representing a far more balanced approach to economic and social factors than either the IMF or World Bank, both heavily influenced by the United States, and more akin to the European management of social and economic policy.

- *The International Labour Organisation* (ILO), based in Geneva, is much more concerned, considering its post-Second World War social democratic traditions, with the pursuit and maintenance of workers' conditions and wage levels than the key Washington 'market'-oriented institutions, which have been hostile since the 1980s to the ILO's monitoring of global social and labour standards. It was consistently engaged in a battle with the World Bank's strategy of 'privatising' pensions and state social security.

- *The World Trade Organisation* (WTO), based in New York, also driven by the neo-liberal agenda (through free trade), has viewed the maintenance of decent labour standards as antithetical to free trade, and has prohibited any free trade agreement clauses that refute cutting social spending.

- *The United Nations* and the plethora of *United Nations* agencies are explicitly committed to the formulation of social policy at the global level. Such agencies include the United Nations Development Programme (UNDP), the World Health Organisation (WHO), and the United Nations Research Institute for Social Development (UNRISD). UN Social Summit conferences have facilitated debate on social policy and social development.

While the WHO has clearly played an important part in overseeing health developments, it has received criticism since the 1990s for its economistic discourse and its close relationship to the WTO (and for trading in health). The Economic and Social Committee (ECOSOC) is the UN body formally responsible for economic and social policies, but the United Nations Department of Economic and Social Affairs (UDESA) produces major reports and is involved in key initiatives. The United Nations Education, Scientific and Cultural Organisation (UNESCO), based in Paris, supports nations in their creation of education policies, prioritising the pursuit of peace and human development over economic growth. The United Nations Children's Fund (UNICEF) is concerned with the World Bank and in influencing their policies. It also feeds into the Millennium Development Goals Project. On the other hand, its commercial ventures with private companies have invited criticism on the grounds of hypocracy and unacceptability.

■ *Non-governmental organisations (NGOs) and international NGOs* are organisations or groups independent of government, promoting the interests of the poor, while protecting the environment, providing basic social services, and undertaking community development (World Bank Operational Directive 14.70). Many maintain official relations with UNESCO, and include Oxfam and the African Network Campaign on Education for All. Among the top global NGOs are Amnesty, Human Rights Watch, Partners in Health, and Save the Children (*Global Journal*, 2013). There are also global knowledge networks, such as the Global Forum for Health Research.

Undoubtedly supportive of the idea of global social policy institutions, Joseph Stiglitz (2002), a former Director of the World Bank, finds the IMF, the World Bank, and the WTO to be 'full of broken promises', and makes the following points. The introduction of the market with ideological fervour has led to deleterious consequences, particularly from the IMF. The most overt of these changes was during the 1980s of the Reagan and Thatcher monetarist policies. The IMF and the World Bank became 'the new missionary institutions' which pushed massive loans and debt onto poor developing nations such as Botswana and a number of Latin American countries. There is no way of unearthing what an ostensible public institution such as the IMF is really doing. Through the 1980s and 1990s, the 'Washington Consensus' advice rested upon privatisation, fiscal austerity, and market liberalisation. Given that under the free market climate poverty rocketed and incomes plummeted, the whole mind-set of interests and ideology has to be challenged (Stiglitz, 2002, pp. 214–52).

Deacon offers a 'Global Policy Strategy for the Future', embracing a global governance reform agenda. His reforms entailed the social regulation of global trade; making the Bretton Woods institutions more accountable and widening their brief; reforming the United Nations so as to enhance the financial support from the United States; strengthening global, political, legal, and social rights (e.g. right to a minimum income) so as to strengthen a real sense of global citizenship; and the associated empowering of international civil society. His revised thinking on the strategy (Deacon, 2007) reflected an emphasis upon global advocacy organisations, but also a serious engagement in encouraging the powerful private multinational corporations to be socially responsible, and facilitating debates with the anti-globalisation movement regarding global alternatives.

David Held, in his *Global Covenant* (2004), prioritises the institutional structure of global decision-making, but does not see globalisation as heralding an end to the nation-state. Rather, he perceives globalisation as allowing the continuation of politics by a new set of methods operating at many diverse levels. His proposed reforms of the global governance aim at promoting coordinated state action for dealing with common issues; strengthening the institutions capable of functioning in an effective manner; and developing multicultural rules and procedures that commit both minor and major political powers to such a multicultural framework. Held's detailed proposals for creating social democratic world governance bodies include:

- the inauguration of a completely reformed General Assembly of the United Nations, embracing states, IGOs, social movements and citizen groups, etc.;
- setting up regional parliaments, and enhancing existing ones such as the EU's European Parliament (see Chapter 24);
- making the Bretton Woods institutions specifically more open and accountable to the respective global and regional bodies;
- by directly engaging with a social policy agenda, forming new global governance structures;
- the application of general referenda at global and regional levels which cross-cut nation-states and nations in the event of 'contested priorities'.

However, critics of international social policy institutions have questioned their very notion. Hirst and Thompson's position (1999) is central in this respect. They argue that the internationalised economy is far from novel, and even less integrated and open than in the Victorian era. Furthermore, few multinational companies are essentially transnational, since the majority are based nationally and trade multinationally. Again, the international economy is not fully global, being concentrated until recently in Europe, Japan, and the USA (and now China in 2013?). The leading capitalist economic powers, constituting the G8, are in a position to pressurise financial markets and their networks, meaning that regulation and control of markets and market-based economies is not out of the question. More likely, Hirst and Thompson continue, 'globalization' is more of an ideological myth (see the debates on the nature of globalisation). 'The opposite of a globalized economy', they contend, 'is not . . . a nationally inward-looking one, but an open world market based on trading nations and regulated to a greater or lesser degree by both the public policies of nation-states and supranational agencies' (Hirst and Thompson, 1999, p. 16).

In summary, the Bretton Woods global institutions continue to represent the institutional power locus of Western capitalism, placing economic criteria before human factors, while the United Nations, the OECD, and the ILO have ostensibly reflected a more socially orientated practice. But the effectiveness of the UN and its agencies has also come into question. In the face of such seemingly unaccountable global bodies, the actual notion of truly democratic global decision-making organisations may be countered by arguments that strong nation-states are still able to control and modify market and financial mechanisms (yet consider the case of the 2008 global crisis!). In the following section, however, we trace the ways in which global resources remain uneasily distributed between rich and poor nations, and between rich and poor populations.

> **STOP AND THINK**
>
> How may we distinguish between the respective roles of the IMF and the World Bank? How might they be made more accountable?

Wealth distribution and income inequality

Wealth distribution

The figures for the world's distribution of wealth between individuals at the start of the twenty-first century are stark (*The Guardian*, 2006; UNU-WIDER, 2006) (see Figure 23.1):

- 1 per cent of adults own 40 per cent of all global wealth;
- 10 per cent of adults own 85 per cent of total global assets;

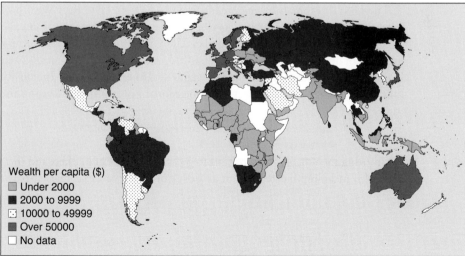

World Wealth Levels in Year 2000

Wealth per capita ($)
- Under 2000
- 2000 to 9999
- 10000 to 49999
- Over 50000
- No data

Figure 23.1 The world distribution of household wealth, wealth per capita, 2000

Source: UNU-WIDER (2006)

- 50 per cent of the world's adults own 1 per cent of global wealth;
- the top 1 per cent own almost 40 times as much as the bottom 50 per cent.

Focusing on the geographical distribution of wealth, *Global Outlook*'s 2012 rankings of estimated purchasing power include those shown in Table 23.1

Income distribution

Global income distribution is less marked, but still seen by many as being morally unacceptable. From research conducted at the World Bank in the early twenty-first century (figures from Milanovic, 2011):

- approximately 9 per cent of the world's population receives 50 per cent of global income;
- the top 1 per cent of population receives 13 per cent of total income;
- the bottom 50 per cent of population receives 6.6 per cent of total income;
- citizenship (roughly location) explains some 60 per cent of variability in personal incomes globally.

Over the past 10 years, economic inequality has been growing, particularly in developed countries. According to World Bank data, income inequality tends to be lower in Northern Europe, especially nations such as Sweden, Norway, and Finland. But it is also low in countries like Ethiopia and Afghanistan. The highest levels during the 2000s have been in areas such the Central African Republic, Angola, South Africa, and Haiti. In most OECD countries, household incomes grew faster for the richest 10 per cent than for the poorest 10 per cent in 2011.

The UNDP Human Development Report of 2010, 'The Real Wealth of Nations: Pathways to Human Development', is especially revealing on the incidence of inequality across the globe. The UNDP now applies three new measures of human development in the world: inequality, through an adjusted Human Development Index (HDI); gender, through a Gender Inequality Index; and poverty, through a Multidimensional Poverty Index. During the

Table 23.1 Purchasing power per capita from GDP in 2012, selected countries (US dollars)

1 Qatar – 106,284
2 Luxembourg – 79,649
7 USA – 49,601
15 Sweden – 41,129
23 United Kingdom – 36,605
115 Paraguay – 5293
181 Democratic Republic of Congo – 364

Source: Figures and estimates from the IMF's *World Economic Outlook Database* (2012).

past two decades, clear improvements have occurred globally. People were generally healthier over the period, had more wealth, and were better educated. From 1990 to 2010, the average HDI grew by 18 per cent, reflecting transparent gains in literacy and income, school enrolments, and life expectancy.

Notwithstanding this seemingly optimistic scenario, a notable volatility was detected in people's experiences. Ninety per cent of the 135 countries from the UNDP's sample had enjoyed progress. Yet the inequalities were striking. The HIV epidemic had a huge impact in Sub-Saharan Africa. Adult mortality rose in the former Soviet Union nations. Most progress took place in China, Indonesia, South Korea, and Tunisia. There were big improvements in health and education; but in the case of health, improvements were substantial, although slowing down. Viewing the broad picture, the divide between developed and developing nations has continued; economic growth remains vastly uneven. While narrowing, the gaps in human development across the two decades remained startling. Since the 1980s, income inequality grew in many more countries (most notably in former Soviet countries, and in the majority of countries in the Pacific region and East Asia) than in those experiencing a reduction.

Of course, since the 2010 Report, global economic conditions have considerably negated advances made by nations with positive human development. The 2012 mid year report notes the natural disasters and the global financial crisis, which has slowed progress. The 'Millennium Development Goals Report' (UNDESA, 2012) notes that a particular area of concern includes the slow decrease in levels of '[v]ulnerable employment – defined as the share of unpaid family workers and own-account workers in total employment'. Global economic growth was beginning to slow down generally in mid 2011, by an estimated average 2.8 per cent over the previous year. This trend was expected to continue into 2013.

Social inequalities

The UNDP's Human Development Index (HDI) adjusted for inequality measures the level of human development of people in a society that accounts for inequality. Results show that:

- The average loss in the HDI due to inequality is some 22 per cent.
- Nations with less human development tend to show greater inequality in more dimensions.
- Citizens of Sub-Saharan Africa suffer the greatest HDI losses due to major inequalities across all three dimensions (inequality, gender, poverty). The new measure of gender inequality was introduced because the disadvantages women and girls encounter constitute a prime source of inequality.
- Losses in achievement due to gender inequalities vary from 17 to 85 per cent. The most equal nations are Denmark, Sweden, Switzerland, and the Netherlands.

- Countries with an unequal distribution of human development also experience high measures of inequality between women and men, and vice versa (e.g. the Central African Republic, Haiti, Mozambique).

On the Multidimensional Poverty Index (MPI), findings were as follows:

- Approximately 1.75 billion in the 104 nations surveyed live in multi-dimensional poverty.
- Sub-Saharan Africa contains the highest level of multidimensional poverty. However, 50 cent of the globe's multidimensionally poor reside in South Asia (51 per cent or 844 million people), and more than 28 per cent (or 458 million) live in Africa.
- A high MPI coinciding with low-income poverty (or higher) suggests that there is a lot to gain from enhancing the delivery of basic public services.

The 2012 'World Development Report' (World Bank, 2012) states that globalisation has removed some of the constraints to greater equality for women. However, not all females have benefited. Often women are the ones for whom existing constraints are most binding. In the absence of public policy and despite changing perceptions through greater access to information, globalization alone cannot and will not make gender inequality go away. 'Wide gaps are still prominent in various areas. Public action aimed at closing existing gender gaps in endowments, agency, and access to economic opportunities is therefore necessary ...' (World Bank, 2012, p. 271). A 'Global Wage Report 2008/9' (ILO, 2009), a study of wage differentials between men and women, indicates parallel findings.

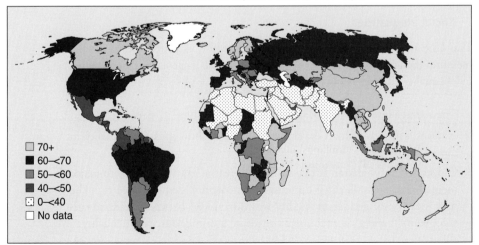

Female Labour Force Participation Rates (Percentage)

Figure 23.2 Female labour force participation rates (percentages)

Source: World Bank (2012, p. 199), ILO (2010)

Income growth is weighted towards the richest. Improvements have occurred, but the income gap, especially between North and South, is wide. Close to 2 billion people are living in poverty. Gender inequalities have certainly decreased, but only marginally so. There is little evidence that globalisation is reducing inequalities.

In the next section, we examine the activities of transnational corporation, one of the foremost agents of globalisation.

Transnational corporations and global inequalities

What are transnational corporations?

Transnational corporation (TNCs) may be defined in the following way: they tend to control what goes on in an economy in two or more countries; they profit from differences in such aspects as the price of labour, market conditions, and state fiscal practices in different countries; they possess an element of geographical mobility, and are often able to move their resources across the globe; they boost consumerism globally; and they are able to exert considerable economic and social power on a global scale.

The economic and social power of transnational corporations

The wealth and resources of the TNCs are such that they dwarf those of some nation-states, endowing the corporations with enormous economic and social power globally, as witnessed in Table 23.2.

Adverse effects of transnational corporations on nation-states

It is argued here that TNCs exert a negative effect upon nation-states' policy decisions, divesting nations of their traditional sovereignty. This is the case for

Table 23.2 Selective figures comparing economic power of assets (measured in sales) of transnational corporations and the GDP of countries, 2009–10

USA GDP ($millions) 14,256,300
Switzerland GDP ($millions) 500,260
Walmart sales ($millions) 408,214
Greece GDP ($millions) 329,924
Bank of America sales ($millions) 150,450
Kuwait GDP ($millions) 148,024
Royal Bank of Scotland sales ($millions) 91,767
Morocco GDP ($millions) 90,859
Bangladesh GDP ($millions) 89,378
United Health Group sales ($ millions) 87,138

Source: Cohen and Kennedy (2013) from *Fortune 500* and World Bank.

a number of reasons. First, local capital finds it difficult to compete with corporations' global production and selling resources, causing local employers to lower their wage costs, worsening general employment conditions and lowering the quality of goods or services offered. Second, the strategies of TNCs do not necessarily coincide with a government's policies, such as those on employment or regional development. Finally, many TNCs may exact a powerful negative influence on modes of consumption, including lethal cigarette smoking encouraged by global cigarette manufacturers through the aegis of advertising and mass promotional techniques. They also have a direct influence on a population's health care, as in the case of multinational or transnational pharmaceutical corporations.

The huge size of these pharmaceutical corporations places them in an almost unassailable position regarding developments in medicine. Some of them are listed among the world's largest corporations in any industrial sector. Given their private market positioning they are, of course, obliged to focus upon profit maximisation, arguably the very antithesis of health care (Goldacre, 2009). The American corporation, Johnson and Johnson, received total revenues of $61.9 billion in 2010, ranking it 103 globally on Fortune's top 200 list. UK-based GlaxoSmithKline declared total revenues of $45.3 billion (£28.3 billion), ranking it 168th on the list. Bayer Health Care, Germany, declared $22.3 billion, ranking it 154th on the list, while Roche, Switzerland showed revenues of $47.35 billion, ranking it 171st on the list. Finally, Sanofi, France, with $41.99 billion, ranked 181 on Fortune. It is estimated that the pharmaceutical industry globally is worth some £150 billion. In the United Kingdom, the industry is the third most profitable commercial activity, following in the wake of only the finance and tourist industries. The population spends around £7 billion per annum in purchasing pharmaceutical drugs (Goldacre, 2009, pp. 201–2).

A significant part of the market for medical drugs is for cancer care and cancer research. The estimated global market for all cancer drugs in 2008 was $48 billion. The annual expenditure on research and development of cancer drugs varies from $6.5 billion to $8 billion, way above those of any government or research charities such as Cancer Research UK or Cancer America on the development of drugs. This indicates that any new drugs tend to be those with the highest commercial outcome rather than those likely to yield the greatest public health benefits (James, 2011, p. 2). Sales on approximately 19 anti-cancer drugs were in excess of $1 billion in 2009. As James (2011, p. 2) suggests, any national health system in the world is going to experience gross difficulty in consistently having to purchase these drugs for their patients. And in many of the poorest nations, access to the most effective treatments, considering the burgeoning price of the drugs, is limited.

STOP AND THINK

To what extent do TNCs hold ultimate power in determining global social policy?

To recap, the global economic power of the TNCs, in terms of resources and turnover, exceeds that of many nation-states' gross domestic product, and provides them with immense political leverage in the global marketplace, often juxtaposed to the interests of nations, and often in tandem with governmental interests. They affect the health and welfare of millions of citizens. The drug TNCs are a case in point of corporate power pressing for profits over human needs, including cancer patients' care and recovery. How one responds to these developments of 'globalisation' and transnational power and their effects on social policy, depends upon the perspective adopted. The theorisation of perspectives is discussed in the following section.

The contending perspectives on globalisation

The social policy literature has produced various typologies of contending, sometimes overlapping perspectives. Goldblatt *et al.* (1999) suggest three fundamental ones, namely the hyper-globalist perspective, the transformationalist-globalist perspective, and the sceptical perspective. Another typology identifies the sponsors' camp, the sceptics' camp, the doubters' camp, and the hecklers' camp (Fitzpatrick, 2001), while a basic division of 'hyper-globalisers' and 'globalisation sceptics' replaces the traditional political divide of 'right' versus 'left' (Steger, 2009). Whereas the hyper-globalisers argue that since the 1960s a 'de-territorialisation' of politics, rule, and governance has transpired, the globalisation sceptics have emphasised the continuance and significance of the nation-state and the growth of regional blocs.

George and Wilding's (2002) comprehensively annotated typology, incorporating all of the above, identifies five types of overarching perspectives: the technological enthusiasts, Marxian pessimists, the plural pragmatists, the sceptic internationalists, and the political economists. Most favourably disposed towards globalisation, the technological enthusiasts (e.g. economist W.W. Rostow, sociologist Manuel Castells, political theorist Francis Fukuyama) tend to construe globalisation as a post-Second World War process deriving from the new technologies in telecommunications and transport, which constitute globalisation's driving force. Furthermore, they argue, technology and economics determine the political and the cultural: the dynamics of technology are irresistible. The nation-state may lose most of its powers to the multinational corporations, but the results of new technology are undeniably socially desirable.

Diametrically opposed to the enthusiasts is the 'Marxist' perspective (Harvey, 2011, 2012), which contends that the prime driving force of globalisation is the very logic of capitalism, a system in constant pursuit of increased profitability; it is a process stretching back through the centuries to the birth of Western European capitalism, along with the whole system of finance, production, and consumption. The social consequences are adverse: capitalist globalisation is resulting in a permanent increase in poverty and inequality; people's values and behaviour are moulded by materialist global media.

George and Wilding's plural pragmatists, such as Robertson (1992) and Giddens (1999), interpret globalisation's thrust as pluralistic rather than engaged with a factor such as technology or the economic system: they also include political forces, ideology, and cultural facets. The results of globalisation are nothing so dramatic as the enthusiasts or Marxists claim, and there is no inevitable convergence of West and East under the former's domination. The sceptic internationalists generally react to the technological optimists, challenging their premises on empirical grounds; they are sceptical that national borders have lost their *raison d'etre*, and argue that globalisation is an ideological tool (i.e. it is the neo-liberal market writ large).

Political economy, the final approach in George and Wilding's typology, holds that an inter-connected series of driving forces encompass: the expansion of knowledge, the logic of capitalism, the power of technology, and the policies of governments. Globalisation's impacts may be viewed as economic, with uneven growth trajectories; political, whereby supranational institutions such as the World Bank constrain the role of the state in economic and social policy formulation; and socio-economic, given the continued uneven economic development between and within nations. As this whole area is a greatly contested one, the following section probes a more detailed rationale of the discrete perspectives.

CONTROVERSY AND DEBATE

Perspectives on globalisation

The most trenchant controversy surrounding political perspectives on globalisation, extending beyond academic analysis to the defensive barriers of the international conference hall and forceful street protest, is the one between the enthusiastic supporters of global capitalism and those advocating its displacement. Such conflict is here captured in snapshot by statements from Friedman and Callinicos.

The hyper-globaliser: Thomas Friedman

'So then what does the Lexus (Japanese car – *sic*.) represent? It represents a . . . fundamental age-old human drive – the drive for sustenance, improvement, prosperity and modernization – as it is played out in today's globalization system. The Lexus represents all the burgeoning global markets, financial institutions and computer technologies with which we pursue higher living standards today . . . (While) different people have different access to the new markets and technologies that characterize the globalization system, and derive highly unequal benefits from them, this doesn't change the fact that these markets and technologies are the defining economic tools of the day and everyone is either directly or indirectly affected by them.' (Friedman, 2000, pp. 32–3)

The anti-globaliser: Alex Callinicos

'Neo-liberalism has failed even to restore the rates of economic growth ... during the Long Boom of the 1950s and 1960s ... let alone to reduce poverty and inequality ... The process of competitive accumulation is responsible for capitalism's chronic tendency towards crises of over-investment and profitability. The competitive struggle among the multinational corporations that dominate the contemporary world economy is also the main driving force behind processes of environmental destruction ... The major problems facing humankind – poverty, social injustice, economic instability, environmental destruction, and war – have the same source, in the capitalist system: the solution to these problems must, accordingly, be a radical one.' (Callinicos, 2003, pp. 65–6)

A key figure among the pro-globalisers or 'hyper-globalisers' is Martin Wolf (2004). Wolf's argument proceeds in the following way. The liberal market economy should be upheld because of its long-term track record in supporting democracy and freedom and enabling prosperity. The democratic state and the market interdependently reinforce each other. This is not to deny the limitations of global neo-liberalism. Notwithstanding technological advances, the global institutions' performance has been inadequate, especially in the financial arena. Political will is crucial, so there is cause for optimism over globalisation. Political fragmentation, rather than economic integration, has acted as a barrier to all-round success for globalisation. The persistence of inequality incurred by individuals across the world rests on the institutional quality of institutions. International economic integration – that is, better politics – is the most viable counterforce to the vastly unequal division of states.

Thomas Friedman's pro-global *The Lexus and the Olive Tree* (2000) fixes the period of globalisation (inaccurately) from 1989 onwards. For Friedman, the interconnected technological system of globalisation has replaced that of the Cold War years (from 1948) but is more intense and incorporates more of the world's population. Where it is completely dissimilar from the international economy of the 1900s is in its complete domination by American power, by American culture, and 'the American dollar'. Hence, proclaims Friedman, global = America. In similar vein to Wolf's, his perspective is not one supportive of a perfect system, but nevertheless one in support of the WTO, the IMF, and the other major capitalist transnational institutions. Globalisation is a new technological, contemporaneous system, but it unarguably possesses defects. The challenge is to discover a balance between community awareness and the ability to survive within the system: 'America has more assets, and fewer liabilities, in relation to this system than any other major country. Globalization is "almost" irreversible (p. 407) ... However, from banks to mutual funds to hedge funds ... bad lending on a global scale poses a real financial threat to the system' (p. 457).

The globalisation sceptics

Sceptics argue that the image of the 'twilight of the nation-state' is an over-statement of globalisation's political weight. Supranational bodies may have become equated with the global environment, yet many of these supranational bodies are about inter-governmental cooperation, and tend to vary widely. Hirst and Thompson view the hyper-globalisers' globalisation as myth: more, it is an ideological product, uncritical of what is actually taking place in the world. Any substantial shift of investment and employment towards the developing nations has not transpired. And the process is hardly deterministic. The major economic powers 'have the capacity to exert powerful government pressures over financial markets and other economic tendencies ... Global markets are thus by no means beyond regulation and control' (Hirst and Thompson, 1999, p. 4). The nation-state retains its importance as a world political actor and decision-maker.

The transformationalists

John Keane (2009) opts for a global civil society, produced without violent power: a new political vision. A global civil society implies new democratic ways of living and a fresh manner of viewing global institutions. His critique of current globalisation is that 'our world is today coming under the influence of a new form of governmental power: cosmocracy'. This 'describes in simplified form a type of institutionalised power that defies all previous accounts of different governmental forms ... an emergent system of political power ... without precedent' (Keane, 2003, p. 97). Its predominant features are:

- the first ever world polity, with its web of inter-dependence;
- 'a conglomeration of interlocking and overlapping sub-state, state and supra-state institutions and multi-dimensional processes that interact, and have political and social effects, on a global scale' (Keane, 2003, p. 98);
- a dynamic polity: a 'conglomeration of institutions shaped by several structural principles' (Keane, 2003, p. 102);
- but still problematic, because of: the unaccountability of a number of its institutions, and the USA's dominant power; the lack of democracy; the accompanying encouragement of 'fatalism' due to cosmocracy's complexity, a fatalism as 'enemy of both global civil society and of the goal of injecting positive sum-powers and public accountability into the system of cosmocracy that frames it' (Keane, 2003, p. 127).

The Marxists

David Harvey (2011) emphasises capital flows as the mainspring of the capitalist system which determines globalisation: the capitalist thrust to accumulate capital and multiply profits. Permanent accumulation is unfeasible (since capitalists compete against each other for better sites and superior technologies), hence the system's susceptibility to periodic crises. Such crises can spiral out of control, creating global crisis. Therefore, we extend Harvey's prognosis in the section on 'explanations of the global crisis' below.

Ferguson *et al.* (2002) contend that the system has indeed become 'welfare' capitalism'. The immiseration of a workforce is no longer viewed as automatically benefiting the capitalists, who need healthy workers with sufficient education and training geared to a technological society, supplemented by the delivery of social, welfare, and educational services benefiting labour. On the other hand, social control is another motivation behind welfare within the system, the goal being to minimise the very costs of state welfare leads to policies for controlling industrial action such as withholding entitlements and benefits and to cutting back on expenditure for social welfare services. Finally, suggest Ferguson *et al.*, the level of 'class' response retains its significance, since the potential of working-class collective action motivates social policy.

In summary, typologies appear to gravitate around the support, opposition to or modification of globalisation. We have seen that the avid supporters of globalisation and its technological creativity nevertheless concede the recurrence of negative outcomes, but for pro-globalisers the latter become an occasion for painful hand-wrenching if not much else. Those who call for a civil society deliver a plea for a complete change of 'mind-set' in breaking down the determinism of global thinking, whereas Marxists will not countenance such 'idealism' unless the unstable capitalist system itself (of which its modern form is globali-

> **STOP AND THINK**
>
> Why do you think the contending perspectives on globalisation are in the end political?

sation) is replaced. Which is not to deny that the system does provide health and welfare facilities (to keep workers productive): it does, but generally when times are good. When they are not, social welfare is dispensable and class conflicts re-emerge. We now turn in the next section to a current, wholesale manifestation of globalisation in bad times, namely the recent global financial crisis and its redoubtable consequences for social policy.

Global recession and social welfare

Undoubtedly, the latest global economic recession (2008) is the seminal event bearing upon social welfare provision and contemporary social policy, and this situation will continue in a number of countries well into the current decade. Also, as covered in the chapter on the European Union (Chapter 24), the negative fallout for human welfare has been compounded for certain European nations by the more recent crisis over the euro currency (the Eurozone crisis) in 2012. However, it is pertinent to note that preceding the latest global recession, a world economic crisis occurred at the beginning of the new century, leading to the collapse of Enron and the media corporation WorldCom in the USA; following this crisis, the world economy was the recipient of voluminous tranches of debt created by the practice of 'sub-prime lending' in the financial sector (explained in greater detail below), as it moved into a new wave of expansion, considered dangerous by a few but hastily dismissed by the official global institutions. Indeed, the IMF's 2007 Report confidently stated that the 'strong global economy' was likely to continue! The recession commenced in the United States, with the collapse of major financial traders on the New York Stock Exchange (Wall Street). These financial corporations, buoyed up by the neo-liberal market climate, had been involved in high-risk speculation and the 'sub-prime' lending. The purpose of their sub-prime loans was to maintain the housing boom from 1995 to the mid 2000s. This entailed agreeing to high-risk loans to applicants with poor or without any credit records; however, investment banks (in the business of buying or selling securities on the stock market) were handed the task by government of delivering the mortgage lending policy. These financial institutions transformed the mortgage loan assets into investment bonds, and sold them on to other financial concerns, which proved problematic in that the borrowers who had taken out the loans in the first place were unable to keep up with payments when interest rates rose rapidly after 2004 (Gamble, 2009). The myriad financial speculations were simultaneously reinforced by a near absence of consistent regulation to protect vulnerable groups and the whole community. Such ideological myopia was not the exclusive preserve of the traders. Alan Greenspan, Chairman of the US Federal Reserve from 1987 to 2006, was impressed by the irrational ebullience of the markets, but took no preventative action.

The whole of the US financial sector was soon in recession. The housing bubble burst in 2008. Of concern for social policy was the immediate and shattering impact on ordinary Americans' housing, and the consequential increase in homelessness. The crisis spread globally, necessitating huge government packages to rescue national banks, as in the UK and Europe, while China, cognisant of the ramifications of global collapse, made available billions of dollars for financial bailouts. Even Australia, through its unusually high rise in house prices, became an early victim of the credit crisis.

To briefly review the cataclysmic turn of events, the global economic system, not without precedent, was thrown into major crisis as a result of unregulated financial speculation and lending in the United States, in the wake of neo-liberal boom conditions for up to a decade, producing mass homelessness in the globe's wealthiest society and grave uncertainty for millions regarding their future welfare. So what were the social policy responses to the global crisis on the part of the global social policy institutions, a theme to which we now turn?

Global social policy response to crisis

One might have expected a powerful redirection of the IMF's and World Bank's social policies and practices in their response to the deepest financial crisis of modern times, yet redirections were minimal: at the most, they have targeted poverty alleviation in the global South. From 2008, agreements were made with Eastern European nations, Pakistan, and El Salvador, entailing economy contractions, public sector wage freezes, and cutbacks in budgets, rather than growth and welfare protection. The global institutions' lending policies continued more or less undisturbed. A 'minimum social protection package' was agreed by the UN Chief Executive Board for Co-ordination. More directly, however, the G20 summit of 2009 made $1.1 trillion available for nations in crisis, although only $100 billion was for development, including social development (Deacon, 2011). In Chapter 22, we look at the social policy responses of particular nation-states to the global crisis and recession. Having outlined the series of events leading to global crisis, we examine below the competing reasons as to why the crisis developed in the first place.

Competing explanations of the global crisis

Once appraised of the facts as to the current recession's events, it is just as prudent for social policy practitioners and researchers to comprehend why they happened. Explanations vary from right to left of the political spectrum, as well as from partial to overarching causes.

Marglin (2008) proffers a critique of the 'market' and neo-liberalism. He focuses on the ideological aspects of capitalist economies, specifically the economist's individualism and the perpetuated myths of free market economics. Economists have signalled a free-for-all in the self-enhancement of individual fortunes through the market. Market relationships justify the isolation of self-motivated individuals, a situation antithetical to conceptions of community and strategies involving caring for others. Where individual consumption patterns assume priority, social connections prove worthless.

Political theorist Michael Sandel (2012) avoids challenging the idea of the market *per se*, but his empirically rich, moral assault on how markets have in fact functioned through recent decades does place market relationships in a questionable light. Everything is a saleable commodity, including citizenship for immigrants with an ability to pay. Market values take precedence; they have marginalised non-market values in every sphere of society, including family life and even personal relationships. A climate is created for the acceptance of non-caring, non-communal values and behaviour: 'sometimes, market values crowd out nonmarket norms worth caring about' (Sandel, 2012, p. 155). Behind the crisis lies the death of morality. For instance, the insurance industry became a speculative investment arena, where life insurance policies were purchased from retired people and sold on to investors, a practice tantamount to gambling on the life expectancy of older people. By the mid 2000s, a prodigious secondary market in life insurance had become big business carried out by hedge funds and major financial institutions engaged in 'spin-life' policies. From 2007, key investment banks such as Goldman Sachs and Bear Stearns (both of which collapsed) were promoting such policies and resisting state regulation. Yet even by 2009 the millions rendered jobless, 'did not prompt a fundamental rethinking of markets . . . Notwithstanding . . . voices of protest, serious debate about the role and reach of markets remains largely absent from our political life' (pp. 12–13).

Hancock and Zahawi (2011) present a guarded defence of the capitalist market. Their theme is our actual behaviour, and the explanation rests in the realms of human nature: the failure to understand human nature resulted in the massive global crisis. The 'Masters of Nothing' extremists, in their greed, their irrational behaviour, and their reckless dealings, accumulated mistakes in financial policy that exacerbated the scale of the crisis. They predict a recurrence of the crisis failing any overt challenge to the irrational behaviour, although they cautiously state as a caveat that change will not be easy, 'human nature being what it is' (Hancock and Zahawi, 2011, p. 219). In common with a host of mainstream economists (now wise after the event?), they restate the inadequacies of mathematical economic models. On the surface, the authors' implicit support of global neo-liberalism is tempered by their misgivings: 'Free market capitalism can only work effectively if it enjoys public trust. That trust is undermined unless the financial industry – a symbol of capitalism – shows it is founded on trust, mutual respect, and an honourable relationship between debtor and creditor' (ibid.).

Paul Krugman, the Keynesian economist, claims that any explanation of global depression must stress the historical dimension, and grasp the transformations in the financial system as witnessed by events relating to 'the huge turnaround of fortunes' in the Asian, Latin American, and Japanese economies. When the bubble burst, the consequences were more severe than anyone imagined, because 'the financial system had changed in ways that nobody appreciated' (Krugman, 2008, p. 152). The sheer size of the US housing bubble influenced the economic depression. Housing, by 2006, 'probably overvalued by more than 50 per cent', culminated in negative equity. In turn, this affected the lenders, and 'triggered the collapse of the shadow banking system' (p. 169). Why did this take on a global dimension? The character of the financial system over the previous decade and a half had been transformed by the rise of financial globalisation, with investors in each nation holding substantial stakes in other countries. The demand side of economics, for Krugman, has received insufficient attention from economic theorists and policy makers due to the politics of economic policy. Neo-liberalism's adoption of monetarism has illequipped the Western capitalist policy-makers to deal with failures on the demand side. Yet '(depression) economics is back' (p. 184).

Graham Turner's (2008) main explanation of the crisis hinges upon the liberalist surge for free trade and economic expansion, at the expense of social criteria. For Turner, globalisation, predicated on unfettered markets, is going awry. The housing bubbles were not accidental, spawned simply by careless regulatory oversight. They were a necessary component of the incessant drive to expand free trade at all times. Dominant corporate power was the engine of economic expansion. Profits were allowed to soar. A growing share of the national income was absorbed by companies at the expense of workers. And the record borrowing provided a short-term panacea to bridge the yawning gap that inevitably ensued. Government fostered housing bubbles so as to stay in power. Consumers were encouraged to borrow, to ensure there would be enough economic growth. Turner's imperative is to halt the concentration of corporate power and the TNCs' ability to control and drive labour costs down. If not, then housing bubbles will continue in the West.

Harvey (2011) is perhaps the best known contemporary representative of Marxist explanations of the credit crisis, approaching economic crisis in terms of the dysfunctional nature of the total capitalist system: 'In trying to deal with serious tremors in the heart of the body politic . . . (the) central bankers are flooding their economies and inflating the global body politic with excess liquidity in the hope that such emergency transfusions will cure a malady that calls for far more radical diagnosis and interventions' (Harvey, 2011, p. vii). Harvey demonstrates that capital crises are not new. The 2008 disruption to the system was the 'mother of crises' (the sub-prime mortgage crisis) but not exceptional. Neo-liberalism has constituted a global class-based capitalist project, entailing the centralisation of wealth and power. The crash of the US financial sector in 2008 has thrown the long-term American global hegemony into disarray. The global crisis displays all the uneven characteristics of the finance capitalist system. Its effects on housing, low wages, and transport systems have been crushing. Capitalism is transparently a crisis-prone system. Furthermore, the impacts have also led to waves of popular protest, announcing that not all human beings are submissive in the face of globalisation.

To summarise the above explanations of the global crisis, they include the recognition of the ideological, individualistic leanings of the financiers ('greed', in other words); the blind, uncritical faith in the market; the worship of a positivistic, academy-inspired mathematical methodology that has proven inoperable; the irrationality and frailty of human behaviour (human nature); a failure to understand the economic system's historical changes in the direction of global finance; and the neo-liberal monetarists' inability to recognise problems of demand. Finally, the Marxist prognosis, in accord with the perspective outlined above, views the crisis and concomitant recession as the predictable consequence of the system's instability, unevenness, and susceptibility to crisis, creating its own opposition in the process. In the next section, we move to an assessment of the foremost contemporary global protests in the wake of crisis.

The politics of globalisation and the anti-globalisation movement

The anti-globalisation movement was born approximately 15 years ago, when a rather diverse set of organisations and protest groups mobilised across the world against the socially unjust and inhumane policies and practices of the powerful transnational bodies discussed above: namely, the World Bank, the World Trade Organisation (WTO), the G8 (the original G7 nations plus Russia), the EU, and the transnational corporations. After the first demonstration in 1999 in Seattle, others in Gothenburg, Genoa, and Brussels in 2001 exceeded 25,000 participants. A number of the demonstrations turned violent with brutal responses according to many from riot police and a number of deaths. Despite the growth of the movement, institutional policies scarcely changed, except for slight shifts in the pricing of drugs for AIDS by the transnational pharmaceutical companies. The World Bank's social provision and protection remained basic; the WTO contributed to the global market in private insurance services, private education, private health, and social care (Deacon, 2007). On the other hand, the ideas of the movement reached a mass audience beyond a few interested parties and made social policy commentators more sensitive to the impacts of international organisations upon health and national health and social welfare policies (Yeates, 2001).

More recently, the global credit crisis and accompanying economic recession appear to have engendered a new stage for the anti-global movement, directly addressing the central private corporate financial institutions and their negative consequences for the welfare of 99 per cent of the population. Occupy Wall Street was initiated in New York City in September 2011, outside the New York Stock Exchange; it was imitated in London, and spread to other parts of the world. The movement's basic tactic is the occupation of a public space close to the headquarters of economic and political power, so as to galvanise discussion and debate over the activities and morality of the financial institutions. Their methods, bolstered by the latest forms of information technology, have enabled the youth-led movement to confront 'the old order on its own terms' (Mason, 2012, p. 139). The London 'Occupy' movement was legally prevented from occupying a space close to the London Stock Exchange. Protestors occupied the public square adjacent to St. Paul's Cathedral for up to eight months, on a platform against financial greed and social injustice. The protestors' list of demands included an alternative to the current unsustainable system: 'we support . . . actions to defend our health services, welfare, education and employment'; and 'we want structural change towards authentic global equality' (*The Guardian*, 2011).

Unexpectedly, the spirit of the 'occupy' global campaign was picked up in the Middle East, defying the activists' own singularly autocratic economic elites and rulers. At the beginning of 2011, the Middle Eastern movement's protests against poor living conditions, rising food prices, and lack of freedoms culminated in the fall of President Ben Ali in Tunisia; soon afterwards President Mubarek's regime in Egypt collapsed, followed by similar protests in Bahrain, Yemen, Libya and Syria, and once again, demonstrations at the end of 2012 against President Morsi's new Muslim Egyptian regime. The rapid proliferation of these initially revolutionary events echoed the Central European events of 1989, which were amplified by the ubiquitous television cameras. However, the likely long-term results remain somewhat uncertain in the context of the contemporary oscillations in Middle Eastern political developments.

In Europe, thousands of Greek youths occupied Athens' main square in June 2011; 400 of them encamped, protesting against the austerity cuts. During the whole of 2012, a series of protests and demonstrations took place in the marginalised Mediterranean economies of Greece, Italy, Spain, and

Portugal, each constrained by unmanageable debt arising first from the global credit crisis and then from the Eurozone crisis (see Chapter 24). A general strike took place in November 2012, in the capital cities of Athens, Rome, Madrid, and Lisbon, supported too by 'sympathy' strikes in France and Germany. This was one of the largest ever coordinated across Europe, drawing in millions of participants (*The Guardian*, 2012).

To recount, it is clear that the anti-globalisation movement grew out of the neo-liberal policies of the global economic institutions and their divisive impacts. In a sense, the global crisis revitalised the movement via the latter's revisiting of non-violent tactics in a face-to-face spatial occupation, and certainly amplified the public voice of anti-financial corporate sector dissent by articulating alternative (though generalised) social policy priorities. Furthermore, the very act of defiance was taken up by populations in the Arab countries, against their own oppressive regimes (many of them cynically aided by Western governmental interests in recent years), while the major revolts of the worst affected European economies reflected growing global anger at the human effects of 'austerity budgets', and their socially unequal cutbacks in state social expenditure.

Conclusion

From focusing upon these issues, we have arrived at a set of conclusions. The institutional framework of global social policy is US-dominated, exercising unharnessed economic and financial power over capitalist aid markets, often at the expense of many nation-states, and, on the whole, lacking in accountability. And, although UN bodies provide more socially orientated support for poverty stricken economies, they too have been drawn in by the forces of neo-liberalism. But the continued influence of wealthy nation-states still leaves open the question of the viability of global social bodies. The global context in which the institutions have to operate does not give great cause for optimism: a world of mammoth economic and social inequalities, where 1 per cent own 40 per cent of the world's wealth; where incomes, admittedly more widely distributed, are still unquestionably unequal; where millions across the global South exist in multiple poverty; and where the inequality gap continues to widen.

Such gaping inequalities may be grasped by examining the role of transnational corporations in the politics of globalisation and their command over economic resources far in excess of many nation-states. The power of pharmaceutical corporations provides one illustration of how the pursuit of corporate profit frequently subverts health care needs. Yet one must incorporate the significance of political perspectives and ideological frameworks in arriving at an assessment of globalisation's developments. Is it so that all nations' fortunes are determined by an unassailable megalith? Or does the international arena comprise an amalgamation of proactive national decisions and policies? The 2008 credit crisis turned recession throws a number of these issues into sharp relief. Emanating in the United States, the epicentre of global neo-liberalism, the unregulated financial speculation has been acted out in a distinctly social arena: housing. Although the global ramifications are geographically uneven, suffering is now the experience in many parts of the world. But how may such catastrophic events be explained? The most influential accounts emphasise the holding of uncritical faith in the market mechanism; the application of inappropriate mathematical models for lending; the historical lack of understanding of irrationality in human nature; the monetarist economists' incompetence in dealing with the collapse of demand; and the clash of contradictions in a crisis-prone, economically and socially unequal capitalist system. Certainly, a system that allows profit to push aside human needs must cause alarm in the social policy community. Such untrammelled neo-liberal globalisation has led to the genesis of the anti-globalisation movement, the rise of the 'occupy' movement in response to the policies of the financial corporations, the highly unexpected explosion of ostensibly revolutionary uprisings in the Middle East against long-standing dictatorships, and the desperate but predictable demonstrations against 'austerity' budgets in the Mediterranean economies of Europe, which have been skewed towards cutting back on welfare payments and social provision.

Summary

In this chapter, you have been introduced to:

- the institutional framework of global social policy and the ideas of global governance;
- the global context of economic and social inequality in which global institutions operate;
- the activities and economic power of transnational corporations;
- a typology of perspectives on globalisation as a process;
- the events and competing explanations of the 2008 global financial crisis;
- the development of an anti-globalisation movement.

Discussion and review

- To what extent have global and social bodies proved inadequate for dealing with the social impacts of global economic crisis?
- Are the economic and social objectives of global institutions irreconcilable with those of national states?
- Which explanation(s) of the current crisis in the global financial might seem most plausible to social policy-makers and practitioners?

References

Callinicos, A. (2003) *The Anti-Capitalist Manifesto*, Polity, Cambridge.

Cohen, R. and Kennedy, P. with Perrier, M. (2013) *Global Sociology* (3rd edn.), Palgrave Macmillan, London.

Deacon, B. (2007) *Global Social Policy and Governance*, Sage, London.

Deacon, B. (2011) 'Global social policy responses to the economic crisis', in K. Farnworth and Z. Irving (eds.) *Social Policy in Challenging Times: Economic Crisis and Welfare Systems*, Policy Press, Bristol.

Deacon, B. with Stubbs, P. and Hulse, M. (1997) *Global Social Policy: International Organisations and the Future of Welfare*, Sage, London.

Ferguson, I., Lavalette, M. and Mooney, G. (2002) *Rethinking Welfare: A Critical Perspective*, Sage, London.

Fitzpatrick, T. (2001) *Welfare Theory: An Introduction*, Palgrave, London.

Friedman, T. (2000) *The Lexus and the Olive Tree* (new edition), Anchor Books, New York.

Gamble, A. (2009) *Spectre of the Feast: Capitalist Crisis and the Politics of Recession*, Palgrave Macmillan, London.

George, V. and Wilding, P. (2002) *Globalization and Human Welfare*, Palgrave, London.

Giddens, A. (1999) *Runaway World: How Globalization is Reshaping Our Lives*, Profile Books, London.

Giddens, A. (2007) *Europe in the Global Age*, Polity, Cambridge.

Global Journal (2013) *The Top NGOs, Global Journal*, 22 January.

Goldacre, B. (2009) *Bad Science*, Fourth Estate, London.

Goldblatt, D., Perritan, J., Held, D. and McGrew, A. (1999) *Global Transformations: Politics, Economics, Culture*, Polity, Cambridge.

Hancock, M. and Zahawi, N. (2011) *Masters of Nothing: How the Crash will Happen Again Unless We Understand Human Nature*, London: Biteback, London.

Harvey, D. (2011) *The Enigma of Capital and the Crises of Capitalism*, Profile Books, London.

Harvey, D. (2012) *Rebel Cities: From the Right to the City to the Urban Revolution*, Verso, London.

Held, D. (2004) *Global Covenant: The Social Democratic Alternative to the Washington Consensus*, Polity, Cambridge.

Hirst, P. and Thompson, G. (1999) *Globalization in Question*, Polity, Cambridge.

International Labour Office (ILO) (2009) *Global Wage Report, 2008/9*, ILO, Geneva.

International Labour Office (ILO) (2010) *Key Indicators of the Labour Market*, ILO, Geneva.

International Monetary Fund (IMF) (2007) *Annual Report 2007: Making the Global Economy Work for All*, IMF, Washington, DC.

International Monetary Fund (IMF) (2012) 'Estimated purchasing power per capita from GDP, countries', *World Economic Outlook Database.*

James, N. (2011) *Cancer: A Very Short Introduction*, Oxford University Press, Oxford.

Keane, J. (2003) *Global Civil Society?*, Cambridge University Press, Cambridge.

Keane, J. (2009) *The Life and Death of Democracy*, Simon & Schuster, London.

Krugman, P. (2008) *The Return of Depression Economics and the Crisis of 2008* (2nd edn.), Penguin, London.

Marglin, S.A. (2008) *The Dismal Science: How Thinking Like an Economist Undermines Community*, Harvard University Press, Cambridge, MA.

Mason, P. (2012) *Why it's Kicking Off Everywhere: The New Global Revolutions*, Verso, London.

Milanovic, B. (2011) 'Global income inequality; the past two centuries and implications for 21st century', available at http://www.ub.edu/histeco/pdf/milanovic.pdf.

Monbiot, G. (2003) *The Age of Consent: A Manifesto for a New World Order*, Flamingo, London.

Robertson, R. (1992) *Globalization: Social Theory and Global Culture*, Sage, London.

Sandel, M. (2012) *The Moral Limits of Markets*, Allen Lane, London.

Steger, M.B. (2009) *Globalization: A Very Short Introduction*, Oxford University Press, Oxford.

Stiglitz, J. (2002) *Globalization and its Discontents*, Penguin, London.

The Guardian (2006) 'World's richest 1% own 40% of all wealth, UN report discovers', 6 December.

The Guardian (2011) 'Occupy London Stock Exchange – the initial statement', 19 October.

The Guardian (2012) 'Europe's day of anti-austerity strikes and protests turns violent', 15 November.

Turner, G. (2008) *The Credit Crunch: Housing Bubbles, Globalisation and the Worldwide Economic Crisis*, Pluto Press, London.

United Nations Department of Economic and Social Affairs (UNDESA) (2012) *The Millennium Development Goals Report*, July, UNDESA, New York.

United Nations Development Programme (UNDP) (2010) *The Real Wealth of Nations: Pathways to Human Development*, Human Development Report 2010, UNDP, New York.

United Nations University/World Institute for Development Economics Research (UNU-WIDER) (2006) *Wealth Levels, 2000*, UNU-WIDER, Helsinki.

Wolf, M. (2004) *Why Globalization Works (Yale Nota Bene)*, Yale University Press, New Haven, CT.

World Bank (2012) *The World Development Report*, available at siteresources. http://www.worldbank.org/INWDR2012.

Yeates, N. (2001) *Globalization and Social Policy*, Open University Press, Maidenhead.

Further reading

Bob Deacon's *Global Social Policy and Governance* (Sage, London, 2007) is the seminal work in the field, delivering a research-rich overview of the major global institutions, the key issues and their impacts upon contemporary social policy. The related journal, *Global Social Policy*, is also an indispensable research tool. George and Wilding's *Globalization and Human Welfare* (Palgrave, London, 2002) is a lively and accessible text charting the connections between perspectives, social policy, and globalisation. Gamble's *Spectre of the Feast: Capitalist Crisis and the Politics of Recession* (Palgrave Macmillan, London, 2009) gives a sharp assessment of the developments of the global crisis. An alternative is Stiglitz's *Free Fall: Free Markets and the Sinking of the Global Economy* (Penguin, London, 2010). *Understanding Global Social Policy* (Policy Press, Bristol, 2008), edited by Nicola Yeates, is a useful reader on social policy issues such as pensions, employment, and health.

Useful websites

Eurofound (http://www.eurofound.europe.eu)
EU (http://www.Europa.eu)
European Commission (http://www.ec.europa.eu)
IMF (http://www.imf.org/external/index.htm)
World Economic Outlook (WEO) for Data and Statistics (http://www.imf.org/external/data.htm)
United Nations (http://www.un.org)
World Bank (http://www.worldbank.org)
UK Politics/Government (http://www.politics.co.uk)
BBC News (http://www.bbc.co.uk/news/business)
BBC News Europe (http://www.bbc.co.uk/news/Europe)
The Guardian (http://www.guardian.co.uk)
Economist (http://www.Economist.com)

CHAPTER 24

The European Union and Social Policy

Harry Cowen

Learning objectives

- To outline the origins and structures of the European Union
- To investigate key areas and topics in European social policy
- To identify historical tensions between UK and EU social policy
- To assess the social and economic impacts of the Eurozone crisis
- To discuss competing explanations of the Eurozone crisis
- To evaluate the EU policies in response to the euro crisis

Chapter overview

The European Union represents the foremost example of a global regional bloc. It is a huge organisation comprising a growing number of nation-states that delegate some of their sovereignty to the EU so as to support economic, political, and social decision-making at the European level. Yet it has invited a myriad of alternative perspectives. While its economic policies have remained overtly driven by neo-liberalism, it has been far more socially orientated than any other contending regional bloc: thus, the presentation of the 2012 Nobel Peace Prize to the European Union. In contrast, it has been perceived as no more than the slave of the United States, yet it has also been construed as a powerful entity independent of the USA; it has been portrayed as 'fortress Europe' in its immigration policies, but also as the champion of freedom of movement of labour and of human rights; it has been perceived as possessing no social policies of its own except for labour legislation, leaving social policy formulation to the nation-state governments with its own role as basic support and coordination; on the other hand, its social policy inventory now covers a wide area. This chapter outlines the key developments and issues of the European Union as the prime global supranational organisation in relation to social policy. The chapter begins with a focus on origins and structures over the past half-century, and the accompanying historical treaties that guide the social framework. It engages with seminal structural and political issues, such as the enlargement of the Union whose more recent growth in membership has turned it into the world's biggest regional organisation, while harbouring substantial internal opposition. Next, we cover specific areas of EU social policy and its progressively widening definition of social policy. The analysis deals with the workforce, the social charter and social rights, family policy, policies for older people, and education. We then address the UK Government's political equivocations relating to EU social policy. The following section concentrates upon the Eurozone crisis, the social and economic impacts on social welfare policy, not least in the Mediterranean economies. We next look at selective explanations of the euro crisis before addressing the specific policy responses from the EU's institutions in order to assuage the worst effects of member states' austerity budgets. The chapter concludes by speculating on the future viability of a European social policy and the EU's institutional resilience in the face of further financial crisis.

SPOTLIGHT

The purpose and shape of the Economic Community/European Union

As reflected in the extracts below, major issues since the inception of the European Community have embraced the themes of political democratic representation, the role of the market, the augmenting of a powerful bureaucracy, and the EU's relationship to the United States.

'My objective is that before the end of the millennium Europe should have a true federation. The Commission should have a true federation. The Commission should become a political executive which can define essential common interests . . . responsible before the European Parliament and before the nation states represented how you will, by the European Council or by a second chamber of national parliaments.'
(Architect of the European Commission, Jacques Delors, 1990)

'It is impossible to build Europe on only deregulation . . . 1992 is much more than the creation of an internal market abolishing barriers to the free movement of goods, services and investment . . . The internal market should be designed to benefit each and every citizen of the Community.' (Delors, Speech to the British TUC, 8 September 1988)

'To try to suppress nationhood and concentrate power at the centre of a European conglomerate would be highly damaging and would jeopardise the objectives we seek to achieve.' (British Prime Minister Margaret Thatcher, Bruges speech on the European Community, September 1988)

'Against the notable gains . . . I had to set a more powerful Commission ambitious for power, an inclination towards bureaucratic rather than market solutions . . . with its own federalist and protectionist agenda.' (Thatcher, 1993)

'The US is hostile to all forms of international co-operation and multilateralist endeavour. It is wedded to the exercise of autonomous power guaranteed by its military superiority; and its world view is supported and entrenched by the vigorous conservative ideology that dominates its politics and economics. Without a countervailing power of sufficient strength prepared to provide finance and political muscle, the development of multilateral institutions and processes by which a rampant globalisation may be governed will cease. Only the EU has the weight in the world to assume this role.' (Will Hutton, 2002, p. 365)

The European Union's global significance today

In a major post-war history of Europe since 1945, Judt (2007, p. 7) proclaimed the EU as '(e)mbracing everything from child-care to inter-state legal norms . . . (This) European approach stood for more than just the bureaucratic practices of the European Union and its member states; by the beginning of the twenty-first century it had become a beacon and example for aspirant EU members and a global challenge to the United States and the competing appeal of the American way of life.' Similarly, Hutton (2002, p. 2) deems the EU the only feasible antidote to American dominance: '(The) quest for European union is one of the great rousing and political projects of our time. It is vital in providing a counterweight to the US and thus offering genuine multilateral leadership in the search for securing global public goods. It is a means of advancing core European values. It is also the way to reanimate our politics and the public realm.'

Such a position was countered by Anderson (2011): 'Today's EU, with its pinched spending . . . miniscule bureaucracy (around 16,000 officials, excluding translators), absence of independent taxation, and lack of any means of administrative enforcement, could in many ways be regarded as a *ne plus ultra* of the minimal state, beyond the most dramatic imaginings of classical liberalism: less even than the dream of a nightwatchman' (p. 66). And indeed, 'The EU is basically about business . . . overwhelmingly about the promotion of free markets' (p. 67).

The origins and structures of the European Union

One may trace the EU's beginnings back to the Second World War. The idea of the continent's integration was mooted as a preventative measure against further war and human devastation. The European Community, formed in 1950 by the French Foreign Minister, Robert Schuman, originally comprised France, the Netherlands, Germany, Luxembourg, Belgium, and Italy. Ever since, the European organisation has witnessed constant competition among key nations for political leadership so as to hold on to their own national interests.

In the 1960s, France's President General de Gaulle, in the pursuit of French power, was opposed to the idea of federalism, which was supported by the majority of the other member states. Hence, he blocked attempts by Britain to join the organisation (delayed until 1973). Jacques Delors' presidency of the European Commission moved it towards federalism, adopting the idea of institutional reform, a European single market, and a single currency in the form of the euro. The United Kingdom Government, under the premiership of Margaret Thatcher (personally vociferous over the UK's share of the budget), declared its own opposition to much of Delors' programme. A series of reforms has shaped the impressive growth of the European bloc up to the present day. Both the European Coal and Steel Community (ECSC) and the European Atomic Community (Euratom) were inaugurated by the Treaty of Paris in 1951. In 1958, the Treaty of Rome created the European Economic Community (the EEC), largely a trading bloc and still containing the same constituent members as in 1951. The organisation was enlarged when Ireland, Denmark, and the UK joined in 1973, followed by Greece in 1981, Spain and Portugal in 1986, and Sweden, Finland, and Austria in 1995. In the first decade of the twenty-first century, 12 more countries drawn from Central and Eastern Europe acceded. The present European Union was formed in 1992 by the Treaty of Maastricht, with the aim of strengthening the inter-relationships of the member states both politically and economically. Furthermore, the introduction of the European Monetary Institute prepared the way for the new euro currency. In the next section, we look at the European Union's prime institutions, all of which play a significant part in the Union's execution of social policy.

BOX 24.1 TREATIES OF THE EUROPEAN UNION

- 1951 – *Treaty of Paris*: creation of the European Coal and Steel Community (ECSC) and the European Atomic Community (Euratom)

- 1958 – *Treaty of Rome*: formation of EEC

- 1991 – *Treaty of Maastricht*: launch of EU and beginnings of social policy; established economic and monetary union

- 1997 – *Treaty of Amsterdam*: enhanced the status of social policy and citizenship rights in the EU

- 2001 – *Treaty of Nice*: prepared the EU for further enlargement; extended Qualified Majority Voting

- 2007 – *Treaty of Lisbon ratified*: replacement of the European Constitution, appropriate to major enlargement of EU; set out strategy for Union in context of globalisation

---

Institutionally, the Union is made up in the first instance of five major bodies: the European Commission, the Council of the European Union, the European Parliament, the European Court of Justice, and the European Court of Auditors.

The European Commission

The Commission is the central policy-making and executive body of the EU. Sitting in Brussels, it comprises 20 commissioners who are nominated by the individual member governments for a five-year term. Germany, France, the UK, Spain, and Italy, by dint of their demographic power, are entitled to two commissioners each. In turn, a number of Directors General (like Departments), such as 'Education, Training and Youth' and 'Employment, Industrial Relations and Social', back up the Commission.

The Council of Europe

The Council acts as the representative of the Council of the European Union member states, formulating the agenda for the Union's policies at its meetings held in Brussels, while the Council of Ministers meets in Brussels and Luxembourg. The representative of the nation that happens to hold the Presidency at the time chairs the Council for a six-month period.

The Council of Ministers draws up the Union's political objectives and tries to coordinate the discrete national policies and integrate them into the Union's overarching objectives, making its decisions through unanimous or Qualified Majority Voting procedures.

The European Parliament

The member states' citizens elect the 732 Members of the European Parliament (MEPs) who meet in Strasbourg. The members, of which 78 are elected by the UK, sit for five years. The Parliament's main mission is the protection of the interests of European citizens, and accordingly it supervises the Commission's and the Council's actions. There are, however, differences with the British Parliamentary system, since the European Union may exercise little jurisdiction for passing laws. In addition, the European Parliament possesses no real control over finances or for raising funds. Member states have also effectively countered any moves to enhance the Parliament's own legislative powers, although it may engage in decision-making on matters pertinent to spending, or to social policy, or communicating with the European Council on issues concerned, for instance, with social programmes and educational issues; finally, it is even able to reject the whole budget, but on rare occasions.

The European Court of Justice

The Court is located at the top of the Union's legal system, required by the treaties to make certain that the European Union's law, made up of legislation and the cumulative treaties passed by the particular bodies, is respected. Based in Luxembourg, the Court of Justice rules on cases pertaining to freedom, justice, and security. One judge, appointed for a six-year term, is provided by each member state. The Court adjudicates over the European Commission's actions against a member state or by one state against another state, where it is claimed that a treaty obligation has not been fulfilled. Most of the cases, however, stem from claims by companies or individuals against governments or other companies or individuals, initially heard in the courts of the appropriate member state, and then dealt with by the Court of Justice as the final court on matters of interpretation. By the end of the century's first decade, the Court had deliberated on well over 7000 cases.

The European Court of Auditors

Sitting in Luxembourg, this Court exercises control and management of the Union's budget, takes actions to the Court of Justice, and possesses jurisdiction over any institution in receipt of Union funds.

The European Central Bank

The Bank, established in 1999 under the Maastricht Treaty, carries out the European Union's monetary policy and manages the euro, largely by attempting to maintain the euro's purchasing power (and hence price stability in the euro area). As discussed later in this chapter, the stability of the euro has seriously plummeted, with deleterious consequences for the welfare of many European citizens and for related social policy. When the euro area was first set up, it constituted 11 countries; by 2012, there were 17 members.

The European Investment Bank (EIB)

The EIB is responsible for the financing of investment projects in the European Union. Its declared corporate aim is 'to achieve a balance between economic growth, social well-being and the protection of the environment', taking into account the Lisbon Strategy framework.

From small beginnings, then as the EEC (European Economic Community), the European Union has become the major coordinated economic and social global bloc, incorporating 27 member states.

BOX 24.2 GROWTH OF THE EUROPEAN UNION

- 1952 – the founding members of the ECSC were Belgium, the Netherlands, Luxembourg, France, Italy, and West Germany.

- 1958 – Formation of European Economic Community (EEC) with above members

- 1973 – UK, Denmark, and Ireland join European Community (EC)

- 1981 – Greece joins EC

- 1986 – Portugal and Spain join EC

- 1995 – Austria, Finland, and Sweden accede to the European Union (EU)

- 2004 – accession to the EU of Czech Republic, Estonia, Hungary, Latvia, Lithuania, Poland, Slovakia, Slovenia, Malta, and Cyprus – EU up to 25 members

- 2007 – accession of Bulgaria and Romania – EU now 27 members

---

But it is this very growth in the number of participatory states that has led to one of the most controversial debates surrounding the development of the European Union: the enlargement debate (to be discussed below).

In summary, the EU's structure and institutions evolved over a half-century, from a relatively minor economic trading bloc to the current regional organisation comprising a vast parliament, executive body, and a plethora of committees, with a constitution supported by a series of major treaties regulating a range of policies, including social policy and the processes of economic growth. The next section proceeds to discuss the central EU issue of membership growth.

The enlargement debate

In the years preceding 2000, debate was lively regarding future enlargement of the EU, how the new countries might align their national social legislation with that of other member nations, and institute viable systems of social protection (Hantrais, 2007, p. 14). By 2000, it was evident that institutional change and reform was called for because of the Union's rapid enlargement (Laursen, 2001). Soon after the turn of the century, the Union prepared for material expansion into Central and Eastern Europe by a comprehensive reform of its institutions, including extension of voting rights. The 12 new members were: Cyprus, the Czech Republic, Estonia, Hungary, Latvia, Lithuania, Malta, Poland, Slovakia, and Slovenia (all 2004) together with Bulgaria and Romania (2007). With these additional countries bringing a diversity of welfare situations into the Union, it was expected that they would have a heavy bearing on social policy. Most seriously, it was predicted that they would import mass poverty, deprivation and unemployment, and generally lower standards. However, studies in the early years of the new century demonstrated such fears to be over-generalised (Hantrais, 2007, pp. 261–2). For example, according to data for 2003–04, Slovenia and the Czech Republic were the nations least 'at-risk-from-poverty'. None of the CEE (Central and Eastern Europe) nations had the lowest long-term unemployment rates, but Poland, Latvia, and Slovakia had the highest.

In the sphere of economic policy, the Commission found that the enlargement had boosted the additional members' agriculture sector through the CAP (Community Agricultural Policy), which led to an enlarged EU market (expanding from 380 million to almost 500 million people) and strengthened the European Union in international markets (European Commission, http:www.ec.europa.eu/ag). Another economic study showed that 'the EU enlargement significantly contributed to economic growth of the ten new Central and Eastern European economies' (Rapacki and Prochniak, 2009).

Andrew Duff, an expert on the EU's Constitution and one of the UK's MEPs, drew attention, however, to its repeated setbacks, including rejection of the Constitutional Treaty by the Netherlands and France in 2005. Accordingly, Duff called for a complete renegotiation of the Constitution. In 2007, a European Union Reform Treaty was finally ratified in Lisbon (discussed further below). By the end of 2007, the European Commission felt that on the whole, enlargement had been successful and was in the EU's interest (European Commission, 2007).

While the enlargement of the EU has also raised the question of weakening democracy in an expanded European Parliament, fuelling the anti-EU campaigns of political parties in Denmark, the Netherlands, and UKIP in the UK, the traditional right of the Conservative Party, as well as frustrated MEPs (plus practitioners and researchers requiring timely decisions on their applications for funding), the European Parliament is the first attempt to create an elected regional parliament beyond the level of the nation-state (Keane, 2009). It has been demonstrated that the European Parliament possesses the potential to influence similar structures globally, and thus may offer the most promising route to Held's (2004) global governance. An academic enquiry into the European Parliament and democracy concluded: 'Despite the

STOP AND THINK

Is the current 27-strong membership
of the EU simply too unwieldy to
provide efficiency and equity?

continued inability of the Parliament to initiate legislation, the progress made in integrating it into the
governance structures of the Union has been positive
for increasing the role of democratic politics in decision making' (Hobson, 2011, p. 239).

Challenge to the Constitution and the Lisbon EU Reform Treaty

The Lisbon Treaty, ratified in 2007 and effective from 2009, acted as a
replacement for the European Constitution that the referenda in the
Netherlands and France had rejected in 2005. A predominant goal was to
accelerate decision-making in the greatly expanded Union:

- It amended, but did not replace, the earlier treaties, enabling more effective
  decision-making within a massive organisation of 27 nations and a sharper
  focus than previously upon the ways international competition and globalisation were affecting the total bloc *per se*.
- For the first time, it included the particular national parliaments in the
  formulation of new legislation. They were now able to assess the extent to
  which European Union proposals conformed to the 'subsidiarity principle'
  (which states that the EU should only take action where the latter adds value).
- The Treaty introduced a new majority voting system for the Council's
  national ministers. Thus, any new legislation now must have, as a
  minimum, the support of 65 per cent of the Union's population.
- 'Enhanced cooperation' rulings enabled individual member states to work
  more closely together without the involvement of those reluctant to take part.
- The Charter of Fundamental Rights was finally incorporated into European
  law, and collated those rights enjoyed by European Union citizens to date;
  such rights were also applied to each of the member states (http:www.
  Europa.eu).
- Within the rapid changes in the world outside the boundaries of the
  European Union, the Lisbon Treaty was a call for the Union to look
  outwards. The EU's negotiations, slowly built up over half a century to
  protect its economic and political barriers, had come under pressure from
  the forces of globalisation, which, in the first decade of the twenty-first
  century, had eased the cross-border movements of work and trade.

The United Kingdom and the Lisbon Treaty

The UK Government, keen on maintaining its national rights of sovereignty,
was pro-active in the Lisbon proceedings. New Labour Prime Minister

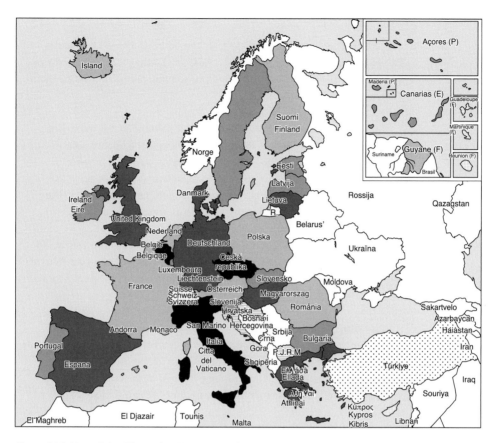

Figure 24.1 Map of the 27-member European Union

Gordon Brown, who had repeatedly refused to hold a referendum on the new treaty, was highly sensitive to the mounting hostility towards the European constitution. Of course, continued demands for a referendum were made once the Treaty had been finalised. The politically right-wing UK Independence Party (UKIP) and the Democracy Movement campaigned for a complete withdrawal from the Union, essentially on the grounds of the assumed loss of national sovereignty. Interest groups opposing the Treaty, such as the Institute of Directors and the 'popular' press claimed that it had removed all significant powers from the hands of individual governments.

CONTROVERSY AND DEBATE

The EU and the long-standing membership controversy

Since the early years of the Community and then the Union's formation, the UK has adopted an equivocal, to say the least, position towards membership of the EU. The latest example came in the form of Prime Minister David Cameron's controversial 'Referendum' Plan. On 2 July 2012, David Cameron addressed the House of Commons on the EU summit, promising a referendum (http:www.politics.co.uk, 2012):

'(It) would be wrong to rule out any type of referendum for the future. The right path for Britain is this . . . Over time take the opportunities for Britain to shape its relationship with Europe in ways that advance our national interest in free trade, open markets and co-operation. That should mean . . . less Europe, not more Europe. Less bureaucracy, less meddling in issues that belong to nation states.' (http:www. politics.co.uk)

Closer to 2013, responding to news that within weeks Cameron was to indicate his plans to hold a referendum on a new EU settlement, Lord Kerr of Kinlochard (a British team member of the 1991 Maastricht Treaty negotiations) issued the following statement:

'I think that the Cameron strategy . . . could lead to our leaving by accident. I think there is an analytical error . . . I think they genuinely believe people are going to leap to their feet to sing . . . Rule Britannia and it is a done deal . . . But supposing the rest of the EU don't leap to their feet . . . It sounds more like bust-up time.' (*The Guardian*, 2012d)

Do you think the 'dangers' to the EU are rather exaggerated? Has the history of the UK in Europe been tantamount to 'little Englandism'?

The Conservative-led Coalition government has once again turned back the clock towards the early years of the Economic Community. The UK's membership has always been controversial since its first application to join in 1961. The government's position has remained equivocal, and the UK's membership remains under challenge, at least from the Conservative Party and specifically its more traditional right wing. In 1989, Prime Minister Margaret Thatcher's government refused to sign the EU Social Charter, the only government to do so. The Charter set out 30 general principles embracing health and safety at work, improvements of living conditions, workers' rights, fair wages, rights for elderly and for disabled persons, and gender equality. In 1992, Prime Minister John Major refused on behalf of the Conservative Government to sign the EU's provisions on social policy and other social issues (its 'social chapter'), according to the Maastricht Treaty, which set up the new EU, on the grounds that the requirements for workplace conditions would tie the hands of business. Major then opted out of EU social policy completely. When the New Labour government took power in 1997, Prime Minister Tony Blair signed the social chapter aligned with the Amsterdam Treaty. The position as at 2012 was that the Conservatives, with 26 MEPs, stood opposed to further EU integration, yet

Table 24.1 Number of European Parliament seats per country, 2009–14 parliamentary term (total = 736)

Germany, 99	France 72	Italy, 72	UK, 72
Poland, 50	Spain, 50	Romania, 33	Netherlands, 25
Belgium, 22	Greece, 22	Hungary, 22	Portugal, 22
Czech Republic, 22	Sweden, 18	Austria, 17	Bulgaria, 17
Denmark, 13	Finland, 13	Slovakia, 13	Ireland, 12
Lithuania, 12	Latvia, 8	Slovenia, 7	Cyprus, 6
Estonia, 6	Luxembourg, 6	Malta, 5	

Source: Europa (2010), in Hobson (2012).

were not in favour of withdrawing from the Union. In 2007, David Cameron made a pledge to prioritise withdrawal from the EU's social chapter under a forthcoming Conservative government, and reiterated the pledge on taking office in 2010, stating his position to withdraw the Conservative MEPs from cooperating with the European People's Party in the European Parliament. On the other hand, the right wing of his Party increased its pressure for totally seceding from membership of the EU itself. The Liberal Democratic Party, the other party to the UK Coalition government, with 12 MEPs, remained traditionally supportive of European Union membership, but had adjusted its perspective on Europe since achieving coalition government status.

At the end of 2012, Prime Minister Cameron was calling for the EU budget to be frozen at 2011 levels, compared with an actual increase suggested by the European Commission and the European Parliament, although general disagreement over the budget caused disarray of the Summit and its postponement until mid December, when the EU decided upon a 2.4 per cent increase on the 2012 budget.

To summarise, since the early formations of the EEC, the new century has witnessed an 'opening out' of membership, particularly to the Central and Eastern European nations. The inter-governmental, Council of Ministers and European Parliament deliberations, culminating in the Lisbon Treaty's new constitution, may well have heightened the continuous right-wing dissent in the UK and elsewhere. Yet evidence up to the point of the financial crises indicated that the expansion was substantially less dysfunctional than argued in some quarters. In the same vein, the European Parliament arguably remains an essentially progressive democratic decision-making organ. In the following section, we focus directly on specific social policies, the European Union's approach, and the key issues that have confronted its policy-makers.

European social policy

It is undeniably the case that the EU, of all the global regional blocs, boasts the most mature social policy framework. At the same time, its formal definition of social policy is still somewhat narrowly conservative, although now rather outdated, and the limits of the Union's intervention in certain social spheres remain in dispute. The 1957 Treaty of Rome, more of a trade agreement, contained no reference to social policy. The 1991 Maastricht Treaty occasioned the first developments of social policy in the category of employment and labour relations. The EU's contemporary social policy basically handles working conditions; improvement of the working environment to protect workers' health and safety; the provision of information and the consultation of workers; equality between women and men in the workplace; and the integration of people excluded from the labour market. While the structure of employment services is variable between the EU nations, depending upon the specific political and social culture, consistent efforts have been made to harmonise the separate policies without watering down the higher standards pertaining in the more socially aware welfare states.

European social policy supports and coordinates national policies, and passes laws implemented by the Council and Parliament in consultation with each other. In addition, the European Commission has to encourage member states to cooperate with each other on issues, including social security and training. The 1997 Treaty of Amsterdam gave the Council powers of unilateral action against all forms of discrimination. However, in spite of the overt orientation in the labour policy direction, the EU has made moderate progress towards a more inclusive social welfare policy.

The Community Charter of Fundamental Social Rights of Workers (The Social Charter)

This Charter gave rights of social protection to those without subsistence means, retired people, and disabled persons. Disquiet, though, was articulated over the possibilities of the newly joined Mediterranean economies, who were poorer on the whole than early EU members (hence enjoying lower labour costs), and who possessed unfair advantages. Notwithstanding, the 1991 Maastricht Treaty was highly influential in spreading the idea of a European social policy. It promoted the practicality of working together in such areas as public health, youth policy, and education. Maastricht also reiterated European citizenship rights, such as health care access, greater choice for university students, and social security support for migrants.

The Amsterdam Treaty was also a turning point in the interpretation of social policy, with the further advancement of European citizenship rights: workers now held the right of residence in any EU country; additionally, gender equality became a prime goal. At the beginning of the new century, the EU announced anti-discrimination directives on racism, sexual orientation, age, disability, and belief in the employment arena.

One long-standing concern has been over poverty and social exclusion. The European Commission pressured the European Council to accept key objectives of more secure income levels, social integration, sustainable pensions, and sustainable health care of a high quality. In spite of the Charter of Fundamental Rights for social policies not being actionable in law, the principles have served as a litmus test for refuting unacceptable practices across the member states. Clearly, the European Union does behave as a kind of welfare state. Structural communication takes place between nations and in turn between the nations and the European Commission about pensions, social exclusion, and health care, via what is known as the Open Method of Coordination (OMC) (Deacon, 2007). What of other particular social policy areas operational in the Union? Below, we consider three: family policy, policy for older and disabled people, and education and training.

Family policy

Family policy figures more prominently now than in the past. For instance, the Commission published a report on demographic change in Europe, calling for increased support for families taken up with caring. The Charter of Fundamental Rights began to include articles on 'rights of the child' and 'respect for private and family life'. A drawback, however, has been that the European Union, because of its strong commitment to respecting national diversity in family policy, found it virtually impossible and indeed undesirable to attempt a coordinated EU policy. The European Union's social policy principle has forged a distancing of national approaches towards social protection issues. The Commission was also reluctant to interfere in family matters. Hence, commentaries on EU social policy have tended to chart 'indirect' social policies. The first real European Community reference to family policy, that it should become integral to all Community policies, appeared in the 1980s. The subject was incorporated onto the European Union agenda in 1994, with the signing of the Treaty on European Union, which states as an objective to develop targeted benefits for certain groups of families in need. However, the rights and benefits remained employment-related; many of the nations were not prepared to recognise the crucial changes that were occurring in the 'family' structure, so that both the EU's Council and the Commission felt unable and unwilling to attempt to synthesise the discrete policies into an EU-wide family policy. In the case of the UK, although its governments had administered a seemingly 'negative' policy, as reflected in their rejection of the notion of 'family policy', they actually put in train policies implicitly affecting families.

The EU, then, has encountered conflicts of interest that imply moral and political issues, such as whether policy should support the 'traditional' family (i.e. married couples and their legitimate children) or recognise different family structures such as co-habiting couples and lone parents and other family arrangements. During the 2000s, the majority of the EU's member governments avoided prohibitive laws, such as those legislating against divorce or abortion, and in addition recognised non-traditional family structures. In the early part of the decade, the majority of members increased child benefits, but again there was a disparity of approaches, such as between Scandinavian and Mediterranean countries, to families experiencing financial hardship and those on the edge of poverty. Given the 'indirect' route pursued by the EU, it is not easy to form an assessment of the Union's or the Commission's impact on the member states' individual family policies, and indeed whether the reverse is feasible.

Policy for older and disabled persons

European social policy has undoubtedly undergone an impressive transformation, considering the movements of declining populations on the European continent, accelerated demographic ageing, and a notable imbalance between the generations. However, a substantial issue for policy coordinators is the dissimilarities in trends and impacts between the member states. For example, in the early 2000s, Greece, Italy, Germany, and Austria were the most affected by population decline alongside the ageing of their respective populations. In comparison, by dint of lower longevity rates, the poorer economies of Central and Eastern Europe were more anxious about the fall in their populations. Whereas retirement age hardly varies between the European countries, social tensions have appeared among the different generations. It is for this reason that European documentation is often focused upon the extent to which pensions are adequate, and on the need for inter-generational solidarity (Hantrais, 2007).

An important aspect of policy's impact on older people is the question of how treatment of older people was affected by the 2008 crisis in EU member states. A study on the 'Impact of the recession on age management policies' (Eurofound, 2012b) investigated policy in relation to the retention of older workers (age 50+) in employment and establishment levels in Austria, Belgium, Czech Republic, Hungary, Latvia, Netherlands, Spain, Sweden, and the UK. The survey found that in general, early retirement was used as a tool; partial retirement schemes were extended and reformed; in a number of countries, the pension age was raised, while the requisite contributions from workers were increased. Nation-states made a distinct move towards part-privatisation or towards defined contribution schemes where private provision is predominant (as in the UK). Some expanded or introduced tax and social security incentives for employers and employees to keep older workers in employment. The study concluded that in some cases during the crisis period, older workers were not often treated as a priority in the face of younger workers' greater employability, but the 2008 crisis did not unduly affect older workers' employment. Age-related policy reforms took place in Hungary, Latvia, and Spain, nations badly affected financially, but mostly along the lines of cost-cutting.

Education and training

On viewing the changes in educational standards in the European Union through the first decade of the present century, the statistical picture is a positive one. The EU average 'percentage of persons of age 20–24 having completed at least upper secondary education' rose from 76.6 per cent in 2000 to 79.5 per cent in 2011. The EU average 'percentage of tertiary education attainment, persons of age 30–34' was 22.4 per cent in 2000, but grew to 34.6 per cent in 2011. The EU average 'percentage of low reading literacy performance of pupils' (15-year-olds) was 19.8 per cent in 2000, but by 2009 it had fallen slightly to 19.6 per cent. Since the gestation period of the EU, European Council and Commission pronouncements on education and training have re-emphasised the prominence of the European dimension and the inculcation of how to respect and understand other cultures, hence the variety of programmes in this area. But enhancing opportunities for vocational training has resulted in programmes for encouraging mobility among students. By the early 2000s, all EU member states provided vocational training through the school system, rather than in the workplace. Lifetime learning was also stressed such that the EU set guidelines of a 12.5 per cent average EU participation in lifetime learning for the working population for the period 2005–08. Despite the guidelines, what kind of influence has EU policy been able to wield over the national educational systems? There was a growing acceptance across Europe of the need to cross boundaries (e.g. regarding the recognition of qualifications). However, as with EU social policy *per se*, it is difficult to gauge the success of these policies at EU level or their impact upon national policy-making. The EU's Education Council adopted 16 core indicators 'for monitoring progress towards the Lisbon objectives in education and training' in 2007. *Education and Training 2020* (Eurostat, 2009) outlined eight benchmarks defined for 2020, including that 'an average of at least 15 per cent of adults should participate in lifelong learning' (synonymous with 'lifetime learning'); 'the share of low-achieving 15-year olds in reading, mathematics and science should be less than 15 per cent'; and 'by 2020, the share of employed graduates (20–34 year olds) having left education and training no more than three years before the reference year should be at least 82 per cent'.

In spite of the EU's social policy trajectory being somewhat inconsistent and uneven, it has nevertheless made considerable headway since its early beginnings by formulating appropriate standards and principles for the member states to adopt. It has inaugurated in addition the social charter acceding fundamental social rights to workers; the EU family policy has become more direct, although many member states cling to their traditional family structures; educational and training quality has universally improved with the Union's cooperative measures; and an impressive array of social policies is available for older and disabled persons, yet this is in danger of being totally nullified by the impact of and the response to the global financial crises (discussed below). In the following section, we consider precisely how global and regional financial crises have cut deeply, perhaps irretrievably, into the organisation's welfare objectives.

STOP AND THINK

How much, do you feel, has social policy now become part of mainstream EU policy?

The social and economic impact of the Eurozone crisis on the EU

The impact of the global 2008 crisis has been a powerful one in those member states categorised as the Mediterranean economies (Spain, Italy, Portugal, and Greece) by Perrera's and by Giddens' modification of Esping-Andersen's capitalist welfare states model. The developing recession hit Portugal, Spain, Italy, Greece, and Ireland most severely, each experiencing vast national debt and bankruptcy. The European Union economies have been pressured by the wealthier Western EU economies, particularly Germany, to employ vast cutbacks in their economic and social infrastructures (now commonly termed 'austerity budgeting'), not least in social welfare. This has resulted in a number of social problems bearing upon social policy, including mass unemployment, poverty, and reduced social benefits. But the problems were multiplied for the EU states by the later Eurozone crisis. The individual prognoses are analysed in detail in Chapter 22. Our immediate concern in this chapter is to provide an assessment of the social ramifications of this most recent Eurozone crisis.

The initial euro crisis and its development

The Eurozone (also known as 'Euroland') is an economic and monetary union (EMU), comprising 17 EU member states that have adopted the euro as their currency: Austria, Belgium, Cyprus, Estonia, Finland, France, Germany, Greece, Ireland, Italy, Luxembourg, Malta, Netherlands, Portugal, Slovakia, Slovenia, and Spain. The European Central Bank, based in Germany, exercises overarching responsibility for monetary policy. The Eurozone crisis, although adding to the earlier and continuing stresses from the global recession, is affecting the social policies of these countries more than anything else. The Eurozone crisis is usually regarded as a sovereign debt crisis, currently in Greece and Ireland. A debt crisis even in small peripheral economies can affect the whole monetary system, given that the euro's financial system is overstretched and highly integrated.

The Eurozone crisis originated in Greece, whose national sovereign debt had accumulated by 2009. (Explanations are discussed later in this chapter as to why the national crisis was allowed to affect the Eurozone more widely on such a massive scale and for such an indeterminate period.) Greece had entered the European Community in accord with the Maastricht Treaty in 1992, and was allowed to enter the Eurozone, evidently a political decision since its GDP was less than 1 per cent of Europe as a whole. However, the profile of the Greek state was atypical in the Eurozone: powerful private interests, such as the shipowners, were not subject to tax; nor were thousands of workers reliant upon the nation's tourist industry. Consequently, the private and public debt grew uncontrollably, a situation only revealed in 2009 by an incoming Papandreou government announcement that the state accounts had been consciously falsified. The crisis affected both the banks and the public sector. Interest rates began to rise in response to the clear unsustainability of the public debt. This set in train a snowball effect, as the Greek and European leaders countered the possibility of any default by Greece in paying its debt, in tandem with measures imposed by international fiscal bodies (the European Commission, the European Central Bank, the IMF). In 2010, cutbacks of 25 per cent were made to public sector wages, complementing huge public sector spending reductions, regressive tax increases, and pressures for privatisation. By the end of 2011, the accumulation of austerity policies had pushed the national debt up to 160 per cent of GDP. These policies led to sizeable demonstrations in the Greek capital, Athens. In early 2012, the Greek Government accepted a new 'bailout' plan of 174 billion euros, on top of involvement from the private sector. The result was a further economic recession in the Eurozone, a culmination of its persistently poor economic growth over the decades.

The social impact

Pay restraint and reductions in workers' earnings were continuing even in 2012, notwithstanding various governmental measures such as increased flexible employment, which were scarcely activated (Eurofound, 2012a). Greece's economy was close to financial collapse by 2012 in the wake of total uncertainty; unemployment was as high as 23 per cent, and the health care system was suffering from lack of medical equipment (*The Guardian*, 2012a). The health service had already suffered from the global crisis cutbacks in 2010 (with a 40 per cent reduction in its hospital budget), yet was faced with a rise in admissions to public hospitals from 2009. Health outcomes had worsened, particularly among vulnerable groups; suicides had risen by 17 per cent. Yet Greece's membership of the Eurozone made its debt crisis worse: the government had been unable to leave the euro, and thus could not devalue the Greek currency. Instead, Greece had been forced to borrow 110 billion euros from the IMF (*Lancet*, 2011).

Spain was badly hit by the later Eurozone crisis, having already suffered from the demise of its massive property bubble in 2007–08. Its banking sector was hugely indebted, and one of its largest banks, Bankia, called for a 19 billion euros bailout (*Economist*, 2012). By 2012, Spain's unemployment rate of 25 per cent was the highest in the European Union. The majority of young adults (21.5 per cent of the population) were unemployed. Whereas the general unemployment rate of 8.5 per cent in 2006 had been close to the EU average, it was twice as high at 21.7 per cent by 2011. One in four Spaniards had become at risk of poverty or social exclusion since 2010. In addition, Spain's regional administrations were struggling financially, and approaching the central government for assistance (BBC News Europe, 2012; Eurostat, 2012).

Italy's austerity measures of 2010 in response to the global credit crisis and mass accumulated debt did put a brake on the country's economic growth. Because of its continued debt crisis (up to 2 trillion euros) and the Eurozone crisis, Italy had ended up deeper in recession. A further contraction of the economy sent its GDP spiralling downwards by 2.5 per cent from only the previous year, leading to extra cutbacks of 4.5 billion euros. The social policy repercussions were grave. Some 10.3 million Italians were living in poverty. Many poorly paid youths were leaving Italy (*Der Spiegel*, 2012). Families in the south were in basic poverty: 'scavenging and scraping by without gas or electricity' (*Daily Beast*, 2012). Ten of Italy's cities, responsible for the provision of domestic services, were almost deplete of funds by late 2012, yet the national government was planning to wipe another 500 million euros off its provincial budget (*The Telegraph*, 2012a).

Like the Eurozone member states referred to above, Portugal was one of those most affected by global recession, and its population's hardships were exacerbated by the Eurozone crisis. Unemployment was at 15 per cent in 2012, and still rising. Its debt was predicted to grow to 124 per cent of GDP by 2014; its recession was expected to last until 2013 (IMF *et al.*, 2012), perhaps an overly optimistic prediction at the time of writing. The government's social policy response to hardship was to attempt to enlarge social contributions for workers from 11 per cent to 18 per cent, and to lower them for companies from 25 per cent to 18 per cent (EUobserver.com, 2012). In October 2012, the government's proposed large tax increases for 2013 were received by warnings from the unions that they would lead to a drastic worsening of living conditions and life expectancy (*The Telegraph*, 2012b).

In 2013, later than in the case of the above economies, Cyprus, a Eurozone member and ironic location of the European Council's new Presidency (while also an investment haven for Russian billionaires) ran into grave financial crisis, re-igniting the euro crisis. Following temporary closure of its banks, a last-minute bailout of 17 billion euros was sanctioned by the European Central Bank, IMF, and the European Commission.

To summarise, the Eurozone crisis is yet one more major financial crisis bearing upon the economic stability of EU member states, the viability of their social policies, and the social wellbeing of their populations. The crisis, originating in the sovereign debt of a member state, Greece, has produced unequal effects within the European Union, with the Mediterranean countries most extensively affected. In each case, the euro crisis compounded the problems from the earlier global crisis. The resultant unemployment, family poverty, reduced social benefits, and general poverty conditions have persisted, contributing to rising inequality. The next section presents alternative prognoses as to why the crisis occurred in the first place.

STOP AND THINK

To what extent do 'austerity' policies, incurred due to the impact of financial crises on the EU economy, imply welfare cutbacks and further economic and social inequalities?

Explanations of the Eurozone crisis

The BBC's 'online' explanation was that the earlier global financial crisis and the later, more specific Eurozone crisis (focused upon the Eurozone member states) were closely connected. In Spain and Italy there had been a sizeable accumulation of debt, but this was scarcely due to the governments' actions. Instead, as noted in Chapter 22, it was attributable to the activities of the private sector, namely financial companies and the mortgage borrowers who were taking out loans. Interest rates had plummeted in southern European countries when they 'pinned' the euro, encouraging a boom driven by the cumulative debt. Germany had created the Eurozone in 1991 and acted as the EU's driving force from its abundant funds loaned to the southern Mediterranean economies. But this left Spanish and Italian employers with a huge competitive price disadvantage. Which is why it became far more prohibitive for the southern Mediterranean nations to export to Germany. The outcome of the resultant cutbacks was to deepen the 2008 recession, so that wage levels declined, unemployment rose, and the debts were increasingly difficult to pay back (BBC News, 2012a). A critical interpretation of this scenario, which portrays why the Eurozone economies have ended up with this seemingly immovable debt burden, is that in 2007–08 they had spent hundreds of billions of euros in rescuing the banks (Callinicos, 2012). This series of events also needs to be placed in the context of the whole financial system still in a precariously weak condition following the 2008 capitalist crisis.

In summary, the 'empirical' explanations testify to the accumulation of debts from the private sector, affecting those southern European economies most in debt to the relatively booming German economy, and also to the linkages with the preceding global crisis. But according to the anti-capitalist critique, the close associations with the earlier crisis in global capitalism, which forced EU members into the unprecedented outflow of euros towards the financial corporate sector, forced the susceptible Eurozone member states into a sovereign debt crisis. At this juncture, it is appropriate to scrutinise the policy responses within the EU to this European crisis.

The European Union policies in response to the euro crisis

How have governments, and indeed the EU's own financial institutions, managed to deal with the euro crisis, which, at the time of writing, has lasted some three years? It is evident that the Eurozone has become the new epicentre of the global financial sector. The euro crisis has exerted a corrosive effect on the growth of the world economy, implicating China, Brazil, and India, resulting from the reduced trade to Western countries. In spite of a series of meetings held by the G20, recovery to date is inconspicuous. 'The crisis has struck at the heart of the financial system – the banks – but it is systemic affecting every part of the economy: banks, firms, households, states' (Aglietta, 2012, p. 15). Significantly, and mirroring the initial differential power bases, massive imbalances developed between the member states within the European Union. While the large European banks became global operators, EU policy was only capable of delivering 'half-measures' thanks to a 'deep-seated conservatism' that may be construed as 'disastrous in times of turbulence'. Added to which, suggests Aglietta, the Eurozone suffers from profound structural faults attributable to how it was initially constituted. For example, the French and German banks helped to pour funds into Spain's housing sector, fuelling Spain's own housing bubble, which subsequently burst, leaving massive private debt.

Germany and the Eurozone crisis

As implied above, Germany has been the dominant actor within the zone, with the zone itself modelled on Germany's own monetarist doctrine (that is, a belief in the regulation of the amount of money in an economy, as opposed to fiscal/taxation changes to control an economy). Two-thirds of the country's trade surplus is derived at the cost of Germany's partners in the Eurozone. The nation's political rulers adopt an anti-market stance, and emphasise rules and regulations. Furthermore, and relating back to the connections between this crisis and its 2008 predecessor, German banks are 'loaded with toxic assets deriving from the American subprime mortgage crisis' (Aglietta, 2012, pp. 33–5). It was unsurprising, then, that tentative solutions were 'incremental, homeopathic', and ineffective, offering no real hope for European growth. What of the role of the Union's own bank? The Eurozone possessed a further barrier in its very institutional design, dominated by the European Central Bank (ECB; see above), which is the only federal organ within a non-federal Europe. Aglietta (2012) concludes that this 'contradiction lies at the heart of the present crisis'. Until July 2012, the ECB appeared unable to act. In September 2012, the President of the ECB, Italian economist Mario Draghi, intervened in the crisis to enhance the status of the bank by buying bonds in the Eurozone countries (*The Guardian*, 2012b).

Although the ECB's constitutional weaknesses (both the Maastricht and the Lisbon treaties forbade the ECB from lending money to governments) inhibited financial proactivity, George Soros's attempt to intercede in the Eurozone crisis, subsequently rejected by the German Government, pointed to the defective stance of Germany (Soros, 2012). Soros was formerly a successful billionaire speculator on global markets and currencies. He claimed that the policies pursued by Germany's leadership were capable of holding together the euro for an long period of time, but not permanently. The continued division of the EU into creditor and debtor nations was politically unacceptable. Germany, declared Soros, bore a big responsibility. The best alternative was to persuade Germany to make a choice between benevolent hegemony and leaving the euro. The German Bundesbank was continuing with an outmoded set of monetarist tenets. The climate of austerity in the European Union was now to be distinguished from that in the late 'seventies. Greece could have been rescued at the outset of the Greek crisis through extension of credit.' At the end of 2012, the EU made an agreement, despite strong resistance from Germany, to empower the ECB with authority over the Eurozone's 6000 banks, a step towards a Eurozone fiscal and political federation, while the UK

Government, as a non-member of the Eurozone, negotiated for UK banks to remain outside of the agreement (BBC News, 2012b; *The Guardian*, 2012c).

To recap, although the Eurozone crisis affected the global economy, including the financial and banking system, the European Union, a crucial institutional actor in global economic and social policy has not proactively countered the Eurozone crisis, unlike the big European banks. What is arguably so apparent from this second course of events is first, the worrying disparities between the southern Mediterranean regimes and the Western European economies (particularly the ascendant, monetarist Germany) within both the Eurozone and the Union, and second, the immanent structural and constitutional weaknesses of the EU's central financial institutions. In these respects, the politics of the European Union remain as charged as ever.

Conclusion

From researching these issues, we are able to formulate a set of conclusions. The European Union's brief history as a complex organisational network of structures, treaties, and constitutions is unique. A central concern of the Union revolves around the limits of the organisation's enlargement, not least during the past decade and the removal of barriers so as to encompass middle European member states, a process culminating in the historic Lisbon Constitution. Regardless of repeated conservative attacks on the unwieldy nature of the enhanced EU, the organisation survives intact, even in the midst of the global and euro crises. European social policy, emergent from its traditionally minor role in the spheres of family policy, policies for older people, and education and training, is of contemporary significance. Notwithstanding the overt tensions between the Commission and the individual states, the Union has managed to establish a set of policy directives accepted by a majority of the states, leading to rising standards of equity. But the Eurozone crisis is a key moment for the European Union as a whole, coming immediately after the global financial crisis, given the ramifications for member states, and that the continued existence of the EU was thrown into doubt by media commentators at least until the beginning of 2013. The Eurozone crisis imposes yet a further social burden upon the Mediterranean economies (and the majority of their respective citizens) and renders visible the gap in economic and political power between them and the affluent Western European nation-states. Whereas the origins of the crisis resided in the sovereign debt of Greece, the accumulation of previously unthinkable Mediterranean debt was not only caused by private sector exhortations and the interests of an economically booming Germany, but also by having to pay for the earlier and indisputably related global financial crisis. Finally, the European Union's singular response to the Eurozone crisis is a disappointing one, compared with those of the member states' own banks. The European Central Bank lacks 'weight', by dint of its historical constitutional weaknesses, while the circumstances of the latest crisis testify to the European Union's lack of an effective, centralised financial authority.

Summary

In this chapter, you have been introduced to:

- an overview of the European Union's history, structures, treaties, and constitutions;
- the 'enlargement debate' in the European Union;
- the development and current status of European Union social policy;
- the events and explanations of the Eurozone crisis, and the concomitant social impacts on member states;
- the EU's response to the euro crisis.

Discussion and review

To what extent has the combination of 'global capitalist crisis' and 'euro zone crisis':

- signalled the possible future demise of the EU?
- heightened the inequalities of power and wealth between and within EU member states?
- strengthened the UK Coalition government's arguments for maintaining a sceptical distance from full participation in the EU?

References

Aglietta, M. (2012) 'The European vortex', *New Left Review*, May/June, pp. 15–36.

Anderson, P. (2011) *The New Old World*, Verso, London.

BBC News (2012a) 'Eurozone crisis explained', 19 June.

BBC News (2012b) 'UK agreement with EU re: banks', 13 December.

BBC News Europe (2012) 'Eurozone crisis: Spain in numbers', 25 July.

Callinicos, A. (2012) 'The crisis of our time', *International Socialism*, 11 October.

Daily Beast (2012) 'Europe's austerity crisis ravages Italy's south', 2 October.

Deacon, B. (2007) *Global Social Policy and Governance*, Sage, London.

Delors, J. (1988) Speech to the British TUC, September.

Der Spiegel (2012) 'Italy cities in crisis', 6 August.

Economist (2012) 'Spain', 1 December.

EUobserver.com (2012) 'Portugal in crisis after 1 million say No to austerity', 20 September.

Eurofound (2012a) *Wages and Working Conditions in the Crisis – A Comparative Study*, European Working Conditions Observatory (EWCO), available at http://www.eurofound.europa.eu/docs/ewco/tn1203015s/tn1203015s.pdf.

Eurofound (2012b) 'Impact of the recession on age management policies (résumé)', January, available at http://www.eurofound.europa.eu/pubdocs/2011/75/en/4/EF1175EN.pdf.

European Commission (2007) 'Communication from the Commission to the European Parliament and the Council on Enlargement Strategy, 2007–8', 6 November (http:ec.europa.eu/enlargement).

Eurostat (2009) *Education and Training 2020 (ET 2020)*, available at http://europa.eu/legislation_summaries/education_training_youth/general_framework/ef0016_en.htm.

Eurostat (2012) 'Spain and crisis', Eurostat, Luxembourg.

Hantrais, L. (2007) *Social Policy in the European Union* (3rd edn.), Macmillan, London.

Held, D. (2004) *Global Covenant: The Social Democratic Alternative to the Washington Consensus*, Polity, Cambridge.

Hobson, J. (2011) *Democratic governance beyond the nation state: An explanation of democracy and governance in the European Parliament*, unpublished PhD thesis, University of Gloucestershire, Cheltenham.

Hutton, W. (2002) *The World We're In*, Little Brown, London.

IMF, European Central Bank, European Commission (2012) 'Joint statement on Eurozone crisis', 11 September.

Judt, T. (2007) *Postwar: A History of Europe Since 1945*, Pimlico, London.

Keane, J. (2009) *The Life and Death of Democracy*, Simon & Schuster, London.

Lancet (2011) 'On Greece and health', 22 October.

Laursen, F. (2001) 'EU enlargement: interests, issues and the need for institutional reform', in S.S. Andersen and K.A. Eliasen (eds.) *Making Policy in Europe* (2nd edn.), Sage, London.

politics.co.uk (2012) 'UK Prime Minister David Cameron addresses House of Commons on EU Summit', 2 July.

Rapacki, R. and Prochniak, M. (2009) *The EU Enlargement and Economic Growth in the CEE New Member Countries*, European Commission, March.

Soros, G. (2012) 'The tragedy of the European Union and how to resolve it', *New York Review of Books*, 27 September.

Thatcher, M. (1988) 'Bruges speech on the European Community', September.

Thatcher, M. (1993) *The Downing Street Years*, Harper Collins, London.

The Guardian (2012a) 'Greece', 15 June.

The Guardian (2012b) 'Eurozone crisis', 8 September.

The Guardian (2012c) 'Eurozone and UK Government agreement', 14 December.

The Guardian (2012d) 'Cameron's announcement of Government referendum on EU', 29 December.

The Telegraph (2012a) 'Italian cities in crisis', 23 July.

The Telegraph (2012b) 'Debt crisis: Portugal to raise taxes to meet austerity', 3 October.

Further reading

Currently, a surfeit of literature abounds on the EU in general, less so on social policy in particular, but the latter is likely to change through expected further commentaries on the global and euro crises. Pinder and Usherwood's *The European Union: A Very Short Introduction* (Oxford University Press, Oxford, 2007, 2nd edn.) is a useful overview on structures while less attentive to social policy. However, Hantrais' *Social Policy in the European Union* (Macmillan, London, 2007, 3rd edn.) is an indispensable scholarly guide, touching on all the pertinent controversies. McCormick's *Understanding the European Union: A Concise Introduction* (Palgrave Macmillan, London, 2011, 5th edn.) is an up-to-date representation of the Union's institutional and political framework. Giddens' *Europe in the Global Age* (Polity, Cambridge, 2007) presents a sociological assessment of European developments, locating EU issues within the wider global context and the challenges to the organisation's welfare state 'social model'. Taylor-Gooby's (ed.) *Making a European Welfare State? Convergence and Conflict Over European Social Policy* (Blackwell, Oxford, 2004) examines open markets versus welfare state, ranging from pensions and social welfare to labour markets, in Germany, Finland, UK, Bulgaria, Romania, and the Mediterranean economies.

Useful websites

Eurofound (http://www.eurofound.europe.eu)
EU (http://www.Europa.eu)
European Commission (http://www.ec.europa.eu)
IMF (http://www.imf.org/external/index.htm)
World Economic Outlook (WEO) for Data and Statistics (http://www.imf.org/external/data.htm)
United Nations (http://www.un.org)
World Bank (http://www.worldbank.org)
UK Politics/Government (http://www.politics.co.uk)
BBC News (http://www.bbc.co.uk/news/business)
BBC News Europe (http://www.bbc.co.uk/news/Europe)
The Guardian (http://www.guardian.co.uk)
Economist (http://www.Economist.com)

CHAPTER 25

Conclusions

Hugh Bochel and Guy Daly

Chapter overview

This book has outlined some of the many areas of debate in contemporary social policy. This chapter reflects briefly upon:

- trends in social policy;
- changes that may affect the subject;
- the broad approaches of the Labour and Conservative-Liberal Democrat coalition governments to social policy since 1997.

As outlined in Chapter 1, and repeatedly evident in other chapters throughout this book, social policy is an academic subject that is founded in the social sciences and which relates to other social science and related subjects such as economics, history, politics, and sociology. It is a subject that continues to have major relevance to and links with a range of professions, such as nursing, social work, and housing. Yet, at the same time, social policy is also something that goes on in the real world and which affects real people on a daily basis. It is sometimes therefore necessary to take all of these actualities into account when discussing 'social policy'. To some extent, this chapter reflects this: its primary purpose is to focus upon developments in the real world, but at the same time it seeks to point out a number of areas where the academic subject is concerned, and where the two may come together, to point this out.

Any reading of this volume will have made clear that social policy is continually developing, and that there are inevitably a wide range of interactions with many other policy areas and with economic, political, ideological, and social imperatives. Chapters 2, 3, and 4 serve to highlight the ways in which social policy is both affected by and impacts upon wide swathes of economic, social, and political life, and Chapter 5 reflects this in discussing the impact of devolved legislatures in Northern Ireland, Scotland, and Wales since they were created in 1999.

Chapter 6 provides a vital underpinning for our understanding of policy change through a consideration of the development of social policy historically, and in particular the ways in which governments increasingly became involved in the provision of welfare services. Building upon this, for three-quarters of the twentieth century it was possible to argue that the key social policy development in the United Kingdom was the gradual extension of state welfare and the establishment of a welfare state, closely linked with the rise of organised labour, and in particular the 1945 Labour government, which was strongly influenced by social democratic and democratic socialist thinking, including the Fabian tradition. Following the Second World War, there was a broad consensus on the idea of the welfare state, together with a commitment to full employment, and to a mixed economy, managed by governments using Keynesian techniques.

However, by the 1970s this consensus was coming to an end, shaken by a variety of criticisms from different parts of the political spectrum, as outlined in Chapters 7 and 8, and by a recognition that the welfare state had not achieved all that many of its supporters would have wished. Indeed, from 1979, with the election of the Conservative government led by Margaret Thatcher, elements of previously widely accepted social policy were being seriously questioned, with a new emphasis upon individualism, selection, and the market replacing that on collectivism, universalism, and the state. At the same time, within the academic subject of social policy, there was a much greater recognition of the diversity of the subject, with the development of a variety of critiques of past approaches and the incorporation of new ideas from both domestic and comparative approaches to the study of social policy. Many of these changes are reflected in the topics considered in Chapters 9 to 21.

Despite much of the rhetoric, and some significant reforms, after 18 years of Conservative government substantial parts of the welfare state remained largely intact when Labour returned to power in 1997. However, by the late 1990s Labour's approach to social policy was not the same as it had been (see Chapter 8). There was now a much greater commitment to the use of a diversity of forms of provision, from public, private, and voluntary sectors, and a view that was expressed by the New Labour government was that what mattered was 'what works', rather than who provides services and benefits. Public opinion, which, as measured by opinion polls and surveys, had frequently favoured increased expenditure for improved public services (and particularly for services used by the bulk of the population), but did not always match this with a willingness to pay the higher taxes necessary for this, made the government's position more difficult, although it was to some extent aided by the failure of the Conservative Party to offer effective electoral opposition until 2005. In addition, the rising costs of welfare were encouraging governments to seek to control levels of expenditure and to spread the financial burden, whether through reliance upon informal and voluntary provision, or through encouraging people to make provision for themselves and their families, for example through insurance or pensions provision by the private sector.

After more than a decade of a buoyant UK economy, the economic crisis of 2008 meant that, whatever the complexion of the next government, cuts in public expenditure were inevitable. Following David Cameron's election to the leadership of the Conservative Party he had sought, in some respects at least, to soften the position of his party and to talk about the need to fight poverty, although at the same time he took up the idea that British society was 'broken', including in relation to family breakdown, unemployment, and welfare dependency. At the same time, among the leadership of the Liberal Democrats there had been a shift away from those with more social democratic leanings to those who favoured a more economic liberal approach. When no party won an overall majority at the 2010 general election, it was perhaps less surprising than it might have been that, after several days of negotiation, a Conservative-Liberal Democrat Coalition government emerged.

Given the economic crisis, the scale of the United Kingdom's fiscal deficit, and the implications of different ideological positions, it is understandable that one of the major questions for the future remains how social welfare should be paid for. However, equally important is how resources should be used. Questions of government income and expenditure therefore relate strongly to issues around the distribution, and potentially the *re*-distribution, of resources. For much of the post-war period there had been a broad commitment, particularly from the political left, to a degree of redistribution from the wealthier in society to the poorer, to be achieved primarily through higher taxes on the former and the provision of benefits and services to the latter. By the 1990s, this had largely been replaced by a desire by New Labour to keep 'middle England' happy and, in particular, to do so by avoiding increases in income tax. Labour's attempts at a degree of redistribution were therefore very different from those of the post-war years (see, for example, Chapter 9). For the Coalition, and particularly for those who favoured neo-liberal approaches to economic and social policy, the economic crisis inevitably meant large-scale reductions in public expenditure, going beyond those planned by the previous government, and frequently justified by the perceived need to reduce the government's borrowing and to keep the markets happy, although by the third year of the Coalition government there was increasing questioning of the impact of the cuts on economic growth and of the failure to reduce public borrowing and the budget deficit. Critics also noted that the scale of the cuts meant that parts of the welfare state were likely to be altered to an unprecedented degree, meaning that neo-liberal policies were having a greater impact than even during the Thatcher period.

For social policy the impacts of the Coalition government were therefore obvious not only in terms of substantive policy change, but also in relation to changes in public expenditure, even in areas such as the NHS and education, which the Coalition had promised to protect in real terms, while the implications of protection for some areas meant that others, such as the benefits system, suffered much deeper reductions in spending. The chapters in Part 3 of the book explore these further. It is clear, overall, that the combination of policy change and major cuts in public expenditure are posing significant challenges for many areas of the welfare state. For example, the introduction of universal credit and the capping of some benefits were argued by the Coalition government to be both a response to the needs of the economy and to welfare dependency, but are likely to have the greatest impact upon some of the most vulnerable members of society (see Chapters 9 and 10).

One of the other developments under New Labour, although not unique, was an attention to the mechanisms of policy-making and implementation, not seen since the 1960s, if then (see Chapters 3, 4, and 5). This helps to remind us of the importance of politics and decision-making for social policy. Social policy is not technocratic: it is not simply a question of making minor adjustments to ensure the smooth running of mechanisms. As noted above, there are fundamental decisions to be made that affect society, including over how resources are raised and distributed. To these traditional social policy concerns have been added – as has been highlighted, particularly following the introduction of devolved administrations in Northern Ireland, Scotland, and Wales since 1997 – an awareness of the importance of the mechanisms that are used to make and implement social policy, and there is now the potential for even greater diversity within the United Kingdom. Yet, as has frequently been noted by many commentators, like the Conservatives before them and the Coalition government after them, Labour's apparent desire to devolve some aspects of decision-making was matched by a high degree of centralisation and control, again reflected in many chapters of this book, particularly in England, where there has been little evidence of localism actually empowering local communities or councils.

While the domestic agenda remains important, Chapters 22, 23, and 24 remind us that international developments, including the United Kingdom's membership of the European Union, are also having an impact upon social policy. Yet the discussions within these chapters also make clear that the same phenomenon can be interpreted very differently from different analytical or ideological perspectives. In the same way, the realm of social policy has also been broadened by other debates, including those that continue over the boundaries of the subject (Chapters 20 and 21).

Looking to the broader political debate, since 1997 some have argued that within the major political parties there is again something approaching a general consensus upon social policy. This new consensus could be said to be founded: in a belief that there should be a mixture of providers, drawn from across the sectors, but with regulation by the state; in some commitment to public provision, but with a significant emphasis upon provision by the private sectors, and to encouraging individuals to make provision for themselves; and in a greater concern by the state with tackling social problems and exclusion through attempts to create more equal opportunities for individuals, rather than through financial redistribution from the richer to the poorer. However, particularly given the enthusiasm of the Coalition government for major reductions in public expenditure and for quite radical change in areas such as benefits reform and education, and changes such as opening up the NHS to greater provision by the private and not-for-profit sectors, the extent to which such a consensus actually exists – either within the political parties or the wider public – is unclear. As always in social policy, one of the few certainties is that both the subject that is social policy, and social policies themselves, will continue to change and develop.

Discussion and review

- Do you agree that there is a broad political consensus on social policy? What evidence would you use to support or refute such a view?
- What do you believe should be the balance of welfare provision across informal, public, private, and informal sectors? Why?

Abolitionism   Used as shorthand to describe the scrapping of, for example, hanging, prison or corporal punishment. It is allied also to attempts to substantially limit the use of prison or, more loosely, to move away from the punitive fixation of the criminal justice system towards restorative/restitutive forms of justice.

Academy schools   These originated under the Labour governments of 1997–2010 but were developed and expanded (arguably in a way that Labour never intended) by the Coalition government from 2010. They are publicly funded schools that have freedom from local authority control and greater freedoms, including over the delivery of the curriculum, the lengths of days and terms, and the pay and conditions of their staff.

Activation policies   Government programmes that intervene in the labour market to help the unemployed find work.

Active ageing   Active ageing is a policy or set of polices that aims to maximise the opportunities for older people to live, work, and participate in society as fully as possible and for as long as possible in order that they can enjoy healthy and secure lives.

Acts of Settlement   The name given to a number of Acts of Parliament passed from the sixteenth century that defined who was eligible for parish relief. In order to try to keep Poor Law costs down, the parish was only responsible for paupers who were born within a parish or who had some other connection, for example through marriage.

Actus reus   The type of offence committed.

Anti-social behaviour   Technically defined in the Crime and Disorder Act 1998 as behaviour that has 'caused or was likely to cause harassment, alarm or distress to one or more persons not of the same household'. However, it has come to be understood as a catch-all category for nuisance behaviour, which may or may not be criminal, and which is most commonly associated with youth.

Anti-social behaviour order (ASBO)   A hybrid legal instrument in that it spans both civil and criminal law. Orders are granted in a civil court (rather like an injunction) and impose a number of prohibitive conditions on an individual to prevent them from engaging in 'anti-social behaviour'. Breach of these conditions, however, is a criminal offence, which is punishable with a maximum of five years' imprisonment.

'Back to Basics'   A campaign launched by John Major at the Conservative Party conference in 1993, aimed at raising moral standards, it became focused particularly on lone parenthood.

'**Basic income**' or '**Citizen's income**' An idea which, in various forms, has been around for a long time. It involves a critique of existing social security systems, based on social insurance or social assistance principles, as exclusionary, and proposes their replacement by a universal tax-financed cash grant, payable to all individuals regardless of labour market position, marital status, etc. It involves removing the link between work and entitlement, which is so important in most contemporary social security systems.

Bedroom tax The Coalition government decided to cut housing benefit from 2013 for recipients who were deemed to be living in a house with too many bedrooms for their needs. This was soon dubbed the 'bedroom tax'.

Behavioural economics Aims to draw upon psychological insights to provide a better understanding of economic behaviour.

Beveridge Sir William Beveridge, a civil servant/academic responsible for the publication of the Social Insurance and Allied Services Report of 1942 – the Beveridge Report – often considered the blueprint for much of the development of the post-war British welfare state.

Big Society The idea of the 'Big Society' was launched by David Cameron around ideas such as empowering communities and fostering a culture of volunteerism. Despite a number of relaunches between 2010 and 2012, it largely failed to capture the imagination of the public or those organisations that were intended to be at its heart.

Bretton Woods Refers to the Bretton Woods system of monetary management regulations for the western capitalist states. A series of Bretton Woods agreements were signed in 1944 at Bretton Woods, New Hampshire, USA, and created the World Bank and the International Monetary Fund.

British Social Attitudes Survey A long-running (since 1983) set of annual surveys looking at changes in attitudes within society. Run by the National Centre for Social Research.

'**Broken Britain**' An idea that largely originated from the right-leaning think tank the Centre for Social Justice, it suggested that Britain was experiencing social breakdown.

Brown field sites Term loosely used to describe land that has previously been developed, as opposed to green field sites, which have not.

BSE crisis In 1996, fears over an epidemic of bovine spongiform encephalopathy and over vCJD (new variant Creutzfeldt-Jakob disease, the human equivalent of BSE) led to a crisis in British farming, with the slaughter of millions of cattle and the introduction of new regulations on the slaughter and consumption of beef.

Children's Commissioner Following the Children Act 2004, the post of Children's Commissioner for England was appointed to act as an independent voice for children and young people. Scotland, Wales, and Northern Ireland each have their own Commissioner.

Children's Fund Focused on developing services that support multi-agency working, the Fund was targeted at 5- to 13-year-olds and was a key part of the Labour government's strategy to tackle disadvantages and inequalities that derive from child poverty and social exclusion. However, from 2008 these were absorbed into local authority mainstream provision.

Classical liberalism Descriptive of a political doctrine usually associated with the nineteenth century and with early formulations of social policy. An interventionist role for the state may be justified where other social structures (markets) are seen to be failing and wherein state activity is minimal or residual.

Clinical commissioning groups (CCGs) Established by the Coalition Government's 2012 Health and Social Care Act and replaced primary care trusts (PCTs) as the local commissioners (or purchasers) of health services. They are led by clinicians (mostly GPs) who are believed to be better placed than managers or administrators to determine the health service needs of local populations.

Commodity A good or service regarded as having no intrinsic merit. Its value is its exchange price, as determined by the interaction between supply and demand.

Communitarianism Range of ideas expressing the desire to re-establish or rediscover 'civil society', in which collective welfare is expressed through the agency of the active community and active citizen rather than that of a centralised state machinery.

Community care A term that can be understood in many different ways, but is generally applicable to a range of policies applied to looking after people with particular needs in the community, including the movement of people from long-stay institutions to living in the community.

Community charge In 1989 (in Scotland) and 1990 (in England and Wales), the Conservative government replaced the existing system of local taxation, known as 'rates' with the community charge (widely known as the 'poll tax'), a charge on each member of a household. Following widespread protests and significant problems with collection, it was replaced by council tax in 1993.

Comprehensive education System of state secondary schools designed to ensure that all children receive similar education, thus increasing equality of opportunity.

Comprehensive schools Schools offering education without attempting to differentiate between abilities of pupils along arbitrary academic or technical lines. Developed as the preferred method of state schooling during the 1960s and 1970s.

Comprehensive Spending Review   Introduced by Gordon Brown when he was Chancellor of the Exchequer, this involves government departments justifying their expenditure plans to the Treasury for a three-year period, rather than the previous annual spending allocations. It also gave the Treasury a greater role in coordinating and controlling government expenditure.

Consensus/welfare consensus   Term applied to the post-war political settlement characterised by the similarities exhibited in the economic policies of successive Labour (Gaitskell) and Conservative (Butler) Chancellors of the Exchequer. In particular, the consensus was built upon the acceptance of the role of the state in the pursuit of welfare and greater equality together with the pursuit of full employment as an economic principle.

Consumerism   A neo-liberal doctrine that stresses the role of the individual as a consumer of welfare services within a market- or quasi-market-oriented welfare state. It regards consumers as having sovereignty within markets which individuals lack in any state-dominated system of welfare provision.

Corporate crime   Crime committed in some form of organisational context. This highlights the problem of attributing individual human agency to the 'author' of the crime, and thus the problem of exacting appropriate punishment. Recent attempts to upgrade the law on 'corporate killing' testify to some of the problems here. Sutherland uses this interchangeably with white-collar crime as a rhetorical challenge to criminology.

CRASBO   Criminal ASBO, which the court can impose upon conviction of a criminal offence in addition to the punishment. Conditions of the CRASBO are intended to help prevent re-offending, but extend further than merely desisting from committing the offence in future.

Crime control   Model of criminal justice policy that is concerned with attempts to suppress crime and criminal activity, often without regard to the consequences for civil rights.

Criminalisation   Refers to a range of social and criminal justice processes (including policing, prosecution, punishment, penalisation, stigmatisation, and blame) through which an individual or group is accorded the 'label' of criminal.

Crown Prosecution Service (CPS)   Government agency with responsibility for deciding whether to instigate, and pursue, criminal proceedings through the courts.

Cycle of deprivation thesis   Conservative Minister Keith Joseph, in a speech to the Pre-School Playgroup Association, propounded the view that deprivation was transmitted through the family.

'Decline', 'declinism'   An influential view, mood or feeling held by opinion-formers, journalists, and to some extent politicians and the public about the state of the UK from the 1950s to the 1980s, namely that it was 'in decline'. The UK appeared to be relatively economically unsuccessful compared with, for example, many European countries and Japan. Growth rates were low compared with other countries, and there were endemic industrial relations problems and balance of payments crises. (In fact, the UK's economic growth performance was quite respectable compared with its own past history.) This pessimistic mood or feeling was enhanced by two things: the UK's having 'won the war' in 1945 but then appearing much less successful than its defeated rivals; and the disappearance of the Empire between the 1940s and 1960s. 'Declinism' was in fact widely shared by left and right, but can be seen as underpinning the views particularly of the Thatcher governments in the 1980s, which went on to claim that they had solved the problem of the UK's decline.

Demand-side   Stimulation of demand for goods and services.

Democracy Movement   This is a non-party pressure group, set up to prevent the British Government from adopting the euro as its currency, thereby replacing the pound sterling. The organisation is against an EU constitution, viewing the EU as an undemocratic superstate.

Democratic deficit   Term describing the lack or weakness of traditional democratic forms of control and scrutiny of the Executive.

Dependency culture   Often used to describe a situation where people are seen to have become passive recipients of welfare, dependent upon benefits.

Dependency ratio   Dependency rates or ratios focus on the relative sizes of the economically active part of the population and those who are designated as dependent (primarily children and older people). Generally, a lower dependency ratio implies relatively more workers and less need to support dependent populations, while a higher dependency ratio suggests that a higher proportion of a population is dependent and a smaller proportion economically active.

Deregulation   The process by which governments have sought to reduce and remove regulations on businesses in order to improve the theoretical efficiency of markets. The theory is that deregulation will lead to greater competitiveness and efficiency.

Deserving poor   Term applied to paupers thought to be more genuine and therefore deserving of parish relief. This might include those people who find themselves in poverty by virtue of illness, disability or old age.

Deviance   A term used to refer to 'rule-breaking behaviour' and, more controversially, to deviations from the normal, that is, pathological states.

Discrimination   The act of making distinctions – usually with reference to particular social groups, for example based on race or ethnicity, gender, class, sexual orientation – and treating differently (and less or more favourably) because of such distinctions. Direct discrimination is where an individual or group is treated differently (and less favourably) directly, such as because of their ethnicity, gender or sexual orientation; indirect discrimination is where an individual or group is treated differently (and less favourably) as an indirect consequence of a policy or practice.

Due process   Model of criminal justice policy that is concerned with the pursuit of justice within the criminal legal system based upon a set of procedural rules that should be followed.

Earth Summit   An attempt to bring together participants, including heads of state and government, national delegates, non-governmental organisations, businesses, and other major groups to focus upon improving people's lives and conserving natural resources.

Economic inactivity   Refers to people not looking for, or not available for, work.

Enabling authority   The job of a local authority, for example its adult social care department, is increasingly to coordinate and monitor the quality of social care provision within its locale rather than to act as a provider of such services. The 'enabling authority' was to be key in the development of an internal market in social care following the passage of the NHS and Community Care Act 1990.

Enlightenment   This term describes the historical period at the end of the Middle Ages during which rational and scientific methods of thought and investigation were developed.

Equal opportunities policies   A range of policies designed to narrow gender or other inequalities within society, either by equalising outcomes of policy initiatives or equalising the environment within which policy operates.

Ethnicity   The identification of individuals as members of a particular group on the basis of their origin in a community, which may be mythical or real, with a historical, territorial, cultural, and/or racial basis.

Ethnocentrism   Term describing attitudes and the development of policies that explicitly or implicitly discriminate against minority ethnic groups.

European Community/European Union (EC/EU)   The economic association developed among European countries following the Second World War, with the aim of creating a single market on the continent of Europe and guaranteeing economic progress.

European Free Trade Association   Alternative form of economic association to the EU designed around bilateral agreement between member states rather than common agreements across all member states.

Exchange rate mechanism   Monetary system established within the EU designed to tie the rate of currency exchange of its member nations more closely and to minimise rapid and wild currency fluctuations.

Externality   A side-effect of an activity that affects other parties without being reflected in the price of the good or service involved.

Fabianism   The Fabian Society has existed for more than 150 years. Fabians have believed that the free market system was inappropriate for the solution of social problems and that instead there should be collective provision. Closely linked with the Labour Party and with social democratic and democratic socialist thinking, Fabian ideas were influential in the development of the post-war welfare state.

Five giants   The most pressing social problems – Want, Ignorance, Disease, Idleness, and Squalor – as defined by the Beveridge Report.

Fordist   A range of processes associated with industrial mass production, named after Henry Ford's approach in the car industry.

Free schools   Publicly funded schools set up as a response to local demand. They were enthusiastically supported by the Secretary of State for Education, Michael Gove under the Coalition government from 2010. Critics argued that many free schools were undersubscribed and were established in areas where there was no evidence of need.

Full employment   Unwritten government goal throughout much of the post-war era up to the late 1970s which sought to maintain consistently low levels of (male manufacturing) unemployment.

Further education   Education often provided by further education colleges, sometimes available to children aged 16–19, but also aimed at adults. Although often linked to qualifications or careers, it can also be used solely to enhance knowledge and skills.

Genetically modified (GM) crops   These crops are from plants that have had their genes modified, for example, to make them more tolerant of particular conditions or resistant to certain herbicides.

Gini coefficient   A measure of inequality ranging from 0 (complete equality) to 1 (one person has all the income or wealth, depending on what is being measured). Sometimes expressed as a percentage (0–100 per cent).

Globalisation   While there are different perspectives, globalisation recognises that a variety of forces are leading to similar cultural, economic, social, political, and technical developments around the world.

GP fundholders   As part of the internal market within the health service created by the Conservatives in the 1990s, GP practices were able to opt to receive a budget (become fundholders) with which they could then establish contracts with their chosen providers.

Grant-maintained schools   Schools that opt out of local education authority control, are self-governing, and receive their funding directly from central government.

Grant-maintained status   Also known as 'opting out', such schools are managed independently of their local authority and financed directly by the Department for Education.

Gross domestic product   The total value of goods and services produced by a nation. The GDP includes consumer and government purchases, private domestic investments, and net exports of goods and services. It therefore measures national output.

Health promotion   Describes a set of policies designed to induce personal and individual responsibility for health issues. Usually involves a programme of health education to promote healthier lifestyles, for example by discouraging health-damaging behaviour such as smoking, heavy drinking or poor diet or by promoting particular health issues such as more careful sexual behaviour.

Higher education   More specialist provision through universities and colleges of higher education, including undergraduate degrees (BA, BSc, LLB, etc.), taught postgraduate awards (MA, MSc), and research degrees (frequently a PhD, or Doctor of Philosophy).

Historical materialism   Marx's theory of social development in which he suggested that all human societies were governed, in their development, by immutable historical laws.

Housing associations   Non-profit-making bodies that specialise in housing and plough any surplus back into maintaining existing homes and helping to finance new ones. They provide homes to rent and also run low-cost home ownership schemes.

Human development index   The HDI provides a composite measure of three dimensions of human development: living a long and healthy life (measured by life expectancy), being educated (measured by adult literacy and enrolment at the primary, secondary, and tertiary level), and having a decent standard of living (measured by **purchasing power parity**, PPP, income). Based on this composite measure, the countries of the world are ranked in terms of their relative development.

Independent sector treatment centres   Treatment centres owned by the private sector or by social enterprises that are contracted to work within the NHS in England. They generally perform common elective surgery and diagnostic tests.

Informal economy   Those economic activities conducted mostly outside of the legal and administrative institutions of the formal economy.

Institutional racism   Processes within an organisation that lead to differentially adverse outcomes for minority ethnic persons, going beyond prejudicial behaviour of individuals within the organisation.

Integrated care   The desire or attempt to bring together the various multiple parts of (health and social) care in order that patients and/or service users receive care that is coordinated and 'joined up', as opposed to fragmented or disjointed.

Integration, integrationism   The notion that members of minority ethnic groups should feel and be seen to be participant in the culture, economy, and politics of society as a whole, while having their own particular ethnic identity.

Inter alia   Literally meaning 'among other things'.

Inter-governmental organisations   Organisations that are generally created by treaties or agreements between states, such as the World Bank; these have a legal status and often have mechanisms for resolving disputes between members.

Internal markets   The Conservative governments of 1979–97 sought to improve the efficiency and responsiveness of services such as health and social care through the introduction of internal markets, based on the separation of the functions of purchasing and provision of services.

Invisible hand   Term coined by the economist Adam Smith to describe the 'natural' operation of the free market and its tendency to self-regulation.

Keynesianism   The economist John Maynard Keynes argued that governments could successfully intervene in the economy to stimulate demand (and therefore to achieve full employment) and to reduce demand (and therefore achieve lower inflation). Keynesianism provided the basis for economic policy in most Western states from 1945 to the 1970s. This is complemented by the development of a comprehensive range of high-quality universalist welfare services. The Keynesian welfare state concept is also typically associated with the concept of the post-war 'consensus'.

'Keynesian social democracy', 'Keynesian welfare state'   These are short-hand terms used to describe or refer to, typically, European welfare systems and states such as that of the UK from the 1940s until the 1970s, underpinned by a combination of economic policy and social policy in order to promote social goals. 'Keynesian' (which refers to the economist John Maynard Keynes, who developed a new theory about unemployment and economic policy in the 1930s) in this context refers to the commitment to use economic policy tools to maintain high or 'full' employment and to the belief that governments can effectively manage the economy to achieve this and other economic policy goals, including low inflation, balance of payments stability, and a reasonable rate of economic growth. This is complemented by the development of a comprehensive range of high-quality universalist welfare services. The Keynesian welfare state concept is also typically associated with the concept of the post-war 'consensus'.

Kyoto Protocol   Signed in Kyoto in 1997 this committed the industrialised nations to reducing worldwide emissions of greenhouse gases by an average of 5.2 per cent below 1990 levels over the next decade.

Labelling theory A convenient shorthand for the social reaction perspective based on the premise that a situation, if defined as real, will be real in its consequences. The area is contested, but ranges from a focus upon the interaction between the potential deviant and those who so label him/her, through to the idea that if you call someone deviant/criminal this will confirm and reproduce their problem behaviour and thus make things worse. For example, the idea that the criminal justice system is part of the problem of crime in that it makes things worse, and is not necessarily the best solution.

Labour intensification Refers to how some people are working harder.

Labour market segmentation A situation in which there are so-called 'insiders', the workers with a protected job requiring high skills, and 'outsiders', who are low-skilled people that are either unemployed or employed as fixed-term, part-time or temporary with little chance to climb the career ladder.

Laissez-faire The economic doctrine that urges abstention by governments from interfering in the workings of the free market.

Laissez-faire capitalism Seen as a pure form of capitalism, it implies that governments should not intervene in the workings of the economy (laisser faire: to leave alone), and leave all to the workings of the 'market'. This school of thought believes business operations should be unimpeded.

Lease Lend A programme that allowed the United States to provide the United Kingdom (and other allies) with material for the Second World War in return for military bases.

Legitimacy, legitimation This involves a reference to states, governments, social orders, and institutions (such as welfare institutions) and the degree to which they command the loyalty and support of the population and their authority is accepted.

Less eligibility A principle of the Poor Law that suggested that the relief given to the poor should be at a level below that of the lowest paid of labourers to ensure that the poor would choose work rather than relief.

Liberal feminists Seek the same rights and opportunities for women as for men and focus largely on inequalities caused by prejudice and stereotyping, calling for legislation that outlaws discrimination.

Life expectancy The average period a person, of a given age, may expect to live.

Local management of schools A system of management in schools brought in following the 1988 Education Reform Act in which much decision-making was devolved to head teachers and boards of governors rather than local education authorities.

Male breadwinner Model of the family where the husband works (the breadwinner) and earns the family income while the wife provides care for the family.

Managerialism   An approach to criminal justice that emphasises the management of the system as a whole, with a focus on effective service delivery, efficiency, and value for money. It also reflects a concern with identifying and managing 'risk' through the collection of aggregate data on offending and calculation of statistical probabilities.

Means test   A test of income or wealth that determines entitlements to welfare benefits. Not all benefits, however, are subject to a means test.

Mens rea   Intention to commit a criminal act.

Micro-economics, macro-economics   Micro-economics refers to the sphere of economic activity, markets, and market exchanges in particular sectors of the economy, including the behaviour of firms and enterprises in innovating, setting prices, determining output and production; the labour market and the processes of determining wages and labour supply; and families and households in making decisions about consuming, working, and so on. Macro-economics is concerned with the level of the whole economy, rather than particular sectors or markets. It is concerned with such issues as price stability and inflation and the balance of payments. It is typically associated with such issues as monetary policy, e.g. whether the central bank should pursue price stability through inflation targeting, and with fiscal balance and fiscal policy – the appropriate level of taxes and the volume of public spending.

'Mixed economy of welfare' or 'welfare pluralism'   Descriptive terms that refer to the fact that welfare in any society is a product of a variety of agencies and institutions, including voluntary, commercial, and informal ones (such as the family), as well as statutory (public) agencies. The terms may also have a programmatic aspect to them, namely, that policy should seek to develop a plurality of welfare-providing institutions and try to move away from an exclusive reliance on one, such as statutory agencies.

Mode of production   Marx's term describing the organisation within a society of resources (forces of production) – capital, labour, land, and raw materials.

Monetarism   An economic theory that emphasises the control of the money supply as a method of managing the economy and in particular of controlling inflation.

Morbidity   Measure of the rate of disease or illness in a society within a given period.

Mortality   Measure of the rate of death in a society within a given period.

Multiculturalism   The notion that a multi-ethnic society should respect, protect the rights of, and even foster distinct minority ethnic cultures.

National Assistance   A system of welfare (mostly cash) benefits to which entitlement is most usually determined by the administration of a means test. This system has operated under various guises over the past 50 years, developed as supplementary benefits and latterly income support.

National Curriculum   A standardised curriculum approved by the Department for Education, which specifies what subjects must be taught to children of compulsory school age in virtually all state schools and stresses the development of literacy and numeracy and allows for comparisons of achievement between schools.

National Insurance   A system of welfare (cash) benefits to which entitlement is determined by a National Insurance contributions record.

Nationalisation   Taking into public (state) ownership, as happened with major industries such as coal, gas, electricity, and iron and steel in the post-war years.

National minimum wage   Introduced from April 1999, the national minimum wage began as a key element of Labour's Welfare to Work strategy, including by making low-paid employment more attractive. Since its introduction, it has been widely seen as a positive development.

Negative equity   A term coined after the slump in the private housing market in the early 1990s. Describes a situation wherein the market value of a property is less than the outstanding mortgage liability.

Neo-liberalism   A political ideology promoting economic liberalism, partly as a means to political liberty.

New public management   A phrase used to describe a set of ideas widely implemented by governments, particularly in English-speaking countries, from the 1980s, which emphasised marketisation and drew on private sector practices.

New Right   The ideas of a group of right-wing thinkers, often associated with the Thatcher governments. Neo-liberalism and neo-conservatism were important elements of this political position.

NHS trusts   Created by the Conservative government in the 1990s as part of the internal market within the NHS, the trusts run hospitals and/or community health services as self-governing bodies.

Non-contributory benefits   Range of cash benefits to which entitlement is determined by criteria other than National Insurance contributions.

Non-governmental organisations   Organisations established by individuals or associations of individuals and not possessing governmental powers; NGOs vary widely in size and influence.

Nursery education   Pre-school education for children below the age of formal compulsory education.

Occupational pension   A company pension to which both the employer and the employee make contributions.

Outdoor relief   Following the 1601 Poor Law, this was provision (such as money, food or clothing) given to help individuals avoid poverty without the need to enter an institution.

People's Budget   Lloyd-George's redistributive Budget of 1909, which imposed higher levels of taxation on the rich in order to finance spending on social policies, including pensions and contributions to the National Insurance fund.

Performance measurement   The use of measures of performance for organisations, such as schools, hospitals or even local authorities, sometimes linked with the use of 'league tables'.

Pluralism   A view that believes that power is or should be shared among the diverse groups and interests in society, and that political decision-making should reflect bargains and compromises between these groups.

Police and Crime Commissioners   Established by the Coalition government in 2013, they were intended to make the police more responsive and accountable to local communities. The first elections were, however, notable for a turnout of only 15 per cent.

Policy transfer   The practice of governments learning from approaches in other states and implementing them in their own jurisdiction.

Polytechnic   A type of higher education institution developed in the 1960s offering degree-level study but specialising in the teaching of technical and vocational subjects. Polytechnics ceased to exist in Britain in 1991 as they were granted full university status.

Poor Law   A system of pauper relief developed in Britain between the sixteenth and nineteenth centuries. In its earliest form, the parish was charged with responsibility for the poor living within its boundaries who would be helped with either outdoor relief – money, or food and goods – which allowed the poor to carry on living and working within the parish. Alternatively, the parish could provide indoor relief through workhouses, which would put the poor to work in return for assistance. The New Poor Law, which operated from 1834, did away with most outdoor relief and depended much more on the provision of help within the workhouse. The workhouse was intended to act as a deterrent and to encourage the poor to find work rather than rely on the help granted by the local Board of Guardians of the Poor who administered the new system.

Post-Fordist   Used to describe a perceived contrast with Fordist methods of production, with an emphasis on flexible systems of production and a flexible workforce.

Post-Fordism   A term used in industrial sociology and political economy. 'Fordism' is named after Henry Ford, the American creator of a mass-production car industry. Fordism refers to industrial processes – the mass-production of standardised products and components in large-scale manufacturing firms and enterprises – that developed in the twentieth century for a mass market with supposedly uniform and standardised tastes. 'Post-Fordism' refers to an alleged decline of such standardised mass production and its replacement by a diversified model of smaller-scale production for a much more diversified market, perhaps involving a decline in the giant manufacturing firm, 'lean' production processes, and outsourcing.

Power (dominance) and new criminology A model of criminal justice that sees crime as a 'social construct' such that neither individuals nor their behaviour should be regarded as inherently criminal.

Predictive genetic testing The ability to test or screen using genetic tests which may suggest that individuals are likely to develop one or more particular condition, such as Huntington's disease.

Pre-fabrication Method of rapid housing construction in which house components were constructed in factories and assembled on site.

Pre-sentence reports Documents prepared for a criminal trial that provide the court with background information about the accused person.

Primary education Education from the age of 5 to 11, designed to provide children with basic skills.

Primary health care Health services provided often as the first point of treatment. Examples include general practice, dentistry, health visiting services, and locally based health clinics.

Private Finance Initiative The Private Finance Initiative is a method of injecting private capital into the provision of public services. It can take the form of an agreement between a public body and a private company for the supply of buildings or services over a period of time, often 30 years. The public body sets the standards and pays a fee to the private company for the services provided, such as a hospital or school building, or the repair and improvement of local authority dwellings. Borrowing by the private company does not count as part of the Public Sector Borrowing Requirement.

Public health The health of the population as a whole, initially concerned with issues such as sanitation, but more recently focused on areas around the prevention of illness, such as immunisation.

Public schools Independent schools that charge fees; they do not have to teach the National Curriculum.

Public Sector Borrowing Requirement (PSBR) The difference between government spending and its income. It is regarded as an important indicator of the Chancellor of the Exchequer's prudence in managing the economy.

Public service agreements Established between the Treasury and central government departments, public service agreements set out what the department aims to achieve with a given level of resources.

Qualified majority voting (QMV) Refers to the simplified system of voting in the European Union. Under this system of Council decision-making, a qualified majority is achieved only if a decision is supported by 55 per cent of member states, including at least 15 of them, representing at least 65 per cent of the Union's population. Unanimity is not required.

Quangos Although not entirely accurate, the term quasi-autonomous non-governmental organisation (quango) is widely used to describe organisations that are not directly accountable to elected bodies, such as Parliament or local government.

'Quasi-market' or 'internal market' Kind of market associated with reforms of UK welfare agencies in the 1990s. Depends on the idea that there are two important elements in the organisation and delivery of welfare services – financing the service and providing or delivering it – and that these two elements can be separated to some extent. The agency remains part of the public sector, but an element of competition is injected into their operations by separating the function of purchasing the service from that of providing it. Henceforth, two different agencies are involved – a purchasing (or 'commissioning') agency (such as, in the NHS, a clinical commissioning group) and a providing agency (such as, in the NHS, a foundation hospital trust). The purchasing/commissioning agency, working on behalf of their local resident population, may select any provider on grounds of quality, cost, accessibility, and so on. Versions of the idea have been applied to health, social care, housing, and education in an attempt to improve quality, efficiency, and responsiveness.

Queen's Counsel (QC) Senior barristers who usually work in the higher levels of the court system – High Court, Court of Appeal, House of Lords.

Race The identification of individuals as members of a particular group on the basis of some physical difference of 'skin, hair, and bone'.

Racialisation A descriptive process in which **race** and/or **ethnicity** are used to categorise people into groups.

Radical feminists They see women as a group oppressed by men as a group, including through male dominance of the state, and tend to call for a radical transformation of all spheres of life, with some calling for political, and in some cases personal, separation from men.

Rational choice theory (also known as **public choice theory**) The application of economic concepts and methodology to other areas of social life. It involves the idea that social life and social institutions, including the state and politics, can be understood as the outcome of behaviour by rationally choosing individuals seeking to maximise advantage.

Relative deprivation A term, made famous by the work of Peter Townsend, used in poverty research and policy. Above the level of destitution or absolute subsistence, poverty is only meaningful if defined in terms of a relationship, between a norm of an average or generally acceptable or 'decent' standard of living in a particular society, shared by most people, and groups unable, because of lack of income, to share in this. Such groups may be described as 'relatively deprived'. The concept acknowledges the constantly evolving nature of poverty and of the societal norm of decency.

Rent control   State control of the rents charged by private landlords. The Conservatives attempted to phase out rent control in the 1930s and 1950s. By the 1970s, the major form of rent control was the determination of 'fair' rents by rent officers.

Replacement ratio   The ratio of the amount a person could receive in social security benefits while out of work relative to the amount they could receive if they were earning.

Reserve army of labour   Groups of workers maintained in capitalist societies who are available to work when the economic system enters one of its periodic boom cycles.

Restructuring   This can refer to one of two things: (1) A general process of economic and industrial change, such as that accompanying the decline of manufacturing industry and rise of service industries, as in the UK from the 1970s to the 1990s, or with 'post-Fordist' transformations of the industrial sphere. (2) Changes in public sector organisations, such as welfare delivery agencies, particularly associated with the decline of the traditional post-war rational-bureaucratic public administration model and development of so-called 'new public management', involving new forms of management, 'quasi'-markets, and purchaser–provider separation.

Rio Earth Summit   Held in Rio de Janeiro in June 1992, the Rio Earth Summit was the largest environmental conference ever held, attracting over 30,000 people and more than 100 heads of state.

Secondary education   Education from 11 to the minimum school leaving age of 16, or to 18.

Security of tenure   Refers to the legal presumption that a tenant should remain in a dwelling unless the landlord can convince a court that there are very good reasons to evict the tenant.

Serious Fraud Office   A state-sponsored organisation responsible for the investigation of commercial malpractice, such as insider trading.

Skills shortage/skills mismatch   Two terms used to describe shortfalls in education and training policy. Skills shortage is a term particularly related to school leavers, who lack education in the skills relevant to and required by industry and the economy generally. Skills mismatch is a term that refers to the type of skills possessed by workers and their inapplicability to the needs of the economy. An example would be where there have been redundancies in traditional industries, say engineering, and a rise in new technologies, computing, and telecommunications, and the skills of the traditional industry are not readily transferred to the new.

Social Charter More correctly called the Community Charter of the Fundamental Rights of Workers, this represents a key stage in the widening of the concept of European social policy beyond simply the rights attributed to those in employment.

Social control A sociological concept that refers to the achievement of social order through the regulation of society and social life by various means, including, in complex, differentiated, modern societies, the exercise of state power, behaviour-regulating law and legislation, agencies of coercion such as armed forces and police, and also such means as religion and education.

Social democracy This position has historically encompassed both socialism and democracy as essential components. Social democrats see capitalism as capable of transformation and reform through democratic action including the welfare state. However, from the 1980s some social democratic parties have adjusted their positions in response to critiques from the New Right and others.

Social exclusion Often used to describe the wider processes and outcomes that prevent people from participating in society and from accessing services.

Social housing The term was invented in the 1980s as a way to blur the distinction between local authority housing and accommodation provided by housing associations. It has been associated with accommodation let at a rent below the market price

Social inclusion A situation whereby people do not suffer the problems associated with social exclusion.

Social investment Social investment is seen by many as being concerned with investment in human capital, particularly for the future, with the social investment welfare state being one that invests in its people, and in particular its children. However, the Coalition government has used the term social investment to describe the provision of capital that gives social sector organisations the capacity to deliver social or financial returns or both.

Socialist feminists Socialist feminists aspire to an economically just society, with both women and men having the opportunity to fulfil their potential.

Social mobility The degree to which an individual's, family's or group's social status can change throughout the course of their life.

Social model of disability Developed by disabled people as an alternative to the 'medical model', it argues that disability is caused by the society in which we live and is not the 'fault' of an individual, or an inevitable consequence of their limitations. Instead, it arises from physical, organizational, and attitudinal barriers that lead to discrimination.

Standard Attainment Tests (SATs)   A system of assessing school children at ages 7, 11, and 14 that is used to measure a child's progress and upon which school league tables have been based.

Stealth taxes   Taxes of which the population is supposedly unaware (or at least are only partially aware) of their existence and function.

Stigma   A term made famous by the American sociologist Erving Goffman in his book of that title (1963). Stigma involves the idea of 'spoiled identity'. It involves loss of status or dignity in some sense. Students of social policy in the 1960s and 1970s such as Richard Titmuss were particularly concerned with the issue of how and to what extent social policies and services might engender stigma among service users. The issue was perhaps most serious for long-term recipients of services in the social care sector and some parts of means-tested social security, but was important wherever distinctions were made between service beneficiaries or users on, for example, income grounds. Examples include school children receiving free school meals who could be identified as such. The Poor Law was an example of a social policy that was, to some extent, deliberately designed to stigmatise.

Sub-regional governance   Refers to the regional groupings of national states engaged in applying supranational economic and political policies and regulation, such as the European Union (EU), the North American Free Trade Association (NAFTA), and the Organisation of African Unity (OAU).

Subsidiarity   A doctrine of policy-making in the European Union which holds that policy decisions should be taken at the lowest appropriate level and national governments should take precedence over the European Commission.

Subsistence   The minimum required to maintain life, but often used to refer to the lowest level at which benefits should be set.

Sure Start   A programme introduced by the Labour government designed to address the social and health needs of children and families, including the availability of childcare.

Tax credits   These were introduced by New Labour and used to reduce the amount of taxation paid by subtracting a sum from an individual's tax bill, but where people are not paying tax can lead to a cash payment.

Tenure   Set of legal rights to occupy property whether a rented, leased or owner-occupied property.

Thatcherism   The ideas and policies of Margaret Thatcher, the British Prime Minister from 1979 to 1990.

Think tanks   Arguably a special type of pressure group that often has close (usually informal) links with a particular political party (such as those of the Adam Smith Institute, the Institute for Economic Affairs, and the Social Affairs Unit with the Conservatives, particularly from 1979 to 1997, and the Institute for Public Policy Research with Labour).

Toryism   Essentially a form of paternalistic Conservatism, with a better-off minority having a responsibility to the poorer majority.

Transferable married person's allowance   Proposal by the Conservative Party to allow married couples to transfer the personal tax allowance, worth about £20 per week, if one partner was not working.

Tripartism   A term denoting the 'three-way' organisation and management of compulsory and secondary education in Britain after the Second World War. Secondary schooling was split between the grammar, modern, and technical schools, entry for which would be determined by assessment – the eleven-plus examination. Management in the education system was divided between the Ministry for Education, local education authorities, and teachers in schools.

Underclass   Often used to denote a class of people dependent on welfare, and in particular state assistance, for survival. The term has been associated, by thinkers on the right, with dependency (and a stratum of the poor within a population, which is said to be reliant upon the welfare benefits system and to be living outside and detached from established social norms), while some on the left have made a link with social exclusion.

Undeserving or indolent poor   Term applied to paupers thought to be less genuine and therefore not deserving of parish relief. This might include those simply unemployed and regarded as indolent or lazy, beggars and 'tramps' who moved about the country in search of work.

United Kingdom Independence Party (UKIP)   A libertarian political party, founded in 1993, whose main goal is the UK's withdrawal from the EU, on the basis that the latter has destroyed the country's political sovereignty.

Universal, universalism   These terms refer to welfare services and programmes that are in some sense available to all, not just some section of the population. Child benefit, for example, was, until 2013, available to all mothers with dependent children, regardless of income level. Universal may be contrasted with 'selective' social services or benefits, but the distinction is a difficult one. Means-tested social security benefits (income support, jobseekers' allowance) might be regarded as 'selective' benefits, but in reality anyone meeting the eligibility criteria is entitled. Perhaps the distinction is better thought of in terms of a distinction between benefits and services that are only available on the basis of a means test (selective) and those which are not, such as child benefit, the state retirement pension, and NHS care (universal). Universalism and universal benefits are often associated with an equality-promoting, 'institutional' model of the welfare state, in the sense of one that promotes universal equal citizenship, selectivism, and selective benefits versus a welfare system merely focused on relieving poverty, but the reality is more complex.

Universal credit Introduced by the Coalition government from 2013, universal credit was intended to simplify the benefits system by bringing a range of working-age benefits together. There were, however, significant uncertainties over the administrative effectiveness and practical implications of its introduction.

Victimless crime Crime in which there is no 'obvious' direct victim of the criminal act, but instead the victim may be public morality/decency, or the criminal him/herself, for example, in relation to personal drug use.

Welfare dependency Relying on social security benefits for financial support (see also **dependency culture**).

Welfare and rehabilitation Model of criminal justice that seeks to rehabilitate the 'criminal' back into wider society.

Welfare state The state takes responsibility for providing at least minimal levels of economic and social security through the provision of public services (such as education, health, housing, and income maintenance).

Welfare to Work A programme of employment assistance, more widely available than previous targeted schemes, which employs a system of subsidy for employers who create permanent jobs for the unemployed. Initially targeted at the younger unemployed, it was later extended to include the long-term unemployed, single parents and the disabled.

White-collar crime May be defined as those offences committed by people of relatively high status in the course of their occupation and so could include (for example) fraud, embezzlement, tax evasion, and corporate crimes involving health and safety violations and pollution.

Winter of Discontent Period of industrial unrest, particularly in the public sector, between the autumn of 1978 and spring of 1979, which marked the end of the Labour government's policy of wages control used to control the economy.

Workers' Education Association A voluntary movement, founded in the early twentieth century, to support the educational needs of working people.

Workfare The requirement to work, or to engage in other work-related activity, in return for welfare.

INDEX